Strategic Marketing

The Irwin Series in Marketing
Consulting Editor
Gilbert A. Churchill, Jr.
University of Wisconsin, Madison

Strategic Marketing

David W. Cravens

M. J. Neeley School of Business
Texas Christian University

Second Edition   1987

Homewood, Illinois 60430

ISBN 0-256-03370-6

Library of Congress Catalog Card No. 86-82214

Printed in the United States of America

1 2 3 4 5 6 7 8 9 MP 4 3 2 1 0 9 8 7

To Sue and Karen

Preface

Marketing strategy is a challenging, exciting, and important activity in contemporary business practice. Rapid changes in markets, intense global competition, and slow economic growth require the development of market-driven business strategies. *Strategic Marketing* integrates marketing strategy with business strategy, examining marketing from the point of view of the enterprise rather than using a business function perspective.

A MARKET-DRIVEN ENVIRONMENT

The central role of markets and competition in business practice is demonstrated in various ways. Economic, social, governmental, and technological changes affect markets, creating opportunities in some and threats in others. The deregulation of transportation, financial services, and telecommunications, the intense competition in such mature industries as automobiles, consumer electronics, and household appliances, and the fluctuations in the supply and prices of oil have all been instrumental in altering market opportunities for many businesses. Market changes and new forms of competition have led to impressive growth and performance for those firms where management has incorporated strategic marketing concepts and analyses into business strategy development and implementation. The marketing challenge is apparent in a variety of industries in the United States and around the world.

Marketing planning is essential to companies' survival and growth in the rapidly changing business environment of the 1990s. To a much greater degree than in the past, organizations' strategies are being influenced by forces in the marketplace. Analyzing market behavior and adjusting strategies to changing conditions require a hands-on approach to marketing planning. Due to the frequent need to alter strategies for products and markets, decision-based planning has become increasingly critical. Seat-of-the-pants approaches to marketing strategy are ineffective in the current environment.

This book provides a complete examination of marketing strategy and is appropriate for use in advanced undergraduate marketing strategy and marketing management courses and MBA marketing core and advanced strategy courses.

THE NATURE AND APPROACH OF THE BOOK

Strategy development is the purpose of this book. The book is concerned with how to identify the key issues and the important factors in selecting a strategy. While considerable attention is given to such areas as portfolio and screening analysis, profit impact of marketing strategy (PIMS), market segmentation, and positioning strategies, our primary objective is to weave the various areas into a strategic framework rather than to provide in-depth coverage of each analysis area. A depth treatment of each area would require far more space than is feasible in one book. When more depth is required, the end notes identify various sources. Nevertheless, I have attempted to provide adequate coverage of several important research and analysis tools for the book's target audience.

Since the publication of the first edition, it has become increasingly apparent that instructors desire more emphasis on marketing strategy that incorporates business strategy issues. Importantly, discussions with various instructors indicate a desire to provide a strategy perspective and emphasis that extends beyond the traditional focus on managing the marketing function.

The book is designed around a strategic marketing planning approach with a clear emphasis on how to do strategic analysis and planning. A step-by-step approach to building a strategic marketing plan is developed in the first chapter, and each step is covered in subsequent chapters. The book is divided into five parts. The first examines corporate and business unit strategy. Next, marketing situation analysis is discussed. In Part 3, marketing strategy development is covered. In Part 4 strategic marketing programming is considered. Finally, in Part 5, preparation, implementation, and control of the strategic marketing plan are discussed. Numerous how-to guides are provided throughout the book to assist the reader in applying the analysis and planning approaches developed in the text.

CHANGES IN THE SECOND EDITION

The concept and general approach to *Strategic Marketing* are retained in the second edition. Nevertheless, several important changes, additions, and major updating of examples have been incorporated into the revision. Every chapter has been substantially revised to include new material and expanded treatment of important topics. Several new chapters provide a more complete coverage of marketing strategy. The second edition contains these new features:

There are five new chapters: Chapter 4, Financial Analysis; Chapter 6, Analyzing Buyers; Chapter 7, Analyzing Strategic Situation and Competition; Chapter 11, New Product Planning; and Chapter 15, Selling and Sales Promotion Strategies.

New and expanded material has been incorporated, including financial analysis, buyer behavior, product and branding strategy, competitive marketing strategies, organizational design, implementing marketing strategy, international marketing, and the marketing of services.

Strategic applications have been added to each chapter. These short case situations involving a cross-section of consumer and industrial products, goods and services, firms of various sizes, and organizations at different levels of the distribution channel can be used to apply strategy concepts and illustrate various marketing strategy applications.

Substantial revision of chapter design and writing style have been accomplished to improve flow and reader interest.

A complete teaching-learning package is available in the Instructor's Manual. It includes answers to end-of-chapter questions, instructor's notes for strategic applications, a multiple-choice question bank, and a complete set of transparency masters.

ACKNOWLEDGMENTS

The book incorporates the contributions and experiences of many different people and organizations. Various business executives and colleagues at universities throughout the country have influenced the development of *Strategic Marketing*. While space does not permit thanking each person, a special note of appreciation is extended to all. I shall identify several whose assistance was particularly important. A special note of appreciation is extended to consulting editor Gilbert A. Churchill, Jr., University of Wisconsin. The following individuals reviewed the manuscript and offered valuable suggestions.

Benny Barak, *CUNY-Bernard M. Baruch College;* David K. Chowdhury, *British Columbia Institute of Technology;* Barbara Coe, *North Texas State University;* Stanton G. Court, *Case Western University;* Eddie Easley, *Drake University;* John S. Ewing, *California State University;* Roberto Friedmann, *University of Georgia;* Roy Howell, *Texas Tech University;* Allan D. Shocker, *University of Washington;* John E. Van Kirk, *Xavier University;* Dale Varble, *Indiana State University;* and Ken Williamson, *James Madison University.*

Student assistants provided various kinds of support that were essential to completing the revision. Nancy Robbins typed the complete manuscript, and she is due a special note of thanks for a job well done. I also want to thank Mrs. West for the generous support provided to me by the Eunice and James L. West Chair. I sincerely appreciate the continuous support of my research and writing by Charles W. Lamb, Jr., Chairman of the Department of Marketing, and Edward Johnson, Dean of the M. J. Neeley School of Business, Texas Christian University. Finally, permission to use material from Dow Jones & Co. publications and numerous other publications and organizations enabled me to include a wide variety of illustrations and examples.

David W. Cravens

Contents

Part 5 Strategic Marketing in Action

PART 1

Corporate and Business Unit Strategy

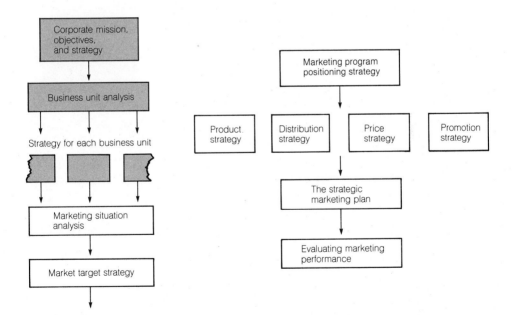

CHAPTER 1

Strategic Marketing

The Limited, the largest women's apparel specialty store and mail-order retailer in the United States, is expanding through acquisitions into related retail businesses. It is a market-driven, mission-focused enterprise that has experienced rapid and profitable growth. The company's corporate strategy demonstrates the close link between strategic planning and marketing strategy. The Limited opened its first store in 1963, and has evolved into a $2.5 billion company. Chairman Leslie H. Wexner explains The Limited's approach to business:

> We expect change and try to anticipate as well as manage it. We are not "locked into" any retailing concept or point of view. We see ourselves as trying to satisfy customer needs. These needs and the most appropriate responses for satisfying them always change. Consequently, we are always testing, refining, and revising because we seek success. We are entrepreneurial and create our own opportunities, and then exploit them to the limit of our abilities.[1]

The Limited has diversified into *(a)* women's special-size clothing with Lane Bryant and Roaman's, *(b)* Victoria's Secret lingerie through mail-order and retail stores, *(c)* women's off-priced apparel by acquiring Pic-A-Dilly, Inc., and *(d)* women's budget apparel with the acquisition of 800 Lerner Stores. Further expansion in the future of this rapidly growing retail empire is likely. The Limited's movement into these specific segments provides a strong base for growth. Offering fashion, quality, and value to the American woman through multiple retail formats, in 1985 The Limited had over 1,400 retail outlets and 6 nationally distributed mail-order catalogues. Strategic marketing actions such as analyzing markets, targeting specific segments, and developing effective product, distribution, price, and promotion strategies are central to The Limited's approach to business.

This book is about *strategic marketing planning, implementation, and control.* It presents an approach to marketing strategy as well as various applications that illustrate how this approach can be applied in business firms and not-for-profit organizations. *Strategic Marketing* examines the strategic analyses and decisions that management must make in any organization in order to satisfy customer needs and wants. This chapter sets the stage for the remainder of the book by first describing marketing's important strategic challenge. Next, we consider the enterprise-spanning significance of the marketing concept. The discussion shows how adopting the marketing concept leads to customer satisfaction. Finally, we present a step-by-step approach to strategic marketing planning, implementation, and control. The approach is developed within the guidelines provided by corporate and business unit strategies.

MARKETING'S STRATEGIC CHALLENGE

Marketing has been assigned a new priority in many companies as chief executives increasingly recognize the central role of the market in corporate strategy. The broad consumer market has separated into many different consumer groups, each with specific needs and wants:

> The emergence of this fragmented consumer population, together with an array of economic factors—intense international competition, the impact of rapid technological change, the maturing or stagnation of certain markets, and deregulation—has altered the shape of competition.
>
> The realization that marketing will provide the cutting edge in the 1980s not only has hit well-known packaged goods marketers—such as Procter & Gamble, Coca-Cola, and General Foods—but is affecting industries that used to be protected from the vagaries of consumer selling by regulatory statutes. Airlines, banks, and financial-services groups are looking for ways to grow and prosper in an environment of product proliferation, advertising clutter, escalating marketing costs, and—despite advances in research and testing—a dauntingly high rate of new-product failures.[2]

The rapidly expanding importance of marketing as a business activity is illustrated by the adoption of marketing concepts and methods in various professional services, such as law, medicine, dentistry, architecture, and public accounting. Until recently the marketing of medical services was considered unnecessary and inappropriate by hospitals, physicians, dentists, and other suppliers of medical services. This same point of view was characteristic of professionals representing a wide range of services.

Marketing's Expanded Strategic Role

Strategic marketing extends beyond the arena of traditional marketing management. Until the 1970s marketing executives were preoccupied with pulling together the components of marketing (product, distribution, price, and promotion) into an integrated marketing program. During the 1970s marketing professionals began to direct attention to market target strategies, placing considerable emphasis upon segmenting markets. It became important to identify a promising niche in a product market because of competitive pressures, particularly in mature markets. The profit potential of gaining a strong market position in one or more market segments increased the strategic importance of market analysis and targeting.

Until the late 1970s marketing executives in many firms had little involvement in corporate strategic planning. As firms began to implement strategic planning programs, however, their managements found that many aspects of strategic analysis involve marketing strategy. Decisions to diversify, the evaluation of product-market opportunities, the selecting of market target strategies, and the evaluation of new product ideas—all these developments illustrate the many strategic decisions that require the skills, experience, and analytical tools of marketing professionals.

As a result of these developments, marketing management is being asked to fulfill an expanded strategic role in an increasing number of companies. Two kinds of demands are being placed upon business executives. First, top management and all others involved in strategic planning must increase their understanding of strategic marketing in order to identify the aspects of marketing strategy that are to be incorporated into corporate strategy. Strategic planners must also determine where gaps exist in strategic analysis skills that can be eliminated through greater involvement of marketing professionals. Second, marketing professionals must expand their knowledge of corporate strategic planning in order to properly link marketing strategies to business strategies.

Achieving Excellence in Marketing

While many factors ultimately determine the success of a particular marketing strategy, satisfying the key requirements listed below is essential. A brief examination of these requirements provides a useful overview of strategic marketing.

Developing Market-Driven Business Strategies. In today's complex and highly competitive business environment, it is important to guide the mission, objectives, and strategies of a business on the basis of the needs and wants of the marketplace. A strong market-centered focus to business strategy is the starting point. The Limited follows a market-centered strategy in women's specialty retailing by uncovering customer needs and responding to changes in needs. Management's movement into mail-order retailing is illustrative of its responsiveness to change. Mail-order sales of a wide variety of consumer goods experienced explosive growth during the first half of the 1980s.

Finding Business Advantage.   Understanding the strengths and weaknesses of a business is the starting point in identifying business advantage. What is the firm's strategic advantage? What can it do better than its competition? Nucor, a "minimill" steelmaker has concentrated on producing steel joists and other specialty items, avoiding head-on competition with giants like U.S. Steel. In 1985 Nucor's profits totaled $59 million, with sales of $759 million. The firm's growth and financial performance for the previous decade were very strong, particularly in light of the major financial problems present throughout the steel industry.

Listening to the Marketplace.   An incredible failure to listen to the marketplace occurred as the United States entered the 1980s. While the following example concerns a government program, we can see how critical the understanding of customer needs can be to the success of any organization, public or private. Consider a 1980 report in *The Wall Street Journal* on the Susan B. Anthony dollar:

> The U.S. Mint, faced with a growing mountain of Susan B. Anthony dollars, will temporarily stop producing the coin at the end of March.
> Stella Hackel, director of the Mint, said in an interview that the government by the end of January had produced about 780 million of the dollar coins, which were introduced last July. Only about 270 million currently are in circulation, however. Mrs. Hackel said that officials decided "to discontinue production until our inventories are depleted." She wouldn't estimate when production would resume.
> The Mint hasn't given up on the Anthony dollar, she said, and it plans to continue to promote the coin. The coin hasn't been accepted by the public in part because it is about the same size as a quarter and thus causes confusion. But Mrs. Hackel said, "We aren't disappointed. We expected that it would take about three to five years to achieve widespread circulation."
> At the beginning of this month, the U.S. Postal Service agreed to use the Anthony dollars in making change unless customers objected. A spokesman for the Mint said that during the week ended Feb. 8, 1.6 million of the Anthony dollars were put in circulation. He said it was the highest weekly circulation figure since the coin was introduced, and compared with a weekly average of about 190,000 during the four prior weeks.[3]

One has only to look at the coin to see why people do not want to use it. It looks like a quarter. The logic of the coin from the Mint's point of view is clear; its estimated life is far greater than a paper dollar, thus offering huge savings over the printing and replacement costs of paper dollars. But for the Mint to realize these benefits, people must use the coins. Retailers did not want to use the new coin and consumers also did not accept it. Most of the 780 million coins were never placed in circulation.

Competitor Analysis. Gaining strategic advantage begins by identifying and analyzing the competition. Competitor analysis has become very important because of the complexity of market structure, the scrambled arena of competition, and the blurring of competitive boundaries. Changes occurring in the financial services industry illustrate how important it is to identify competitors and assess their strengths and weaknesses. Bankers are becoming brokers, and retailers like Kmart Corporation and Sears Roebuck & Co. are moving into financial services. Organizations traditionally identified as banks, savings and loan associations, credit unions, brokerage houses, and consumer goods retailers all face a common strategic challenge. They must cope with, and capitalize on, the uncertainty and intense competition that is developing in the once well-ordered financial services industry.

Targeting Customers. The increasing diversity of needs and wants in markets is creating subgroups of buyers within the total market, each displaying different needs and wants. Such differentiation provides an opportunity for businesses to design product offerings to meet the needs of various customer groups. Targeting *all* people (or organizations) in a market is not a typical strategy for most firms. Instead, many firms target one or more segments within the total market. Deciding what people (or organizations) to target is an important strategic decision. The traveler-lodging market illustrates how hotel chains are targeting different customer groups. Factors such as price, hotel size, location, and use (e.g., for vacation or business) help identify user groups. Exhibit 1–1 shows the lodging market separated into three customer groups.

Positioning. A product, line of products, or a company is positioned in the eyes and minds of buyers. This "positioning" of a firm's offering is influenced by the marketing actions of a company as well as by the marketing efforts of competitors. For example, one of the challenges the Tandy Corporation encountered in trying to expand its market for personal computers in 1984 was the "discount-store image" many buyers held of the Radio Shack chain. Management's plans to improve the Radio Shack image included an expanded campaign of advertising and public relations. This campaign focused on the high-quality technology of its products and upscaled the look of the firm's print advertising.[4] Positioning a company and its products in the eyes and minds of buyers is an important strategic concern for many organizations.

EXHIBIT 1-1 Illustrative Targets in the Lodging Market

Customer Group	Examples
High-priced ($65–100 +), large hotels (300 + rooms), luxury accomodations for the convention and/or business traveler.	Hyatt Regency, Mariott Corporation
Mid-priced ($45–65), medium-size (100–300 rooms), hotels and motels for the commercial and/or family traveler.	Holiday Inns, Inc., Ramada Inns, Inc., Howard Johnson's
Low-priced (below $45), smaller hotels and motels for the commercial and family traveler.	Days Inn of America, Inc., Independents

---

Managing for Results. Traditionally marketing executives have been primarily concerned with expanding revenues (sales) and market share. But today profit performance has also become a critical concern. Both costs and revenues are important in managing for results. Consider, for example, the success of The Price Clubs, a chain of membership-only warehouse outlets in California, Arizona, and Virginia. The company began business in 1976 with one store. By 1985 it had 20 warehouses and annual sales of nearly $2 billion. Interestingly, net profit margins are in the 2 percent plus range. Low prices, expense control, and warehouse facilities have enabled the firm to expand rapidly and profitably.

Adding Marketing Value. A final requirement for achieving top performance in marketing is to provide customers with marketing value. The use of services as an active marketing tool shows the value-added concept. Service has become a serious concern for U.S. car makers:

> Product quality and service are closely intertwined in the car business, according to J. David Power, president of J. D. Power & Associates in Westlake Village, California. Power has conducted market research for Japanese and domestic auto makers since 1968, and he currently produces an annual Customer Satisfaction Index that tracks, among other things, service-related issues. Mercedes-Benz gets the highest rating. Toyota Motor Corp. is second-best, and Ford Motor Co. is the only U.S. auto company to garner an above-average rating. American Motors Corp. comes in last.[5]

The primary objective of this book is to develop an approach to marketing strategy planning, implementation, and control that incorporates these eight key requirements for marketing success.

ACHIEVING CUSTOMER SATISFACTION

The effectiveness of a marketing strategy ultimately depends upon achieving customer satisfaction. Earlier in this chapter we discussed the commitment of The Limited's top management to satisfying customer needs. The marketing concept is a basic guide to reaching this objective.

The Marketing Concept

The essence of the *marketing concept* is that if people do not want or need what you are marketing, they will not buy it. This applies to Susan B. Anthony dollars, toothpaste, industrial cranes, and any other product or service. This simple, yet critical, logic is at the heart of business success. And it also applies to not-for-profit organizations. The marketing concept consists of three vital cornerstones:

Start with the customer's needs and wants as the foundation of business purpose. An organization must identify these needs and wants and then decide which ones it should try to satisfy.

Next, an organization must determine how it will satisfy these needs and wants. This is the responsibility of all members of the enterprise, not just those assigned to the marketing function.

Finally, the opportunity to meet organizational objectives will occur through the enterprise's efforts to deliver customer satisfaction.

While the marketing concept represents nothing really new to perceptive executives and its commonsense logic is clear, many businesses have never put the concept into practice. Consider, for example, the failure of the U.S. Treasury's efforts to force people to use a coin that did not correspond to their needs and wants.

Adopting the Marketing Concept

Applying the marketing concept is a continuing activity. We need to develop, implement, and evaluate strategies that use the four guidelines described below. Management cannot identify customer needs and wants at one point and expect them to never change. It is not always an easy task to determine these needs. An organization must adapt to changing conditions that may generate new opportunities and problems. Once these opportunities and problems are identified, it is a major challenge for management to select an effective business strategy. Management must also make wise choices among the available resources and capabilities. Since well-planned and well-executed business strategies do not always result in the expected levels of performance, management must continue making changes until a satisfactory performance is reached. In adapting the marketing concept, management should consider the four guidelines we shall now describe.

Selecting Needs and Wants. Since there are many different needs and wants in the marketplace, management must decide which of them the firm should try to satisfy. Central to this decision is finding a competitive advantage. This advantage may be gained by meeting a need or want more effectively than the competition or by identifying a need or want that is not being met by other firms. Domino's Pizza found a set of consumer wants that were not being served very well—people who want a free pizza delivery that is fast and effective. Domino's competition is primarily mom-and-pop pizza stores whose home delivery service is often unreliable and slow. Domino's primary market target is the 18–34 age-group and the secondary target is the 35+ age-group. Customers are promised 30-minute service through the use of experienced, highly motivated delivery people. Domino's 1984 sales were $600 million through 2,000 retail outlets. Home delivery represents 90 percent of Domino's sales compared to only 16 percent of industry sales in the $7 billion total pizza market.[6]

Corporate Teamwork. The success of the customer-oriented approach to marketing advocated by the marketing concept depends on everyone in an organization, not just on those assigned specific marketing responsibilities. Management needs to develop an appropriate organizational structure as an essential means of establishing linkages within a company. Hewlett-Packard Company, the giant manufacturer of electronic instruments and computers, made a major overhaul in its organization in 1984, in an attempt to make the company more customer-driven rather than technology-driven.[7] A key objective in the organizational changes was to make the company and its employees more sensitive to customers. The firm's market base needed to be expanded. The new structure grouped dozens of product divisions under market sectors instead of product lines. For example, two of the sectors will market computers, one concentrating on business customers. The other sector will target scientific and manufacturing customers, offering both computers and instruments. As a result of this change, HP can now offer a complete process control and testing capability that links computers and measurement and control devices. A major element in HP's new organizational structure encourages corporate teamwork by offering customers integrated solutions to their problems. Adopting the marketing concept calls for a blending of corporate and marketing strategy. Strategic marketing requires the assembly and integration of the enterprise's capabilities on the basis of management's choice of the customers' needs and wants it has decided to serve. Marketing strategy integrates all the firm's customer-influencing activities, rather than representing a specialized function. As in the Hewlett-Packard illustration, everyone in the company must work together as a team to achieve customer satisfaction. While this does not mean that the marketing function should take over corporate strategy, it argues strongly for heavy participation by the chief marketing executive in strategic analysis and planning.

Information, Analysis, and Action.   Successful adoption of the marketing concept requires sound planning and implementation. Management must do its homework before launching new strategies, beginning by listening to the voice of the marketplace:

> Intecolor Corp., a 10-year-old Atlanta maker of color video display terminals for process control and computer graphics systems, believes that an about-face in its new product tactics was needed to maintain its leading share in niche markets, says President David M. Deans. "When the company was founded, we were engineering-driven. We came up with good products and hoped the world would beat a path to our door. Today we spend much more time talking to our marketing people and customers to find out what they—not the engineers—want."[8]

Marketing strategy begins with obtaining information relevant to the strategy situation, analyzing it, and then taking action consistent with the results of the analysis.

Rethinking the Marketing Concept.   One authority argues convincingly that the marketing concept is moving into a new era called *megamarketing*. This expanded view of strategic thinking includes government officials, public-interest groups, and the news media as marketing targets. In addition, it includes the addition of political power and public-opinion formation as concerns of marketing strategy. The key implication is that the environment must be managed as well as a firm's marketing strategy. This new view of the marketing concept advocates a more active societal role of marketers.[9]

While the marketing concept offers considerable direction to management in charting the course of an enterprise into the future, its implementation requires carefully selected strategies and effective management of the strategies over time. The marketing concept contains the supporting logic for developing corporate and marketing strategies. It does not indicate *how* these strategies should be developed, but rather *what* should occur when the strategies have been properly planned and implemented. Thus the major distinction between the marketing concept and marketing strategy is that the former expresses a desired outcome while the latter delineates the strategic actions necessary to implement the marketing concept.

STRATEGIC MARKETING PLANNING

The relationship between strategic planning for the corporation, the business units within the corporation, and marketing strategy is

---

EXHIBIT 1-2 Strategic Linkages

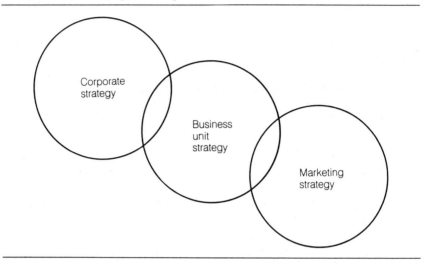

---

shown in Exhibit 1-2. Strategic planning for a corporation is a continuing process consisting of:

Analyzing corporate performance and identifying future opportunities and threats.

Determining corporate mission, objectives, and strategies.

Setting objectives and developing strategies for each unit of the business unit portfolio of the corporation.

Implementing, managing, and adjusting mission and strategies to achieve corporate and business unit objectives.

A former manager of strategic planning for General Electric Company's Housewares and Audio Business Division describes marketing's role in strategic planning at General Electric:

> The marketing manager is the most significant functional contributor to the strategic planning process, with leadership roles in defining the business mission; analysis of the environmental, competitive, and business situations; developing objectives, goals, and strategies; and defining product, market, distribution, and quality plans to implement the business' strategies. This involvement extends to the development of program and operating plans that are fully linked with the strategic plan.[10]

The chief marketing executive's strategic planning responsibility includes: (1) participating in corporate strategy formulation, and (2) developing business unit marketing strategies in accordance with corporate priorities. Since these two areas are closely interrelated, it is important to examine marketing's role and functions in both areas to gain more insight into marketing's responsibilities and contributions. Peter F. Drucker describes this role:

> Marketing is so basic that it cannot be considered a separate function (i.e., a separate skill or work) within the business, on a par with others such as manufacturing or personnel. Marketing requires separate work, and a distinct group of activities. But it is, first, a central dimension of the entire business. It is the whole business seen from the point of view of its final result, that is, from the customer's point of view.[11]

This perspective of marketing's role in an organization can be combined with the traditional view of marketing management to define *strategic marketing*—a process of:

Strategic analysis of environmental, market, competitive, and business factors affecting the corporation and its business units and forecasting future trends in business areas of interest to the enterprise.

Participating in setting objectives and formulating corporate and business unit strategies.

Selecting market target strategies for the product-markets in each business unit, establishing marketing objectives as well as developing, implementing, and managing the positioning strategies of the marketing program in order to meet market target needs.

This strategic marketing planning process is shown in Exhibit 1–3. An examination of each step in the process will highlight the nature and scope of the strategic marketing tasks.

Corporate Mission and Objectives

Corporate mission is what the management of a company wants it to be and what available resources will allow it to be. The Limited's corporate purpose is to be one of the leading retailers in the world. The crux of mission determination is deciding the product and market areas the firm should pursue. Mission and objectives provide a framework for strategic planning. Over time, strategic analysis may indicate a need to alter mission and objectives. While changes in mission are not made frequently, adjustments to new conditions may be necessary. For example, Burlington Northern, Inc., as a consequence of deregulation of railroad and transportation services, is moving aggressively into developing a broad base of transportation capabilities. The firm's intermodal business unit has experienced rapid growth during the last few years.

EXHIBIT 1-3   The Strategic Marketing Planning Process

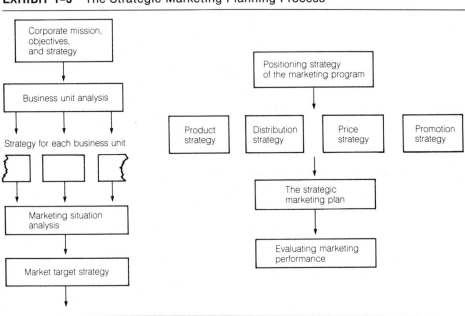

Business Unit Analysis and Strategy

George A. Steiner describes this part of the strategic planning process:

> The essence of formal strategic planning is the systematic identification of opportunities and threats that lie in the future, which in combination with other relevant data provide a basis for a company's making better current decisions to exploit the opportunities and to avoid the threats. Planning means designing a desired future and identifying ways to bring it about.[12]

Strategic analysis involves assessments of present financial and market performance of the firm in the *product* and *market* areas that it serves and an evaluation of the future opportunities and threats in these areas. It also includes finding and evaluating product and market opportunities outside the present scope of the business. One of the major developments in strategic planning during the last decade is that management should analyze strategically a corporation comprised of two or more business activities (e.g., sewing products and power tools) as a portfolio of business units. Each business unit will reflect its unique characteristics as to its future attractiveness to the firm. The strategic planner studies the composition of the business as well as the product and market interrelationships among the units. He or she then pinpoints future threats and opportunities. Financial and market analysis capabilities are essential in performing these strategic analyses. Typically we should focus upon each unit of the business designated by many firms as a strategic business unit (SBU). As a result of our strategic analysis, we can decide how each unit should be managed. Some business units face slow growth while others may offer exciting future opportunities. A firm's strength over competition will also vary among business areas. Thus strategic planning activities should indicate how to allocate financial resources among units and what to expect in the way of financial and market performance for each business unit:

> This concept of the organization as a collection of units and subunits having different objectives is at the very root of contemporary approaches to strategic market planning. The term *portfolio* is commonly used to describe such a collection. Differences are expressed in terms of whether the unit is a net source of cash or a user of cash, as well as goals for growth, market share, net income, or return on investment.[13]

Business unit objectives set the stage for developing strategic plans for each unit. These plans include such supporting strategies as marketing, finance, and operations.

Plans must lead to actions, and strategic plans must be translated into short-term (e.g., annual) budgets and operating plans. Planning structure consists of a formal strategic planning system that connects three major types of plans: strategic plans, medium-range programs, and short-range budgets and operating plans.[14]

Marketing decision makers are involved in the strategic planning process in three important ways: (1) they participate in strategic analysis and planning for an enterprise; (2) they serve with other functional managers as members of the business unit strategic planning team; and (3) they develop and implement strategic marketing plans for the markets served by the business unit. Moving from this overview of corporate and business unit strategic planning, we now consider the strategic marketing activities and decisions of the chief marketing executive and staff (see Exhibit 1–3).

Marketing Situation Analysis

It is important to place correct boundaries around markets in order to analyze buyers and competition and to forecast future trends. In strategic analysis and planning it is not very useful to refer to the Toronto market, the United Kingdom market, or some other geographical area that contains people and organizations with diverse needs and wants. More specific identification of needs and wants is necessary. In order for a market to exist, there must be people with particular needs and wants and one or more products that can satisfy these needs. Additionally, the people in the market must be willing and able to purchase the product that satisfies their needs and wants. Thus the concept of a product-market lends considerable direction to the task of definition.

A *product-market* is a specific product (or line of related products) that can satisfy a particular set of needs and wants for all people or organizations willing and able to purchase the product or service. This definition matches people or organizations with a particular set of similar needs and wants to a product or service category that can satisfy those needs and wants. Of course, depending upon how specific or general the needs are, the corresponding product category will likewise be specific or general. In defining a product-market, we need to satisfy two important objectives. First, we need to define the product-market in such a way as to include all products or brands that offer solutions to the same set of needs. Second, the definition should not be so broad that it is not operationally useful in analysis and forecasting.

Analyzing product-markets and forecasting how they will change in the future are essential aspects of corporate and marketing planning. Decisions about entering new product-markets, about how to serve existing product markets, and about when to get out of unattractive product-markets are critical to strategic marketing. More so than any other area in the enterprise, marketing professionals have the skills, experience, and tools essential to: (1) conducting product-market analysis; (2) interpreting the strategic consequences of the results; and (3) choosing strategies for serving product-markets. Marketing's role in analyzing product-markets consists of the following activities:

1. Locating and defining new product-markets that offer opportunities for a company.
2. Evaluating existing product-markets to determine strategic priorities.
3. Scanning the environment and forecasting future trends in product-markets.

Marketing situation analysis should extend beyond the analysis of markets and buyers to include the determination of the strategic marketing situation confronting a company. Assessment of competition is an important part of strategic situation analysis. Other factors affecting the strategic situation are the organization, market, and environmental factors. Through understanding the strategic marketing situation, management is provided with important guidelines for the development of a marketing strategy.

An illustration will demonstrate the impact on corporate performance of an effective analysis of a marketing situation. RCA Corporation's videodisk player venture, a consumer electronics product projected to be a major new product success, was in serious trouble by late 1983. When it was introduced in 1981, an early forecast held that industry sales of the player could reach $1 billion in 1982.[15] As of late 1983 the situation was as follows:

RCA originally expected to sell 500,000 players in the first year. Competitors projected sales of an additional 250,000. Instead, total sales of the machines, used by consumers to play movies, won't reach their first 500,000 units until the end of 1983, even though prices have been cut in half since 1981 and more advanced models have been introduced. In contrast, videocassette recorders, which can record programs as well as play them, are selling very well. And low-priced home computers have pushed aside any possible claims by videodisk players to being the hot new electronic gadget of the decade.

The company hurt most by the machine's problems is RCA, which accounts for about 75% of all videodisk player sales. Former RCA chief executive officer Edgar Griffiths once called the videodisk player RCA's "priority project for the decade." But the company's biggest priority now is halting losses on the product—$288.2 million from 1979 through 1982—and making the players profitable by 1986.[16]

RCA stopped production of the videodisk player in 1984. Sale of videodisk recorders (VCRs) and videodisk players from 1979 to 1984 are shown in Exhibit 1–4. Several factors apparently led to the poor sales performance of the product. Prices of VCRs declined much faster than originally estimated by RCA, and picture quality improved. Prices of VCR tapes fell rapidly during the period of introduction of the videodisk player. The availability of inexpensive rental tape offering a wide variety of movies further enhanced the attractiveness of VCRs. Perhaps even more significant was the desire of RCA's management "to do something big to regain its technical reputation."[17] The overall consequence of these factors was that the videodisk player did not offer a marketable advantage over the VCR. Interestingly, by 1985 use of videodisks for business and other special applications was expanding rapidly. These special uses include employee training, conferences, and instructional programs. These applications utilize a type of laser player rather than the type of stylus offered by RCA.

Market Target Strategy

Once a company's product-markets have been identified and their relative importance to the firm determined, management must decide which people (or organizations) to target in each product-market. This is the *market target* decision. As an illustration, consider Magnavox's market target strategy for its laser videodisk player.

In early 1980 Magnavox, a subsidiary of North American Phillips, was marketing a new videodisk player in selected cities throughout the United States. The player uses a laser beam to read from a disk similar to a long-playing record album. The player retailed at $775, and prices for the disks ranged from $6 to $25. RCA's player introduced in 1981 used a diamond-tipped stylus rather than a laser. RCA's unit was to sell for under $500. Considering RCA's much lower price and position in the

---

EXHIBIT 1-4 Sales of Home Video Machines (in millions of units, to dealers)

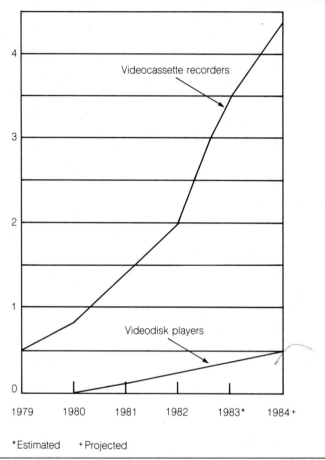

*Estimated   + Projected

SOURCE: Electronic Industries Association and Laura Landro, "RCA Reaches Crossroads on Future of Its Troubled Videodisk Player," *The Wall Street Journal,* September 13, 1983, 35.

---

home entertainment market versus Magnavox's more expensive (and versatile) unit and its more limited distribution network, what would be the best market target strategy for Magnavox to follow?

At least two possibilities could have been considered. Magnavox could meet RCA head-on, using its lead position to provide momentum for going after the mass market. Alternatively, Magnavox could attempt to appeal to people (and organizations) in a particular niche of the market that might find the higher price acceptable in return for the unit's innovative player technology and added features. By 1985 it was clear that Magnavox's management had adopted a niche strategy. The industrial videodisk market was about $500 million in 1985, including hardware and computer peripherals, and was expected to reach $3 billion by 1990.[18]

In a given product-market management may decide to serve all people in it by using a mass strategy. Alternatively, management may seek to serve one or more subgroups (niches or segments) of people in the product-market by using a different marketing strategy for each subgroup. How are subgroups formed in a given market? Usually subgroups reflect the various characteristics of people, the reasons that they buy or use certain products, and their preferences for certain products. Likewise, segments of industrial product-markets may be formed according to the type of industry, the uses for the product, and various other factors.

Marketing Program Positioning Strategy

A *marketing program positioning strategy* is the combination of the product, channel of distribution, price, and promotion strategies selected by management to position a firm against its key competitors in meeting the needs and wants of the market target. The first step in developing a positioning strategy is deciding what is to be accomplished for each market target. We should often establish marketing objectives at several levels in an organization. The corporate objectives—for which the marketing function is totally or partially responsible—indicate overall performance targets (e.g., growth, profit, employee development, and other broad objectives). We need to set specific objectives for each market target. For example, suppose as one of its objectives a corporation wishes to double sales (in constant dollars) over the next six years. Management should then allocate this objective to the firm's market targets since it is unlikely that each market target will account for the same proportion of sales. Similarly, the profit contributions that are feasible for different market targets often vary; management must take this into consideration in setting objectives. Objectives form a hierarchy ranging from very broad corporate objectives to the very specific objectives of a particular salesperson. Examples of marketing objectives are shown in Exhibit 1-5.

After selecting a market target and formulating marketing objectives, the final step in developing a marketing strategy is to decide how to fit together product, distribution, pricing, and promotion strategies into an integrated marketing program for each market target. Management has considerable latitude in deciding the strategic role of these marketing program components. Programming is an attempt to blend the strategies so that sales, market share, profit contribution, and other market target objectives are met. Consider a successful marketing pro-

---

Exhibit 1-5   Illustrative Marketing Objectives

Corporate: Achieve a net profit growth rate (in constant dollars) of 20 percent per year for the next five years.

Marketing: Maintain a marketing expense to sales ratio of 15 percent or less for 1987.

Market Target: Increase our market share in the video tape recorder product-market from 13 percent to 18 percent during the next 24 months.

Advertising: Increase consumer brand awareness in the Southeastern region from 42 percent to 50 percent by one year from now.

Salesperson: Increase our share of sales to the Apex Company from last year's 30 percent to 45 percent by the end of next year.

---

gram strategy used by Palm Beach, Inc. in building its Evan-Picone line of tailored apparel for career women:

> Acquired in 1973, sales increased over 10-fold to more than $60 million in 1979. Central to the Palm Beach strategy was strengthening relationships with a select group of department stores. The number of stores was reduced from nearly 5,000 to less than 900 and only 80 account for most of Evan-Picone's sales. By providing a high-fashion label that can be mass produced at reasonable costs, developing a team of capable merchandising representatives to work with retailers, and using a selective distribution strategy, Evan-Picone is one of the few success stories in a sluggish industry.[19]

Choice of a good marketing program strategy is complicated by the wide range of options that confront management. Yet often there is a clear logic as to how the marketing program components should fit together in a given situation. For example, Palm Beach, Inc.'s decision to move toward a selective distribution strategy was consistent with building a strong network of key retailers that could attract fashion-conscious women and could serve them with designer label clothing at reasonable prices. Decisions about products, distribution channels, price, advertising, and personal selling must lead to a cohesive marketing program aimed at meeting the needs and wants of customers in the firm's target market. Designing the marketing program combines the firm's marketing capabilities into a package of actions intended to position the firm against its competition in order to compete for the customers that comprise its market target.

Management must decide both the role and amount of resources it wishes to use for each marketing program component. These decisions determine the total amount to be spent on the marketing program during the planning period, and also indicate how the resources will be allocated among the various program activities, such as advertising and personal selling. When we decide the strategic role of each marketing program component, this amounts to deciding what management wants it to accomplish. For example, when Palm Beach acquired Evan-Picone, the 25 salespeople who had been calling on retail store executives were replaced by 5 merchandising representatives who did not take orders, but rather worked closely with the retail salesclerks.[20] Thus the personal selling role for the Evan-Picone line was changed to provide assistance and support to salesclerks.

The Strategic Marketing Plan

As shown earlier in Exhibit 1–3, we need to place the various strategic marketing decisions into a strategic marketing plan. Each part of the strategic planning process outlined in Exhibit 1–3 provides a building block for the strategic marketing plan. One important planning issue is deciding how to fit together strategic plans from different levels in a company. Several planning levels within a business firm are shown in Exhibit 1–6. Each type of plan is described below:

Corporate Strategic Plan.   This plan should indicate the business mission, objectives, and major strategies for achieving business objectives. Financial analyses and projections are an important part of the corporate plan.

Business Unit Strategic Plan.   Included here are the mission and objectives of the business unit and the functional plans that show how the unit will achieve its objectives.

Strategic Marketing Plan.   In this plan market target strategies, objectives, and marketing program positioning strategies are specified. Also included are the design of the marketing organization and supporting financial analyses.

Short-Term Marketing Plan.   This plan is used to translate the major strategies that are delineated in the strategic marketing plan into short-term or annual plans. This plan contains specific actions, responsibilities, time schedules, and deadlines.

How a company assigns planning responsibility for the above types of plans may vary considerably according to its size, planning complexity, and the management's preferences. For example, in some companies the business unit and strategic marketing plan are combined. The approach to strategic marketing planning taken in this book is applicable to planning at the four levels of plans shown in Exhibit 1–6 or, alternatively, to planning situations where business unit and strategic marketing plans are combined. In small or single-business firms the top three planning levels of Exhibit 1–6 are sometimes combined into one strategic plan.

Exhibit 1-6 Planning Levels in a Multibusiness Company

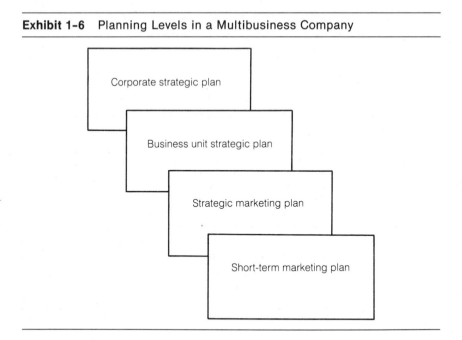

Corporate strategic plan

Business unit strategic plan

Strategic marketing plan

Short-term marketing plan

Evaluation of Marketing Performance

Strategic marketing planning is a continuing process of making strategic decisions, implementing them, and gauging their effectiveness over time. Planning is adaptive, not fixed. In terms of its time requirements, strategic evaluation is far more demanding than planning. To be meaningful and effective, plans must contain commitments. Strategic evaluation is concerned with tracking performance and, when necessary, altering plans to keep performance on track. Strategic evaluation also includes looking for new opportunities and potential threats in the future. It is critically important for management to evaluate changing conditions in business planning:

> Any business plan that is over 12 months old in today's rapidly changing state of economic and social affairs is an extraordinarily dangerous document. At the very least, management should review *all* the basic assumptions and trends underlying the overall strategic plan annually. Then it should conduct a careful review of the interim progress that has been made and clearly identify the reasons for underperformance or overperformance.[21]

This statement highlights the importance of evaluation in the strategic planning process. Strategic evaluation is the connecting link in the strategic marketing planning process shown in Exhibit 1-3. By serving as both the last stage and the first stage (strategic evaluation before taking action) in the planning process, strategic evaluation assures that planning will be a continuous process.

PLAN OF THE BOOK

The exciting new challenge confronting the practice of marketing today has never been greater in the history of business. As the world moves toward 1990, a new era is unfolding for marketing professionals. There is a shift toward a much greater emphasis upon strategic decisions and a more active participation of marketing professionals in corporate strategic analysis and planning. Matching product and service offerings with customers' needs and wants is what the practice of business is all about. To be successful, management must develop capabilities for identifying, analyzing, and deciding how to serve markets. In the past, companies could sometimes successfully enter new markets with only very general information about the people or organizations that comprised their markets for goods and services. But superficial assessments of market opportunities in today's highly complex and competitive marketplace often lead to failure or substandard performance. Management is finding that a key strategic challenge is deciding how to best position a company in a market to gain the greatest advantage over the competition. And, in some instances, management may decide not to enter but instead to exit from a particular market. At the heart of these decisions is gaining the necessary information about each market opportunity.

The purpose of *Strategic Marketing* is to expand your understanding of strategic marketing decisions, analyses, and issues. The book should be of value to students, marketing professionals, and other executives interested in marketing strategy. Throughout the book we concentrate heavily upon the *how* of strategic planning. Emphasis is placed upon integrating corporate and marketing strategic planning. Guidelines for strategic marketing planning are developed and applied. We make a wide use of how-to-do-it guides to analysis and planning. Various techniques and methods used in corporate and marketing strategic planning are explored throughout the book to illustrate their usefulness in business analysis and screening, product-market definition and analysis, segmentation, product positioning, new product planning, price analysis, financial planning, and many other application areas. We have also made extensive use of company applications of strategic marketing.

The book is organized around the strategic marketing planning process shown in Exhibit 1-7. The chapters have been grouped into five parts. Part 1 is concerned with corporate and business unit strategy. Product-market analysis, analyzing buyers, analysis of strategic situa-

EXHIBIT 1-7 Plan of the Book

Part	Chapter
1: Corporate and Business Unit Strategy	1. Strategic Marketing 2. Corporate Strategic Planning 3. Business Unit Analysis and Strategy 4. Financial Analysis
2: Marketing Situation Analysis	5. Defining and Analyzing Markets 6. Analyzing Consumer and Organizational Buyers 7. Analyzing the Strategic Situation and the Competition
3: Marketing Strategy Development	8. Market Target Strategy 9. Marketing Program Positioning Strategy
4: Strategic Marketing Programming	10. Product Strategy 11. New Product Planning 12. Distribution Strategy 13. Price Strategy 14. Promotion and Advertising Strategies 15. Selling and Sales Promotion Strategies
5: Strategic Marketing in Action	16. The Strategic Marketing Plan 17. Moving from Plans to Implementation 18. Strategic Evaluation and Control

tion and competition, and financial analysis are considered in Part 2, Marketing Situation Analysis. In Part 3, Marketing Strategy Development, market target and marketing program positioning strategies are examined. Strategic marketing programming is covered in Part 4, where strategies for products, distribution, price, and promotion are outlined. Finally, in Part 5, Strategic Planning in Action, strategic marketing decisions are pulled together to show how to prepare the strategic marketing plan, how to implement and manage the plan, and how to perform strategic evaluation and control. While moving through the book, we will discuss several strategic issues that promise to be important in the future.

Often we can learn as much by analyzing mistakes as by studying the successes of business firms. In this book the corporate and marketing strategies of a variety of companies are examined to illustrate both successful and unsuccessful decisions involving consumer and industrial product and service firms. The objective is *not* to praise or criticize the management of any company. Rather, their experiences can assist other firms to develop successful strategies for capitalizing upon opportunities and avoiding threats. Moreover, some companies that are in trouble today may be very successful in the future, and vice versa. By retaining our objectivity we can learn a great deal from these successes and failures.

CONCLUDING NOTE

Strategic marketing consists of the strategic analyses and decisions that management must accomplish in order to satisfy customer needs and wants. Marketing is playing an expanded strategic role in many firms. If we are to achieve excellence in marketing, we must satisfy a number of requirements, such as developing market-driven business strategies, finding business advantage, listening to the marketplace, identifying and evaluating competition, selecting target customers, developing effective positioning strategies of the marketing program, managing marketing strategy for results, and providing customers with marketing value.

The effectiveness of a marketing strategy ultimately depends on achieving customer satisfaction. Adoption of the marketing concept provides a logical basis for achieving this objective. The three cornerstones of the marketing concept are: (1) start with the customer's needs and wants as the foundation of business purpose, (2) develop an organizational approach to satisfying these needs and wants, and (3) meet the organization's objectives by delivering customer satisfaction. Success in following the guidelines of the marketing concept depends mainly on selecting the needs and wants the organization is best suited to satisfy, developing an effective corporate marketing effort, and accomplishing sound marketing planning and implementation.

Strategic marketing planning starts with an understanding of the corporate mission, objectives, and strategy of each business unit. Next the marketing situation analysis considers market opportunities, buyers, competition, and the strategic marketing situation confronting the organization. The selection of the people (or organizations) to be targeted by the company follows the situation analysis. The market target decision indicates the needs to be satisfied by the marketing program positioning strategy. Positioning is the combination of product, channel of distribution, price, and promotion strategies selected by management to position the firm against its key competitors in meeting the needs of the market target. Finally, the strategic marketing plan assembles the various decisions in targeting, setting objectives, and marketing program positioning. Strategic marketing planning is a continuing process of making strategic decisions, implementing them, and evaluating and managing the marketing strategy.

NOTES

1. The Limited, Inc., *1983 Annual Report*, 4–5.
2. "Marketing: The New Priority," *Business Week*, November 21, 1983, 96.
3. "U.S. Mint to Suspend Production in March of Anthony Dollars," *The Wall Street Journal*, February 20, 1980, 48.
4. Jeff Guinn, "Image Problem Is Under Attack at Radio Shack," *Fort Worth Star-Telegram*, January 13, 1984, D1 and 2.
5. "Making Service a Potent Marketing Tool," *Business Week*, June 11, 1984, 170.
6. Bernie Whalen, "People-Oriented Marketing Delivers a Lot of Dough for Domino's," *Marketing News*, March 16, 1984, 4 and 5.
7. "Why Hewlett-Packard Overhauled Its Management," *Business Week*, July 30, 1984, 111–12.
8. "Listening to the Voice of the Marketplace," *Business Week*, February 21, 1983, 94.
9. "Kotler: Rethink the Marketing Concept," *Marketing News*, September 14, 1984, 1 and 22.
10. Steve Harrell, in a speech at the Plenary Session of American Marketing Association's Educators' Meeting, Chicago, August 5, 1980.
11. Peter F. Drucker, *Management: Tasks, Responsibilities, Practices* (New York: Harper & Row, 1974), 63.
12. George A. Steiner, *Strategic Planning* (New York: Free Press, 1979), 13–14.
13. Derek F. Abell and John S. Hammond, *Strategic Market Planning* (Englewood Cliffs, N.J.: Prentice-Hall, 1979), 6–7.
14. Steiner, *Strategic Planning*, 15.
15. "RCA Makes the Long-Expected Decision to Market Its Home Video-Disk System," *The Wall Street Journal*, January 10, 1979, 6.
16. Laura Landro, "RCA Reaches Crossroads on Future of Its Troubled Videodisk Player," *The Wall Street Journal*, September 13, 1983, 35. 35.
17. "The Anatomy of RCA's Videodisc Failure," *Business Week*, April 23, 1984, 89–90.
18. "Viva Videodisks!" *Forbes*, March 11, 1985, 13.
19. Adapted from Louis Kraar, "Palm Beach, Inc.'s Lucrative Labels," *Fortune*, January 15, 1979, 104–7.
20. Ibid., 106.
21. Ronald N. Paul, Neil B. Donavan, and James W. Taylor, "The Reality Gap in Strategic Planning," *Harvard Business Review*, May–June 1978, 129.

QUESTIONS FOR REVIEW AND DISCUSSION

1. Suggest some methods that U.S. Mint officials could have used to determine consumers' reactions to the Susan B. Anthony dollar *before* placing it into circulation.
2. Discuss the use of the marketing concept as a guiding philosophy for a social service organization, giving particular attention to user needs and wants.
3. Compare and contrast the corporate mission of The Limited with that of Hewlett-Packard Company.
4. Identify and discuss the various problems a company may encounter

if management does not develop and implement strategic plans.

5. Indicate the strategic planning role and functions you feel the chief marketing executive and staff should be responsible for in a company (or division). Support your arguments, showing why these responsibilities should be assigned to marketing.

6. Suppose you have been appointed to the top marketing post of a corporation and the president has asked you to explain strategic marketing planning to the board of directors. Develop an outline of your presentation.

7. How can a firm best identify a business advantage?

8. A company manufactures single-edged disposable razors. Define and describe the product-market.

9. Discuss the importance of strategic evaluation in today's marketing environment.

10. What types of technological advances can you suggest that might have enabled the RCA videodisk player to gain a marketable advantage over the videocassette recorder? What market target strategies could be used by RCA, given these advantages?

STRATEGIC APPLICATION 1-1

E. T. WRIGHT & CO.

Five years ago, E. T. Wright & Co. couldn't sell enough shoes to keep its factory in Rockland, Mass., busy. Wright's stodgy but durable dress shoes appealed mostly to an aging group of well-off men who bought them only when an old pair wore out. Department stores, which once accounted for 30% of Wright's sales, had lost interest in stocking the expensive footwear because of inventory costs.

Today, Wright's employees are working overtime, sales are about $19 million a year and growing at about a 6% annual rate; management is seeking ways to expand capacity. "They're strong as horseradish," says Ivor Olson, an industry consultant who has advised the company.

Wright, still owned by the families of those who founded it in 1895, is a survivor in an ailing industry. The expensive men's shoe market hasn't been as hard hit by imports as have other segments—less than a third of it, Wright estimates, has been captured by foreign companies,

compared to 74% of the entire U.S. footwear market. Still, dozens of Wright's peers have sold their brand names or folded altogether, victims of poor management, financial weakness, changing fashions or distribution problems.

Wright's better times reflect the success of two risky marketing moves the company made at the beginning of the decade. It broadened its product line to include the unfamiliar: both more stylish and less expensive shoes. And, despite grousing from some retailers, it began selling shoes by mail.

Meanwhile, Wright didn't try to cheapen its traditional shoes. Instead, it kept raising the price—now at $130 a pair. Says John Quelch, a Harvard Business School marketing professor who joined Wright's board two years ago: "If one religiously follows a path of developing and sustaining a premium, quality position in the market, then a domestic manufacturer can prosper in a declining industry."

Wright's first new products were so slightly different from its old ones that only a shoemaker could appreciate the changes, but soon it added shoes without laces, shoes with tassels, shoes with crepe soles. It began to make lighter, more flexible shoes and hand-sewn shoes that appealed to younger men.

The tactic worked. Wright shoes, which had been popular only with men older than 55, began to catch on with younger customers. "We're getting nice young men, 30 to 35, who are just beginning to make good money so they can afford $130 shoes," says Herbert Sherman, a Philadelphia shoe retailer.

"Young men are less price conscious today about footwear than they used to be," says Alfred L. Donovan, Wright's president and grandson of one of its founders. "After all, they pay $120 for a pair of sneakers."

Nevertheless, Wright figures that only 2% of adult American men buy high-priced shoes. So Wright recently began to sell $80 rubber-sole casual shoes made to its specifications by two other small companies. "If you're geared to make $130 footwear, you really can't make $80 footwear in the same factory," says Joseph Morocco, Wright vice president.

Wright's move into mail order was as unpopular with some retailers as its new products were popular. "I just don't like the idea of them competing with us," says Mr. Sherman in Philadelphia. But, he adds, "If I were in their boots, I would have done the same thing."

Mr. Olson, the consultant, says Wright "was clinging to one channel of distribution, the independent shoe store and key department stores." Some shoe manufacturers addressed the distribution problem by opening their own stores, but Wright felt it didn't have the expertise for that and it feared the expense of spreading inventory across the country. Inventory is no small consideration for a shoemaker. Wright stocks about 45,000 pairs worth $2.25 million at wholesale. For one style, the company has 84 different sizes.

Wright figured a mail-order business could share its central inventory. So in 1979, the company hired a direct-mail whiz and began mailing catalogs. The business grew slowly, in part because Wright built its mailing list of about 200,000 names mostly through its own ads.

"We didn't make any money for the first three years," Mr. Donovan says. But now 25% of Wright's sales come by mail, and the company says that most of the retailers have stopped complaining. Even Mr. Sherman, the Philadelphia retailer, admits his sales haven't suffered since Wright began selling by mail.

Now Mr. Donovan and Mr. Morocco, who constitute half of the Wright's management team, are worrying about ways to make more shoes. Expansion of the Rockland factory isn't likely; factory workers are hard to come by in Boston's high-tech suburbs and Wright's wages average a relatively low $7 an hour. Instead, Wright is experimenting with contract manufacturing—providing leather to other companies to see if they can stitch the pieces together to Wright's standards for its high-priced shoes.

One potential problem has eased, however. Six months ago, Wright was worrying about the steady disappearance of the New England companies that sell insoles, heels, eyelets and other parts. But recent government moves to protect domestic shoemakers should help keep suppliers in business, Wright believes.

That's a relief. Says Mr. Donovan: "You can't have a cab go into Boston and pick up some eyelets if the factory is in Manila."

DISCUSSION QUESTIONS

1. Prepare a detailed description and assessment of Wright's marketing strategy.
2. Is the company following the guidelines of the marketing concept?
3. Why might distribution by mail as well as through retail stores antagonize retailers?
4. What changes do you recommend be made in Wright's marketing strategy?

STRATEGIC APPLICATION 1-2

ORE-IDA FOODS

Campbell Soup Co. built its empire by giving the consumer easy-to-prepare soups, and General Mills did the same with cake mixes. So it is with Ore-Ida Foods.

This Boise, Ida.-based subsidiary of H. J. Heinz Co. has grown to become one of the most successful brands in U.S. grocery stores by turning a huge homemade market into one in which customers would just as soon grab the product from supermarket shelves.

Ore-Ida has been so successful, in fact, that it dominates what competition it has, holding a 50% share of the U.S. frozen potato market in pounds at retail and about 61% in dollars. In 1983, the Ore-Ida brand ranked 10th among all food brands in dollar sales at retail (Campbell's condensed soups were first) and third among all frozen brands (after Stouffer's single dishes and Minute Maid orange juice).

Also, Ore-Ida holds about a 12% share of the huge foodservice market for frozen potatoes, which is estimated at 3.7 billion lbs., or about four times the size of the retail market.

It's this foodservice market, driven by fast-food giants such as McDonald's Corp. and Burger King Corp. and the vast sums they've spent to convince a generation of kids that a hot serving of french fries is a right, that has helped Ore-Ida's development of the home market.

U.S. Department of Agriculture statistics tell the story: Per-capita consumption of frozen potatoes—almost all of which are fried—in the U.S. went from 2.7 lbs. in 1960 to 11.7 lbs. in 1970 to 16.9 lbs. in 1980. In 1983, it is estimated, it went up to 19.8 lbs.

Ironically, this was going on while many food processors were rushing in to ride the low-calorie, health-food crest. (Ore-Ida hedged its bets; in 1978 it acquired Foodways National, packers of the frozen Weight Watchers brand.)

In a given month, according to Ore-Ida research, 65% of U.S. households will prepare fried potatoes, either from scratch or from a commercial frozen product. As for away-from-home consumption, NPD Research shows that fries are served as part of 23% of all restaurant meals. (The only item that tops that penetration is soft drinks, with 29%.)

McDonald's alone, it is estimated, prepares 650 million lbs. of frozen fried potatoes a year; Burger King, for whom Ore-Ida is a major supplier, fries between 280 million and 300 million lbs.

Many factors influenced Ore-Ida's growth from a nearly defunct frozen-vegetable processor to the top of the in-home frozen potato industry. Those factors include Heinz' purchase of Ore-Ida, the overhaul of Ore-Ida's top management, the painful transition from a sales-driven to a marketing-driven organization, the push into national distribution, inept competition, Doyle Dane Bernbach's "All-righta" campaign, the launch of numerous flanker items and Ore-Ida's latest expansion—opening the in-home fried potato market in Japan.

But long before all this occurred, brothers Nephi and Golden Grigg bought a small freezing factory in 1951 in Ontario, Ore., a town of 8,800 on the Idaho border and smack in the middle of America's most fertile potato growing region.

The Griggs organized Oregon Frozen Foods and emphasized corn, but in 1952 they started processing frozen french fried potatoes and became a pioneer in that business. A major breakthrough came in 1958 when the company developed Tater Tots, an extruded product that uses scraps left from making french fries, thereby increasing over-all efficiency and processing profitability.

Oregon Frozen Foods prospered. In 1961, it changed its name to Ore-Ida Foods, went public, and opened a second potato processing plant, in Burley, Ida.

A master broker, D. B. Berelson & Co. of San Francisco, purchased the sales rights to Ore-Ida brands at retail, and through a growing network of frozen food brokers, a line of frozen potatoes, corn on the cob, onion rings and chopped onions was being pushed into national distribution.

But distribution was still weak and spotty in the Northeast, a strong area for fried potato consumption and the bastion of the Birds Eye division of General Foods, Ore-Ida's main competitor at the time.

Packaging for the retail line of frozen potatoes was paper carton with a prominent Idaho-shaped logo—the better to identify with that state's growing reputation for quality potatoes. Consumer awareness of the Ore-Ida brand name was 20% at the time.

This was the market status at Ore-Ida when Frank B. Armour, then vice-chairman of Heinz, fingered it for acqui-

sition, about a year after he had engineered the purchase of Star-Kist Foods.

Ore-Ida had annual sales of $30.8 million and about a 23% share of the U.S. frozen potato market at retail when, in 1965, it was sold to Heinz for stock valued at $29.7 million.

McKinsey & Co. was brought in to study efficiency possibilities, and things seemed to be proceeding normally until 22 months later.

"A lot of things were chaotic when we came into this company," says Robert K. Pedersen, who was brought in by Mr. Armour from Star-Kist, where he was vp-operations, to head Ore-Ida. "On a Monday in August, 1967—it's called Black Monday by some of the people who are still around—the Heinz board, and Burt Gookin [at the time, ceo of Heinz] particularly, decided it had to change management.

"So they came out here and summarily fired the top seven people," he says. Three days later, the call went out to Mr. Pedersen, who came with the understanding that in a short while he would become president-ceo of Ore-Ida, a post he held until retirement in 1977.

McKinsey's study uncovered two main problems: Possible conflicts of interest and rundown plants.

Top executives of the old management were also potato farmers contracting their crops to Ore-Ida. Also, a year earlier, with the idea that Ore-Ida should raise its own raw material, the company had purchased the 10,000-acre Skyline Farms near Ontario, Ore.

"Skyline never did make it because it was poor soil," Mr. Pedersen says, "and we were losing a million and a half bucks a year on it."

Also, the Skyline purchase had angered local farmers.

The other main problem was that Ore-Ida's plants were rundown. "They [the previous management] had set the company up to sell," Mr. Pedersen says.

"They had capitalized pencils, but they had spent very little money on repair or maintenance for two or three years. We had a few problems on quality, too. Things were sloppy."

To solve these and other problems, Mr. Armour recruited a new Ore-Ida management board, and it met every morning. All board members except Mr. Pedersen, who was in his mid-40s at the time, were in their early 30s. (One, J. Wray Connolly, a 32-year-old lawyer from Heinz brought in to clean up procurement, is today president of Heinz U.S.A.)

"Frank Armour realized we needed marketing skills," Mr. Pedersen says, "and he had a fellow he liked in Pittsburgh, Paul Corddry, the brand manager on ketchup."

Mr. Corddry, 32 at the time, joined Ore-Ida's sales operation, which was then in San Francisco, as general manager-product marketing; he became vp-marketing a year later.

Also in 1968, the new management bought out D. B. Berelson's rights to sell Ore-Ida products and brought in an ex-Berelson executive, William Moseley, to be vp-sales.

Attracting and holding the bright new team of young executives to Ontario, Ore., was proving a real problem, and the decision was made to move corporate headquarters to Boise.

Then in mid-1969, Ore-Ida's main plant in Ontario was destroyed by fire. This gave Gerald D. Herrick, the new vp-operations, the opportunity to build a modern, efficient plant—a job he finished in six months. This set the stage to standardize equipment and procedures in all plants and was a big step toward a key Ore-Ida goal: Low cost production and high quality control.

"Our yield was below 45% then," Mr. Pedersen says in discussing the amount of salable product derived from raw potatoes on the dock, "and Gerry was able to get it well above 50%."

The capital expenditure authorization from Heinz was symbolic; it helped quell rumors that Heinz was thinking of selling Ore-Ida.

With operational problems on the mend, attention at Ore-Ida increasingly turned to marketing expansion—increased distribution and new products—and this threw the spotlight on Mr. Corddry.

"Heinz, Burt Gookin especially, dictated that Ore-Ida was to be a consumer-driven company, marketing directed," Mr. Pedersen says, "and I've always felt it was smart to do what your boss wants."

Mr. Corddry had started the marketing ball rolling in 1967 when he joined the company by retaining Glendinning Associates, a Westport, Conn., marketing consulting company. Then Mr. Corddry retained Doyle Dane Bernbach, Los Angeles, as Ore-Ida's first agency of record.

The next step was to recruit a marketing staff, and five young assistant product managers were hired; none had package goods experience, and a training program was instigated.

In 1969, a crucial decision in Ore-Ida marketing history was made: "We followed the dictates of Heinz," Mr. Pedersen says. "Give the profit responsibility to marketing, the volume responsibility to sales. So, marketing controlled the budget—and if you don't think that didn't lead to problems! In the past, sales managers in the field could make some expenditures on their own, trade deals; now marketing had to approve trade deals."

Concurrent with this was marketing's need to educate Ore-Ida's new management board, most of whom did not have a marketing background and didn't know what to expect from a consumer-driven organization.

"I found out that in marketing you need to crunch a lot of numbers; you don't wing anything," Mr. Pedersen says.

In 1969, in what was a momentous move, Mr. Corddry recommended Ore-Ida change its retail packaging and its corporate image. Landor Associates in San Francisco was retained to come up with a new design.

One reason for the change was to get out from under the Idaho-shaped logo on existing packaging that implied all Ore-Ida products were made from potatoes grown in Idaho, which was not true.

Also, there was a desire to have packaging that would create a dramatic billboard effect in retail freezers and to get away from the "commodity look" believed to be associated with existing packaging.

Consumer research indicated that there was not even a consistency in the way people pronounced the word "Ore-Ida," particularly on the East Coast, and only one-third of the respondents associated the word with potatoes.

Landor came up with a bold design and a new double-leaf logo printed in orange and brown to depict the company's earthy primary product—potatoes. This recommendation led to what Mr. Corddry now recalls as "major battles."

For one, sales of Ore-Ida products were growing and the traditionalists said, "Why fix something that isn't broken?" Second, it would cost $300,000 to switch to polyethylene bagging, and, "That was $300,000 we didn't have," Mr. Pedersen says.

More important, sales opposed the move, and that focused the hostility. "It got to the point where they [sales and marketing] weren't talking," Mr. Pedersen says. "Bill Mosely was a traditionalist, one hell of a salesman—a volume salesman, but I finally had to make a decision—one of the toughest I had to make there—to let Mosely go."

In 1971 sales and marketing at Ore-Ida were combined into one division under the direction of Mr. Corddry. "You've got to make marketing predominant in that they control the budget, but you've got to make sure you have sales people who appreciate that."

To make it work harmoniously, he says, sales must be given a lot of input into the marketing decision making process.

After beefing up East Coast distribution, Mr. Corddry was ready in 1972 to make a proud announcement: After years of local market tv and newspaper advertising, Ore-Ida would have its first national campaign—a seven-page schedule in six consumer magazines, including *Family Circle, Good Housekeeping* and *Reader's Digest.* Six potato items would be featured.

"The purpose of the new campaign," Mr. Corddry wrote at the time, "is to build awareness of the Ore-Ida brand name and link our name with quality. We hope to accomplish this by clearly establishing the company and its people as potato people who really know their business."

Earlier, in February, 1970, Ore-Ida marketing had started another project that had considerable potential to expand in-home consumption of frozen fried potatoes. It proved to be a drawn-out project that was never successful.

It was common at the time for people at home to cook frozen french fries in a skillet. The way around this messy, sales-inhibiting procedure, Ore-Ida figured, was a line of products that could be cooked in an oven, but still would have the attributes of a product that had been deep fried. Research showed some consumers would be willing to pay a premium price for such a product.

The product was called Deep Fries, and the slogan was, "The frozen french fries that actually fry."

Deep Fries went into test market under that name with no Ore-Ida identification and at a premium price over regular Ore-Ida fries. This was done to minimize cannibalization of existing Ore-Ida products, a continuing concern as Ore-Ida's line extensions and flanker items grew.

Deep Fries did well enough in three test markets to justify a rollout, but that fell flat because, Mr. Kluth says, "We didn't provide enough ad support." One consequence, according to Stephen J. Encarnacacao, who was product manager on the line, was that brand name recall was low.

In 1974, Ore-Ida tried again, but with a much different approach. This time Deep Fries went into seven test markets with a new name: Heinz Deep Fries, the first time an Ore-Ida product had leaned on its parent's name for consumer recognition.

Advertising had been shifted from Doyle Dane Bernbach to Foote, Cone & Belding/Honig, Los Angeles, and there was a new "self-sizzling" slogan.

The result is that today Heinz Deep Fries distribution is limited to a few northeastern markets, but it is still a major brand with a 7% or 8% share in New York and Boston.

The experience had another impact: The Ore-Ida account was moved from the San Francisco office of Doyle Dane to the New York office, where it's been since, and the development of Ore-Ida's first national tv ad program was in the works.

SOURCE: Jack J. Honomichl, "Spud-King Ore-Ida Turns Tatters into Taters," *Advertising Age,* November 12, 1984, 4, 58, and 60.

DISCUSSION QUESTIONS

1. Is Ore-Ida following the guidelines advocated by the marketing concept?
2. Analyze demographic and socioeconomic trends that may affect sales of Ore-Ida products in the future.
3. Discuss other frozen potato innovations that Ore-Ida might consider.
4. Discuss the decision to "revamp" the Ore-Ida logo and packaging.

CHAPTER 2

Corporate Strategic Planning

The turbulent 1980s have forced many corporate managements to alter their future strategies in attempting to take advantage of opportunities, counter threats, and improve performance. General Mills, Inc. began an aggressive diversification program in the early 1970s, expanding from its food processing business. It was growing slowly and was generating cash that could be used to invest in other business areas. By the early 1980s the company was operating in five major business areas: consumer foods, restaurants, toys, fashions, and specialty retailing. Sales in 1985 were $4.3 billion. In early 1985 management announced plans to move out of toys and fashions, concentrating instead on consumer foods and restaurants.[1] Other food processing companies, including Quaker Oats Co., Beatrice Companies, Inc., and Ralston Purina Company, had already eliminated their nonfood business units. General Mills's management found that businesses such as the toys and fashion groups were too different from the food business. These ventures proved to be high in risk, cyclical, and capital-intensive, requiring a more entrepreneurial management style than provided by the food company. The units to be eliminated included Kenner Products, Parker Brothers, Izod Ltd., Monet Jewelry, Ship 'n Shore, and Foot-Joy Inc. Interestingly, while General Mills was moving into nonfood businesses, its competitors were expanding their basic food businesses. General Mills diversification and return to concentration on the basic business illustrates the kinds of decisions that are involved in developing and implementing strategies for a large corporation. Corporate strategic planning is a challenging responsibility for top management. The decisions that are made establish the strategy guidelines for the corporation.

This chapter examines the strategic decisions that the managements of companies like General Mills must make in planning the future of their organizations. The chapter begins with an overview of the planning process, consideration of business mission, and a description of the possible paths of corporate development. A discussion of the company situation assessment and corporate strategy follows. Next, the task of forming strategic business units is considered. Finally, the issues and decisions in establishing planning guidelines for strategic planning are examined and illustrated.

STRATEGIC PLANNING PROCESS

Top management of a corporation must decide the nature and scope of the business, its objectives, the directions of future development, and strategies for each part of the business. The General Mills example illustrates several corporate strategic planning activities, such as altering business scope, objectives, strategy, and the composition of a multiunit corporation. The major stages in strategic planning for a business like General Mills are shown in Exhibit 2-1. A brief description follows:

EXHIBIT 2-1   Corporate Strategic Planning Process

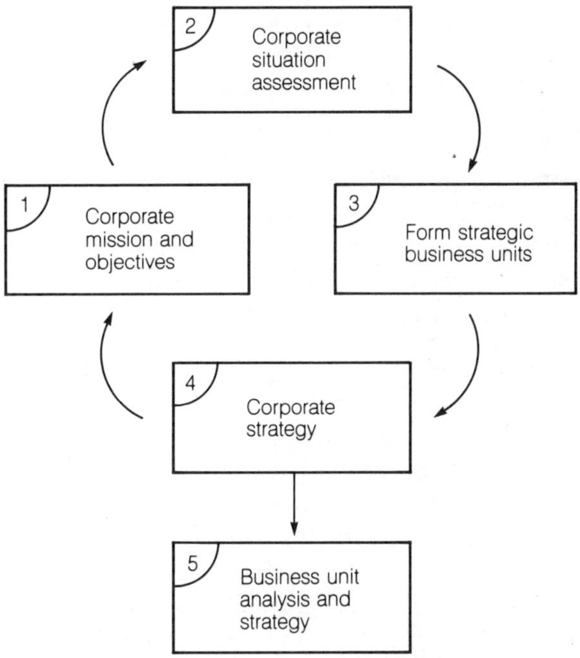

Corporate Mission and Objectives Deciding the nature and scope of the business, its future direction of development, and performance objectives is the starting point in corporate strategy. Business definition establishes the strategic arena of the firm.

Situation Assessment This activity consists of evaluating relevant environmental influences, market opportunities and threats, competitive situation, and company strengths and weaknesses.

Form Strategic Business Units Since many corporations are operating in more than one category of business, the components must be identified. Each part of the corporation is called a strategic business unit (SBU). An SBU performs all or many of the business functions, such as marketing, production, and finance.

Corporate Strategy Management must decide the overall strategy for the corporation, indicating guidelines for SBU strategy development.

Business Unit Analysis and Strategy This part of the planning process consists of the SBU situation analysis, strategy determination, and implementation and control of strategy for each SBU.

The strategic planning process is a continuing one; it begins by defining the mission of the business. We should conduct on a regular basis an assessment of the situation faced by a corporation. The corporate mission may, over time, be changed to respond to the findings of such an assessment; for example, General Mills' decision to focus on the food business. Strategies need to be developed for the product and market areas that determine the composition of a business. An important part of the strategic planning process in a firm made up of more than one business unit is a periodic analysis of the different business areas. These business units often have different objectives and strategies. The strategic plan for each unit spells out how the unit will fulfill its assigned role in the corporation. Underlying each unit's strategic plan are functional strategies for such supporting areas as marketing, finance, and operations. Strategies are then implemented and managed. Corporate strategic planning is examined in this chapter, while business unit analysis and strategy are considered in Chapter 3.

Before moving into an expanded discussion of Exhibit 2-1, we need to consider two issues. First, compare Exhibit 1-3, which shows the strategic marketing planning process around which this book is organized, and Exhibit 2-1, which indicates the major stages in corporate strategic planning. Since the primary concern of this book is strategic marketing, the steps in corporate strategic planning were first shown in Exhibit 1-3 in an abbreviated form. Exhibit 2-1 provides additional details on this topic in order to guide their discussion in Chapters 2 and 3. In a similar manner, we will provide more details about the other strategic marketing planning stages of Exhibit 1-3 when we examine these stages in Chapters 5 through 18. Second, consider the sequence of decisions and activities shown in Exhibits 1–3 and 2–1. While these diagrams attempt to indicate the sequence of planning activities, we need to keep in mind that many activities shown later in the process also bear upon the earlier stages. For example, defining and analyzing product-markets are important to SBU analysis, the corporate situation assessment, and other strategic planning activities. This factor highlights the close tie between corporate strategic planning and marketing strategic planning. The important point to recognize is that strategic planning is a process in which the various stages are closely related.

Deciding Corporate Mission

The corporate mission statement defines the nature and scope of a business and provides important guidelines for managing the corporation. Management must initially establish the nature and scope of a firm's operations and adjust these decisions as necessary over time. Strategic choices about where the firm is going in the future—choices that take into account company capabilities, resources, opportunities, and problems—establish the mission of the enterprise.

Early in the planning process we need to examine the corporate mission and develop a statement of mission. This statement is reviewed and updated as shifts in the strategic direction of the enterprise occur over time. The mission statement spells out what management of the corporation wants it to be, and it establishes the following important guidelines for strategic planning:

1. The reason for the company's existence and its responsibilities to stockholders, employees, society, and various other stakeholders.
2. The customer needs that are satisfied by the firm's products or services (areas of product and market involvement).
3. The extent of specialization within each product-market area.
4. The amount and types of product-market diversification desired by management.
5. Management's performance expectations for the company.
6. Other general guidelines for overall business strategy, such as technologies to be used and the role of research and development in the corporation.

Exhibit 2–2 shows the corporate mission statement for Northern Indiana Public Service Company. NIPSCO supplies electricity and natural gas in northern Indiana. The utility's 1986 revenues were about $2.1 billion.[2] Note that NIPSCO's management has not restricted its mission to supplying electricity and gas. Instead, the energy and energy-related services could extend into other services.

EXHIBIT 2-2   Corporate Mission Statement—Northern Indiana Public
Service Company

NIPSCO is an energy company committed to profitability on the basis
of providing fair values and competitive products in energy and energy-
related services.

THE COMPANY is dedicated to rendering quality service and will strive
to achieve customer satisfaction.

THE COMPANY will maximize productivity of its human and capital
resources for the benefit of its customers, investors, and employees.

THE COMPANY will provide efficient, reliable, and modern energy
capability to all customers and will support the growth, vitality, and
diversity of its markets.

THE COMPANY will also pursue other energy-related business ventures
that offer a profit opportunity and that can better utilize its service
organization and other resources.

THE COMPANY is committed to providing an environment for its
employees that includes training and career development, compensation
programs, and workplace facilities necessary to achieve job satisfaction
and high productivity.

THE COMPANY will communicate actively with customers, investors,
employees, and the public, and will encourage responsible community
leadership in its service area.

SOURCE: NIPSCO *1984 Annual Report*, 2.

Factors Affecting Mission.   Several factors help determine the nature and scope of the business mission. Among these factors are the following:

> *benefits provided to the customer,*
> *technologies used* (to perform particular customer functions),
> *customer segments served* (market targets), and
> *level in the distribution system* (level of participation in the se-
> quence of stages in the value-added system from raw materials to
> the end user).[3]

An illustration will highlight how each of the factors contributes to
business definition. Durr-Fillauer Medical, Inc. distributes pharmaceuticals, drugstore sundries, medical products, and orthotic-prosthetic
devices to hospitals, pharmacies, nursing homes, physician offices, and
laboratories.[4] The company also manufacturers, fabricates, and distributes components for artificial limbs and braces. The customer benefits consist of supplying various medical products and offering assistance in product use; the technologies used are various distribution
capabilities, such as transportation, storage, and communications; the
customer segments consist of hospitals, physicians, and other medical

facilities; and the distribution is at the wholesale level (and the manufacturing level for limb and brace components). Durr-Fillauer's 1985 sales were $427 million and net income after taxes was $6.1 million.

An overriding influence on the mission decision is what management wants the business to be. Acknowledging the constraining nature of capabilities, resources, opportunities, and problems, management is left with a considerable degree of flexibility in making the decision as well as changing it in the future. Uncontrollable factors may create the need for alteration of mission. Management must decide how to solve a problem or capitalize upon an opportunity. A leading management authority describes the task: "Defining the purpose and mission of the business is difficult, painful, and risky. But it alone enables business to set objectives, to develop strategies, to concentrate its resources and to go to work. It alone enables a business to be managed for performance."[5]

Corporate Objectives. In addition to a mission statement, objectives should be indicated so that the performance of the enterprise can be gauged. The mission statement does not change very often, if at all. Objectives are more likely to be altered as conditions and performance change over time. Corporate objectives are often established in the following areas: *marketing, innovation, resources, productivity, social responsibility,* and *finances.*[6] Examples include growth and market share expectations, employee training and development, new product targets, return on invested capital, earnings growth rates, debt limits, energy reduction objectives, and pollution standards. When corporate objectives are general, it is important that they be made more specific at lower levels in the organization. Recall from Chapter 1 that objectives are set at several levels in an organization beginning with those indicating the enterprise's overall performance targets. Each major business component should also have objectives since one business area, such as the General Mills retail chain, may not have the same objectives as one of the firm's other units. Objectives should be realistic and specific to the extent that management can measure progress toward them.

Corporate Development Alternatives

The major corporate development options are shown in Exhibit 2-3. There are, of course, many specific combinations of these major options. Most companies start a business in some core area. Success often leads to expanding into related areas and sometimes entirely new product-market areas. An examination of each alternative will provide an understanding of corporate expansion activities.

Core Business. The initial venture of an enterprise is designated the core business, as food processing is for General Mills. Many firms start

---

EXHIBIT 2-3 Corporate Development Options

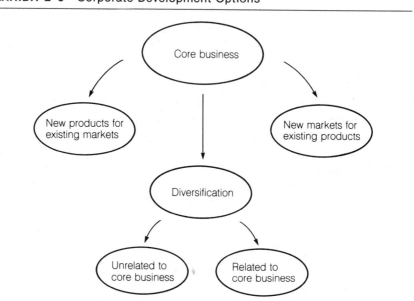

---

out serving one product-market. The product or service offered may be a single product or line of products. This strategy, when it involves a single product-market, offers the advantages of specialization but contains the risks of being dependent on one set of customer needs. As a corporation grows and prospers, management often decides to move into other product and market areas, as shown in Exhibit 2-3. One company that has stayed close to the core business since its founding in 1896 is Tootsie Roll Industries. "Fully 93 percent of its sale still come from the basic Tootsie Roll and its permutations such as Tootsie Pops, Flavor Rolls, Caramel Pops, and Tootsie Squares."[7] This single-product business continues to prosper although management recognizes the risks of having all its eggs in the Tootsie Roll basket. The chief executive officer has publicly stated a desire to diversify out of the candy field. With no long-term debt and a strong cash position, the money is available. Management's criteria for an acquisition include companies in a related field, located in the Midwest or East, sales from $5 to $15 million, and a capable management willing to stay with the firm.[8]

Rarely does a successful single product-market firm stay with the original business. Instead, management decides to pursue at some point one or more of the alternatives shown in Exhibit 2-3. Reduction of the dependence on the core business is a major factor in corporate development. Of course, financial resources are necessary to expand into related or new areas. In some situations, selling the business may offer management an attractive opportunity for expansion. For example, Entenmann's Inc., a small but highly successful bakery in the Northeast and Florida, lacked the capital needed to expand at a rate desired by its owner-managers. They sold the company in 1978 to Warner-Lambert, remaining with the company to move it toward national status. Subsequently the bakery was sold to a food-processing company.

New Markets for Existing Products.   One way to expand away from serving a single product-market is to serve other needs and wants by using the same product or a similar product. Northern Indiana Public Service Company, for example, supplies electricity and natural gas to both commercial and household customers. For many companies, expanding into new markets is a natural line of development. This strategy reduces the risks of depending upon a single market yet it allows the use of existing technical and production capabilities. If we decide to pursue this strategy, we must have adequate resources for expansion and be able to develop a new marketing strategy. Since it may be difficult to acquire a marketing capability or to turn it over to a marketing intermediary, we need to recognize the requirements for internal marketing strategy development if we adopt this alternative. The primary caution to be exercised is to be sure to make a careful evaluation of the new market opportunity's feasibility and attractiveness.

New Products for Existing Markets.   Another strategy for shifting away from dependence on one product is to expand the product mix offered to the firm's target market. Magic Chef, the range and oven manufacturer, in 1979 added to its appliance offering by acquiring lines of washers and dryers and refrigerators and freezers. Use of common distribution channels, promotional support, and research and development are among the possible advantages of this strategy. New products can be developed internally, although acquisition is faster. Resources are necessary to support either alternative. A disadvantage of this strategy is that the company will continue to depend on a particular product-market area, such as household appliances.

Diversification.   Finally, diversification is a popular option for corporate development by many firms. The distinction between diversification and product or market expansion is that diversification involves movement into a new product-market area either by internal development or acquisition. This option is often the riskiest and costliest of all those shown in Exhibit 2–3. Yet it may be an attractive avenue for growth if existing product-market areas face slow growth, if resources for diversification are available, and if good choices are made. For example, General Mills benefited from some of its diversifications, such as restaurants, but the venture into toys and fashions did not prove to be an attractive growth opportunity. Diversification, once it has been successfully implemented, offers the advantage of spreading risks over two or more segments of the business. Diversification may follow one of two avenues: (1) movement into different, yet related product-market areas, or (2) building the corporation into a conglomerate that consists of a few or several unrelated product-market areas.

While the risks of bad diversifications are clear, the rewards of good diversification strategies can be substantial. Consider, for example, General Signal Corp., one of the fastest-growing conglomerates in the United States. The company's development under the leadership of Nathan R. Owen, chairman and CEO is impressive:

> Thanks to 27 deals, all cut by the chairman himself over the past two decades, General Signal has been transformed from a doddering maker of railroad signals into a thriving company that also produces electric instruments, water-treatment equipment, and other kinds of sophisticated controls. The company's sales, stuck at around $20 million in the late 1950s before Owen appeared on the scene, are expected to reach $1.5 billion in 1980. General Signal's latest foray is into the fast-growing semiconductor industry.[9]

The title of the cover story in the June 3, 1985 issue of *Business Week* was: "Do Mergers Really Work?" The story then replied, "No, not very often. And that raises even more questions about the current merger mania." Acquisitions sometimes are logical, such as Nabisco and Standard Brands, Allied and Bendix, and Heinz and Weight Watchers. Nevertheless, the track record of mergers in general is not impressive. Examples of unsuccessful acquisitions include Mobil Oil Corp.'s purchase of Marcor Inc. (Montgomery Ward & Co., Inc. and Container Corp. of America), The Greyhound Corporation's purchase of Armour, and Exxon Corporation's acquisition of Reliance Electric.)

What are the characteristics of a sound diversification strategy? Analysis of successful diversification strategies suggests that the following factors are often important:

1. Top management has the capabilities to manage a portfolio of businesses, including a proven record of sound strategic planning. Adequate cash for diversification is also essential.
2. The new business areas are in attractive (fast-growing) product-markets and business strength is high compared to competition.
3. The diversification candidate has one or more key advantages over competing firms such as low-production costs, strong acceptance by customers, proprietary products, marketing strengths, and technical strengths.
4. The business has good internal management and technical people that are strongly committed to the success of the business.
5. Acquisition prospects have a strong financial performance record over several years.

6. The costs of internal development or acquisition are not so high that profitable operation of the business area will be jeopardized.

Clearly, satisfying all of these criteria is difficult, if not impossible. Nevertheless, if a new business area does not offer distinct strategic advantages in terms of the six factors as well as other situation specific factors, success is doubtful. Of course, each situation must be assessed as to its unique characteristics. Regardless of the advantages, movement into entirely new fields is often riskier than expanding into business areas related to a company's existing business activities.

The options shown in Exhibit 2–3 are not mutually exclusive. Movement beyond the core business is typical as businesses grow and mature. A firm may be involved in all the options shown, such as product and market expansion, diversification, and possible divestment of business units. As we have seen, several factors may influence the rate and direction of corporate development activities, including available resources, management's preferences, pending opportunities and threats, corporate management and technical capabilities, and the desire to reduce total dependence of the corporation upon a single product-market area.

SITUATION ASSESSMENT

The corporate situation assessment (sometimes called an *audit*) is "an analysis of data, past, present, and future, that provides a base for pursuing the strategic planning process."[10] The assessment consists of two stages: (1) analyses of environmental influences, market situation, and competition, and (2) a delineation of the strategic opportunities and threats facing the corporation as well as the corporation's strengths and weaknesses. This information is then used as a basis for preparing and implementing strategic plans. Consider, for example, American Hospital Supply Corp.'s analysis of the troubled hospital industry in the mid-1980s that helped to establish the firm's strategic guidelines for becoming the dominant force among its competitors.[11] Cost cutting and higher efficiency placed severe pressures on suppliers. American Hospital adapted quickly to the situation with its pioneering corporate marketing program. From 1979 to 1984 it gained a 10 percent market share based on per-bed sales. Offering the industry's broadest product line and most extensive distribution network, American Hospital also included rebates and price freezes based on volume, low-cost consulting and management programs, a computerized order-entry network connected to 122 distribution centers, inventory control software, and other cost-effective services. This is how the American Hospital corporate customer program works:

Maimonides Medical Center, for example, a 700-bed hospital in Brooklyn, N.Y., will buy about 70% of its supplies—$6 million this year—under a corporate agreement with American Hospital. And it hopes to transfer most of the rest of its business to American Hospital in coming years. Why not? The hospital reduced average supply prices 1.2% last year while hospitals nationwide absorbed an average 5% increase. With almost immediate delivery available from a nearby New Jersey warehouse, Maimonides has pared inventories to $150 a bed from about $1,200 since becoming a corporate customer in 1979.

American Hospital supplied the center's inventory control software. An American Hospital consultant helped streamline inventory procedures. American Hospital has joined Maimonides in a home health-care business—knowing full well the hospital intends to dump its partner as soon as it learns the operation (American Hospital will still get the venture's supply business, however). Does the hospital need a computer program that plots diversification strategy or a briefing on the effect of the new federal prospective payment system for medical treatment? It has but to ask.[12]

Analysis of Environmental Influences

Environmental analysis and forecasting are major activities in the corporate situation assessment. Economic, technical, legal, political, and social factors relevant to the enterprise must be identified and analyzed and their effects on the corporation forecasted. Two kinds of problems may occur in environmental analysis. First, we may not identify soon enough the relevant environmental forces, and it may be too late for us to develop counterstrategies when those forces impact a corporation. The second problem is concerned with interpreting the significance of forecasts of future events and trends. A planned approach to environmental analysis will help to avoid these problems. This process consists of selecting relevant environmental factors, analyzing them, and forecasting their future impact on the business.

Select Relevant Environmental Factors.   While there is a danger in leaving out a potentially important factor, trying to track too many possible influences can be confusing and expensive. We need to identify these factors in the context of corporate areas of present and future interest. Several examples of environmental forces and their impacts upon companies and industries are shown in Exhibit 2–4. Often environmental forces impact a firm in its product-markets so examination of the key factors that can affect each product-market is a good starting point. A useful technique for determining which environmental factors are related to potential strategic actions is to place the factors and actions in a matrix like the one shown in Exhibit 2–5. This matrix is for use by a large credit card company. The idea is to examine the impact linkages between each factor and the various strategic actions. Where

---

EXHIBIT 2-4 Some Illustrative Environmental Forces and Impacts upon Corporations and Industries

Environmental Force		Consequences of the Impact of the Force
Economic		
High interest rates	→	Drastic slowdown in homebuilding
High prices and shortages of oil	→	Reduction in purchases of automobiles and changes in types of automobiles purchased
Technical		
Development of quartz crystal technology by Seiko and others	→	Major alterations in the composition of the watch industry including the demise of several traditional watchmakers
Political		
Changes in the regulations of financial institutions	→	Creation of a new competitive structure in banking and savings institutions including the authority to offer checking accounts and other services by savings institutions
Social		
Changing age-group composition of the population over the next 10 to 20 years	→	Creation of opportunities for some firms and threats for others; for example, the huge increase in the number of adults in the furniture-buying range over the next decade will be a strong stimulus to furniture sales

---

potentially significant linkages exist, we should conduct analyses to forecast the probability of their occurrence.

Analysis and Forecasting. The methods used to analyze and forecast environmental changes range from executive judgment to formal forecasting techniques. We can conduct studies, pool the results, and then feed back the opinions of participants to the panel of experts several times until a consensus is reached. These are called *Delphi studies,* and they have been quite popular in estimating the future impact of environmental factors. Trend extrapolation is also widely used in technological forecasting. Computer models are important tools in economic analyses. We can forecast demographic and socioeconomic changes, such as the future age-group composition of the population, by projecting changes from present levels.

Consider this illustration. Some dramatic changes will occur in the size of different population age-group segments in the United States as we move toward the year 2000. We can also make similar projections for other nations throughout the world. Only two factors affect the age-group distribution in the population: births and deaths—and both can be estimated with high accuracy. Moreover, for many age-groups, estimating births is not necessary. Exhibit 2-6 shows the size and trends

EXHIBIT 2-5 Preliminary Matrix Relating Environmental Change to Potential Strategic Action

Likely external changes

Strategic Planning Components \ Environmental Factors:	National banking chains	Federal Reserve restraints on credit	Computer/ satellite credit data	"Finger-print" identification via satellite	Two-way TV shopping	Anti-discrimination laws (color, sex, age, marital status, etc.)
Emphasis on travellers						
Liberal credit for "good" customers			⊕	⊕		⊕
Fees for use		⊕				
Profit from interest on unpaid balances		⊕				
Integrate with check less banking account	⊕					
Finance buying from home					⊕	

(Potential strategic actions)

⊕ = Important "impact linkages"

source: Harold E. Klein and William H. Newman, "How to Integrate New Environmental Forces into Strategic Planning," *Management Review*, July 1980, 43.

for various age-groups in the United States. Consider the following changes in age-group composition from 1980 to 1990, when the U.S. population will be nearing a quarter of a billion:

During this decade the number of teenagers aged 15 to 19 will decline by 18 percent.
The young adult (20–34) segment will experience slow growth.
The middle-aged (35–49) segment will experience rapid growth.
The senior citizen segment will expand significantly.

After forecasts are made, we need to estimate the consequence of each change to determine strategic opportunities and threats. This final step in strategic situation assessment is considered further after discussing the other components of the analysis.

Product-Market and Competition Analyses

The situation assessment should examine markets and competition in depth. Product-market analyses should highlight trends that may ne-

EXHIBIT 2-6   Age Group Trends in the United States Population

Age	1970 Population	1980 Population	Percent Change 1970–1980	1990 Population	Percent Change 1980–1990
0–4	17,154,337	16,348,254	− 4.7	19,199,700	17.5
5–9	19,956,247	16,699,956	− 16.3	18,599,300	13.8
10–14	20,789,468	18,242,129	− 12.3	16,776,400	− 6.1
15–19	19,070,348	21,168,124	11.0	16,895,000	− 18.4
20–24	16,371,021	21,318,704	30.2	18,352,000	− 12.1
25–29	13,476,993	19,520,919	44.8	21,392,700	11.9
30–34	11,430,436	17,560,920	53.6	21,932,600	27.5
35–39	11,106,851	13,965,302	25.7	19,959,900	46.0
40–44	11,980,954	11,669,408	− 2.6	17,822,400	56.1
45–49	12,115,939	11,089,755	− 8.5	13,968,000	28.8
50–54	11,104,018	11,710,032	5.5	11,416,800	− 0.3
55–59	9,973,028	11,615,254	16.5	10,450,900	− 8.0
60–64	8,616,784	10,087,621	17.1	10,638,700	7.9
65–69	6,991,625	8,782,481	25.6	10,006,400	16.7
70–74	5,443,831	6,798,124	24.9	8,048,100	21.5
75–79	3,834,834	4,793,722	25.0	6,223,900	33.4
80–84	2,284,311	2,935,033	28.5	4,060,500	42.2
85 +	1,510,901	2,240,067	48.3	3,460,900	58.9
Median age	28.1	30.0			

SOURCE: *State Demographics* (Homewood, Ill. Dow Jones-Irwin, 1984), 2.

cessitate changes in corporate strategies. These analyses should include information about demand, customer characteristics, industry, and distribution channels. Since Chapter 5 is devoted to product-market definition and analysis, we will delay further discussion of this area until then.

Like markets, competitors must be monitored on a regular basis. Spotting potential competitors is as important as following what present competitors are doing. In many ways competitor tracking is similar to intelligence gathering and analysis. The following information is often included in competitor analysis:

Identification of actual and potential competitors.
Key competitors' missions, objectives, and strategies.
Position and performance of each competitor in the product-market.
Strengths and limitations with respect to management, finances, marketing, technology, and operations.
Financial performance.
Possible corporation strategy changes in the future.[13]

Our analysis should indicate a profile of each competitor for the above and other relevant areas. Both competitive threats and opportunities should be summarized from the analysis. Estimated future strategies of competitors are important. We will consider in depth competitor analysis in Chapter 7.

Summary of Weaknesses, Opportunities, Threats, and Strengths (WOTS)

A critical and realistic look inside the corporation is also a key part of the situation assessment. We should prepare much of the same information obtained about competitors about our own company with particular emphasis on its strengths and limitations. Exhibit 2–7 shows an illustrative guide to company evaluation. This form can be expanded or modified to fit a particular firm's needs. An essential aspect of the evaluation is to show how our firm measures up to the competition. Exhibit 2–7 can be expanded to compare the factors shown against each key competitor. The purpose of the entire evaluation is to find out where a firm is weak and where it is strong. In a corporation made up of two or more business units, we might make an evaluation for each unit and the entire corporation, unless the corporation is so diversified that a composite would not be meaningful.

The WOTS summary combines all the information obtained from our analysis of environmental factors, product-markets, competitors, and the corporation's strengths and limitations. This summary, in turn, guides the firm's strategic plans. Exhibit 2–8 is an example of a situation assessment summary. As indicated, the summary should also state the strategic implications of each finding in the situation assessment.

EXHIBIT 2–7 Critical Evaluation of the Corporation or a Business Unit

Check off in each category how you evaluate your organization according to:

Column I   Better than anyone else. Substantially in excess of present needs. Definitely leaders.

Column II   Better than average. Good strong performance. No problems.

Column III   Average. Adequate. Competitive. Solid.

Column IV   Should be better. Deteriorating. Cause for concern.

Column V   Definitely worrisome. Must be improved. Bad. Crisis. "We are being clobbered."

Category	I	II	III	IV	V
Finance					
Debit-equity structure	___	___	___	___	___
Inventory turnover	___	___	___	___	___
Customer credit	___	___	___	___	___
Capital resources	___	___	___	___	___
Available cash flow	___	___	___	___	___
Break-even points	___	___	___	___	___
Sales per assets employed	___	___	___	___	___
Ratio fixed to liquid assets	___	___	___	___	___
Performance versus budget	___	___	___	___	___
Return on new investments	___	___	___	___	___
Ownership	___	___	___	___	___
Dividend history	___	___	___	___	___

EXHIBIT 2-7 *(concluded)*

Category	I	II	III	IV	V
Production					
Capacity	___	___	___	___	___
Production processes	___	___	___	___	___
Conversion efficiency	___	___	___	___	___
Labor supply	___	___	___	___	___
Labor productivity	___	___	___	___	___
Raw material supply	___	___	___	___	___
Sales per employee	___	___	___	___	___
Sales per fixed investment	___	___	___	___	___
Age of plant equipment	___	___	___	___	___
Quality control	___	___	___	___	___
On-time shipments	___	___	___	___	___
Downtime	___	___	___	___	___
Space for expansion	___	___	___	___	___
Plant location	___	___	___	___	___
Organization and administration					
Ratio of administrative to production personnel	___	___	___	___	___
Communications	___	___	___	___	___
Clear-cut responsibilities	___	___	___	___	___
Management turnover	___	___	___	___	___
Management information	___	___	___	___	___
Speed of reaction	___	___	___	___	___
Marketing					
Share of market	___	___	___	___	___
Product reputation	___	___	___	___	___
Brand acceptance	___	___	___	___	___
Selling expense	___	___	___	___	___
Customer service	___	___	___	___	___
Distribution facilities	___	___	___	___	___
Sales organization	___	___	___	___	___
Prices	___	___	___	___	___
Number of customers	___	___	___	___	___
Distribution costs	___	___	___	___	___
Market information	___	___	___	___	___
Work force					
Hourly labor	___	___	___	___	___
Clerical labor	___	___	___	___	___
Salespeople	___	___	___	___	___
Scientists and engineers	___	___	___	___	___
Supervisors	___	___	___	___	___
Middle management	___	___	___	___	___
Top management	___	___	___	___	___
Training costs	___	___	___	___	___
Management depth	___	___	___	___	___
Turnover	___	___	___	___	___
Technology					
Product technology	___	___	___	___	___
New products	___	___	___	___	___
Patent position	___	___	___	___	___
R&D organization	___	___	___	___	___
Engineering design capability	___	___	___	___	___

SOURCE: Reprinted by permission of the publisher, from *Long Range Planning for Your Business,* by Merritt L. Kastens, © 1976 by AMACOM, a division of American Management Associations, pp. 52–53. All rights reserved.

EXHIBIT 2-8   Situation Assessment Summary

Factor	*Strategic Implication*
Weaknesses	
Managerial	
We have six different products and continue with a centralized organization that is not working well.	Decentralize.
Too many middle managers have a poor performance rating.	a. In acquiring companies insist on strong management.
	b. Begin management development program.
Markets and products	
Product A is losing market share because it is becoming obsolete.	Redesign product A.
One customer buys 50 percent of product B.	Find new markets for product B to reduce reliance on one customer.
Strengths	
Managerial	
Strong research and development group.	Rely on in-house product development as well as acquisition for expansion.
Markets and products	
Product C has a growing share in a growing market.	Invest to expand market shares and increase return on investment.
Threats	
Competition	
New government safety standards are likely at plant B and cannot be met easily.	Begin now to devise methods to meet the standards to avoid a shutdown.
Facilities	
Chile threatens to nationalize and expropriate our plants.	Begin negotiations with the U.S. state department and the government of Chile.
Opportunities	
Market and products	
Strong growth is forecast for product D in South America	Prepare studies as to whether we should build plants, export, or license in South America.
Finance	
We have a strong cash position, low debt/equity ratio, and a high price/ earnings ratio.	Search for new acquisitions.

SOURCE: Reprinted with permission of Macmillan Publishing Co., Inc. from *Strategic Planning* by George A. Steiner, Copyright © 1979 by The Free Press, a Division of Macmillan Publishing Co., Inc.

The summary should be specific so that it can be used to guide the development of strategic plans. Our assessment should point to areas that may affect our firm's mission and objectives, the strategic analysis of business units, and other aspects of strategic planning.

FORMING STRATEGIC BUSINESS UNITS

Understanding the composition of a business is of vital importance in both corporate and marketing strategic planning. In single-product firms, such as Tootsie Roll Industries, it is easy to determine the composition of the business. In many other firms we need to separate the business into parts to facilitate strategic analysis and planning. When firms are serving multiple markets with different products, grouping similar business areas together facilitates planning. The importance of organizing a large corporation along strategic lines is illustrated by the following statement by the chairman of the board of directors of Manufacturers Hanover Corporation:

> The creation of five strategic business sectors means not only a change in structure, but a change in style—a shift from a *centralized* to a *decentralized* approach to managing your corporation. The new structure also recognizes that we are no longer a bank, per se, but indeed, a financial services corporation.[14]

The five strategic business sectors correspond to the five major customer groups served by Manufacturers Hanover: investment banking, asset-based financing, banking and international, corporate banking, and retail banking. Each sector operates as a stand-alone business with responsibility for meeting targeted objectives. The business functions of each unit include pertinent support groups, such as personnel, financial reporting, planning, operations, and marketing.

Some Definitions

Business Segment, Group, or Division. These terms typically designate the major areas of business of a diversified corporation. Each segment, group, or division often contains a mix of related products (or services), although a single product could be assigned such a designation. Note that this use of the term *segment* does not correspond to a market segment (subgroup of end users in a product-market), which is discussed later in the book. Most large corporations break out their financial reports into business or industry segments according to the guidelines of the Financial Accounting Standards Board. Some firms may establish subgroups of related products within a business segment targeted to different customer groups. The five strategic sectors established by Manufacturers Hanover fall into this category.

Strategic Business Unit. A business segment, group, or division is often too large in terms of product and market composition for use in strategic analysis and planning, and should be divided into more specific strategic units. One of the most popular names for these units is the *strategic business unit* (SBU). Typically these strategy units represent groupings based on product-market similarities:

> Ideally, an SBU should have primary responsibility and authority for managing its basic business functions: engineering, manufacturing, marketing, and distribution. In practice, however, traditions, shared facilities and distribution channels, manpower constraints, and business judgments have resulted in significant deviations from this concept of autonomy. In General Foods, for instance, strategic business units were originally defined on a product line basis, even though several products served overlapping markets and were produced in shared facilities. Later, these product-oriented SBU's were redefined into menu segments, with SBU's like breakfast food, beverage, main meal, dessert, and pet foods targeted toward specific markets, even though these, too, shared common manufacturing and distribution resources.[15]

A strategic business unit is a single product or brand, a line of products, or a mix of related products that meets a common market need or a group of related needs, and the unit's management is responsible for all (or most of the basic business functions). The SBU has its own strategy rather than a shared strategy. Units that do not satisfy these requirements are instead subunits within an SBU.

Often an SBU is comprised of a portfolio itself rather than being a single homogenous unit. In a large study of portfolio planning in corporations, many of the participants indicated that they consider an SBU as being comprised of product-market segments that occupy very different market attractiveness/business strength positions and strategic missions.[16] This finding is logical in that the rationale for SBU formation at the corporate level focuses on the management of shared resources. These businesses often cut across market segments with very different characteristics and opportunities. Consider for example a medium-size bank in a holding company's portfolio. The bank can be considered an SBU that serves retail and commercial customers, each containing market segments.

As an illustration of the business composition of a medium-size corporation, the medical supplies wholesaler, Durr-Fillauer Medical, Inc. is organized into three business segments, as shown in Exhibit 2–9. A business segment is typically made up of products and customer segments that possess some degree of similarity, such as distributing pharmaceuticals and drugstore sundries. A business segment may contain one or more strategic business units. In the case of Durr-Fillauer, each business segment consists of one SBU. In a larger firm a segment might contain several SBUs. For example, General Mills's restaurant segment contains the Red Lobster chain and York Steak Houses SBUs.

Subunits. Various subunits may be formed within a strategic business unit such as marketing planning units. For example, a product line

EXHIBIT 2-9   Business Composition of Durr-Fillauer Medical, Inc.

Business Segments		
Medical-Surgical Division	*Wholesale Drug Division*	*Orthopedic Division*
Supplies over 20,000 items and related services to independent and group-related hospitals, physician offices, nursing homes, clinics, laboratories and other alternate site providers. The division operates 16 sales, service, and distribution centers in seven states.	One of the largest distributors of pharmaceuticals and drugstore sundries in the Southeast. The division distributes products to approximately 2,000 independent and chain drugstores and hospital pharmacies through five distribution centers.	The Orthopedic Division manufactures fabricates, and sells a full line of components for artificial limbs, braces, and other orthotic-prosthetic devices.
Customer Segments		
Hospitals, 68%	Independent drugstores, 52%	Catalog, 69%
Nursing homes, outpatient centers, and other, 17%	Hospital pharmacies, 34%	Retail, 24%
Physicians, 15%	Chain drugstores, 14%	International, 7%
Total Revenues, 1984		
$145 million	$188 million	$7 million

SOURCE: Durr-Fillauer Medical, Inc., *1984 Annual Report.*

produced for a private-label customer and also marketed through separate distribution channels under a company's brand name could represent two marketing planning units within an SBU. Planning by specific brands is also popular, particularly in consumer products firms. For example, the customer categories (e.g. hospitals, nursing homes, and physicians) of Durr-Fillauer Medical, Inc. shown in Exhibit 2-9 represent different marketing strategy units.

Establishing Business Boundaries

Traditionally, product or industry designations were used to designate the nature and scope of business operations. A company might be described as a steel processor, a candy maker, or a heavy equipment manufacturer. Use of only the product or service to establish boundaries between areas of business activity is incomplete because consideration of the end user of the product or service is excluded. Three important dimensions should be considered in defining business activities:

1. What *need* or *want* is the enterprise attempting to meet?
2. What *end-user customers* does the firm want to serve?

3. What *product or service* offering will be used to meet the needs of customers?[17]

An example will help illustrate each dimension. Suppose that there is need to photograph action scenes, such as a swimming race, so that the scenes can be shown in movie format. Look at the three dimensions shown in Exhibit 2–10. Notice that the needs for a particular product function vary, that different end-user groups are involved, and that the need can be met using two different product offerings. By considering the three dimensions we have a useful basis for establishing business boundaries for those firms serving a range of needs with several products or services. Even in a company serving a single product-market, use of the three dimensions adds considerable direction to strategic planning by showing how competing product-market categories (and the firms that serve them) must be considered in developing strategies.

As a company attempts to meet more and more needs by offering various products and services, the more diversified it becomes. When the needs of different user groups are met with the same product or service, this may position a firm in more than one product-market, each requiring a different marketing strategy. So we need to consider all three dimensions in defining a business and grouping together similar product-market activities.

A clarification is needed concerning the end-user customer. In many situations manufacturers sell their products to distributors, retailers, and other agents. While these firms are often referred to as *customers*, they are not end users. We shall reserve this term for the organization or individual that *consumes* the product or service. The companies working between the producer and final user are providing valuable functions that are essential in linking end users with products and services that meet the end-users' needs and wants. Thus a grocery wholesaler who purchases Wheaties, Cheerios, or Gold Medal Flour from the manufacturer provides services that help General Mills meet consumers' needs for these products.

Forming Strategic Units

Hall describes the formation of an SBU:

> The fundamental concept in the identification of SBUs is to identify the discrete, independent product-market segments served by the firm. In essence, the idea is to decentralize on the basis of strategic elements, not on the basis of size or span of control.[18]

Thus the SBU represents an attempt to form strategic building blocks, each of which represents one or more product-markets comprised of end users with a set of needs that can be met by a product or service of-

EXHIBIT 2-10 Meeting a Need to Photograph and Replay Action Scenes

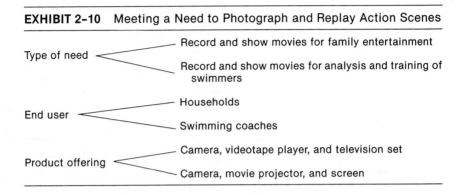

Type of need
- Record and show movies for family entertainment
- Record and show movies for analysis and training of swimmers

End user
- Households
- Swimming coaches

Product offering
- Camera, videotape player, and television set
- Camera, movie projector, and screen

fering. Both product and market considerations are important in forming strategic planning units.

How broadly or narrowly defined is the product-market served by an SBU? Should an SBU be composed of only one product-market or more than one? There are various product-market levels ranging from a generic group of products or services serving a very general need to a product seeking to meet the specific needs of a market segment.

An SBU may include one or more specific product-market from a generic product-market. Management has a great deal of flexibility in deciding what boundaries to establish for the firm's business segments and SBUs.

In illustrating SBU formation, it is informative to examine how General Foods Corporation, a leading producer of packaged foods, has regrouped its divisional structure into strategic business units. James L. Ferguson describes how the firm's products were repositioned into menu segments:

> We started out with four divisions: Kool-Aid, Bird's Eye, Jello, and Post. Among the products in those four divisions, we saw five basic menu segments in addition to coffee: dessert, main meal, breakfast beverage, and pet food. We combined these five strategic business units—SBUs—into three new divisions: main meal and dessert SBUs became the food products division; beverage and breakfast SBUs were combined into one division, and pet foods—which we considered a major growth opportunity—was put into a third division.[19]

The General Foods approach to SBU formation consists of a group of brands linked together by their natural interrelationship on the consumer's menu. It is not concerned with the fact that certain brands may share a common manufacturing process (e.g., frozen foods) or method of distribution. Thus, in this instance the type of need being satisfied is an essential factor in defining SBUs. For example, the company's main meal SBU includes frozen vegetables, instant rice, seasoned coating mix, and salad dressing mixes.[20] While all of these brands are foods, several different manufacturing processes are involved.

As we take up business unit analysis in Chapter 3, product-market analysis in Chapter 5, and market target strategy in Chapter 8, it is important to identify the specific product-markets that constitute an SBU. For example, in estimating business strength and market attractiveness for General Foods's main meal SBU, we should analyze each of the product-market categories within the SBU, such as frozen vegetables, instant rice, and the other product categories. Often each specific brand will require a separate analysis. Preparing forecasts of demand and growth rates for the main meal SBU would amount to summing up these estimates for each of the specific product-markets or brand-markets within the SBU. Development of marketing strategy for an SBU also requires analysis at the specific product-market level. Thus the specific product-market represents a basic unit of analysis in corporate, business unit, and marketing strategy development.

Grid Analysis to Determine SBUs

While management may have certain situation specific factors that influence how SBUs are formed, grid analysis provides a useful starting point. The first step is to create a product and market target grid. It is necessary to identify the products offered by the corporation, including specific products, product lines, and mixes of product lines. Next, identify the market segments targeted by each product. This can be accomplished using a grid similar to Exhibit 2–11. After creating the grid, the next step is to group product line/market target cells to form SBUs.

The basis for forming an SBU is grouping cells with similar product and market characteristics. The cells that comprise an SBU should have common strategic features, such as distribution channels, market targets, technology, and/or advertising and sales force strategies. Exhibit 2–11 shows an illustrative combination of cells into five SBUs. Further analysis by management can incorporate company-specific factors into the process. We should also make an assessment of the proposed scheme to determine if the SBUs offer both operational and strategic advantages to the corporation. Do the potential benefits provided by the organizational scheme exceed the costs?

Note that building up from specific product and market categories offers a more useful scheme for forming SBUs than starting from the top and breaking it down. A note of caution is in order. Too many SBUs may be more harmful than useful. The creation of a strategic planning unit signifies that we will develop a strategic plan for the unit. A large number of units requires a correspondingly large number of strategies and management structures that are expensive and probably not cost-effective. From top management's perspective, keeping track of SBUs

---

EXHIBIT 2-11   Product and Market Target Grid for SBU Determination

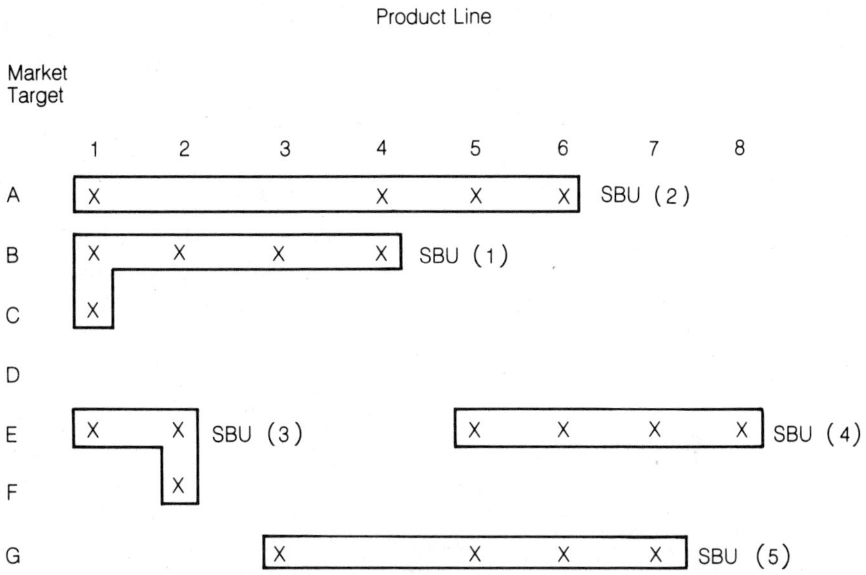

Product Line

Market
Target

	1	2	3	4	5	6	7	8
A	X			X	X	X	SBU (2)	
B	X	X	X	X	SBU (1)			
C	X							
D								
E	X	X	SBU (3)		X	X	X	X	SBU (4)
F		X						
G			X		X	X	X	SBU (5)

---

can be both confusing and difficult when too much proliferation has occurred. Moreover, a large number of planning units may indicate that the firm is going after many small business opportunities that will be overly demanding on the firm's management and financial resources.

Another danger is not recognizing that a new product may place the firm into a new business area. If the decision pushes the firm into a new product-market, unrelated to its present business mix, then management must recognize the consequences of this decision. The mission of our firm will be altered, and substantial resources may be required to support the venture. In other instances the existence of an attractive opportunity may cause management to purchase another firm and thus create a new planning unit; this was the case when General Mills acquired Red Lobster. Regardless of the origin of new product-market opportunities, the important issue is to recognize which ones involve pushing the firm into a new strategic segment. Such decisions should be carefully analyzed and evaluated to determine the overall impact upon our corporate mission and objectives.

Criteria for Selecting SBUs[21]

Several criteria may be relevant in deciding how to form SBUs in a particular corporation. These include the strategic relevance of the unit, administrative requirements, the applicability of analysis methods, flexibility, and the costs and benefits of alternative SBU schemes.

Strategic Relevance.   The purpose for establishing an SBU and the organizational level of use affect its strategic relevance. Top management is more concerned with relatively aggregate units whereas marketing executives must plan and manage market targets. The use of the SBU as a unit for analysis and planning may include strategy formulation, diagnosis and control, and exit or entry.

Administrative Requirements.   There are both internal and external factors that affect the usefulness of an SBU as an administrative unit. These include financial planning, reporting, and control; organizational arrangements; range of products; manufacturing responsibilities; and market(s) served. The choice of SBUs should take into account relevant internal and external administrative factors.

Strategic Analysis Methods.   The analysis methods discussed in Chapter 3 require various kinds of information. The availability of information on finances, the competition, and the market may affect the choice of SBUs. In choosing the SBU formation scheme, we should consider information needs for analysis and planning.

Flexibility.   It is likely that a particular SBU scheme will not meet the needs of all the strategists in an organization. Thus it is desirable to select an SBU that can be aggregated or disaggregated to meet the needs of various organizational levels.

Cost/Benefits.   In making the final selection of an SBU scheme, management should evaluate the costs and benefits of the approach under consideration. Our objective should be to define SBUs that are large enough to represent operationally useful components for strategy development and performance tracking, yet small enough to clearly identify differences in strategy and management.

CORPORATE STRATEGY

Top management should establish guidelines for long-term strategic planning. In a business that has two or more strategic business units, decisions must be made at two levels. Top management must first decide what business areas to pursue, and then establish priorities for allocating resources to each SBU. Decision makers within each SBU must determine the appropriate strategies for delivering the results that management expects. Corporate level management should assist SBUs in achieving their missions.

Developing Strategic Guidelines

Determining a set of strategic guidelines can facilitate planning at both the corporate and SBU levels. Dayton Hudson Corporation, one of the more successful retail conglomerates of the 1980s, operates a chain of department stores, Target stores, Mervyn's, B. Dalton Booksellers, and other retail businesses. Strategic planning is an essential part of the company's management process. Dayton Hudson has five strategic guidelines:[22]

Operating Strategy. This guideline highlights the importance of the customer and the prevailing trend of the importance of value to the retail shopper.

Management Strategies. This guideline emphasizes managing the business for growth in an environment that is rapidly and continually changing.

Trend Management. This strategy recognizes that distinct phases exist in the life cycles of major fashion trends. Programs are established to deal with trends effectively at each point in their development.

Capital Investment Strategy. The principles of portfolio management are applied in the retail businesses, considering the operating companies from a financial perspective. The portfolio of businesses is managed to achieve the greatest degree of consistency in earnings growth and return on investment.

New Businesses. Management recognizes the importance of new ventures to the company. At least one new business is under study or development at all times at the corporate level.

These strategic guidelines indicate direction and focus for the corporation and its business units. Corporate management is providing its SBU managers with appropriate inputs to strategically managing their units. While the Dayton Hudson strategic guidelines are illustrative, they emphasize the types of strategy issues that should be considered by top management. The decisions that must be made on a continuing basis include managing the existing portfolio, adding new business components, and divesting unsatisfactory business units.

Corporate strategy and capabilities should enhance the capacity of an SBU to compete more effectively than if it were operating on a completely independent basis. "To remain competitive, corporations must provide their business units with low-cost capital, outstanding executives, corporate R&D, centralized marketing where appropriate and other resources in the corporate arsenal."[23] The SBU has its product and market domain that is shaped by the corporate portfolio. Corporate resources and synergies help the SBU establish its differential advantage over competition. The strategic focus and priorities of corporate strategy help determine SBU strategic thrusts. Finally, top management's expectations for the corporation indicate the results expected from an SBU, including both financial and nonfinancial objectives. When viewed in this context, the SBUs become the action instruments of the corporation.

Responsibility for Strategic Planning

While most executives do not question the importance of strategic planning to the performance of a business, there are different views as to how strategy should be developed and who should do it. By the mid-1980s planning by decision makers rather than professional planners was widely advocated. Not surprisingly, many companies had not found strategic planning professionals effective in prescribing strategies for the enterprise. Since these professionals were removed from operating management and not involved in implementation, far too many of their strategies did not succeed. Criticism was also directed at the planning tools that became popular in the mid-1970s, such as the Boston Consulting Group growth-share matrix, which was used to analyze the various business units of a corporation. Documenting the difficulty of strategy development, a *Business Week* reassessment in 1984 of 33 strategies analyzed in 1979 and 1980 found that 19 had failed, run into trouble, or been abandoned.[24] Only 14 were considered successful. Cited as unsuccessful was Adolph Coors's strategy to become a national force in the beer industry. Hershey Foods's diversification into non-candy foods and other areas was one of the success stories.

Top management must share responsibility for faulty strategic plans. Too much dependence was apparently placed on both the planners and their analytical methods. Compounding the problem was the tough, demanding, and turbulent global business environment experienced in the first half of the 1980s. As we shall see in Chapter 3, both professional planners and their tools have useful contributions to make to corporate strategy.

CONCLUDING NOTE

In this overview of strategic planning, we have considered the major steps in building a plan for the corporation. The strategic planning process for a firm consists of: (1) defining the corporate mission and setting objectives; (2) conducting the corporate situation assessment; (3) forming strategic business units; and (4) establishing guidelines for long-term strategic planning of the corporation and its business units. Top management must decide what corporate strategies will move the firm toward its objectives. After implementation of a strategy, management must determine how the strategy is progressing and what adjustments are needed. Successfully executing these steps requires penetrating and insightful analyses. Strategic planning is essential to corporate survival and performance.

The corporate mission statement defines the nature and scope of the business and provides essential strategic direction for the corporation. Decisions about the needs or benefits provided to customers, about the technologies to be used, about market targets, and about the firm's level in the distribution system assist management in defining the business. The firm's objectives indicate the performance desired by management. In moving away from the core business, several paths of corporate development are possible, including expansion into new products and/or markets as well as diversification.

To evaluate the corporate situation we need to begin by assessing the relevant economic, technical, legal and political, and social forces as well as their estimated impact on the enterprise. Next, we need to conduct product-market and competition analyses in order to identify potential opportunities and threats for the corporation. An analysis of company strengths and limitations follows. The last step in the situation assessment is to synthesize all these findings into a summary of the strategic situation confronting the corporation.

To form strategic business units, we need to divide the corporation into operational strategic components that can be effectively managed. An SBU contains related products and market segments that perform all or most of the basic business functions. We should consider both the markets served and the products offered in SBU formation. Product and market grid analysis provides a useful basis for defining SBUs.

In corporations involving two or more SBUs, strategic guidelines should be developed for managing the business portfolio. These guides include operating strategy, management strategies, trend management, capital investment strategy, corporate development, and other strategic considerations important to a particular corporation. Responsibility for strategic planning should be assigned to operating management rather than staff planners.

Mission determination, the assessment of the corporate situation, the definition of a business unit, and the establishment of strategy guidelines all set the stage for Chapter 3, which will consider business unit analysis and planning, implementation, and the control of strategy. As we shall see, a corporation's strategy is implemented through its business units.

NOTES

1. "General Mills Outlines Plan of Divestiture," *The Wall Street Journal,* March 27, 1985, 2.
2. *The Value Line Investment Survey,* January 24, 1986, 732.
3. George S. Day, *Strategic Marketing Planning* (St. Paul, Minn.: West Publishing, 1984), 18–22.
4. Durr-Fillauer Medical, Inc., *1984 Annual Report.*
5. Peter F. Drucker, *Management* (New York: Harper & Row, 1974), 94.
6. Ibid., 100.
7. John Brimelow, "Toot, Toot Tootsie Roll," *Barron's,* September 17, 1979, 9.
8. Ibid., 9.
9. Bro Uttal, "Knighthood Is Still in Flower at General Signal," *Fortune,* October 6, 1980, 58.
10. George A. Steiner, *Strategic Planning* (New York: Free Press, 1979), 122.
11. This illustration is based on Hal Lancaster, "American Hospital's Marketing Program Places Company Atop a Troubled Industry," *The Wall Street Journal,* August 24, 1984, 23.
12. Ibid.
13. A discussion of competitor analysis is provided in William E. Rothschild, "Competitor Analysis: The Missing Link in Strategy," *Management Review,* July 1979, 22–28, 37–39.
14. Manufacturers Hanover Corporation, *1985 First Quarter Report,* cover.
15. William K. Hall, "SBUs: Hot, New Topic in the Management of Diversi-fication," *Business Horizons,* February 1978, 19.
16. Philippe Haspeslagh, "Portfolio Planning: Uses and Limits," *Harvard Business Review,* January–February 1982, 65.
17. These are similar to the customer group, function, and technology dimensions recommended by Derek F. Abell and John S. Hammond, *Strategic Marketing Planning* (Englewood Cliffs, N.J.: Prentice-Hall, 1979), 392.
18. Hall, "SBUs: Hot, New Topic in the Management of Diversification," 19.
19. "James L. Ferguson: General Food's Super-Marketer," *MBA Executive* (March/April 1980), 6.
20. Ibid., 6.
21. An expanded discussion of this topic is provided in David W. Cravens and Charles W. Lamb, Jr., "Defining and Selecting Strategic Marketing Planning and Control Units," in *Strategic Marketing and Management,* ed. H. Thomas and D. Gardner (Chichester, England: John Wiley & Sons, 1985), 97–99.
22. Dayton Hudson Corporation, *1982 Annual Report,* 4 and 6.
23. This discussion is based on Boris Yavitz and William H. Newman, "What the Corporation Should Provide Its Business Units," *Journal of Business Strategy* 3, no. 1 (Summer 1982), 14.
24. "The New Breed of Strategic Planner," *Business Week,* September 17, 1984, 64–68.

QUESTIONS FOR REVIEW AND DISCUSSION

1. As staff assistant to the vice president of marketing for a regional bank holding company you have been asked to prepare a corporate situation assessment. Identify and briefly discuss the major factors to be covered in the assessment.

2. One important part of a situation assessment is the identification and evaluation of competitors. Finding potential competitors is a key problem in preparing such a situation assessment. Suggest several ways to determine potential competitors of a company.

3. Top management of companies probably devoted more time to reviewing (and sometimes changing) their corporate mission in the early 1980s than in any other period in the past. Discuss the major reasons for this increased concern with the business mission.

4. What advantages do you see in defining a corporate mission in a very specific way? Are there any disadvantages to clearly describing the corporate purpose?

5. Discuss the major issues that top management should consider in deciding whether or not to expand business operations beyond the core business.

6. Discuss the environmental factors that should be assessed on a regular basis by a large retail corporation like Dayton Hudson Corporation.

7. What are the advantages of combining two or more strategic planning units into a division or business group, compared to keeping the planning units as separate organizational units?

8. Discuss what you consider to be the major issues in trying to divide a corporation into strategic business units, indicating for each problem suggestions for overcoming it.

STRATEGIC APPLICATION 2-1

GILLETTE CO.

Boston—King C. Gillette, still sporting a mustache, smiles benevolently from his official portrait. All around the turn-of-the-century traveling salesman and entrepreneur, a certain amount of confusion reigns. Sawdust, half-painted walls and detour signs testify to a mammoth remodeling of Gillette Co.'s safety razor headquarters. Outside, the company's softball fields are being swept for an evening game, and the rusty neon "Shaving World Headquarters" sign stands high above South Boston, as it has since the early 1960s.

If portraits could see and hear, King Gillette likely would nod in approval.

The safety razor division, the cornerstone on which he founded his company in 1901, not only is modernizing the 15-building, 27-acre facility that already produces 5.4 million blade edges a day, it's also galloping into a period of new-product development and growth that should only strengthen Gillette's position as the premier purveyor of materials for that daily male ritual, the close, wet shave.

Gillette is moving in other ways as well. The personal care division, which began the 1980s on a binge of new products, is rethinking *its* strategy after a series of disappointing clinkers, such as For Oily Hair Only, Mink Difference shampoo and Silkience moisturizer. The division has by no means abandoned innovation; personal care division president Bill Ryan tantalizingly alludes to "something exciting" due later this summer. But it now plans to go more slowly and be far more selective in bringing new products to market, an approach that pleases many Wall Street analysts.

And that's not all. Derwyn Phillips, exec vp, Gillette N.A., is running a special ventures group investigating entirely fresh, outside avenues for Gillette's en-

Gillette's Net Income

Anticipating a flat domestic shaving market, Gillette Co. hopes to build on a solid bottom line with new shaving products, more judicious activity in the toiletries market and selective investments in small growth-oriented companies.

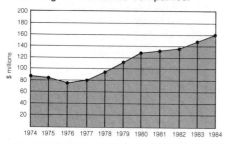

SOURCE: Gillette

terprise. As president of the personal care division during the late 1970s, Mr. Phillips spearheaded that division's rise in the Gillette galaxy.

Why the need to diversify, and why now? During the next decade, the domestic shaving market is expected to remain flat; the already grueling competition in toiletries should only get more so.

Gillette's management, therefore, is committed to stretching its considerable distribution, marketing, and manpower resources onto virgin turf.

Under the auspices of Mr. Phillips, the company is examining partial equity investments in low-capital, fast-growth companies whose businesses hold promise of long-range return for Gillette.

"It's very much like a venture-capital situation," said Mr. Phillips, whose 16-year career at Gillette has spanned two continents and a wide range of marketing positions. "Right now our tendency is to invest in companies that have less than $5 million in sales and are largely in start-up situations. Hopefully, within the next five to ten years, these concerns will have grown to about $50 million-to-$100 million. All of this gives us an opportunity to learn about a company and

the people who run it, without hurting Gillette stockholders.

"It's also an excellent means of stimulating younger, bright people within the company," he added. "I have often said that if I could turn back the clock 20 years, I would get involved in this work early on. That may be why I am doing it now."

So far, Wall Street analysts have yet to match Mr. Phillips' enthusiasm on this issue, instead remaining cautious about Gillette's involvement with embryonic ventures. "I tend to be less sanguine about some of these forays," said Diana Temple of Salomon Bros. "The fields may be growing rapidly and look very attractive at first glance, but the question will be how much return on investment can they make over time. I only hope Gillette goes very carefully."

For the most part, the degree to which these enterprises prove compatible with Gillette—in terms of corporate personality, strategy and product portfolio—will determine how long they live together. To date, Gillette has been quite selective in picking partners. It owns 100% of Mislo Corp., a Homedale, N.J.–based marketer, via catalog, of computer supplies and accessories. It also has purchased part ownership in two other computer companies and has invested in a hearing-aid marketer, Audiological Consultants, Milwaukee.

Mr. Phillips is particularly excited about Gillette's budding participation in specialty retail eye stores, where glasses can be fitted, prescribed, and produced on premise. Last September, Gillette bought 40% of Eye World in neighboring Framingham, Mass., with the option to acquire more if the company performs well. Gillette also has invested in Houston-based Eye & Tech.

Overall, the eyeglass field is predicted to vault from $6 billion to $20 billion during the next decade. The superstore segment being explored by Gillette is expected to grow 15%-to-20% faster than the market in general. "There's something of a revolution going on in the marketing of eyeware and contacts," Mr. Phillips said. "Two trends are coming to bear—the aging population and a growing fashion awareness. People are beginning to have multiple pairs of glasses to wear with various outfits."

Gillette also is toying with day spas, places where customers can trim pounds and inches through both exercise and diet plans. Gillette's idea goes further than the traditional health club, though, as the company hopes to sell a wide array of Gillette products within the spa itself and offer on-site beauty treatments as well.

In addition to venture activity, Gillette has rid itself of at least one ailing business, Cricket Lighters, which it sold to Stockholm-based Swedish Match Co. in October. . . . On the flip side, Gillette has been making noises on the acquisitions front, having in March, 1984, surprised the investment community by purchasing Oral-B Laboratories Inc., a Palo Alto, Cal.–based company with a strong presence in the ethical over-the-counter market through toothpastes, toothbrushes, flourides and dental flosses—all of which it markets mainly through professionals.

According to Oral-B's exec vp, Harris Goodman, this marriage has been made in heaven, with Gillette allowing Oral-B the freedom to chart its traditional paths with more gusto than ever. "Gillette bought this company for our entrepreneurial spirit," Dr. Goodman said. "They said they would let us continue much as we had been and they're keeping their word. With Gillette's backing, we now have the ability to spend more money than before—whether it be for capital formation for new plants, marketing, whatever. It's been all across the board."

Oral-B is using Gillette's well-honed and far-reaching distribution system to broaden its strength overseas, most notably in Germany, Australia, and the U.K., where it is using foodservice outlets for the first time. With the Gillette go-ahead, Oral-B also plans to nurture the Oral-B Zendium toothpaste line, which fights "problem deposit buildup," a point of difference now being touted by Minnetonka's Check Up and Lever Bros.' Aim toothpastes.

All well and good, but if Gillette plans to double its sales by the end of the decade—something it has said it plans to do—the company must milk its existing mainstays: shaving instruments, toiletries, and writing utensils.

These days, analysts are particularly applauding Gillette's renewed concentration on what it does best: The development, manufacture and marketing of razors and blades. Indeed, some 60% of Americans who shave do so with Gillette products.

Shaving entries generate two-thirds of the company's total profits and one-third of total sales. In 1984, for example, sales of razors and blades reached $768 million, up from $755 million the previous year, and thus comprising 34% of total Gillette sales.

All this has proven very good for Gillette's bottom line. "In the last couple of years, Gillette has shown a solid increase in profits," said Morgan Stanley analyst Brenda Landry. "They have gone from a 5% after-tax margin in 1977 to 7% last year, which is not bad at all. Gillette is currently carrying some of the best profit ratios in the cosmetics/toiletries business."

To continue doing do, Gillette recently ended an eight-year lull in new shaving products. In the last three months, the safety razor division has christened two items with decidedly different appeals and market objectives: The premium Atra-Plus refillable system with a lubricating strip, for beards requiring a softer touch, and, more recently, the Micro-

Trac, an inexpensive twin-blade disposable that the company says grants a close shave with the slimmest shaving head around. . . .

"Gillette is definitely reemphasizing their razor and blade business," said Salomon Bros.' Ms. Temple. "In addition to stressing innovation, they are also working hard on manufacturing efficiencies, which can only help profits."

Indeed, one of the MicroTrac's pluses is the fact that it uses less plastic, and thus is relatively cheap to produce. "We have designed a state-of-the-art manufacturing process," explained David Preston, president of the safety razor division. "Because of the advanced technology, [we] will be able to sell the MicroTrac razor at a lower price than any other Gillette disposable. This means an excellent product at a lower price."

Mr. Preston, a stocky, smiling Canadian whose office overlooks South Boston and Gillette's softball fields, promises more such products. "We don't want to go for another seven-to-ten-year period where there are no significant new entries," he said, eyes gleaming.

"Another big question is how do you own a shaving scene," Mr. Preston added. Gillette feels it has found the answer in its current "Essence of shaving" campaign by BBDO, the safety razor division's agency. "Even if you don't use Gillette, you will acknowledge that Gillette is the essence of shaving," Mr. Preston explained. "It's the proper umbrella that nobody else can use."

The next few years should be equally telling for Gillette's personal care division. "The toiletries business is more difficult right now than I have ever seen it," mused division president Bill Ryan, as he sat in Gillette's crisp, efficient corporate offices in Boston's Prudential Bldg., several miles across town from the safety razor division. "For one thing, the market has slowed down considerably. For another, competition has increased, as

it is fairly easy for people to get into this business because it is low-capital-intensive."

Consider the figures for the shampoo market, which was growing at some 8% annually in the late 1970s, the heyday of the personal care division's new-product streak, with such winners as Silkience shampoo and conditioner, Dry Idea and Aapri facial scrub; it now charts 2% per annum gains, at best.

To cope with a combative, flat market in not just shampoo, but other hair and skin products as well, Gillette has "moved away from the wave concept of new-product introduction," explained Goldman Sachs' Jack Salzman, a longtime Gillette watcher. "With that, they would keep spewing forth new products, one after another, so that the wave never crested. It tended to work best as a short-term strategy."

These days, Gillette will be far more choosy when it comes to toiletries launches, Mr. Ryan assured. "We are looking for items that are *genuinely* different," he stressed. "Things that have a real point of difference, that can stand away from the pack." Gone are the days when Gillette literally would split hairs with new products that added just another twist to those already on the market. One example is For Oily Hair Only, a product Gillette believed would be the perfect astringent for the working girl, but which has dwindled to only minimal share levels.

In addition to selective new-product development, Mr. Ryan and crew are looking for ways to maximize what they increasingly believe may be their best weapon: longstanding Gillette names that consumers instantly identify and feel comfortable with. Consequently, the company this spring has made two interesting moves, both of which also indicate Gillette's desire to cash in on the growing economy segment.

First, and most immediately, Gillette has quietly lent one of its better-known razor names, Good News!, to a new group of unisex toiletries testing on the West Coast. ... The line, Gillette's first entry aimed at both sexes, includes a regular and concentrate shampoo, deodorant stick, antiperspirant, hair conditioner and shaving cream. Ads by Young & Rubicam brandish the Gillette name, and in doing so take on a decidedly upbeat, lifestyle, soft-drink-type advertising style.

"This is a perfect example of how we plan to work existing Gillette equities harder," Mr. Ryan said. "It's not just Good News!, it's Good News! from Gillette, and we think people will respond favorably."

Next month, the personal care division will inaugurate the national launch of White Rain shampoo and conditioner. Like Good News!, they are low-price entries that will capitalize on the Gillette tradition of quality. They also are the direct descendents of White Rain hair spray, which has been around for nearly 25 years, but fell by the wayside a decade ago when Gillette began concentrating on premium, highly segmented products offering more immediate profits.

Things do go full circle. "It's going to be very interesting to watch Gillette," said Allan Mottus, a consultant familiar with the company. "For the time being, they will be sticking more to the commodities business, largely because the market is saturated and consumers are becoming more and more price conscious. And you never know. They have some marginal brands—like, say, Deep Magic and Tony—that still have a big middle-America draw. They could do something with those."

"Let's just say we're rising admirably to new market conditions," grinned Mr. Ryan, with a sweep of his arm taking in the panorama of Boston below him—not to mention the bottles of White Rain and Good News! stacked neatly on the window sill.

SOURCE: Gay Jervey, "Gillette Sharpens Edge with New Ventures," *Advertising Age,* June 24, 1985, 4 and 94.

DISCUSSION QUESTIONS

1. Define Gillette's corporate mission.
2. Critically evaluate the corporate development paths selected by Gillette's top management.
3. What criteria do you recommend to management to evaluate proposed new ventures?
4. Evaluate the pros and cons of Gillette's management approach to new ventures.

STRATEGIC APPLICATION 2-2

BERKEY PHOTO INC.

White Plains, N.Y.—In January 1984, Berkey Photo Inc.'s top executives, armed with purple markers and oversized tablets, flew to Key West, Fla., to develop a strategic plan for the recovering photo-finishing and distribution company.

After years of teetering on a financial tightrope, Berkey again was financially stable, though performance was lackluster and growth was evasive. "We decided that Berkey's skills weren't in the management of R&D (research and development) or manufacturing, but in marketing and service," says Jerry J. Burgdoerfer, president and chief executive officer. That decision—and the strategic plan threshed out in two days of tropical brainstorming—effectively changed the nature of Berkey's business over the past 18 months.

During that period, Berkey has acquired two marketing and promotion companies and, in its most significant move, agreed to sell its big photofinishing business—around which the company was established—to Colorcraft Corp., a unit of Atlanta-based Fuqua Industries Inc., for $40 million.

In 1984, Berkey's film processing group, which includes both amateur film processing and K&L Custom Services for professionals, contributed 58% of Berkey's $216 million in sales and 66% of pre-tax operating profit of $11.1 million. The sale of the photofinishing business, which is expected to be completed in late August or early September, leaves the company with its Berkey Marketing Cos. wholesale distribution business and Willoughby's, its big camera and electronics store in New York City, as well as the two new marketing acquisitions, Marden-Kane Inc. and B&E Sales Co. Berkey also has expanded its distribution business.

Proposed Name Change

In what may be a final pronouncement of Berkey Photo's new mission, shareholders will vote at the annual meeting scheduled for Sept. 6 on a proposal to change the company's name to Berkey Inc.

The new Berkey is the culmination of a six-year effort to transform it from a family-operated business burdened by huge losses and a mishmash of manufacturing operations to a more profitable, growth-oriented marketing and distribution company that handles varied retail products, seeks out vendors and manufacturers—primarily abroad—for products, and helps companies sell them.

Whether the marketing and distribution businesses will be more successful for Berkey isn't yet clear. Among the biggest risks for distribution companies is being in businesses where prices of the products they sell are going down instead of up, says James Ruf, an analyst at Wertheim & Co. who follows the distribution business.

Moreover, because distributors' margins are narrower than those in manufacturing, "if you make mistakes, they are likely to be more pronounced," Mr. Ruf says. But "there aren't a lot of pitfalls if the company is run properly," he says.

Expansion is Planned

Mr. Burgdoerfer declines to predict 1985 earnings for Berkey but says he expects 1986 pre-tax earnings of $5 million to $6 million on sales of $200 million. Further acquisitions are a strong possibility, he says. After allowing for some time to adjust to the recent transactions—the 2,000 Berkey photofinishing employees will move to Colorcraft, while only 300 or 400 B&E Sales employees will join Berkey—"the balance sheet will allow for the expansion of our existing businesses," he says.

Mr. Burgdoerfer, formerly Hertz Corp. executive vice president responsible for world-wide marketing for the RCA Corp. unit, says that when he succeeded founder Benjamin Berkey as president in 1979, "the banks were ready to close this company down." Between 1974 and 1978, Berkey had posted losses totaling $40.2 million and was in danger of failing. "Management believed that in order to be a major company, you had to have manufacturing, that service wouldn't win enough respect from the financial community," Mr. Burgdoerfer says.

He immediately began to pare the poor performers from Berkey's balance sheet. Graphic arts equipment, business machines and professional lighting equipment businesses were sold. Meanwhile, the founder, Mr. Berkey, resigned as chairman and director in 1982 after selling all his stock in the company; he died in December 1984.

By the end of 1983, Berkey was a financially stable if mediocre performer, burdened by $30.7 million of long-term debt and stymied by limited prospects for growth. Earnings in 1983 rose to $2.3 million, or 50 cents a share, including an extraordinary credit of almost $1.2 million, from $488,000, or 10 cents a share, a year earlier; sales increased to $203.3 million from $190 million. "We could support ourselves, but there wasn't a lot of room to grow," Mr. Burgdoerfer says. "It wasn't very exciting."

Changes in the Industry

The problem stemmed from the slowing growth of camera and film sales for conventional photography and from the changing nature of the photofinishing business. From 1980 to 1984, the number of on-site, quick-service minilab processors jumped to 5,600 from 600, claiming a 10% market share last year, according to a Berkey analysis of the U.S. amateur photofinishing market. "Before minilabs, there was more capacity than demand, and the minilabs compounded that," Mr. Burgdoerfer says.

Furthermore, mass merchandisers had discovered that offering a film processing service brought customers into their stores twice. The big, multistore contracts mass merchandisers wielded gave them enormous clout with photofinishers and sparked intense competition. One industry analyst says that even the beleaguered steel industry "has a better outlook than photofinishing." Berkey was hindered further by gaps in its nationwide photofinishing distribution.

Two Options

At the Key West gathering, Berkey executives had reached a similar conclusion. The company had two options, they decided: expand the photofinishing operation through acquisition to benefit from economies of scale, or sell it. "If we could have found something large enough and funded it, we would have stayed in photofinishing," Mr. Burgdoerfer says.

But when an affordable target didn't appear, Berkey—despite its 53-year history in photofinishing—proceeded to sell. "There wasn't much reluctance to part with photofinishing," Mr. Burgdoerfer says. "The people involved are professional managers, not entrepreneurs who started the business."

Even longtime board members concurred, says Edward A. Smith, the senior director who has served since 1965. "Many things were happening in the industry that led the board to believe we could use the funds from the sale more advantageously," Mr. Smith says. Other assets, including two buildings, also went on the block to raise $11 million for anticipated marketing and distribution acquisitions.

The wholesale distribution group, Berkey Marketing Cos., which had been added in the 1950s, already was the leading independent U.S. distributor of cameras and accessories, but company strategists wanted to expand the product mix and move beyond camera retailers. Berkey decided to distribute General Electric Co. video products, and added video accessories, binoculars and telescopes to the product mix.

In December 1984, Berkey bought Marden-Kane, a creator and administrator of sales promotion programs such as cereal box offers and newspaper contests, for $2.2 million and $600,000 of Berkey common stock. The April 1985 acquisition of B&E Sales, for $22.5 million and as much as $6 million in earnings bonuses, accomplished another objective by giving Berkey an opening into drugstores and supermarkets, Mr. Burgdoerfer says. B&E sells promotional packages of name brand and other household and personal goods, which it either buys in large quantity or orders to meet its specifications, to build traffic in drugstore chains.

As a result of the transactions, Berkey will be able to repay almost all of its $14 million of long-term and short-term bank debt, Mr. Burgdoerfer says, adding that the company still has about $3 million left to pay on 5¾% subordinated debentures and owes $8.5 million in long-term capitalized leases.

Completing the sale of the photofinishing operations also will increase Berkey's book value—the difference between corporate assets and liabilities—nearly 45% to $10.20 a share from $6.98 at March 31, he says. Berkey stock, since the announcement of the Fuqua agreement, has been trading in the range of $6.75 to $8, a level it last reached in the 1984 first quarter.

"In one fell swoop, they [Berkey] have cleaned up everything," says Louis Rusitzky, an analyst at Adams, Harkness & Hill Inc. "The current management did turn this company around and they did a magnificent job so far."

"Jerry [Burgdoerfer] always wanted to run a big company, and being in photofinishing was not an area where you're going to be a big company," says one analyst. "Now he has something to work with."

SOURCE: Elaine Johnson, "Berkey Photo Refocuses Its Business: Firm Seeks to Grow as Marketer and Distributor." Reprinted by permission of *The Wall Street Journal.* © Dow Jones & Co., Inc., August 1, 1985. All rights reserved.

DISCUSSION QUESTIONS

1. What were the important environmental and industry influences on Berkey Photo Inc. that led to a change in the corporate mission?
2. Evaluate the decision to follow a new corporate mission.
3. What strategic factors are likely to be important in the strategic planning of the company?
4. Identify some logical new areas of business that management may want to consider in the future.

CHAPTER 3

Business Unit Analysis and Strategy

Cummins Engine Co. is an interesting illustration of how to develop a business unit strategy.[1] After attempting diversification, management decided to concentrate on the core business, diesel truck engines. The reason for trying to diversify was to smooth out the cyclical highs and lows characteristic of the diesel-engine market. Companies were acquired in diverse business areas, such as skis and computer software. While the new units contributed to profits and growth, management underestimated the market opportunity for diesels. In the mid-1970s inflation and the energy crisis rapidly expanded the demand for diesels. Capital was needed to increase diesel production. The nondiesel SBUs were eliminated from Cummins' business portfolio in 1975–76. A Cummins engine costing about $15,000 can be found today in one out of every two large trucks on North American highways. Cummins' single-product strategy continues to be vulnerable to the peaks and valleys of the market. Management has decided to live with the market situation, working to increase productivity and market domination. The strategy is to generate high profits during market peaks to help compensate for low-period performance, such as 1985 when over 2,000 workers were laid off because of lower demand for truck engines. The company has committed $900 million to retool its engine line and develop new low-horsepower models to increase market penetration and discourage Japanese and European competitors.

Business unit analysis and strategy development are continuing challenges for management. This chapter examines how strategic alternatives like those faced by the Cummins Engine Co. are evaluated and how appropriate business strategies are selected. At the heart of strategic analysis is the ability to view a firm's business units as a portfolio representing a range of opportunities, risks, and challenges to management. The strategic task is to decide how to manage each unit so as to enhance the total performance of the enterprise. In a company with more than one business unit, management must allocate scarce resources to each business area. These choices may result in pushing for growth in some business units, managing other units for cash flow, and eliminating units whose future performance is expected to be unacceptable to management.

The chapter begins with a discussion of the SBU planning process, the objectives of SBU analysis, and the role of analysis methods. Next, we explain and evaluate the major analysis and planning methods, including portfolio grids, screening methods, and the profit impact of marketing strategy (PIMS). The determination of strategic alternatives for an SBU and the development of an SBU strategic plan follows. Finally, we examine several issues important in the implementation and control of SBU strategy, including marketing's strategic role.

BUSINESS UNIT PLANNING

The primary objective of strategic analysis is deciding what future strategy to follow for each business unit in order to enhance the overall corporate performance. Sound strategic planning is essential for survival in most businesses today because of the rapidly changing market environment and strong competition. While faulty strategies may not cause strong businesses to fail, strategic errors can drastically alter the performance of firms. An examination of the steps in business unit planning will provide further insights into the process.

SBU Planning Process

The major steps in the business unit planning process are shown in Exhibit 3–1. A brief description of each step follows:

Corporate Strategy Guidelines. This strategic umbrella includes the SBU definition, management's expectations for the SBU, constraints, corporate assistance provided, and the desired strategic focus of the SBU.

Business Unit Analysis. This activity consists of gauging the SBU's past performance, present position, and estimated future position after considering the market opportunity, competition, and other strategic factors.

Strategic Alternatives. Relevant future strategy options for the SBU should emerge from the SBU analysis. Management should select the most promising future strategy after considering objectives and constraints.

Strategic Plan. Management should formulate the objectives and select planned actions for the strategy selected.

Implementation and Control. The plan is placed into operation through implementation, and then managed so as to keep the gap between desired and actual results as narrow as possible.

The SBU planning process is continuous. Plans are adjusted over time for changing external conditions, shifting priorities, and other strategic influences.

Analysis Objectives

Analysis helps to determine the strategic situation of the SBU, indicating the strategic factors that must be considered in identifying the strategy alternatives appropriate for the SBU. The Cummins Engine example illustrates some influences that may affect strategic situation of an SBU. Similar to the corporate situation analysis, the SBU situation analysis is more detailed, focusing on the SBU and its situation relative to other units in the corporate portfolio. The major objectives of the analysis are to evaluate the SBU's product-market attractiveness and its position against competition, to establish its financial situ-

---

EXHIBIT 3-1   Business Unit Planning Process

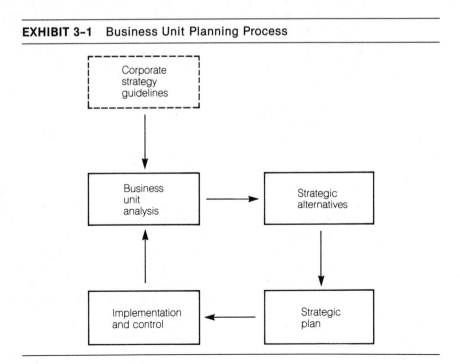

EXHIBIT 3-2   Objectives of SBU Analysis

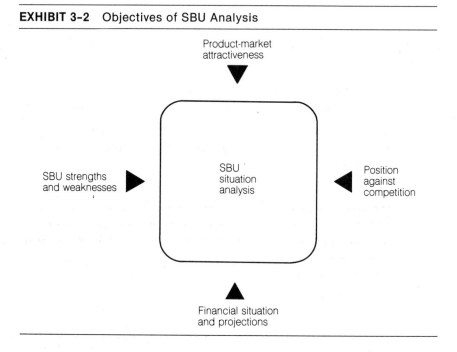

---

ation and projections, and to identify the SBU's strengths and weaknesses, as shown in Exhibit 3–2. The strategic analysis methods discussed in the next section can be used to assist management in evaluating an SBU's strategic situation. Chapter 4 provides guidelines for financial analysis. The chapters in Part Two examine the analysis of the markets, buyers, and competitors in greater depth.

OVERVIEW OF ANALYSIS METHODS

Strategic analysis is concerned with two key activities: (1) *diagnosis* of the SBU's strengths and limitations, and (2) *identification* of alternative strategic actions for maintaining or improving performance. Management must decide what priority to place on each business unit regarding resource allocation; it must then choose the strategic actions necessary to meet the objectives established for the SBU. The choice of a method of analysis depends on how well it serves management in diagnosing the business and identifying appropriate strategic actions. None of the methods completely meets these needs. Each demands a considerable amount of judgment and experience in applying it in a particular firm. After examining the features, strengths, and limitations of each method, we have to make a comparative assessment that takes into account various factors important to management.

First, we consider two very popular grid analysis methods: (1) portfolio analysis based on the growth/share grid developed by the Boston Consulting Group, and (2) business unit screening methods based on the market attractiveness and business strengths grid developed by the General Electric Company. A discussion of the profit impact of marketing strategy (PIMS) model follows. Finally, other analysis and planning tools are briefly discussed.

Portfolio Analysis

The experience curve—the foundation of portfolio analysis—shows that in certain situations, as more units of a product are produced by a firm, costs will drop as a result of experience. Scale of operation, learning by experience, and investment (technology) are the principal causes of the experience curve effect. Bruce Henderson, who founded the Boston Consulting Group (BCG) in the mid-1960s to provide strategic planning assistance to companies, first used the experience curve at the General Instrument Corporation to analyze the probable future cost pattern in the industry.[2] BCG's studies indicated that, for a wide variety of products (such as silicon transistors, integrated circuits, polyvinyl chloride, facial tissues, and gas ranges), total costs decline according to an experience curve.[3] The important part of this finding was that costs and market share seemed to be related. A producer like C whose accumulated volume (market share) is greater than its competitors, A and B, has a distinct cost advantage if the experience curve effect applies as shown in Exhibit 3–3. The relationship is linear in the logarithm. Since the analysis assumes real costs and prices, historical data must be adjusted for the effects of inflation.

When the experience curve applies, the high market share firm should have a distinct cost advantage. By lowering price as costs decline, new competitors can be discouraged while the leading firm strengthens its market position. Higher profits should also prevail for the market leader, because of lower costs.

The Growth-Share Matrix. A company with several business units or products can use experience curve theory to analyze its portfolio by plotting each SBU or product on a two-way matrix as shown in Exhibit 3–4. Market share and market growth rate indicate the position of each product. The names shown in each quadrant, "cash cow," "star," "dog," and "problem child" have become popular with strategic planners to denote the attractiveness of each position and its cash needs. The premise underlying portfolio analysis is that a company with a low

EXHIBIT 3-3   Market Share and Costs for Three Competitors

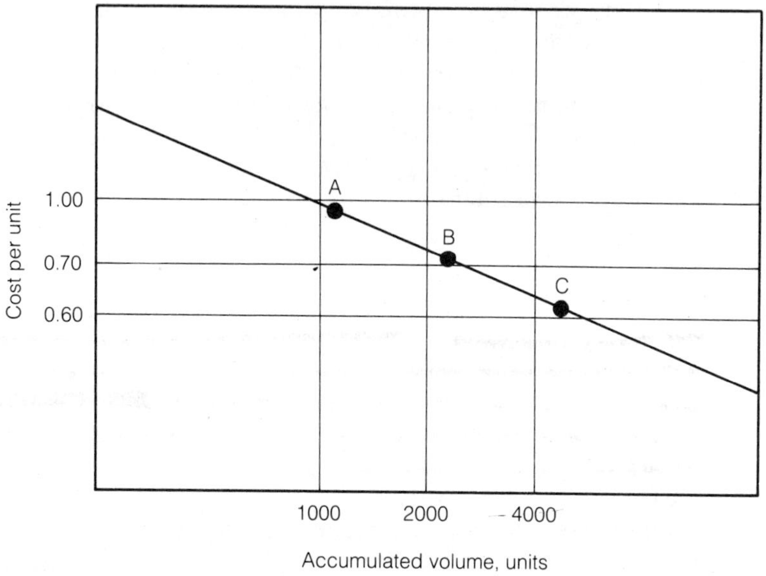

Accumulated volume, units

SOURCE: The Boston Consulting Group, Inc.

market share in a mature, slow-growth market is likely to be attempting an unprofitable battle if it decides to try to gain a market share against entrenched competitors. The other positions vary in their cash needs, with a cash cow generating more cash than is needed and the problem child and star both requiring additional cash.

The experience curve findings in combination with growth-share matrix highlight several important strategic planning implications. The key concept is that costs (exclusive of inflation) decline as volume rises and price also declines. In the opinion of BCG's president, a key strategic point is as follows:

> According to Henderson, the concept is often ignored. U.S. companies, he says, often gain an early leadership in market share of a product and are content simply to ride with it, rather than to spend more and to lower prices to increase their customer base. When price does not follow costs down, aggressive competitors can overwhelm seemingly entrenched leaders.[4]

As a product-market moves through its life cycle, early leaders have an opportunity through cost reduction efforts and price strategies to build their competitive advantages while the product-market is maturing. Future strategic consequences for a particular firm depend upon its present position and actions and the strategies of competing

EXHIBIT 3-4 Balancing the Product Portfolio

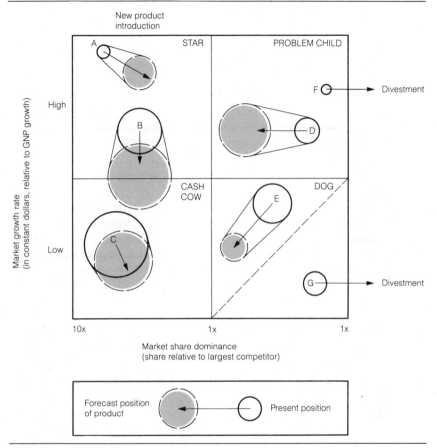

Diameter of circle is proportional to products contribution to total company sales volume.
SOURCE: George S. Day, "Diagnosing the Product Portfolio," *Journal of Marketing,* April 1977, 34.

firms. Depending upon the position a firm occupies on the growth-share matrix, both its market opportunity and its cash needs will vary. Since the opportunity and position of a firm's various product-markets will vary, top management must decide how to develop business unit or product portfolio strategies that will lead to the most favorable overall corporate performance.

Critical Assessment of Portfolio Analysis. Perhaps the greatest contribution of this tool is the emphasis it places on managing a portfolio of business activities, each varying according to risk and opportunity. The grid is helpful in highlighting the difference between the SBUs or products being analyzed. The method is easily understood by management and the data requirements for analysis are not overly demanding.

Analyses for various product categories indicate that costs behave according to an experience curve pattern. The unit under analysis can range from a product to a line or mix of products in a business unit, providing in the latter case, there is some means of combining share and growth information from specific product categories. The planning grid provides a useful springboard for performing more detailed strategic analyses of each unit.

If the effects of scale, learning, and investment do *not* apply to the industry and firm under analysis, the experience curve does not apply. Also the analysis does not apply in a regulated industry or for firms in which the market leaders have made errors in strategy. A patent held by a competitor may adversely affect the analysis. The relationship of cash flow patterns to market share position and product-market growth may be too narrow in focus; as a result, other important strategic factors may be ignored. The BCG matrix does not consider potentially important strategic factors, such as the industry environment, market structure, and specific competitive strengths and weaknesses.[5] Moreover, the emphasis on market position (share) may *inappropriately* suggest divestment of attractive business units. For example, one study of 40 successful low-share businesses found that firms that are not market leaders can nevertheless be successful.[6]

Another key question is whether or not cash flows will occur according to predictions. If our costs behave differently than the predictions or the experience curve, the cash flows will be affected. Such differences may be due to the following factors: (1) our firm may add only a low value to the product; (2) a small competitor of the firm may have access to a low-cost source of materials or to a superior production technology; (3) the experience curves of small competitors may be steeper than those of our firm, or the differences in experience may have little impact on production costs; (4) strategic factors other than the market share may affect our profit margins; or (5) the rates of capacity utilization may be different.[7]

The basis of analysis may affect the results. For example, the industry growth rate may differ from the rate for a market segment served by the firm. As a result, it is important for us to define the product-market that is being analyzed.[8] The steel industry offers a dramatic example of how small, aggressive minimill steelmakers have consistently outperformed the giants in the industry. If Nucor Corp., one of the more successful minimill operators, were placed on the grid shown in Exhibit 3–4 according to its market share position and the market growth rate for the entire steel industry, its position would be in the lower right corner of the grid, reflecting a very weak position. The strategic situation changes drastically when we analyze the steel roof joist segment comprised of commercial building applications. Nucor dominates this growing segment. Interestingly, redefinition of the market being analyzed places Nucor in the star category.

Although the BCG growth-share matrix helped establish the concept of business portfolio analysis, today an increasing number of firms have moved beyond using only market growth and market share measures for positioning SBUs or products on grids. Consider this assessment by Robert Cushman, chairman of the Norton Company:

> There is no question of the value in using the *Portfolio Management* Concept. The Concept attempts to be forward-looking, whereas accounting profit is biased toward past events. The Portfolio Concept attempts to focus on the key variables and the critical businesses that will determine the company's future success. It identifies which businesses provide core strengths, which represent investment opportunities, and which do neither.
>
> Managing the corporation in portfolio terms means more than buying and selling companies. It means setting meaningful measures of competitive advantage, and managing the information, incentive, staff support, and other systems consistent with the role (mode) assigned to the business. The portfolio approach encourages supporting businesses in which fundamental competitive advantages exist, not simply high current profitability. Those that understand the value of their businesses in portfolio terms are better able to enhance corporate value over the long term.[9]

This perspective of portfolio analysis clearly emphasizes the value of managing a corporation as a portfolio of businesses. The Norton Company used growth-share analysis in the mid-1970s. Currently their analyses include a consideration of multiple factors. While the cash flow guidelines suggested by the growth-share matrix provide a useful starting point, additional analysis and evaluation by management are necessary in deciding what strategies to pursue.

Multiple Factor Screening Methods

The screening technique was developed by General Electric Company, working with McKinsey & Co., a management consulting firm. An example of a GE-type screening grid is shown in Exhibit 3–5. Unlike the BCG grid, it uses multiple measures of attractiveness and business strength. The circle areas are proportional to the annual sales volume of each business unit or some other results measure considered important by management. Those units that fall into the high-high categories are in a desirable zone whereas a low-low positioning indicates an undesirable situation. The assumption is that return on investment will be high in a high-high category, and so on.[10]

Screening Criteria. We have to answer two key questions when using multiple factors to position a unit on a screening grid, as shown in Exhibit 3–5. First, what factors should we use to measure business strength and market attractiveness? Second, how are the various factors to be combined to provide a composite measure of each grid dimension?

EXHIBIT 3-5 Business Unit Screening Grid

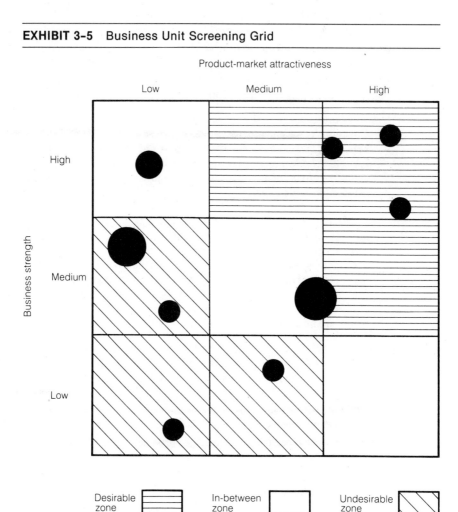

Possible screening factors are shown in Exhibit 3–6. We can modify this list to meet the needs of a particular firm. Care should be exercised in choosing the factors so that the critical ones are identified and the number of factors is not too large. The use of a single factor, such as market share, for assessing business strength may not identify weaknesses that are developing relative to competition and growth rate. In addition, such a factor may not take into account other factors indicating the attractiveness of a product-market. Had A&P's management analyzed its business strengths and weaknesses more carefully in the 1960s when the supermarket chain had the top market share, it might have avoided the firm's loss of market position.

EXHIBIT 3-6 Factors Contributing to Market Attractiveness and Business Position

Attractiveness of Your Market	*Status/Position of Your Business*
Market factors	
Size (dollars, units, or both)	Your share (in equivalent terms)
Size of key segments	Your share of key segments
Growth rate per year:	Your annual growth rate:
Total	Total
Segments	Segments
Diversity of market	Diversity of your participation
Sensitivity to price, service features, and external factors	Your influence on the market
Cyclicality	Lags or leads in your sales
Seasonality	
Bargaining power of upstream suppliers	Bargaining power of your suppliers
Bargaining power of downstream suppliers	Bargaining power of your customers
Competition	
Types of competitors	Where you fit, how you compare in
Degree of concentration	terms of products, marketing
Changes in type and mix	capability, service, production strength, financial strength, management
Entries and exits	Segments you have entered or left
Changes in share	Your relative share change
Substitution by new technology	Your vulnerability to new technology
Degrees and types of integration	Your own level of integration
Financial and economic factors	
Contribution margins	Your margins
Leveraging factors, such as economies of scale and experience	Your scale and experience
Barriers to entry or exit (both financial and nonfinancial)	Barriers to your entry or exit (both financial and nonfinancial)
Capacity utilization	Your capacity utilization
Technological factors	
Maturity and volatity	Your ability to cope with change
Complexity	Depths of your skills
Differentiation	Types of your technological skills
Patents and copyrights	Your patent protection
Manufacturing process technology required	Your manufacturing technology
Sociopolitical factors in your environment	
Social attitudes and trends	Your company's responsiveness and flexibility
Laws and government agency regulations	Your company's ability to cope
Influence with pressure groups and government representatives	Your company's aggressiveness
Human factors, such as unionization and community acceptance	Your company's relationships

SOURCE: Derek F. Abell and John S. Hammond, *Strategic Market Planning: Problems and Analytical Approaches,* © 1979, p. 214. Reprinted by permission of Prentice-Hall, Inc., Englewood Cliffs, New Jersey.

When multiple factors are used to position business units, we need a procedure to combine the measures. One possibility is to weight each factor as to its importance, rate it using a 1–5 or 1–10 scale, and then calculate a total score for business strength and product-market attractiveness. This is done by multiplying the weight by the rating of each factor and summing up the results. Management must then establish a score range for the high, medium, and low categories shown in Exhibit 3–5. Alternatively, we can place a numerical scale on the screening grid and locate each business unit on it according to the unit's total score for business strength and product-market attractiveness. As an alternative, business units (or products) can be screened against a sequence of grids, each comprised of one business strength and one product-market attractiveness factor. Management then judgmentally determines overall positioning on the basis of a review of each screening stage.

The strategic actions indicated by each position on the screening grid are similar to those we discussed for portfolio analysis, although our primary emphasis is upon financial requirements and performance rather than upon cash flow. For example a high-high position in Exhibit 3–5 suggests an investment growth strategy whereas a low-low business unit may be a candidate for harvesting or divestment. These strategy guidelines, while useful in a general way, clearly have some deficiencies. There is no indication of what must be done to achieve a particular strategy (e.g., invest/grow). Firms that occupy the high-high position can lose it through faulty strategies or aggressive competition. For example, the U.S. Surgical Corporation, which entered the surgical stapling market in the late 1960s, was the only producer for a decade until Johnson & Johnson's Ethicon entered the market. By 1980 Ethicon had gained an equal market position to U.S. Surgical's in skin stapling sales. While skin stapling is only part of the total surgical stapling market, U.S. Surgical lost half of the market as a result of misdirected marketing efforts, product performance problems, and Ethicon's strong brand name.[11] U.S. Surgical moved rapidly in 1980 to realign its strategies and strengthen its market position.

Critical Assessment of Screening. Much of strategy development depends upon management judgment and experience. Screening analysis concentrates attention on the differences in products or business units. The underlying analyses necessary to use the screening method provide a detailed diagnosis of the strategic situation. Thus they are more likely than the BCG growth-share grid to reveal strategic gaps and problem areas. The screening methods offer most of the advantages of portfolio analysis, although they are more demanding as to data requirements. Screening is quite flexible in allowing the analyst to select the factors of business strength and market attractiveness that are appropriate for a particular corporation.

Like portfolio analysis, specific guidelines as to appropriate future strategies are not provided by the screening methods. Instead, future strategic actions are suggested in very general terms that may assist management to assign priorities to different business units. Deciding how to combine the screening factors into some type of composite is also challenging and highly dependent upon management judgment and experience. This requires us to think carefully about how to establish the relative importance of different factors. For example, how should we weight a low market share and high technology position in a situation where technical capabilities are key advantages?

While generally acknowledging the usefulness of the GE grid, The Conference Board of Canada's study of strategic planning methods highlighted some problems encountered by users:

> The technique does not explicitly take into account market maturity, and as one executive noted, the GE technique "doesn't distinguish between new, embryonic versus older, attractive but under-resourced units." One respondent pointed out that the value of the technique is impeded if there is one overpowering participant in the market.
>
> Companies described weaknesses in the GE technique parameters as well as some problems in using the technique as part of the planning process. One company reported that the matrix has an excessive centre block concentration. In the words of an executive of a petroleum products firm, this "creates a diversion for senior management in deciding what box to put the SBU in." As a result, "the focus is on the matrix rather than the assumptions used to place the business within the grid," said an executive of an electrical products manufacturer.
>
> Use of the technique requires managers to adopt a long-term focus while acting in the present environment. It is difficult to forecast accurately the long-term prospects necessary for developing strategies. Several companies stressed that the GE matrix is only a tool and should be used not in isolation but rather as a supplement to other methods or processes.[12]

Finally, it is important to recognize that positioning on the grid is subjective; management must decide how to weight the various factors on the grid. In addition, it is necessary to synthesize these factors in establishing a composite value for each grid dimension.

PIMS Data-Based Analysis

The Strategic Planning Institute (SPI) in Cambridge, Massachusetts, has built an extensive data bank of information about business performance and various factors related to performance. The research program, called *profit impact of marketing strategy (PIMS)*, represents the collection and analysis of data over two decades by Sidney Schoeffler and his colleagues at SPI. The data bank contains information on more than 2,400 businesses.

EXHIBIT 3-7   Illustrative Information on Each Business in the PIMS Data Base

---

Characteristics of the business environment
    Long-run growth rate of the market
    Short-run growth rate of the market
    Rate of inflation of selling price levels
    Number and size of customers
    Purchase frequency and magnitude

Competitive position of the business
    Share of the served market
    Share relative to largest competitors
    Product quality relative to competitors
    Prices relative to competitors
    Pay scales relative to competitors
    Marketing efforts relative to competitors
    Pattern of market segmentation
    Rate of new product introductions

Structure of the production process
    Capital intensity (degree of automation, etc.)
    Degree of vertical integration
    Capacity utilization
    Productivity of capital equipment
    Productivity of people
    Inventory levels

Discretionary budget allocations
    R&D budgets
    Advertising and promotion budgets
    Sales force expenditures

Strategic moves
    Patterns of change in the controllable elements above

Operating results
    Profitability results
    Cash flow results
    Growth results

SOURCE: The Strategic Planning Institute, Cambridge, Mass.

Overview of the PIMS Program.   The input data obtained from each participating company consists of about 100 items on each business, as summarized in Exhibit 3-7. Questionnaires are completed by the participating company. A sample page from one of the five PIMS data forms is shown in Exhibit 3-8. As a part of the input data, the firm must supply its assumptions about the "most likely" future rates of change of sales, prices, materials costs, wage rates, and equipment costs. This is done for short-term (1–4 years) and long-term (5–10 years).

The unit of analysis in the PIMS studies is described as follows:

> The unit of observation in PIMS is a *business*. Each business is a division, product line, or other profit center within its parent company, selling a distinct set of *products* and/or *services* to an identifiable group of customers, in competition with a well-defined set of competitors, and for

EXHIBIT 3-8   Sample Page from PIMS Data Forms

103: **"LIFE CYCLE" STAGE OF PRODUCT CATEGORY**

How would you describe the stage of development of the types of products or services sold by this business during the last three years? *(Check one)*

. . . Introductory Stage: Primary demand for product just starting to grow; products or services still unfamiliar to many potential users   ☐ 1

. . . Growth Stage: Demand growing at 10% or more annually in real terms; technology or competitive structure still changing   ☐ 2

. . . Maturity Stage: Products or services familiar to vast majority of prospective users; technology and competitive structure reasonably stable   ☐ 3

. . . Decline Stage: Products viewed as commodities; weaker competitors beginning to exit   ☐ 4

104: What was this business's first year of commercial sales? *(Check one)*

Prior to 1930	1930-1949	1950-1954	1955-1959	1960-1964	1965-1969	1970-1974	1975-
☐ 0	☐ 1	☐ 2	☐ 3	☐ 4	☐ 5	☐ 6	☐ 7

105: At the time this business first entered the market, was it . . . *(Check one)*

. . . One of the pioneers in first developing such products or services?   ☐ 1

. . . An early follower of the pioneer(s) in a still growing, dynamic market?   ☐ 2

. . . A later entrant into a more established market situation?   ☐ 3

106-107: **PATENTS AND TRADE SECRETS**

Does this business benefit *to a significant degree* from patents, trade secrets, or other proprietary methods of production or operation . . .

106: Pertaining to products or services?   NO ☐ 0   YES ☐ 1   **107:** Pertaining to processes?   NO ☐ 0   YES ☐ 1

108: **STANDARDIZATION OF PRODUCTS OR SERVICES**

Are the products or services of this business . . . *(Check one)*

. . . More or less standardized for all customers?   ☐ 0

. . . Designed or produced to order for individual customers?   ☐ 1

109: **FREQUENCY OF PRODUCT CHANGES**

Is it typical practice for the business and its major competitors to change all or part of the line of products or services offered . . . *(Check one)*

. . . Annually (for example, annual model changes)?   ☐ 1

. . . Seasonally?   ☐ 2

. . . Periodically, but at intervals longer than one year?   ☐ 3

. . . No regular, periodic pattern of change?   ☐ 4

110: **TECHNOLOGICAL CHANGE**

Have there been *major* technological changes in the products offered by the business or its major competitors, or in methods of production, during the last 8 years? *(If in doubt about whether a change was "major," answer NO.)*   NO ☐ 0   YES ☐ 1

SOURCE: *PIMS Data Form 1* (Cambridge, Mass.: The Strategic Planning Institute, 1979).

which meaningful separation can be made of revenues, operating costs, investments, and strategic plans.[13]

Thus one company may choose to submit data on an entire division with several products whereas another may select a particular product category. Because a meaningful separation of revenues, operating costs, investments, and strategic plans is required, typically reporting is by division or business unit rather than by specific product-market categories.

The PIMS model identifies nine major strategic influences on profitability and net cash flow. In approximate order of importance, they are as follows:

1. *Investment intensity.* Technology and the chosen way of doing business govern how much fixed capital and working capital are required to produce a dollar of sales or a dollar of value added in the business. Investment intensity generally produces a *negative* impact on percentage measures of profitability or net cash flow; i.e., businesses that are mechanized or automated or inventory-intensive generally show lower returns on investment and sales than businesses that are not.

2. *Productivity.* Businesses producing high value added per employee are *more* profitable than those with low value added per employee. (Definition: "value added" is the amount by which the business increases the market value of the raw materials and components it buys.)

3. *Market position.* A business's share of its served markets (both absolute and relative to its three largest competitors) has a *positive* impact on its profit and net cash flow. (The "served market" is the specific segment of the total potential market—defined in terms of products, customers or areas—in which the business actually competes.)

4. *Growth of the served market.* Growth is generally *favorable* to *dollar* measures of profit, *indifferent* to *percent* measures of profit, and *negative* to all measures of net cash flow.

5. *Quality of the products and/or services offered.* Quality, defined as the customers' evaluation of the business's product/service package as compared to that of competitors, has a generally *favorable* impact on all measures of financial performance.

6. *Innovation/differentiation.* Extensive actions taken by a business in the areas of new product introduction, R&D, marketing effort, and so on, generally produce a *positive* effect on its performance *if* that business has strong market position to begin with. Otherwise, usually not.

7. *Vertical integration.* For businesses located in mature and stable markets, vertical integration (i.e., make rather than buy)

generally impacts *favorably* on performance. In markets that are rapidly growing, declining, or otherwise changing, the opposite is true.

8. **Cost push.** The rates of increase of wages, salaries, and raw material prices, and the presence of a labor union, have *complex* impacts on profit and cash flow, depending on how the business is positioned to pass along the increase to its customers and/or to absorb the higher costs internally.

9. **Current strategic effort.** The current direction of change of any of the above factors has effects on profit and cash flow that are *frequently* opposite to that of the factor itself. For example, *having* strong market share tends to *increase* net cash flow, but *getting* share *drains* cash while the business is making that effort.

Additionally, there is such a thing as being a good or a poor "operator." A good operator can improve the profitability of a strong strategic position or minimize the damage of a weak one; a poor operator does the opposite. The presence of a management team that functions as a good operator is therefore a *favorable* element of a business, and produces a financial result greater than one would expect from the strategic position of the business alone.[14]

Using multiple regression analysis, measures of the nine influences account for up to 80 percent of the observed variation in profitability across the businesses in the data base. "These factors are incorporated into a set of profit-predicting models that assign to each factor its proper weight, judging from the experiences reflected in the data base. The models also indicate how the impact of each profit-determining factor is conditioned by other factors."[15]

Output Reports for PIMS Users. The results of PIMS analyses include both diagnostic and prescriptive information. The four major reports supplied to the participating firm are as follows:

The *"Par" Report* specifies the return on investment that is normal (or "par") for the business, given the characteristics of its market, competition, position, technology, and cost structure. It reports whether this business is the kind that normally earns, say, 3 percent on investment or 30 percent, judging by the experiences of *other* businesses with *similar* characteristics. Also, it identifies the major strengths and weaknesses of the business that count for the high or low "par."

The *Strategy Analysis Report* is a computational pretest of several possible *strategic moves* in the business. It indicates the normal short- and long-term consequences of each such move, judging by the experience of other businesses making a similar move, from a similar starting point and in a similar business environment. It specifies the profit (or loss) likely to be achieved by such projected changes, along with the associated investment and cash flow. This report is used by (a) upper-level managers and planners, for evidence on the potential effects of *broad moves* in market share, margin, capital intensity, and vertical integration; and (b) by middle-level people, for evidence of the potential effects of *specific* action in such areas as programs to improve relative product quality, increases in the ratio of marketing expense to sales, improvements in capacity utilization or employee productivity, or changes in R&D outlays.

The Optimum Strategy Report nominates that *combination* of several strategic moves that promises to give optimal results for the business, also judging by the experiences of other businesses under similar circumstances.

This report offers such an opinion for any of *several different measures of profit performance,* for example: discounted cash flow over 10 years; return on investment for the next 5 years; and short-term earnings dollars.

Report on "Look-Alikes" (ROLA) provides managers with a way to discover effective tactics for accomplishing their strategic objectives (for example, increasing profitability or cash flow, gaining market share, improving productivity or product quality). ROLA retrieves from the data base businesses that are strategically similar to the business being analyzed (its "look-alikes") and reports a large number of the strategic and operating characteristics that helped them to attain the specified objective.[16]

Management can use the PIMS reports in several ways to assist in analyzing business performance and formulating future strategies. The analyses help to focus attention upon possible problems and opportunities. They are useful in examining alternative strategic actions and estimating the consequence of such actions. Business strengths and weaknesses are highlighted in the PIMS comparative analyses.

Critical Assessment of the PIMS Approach.   One of the major strengths of PIMS is that several logical strategic factors, through empirical analysis, are shown to be related to profitability (ROI) and cash flow, using a large cross section of businesses. When using the information generated from pooled business experience data, we need to recognize certain limitations of PIMS. The approach is historical in orientation and so there is no way to be sure that past relationships will hold in the future. Trend analysis can be useful in determining the extent to which these relationships have changed over time. Regression analysis used in the PIMS studies measures *association,* not *causality,* indicating which factors are closely related to performance but not why. Thus the results describe *existing* relationships rather than prescribe what should be done to alter performance. Assuming the relationships hold in the future, PIMS can analyze the impact of alternative strategies, thus helping to identify promising future strategies. The opportunity for analyzing what-if questions is an important feature of the PIMS model. The PIMS analysis is systematic and not subject to the judgments of particular individuals in the firm. The data, of course, are supplied by the firm and can be inaccurate or incorrectly reported. Completion of the PIMS forms may be beneficial to the executive(s) answering them because, in order to answer the questions, one needs to make a comprehensive analysis of business operations.

There is some question as to the possible effects from confounding the dependent and independent variables in the PIMS models.[17] For example, in the Par ROI model, investment, revenue, and cost terms are on both sides of the regression equation. Where this situation occurs, the level of explanation of the predictor variables may to some extent be artificial rather than real.

The PIMS unit of analysis is more aggregate and less flexible in terms of choice by the user than is the case with the grid analysis methods. Also, the variation in units of analysis between firms may affect the results of the analyses. For example, what happens when one firm submits data on a single product in a business area, such as microwave ovens, whereas another firm submits data on a business made of a complete line of major home appliances? Another limitation is that *direct* comparisons with key competitors are not possible. This, of course, is also a strength of PIMS since, if such comparisons were possible, many firms would be unwilling to provide data for analysis. A test of a surrogate of the PIMS model in the brewing industry found that the model behaved in the manner described by the Strategic Planning Institute.[18]

Its limitations acknowledged, the PIMS research has the distinction of being one of the few efforts (the only one of comparable scope) to conduct empirical research in the area of corporate strategy which for so long has been guided primarily by wisdom, simple rules of thumb, and management experience and judgment. The PIMS studies offer convincing evidence of the usefulness of such research—recognizing that management judgment and experience must always decide what strategic actions to take.

Other Strategic Planning Tools

In addition to the three widely publicized methods we have examined, several other strategic planning tools and techniques are used. Many companies have developed procedures that incorporate, in varying degrees, portfolio, screening, and PIMS analyses plus other planning tools. To complete the discussion of strategic analysis, a brief review of two other planning tools is provided, the Shell Chemical Directional Policy Matrix and the Arthur D. Little Life Cycle Matrix. Examples of these methods are shown later in the chapter (see Exhibit 3–10).

Shell Chemical Directional Policy Matrix (DPM). Similar to the GE Screening Grid, this 3×3 matrix evaluates a company's competitive capabilities (strong, average, weak) and profitability prospects (unattractive, average, attractive) for the business sector (industry attractiveness) that is being analyzed.[19] It is used as a framework for evaluating the competitive position of a business. A business (or product) is positioned into one of the nine cells in the matrix, based on the rating for each of the grid dimensions. The analysis can include a firm's SBUs or products as well as those of key competitors. Business sector profitability includes assessment of market growth rate, market quality, industry feedstock situation (raw materials), and environmental factors. Company competitive capabilities include market position, product research and development, and production capability. Strategies are matched to the cell position of a business on the matrix.

Arthur D. Little Life Cycle Matrix. This grid, which considers the product life cycle stage and the company's strengths over its competition, results in a 5×4 matrix.[20] Life cycle stages are embryonic, growing, maturing, and aging. Competitive positions include dominant, strong, favorable, tenable, and weak. The product life cycle stage is evaluated in terms of growth rate, growth potential, distribution and stability of market share, breadth of product line, number of competitors, customer stability, ease of entry, and technological stability. Competitive strengths consider market share, breadth of product line, cost position, management skill, technological advantages, and extent of vertical integration. Each position on the grid corresponds to a different strategy situation. For example, a position suggesting the advisability of divesting or harvesting a particular business unit would be the *aging* stage of the product life cycle and a *weak* competitive situation.

ASSESSMENT OF ANALYSIS METHODS

The basic purpose of the portfolio, screening, PIMS, and other planning tools is to assist management in selecting future strategies for the corporation and its business units. Each method makes a contribution to this objective, primarily in helping to diagnose the strategic situation faced by an SBU. None of the planning tools is very useful in showing what the future strategy should be.

Role of Analysis Methods

By 1985 the analysis methods (portfolio, screening, and PIMS) were receiving negative reactions from some corporate users. Many of these problems were due to the fact that management and consultants were placing too much emphasis upon the strategy guidelines suggested by the analysis methods:

These overly quantitative techniques caused companies to place a great deal of emphasis on market-share growth. As a result, companies were devoting too much time to corporate portfolio planning and too little to hammering out strategies to turn sick operations into healthy ones or ensure that a strong business remained strong. In too many instances, strategic planning degenerated into acquiring growth businesses that the buyers did not know how to manage and selling or milling to death mature ones.[21]

Some observers have placed the responsibility for these problems on consultants who overemphasized the importance of planning tools. Others argue that the role of corporate and business unit planning staffs became too powerful, and that these staffs used planning tools to chart the wrong strategies for businesses. These experiences are unfortunate since the analysis tools can assist in diagnosing the strategic situation confronting an SBU. They are particularly useful in comparing SBUs and competitors. However, when used to map out future strategies, the techniques can be misleading and possibly dangerous. They should never be used to select strategy; this is the responsibility of line management. General Electric's chairman, John F. Welch, Jr., appropriately describes strategy:

> Strategy, says Welch, "is trying to understand where you sit today in today's world. Not where you wish you were and where you hoped you would be, but where you are. And [it's trying to understand] where you want to be in 1990. [It's] assessing with everything in your head the competitive changes, the market changes that you can capitalize on or ward off to go from here to there. It's assessing the realistic chances of getting from here to there."[22]

Strategic planning experiences of many corporations over the last decade are causing users of planning methods to examine the logic of the methods in greater depth. Appropriately, line management is playing a more central role in strategy formulation. These trends are positive since decision makers are encouraged to understand strategic analysis, while relying also on their strategic thinking and intuitive feel for the situation.

One important consequence of the expanded use of strategic analysis techniques was the reorganization of the corporation into SBUs. This concept helped to expand interest and concern about strategy beyond the corporate level. These self-contained businesses have a clearly defined set of competitors, managers responsible for developing and implementing their own strategies, and profitability measured in real income rather than transfer payments between manufacturing divisions.[23] Interestingly, the SBU concept has been adopted by several Japanese companies. Reorganizing into an SBU structure is cited by Toshiba Corp. and Oki Electric Industry Co. as an important factor in increasing their sales and profits. Initially, Toshiba created too many

SBUs, and this was a problem. Starting with 104 units, the number was eventually reduced to 42.

Richard J. Mahoney, president and chief executive officer of Monsanto Co., makes the following comments on strategic analysis:

> Hundreds of U.S. companies, including my own, have engaged in strategic analysis in recent years. In general, despite the trauma, they have found the exercise valuable, particularly when it was done carefully and without mindless adherence to technique. Companies gained a better understanding of what they do well, what they can do better, and what they will never do well. As a result, in the past few years we have seen perhaps the greatest corporate repositioning in recent industrial history—the culmination of the "era of portfolio analysis."
>
> That era has now inevitably, given way to its successor, the "era of post-portfolio analysis," in which we must live with the results of all that strategic planning. Whether we opted for the gain-share strategy (that marvelous euphemism for "cut the price"), the sell-share strategy (meaning "where did all the customers go?"), or some other, we are firmly committed now. The question is: What do corporate managers do after the strategy consultants go home?[24]

As emphasized by Monsanto's experience, strategic planning is far too complex and situation-specific to allow us to use analysis techniques as a substitute for executive decision making. Perhaps the greatest contribution of formal strategic analysis is that it raises vital questions about each unit of a business. The methods highlight the importance of developing a strategy appropriate for the opportunity and competitive situation in each business unit. It simply does not make good strategic sense to treat each business unit the same. Formal analysis forces management to recognize difference in business units and to develop strategies in the best interest of total corporate performance.

Exhibit 3–9 compares the portfolio, screening, and PIMS methods as to their usefulness in various planning activities. With the exception of PIMS, the strategic guidelines are primarily financial (cash flow or ROI). PIMS identifies the key determinants of ROI and cash flow. Yet even this method does not indicate specific strategies for improving the product quality or reducing the cost.

Strategic Relevance of Market Share

Since market share is a key variable in portfolio analysis and is also included as a factor in the GE screening grid and PIMS analyses, a brief discussion of the strategic relevance of market share is appropriate. A major study by Robert Jacobson and David A. Aaker of the market share/return on investment (ROI) relationship (using PIMS data) found that "the direct impact of market share on ROI is substantially less than commonly assumed and, in fact, relatively minor."[25] Market

EXHIBIT 3-9   Usefulness of the Strategic Analysis Methods for Various Planning Activities

Planning Activity	Portfolio Analysis	Screening Methods	PIMS
Comparison of business unit* with:			
Other internal units	Position on the growth-share matrix is the basis of comparison.	Position on the screening grid is the basis of comparison.	The PIMS output provides no direct basis of comparison.
Competition	Competing units (or products) can be plotted on the matrix if market share data are available.	Placing competitive units (or products) on the screen is very difficult as a result of the information needed on business strength.	The PAR and look-alikes reports indicate comparative data for *groups* of firms with similar characteristics.
Present situation analysis:			
Business unit	Desirability of present situation is based upon position on the matrix.	Same as portfolio analysis.	Extensive diagnostic information is provided by the various PIMS reports.
Market segment	Growth-share matrix position.	Screening grid position.	Not applicable.
Product/line	Growth-share matrix position.	Screening grid position.	Not applicable.
Determining future strategies:			
Corporation	Provides resource allocation guidelines based on cash flow requirements.	Provides resource allocation guidelines based on ROI considerations.	Management can use the business unit analyses as an input to corporate strategy.
Business unit	Indicates cash flow strategy.	Strengths and weaknesses of various screening factors may suggest possible future business strategies.	The PIMS reports indicate the projected effect of several possible strategic moves and nominate an optimal strategy.

*Or other appropriate units of analysis.

SOURCE: Portions of this exhibit are based upon Derek F. Abell and John S. Hammond, *Strategic Market Planning* (Englewood Cliffs, N.J.: Prentice-Hall, 1979), 380.

share is more appropriate as a measure of the effectiveness of management's strategies than as a causal factor. There is probably a tendency when using the strategic analysis models and in strategic deliberations to attribute too much strategic relevance to market share.

The implications of the Jacobson and Aaker study are significant in helping to establish how market share relates to strategy.[26] They suggest that emphasis could more appropriately be placed on key factors, such as product quality, customer satisfaction, productivity, corporate culture, product line appropriateness, and management effectiveness. Thus preoccupation with market share position may be inappropriate and possibly misleading. While these research results are from only one study, they reinforce various other questions that have been raised about the usefulness of market share as strategy guideline.

If market share serves better as a measure of performance, this raises important questions as to the usefulness of the BCG portfolio analysis as well as to the general role of market share in strategy development. Caution seems appropriate in the use of market share as a basis of directing strategy. We noted other concerns about the BCG grid earlier in the chapter, such as the success of small market share firms. Since the PIMS data are based on rather aggregate levels of analysis, we need additional studies using the market segment as a unit of analysis to provide a more definitive assessment of market share's strategic role.

Evaluating the Strategic Analysis Methods

Portfolio analysis, screening, and PIMS, respectively, use cash flow, return on investment (ROI), and ROI and cash flow to gauge the performance of an SBU. Since cash flow and ROI are useful guidelines in selecting business unit strategies, a planner might choose both criteria if given the option. Thus the portfolio method falls somewhat short of the other two on this basis of comparison. A major issue is whether the determinants used to predict performance (e.g., market share) are, in fact, *causes* of performance. Let's look closer at the underlying logic of the variables and interrelationships that are used in each method, the research support that exists, and how the validity of analysis results can be evaluated.

Performance Predictors. PIMS comes out best on this basis of comparison, screening is next, and portfolio is last. While the PIMS predictors were selected on the basis of judgment and experience, analysis of data from many firms and business areas within firms indicates which factors (predictors) are most useful in gauging performance. The screening approach assumes that high performance will result in situations with high product-market attractiveness and high business strength. There are some supporting financial data for this assumption. Portfolio analysis bases performance predictions about cash flow upon the analysis of the experience curve (market share position) and considerations of product-market maturity. The data-based approach (PIMS) includes some factors also used in the screening approach so there is an overlap between the two approaches. The PIMS studies offer empirical support in the diagnosis of a particular firm. Both the screening and portfolio approaches depend more heavily upon management judgment.

The user of the PIMS analyses should recognize that the results are deceptively quantitative in that the planner may be inclined to lean more heavily upon the information than is justified. In addition, the comparisons are in terms of groups of firms rather than individual competitors. Finally, the user should be aware that prescriptive guidelines are based on descriptive analyses. This simply means that in analyzing past and existing relationships between ROI and cash flow, we assume that these same relationships will be correct in the future. But it is uncertain whether these relationships will remain stable.

Research Support.   PIMS has a more extensive research base underlying it than do the other two methods. PIMS incorporates several logical factors in terms of their strategic impact on performance, and statistical analysis shows the collective and relative importance of these factors in predicting ROI and cash flow. The regression analysis used in PIMS does not determine that the factors *cause* ROI and cash flow, but instead shows that a strong relationship exists. One should recognize that there is also an extensive base of experience, including performance results, linked to both the portfolio and screening methods. The major distinction is that PIMS includes many more factors while the other methods do not statistically relate performance and its determinants. On the basis of research results, PIMS appears to have somewhat of an edge over the other methods.

Validity of the Results.   There are at least four ways to determine the validity of the results provided by the portfolio, screening, and PIMS models:

1. They can be evaluated by management based on judgment.
2. The user can rely upon the supporting research that exists.
3. The results of two different methods can be compared to see if they yield the same results.
4. Strategies indicated by the analysis can be implemented and then tracked to see how well they work.

Of the four approaches, comparative tests offer an excellent means of evaluation. In a pioneering study Wind, Mahajan, and Swire compared the BCG growth-share, GE screening, Shell, and A. D. Little matrix models, using PIMS data for 15 businesses (SBUs) of a Fortune 500 firm.[27] Using several comparative analyses, differences were found in the classification of an SBU based on the four portfolio approaches. Exhibit 3–10 shows an example of one comparison that illustrates substantial differences in the classification of the 15 businesses. While these results are based on an analysis of one corporation, they clearly suggest caution in the use of the planning models. Variations in definition, cut-off points (for high-low) on the various dimensions, weights of dimensions, or the model used could result in a different classification of SBUs. The consequence of these differences is a variation in diagnosing the strategic situation confronting an SBU.

Two implications emerge from the Wind, Mahagan, and Swire study. First, since each portfolio model emphasizes different objectives (e.g., cash flow versus return on investment), the choice of the model should correspond to management's portfolio objective. Second, the use of more than one model seems appropriate to enable comparative analyses. Multiple models can be used to respond to alternative comparative criteria and to highlight differences for assessment by management. We also need additional comparative studies to gain further insights into the features and limitations of the models.

How Extensively Are the Models Used?

It is of interest to know how widely the planning models are used by companies. A 1979 survey of Fortune 1,000 and Fortune 500 companies found that 36 percent of the firms had used some form of strategic portfolio planning.[28] The industries most apt to use such models included chemicals, farm equipment, electronics and appliances, paper and fiber products, food, metal manufacturing, petroleum refining, glass, concrete, abrasives, and gypsum. Industries reporting rare or no use of the planning tools included aerospace, toys, musical instruments, shipbuilding, railroads, furniture, broadcasting, and several other business categories.

A more recent study conducted by The Conference Board of Canada provides important insights into the use of analytical portfolio models by Canadian companies.[29] A significant portion of major Canadian organizations use one of the techniques shown in Exhibit 3–11. The GE/McKinsey grid was the most popular technique among the companies surveyed. Exhibit 3–12 shows the extent of user satisfaction with the techniques. The index of satisfaction was similar across all methods, even though the extent of use of specific methods varied.

EXHIBIT 3-10 A Comparison of Four Standardized Portfolio Models

---

1. Growth share matrix

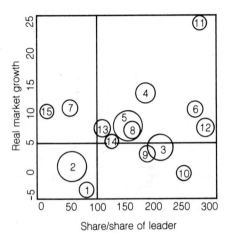

2. Shell international type matrix (weighted)

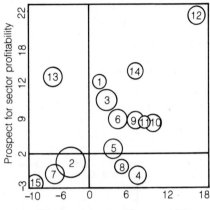

3. Par based indices of business position versus industry attractiveness

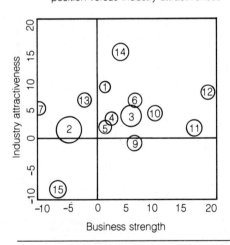

4. A modified A. D. Little type matrix

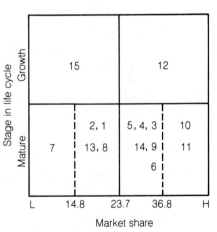

SOURCE: Yoram Wind, Vijay Mahajan, and Donald J. Swire, "An Empirical Comparison of Standardized Portfolio Models," *Journal of Marketing,* Spring 1983, 92.

EXHIBIT 3-11   Usage Patterns by Technique (number of respondents)

Status	Boston Consulting Group Product Portfolio	GE/McKinsey Industry Attractiveness-Business Strengths Array	Shell Chemical Directional Policy Matrix	Arthur D. Little Life Cycle Matrix	Profit Impact of Market Strategies
Used in the past; still being used	26	50	6	22	10
Used in the past; now rejected	6	0	1	1	5
Scheduled for use in the near future	1	4	0	1	2
Considered for use and rejected	11	1	2	5	11
Never seriously considered	41	30	76	56	57
Total	85	85	85	85	85

SOURCE: Carolyn R. Farquhar and Stanley J. Shapiro, *Strategic Business Planning in Canada* (Ottawa: The Conference Board of Canada, 1983), 16.

EXHIBIT 3-12   Users' Degree of Satisfaction—by Technique Used (number of respondents)

	BCG	GE	DPM	ADL	PIMS
(A) With range of available techniques:					
Very satisfied	6	10	1	5	2
Somewhat satisfied	13	29	5	13	6
Half and half	5	7	0	4	1
Somewhat dissatisfied	2	1	0	0	1
Very dissatisfied	0	1	0	0	0
No answer	0	2	0	0	0
Total number of current users	26	50	6	22	10
Index of satisfaction*	72.1	74.0	79.2	76.1	72.5
(B) With entire strategic planning process:					
Very satisfied	2	4	1	2	0
Somewhat satisfied	12	26	3	12	6
Half and half	5	15	2	4	2
Somewhat dissatisfied	7	3	0	4	2
Very dissatisfied	0	1	0	0	0
No answer	0	1	0	0	0
Total number of current users	26	50	6	22	10
Index of satisfaction*	58.7	64.8	70.8	63.6	60.0

Note: BCG—Boston Consulting Group Product Portfolio; GE—GE/McKinsey Industry Attractiveness-Business Strengths Array; DPM—Shell Chemical Directional Policy Matrix; ADL—Arthur D. Little Life Cycle Matrix; PIMS—Profit Impact of Market Strategies.

*The weights assigned to each response are: 100 = very satisfied; 75 = somewhat satisfied; 50 = half and half; 25 = somewhat dissatisfied; and 0 = very dissatisfied.

SOURCE: Carolyn R. Farquhar and Stanley J. Shapiro, *Strategic Business Planning in Canada* (Ottawa: The Conference Board of Canada, 1983), 22.

EXHIBIT 3-13 Advantages and Disadvantages of Strategic Planning

---

Number of Respondents	Advantages Cited
76	Better understanding of the external factors that influence our marketing effort
55	Better understanding of the type of data needed to improve our planning effort
70	Better understanding of the market(s) we serve
27	Better understanding of the type of staff needed for effective planning
48	Better understanding of present and potential customers
48	Better understanding of the products and services sold
0	None

Number of Respondents	Disadvantages Cited
22	Longer lead time needed than was originally expected
7	Difficult to get information on different techniques
4	Difficult to find experts on different techniques
27	Required more management specialist time than was originally expected
28	Required more top management time than was originally expected
14	Higher costs incurred in recovering data than were originally expected
3	Process not as useful as was expected
5	Results achieved after the initial effort did not justify the costs
8	None

SOURCE: Carolyn R. Farquhar and Stanley J. Shapiro, *Strategic Business Planning in Canada* (Ottawa: The Conference Board of Canada, 1983), 87.

A somewhat lower level of satisfaction was found for the entire planning process. Finally, Exhibit 3-13 highlights key advantages and disadvantages of strategic planning by the Canadian survey respondents.

SELECTING AN SBU STRATEGY

Victor Kiam's successful buyout and turnaround of Sperry's Remington Division, a manufacturer of electric shavers, illustrates the importance of selecting the right SBU strategy for the situation that exists. In 1979 Remington had lost money in each of the previous four years.[30] The unit held a strong position in an attractive market niche. The brand name also has a high awareness level among consumers. Kiam was convinced that an aggressive marketing effort would be successful, although profits would depend upon cost reductions. The company's sales increased from $37 million to $150 million in 1984 and a pretax profit of $12 million. Kiam slowed down the introductions of new products and introduced a low-priced shaver. At $19.95 the shaver sold 500,000 units in the first year.

Strategic Options

Decisions about the future strategy of a business unit like Sperry's Remington Divisions are based on an examination of its past performance, the present strategic situation, and its attractiveness as a future product-market. Management must decide whether to: (1) maintain or strengthen its position; (2) attempt to shift into a more desirable position; or (3) exit from the SBU. Of course as a product-market matures, strategic position may be altered because of a decline in the attractiveness of the product-market. While analysis approaches like PIMS and screening offer useful strategic guidelines as to which alternatives to follow, management must select a strategic plan for each business unit while taking into account its strategic position, available resources, forecasts of future competitive and market conditions, and the relative attractiveness of available SBU opportunities. The process is described as follows:

> The end product of the strategic planning process is a future best-yield portfolio composed of individual product-market entries, taking into account risk and short-term versus long-term trade-offs. The decision of which product-market entries to include in the portfolio as well as the extent to which each should be emphasized is a most complex one to make.[31]

Finding a Competitive Advantage

The essence of both corporate and marketing strategy is finding an advantage over competition. Companies can gain competitive advantage in the following ways:

Establishing market power through market share dominance—Goodyear holds this position in the world tire market.

Developing new products—Xerox pioneered a new industry using this strategy as did U.S. Surgical with its line of surgical staplers.

Finding a specialized niche of a product-market that can be dominated—Nucor in steel joists and J. L. Clark in specialized containers have adopted this strategy.

Establishing strong distribution channels—Snap-on-Tools, by concentrating on professional mechanics served by independent dealers in a van, dominates the professional market for socket wrenches and other tools.

Obtaining manufacturing or operating cost advantages due to geographical location, process innovation, or other operating improvements. The cost advantages of Japanese automakers are illustrative.

Developing a strong financial position for growth—Delta Air Lines' low debt compared to other carriers illustrates this advantage in the troubled airline industry, as does Schlumberger in the oil-field service industry.

These are but a few of the many ways that firms establish strong positions in product-markets. Differential advantage is gained by deciding what customer needs to serve and by developing appropriate strategies for meeting the needs of target customers.

Theodore Levitt of the Harvard Business School has a very convincing case for the fact that commodities do not exist; instead, all goods and services are differentiable.[32] He suggests that in addition to the product or service and its attributes, the marketing effort itself can be a powerful basis for building a differential advantage. Levitt observes that a manager, through his/her behavior, becomes an extension of the idea of product differentiation. Here is how he summarizes marketing differentiation:

> While differentiation is most readily apparent in branded, packaged consumer goods, in the design, operating character, or composition of industrial goods, or in the features of "service" intensity of intangible products, differentiation consists as powerfully in how one operates the business. In the way the marketing process is managed may reside the opportunity for many companies, especially those that offer generically undifferentiated products and services, to escape the commodity trap.[33]

In some situations a company may want to establish its brand as a substitute for another rather than to differentiate it. Nevertheless, when this occurs, there are often other aspects of the marketing strategy that vary among firms. The concept of positioning a product is discussed in Chapter 9.

THE STRATEGIC PLAN

The apparel maker, Munsingwear Inc., illustrates the impact that a sequence of faulty decisions can have upon a business performance.[34] Profits started to fall each year after 1977 from $4 million to a loss of nearly $15 million in 1982. Since then, results have been above the break-even level, pulling the company back from near bankruptcy. Contributing to the sales and profit decline was a new management team, which in 1979 started cutting expenses. Because labels were changed on underwear boxes, retailers had problems in finding the boxes in their storerooms. The distinctive waistband with Munsingwear's established brand name was removed from the underwear line. Although the gain was a few cents in production costs, retailers and consumers did not like the blank waistbands. As a result, the label was subsequently placed back on the underwear. Other strategy blunders included new product offerings that did not correspond to the wants of Munsingwear's Middle American segment of the apparel market—for example, a $125 velour warm-up suit aimed at affluent shoppers. A new inventory system was installed but proved to be faulty. Problems with suppliers caused delivery delays to retailers, who shifted their business to Jockey and Izod. A new president, appointed in 1983, found further problems in the finance department, including 40 percent of accounts receivable that were past due, some extending to 18 months! The firm had no objectives or business strategy. No one was apparently responsible for the decisions that were made. A turnaround is now underway, although management faces a major challenge to return the firm to sales and profit levels of the mid-1970s. Expense constraints prevent buying expensive TV time or advertising in major magazines such as *Sports Illustrated* and *People:* the 1984 advertising budget was below $5 million.

Munsingwear clearly illustrates the importance of preparing and implementing a good strategic plan. In this section the development of the strategic business plan is considered, some planning dangers are discussed, and important issues in implementation are examined.

Developing the Strategic Plan

A look at the outline of a strategic plan for a business unit will show what is included in a plan. The following areas are often part of a strategic plan for an SBU:

   I. Strategic situation assessment
  II. Mission statement
 III. Business unit objectives
 IV. Business unit strategy
   V. Functional plans
      a. Business development
      b. Marketing
      c. Quality
      d. Product and technology
      e. Human resources
      f. Manufacturing/facilities
      g. Finance

EXHIBIT 3-14   Appraising the Strategic Situation

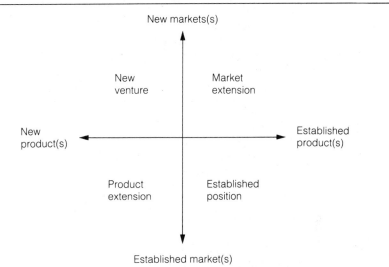

The functional plans section of the strategic plan should correspond to the needs and structure of a particular organization. The above components are illustrative.

The type of strategic situation faced by a business unit should be determined early in the planning process. This situation may range from a new venture involving a new product(s) in a new market to a mature situation with an established product(s) and market. Varying degrees of newness fall between these extremes. We should also indicate both the competitive structure and SBU position. A range of strategic situations is shown in Exhibit 3-14.[35] The two extremes—a new venture and an established position—highlight the differences that may influence management's appraisal of a business unit.

It is often inappropriate to use the same standards to gauge a new venture situation and an established position because of the influence of several factors. The same is true for any of the other strategic situations shown in Exhibit 3-14. For example, if we are at a competitive disadvantage in a new product-market, this problem may be far less critical than in a mature situation since our competition is less firmly entrenched and the market opportunity is growing. Since the strategic situation assessment of an SBU depends mainly on the situation confronting each market target served by an SBU, we shall delay further discussion of this topic until Chapter 7.

In established product and market situations, the chances of a business unit being able to bring about major changes in market position are slim, particularly if we attempt to do so from a weak position.

EXHIBIT 3-15 Outline for the Operations Plan of a Division—Ametek, Inc.

---

1. Executive Summary
   One to two page synopsis of major points covered in plan.

2. Definition of Division's Business Unit
   The most common business unit is a product line.

3. Economic Outlook
   Concise analysis of market growth forecast supported by key assumptions. Also included are inflation forecasts for three most critical cost items.

4. Major Objectives
   Division sales and profits forecast. Broadbrush discussion of major plan objectives following a review of performance to prior year plan's objectives.

   Instructions state:

   Review of Prior Plan Objectives
   a. *Each objective presented in the prior year's plan should be discussed as to its status (particularly if the objective spanned more than one plan year).*
   b. *It is intended the plan be flexible. Therefore, during the plan year an objective may be dropped or changed in response to new opportunities or market conditions.*
   c. *If possible, a table should be prepared comparing in quantitative terms the actual performance to the stated plan objectives.*

   Major Plan Objectives
   a. *Discussion of the major objectives to be undertaken or continued by the division to achieve the above forecast. This is a summary of the discussion to follow in the next section of the plan which will deal with each business unit separately.*
   b. *It is envisioned that each objective will be succinctly defined and couched in a quantitative manner.*
   c. *The rationale behind each objective would be expected to be presented.*
   d. *A statement should be included to assign a probability of successfully meeting the objectives within the prescribed time frame.*
   e. *Also included should be a brief discussion of the opportunities and threats to the success of each objective. Factors of both an external and an internal nature to the division should be listed.*

SOURCE: David S. Hopkins, *The Marketing Plan* (New York: The Conference Board, 1981), 55–56.

The closer the strategic situation is to a new venture, the more likely there is a chance for favorable market opportunity. This greater opportunity, of course, must be weighed against the risks and uncertainties present. When we use one of the strategic analysis approaches for business unit evaluation, the results of our analysis must take into account the strategic situation of the SBU.

The situation assessment provides a basis for establishing the SBU's mission, setting objectives, and determining the strategy to use

5. Financial Analysis
   One-year review and three-year forecast of sales, profits and investment analysis for the total division (financial analysis of individual business units appears in a later section).

6. Individual Business Unit Forecasts
   Brief discussion about each business unit's profit objectives and the strategies planned. Also included here is a discussion of pertinent marketing and other information about the business unit, and a review of obsolete or unprofitable products.

7. Resource Requirements
   Summary of the division's requirements for staffing, plant capacity, marketing expenditures, etc. This should include a presentation of capital investment requirements by manufacturing and may include additional reports if appropriate.

8. Pricing Policy
   Discussion of division's overall pricing policy.
   [Instructions state: This discussion should comment on how pricing actions would change under adverse conditions of falling demand or opportunistic conditions of strong growth. What price actions exist to combat current double-digit inflation?]

9. Contingency Plans
   Discussion of steps planned by division under adverse conditions.
   [Instructions state: Discussion of the steps planned by the division under the four following conditions: (1) labor strike, (2) rapid fall-off in product demand, (3) rapid increase in product demand, and (4) strong competition attack for your share of the market.]

10. Special Subjects
    Discussion of additional subjects or issues deemed important by division general manager.

11. Action Plan
    List of major tasks necessary to fulfill the plan objectives. Estimated start and completion dates are needed for tasks begun in the first year of the plan.

to meet these objectives. The SBU's strategy indicates market target priorities, available resources, financial constraints, and other strategic guidelines needed to develop functional plans. Depending upon the size and diversity of the SBU, the functional plans may either be included in the SBU plan or developed separately. An outline of the plan used by a division of a corporation and its SBUs is shown in Exhibit 3–15. Ametek, Inc. has four product groups, each comprised of one or more SBUs: electromechanical equipment, process equipment, precision instruments, and industrial materials. Sales in 1985 were $0.5 billion.

Implementation Issues

Top management's decisions about areas of business activity, priorities for resource allocation, and business strategies may affect the management team in two ways. First, management's decision about the future of a particular SBU sets the stage for how the unit will be managed (e.g., for cash or for growth). This may create opportunities and, in some instances, threats for the people assigned to a business unit. Second, traditional organizational structures may be inadequate for managing restructured business units.

Once management decides about the future of the firm's business areas, different strategic challenges are created. Some call for growth strategies, while others require managing cash flow and even sometimes deciding to exit from an area. Such differences in business strategies create needs for people with different kinds of experience, technical skills, and preferences. For example, a successful new venture management team may not be effective in managing a mature business unit. While some executives are effective across a wide range of strategic situations, many are not. Consider, for example, the approach taken at General Electric:

> Strategic objectives for the company's wide-ranging products are defined as "grow" and "harvest," depending upon the product life cycle. Now its general managers are being classified by personal style or orientation as "growers," "caretakers," and—tongue-in-cheek—as "undertakers" to match managerial type with the product's status.[36]

In support of GE's approach, Gupta and Guvindarajan studied strategy implementation in diversified corporations and found that for SBU managers of growth SBUs, there was a strong relationship between the willingness to take risks and the effectiveness of strategy implementation.[37] Thus in growth situations managers with a propensity for risk may be better implementors than those who wish to avoid risk. In contrast, managers with greater risk-aversion were more effective for businesses in the harvest category. The study also found that different strategic situations require different functional skills. Not surprisingly, respondents indicated little enthusiasm for managing SBUs with low business strength and low market attractiveness.

Top management must offer proper incentive packages to attract and hold competent executives in all areas of the business. While matching people to jobs is not a recent innovation, the increasing trend toward different treatment of business units expands the importance of the task.

It is important to consider the impact of strategic planning upon organizational design. It seems clear that those responsible for implementing SBU plans should play a major role in strategy formulation. Because of the much greater emphasis placed upon the SBU as a planning unit, its use in organizational design is also logical. Use of the SBU as a basis for organizational design gives consideration to both product and market, and combines all or most business functions into one organizational unit. Increasingly, companies are moving away from manufacturing, brand, and product organizational designs and instead adopting product-market types of organizations.

MARKETING'S STRATEGIC ROLE

Since the remaining chapters of the book are concerned with the development of the strategic marketing plan, a look at marketing's role in building the business unit plan will illustrate the close correspondence between business unit and marketing strategy. Marketing's participation in strategic planning is illustrated in Exhibit 3–16, which is based upon the experience of the General Electric Company. While the marketing manager's role in strategic planning varies from company to company, Exhibit 3–16 highlights the wide range of participation that is possible. The discussion of strategic planning in Chapters 2 and 3 indicates the various planning activities in which the skills and experience of marketing professionals are needed.

Because of marketing's boundary orientation between the organization and its customers, channel members, and competition, the function is central to the strategic planning process.[38] Marketing has the expertise for environmental monitoring, for deciding what customer groups to serve, for product specifications, and for deciding which competitors to position against. Marketing executives must demonstrate the capability to meet these responsibilities of strategic planning. In addition, we need to recognize that corporate and SBU strategies involve integrating marketing and other functional strategies.

AT&T provides an important illustration of the clashes that sometimes occur in corporate power struggles.[39] Deregulation purportedly moved the firm toward a market-driven orientation. Yet three of AT&Ts senior marketing executives left the firm in late 1983 along with several marketing managers. They apparently questioned the role that marketing would play in the new AT&T. Marketing people were convinced that their attempts to meet customer needs were hampered because manufacturing took too long to produce expensive products with limited features. There was a clash between manufacturing and marketing, and the power was centered with manufacturing. Marketing people were edged out of key decisions involving product planning, pricing, and distribution strategy. Thus marketing is not always a central part of corporate and business unit strategy, particularly in industries that historically have been regulated.

EXHIBIT 3-16   Illustrative Role of Marketing Management in Business Unit Planning

---

Planning Activity	Marketing's Role
Mission determination	Key participant with the strategic planner and SBU manager.
Environmental assessment (economic, political, customer, regulatory trends)	Primary contributor and a major beneficiary of the results.
Competitive assessment (actual and potential competitors)	Primary contributor working with the strategic planner.
Situation assessment (industry assessment and company position to identify strengths and weaknesses)	Major contributor working with the strategic planner.
Objectives and goals	Key participant with other functional managers, including responsibility for measuring several performance indicators.
Strategies	Responsible for marketing strategy and for coordination of plans with other functional strategies.
Key Plans	
1. Product/market development	Leadership role.
2. Distribution	Primary responsibility.
3. Business development*	Key supporting role with strategic planning and manufacturing responsible for implementation.
4. Quality	Leading responsibility for quality.
5. Technology	Varies according to the importance of technology to the product or service.
6. Human resources	Responsible for functional area.
7. Manufacturing/facilities	Typically, very limited involvement.

*Decisions to expand, improve, or contract the business.

SOURCE: Based on a speech given by Stephen G. Harrell, General Electric Company, at the American Marketing Association Educator's meeting in Chicago, August 5, 1980.

Exhibit 3-17 shows the relationships among corporate, business unit, and marketing strategies. Corporate and SBU strategy development are discussed in Chapters 2 and 3. Marketing strategy is examined in the remaining chapters of the book.

CONCLUDING NOTE

Planning models became quite popular in the 1970s. The managements of many companies have moved strategic planning to the top of their list of corporate priorities for the 1980s, although some users have experienced problems with the popular planning tools. This chapter examines business unit analysis and strategy development, including the features and limitations of three popular strategic planning models—portfolio, screening, and PIMS. The SBU planning process is guided by corporate strategy guidelines. The process begins with an analysis

EXHIBIT 3-17 Strategy Relationships

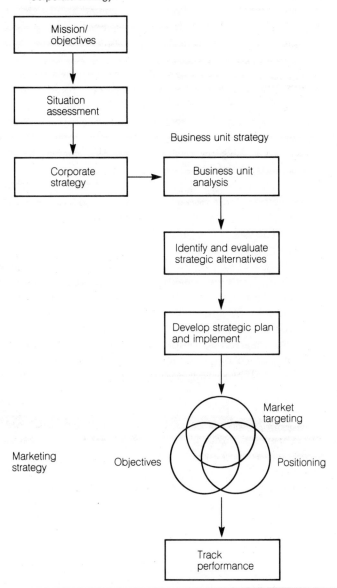

of the firm's market opportunity, position against competition, financial situation and projections, and its strengths and weaknesses. The planning models provide useful frameworks for situation analysis. The end result of the situation analysis is the identification of strategy alternatives for the SBU. Management must select a strategy and develop a strategic plan. The plan is then implemented and managed.

Portfolio analysis, multiple factor screening, PIMS, and other analysis methods offer planners a useful set of tools for diagnosing the strategic situation of an SBU or product. We have examined how each of these techniques is used and have considered the strengths and limitations of each method. The real test of each approach is how well it assists management in *diagnosing* the enterprise's strengths and weaknesses and in helping to define an SBU's strategic situation. Perhaps the most important finding through the use (and misuse) of the planning models during the past decade is the recognition of their limitations and the establishment of their analysis role in business unit planning. Comparative tests of the methods have identified important issues in the use of the planning methods.

Selecting the SBU strategy provides the focus for developing the strategic plan. Management must decide the future strategic direction of the SBU. The options include maintaining or strengthening existing position, shifting position, or exit from the SBU. The central concern is finding (or maintaining) a competitive advantage. The strategic plan indicates the objectives and strategic actions for the SBU, including forecasts, deadlines, responsibilities, and budgets. Implementation puts the plan into operation.

The strategic planning process examined in this and the previous chapter generally corresponds to the approaches utilized in business firms and other goal-directed organizations. This process serves two important purposes. It demonstrates marketing's rapidly expanding role in strategic planning and it provides essential guidelines to the marketing strategist. In moving through the book, we will continue to study the role of marketing in strategic analysis and planning as we work toward our primary objective—the formulation and management of marketing strategy.

NOTES

1. This illustration is based on Harlan S. Byrne, "Cummins Decides to Go with Its Strength as It Pins Hopes on Diesel Truck Engines," *The Wall Street Journal,* July 3, 1984, 21.

2. Bruce D. Henderson, "The Application and Misapplication of the Experience Curve," *Journal of Business Strategy,* Winter 1984, 3.

3. For a discussion of costs as a function of learning, see Patrick Conley, *Experience Curves as a Planning Tool: A Special Commentary* (Boston: Boston Consulting Group, 1970).

4. "Selling Business a Theory of Economics," *Business Week*, September 8, 1973, 85.
5. Carolyn R. Farquhar and Stanley J. Shapiro, *Strategic Business Planning in Canada* (Ottawa: Conference Board of Canada, 1983), 28.
6. Carolyn Y. Woo and Arnold C. Cooper, "The Surprising Case for Low Market Share," *Harvard Business Review*, November-December 1982, 106-13.
7. Derek F. Abell and John S. Hammond, *Strategic Market Planning* (Englewood Cliffs, N.J.: Prentice-Hall, 1979), 192.
8. George S. Day and David B. Montgomery, "Diagnosing the Experience Curve," *Journal of Marketing*, Spring 1983, 55.
9. Phone conversation and letter from Robert Cushman, chairman, Norton Company, November 19, 1984.
10. Abell and Hammond, *Strategic Market Planning*, 374-75.
11. For an extensive strategic and financial analysis of U.S. Surgical, see Kenneth S. Abramowitz, *United States Surgical Corporation* (New York: Sanford C. Bernstein & Co., 1980).
12. Farquhar and Shapiro, *Strategic Business Planning in Canada*, 38.
13. *The PIMS Program* (Cambridge, Mass.: Strategic Planning Institute, 1980), 8.
14. *The PIMSLETTER on Business Strategy, No. 1*, (Cambridge, Mass.: Strategic Planning Institute, 1977), 3-5.
15. *The PIMS Program*, 10.
16. Ibid., 11-12.
17. Barton A. Weitz and Robin Wensley, *Strategic Marketing* (Boston: Kent Publishing, 1984), 216.
18. Michael Lubatkin and Michael Pitts, "PIMS: Fact or Folklore?" *Journal of Business Strategy*, Winter 1983, 38-43.

19. For an expanded discussion of the DPM, see S. J. Q. Robinson, R. E. Hichens, and D. P. Wade, "The Directional Policy Matrix—Tool for Strategic Planning," *Long Range Planning*, June 1978, 8.
20. Farquhar and Shapiro, *Strategic Business Planning in Canada*, 45.
21. "The New Breed of Strategic Planner," *Business Week*, September 17, 1984, 63.
22. Ibid., 66.
23. "A U.S. Concept Revives Oki," *Business Week*, March 1, 1982, 112.
24. Richard J. Mahoney, "What to Do after the Consultants Go Home," *Business Week*, February 13, 1984, 17.
25. Robert Jacobson and David A. Aaker, "Is Market Share All that It's Cracked up to Be?" *Journal of Marketing*, Fall 1985, 11-22.
26. Ibid.
27. Yoram Wind, Vijay Mahajan, and Donald J. Swire, "An Empirical Comparison of Standardized Portfolio Models," *Journal of Marketing* (Spring 1983), 89-99.
28. Philippe Haspeslagh, "Portfolio Planning: Uses and Limits," *Harvard Business Review*, January-February 1982, 59-73.
29. Farquhar and Shapiro, *Strategic Business Planning in Canada*, 1-99.
30. *Business Week*, "Victor Kiam's Guide to Success in a Buyout," July 2, 1984, 74.
31. Harper W. Boyd, Jr., and Jean-Claude Larreche, "The Foundations of Marketing Strategy," in *The Annual Review of Marketing*, ed. Gerald Zaltman and Thomas V. Bonoma (Chicago: American Marketing Association, 1978), 53.
32. Theodore Levitt, "Marketing Success through Differentiation—of Anything," *Harvard Business Review*, January-February 1980, 83-91.

33. Ibid., 91.
34. Frank E. James, "Munsingwear Regains Order and Discipline but Faces a Tough Battle to Restore Profits," *The Wall Street Journal,* September 6, 1983, 31.
35. This approach to arraying strategic positions is similar to the growth vector matrix developed by H. Igor Ansoff, *Corporate Strategy* (New York: McGraw-Hill, 1965), 122–33.
36. "Wanted: A Manager to Fit Each Strategy," *Business Week,* February 25, 1980, 173.
37. Anil K. Gupta and V. Govindarajan, "Build, Hold, Harvest: Converting Strategic Intentions into Reality," *Journal of Business Strategy* (Winter 1984), 34–47.
38. George S. Day, *Strategic Marketing Planning* (St. Paul: West Publishing, 1984), 3.
39. Monica Langley, "AT&T Marketing Men Find Their Star Fails to Ascend as Expected," *The Wall Street Journal,* February 13, 1984, 1 and 12.

QUESTIONS FOR REVIEW AND DISCUSSION

1. A corporation executive has just been briefed by a consultant about the use of portfolio analysis for assessing the corporation's business units. He asks, "How do you know the method applies to my company?" How would you answer his question?

2. Discuss the pros and cons of using *actual* market share versus *relative* market share in portfolio analysis. Which measure do you recommend and why?

3. How would you explain to a corporation chief executive officer the major difference between portfolio analysis and multiple-factor screening methods?

4. The combination of multiple factors into a composite for screening the attractiveness of business units presents a major challenge to the strategic planner. Identify and discuss the issues that should be considered in choosing a way to combine the factors.

5. What do you consider to be the major advantages in using one of the product-market grid methods for strategic analysis of a firm's planning units?

6. Is there any value to a single product-market firm in using one of the strategic analysis methods? Discuss.

7. What considerations may be important in deciding between the use of specific products and lines of products as the unit of analysis in strategic planning?

8. Discuss the relevance and limitations of market share position as a basis for deciding future strategy.

9. Some strategic planners have suggested that data bases, such as the one developed for the PIMS analysis, should be based upon data collected from the industry of which a firm is a part rather than being made up of a broad cross section of firms and industries. Discuss.

10. What are the major deficiencies of all of the strategic analysis methods when they are used to determine future strategies to be followed by a firm?

11. The president of a U.S. corporation with sales in excess of $130 million is interested in selecting a formal method of analysis for use in building strategic plans for the firm's six business units. Select the method of analysis that you consider to be

most appropriate for the needs of the firm. Be sure to support your choice.

12. Identify some logical reasons why top management might decide *not* to adopt a formal method of strategic analysis, and rely instead upon management's judgment and experience as the basis of deciding how to allocate resource to business units.

13. Discuss the importance of finding a competitive advantage. Indicate how a company of your choice has accomplished this objective.

14. In recent years many firms have retained consultants to assist them in strategic planning. Discuss the roles you consider to be appropriate for corporate executives and consultants in strategic planning.

15. Why may some executives be well suited for managing business units in facing favorable market and business-strength situations and not suited for unfavorable market and competitive situations? Discuss.

STRATEGIC APPLICATION 3-1

EXXON CORPORATION

When Exxon Corp. was making facsimile machines in Florida a few years ago, hundreds of old units—some defective and some losing ground to new technologies—had piled up in the warehouse.

A former manager says he urged Exxon to salvage the equipment by selling it to another company. But his idea lost out in the debate. The machines "were just trucked to the dump and bulldozed into the ground," he recalls. "They were literally trashed."

Their fate also more or less befell the rest of Exxon's once-vaunted office-systems business. Last fall, after 10 years and at least a $500 million investment, the world's largest company concluded that oil and office products don't mix.

Exxon says it pulled the plug on its Exxon Office Systems unit because of chronic losses and its disinclination to wager more money on a "highly competitive and rapidly changing" industry. Financially, the decision hit the oil company not much harder than a dry hole—a $30 million charge against record 1984 earnings of $5.5 billion. In fact, given the current shakeout in computers and office equipment, "maybe we recognized earlier

[than most] that the industry wasn't as good as people thought it was going to be," says Lawrence G. Rawl, Exxon Corp.'s president.

A Different View

But the unit's former employees, along with dealers and users of Exxon office products, see it differently. To them, the fiasco reflected a management that took success for granted and focused on what it expected to be a glowing future rather than on dealing with problems at hand. The whole project suffered from Exxon's "delusions of grandeur," says Ian Dowie, former national field-operations manager of the office systems unit. The result was an organization far too costly and cumbersome for what it had to offer customers. And what it offered, apparently, wasn't much.

The fiasco typifies Big Oil's search for life beyond petroleum. Diversification moves by other oil companies into retailing, chemicals, insurance and mining, among other fields, have come a cropper in the past three years. Among the embarrassed companies have been Mobil Corp., Atlantic Richfield Co., Ashland Oil Inc., Standard Oil Co. of Ohio and Chevron Corp.

Exxon's office-equipment blunder also illustrates how a flood of resources can sometimes drown the very entrepreneurial instincts that they are supposed to nurture. "It is a great lesson that you can take all that money and all that talent and still be left holding the bag," says Dennis Morris, former market-analysis director for Exxon Office Systems. "I wouldn't have thought it possible."

Trying Other Fields

For years, Exxon has been bracing for the day of shrinking oil revenues. To that end, it has dabbled in everything from spawning shrimp to fabricating nuclear-fuel rods. But in the early 1970s, the company saw the brightest prospects in electronics. It bankrolled more than a dozen high-technology start-ups, initially with the idea that "we won't tell you how to run the business because chances are we don't know how," says Richard Nelson, the inventor of Exxon's Qwip facsimile machine.

Exxon's venturing seemed to pay off. Its facsimile machine led the market in the mid-1970s. Its Vydec word processor pioneered the full-screen text editor. Its Qyx electronic typewriter bridged the technological gap between conventional typewriters and word processors.

Although profits were slim, the three products were generating roughly $200 million in annual revenue by 1980, and Exxon executives saw a chance to build an information-systems empire. They also wanted greater control as the ventures' cash needs swelled and their ads began alluding to their link to Exxon. They decided that the parent company should take control even at the risk of killing off the ventures.

Ventures Merged

As a first step, Exxon decided to merge the three ventures. The process began in 1980 amid boasts of tackling International Business Machines Corp. and amid forecasts of a multibillion-dollar enterprise by 1990. The new unit abandoned a drab Exxon-owned office building in Pelham, N.Y., for a gleaming complex in Stamford, Conn. It assembled the industry's third-largest sales force and hired dozens of managers from IBM and other competitors.

"While we recognize that some uncertainty will exist during this period, this opportunity to build a strong, competitive office-systems business is truly unique," H. "Ben" Sykes, formerly executive vice president of Exxon Enterprises, told employees in an April 1980 memo. Exxon Enterprises is the Exxon Corp. division that ferrets out new investments and ran the office-systems unit.

Initially, Exxon tried to find jobs for most of the three ventures' roughly 6,000 employees, in the hope of keeping morale up and avoiding bad publicity. But the upshot was a 40-page organization chart, pockets of lingering allegiance to the old ventures and costs too heavy for the new unit to carry. Exxon believed that the bloated structure would ultimately be needed, but others had their doubts.

"We got to be big business before it was ever justified by our products or customer acceptance," says Frank Thomas, a former vice president of the unit's Qwip operation. The strategy, he says, reflected an attitude of "presupposed success."

The new unit first tried to live off the three ventures' old products, but the equipment hit snags, and the ventures' ability to develop new machines was limited. Qwip, for example, was "slow to bring engineering talent on board," having geared itself to selling existing products rather than developing new ones, says K. E. Hassler, a former Qwip vice president. Six years elapsed before it turned out a second-generation product—and the facsimile machine was later scrapped because the paper feeder jammed and the popular technology shifted.

Qwip's sister ventures encountered other glitches. The government banned

Vydec from certain agency work because, the government says, the equipment didn't meet security standards. And at Exxon's New York headquarters, a Qyx machine was burned up in a 1980 fire that some former employees blamed on the typewriter. The company declines comment.

In the spring of 1981, about 30 of the office systems unit's product planners huddled in a New Jersey hotel. They brought test models and blueprints for more than a dozen products, but they found little agreement. "Everybody pumped his pet project, but nothing was decided," says Leon Staciokas, a Qyx vice president who quit that September. "There went a few more million [dollars] out the window."

The heavy spending was partly planned. Originally, Exxon wanted to develop its own technology rather than just market other companies' machines, and it scattered development funds like "seeds in a garden," says John O'Dea, one of the unit's product planners.

Product Problems

But that strategy still left it trailing competitors, who were growing tougher as Exxon's internal-development program plodded on. For its first product, the unit had to scrap a long-delayed Vydec word processor and market one that wasn't even Exxon-made. It kept plugging away on an ink-jet printer, on the drawing board since 1978. The printer hit the market in 1983 but turned out to be a lemon. The ink jets clogged up frequently and the printer didn't work properly, users and dealers say.

The unit's top managers took the problems in stride, relying on five-year plans and Exxon's deep pockets. Many, coming from big companies, were loath to challenge existing strategies, such as building products from scratch, even though rival products were racing ahead.

"Some of us weren't quite creative enough to stand up to the very senior people and say, 'This is stupid, and I

won't do that,' " says a former IBM manager and a senior product planner for the Exxon unit.

The unit's president, Robert A. Contino, was originally hired to head its sales and service operations, on the basis of an IBM career that included a stint as a vice president in IBM's office-products division. But as president, Mr. Contino had trouble sorting out the disparate views on product strategy, several colleagues say. When product problems arose, he didn't get intimately involved. "Bob was a dyed-in-the-wool optimist," a former associate says. . . .

Oilmen's Turn

Exxon then tried populating the unit with old oilmen in key positions such as finance and personnel. Product decisions were increasingly controlled by Exxon Enterprises. But that didn't help. Because of its limited high-tech expertise, Exxon "couldn't figure out what to change or demand of its businesses" when it came to new products, says Calvin Pava, a Harvard Business School professor and one-time Exxon adviser.

Former employees say Mr. Contino's authority was eroded by the insertion, between Mr. Contino and the Exxon Enterprises board, of Lowell Strohl, an Exxon Enterprises official and a former executive in Exxon's oil-trading and European petroleum businesses.

Mr. Strohl soon became an Exxon Office Systems partisan. When, during a 1983 meeting in Houston, Exxon's own oil-marketing division said it preferred Wang Laboratories Inc. equipment over that of its sister company, Mr. Strohl became indignant. He "marched up to the oil guy and said if Exxon wanted to, it could buy that company [Wang] tomorrow," recalls a former Exxon manager who attended. The next year, it was widely rumored that Exxon tried to do just that. Both companies decline comment.

The oil division, meanwhile, bowed to pressure and took Exxon products on the promise that it could always return them. It did so last year.

Unhappy Customers

Other customers weren't so lucky. To many of the estimated 60,000 users of Exxon office products, the Exxon logo stood for faulty machines, spotty service and unfilled promises. Such problems aren't unusual in the computer and office-systems businesses, but Exxon seemed to have more than its share.

Part of the problem reflected Exxon's bent for its own technology. The initial word processor that Exxon bought from another company worked well enough. But the unit Exxonized the product by redesigning the software—to the point that it wasn't compatible with the original machine. The unit also made promises that its engineers couldn't keep. In 1983, Exxon began selling a system that hooked up more than a dozen of its word processors, but adequate software wasn't delivered until almost a year later.

Still, corporate purchasing agents liked Exxon because its products were as much as 25% less expensive than IBM's. But the cost saving doesn't impress many secretaries and other users. "The stuff doesn't work," says Linda Cox, a systems and programming specialist at Dallas-based American Petrofina Inc. However, Robert West, the company's vice president and controller, says he thinks the equipment is "just fine" and adds, "For the money we spent, we got what we paid for."

Lost Documents

Also having problems is the Drug Enforcement Administration's Boston office, which bought six Exxon word processors last year. The machines soon lost documents, and special functions, such as a dictionary that catches misspelled words, broke down. Given the chance, "we would've sent them back and requested something else," says Thomas Hohl, an administrative support specialist there.

Sierra Group, a Phoenix, Arix., information-systems research firm, says its Exxon word processor destroyed $20,000 worth of documents because of poorly designed software. Sierra says Exxon reimbursed it for the trouble.

And Jean Dedekam, a senior secretary at GTE Sprint in Burlingame, Calif., says that last year Exxon replaced a piece of her ailing word processor every day for more than a week. Now, her department is replacing its Exxon word processors with IBM machines. Other GTE Sprint departments have already jettisoned their Exxon word processors.

Word got around. Former salesmen say they became occupied with convincing buyers that Exxon wasn't going to abandon the business—much less selling them on the products' merits. But they didn't always succeed. E-Systems Inc. says it chose Wang's products over Exxon's in 1983 because it wasn't sure Exxon Office Systems would survive.

Unit Sold

Its instincts were correct. Last November, Exxon Corp. disclosed it was selling out, and earlier this year, it sold the unit's remaining assets to Ing. Olivetti & Co. and Harris Corp. for undisclosed sums. Exxon considers the chapter closed and refuses to discuss it in detail.

But in a suit filed last December in federal court in San Diego, 28 former independent Exxon Office Systems dealers are seeking $100 million in damages. They allege that from 1980 to 1984 the company assured them repeatedly of its "long-term commitment" to the office-automation industry. They charge that as late as last October, Exxon denied plans to quit the business and that they were surprised by its announcement the following month. They complain that their business was detroyed and accuse Exxon of fraud and breach of contract. The company declines comment.

The moral of the whole saga, according to a former Exxon Enterprises executive: "Don't get involved where you don't have the skills. It's hard enough to make money at what you're good at."

But Mr. Rawl, Exxon's president, says the company "hasn't completely closed the door in thinking about other things we might do" outside the oil business. However, Exxon now spends most of its extra cash buying back its own stock. Former executives connected with the office-systems foray say they consider the $5.3 billion invested in the stock well-spent.

SOURCE: Richard B. Schmitt and Laurie P. Cohen, "Humbled Giant: Exxon's Flop in Field of Office Gear Shows Diversification Perils." Reprinted by permission of *The Wall Street Journal.* © Dow Jones & Co., Inc., September 3, 1985. All rights reserved.

DISCUSSION QUESTIONS

1. Position Exxon Office Products and its key competitors on a market attractiveness/business-strength grid, indicating the basis for the position of each firm.
2. Prepare a critical assessment of Exxon's diversification into office systems.
3. What strategy alterations could have made the diversification more successful?
4. What changes in the corporate/business unit relationship would you have recommended to management?

STRATEGIC APPLICATION 3-2

DAIMLER-BENZ AG

Stuttgart, West Germany—Werner Breitschwerdt dropped his understated manner for a moment last week when he announced Daimler-Benz AG's surprise bid for majority control of AEG AG.

"We are entering a new dimension," Daimler's 58-year-old chairman said.

On the eve of the 100th anniversary of Karl Benz's patent for his first automobile, the West German prestige auto maker that bears his name is taking a revolutionary new road. By gobbling up three West German high-technology companies for the equivalent of about $1 billion this year, the conservative auto maker is seeking to maintain a technological and competitive edge over its rivals.

The company traditionally has concentrated on the automotive business. Its Mercedes cars have earned the company what one competitor calls "an unassailable reputation for excellence." Its trucks have captured a lion's share of the world market.

But the purchase of AEG, a diversified electrical and electronics group with annual sales of $4.12 billion, will transform Daimler from a narrowly focused automotive company into a sprawling industrial conglomerate with a wide mix of products.

At the heart of Daimler's acquisition policy lies its desire to tap the potential of auto-related technology. Electronic systems that can precisely control functions such as brakes, suspension, steering and air conditioning are finding new importance in cars and trucks.

Competitors are doing the same thing. General Motors Corp. has paid about $7.5 billion in the past year acquiring Hughes Aircraft Corp. and Electronic Data Systems Corp., a computer-services company. Other major U.S. auto concerns are snapping up aircraft makers and high-tech producers.

Heinz Duerr, AEG's chairman, estimates that half of AEG's business can loosely be defined as high tech, although most of this isn't auto-related. But, for example, AEG's factory-automation division could enable Daimler to build robots for use on its own assembly lines. And, speculates one German banker, "It won't be long before Mercedes cars come with AEG car telephones."

AEG also produces some pure automotive equipment, such as cables and small motors, although this amounts to just 2% of its sales. But company officials note that the merger will give Daimler the ability to do a wide range of research with electronic systems thanks to new economies of scale.

The purchase also means that one of West Germany's biggest corporate successes, Daimler, will join hands with the country's biggest corporate insolvency, AEG.

But while most experts say Daimler's management has the ability to make the venture succeed, some wonder what sleek automobiles have in common with ordinary vacuum cleaners.

"This [change of structure] is the extraordinary thing about the deal," says Margot Schoenen, a companies analyst at Westdeutsche Landesbank Girozentrale. Roger Hornett, an analyst at stockbrokers James Capel & Co. in London adds: "The fit is just not that obvious to me." Mr. Breitschwerdt is quick to reassure. "AEG is a good partner," he says. "If we work together with good partners, I can't see any damage being done to our image."

Even though it will produce turbines and typewriters, refrigerators and radar, Daimler stresses that cars and trucks will remain its core business. And the auto maker says it will leave day-to-day management of AEG activities to the present AEG chairman, Heinz Duerr.

Daimler last week purchased a 24.9% stake from AEG for $265 million. A group of banks then offered it a further 30% stake for $314.4 million, and Daimler says it will pay other shareholders the same price, $63.48 a share. The takeover is still subject to clearance by the Federal Cartel Office, but that isn't seen as a problem. Once approval is given, Daimler will become West Germany's largest company, with about 300,000 employees and annual sales of at least $22 billion.

It will also become the country's second largest defense contractor, supplying the military with $1.12 billion of equipment annually. Its engines will be used in the air, on land and at sea, and its space technology might even play a role in President Reagan's Strategic Defense Initiative.

Investors generally view the expansion as a positive and bold step by Daimler, and the company's stock has risen sharply. Purely as an investment, Daimler seems to have picked up a bargain. It gained a majority stake in AEG for less than $600 million.

Moreover, buying the Frankfurt-based company will enable the auto maker to enter large-scale electronics production. And there are several key areas in which the different arms of the Daimler group will be able to work together. "The synergy effects are considerable," says Mr. Breitschwerdt.

But the moves have raised nagging doubts, too. AEG, which emerged from bankruptcy proceedings in September 1984, remains financially weak. Although Daimler's purchase will wipe out its debts, insiders say AEG's assets are probably overvalued. And although AEG has maintained its reputation for innovative research, it has lost some of its brightest employees during the past few years' financial difficulties.

"One of AEG's weaknesses is that it's into a number of areas where prospects for growth are low or uncertain," such as household goods, says a Frankfurt bank analyst who asks not to be named. "The way it spreads out also makes it cumbersome."

Daimler management has steered the company through other crises. At the start of the decade, when many of its competitors languished in the doldrums of world recession, Daimler increased sales and profits. Its luxury limousines are snapped up as fast as the company can produce them, and the popularity of its boxy new 190 model, the Baby Benz, has helped it grab market share away from its main challengers at home, BMW and Audi.

The company says its commercial vehicles division still is profitable, even though it has been hit by falling worldwide demand in recent years, particularly in the Middle East. Overall, Daimler group sales rose 25% to $14.23 billion in the first nine months of this year. No profit figures were given, but in 1984, Daimler's consolidated net income jumped 11% to $412 million on sales of $16.29 billion, up 8.8%.

"We only have two ways to describe our business, 'generally satisfactory' and 'satisfactory,'" says one Daimler manager. "The first means our profits are up, the second means our profits are way up."

It isn't above making mistakes, though. Its U.S. subsidiary Euclid Inc., a maker of heavy off-road haulers it bought in 1977, incurred severe losses for a number of years because of a collapse in demand for heavy equipment, falling oil prices and economic recession. Daimler finally sold the unit last year.

SOURCE: Peter Gumbel, "Daimler-Benz Seeks Technological Edge over Rivals with Its Takeover of AEG." Reprinted by permission of *The Wall Street Journal.* ©Dow Jones & Co., Inc., October 21, 1985. All rights reserved.

DISCUSSION QUESTIONS

1. Discuss some of the reasons why Daimler-Benz's management might feel that it is necessary to diversify the firm from its core business.
2. Evaluate the strategic "fit" of the acquisitions the company has made.
3. Identify several issues that top management must consider in developing a strategy for the company.

CHAPTER 4

Financial Analysis

The critical importance in business success of understanding and applying financial management techniques is illustrated by Leslie H. Wexler, the chairman of The Limited. Several years ago he listened to an intriguing account of how Meshulam Riklis had built Rapid-American Corporation into a $2.4 billion empire. Wexler read Riklis's Ohio State master's thesis—"Expansion through Financial Management"—and used its guidelines to help build one of the exciting growth companies in the 1980s, as described in Chapter 1. Wexler started the company in 1963 with a loan of $5,000 from his aunt. By 1986 sales exceeded $2.5 billion.[1]

While most financial analysis applications are not as dramatic as Wexler's experience with The Limited, all executives in business today need to understand financial basics. Familiarity with the use of basic financial analysis methods is required of executives in most firms. This financial responsibility is described by David S. Hopkins of the Conference Board:

> Today's marketers are finding that strategies designed to forestall product problems often require financial considerations to be held at the forefront of their thinking and planning. Awareness that lack of profitability is so often the surest pointer to a problem means, for them, that costs, prices and profits are key elements in any product situation analysis. A few firms have established a position of marketing auditor or marketing controller who, among other duties, audits marketing costs, prices and profitability. In some other cases, firms are testing the introduction of a product-manager mutation, by making such managers *accountable* for profit to a degree somewhat beyond the looser sense of responsibility for success of the prod-

EXHIBIT 4-1   Marketing Financial Analysis Activities

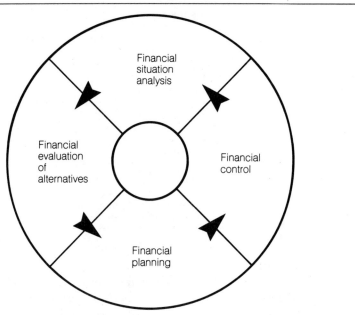

uct that has traditionally been theirs. Moreover, the tendency for market-ing executives to become more financially oriented is being mirrored by the rising frequency with which financial executives are finding themselves much more intimately concerned with questions of product policies and strategies than in the past.[2]

In this chapter we will examine several financial analysis activities and methods in order to (1) gauge how well marketing strategy is work-ing, (2) evaluate alternatives to marketing decision, and (3) develop plans for the future. We shall also discuss some special considerations that may affect marketing financial analyses. The methods covered in this chapter represent a kit of tools and techniques for use in marketing financial analysis. Throughout the discussion it is assumed that you have a basic understanding of accounting and finance fundamentals.

ANALYSIS ACTIVITIES

While many kinds of financial analyses underlie marketing operations, most of these financial analyses fall into the four categories shown in Exhibit 4-1. The *financial situation analysis* determines how well marketing activities are doing. It involves the study of trends, com-

---

EXHIBIT 4-2 Illustrative Financial Analyses

Situation analysis
    Sales and cost analyses
    Profit contribution and net profit analyses
    Liquidity analysis

Evaluation of alternatives
    Sales and cost forecasts
    Break-even analyses
    Profit contribution and net profit projections
    Return on investment

Financial planning
    Sales and cost forecasts
    Budgets
    Pro forma income statement

Financial control
    Sales and cost analyses
    Actual results to budgets
    Profit performance

---

parative analyses, and assessments of present financial strengths and limitations for the entire business or a unit, brand, or some other component of the business. *Financial evaluation of alternatives* uses financial information to evaluate such alternatives as whether to introduce a new product, expand the sales force, eliminate a mature product, or move into a new market. *Financial planning* involves projections concerning activities that marketing management has decided to undertake. For example, if it has been decided to introduce a new product on a national basis, management must prepare sales and cost forecasts, budgets, and other financial planning and control tools. Finally, in *financial control* actual results are compared to planned results. The objective is to keep the gap between actual and planned results as narrow as possible. Several illustrative financial analyses are shown in Exhibit 4-2.

Unit of Financial Analysis

Exhibit 4-3 shows several units that can be used in marketing financial analysis. Two factors often influence the choice of a unit of analysis: (1) the purpose of the analysis, and (2) the cost and availability of the information needed to perform the analysis. We shall briefly examine each influence to see how it affects the choice of a unit of analysis.

In a marketing situation assessment (see Exhibit 4-1), more than one unit of analysis is often needed. Marketing management may be interested in examining the financial performance of several of the units shown in Exhibit 4-3. In contrast, the unit used in the financial evaluation of alternatives should represent the alternative under consideration. For example, if an expansion of the sales force is being analyzed,

---

EXHIBIT 4-3 Alternative Units for Financial Analysis

Market	Product/Service	Organization
Total market	Industry	Company
Market niche(s)	Product mix	Segment/division/unit
Geographic area(s)	Product line	Marketing department
Customer groups	Specific product	Sales unit
Individual customers	Brand	Region
	Model	District branch
		Office/store
		Salesperson

---

the salesperson is a logical basis of analysis. If a product is a candidate for elimination by a firm, an analysis should be performed to assess the revenue and cost impact of dropping the product. The analysis should include the drop candidate plus other products that would be affected. Finally, in financial planning and financial control the unit or units of analysis often correspond to products and/or organizational units (such as branches, departments, and business units) since budgeting and forecasting analyses are typically prepared for these units.

Typically, the most readily available sales and cost information for financial analysis is the information used for formal financial reporting in the given firm. Units used for internal reporting often include product categories, business units, and units of the sales organization (such as regions and districts). When a unit of analysis does not correspond to one included in the firm's information system, both the cost and the difficulty of obtaining information increase significantly. For example, if the cost accounting system has not tabulated costs by individual products, obtaining such information may require a substantial effort. Fortunately, we can often estimate the information needed for marketing financial analysis at accuracy levels suitable for that purpose.

Sales and Cost Information

The data base for marketing financial analysis is obtained by accumulating historical sales and cost data for the various units shown in Exhibit 4-3. The data base can be used in forecasting future sales and costs for these units. In addition to the sales and cost data used in the financial analyses shown in Exhibit 4-2, marketing management often wishes to examine sales and cost trends. Among the widely used bases for the analysis of such trends are dollar and unit sales, percentage growth rates, and market share. Note, for example, the sales analysis for Long John Silver's shown in Exhibit 4-4. We can examine sales trends for each of the four market groups (A, B, C, and D), and then compare these trends to the advertising strategy used in each group.

EXHIBIT 4-4 Long John Silver's Systemwide Sales Analysis

With sales up, Long John Silver's has been able to increase ad expenditures. The chart illustrates the growing number of units in the A and B market groups.

| | Year Ended June 30 | | | |
| | 1981 | | 1980 | |
Market Group*	Number of Shops	Average Annual Sales†	Number of Shops	Average Annual Sales
A. Mature areas with good shop distribution and heavy TV media levels	412	$465,312	334	$431,820
B. Emerging markets with expanding shop distribution and moderate TV media levels	431	447,468	392	398,160
C. Underdeveloped markets with minimal number of shops enabling low levels of TV media‡	207	388,092	241	334,488
D. Pioneer markets with no TV media	75	324,000	66	268,572

*Shops are classified by markets based on actual spot TV advertising media weights experienced during each year.

†Sales of shops not open the entire year have been annualized based on the full months of operations.

‡Markets with only a minimal level of non-prime-time TV media, previously reported as D. TV markets are included in this classification.

SOURCE: Richard Kreisman, "Jerrico Taking Slow Approach to Fast Growth," p. 4. Reprinted with permission from the December 14, 1981 issue of *Advertising Age*. Copyright 1981 by Crain Communications, Inc.

Cost information is not very useful for marketing financial analysis unless it is combined with revenue (sales) data to perform various kinds of profit analyses. While in some instances we can analyze historical costs, such as the average cost required to close a sale, the analysis is incomplete unless we compare costs to what these costs have accomplished.

EVALUATING FINANCIAL PERFORMANCE

Several factors are involved in evaluating financial performance. We begin by discussing some accounting fundamentals. This is followed by a review of the basic financial reports. Next, we define several important financial ratios. Finally, a financial analysis model is presented and some additional marketing performance measures are indicated.

Some Fundamentals

Costs. As we move through the discussion of financial analysis, be sure to recognize the cost category that is being used in the analysis. If we use accounting terminology, costs can be designated as *fixed* or *variable*. From basic accounting you will recall that a cost is fixed if it remains constant over the observation period, even though the volume of activity varies.[3] In contrast, a variable cost is an expense that varies with the volume of a product produced over the observation period. Costs are designated as *semivariable* when they contain both fixed and variable components.

A *direct* cost is a cost incurred for a specific product. An *indirect* cost, often called *overhead*, cannot be assigned to a specific product. Examples of direct costs include labor and material used to manufacture a product. Indirect costs include manager's salaries, office equipment, and utilities.

Break-Even Analysis. This is a technique for examining the relationship between sales and costs as illustrated in Exhibit 4–5. Using sales and cost information, you can easily see from a break-even analysis how many units of a product must be sold in order to break even. In this example 65,056 units at sales of $120,000 are equal to total costs of $120,000. Any additional units sold will produce a profit. The break-even point is calculated as follows:

$$\text{Break-even units} = \frac{\text{Fixed costs}}{\text{Price per unit} - \text{Variable cost per unit}}$$

Price in the illustration shown in Exhibit 4–5 is $1.846 per unit, and variable cost is $0.770 per unit. With fixed costs of $70,000, this results in the break-even calculation:

$$\text{BE units} = \frac{\$70,000}{\$1.846 - \$0.770} = 65,056 \text{ units}$$

Break-even analysis is *not* a forecast. Instead, it indicates how many units of a product at a given price and cost must be sold in order to break even. Some important assumptions are associated with the above break-even analysis:

Fixed costs are constant and variable costs vary at a constant rate. All costs are either fixed or variable.
The analysis considered only one selling price. A higher price will result in a lower break-even point and a lower price will yield a higher break-even point.

When the above assumptions do not apply, the analyst must modify the basic break-even model shown in Exhibit 4–5. The model can be expanded to include nonlinear sales and costs as well as alternative price levels.

Estimates of market demand used in conjunction with traditional break-even analysis can approximate profit-maximizing decisions. An

EXHIBIT 4-5   Illustrative Break-Even Analysis

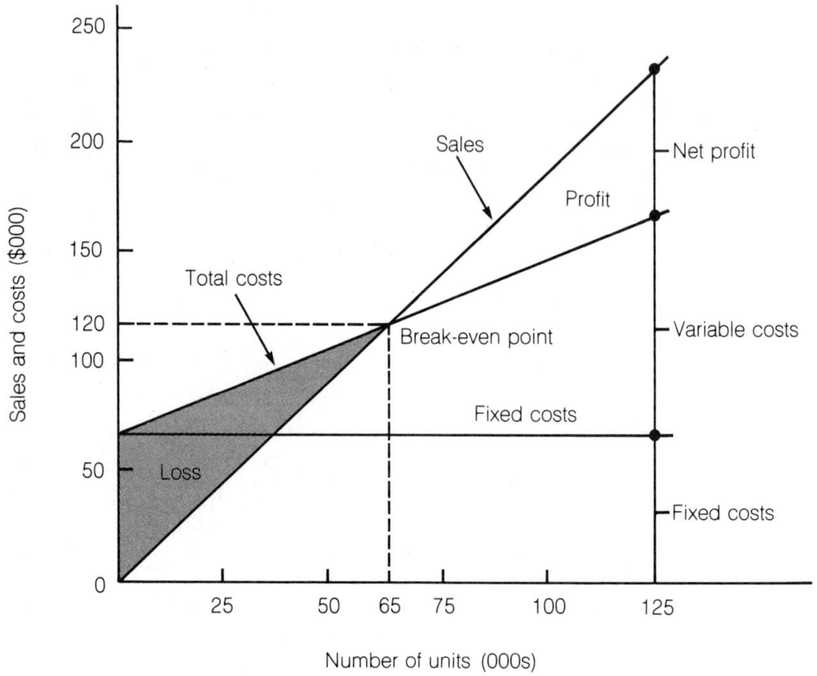

example is presented in Exhibit 4-6, in which the fixed costs are
$200,000, the unit variable costs are $2.50, and demand forecasts are
given for prices of $5, $10, $15, and $20. Of the four prices considered,
the $15 price yields the highest profits ($360,000).[3] You may find it useful to review these calculations.

Contribution Analysis.   When the performance of products, market
segments, and other marketing units is being analyzed, an examination of the profit contribution generated by a unit is often useful to
management. The contribution margin is equal to sales (revenue) less
variable costs. Thus the contribution margin represents the amount of
money available to cover fixed costs. The amount remaining after sub-
tracting fixed costs is net income. An illustration of contribution margin analysis is given in Exhibit 4-7. In this example, if product X were
eliminated, $50,000 of product net income would be lost. If the product
is retained, the $50,000 can be used to contribute to other fixed costs
and/or net income.

EXHIBIT 4-6 Break-Even Analysis with a Market Demand Schedule

Unit Price ($)	Market Demand (units)	Total Revenue ($)	Total Costs ($)	Break-Even Points (units)	Expected Profits ($)
5	65,000	(d') 325,000	362,500	(d) 80,000	(37,500)
10	55,000	(c') 550,000	337,500	(c) 26,667	212,500
15	45,000	(b') 675,000	314,500	(b) 16,000	360,500
20	30,000	(a') 600,000	275,000	(a) 11,429	325,000

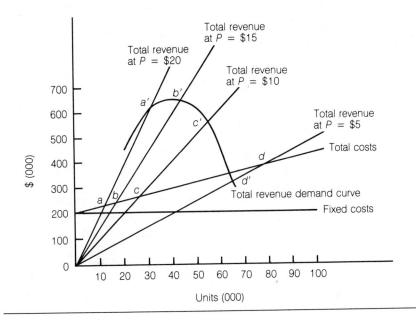

EXHIBIT 4-7 Illustrative Contribution Margin Analysis for Product X ($000)

Sales	$300
Less:	
Variable manufacturing costs	100
Other variable costs traceable to product X	50
Equals: Contribution margin	150
Less: Fixed costs directly traceable to	
product X	100
Equals: Product net income	$ 50

EXHIBIT 4-8   Illustrative Profit and Loss Statement

Sales revenue	$752,000
Less: Cost of goods sold	492,000
Equals: Gross profit margin	260,000
Less: Selling and administrative expenses	140,000
Equals: Net profit before taxes	120,000
Less: Taxes	50,000
Equals: Net profit	$ 70,000

Gross and Net Profit Margins.   Marketing executives should be familiar with the calculation of gross and net profit margins since this information is typically used to gauge company and business unit financial performance and to budget for future operations. Gross and net profit are shown on the profit and loss or income statement. Margins on sales can be calculated by dividing gross or net profit amounts by sales in dollars. The income statement is used to report financial performance to stockholders and to compute taxes. An illustrative statement is shown in Exhibit 4-8.

Basic Financial Reports.   The following reports are typically prepared for a company and its major subdivisions:

1. *Balance sheet.* A statement of financial position at a particular time (e.g., December 31, 1986), indicating total assets by category, short- and long-term liabilities, and stockholder's equity.
2. *Income statement.* This report covers a period of time (e.g., year ending December 31, 1986). It indicates sales minus all relevant costs and the difference is net income (see Exhibit 4-8).
3. *Cash flow statement.* This report starts with a beginning cash balance for a period (e.g., a quarter) plus all cash receipts minus all cash expenditures. It ends with a net cash balance for the period.

Since these reports and future forecasts (pro forma projections) are prepared for a company and its major parts or segments, the reports are normally not part of the marketing plan. Nevertheless, it is important that marketing executives understand the composition and relationships among major financial reports for the enterprise.

Since several financial ratios utilize information from the balance sheet, you should review its composition. An example of a balance sheet is shown in Exhibit 4-9.

EXHIBIT 4-9   Illustrative Balance Sheet ($000)

Cash	$ 100	Current liabilities	$ 75
Accounts receivable	200	Short-term debt	125
Inventory	150	Long-term debt	1,000
Total current assets	450	Total liabilities	1,200
Property and equipment	1,500	Net worth	1,050
Other assets	300	Total liabilities	
Total assets	$2,250	and net worth	$2,250

Key Financial Ratios

Financial information is useful to management if it is prepared so that comparisons can be made. James C. Van Horne comments upon this need:

> To evaluate a firm's financial condition and performance, the financial analyst needs certain yardsticks. The yardstick frequently used is a ratio or index, relating two pieces of financial data to each other. Analysis and interpretation of various ratios should give an experienced and skilled analyst a better understanding of the financial condition and performance of the firm than he would obtain from analysis of the financial data alone.[4]

Typically, a ratio is used to compare historical and/or future trends within the firm or to compare a firm or business unit with an industry or specific firms.

Several useful financial ratios are shown in Exhibit 4-10. These ratios provide a means of comparing the following factors:

1. Ratio values for several time periods for a particular firm.
2. A firm to its key competitors.
3. A firm to an industry or business standard.

There are several sources of ratio data.[5] These include data services such as Dun & Bradstreet business publications, industry and trade associations, government agencies, and investment advisory services.

In using ratio analysis it is important to recognize within industry variations.[6] If all firms in an industry have defined their businesses similarly, then the use of industry classifications and industry data are appropriate. If this is not the case, ratio comparisons between firms within an industry should be used with caution. An alternative is to identify the members of a "strategic group" (based on business definition) for use in both strategy formulation and analytical purposes.

EXHIBIT 4-10 Summary of Key Financial Ratios

Ratio	How Calculated	What It Shows
Profitability ratios		
1. Gross profit margin	$\dfrac{\text{Sales} - \text{Cost of goods sold}}{\text{Sales}}$	An indication of the total margin available to cover operating expenses and yield a profit.
2. Operating profit margin	$\dfrac{\text{Profits before taxes and before interest}}{\text{Sales}}$	An indication of the firm's profitability from current operations without regard to the interest charges accruing from the capital structure.
3. Net profit margin (or return on sales)	$\dfrac{\text{Profits after taxes}}{\text{Sales}}$	Shows after-tax profits per dollar of sales. Subpar-profit margins indicate that the firm's sales prices are relatively low or that its costs are relatively high or both.
4. Return on total assets	$\dfrac{\text{Profits after taxes}}{\text{Total assets}}$ (or) $\dfrac{\text{Profits after taxes} + \text{Interest}}{\text{Total assets}}$	A measure of the return on total investment in the enterprise. It is sometimes desirable to add interest to after-tax profits to form the numerator of the ratio since total assets are financed by creditors as well as by stockholders; hence it is accurate to measure the productivity of assets by the returns provided to both classes of investors.
5. Return on stockholders equity (or return on net worth)	$\dfrac{\text{Profits after taxes}}{\text{Total stockholders equity}}$	A measure of the rate of return on stockholders' investment in the enterprise.
6. Return on common equity	$\dfrac{\text{Profits after taxes} - \text{Preferred stock dividends}}{\text{Total stockholders equity} - \text{Par value of preferred stock}}$	A measure of the rate of return on the investment which the owners of common stock have made in the enterprise.
7. Earnings per share	$\dfrac{\text{Profits after taxes} - \text{Preferred stock dividends}}{\text{Number of shares of common stock outstanding}}$	Shows the earnings available to the owners of common stock.
Liquidity ratios		
1. Current ratio	$\dfrac{\text{Current assets}}{\text{Current liabilities}}$	Indicates the extent to which the claims of short-term creditors are covered by assets that are expected to be converted to cash in a period roughly corresponding to the maturity of the liabilities.
2. Quick ratio (or acid-test ratio)	$\dfrac{\text{Current assets} - \text{Inventory}}{\text{Current liabilities}}$	A measure of the firm's ability to pay off short-term obligations without relying upon the sale of its inventories.
3. Inventory to net working capital	$\dfrac{\text{Inventory}}{\text{Current assets} - \text{Current liabilities}}$	A measure of the extent to which the firm's working capital is tied up in inventory.

Leverage ratios

1. Debt to assets ratio

   $$\frac{\text{Total debt}}{\text{Total assets}}$$

   Measures the extent to which borrowed funds have been used to finance the firm's operations.

2. Debt to equity ratio

   $$\frac{\text{Total debt}}{\text{Total stockholders equity}}$$

   Provides another measure of the funds provided the creditors versus the funds provided by owners.

3. Long-term debt to equity ratio

   $$\frac{\text{Long-term debt}}{\text{Total stockholders equity}}$$

   A widely used measure of the balance between debt and equity in the firm's overall capital structure.

4. Times-interest-earned (or coverage ratios)

   $$\frac{\text{Profits before interest and taxes}}{\text{Total interest charges}}$$

   Measures the extent to which earnings can decline without the firm's becoming unable to meet its annual interest costs.

5. Fixed charge coverage

   $$\frac{\text{Profits before taxes and interest} + \text{Lease obligations}}{\text{Total interest charges} + \text{Lease obligations}}$$

   A more inclusive indication of the firm's ability to meet all of its fixed-charge obligations.

Activity ratios

1. Inventory turnover

   $$\frac{\text{Cost of goods sold}}{\text{Inventory}}$$

   When compared to industry averages, it provides an indication of whether a company has excessive inventory or perhaps inadequate inventory.

2. Fixed assets turnover

   $$\frac{\text{Sales}}{\text{Fixed assets}}$$

   A measure of the sales productivity and utilization of plant and equipment.

3. Total assets turnover

   $$\frac{\text{Sales}}{\text{Total assets}}$$

   A measure of the utilization of all the firm's assets: a ratio below the industry average indicates the company is not generating a sufficient volume of business given the size of its asset investment.

4. Accounts receivable turnover

   $$\frac{\text{Annual credit sales}}{\text{Accounts receivable}}$$

   A measure of the average length of time it takes the firm to collect the sales made on credit.

5. Average collection period

   $$\frac{\text{Accounts receivable}}{\text{Total sales} - 365}$$
   (or)
   $$\frac{\text{Accounts receivable}}{\text{Average daily sales}}$$

   Indicates the average length of time the firm must wait after making a sale before it receives payment.

SOURCE: Adapted from Arthur A. Thompson, Jr., and A. J. Strickland III. *Strategy and Policy* (Plano, Tex.: Business Publications, 1981), 216–18. © BUSINESS PUBLICATIONS, INC., 1978 and 1981.

EXHIBIT 4-11   Financial Analysis Model

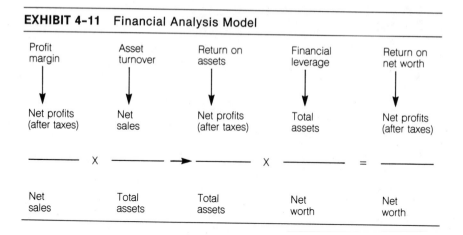

Financial Analysis Model

The financial analysis model shown in Exhibit 4–11 is useful for examining financial performance and identifying possible problem areas. It combines several important financial ratios into one equation. Let's examine the model moving from the far right to the left. Assuming that our performance target is the return on net worth, the product of return on assets and financial leverage determines performance. Increasing either ratio will increase return on net worth. This can be accomplished by increasing leverage (e.g., greater debt) or by increasing profits. Next, note that return on assets is determined by the product of profit margin and asset turnover. Thus greater expense control or faster asset turnover (e.g., inventory turnover) can improve the return on assets. The values of these ratios will vary considerably from one industry to another. In grocery wholesaling, for example, profit margins are typically very low, whereas asset turnover is very high. Through efficient management and high turnover a wholesaler can stack up impressive returns on net worth.

Note how the equation incorporates the major components of the balance sheet and the income statement. An illustration using the model ratios plus other financial ratios is provided in Exhibit 4–12. The variations by type of retailer highlight the importance of comparative analysis of ratios. Comparisons between similar retailers (e.g. home improvement) are more appropriate than comparing an apparel retailer to a drug retailer.

An example of the use of the model to analyze one of the retailers in the speciality apparel store group is shown in Exhibit 4–13. Burlington Coat Factory had a net profits/net worth ratio above several of the retailers shown in Exhibit 4–12.

EXHIBIT 4-12 Profitability Profile of High Performance Retailers, 1982

			Strategic Profit Model Ratios			
Retailer	$\dfrac{Net\ Profits}{Net\ Sales}$ (percent)	×	$\dfrac{Net\ Sales}{Total\ Assets}$ (times)	→ $\dfrac{Net\ Profits}{Total\ Assets}$ (percent)	× $\dfrac{Total\ Assets}{Net\ Worth}$ (times)	= $\dfrac{Net\ Profits}{Net\ Worth}$ (percent)
Price Company	2.2%		6.4×	14.2%	3.0×	43.2%
Home Depot	4.5		3.6	16.1	1.8	29.0
Pic 'N Save	13.9		1.5	21.1	1.2	25.9
Toys "R" Us	6.2		1.9	11.5	1.7	19.8
Burlington Coat Factory	5.3		2.0	10.7	2.7	29.3
Mervyn's	5.3		1.9	10.0	2.6	26.4
Merry-Go-Round	8.5		2.5	21.6	1.6	34.2
Syms	5.1		3.4	17.2	1.4	24.5
General Nutrition	7.0		2.4	16.9	1.6	27.4
Trak Auto	8.8		5.9	52.1	1.9	99.0
Tandy	10.9		1.7	18.3	1.5	27.6
Long's	3.0		3.7	11.1	1.5	17.0
Wal-Mart	3.7		2.9	10.7	2.8	30.6

SOURCE: Burns Fry Limited and Distribution Research Program, The University of Oklahoma.

EXHIBIT 4-13 Financial Profile of Burlington Coat Factory

Strategic Profit Model Ratios (1982)

$$\frac{\text{Net profits}}{\text{Net sales}} \times \frac{\text{Net sales}}{\text{Total assets}} = \frac{\text{Net profits}}{\text{Total assets}} \times \frac{\text{Total assets}}{\text{Net worth}} = \frac{\text{Net profits}}{\text{Net worth}}$$

$$5.3\% \times 2.0\times = 10.7\% \times 2.7\times = 29.3\%$$

Current Size, 1982 (millions of dollars)

Net Sales	$130.5
Net profits	$ 6.9

Composition of Balance Sheet (1982)

Current assets		Current liabilities	
Cash	19.5%	Notes payable	.1%
Accounts receivable	2.7	Accounts payable	46.6
Inventory	66.9	All other	14.5
All other	.2	Total	61.2%
Total	89.3%		
Fixed assets	10.4%	Long-term liabilities	2.2%
All other assets	.3	Net worth	36.6
Total assets	100.0%	Total liabilities and net worth	100.0%

Compound Annual Growth Rates, 1978–1982

Net sales	52.0%
Net profits	—
Earnings per share	—

Liquidity Ratios (1982)

Current assets/current liabilities (times)	1.5×
Current assets (minus inventory)/current liabilities (times)	.4×
Cash/current liabilities (percent)	31.8%
Net profits (before interest and taxes)/interest (times)	118.9×

Growth Potential Ratios (1982)

Net profits (after dividends)/net working capital (percent)	38.3%
Net profits (after dividends)/net worth (percent)	29.3%
Net profits (before interest and taxes)/total assets (percent)	21.7%
Accounts payable/inventory (percent)	69.6%

SOURCE: Distribution Research Program, University of Oklahoma.

EXHIBIT 4-14   Productivity Profile of High Performance Retailers, 1982

Company	Sales per Square Foot of Selling Area	Profits (before taxes) per Square Foot of Selling Area
Price Company	$760.00	$36.00
Cub Warehouse Stores	700.00	28.00
Drug Emporium	500.00	25.00
Home Depot	250.00	25.00
Standard Brands Paint	197.34	22.50
Toys "R" Us	168.95	20.30
Mervyn's	246.25	28.07
Marshall's	212.52	19.52
Crown Books	224.87	15.07
General Nutrition	209.18	29.29
Trak Auto	191.05	33.24
Tandy	155.89	31.96
Long's	269.73	15.97
Rite Aid	189.22	13.13
Eckerd's	167.99	13.93
Target	195.00	12.09
Wal-Mart	169.06	10.99

SOURCE: Distribution Research Program, University of Oklahoma.

Other Performance Measures

A widely used measure of productivity in retail organizations is sales per square foot of retail space. In the following discussion space productivity is used as a basis for comparing the financial performance of two bookstore chains, B. Dalton Bookseller and Waldenbooks:

> Each chain had roughly $250 million in sales in 1980 (the latest year for which comparable information is available), but Dalton sold an estimated $132 worth of books per square foot of store space to Walden's $114. A computerized inventory system installed in 1966 is what gives Dalton its edge—and is a key to why its 10 percent pretax profits are well above Walden's.[7]

Space productivity measures are also obtained for individual departments in retail stores that offer more than one line, such as department stores. Examples of space productivity profiles for several retailers are shown in Exhibit 4–14. Another widely used productivity measure is inventory turnover (Exhibit 4–10).

FINANCIAL PLANNING

Financial planning consists of two major activities: (1) forecasting revenues, and (2) budgeting (estimating future expenses). The financial analyses and forecasts included in the strategic marketing plan vary

EXHIBIT 4-15 Sales-Marketing-Profit Summary

	ACTUAL YEARS PAST					CURRENT YR (EST.)	NEXT YR PLAN	ESTIMATE—FUTURE YEARS			
	19	19	19	19	19	19	19	19	19	19	19
FACTORY SALES IN UNITS (DOZEN OR OUNCES) INCLUDING NEW PRODUCTS											
PERCENT INCREASE OVER PREVIOUS YEAR %											
FACTORY SALES DOLLARS, INCLUDING NEW PRODUCTS (A) ($000)											
PERCENT INCREASE OVER PREVIOUS YEAR %											
INCOME BEFORE MARKETING ($000)											
PERCENT OF SALES %											
MARKETING EXPENDITURE (B) INCLUDING NEW PRODUCTS ($000)											
PERCENT OF SALES %											
ADVERTISING EXPENDITURE ($000)											
MERCHANDISING EXPENDITURE ($000)											
PROFIT AFTER MARKETING (BEFORE ALLOCATIONS) (C) ($000)											
PERCENT OF SALES %											
PROFIT PERCENT INCREASES OVER PREVIOUS YEAR %											

(A) NEW PRODUCTS FACTORY SALES DOLLARS (Included Above) (LIST ITEMS BELOW)	PRODUCTS INTRODUCED THIS YR ($000)			
	PRODUCTS PROPOSED NEXT 5 YRS ($000)			
	TOTAL NEW PRODUCTS ($000)			

(B) EXCLUDE MARKETING RESEARCH, PACKAGING DESIGN, PUBLICITY.

(C) PROFIT AFTER MARKETING: INCOME BEFORE MARKETING LESS MARKETING (EXCLUDES ALLOCATIONS AND CORPORATE ADJUSTMENTS).

SOURCE: David S. Hopkins, *The Marketing Plan*, Report No. 801 (New York: The Conference Board, 1981), 94–95.

considerably from firm to firm. These analyses are often placed in the financial analysis section of the plan:

Sales and market share analyses and forecasts by product, market segment, areas, and other categories.

Budget projections for marketing activities (e.g. advertising, marketing research, salesforce).

Break-even and profit contribution projections by marketing planning unit (e.g., market target, product line, market area, etc.).

Return on investment projections by marketing planning unit.

Capital requirements.

Examples of marketing financial planning forms used by the R. T. French Company, a food-processing firm, are shown in Exhibit 4-15. As is often the case in financial planning, past, present, and future results and forecasts are included. Note how the profit summary compares marketing's impact on the bottom line. The budget proposal illustrates the budget categories accounted for by marketing. The internal financial reporting and budgeting procedures vary widely

EXHIBIT 4-15 *(concluded)*

MARKETING BUDGET PROPOSAL FOR _____

SUMMARY		19___ ACTUAL	19___ ACTUAL	19___ ORIGINAL VOTE	19___ ESTIMATED	19___ PROPOSED	19___ APPROVED
Sales	$						
Income Before Marketing	$						
Income before Marketing to Sales	%						
Marketing (A)	$						
Marketing to Sales	%						
Marketing includ Allocations (B)	$						
Operating Income before Adj. (D)	$						
Operating Income to Sales	%						
Population	M						
Sales Milex ($/1000 pop.)	$						
Marketing Milex ($/1000 pop.)	$						

MARKETING BUDGET CATEGORIES

	ACTUAL	ACTUAL	ORIGINAL VOTE	ESTIMATED	PROPOSED	APPROVED
1 Magazines						
2 Newspaper Rop						
3 Newspaper Supplements						
4 Radio						
5 Television						
6 Posters						
7 Special Media						
8 Agency Fees						
9 Trade Media						
11 Consumer Non-Price Incentive						
13 Consumer Price Incentives						
14 Sales Conferences						
15 Merchandising Materials						
17 Trade Allowances						
18 Trade Free Goods						
19 Sundries						
MARKETING (A)						

Allocations of Publicity						
Alloc. of Fgt. on Un-ident. Merch. Mat.						
Alloc. of Military Food Marketing						
MARKETING INCLUD.ALLOC.(B)						

Package Development (C)						
Market Research (C)						

(A) Marketing — Total of Budget Categories
(B) Marketing including Allocations — Marketing plus Allocations of Publicity, Freight on Un-Identified Merchandising Materials, and Military Food Marketing.
(C) Already deducted via Administration Expense in arriving at Income before Marketing.

(D) Operating Income Before Adjustments — "Income before Marketing" less "Marketing including Allocations", before Corporate Adjustments.

PER _____ DATE _____

among companies so you should consider the French Company's approach as one example rather than a norm.

The choice of the financial information to be used for the marketing plan will depend upon its relationship with the corporate or business unit strategic plan. Another important consideration is the selection of performance measures to be used in gauging marketing performance. Our objective is to indicate the range of possibilities and to suggest some of the more frequently used financial analyses.

IMPORTANT FINANCIAL ANALYSIS ISSUES

Selecting Performance Criteria

Companies vary considerably as to how they gauge marketing performance. Consider these examples of profitability measures used by different firms:

> A diversified manufacturing company currently expects an operating margin on sales of at least 5 percent for all products.
>
> Management in a chemicals company now looks for ROI (return on investment) of at least 15 percent from each product line, and considers an ROI figure of less than 11 percent as calling for close review and possible divestment.
>
> A consumer packaged-goods company has the general objective that any product's marginal profit before advertising and promotional expenditures should be a minimum of 20 percent higher than fixed and variable costs.
>
> A manufacturer of capital equipment demands at least 25 percent ROI from each product or operating unit.
>
> Another capital goods producer, employing the ratio of direct costs to sales price as a means of measuring relative profit performance, classes a ratio of 60 percent as satisfactory and one over 70 percent as unsatisfactory.[8]

How exactly should management measure the financial performance of marketing operations? What criteria should be used—return on investment (ROI), sales, profit contribution, or something else? Many firms use volume attainment and profitability as criteria although surprisingly those using ROI seem to be in the minority.[9] This may be due to several difficulties in attempting to apply the technique to gauge marketing performance:

> Because there are innumerable variations of profit levels, a proper question, initially, is *what return* is being used for the measure? Examples of profit levels are profit before royalties (including or excluding interest pay-

ments), profit before taxes, cash flow, division profit contribution, factory contribution, or sales region or district contribution.

Any of the above are useful, depending upon the investment base being used.

Again, one could ask, "Return on *what investment?*" It may be total parent company investment, total investment of subsidiary, total assets, manipulative assets (excluding intangibles), funds employed (tangible working capital), or selected bases (receivables, inventories, cash, etc.).

The remaining question is, *whose investment?* The investment of the stockholder differs in concept with the operating investment of the firm. Use of each may give startlingly different results, especially in the case where tangible funds employed in a firm are contrasted with the stockholder's investment if large amount of good will have been capitalized.[10]

Once these questions are answered, ROI measures provide an important gauge of marketing performance.

Marketing's decision-making information needs often do not correspond to traditional managerial accounting reporting procedures so some give-and-take negotiations may be necessary among top management, marketing, and accounting. Issues as to how to allocate revenues and costs, the extent of disaggregation of both revenues and costs, and many other questions must be resolved in order to obtain relevant information for financial analysis. Revenue and cost information has two dimensions, the past and the future. We have to accumulate past information and analyze it in order to measure the effectiveness of our past strategies. We need to develop future estimates to evaluate the proposed strategies.

Finally, the time period of analysis must be selected. Because most strategic marketing decisions extend from a few to several years into the future, financial analysis must take into account the time value of money and the flows of revenue and costs over the relevant time horizon. Estimating inflation during the period of analysis adds another complicating factor to financial projections.

Marketing's Influence on Financial Performance

Marketing strategy, once implemented, affects the financial performance of the corporation by generating sales and by incurring costs. An examination of a basic financial analysis system widely known as the Du Pont investment model will highlight marketing's impact upon financial performance. This model is shown in Exhibit 4–16. The shaded boxes indicate that marketing has some effect upon the area. Note that the ROI in Exhibit 4–16 corresponds to net profits (after taxes divided by total assets as shown in Exhibit 4–11). By following the arrows you can trace marketing's influence upon revenues and costs all the way to the return on investment. Exhibit 4–16 can be expanded to include more details.

EXHIBIT 4–16 Financial Analysis Model

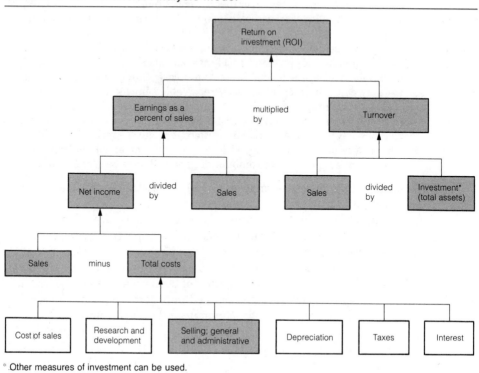

* Other measures of investment can be used.

Eliminating Information Gaps

The following example illustrates how to eliminate information gaps. Suppose a company has three products: A, B, and C. You want to perform a break-even analysis for product B, but the fixed-cost information provided is for the entire company. Since you have sales for each product, one way to proceed is to assume that fixed costs can be allocated to each product on the basis of the percentage of total sales accounted for by that product. For example, if product B represents 20 percent of sales, then it would be assigned 20 percent of fixed costs. Using this fixed-cost estimate and per unit selling price and variable cost, we can estimate the break-even point for product B. While the fixed-cost estimate may not be exact, it is probably adequate to give a close approximation of the break-even point. Other factors for allocating fixed costs may be appropriate in a given situation, such as the profit contribution of a product. The assumptions underlying our estimating procedure have to be logical.

When you estimate the values for information needed in an analysis, proceed with caution. You should have some definite basis for your estimates. Do not make unrealistic guesses about the values. As a general rule, you should be conservative in your estimates. Sometimes we may find it useful to estimate a range of values for the unknown factor. For example, we might make three estimates in projecting sales of a new product over the next three years. One of them might be an optimistic estimate; the second, a pessimistic estimate; and the third, the most likely estimate of sales for each of the three years.

Finally, we have to determine just how sensitive our analysis is to the information that we are estimating. Let us refer again to product B. If our break-even point is not much affected by different assumptions as to how to allocate the fixed costs, we should accept a reasonable assumption about the allocation. Alternatively, if small changes in an estimated value can affect significantly the outcome of the financial analysis, then we should assess the probable accuracy of our estimates.

Impact of Inflation

As a result of the double-digit inflation rates of the late 1970s and early 1980s, we have learned how important a role inflation plays in marketing financial analysis. Here is a summary of the problem:

> Persistent inflation in the American economy has led accounting rule makers to require large firms to report the effects of inflation on certain of their financial statement data. At present, these adjusted data are to be presented as supplementary disclosures under Statement of Financial Accounting Standards No. 33, "Financial Reporting and Changing Prices." One major result will be significant changes in cost estimates and asset valuations. The changes in financial accounting requirements are likely to be reflected almost immediately in managerial accounting procedures, with specific implications for marketing decisions in such areas as new product introduction, pricing strategy, and the valuation of individual customers and market segments.[11]

Conventional financial reporting using historical cost accounting suffers from two inadequacies during inflationary periods: (1) the dollar does not represent a constant or stable measuring unit over time; and (2) prior to sale, no recognition is given to changes in the prices of the assets held by a firm.[12] Some alternative methods of inflation accounting are shown in Exhibit 4–17. The challenge facing marketing decision makers in financial analysis is described by Webster, Largay, and Stickney:

> As corporate managements attempt to cope with and plan for the combined forces of inflation, tight money supply, high interest rates, and low rates of growth in the economy in general and in specific markets, they will need new criteria to evaluate marketing performance. Commonly used measures such as gross margin, return on sales, and changes in market share all have a shortcoming—they do not take into account the financial resources committed to a particular product, customer, sales territory, or

EXHIBIT 4-17 Alternative Inflation Accounting Methods

	Nominal Dollars*	Constant Dollars
Historical Cost	1. Method used in conventional financial reporting	2. Dollars restated to dollars of constant general purchasing power
Current Cost	3. Dollar amounts reported in terms of current replacement cost of specific assets	4. Same as 3 except that all amounts in 3 are restated to a constant-dollar basis

*Actual dollars received at sale of product and expended when inventory and equipment were acquired.

SOURCE: Adapted from Frederick E. Webster, Jr., James A. Largay III, and Clyde P. Stickney. "The Impact of Inflation Accounting in Marketing Decisions," *Journal of Marketing*, Fall 1980, 9–17, published by the American Marketing Association.

market segment. This shortcoming can be corrected by using such measures of performance as return on investment, return on equity, and return on assets employed.

At the same time, management must be prepared to incorporate the new inflation-adjusted accounting information into these additional measures of performance. Costs must be redefined to take into account changes in prices of plant, equipment, raw materials, working capital, and the labor that have gone into inventories of finished goods and work in process. The effect will almost always be to reduce profit estimates below levels indicated by traditional accounting methods. Attractiveness of particular products, customers, sales territories, market segments, and even total businesses may be changed accordingly. The amount of the profit decrease will depend, in general terms, on the amount of capital (plant, equipment, and working capital) committed to a particular marketing unit (product, customer, territory, etc.) and specific price changes of factors such as raw materials and energy used by that marketing unit. Marketing units that look like real "winners" on the basis of traditional accounting methods and measures such as gross margin and return on sales can quickly become "losers" when inflation-adjusted costs and capital requirements are considered.[13]

Perhaps the most significant implication is the apparent emphasis by top management on the total level of asset commitment to specific products and markets. This factor, of course, will have its greatest impact on products and markets requiring heavy capital investments in fixed assets and working capital.[14]

Time Value of Money

The time value of money also influences how we evaluate the financial performance of marketing operations. Since several sources provide extensive coverage of this topic, we shall only note its importance in marketing financial analysis, particularly when dealing with uneven cash flows over long time periods.[15]

Joining Financial Analysis to Marketing Strategy

Finally, in making a financial analysis in marketing, we need to recognize that various marketing strategy decisions can (and should) be viewed as investment decisions.[16] This introduces risk into the decision-making process and establishes a time horizon beyond annual budgeting for evaluating the use of financial resources in marketing. For example, a firm with its own distribution system and/or sales force is faced with more risk than a firm using independent intermediaries and sales agents.

An illustrative simulation of financial analysis for evaluating the interaction of market share and profit indicates that such an analysis can be used in assessing marketing strategy.[17] In this simulation, which uses market share, cost of capacity, net present value, and return on investment, seven marketing strategies are analyzed and compared. While the data and results are only illustrative, the scope and approach to analysis are good examples of joining financial analysis to marketing strategy.

SPREADSHEET ANALYSIS USING PERSONAL COMPUTERS

The increased availability of computers provides us with a powerful tool of analysis. With the most basic of personal computers, the business student can simplify lengthy and repetitive analyses and can evaluate multiple alternatives. Customized programs and graphing features are widely used by businesses along with electronic spreadsheet software.

Spreadsheet Capabilities

The electronic spreadsheet, which is marketed under names such as VisiCalc, Peach Calc, Lotus 1 2 3, and others, provides the basic tools of analysis in a easy-to-use software program. Text, formulas, and numbers can be fed into the computer to develop ratio analyses, sales forecasts, reconciliations, accounting statements, and cost data. The major advantage of the spreadsheet is that it enables us to perform analyses; we can change various assumptions and arrive at an answer or conclusion without manually repeating the calculations.

Some software packages, including Lotus 1 2 3, have computer graphics capabilities. Graphs, pie charts, bar charts, and other visual

EXHIBIT 4-18   Analysis of Customer Shopping Frequency for XYZ Stores

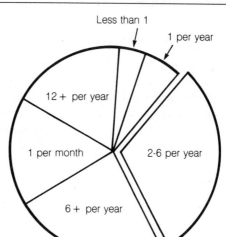

comparisons can be prepared. For example, the analysis shown in Exhibit 4–18, was prepared in less than five minutes on a computer that has built-in graphics capabilities. The person preparing the analysis only needs to type in the number of people for each shopping frequency, instructions for pie-slice shading, and the name of each slice. The slice to be pulled out must also be designated.

How Spreadsheet Analysis Works

To illustrate its features, a more detailed description of the mechanics of spreadsheet analysis is necessary. The spreadsheet is a matrix of cells that can be filled with text, formulas, or numbers. Data can be manipulated by referencing a cell. This includes the row and column location denoted by numbers and letters respectively. This feature allows us to calculate formulas on the basis of whatever number is entered in a cell, and not just upon a number that may need to be replaced should an assumption or key figure be changed.

For example, assume that a firm produces two products, A and B, and that the firm wishes to calculate the total revenue from these products. For each product, one cell would contain the price of the product and another the amount sold. The cell that displays the total revenue would contain the formula: number of units sold of A times the price, added to the number of units sold of B times the price. Let us now enter on the spreadsheet the formula, using the numerical values of the prices and units sold. If any of these values should change, the formula would have to be reentered in the cell to display the correct total revenue accounting for any changes. However, if we entered the formula, using the cell location for the values of the number of units sold of A and B and the prices of A and B, the total revenue figure would be changed automatically. Any change in the price or amount sold of A or B would be entered in the appropriate cell. The computer would recalculate the total revenue on the basis of this change and display the answer in the cell for the total revenue. The accompanying text description would help identify the proper cell and explain the values. If we set up the formulas on the basis of the cell locations rather than on the basis of the values, we will find a spreadsheet analysis especially useful. This is true under the following circumstances: (1) when we have to deal with complex, lengthy formulas; (2) when conditions are likely to change; and (3) when we wish to see the proposed effect of certain changes in variables.

CONCLUDING NOTE

This chapter provides a foundation for marketing financial analysis. We examined a variety of financial analysis methods, such as breakeven analysis, contribution analysis, profit margins, and ratio analyses. Emphasis is placed on application rather than on method since it is assumed that you already have an understanding of basic managerial accounting and finance. To supplement the coverage in the chapter, several sources that cover financial analysis in depth are cited in the notes.

It is clear that the responsibilities of marketing executives in the area of financial analysis are expanding rapidly. We are required to use new concepts and techniques as well as to interpret financial analyses provided by others. Here is how Webster, Largay, and Stickney describe this new orientation:

> Marketing managers will need a better understanding of accounting and financial management than that of their predecessors. The characteristic marketing manager's emphasis in analysis and action on sales volume, gross margin, and market share must be replaced by a more general management focus on bottom-line profitability and return on investment. Top management will think increasingly in terms of total resource allocation across products and markets, assessing the total product portfolio in terms of complex trade-offs between business growth opportunities in markets requiring additional investment for future profitability versus cash generation now in markets with limited or negative investment. Heightened awareness of the impact of inflation on measures of corporate financial performance will undoubtedly sharpen management concern on this dilemma. Marketing management must adopt new attitudes, what

might be called "a general management orientation," as well as make use of the sophisticated measurements, analytical techniques, and strategic planning approaches that are available to help cope with the new pressures and complexities.[18]

Financial analysis activities include situation analysis, evaluation of alternatives, planning, and control. We can use various financial analyses to assess financial performance, examine decision alternatives, and plan and control marketing activities. The information used for marketing financial analysis typically includes sales and cost data.

NOTES

1. "Limited Is Stitching together a Fashion Empire," *Business Week,* February 25, 1985, 78.
2. David S. Hopkins, *Business Strategies for Problem Products* (New York: Conference Board, 1977), 42.
3. This illustration is drawn from David W. Cravens, Gerald E. Hills, and Robert B. Woodruff, *Marketing Decision Making: Concepts and Strategy,* rev. ed. (Homewood, Ill.: Richard D. Irwin, 1980), 335–36.
4. James C. Van Horne, *Fundamentals of Financial Management,* 4th ed. (Englewood Cliffs, N.J.: Prentice-Hall, 1980), 103–4.
5. A useful guide to ratio analysis is provided in Richard Sanzo, *Ratio Analysis for Small Business* (Washington, D.C.: Small Business Administration, 1977).
6. Gary L. Frazier and Roy D. Howell, "Business Definition and Performance," *Journal of Marketing,* Spring 1983, 59–67.
7. Jeff Blyskal, "Dalton, Walden, and the Amazing Money Machine," *Forbes,* January 18, 1982, 47.
8. Hopkins, *Business Strategies,* 11.
9. Sam R. Goodman, *Financial Analysis for Marketing Decisions* (Homewood, Ill.: Dow Jones-Irwin, 1972), 88.
10. Ibid., 102–3.
11. Frederick E. Webster, Jr., James A. Largay III, and Clyde P. Stickney, "The Impact of Inflation Accounting on Marketing Decisions," *Journal of Marketing,* Fall 1980, 9, published by the American Marketing Association.
12. Ibid., 10.
13. Ibid., 13.
14. Ibid., 14.
15. An excellent discussion of evaluating investment opportunities is provided in Robert C. Higgins, *Analysis for Financial Management* (Homewood, Ill.: Dow Jones-Irwin, 1983), Chapters 8 and 9.
16. Adam Finn and Roy Howell, "Marketing Strategy and Finance Theory," in *An Assessment of Marketing Thought and Practice,* eds. Bruce J. Walker et al. (Chicago: American Marketing Association, 1982), 327–31.
17. Victor J. Cook, Jr., "The Net Present Value of Market Share," *Journal of Marketing,* Summer 1985, 49–63.
18. Webster et al., "The Impact of Inflation Accounting, 16–17.

QUESTIONS FOR REVIEW AND DISCUSSION

1. While financial ratio analysis is useful to marketing managers, it does have limitations. Identify and discuss the major limitations of the comparative technique.

2. Return on investment (ROI) is a useful measure of financial performance, but it may be ambiguous under certain conditions. Discuss.

3. Today's marketing managers are becoming increasingly involved with financial analysis in marketing operations. List some of these marketing financial analysis activities and briefly describe how they are used to gauge marketing performance.

4. Typically, two factors often influence the selection of the unit for which a financial analysis is to be performed. Name the two factors and discuss the influence of each unit selection.

5. Snapomatic Camera Company has introduced a new line of low-priced cameras called Click Quick. Below is the information on that product line:

Retail selling price	$25 per unit
Retailer's cost	$20 per unit
Wholesaler's cost	$15 per unit
Manufacturer's variable selling expense as a percentage of selling price	10%
Fixed selling and advertising expense	$800,000
Annual sales for Snapomatic	150,000 units
Estimated market size for low-priced cameras	800,000 units
Variable manufacturing cost	$2.50 per unit
Fixed manufacturing cost	$100,000

    a. What is the variable cost per unit of Click Quick for Snapomatic Camera Company?

    b. What is Snapomatic's contribution margin per unit?

    c. Calculate the break-even volume in units and in dollars.

    d. Estimate the market share that Click Quick has to command in order to (a) break even (b) attain a before-tax target profit of $600,000.

6. The management of Snapomatic Camera Co. is considering the introduction of a new product called Click-O-Matic; it is to be marketed in addition to Click Quick. Click-O-Matic, which is intended for a higher-priced segment of the market, is meant for the more sophisticated photographer. The following information has been compiled for managerial decision making.

Retailer's margin	20%
Jobber's margin	15%
Wholesaler's margin	$5 per unit
Variable selling expense as a percentage of sales	10%
Retailer's selling price	$60
Incremental fixed selling expense	$300,000
Promotion and advertising for Click-O-Matic	$500
New equipment required	$500,000 (to be depreciated over 10 years)
Direct factory labor	$4 per unit
Raw materials	$5 per unit
Factory and administrative overhead	$3 per unit (at a 50,000 unit volume level)

    a. What is the contribution margin per unit for the Click-O-Matic line?

    b. Calculate the break even sales in dollars and in units.

c. How much sales volume in dollars should Snapomatic Camera Company attain on Click-O-Matic to attain a 20 percent return on the equipment?

7. Since customers initially may be sensitive to the higher price of $60 for Click-O-Matic, it is considered worthwhile to perform an analysis by using a unit price of $55 per unit and raising the retail margin to 25 percent. What is the break-even volume in units?

STRATEGIC APPLICATION 4-1

WINKLEMAN MANUFACTURING COMPANY

In a recent staff meeting, John Winkleman, president of Winkleman Manufacturing Company, addressed his managers with this problem:

Intense competitive pressure is beginning to erode our market share in handhelds. I have documented 11 large orders that have been lost to Backman and Wiston within the past three months. On an annual basis this amounts to nearly 10,000 units and $1.5 million in lost opportunities. Within the last 18 months, at least 16 serious competitors have entered the market. Two thirds of these DMMs have continuity indicators. The trend is the same for European and Japanese markets as well. Our sales of handheld DMMs in fiscal year 81 is forecast to grow only 1.7 percent. According to Dataquest projections, the handheld DMM market will grow 20.9 percent for the next five years. I think that figure is conservative. Our competitors are gaining attention and sales with added features, particularly at the present time with continuity indicators. Since a new Winkleman general-purpose, low-cost handheld is two years from introduction, it is important that something be done to retain the profitable position of market leader in our traditional direct and distributor channels. Next meeting I want some ideas.

The Winkleman Manufacturing Company is a major electronics manufacturer in the Northwest, producing many varied products. The three products that most concern Mr. Winkleman are the Series A handheld digital multimeters (DMMs). As an innovator in the field of handheld DMMs, Mr. Winkleman saw his business flourish over the last two years. But now, with his three most successful products in late stages of maturity and a recession in full swing, times are not looking as rosy.

The three multimeters of concern are model numbers 1010, 1020, and 1030. These three models form a complementary family line. The 1010 is a low-cost unit containing all standard measurement functions and having a basic measurement accuracy of .5 percent. The 1020 offers identical measurement functions but has an improved basic measurement accuracy: .1 percent. The top of the line is the 1030. In addition to a basic accuracy of .1 percent, the 1030 offers several additional features, one being an audible continuity indicator. (See Exhibit 1 for sales and projected sales of these three models.)

At the next staff meeting, one of the newer management team members,

EXHIBIT 1 Selected Sales and Projections (number of units)

Model	FY 80 Actual	FY 81 Forecast	Percentage
1020	67,534	61,800	− 8.4%
1010	37,455	35,500	− 5.5
1030	25,602	35,500	+ 39.0
Total	130,591	132,800	+ 1.7%

Dave Haug, presented his ideas for tackling the lost-market problem:

What we need is a face-lift of our existing product line to hold us over the next two years. Changes in color, a new decal, some minor case modifications, and most important an audible continuity indicator in the 1010 and 1020 should give us two more years of product life to tide us over. We can call this Series B to retain continuity in switching from the old to the new. As my analysis indicates, Winkleman's decline in 1010/1020 sales could be reversed and show a modest increase in market share over the next two years with the inclusion of the Series B features [see Exhibit 2]. Discussions with large-order customers indicate that Winkleman could have won 40–60 percent of the lost large orders that were mentioned at our last meeting if our entire handheld family featured audible continuity. As you well know, the popularity of continuity indication has been confirmed in several other studies conducted over the past two years.

An estimate of sales of Series B has been generated from inputs from field sales, distribution managers, and discussions with customers. Conservative estimates indicate that sales of Series B will increase 6.9 percent above current Series A levels, with a marginal revenue increase of $1.5 million at U.S. list and assuming the same list prices as the current Se-

ries A models. During this current period of tight economic conditions, the market is becoming increasingly price sensitive. I am aware that our normal policy dictates multiplying the factory cost by three for pricing purposes and that the added factory cost of an audible continuity indicator is $5.00; but for income purposes we should not tack this on to the current prices. My analysis indicates that an increase of $5.00 would reduce incremental sales by 20 percent, and an increase of $10.00 would reduce incremental sales by 80 percent.

Also remember that we must pay for some nonrecurring engineering costs (NRE) [see Exhibit 3]. These must come out of our contribution margin—which at Winkleman is calculated by taking the total dollar sales less the 28 percent discount to distributors less factory cost for those units. I believe that increasing these prices will reduce our margins significantly, hindering our ability to cover the NRE, let alone make a profit. Therefore I propose we go ahead with Series B and hold the line on prices.

Dennis Cambelot, a longtime Winkleman employee, spoke up with a comment on Dave's proposal:

Dave, I think this Series B idea shows a lot of potential, but pricewise you are way out of line. We have always added the standard markup to our products. We make quality prod-

EXHIBIT 2 Series A and B—Projected Comparison (number of units)

Model	Unit Price	Series A FY 81	Series B FY 81	Change (percentage)	Total Sales* (change)*
1020	$179	61,800	66,000	4,200 (+6.8%)	$ 11.81 (+.75)
1010	139	35,500	40,000	4,500 (+12.6%)	$ 5.56 (+.63)
1030	219	35,500	36,000	500 (+1.4%)	$ 7.88 (+.11)
Total		132,800	142,000	9,200	$ 25.25

*Dollars in millions.

EXHIBIT 3 Engineering Costs and Schedule

The objectives for Series B, Models 1010, 1020, and 1030, are:
All case parts molded in medium gray
New decal for all units
Pulse-stretched beeper for 1010 and 1020
Rubber foot on battery door
Positionable bail
Manuals updated as necessary
For these objectives, NRE costs will be:

Manual (updated schematics for 1010, 1020, along with instructions for operation of beeper; model number and front panel changes for all units)	$ 3,500
Battery door mold (add three units)	12,000
Battery door foot die	3,000
Decal	1,900
Bail improvement	8,600
Photo lab	250
PCB fab (prototypes)	500
Engineering labor (25 man-weeks)	81,000
Hard model run	6,000
Total	$116,750

ucts, and people are willing to pay for quality. The only thing your fancy M.B.A. degree taught you was to be impractical. If you had gotten your experience in the trenches like me, your pricing theories would not be so conservative, and this company could make more money.

At the close of the meeting, Mr. Winkleman asked that each manager consider the Series B proposal. He directed that this consideration include: (1) whether or not to adopt the B series; (2) if

yes, at what price level; (3) alternative suggestions.

This case was prepared by Jim Dooley, under the supervision of Dr. William L. Weis. Albers School of Business, Seattle University.

DISCUSSION QUESTION

1. How would you respond at the next meeting?

STRATEGIC APPLICATION 4-2

SILVERDALE DRUG COMPANY

Scene: Silverdale Drug Company. Office of Preston (Pete) Peterson, president. Meeting with him to discuss company policies and plans are Sheldon (Shell) Summers, sales manager, and Thomas (Tom) Tarkington, treasurer.

Peterson: I've been reading a lot of stuff about return on investment but the idea doesn't seem to apply in its usual form to our particular business. Being wholesalers our real assets are not the normal balance sheet items of buildings, equipment, inventory, bank balances. Rather *our* real assets are our customers. We've invested countless man-hours and a lot of dollars in developing them into loyal customers; and it's from those investments, in the form of continuing business, that we receive our returns—not just in the year we expend the time and money but for many years into the future. Isn't that just as valid as the way manufacturers figure they receive returns on their investments in plant and equipment?

Tarkington: So what?

Peterson: Why can't we, for purposes of making decisions about expenditures designed to increase our sales and/or profitability, look at our customers that way? As if they represented a certain capital value that can be made even more valuable by further or new kinds of expenditures? And if the increase in value is going to be greater than the cost, then that's something we ought to go ahead with.

Summers: How would you do it, Pete?

Peterson: I'm not sure. Any ideas, Tom?

Tarkington: Well, we could calculate their value in terms of their contribution to overhead and profit. That's the way ROI is mostly used with other kinds of investments.

Summers: What would that make them worth?

Tarkington: Let's see. Annual sales are running at $5 million per year. Gross margin—that is, sales minus cost of goods—comes to about 15 percent; and 15 percent of $5 million is $750,000. Now, take off the costs of selling, delivery, a little for postage and telephone and even bad debts—the variable costs associated directly with servicing our customers—which add up to about $350,000. (Consider everything else overhead and profit.) This leaves us with $750,000 minus $350,000, or $400,000—the *annual contribution* that our customers make to our overhead and profit or the *return on investment* represented by our customers. That brings us to the tricky question: How do you translate that into an investment value?

Peterson: Suppose we use 10 percent. That is, consider that in our kind of business, we expect an investment to pay for itself in 10 years; or to put it another way, the standard for judging an investment is whether or not it will return an average of 10 percent per year. Besides, it doesn't really matter what figure we use so long as we are going to be considering alternative uses of our money. So long as the candidates for expenditure all have the same basis, we can compare them against each other.

Tarkington: Using 10 percent, our customers would be equivalent in value to 10 times $400,000, or $4 million. But don't tell the Internal Revenue boys! Our last annual report lists our assets at $1,500,000.

Peterson: Don't worry. There's no reason we can't have a different set of figures designed especially for making management decisions.

Summers: With roughly 400 customers, that makes each one worth about $10,000. Whew! When you realize that, it becomes pretty important to do everything we can to protect our "investments," as you call them, Pete—to see to it that we don't do anything to impair their value.

Peterson: Even more important, to see to it that they increase in value.

Tarkington: If you're going to do that kind of figuring, you'd better remember that they're not all of equal value. Don't forget that 65 to 75 percent of our customers account for 25 to 35 percent of our business.

Summers: Well, let's not get too fancy. The next thing, you'll be telling us that we must consider depreciation—I suppose that would be the rate at which we lose customers per year through death, sellout, defection to another supplier, and so on.

Tarkington: It so happens I have the figures—about 5 percent per year. But that's probably offset by the normal growth of an average customer; otherwise our volume wouldn't remain very stable. So okay, if you really want me to be fancy, what about taking into account the "present value of money" and applying cash-discounted flow techniques?

Summers: What is the name of . . . ?

Tarkington: Okay, okay. It only means that money spent today has a different value—or a different cost—than money spent tomorrow. But forget it. I agree with Pete. That much refinement is meaningless. The important thing is to have a common basis of comparison for alternative uses of money *today*—or any day that you're involved in making such a decision.

Peterson: That's enough—more than enough. Let's look at some of what you fellows are proposing to do with the developmental money we do have at our disposal. I figure that we have up to $35,000 available for investment into a long-range project to improve our sales and/or profitability.

Summers: Well, you know, Pete, I want to add a new salesman, and that would cost about $10,000 per year if it ran the same as for our present salesmen. So the $35,000 we have would cover us for three to four years.

Peterson: How many customers would that add by the end of that time, do you think?

Summers: Maybe 40. Yes, I think it would be 40—that's our present average per man.

Tarkington: What about improving the *effectiveness* of our present salesmen instead? How much would a really good sales training program cost? Certainly, nowhere near as much. And how much would that add to their productivity?

Summers: Not more than 2 percent—if we're lucky, 3 percent. And the cost would be just about the same as adding a new salesman. By the time we got through it, it would be pretty close to $10,000.

Tarkington: But, Shell, that would be a one-time cost, wouldn't it? We'd spend it just once, the first year, and then we'd reap the benefit every year thereafter.

Summers: Sure, but one salesman represents a 10 percent increase in number of customers, and only costs three to four times as much, figuring, as I said, that he could line up 40 customers by the end of three or four years. Furthermore, if you're talking about salesmen's effectiveness, I'd rather take the money available and offer bonuses for the best sales records each year. The prospect of $3,000 or $4,000 to be divided among the top performers at the end of the year would be enough of a carrot to boost total sales 4 or 5 percent, I'd be willing to bet.

Peterson: I'm more interested in improving the effectiveness of our customers, rather than our salesmen. Jim Vigary, who heads up Vigary and Company over in Hopkinton—I talked with him at the Wholesale Druggists Convention I went to last September—has mounted what he says is a very effective program to help his retail drug customers to be better merchants and merchandisers. He figures his payoff comes in two ways: (1) from an increase of sales through better customer performance and (2) from becoming a preferred wholesaler source and increasing his share of the market. Costs him about $20,000 per year,

but he can afford it; he's about twice as big as we are. And he estimates that in two to three years he will be reaching the point where sales of his average retailer are up by 15 percent. Suppose we just spend half as much—say, by using a consultant part time instead of hiring a full-time merchandising specialist the way Vigary is doing it?

Well, let's do a little thinking—and figuring—and see where we come out in terms of contribution to overhead and profit over the next 10 years. In other words, with $30,000 or $40,000 to invest in our customers, which way will we get the best ROI?

SOURCE: Edward C. Bursk, Stephen A. Greyser, *Cases in Marketing Management*, 2d ed., © 1975, 204–7, 208–10. Reprinted by permission of Prentice-Hall, Inc., Englewood Cliffs, N.J.

DISCUSSION QUESTION

1. In what project or projects should Silverdale "invest" $35,000 in order to achieve the best "returns" over the next 10 years?

PART 2

Marketing Situation Analysis

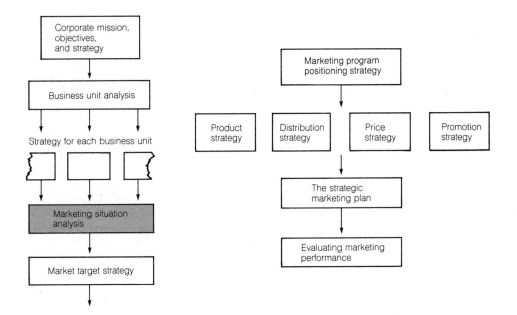

CHAPTER 5

Defining and
Analyzing Markets

The central role of understanding markets and customer needs in developing marketing strategy is dramatically illustrated by the automobile industry. One of the winners in an industry that has been adversely impacted by fuel shortages, intense global competition, environmental pollution, and poor quality control is the Snap-on Tools Corporation. This manufacturer and distributor of hand tools and equipment for the professional automotive mechanic achieved impressive sales and profit growth during the decade ending in 1985.[1] Beginning in the late 1970s, the automotive aftermarket (parts and service) in general and the professional mechanic in particular were influenced by factors such as a weak economy and higher engine speeds (and greater wear) created by small cars. In the face of adverse economic pressures Snap-on expanded its dealer network and benefited from the economic turnaround in 1983 and 1984. Market change, including more business for mechanics and a subsequent rise in their incomes and tool purchases, has provided excellent growth opportunities for Snap-on. Gains in new car sales and moderating gasoline prices have increased maintenance and repair expenditures. The firm's management has responded to the changing market by expanding distribution, speeding up introduction of new products, increasing productivity, improving dealer training, and strengthening the dealer support system. Company executives anticipated and analyzed perceptively changes in the automotive aftermarket. As a result, Snap-on's management has been able to plan and implement effective corporate and marketing strategies. Key strategic plans through 1990 will focus on aggressive marketing, introducing new products, and developing advanced manufacturing processes.

The important role of the market in shaping corporate and marketing strategies is clearly indicated by Snap-on Tools. By defining the market arena, management can guide the analysis of customer needs and the changes over time in these needs. This information provides essential direction to strategies for market targeting, product, distribution, price, and promotion. By tracking the effects of external influences upon a company's product-markets, management can identify opportunities and threats and can develop effective strategies to meet them.

The task of defining and analyzing the structure of product-markets underlies most, if not all, of the strategic decisions that are made in a business. This chapter begins by examining how to define product-markets. Next, we describe and illustrate a step-by-step guide to product-market analysis. A discussion of the forecasts needed to measure the size of an opportunity present in a product-market follows. Finally, research methods for analyzing complex product-market structures are examined.

DEFINING PRODUCT-MARKETS

How a market is defined has an important influence upon various strategic decisions. Corporate and marketing strategists must answer such key questions as the following:

What products should be assigned to a particular business unit?
How should the markets be defined for the SBU so that strategic planning can be facilitated?
What definition will be most useful in guiding market target and other marketing strategy decisions?
What roles should the product and the consumer end user play in establishing product-market boundaries?

The definition of a product-market is the starting point in answering these and other market-related strategic questions.

It is important to recognize the different decision-making needs of executives when defining and analyzing product-markets. Consider, for example, the dessert foods SBU manager at General Foods versus the Jello brand manager at General Foods. The former is concerned with strategy from a total business unit perspective whereas the latter is occupied with marketing strategy and tactical issues for a single brand. Information needs vary substantially between management levels, and it is essential to factor these considerations into product-market definitions.

What Is a Product-Market?

Intuitively, it is easy to grasp the concept of a product-market, although there are some differences in the way in which analysts define the term operationally. Markets are groups of people who have the *ability* and *willingness* to buy something because they have a need of it.[2] Ability and willingness indicate that there is a demand for a particular product or service. People with needs and wants buy the benefits of a product or service. Thus a product-market matches people with needs—needs that lead to a demand for a product or service—to the product benefits that satisfy those needs. Unless the product benefits are available, we have no markets—only people with needs. Likewise, there have to be people who have a demand for what a given product can do for them. Thus a product-market combines the benefits of a product with the market needs that lead people to express a demand for that product. We ought, then, to define markets in terms of *needs* substitutability among different products and brands as well as in terms of the different ways in which people choose to satisfy their needs. "We can define a product-market as the *set of products* judged to be substitutes, within those usage situations in which similar patterns of benefits are sought, and the *customers* for whom such usages are relevant."[3]

For strategic purposes the product is what it does.[4] Digital watches compete with analog watches, although they look and work differently. Steel competes with aluminum, plastics, and other materials in certain uses. One problem in defining product-market boundaries is that competitiveness is a continuum rather than a dichotomy. If two items can perform the same generic function (e.g., relieve pain), they also can compete. Whether they will compete and to what degree they will compete are factors influenced by marketing actions as well as by individual tastes and preferences. Marketing actions, such as the choice of distribution channels, pricing, advertising, and personal selling, can change our perceptions of a product. By so doing, these actions make two alternatives increasingly or decreasingly competitive. Product-market boundaries therefore change as a consequence of changing conditions.

To illustrate the importance of understanding customer needs and the alternative ways (e.g., different products and services) in which these needs can be met, consider the competitive challenge faced by Keuffel & Esser Co. For decades K&E was the leading manufacturer of slide rules, drafting equipment, surveying equipment, and similar supplies. While management's strategic eye was focused on the market for slide rules and other specific products in the mid-1960s, competitors with new technology moved rapidly into the product-market arena long dominated by K&E. In the 1970s hand-held calculators and small computers virtually wiped out the market for slide rules; laser technology had a major impact upon the market for alignment and directional devices; and computers took over many drafting functions. Management finally recognized its new competitive threats, but it was almost too late. The following actions were taken by Thomas R. Hye, K&E's new president:

> K&E had been marketing some 12,000 products of its own and others through a fat catalog that was the bible of the field. Hye cut out more than one third of the items. He began distributing other makers' calculators and small computers. He restructured manufacturing and he bought 79 percent of Laser Systems and Electronics, Inc. to get into electronics; as a result, K&E now has "Vectron"—a device that does surveying with a built-in microprocessor.[5]

Both customer needs and the ways of meeting these needs change. By understanding how a firm's specific products are positioned within more general product-markets, we can monitor and evaluate changes in order to determine whether alternate strategies and product offerings are needed. In defining a product-market, we must establish boundaries that contain all relevant product categories competing for the same needs. The approach to product-market definition and analysis discussed later in the chapter is intended to help us avoid establishing such narrow boundaries that they will exclude products that are potential competitors for the same end-user needs.

Some Definitions

While the general idea of a product-market is widely accepted, there are some differences as to how to define a product-market. These differences can be resolved by recognizing that: (1) terms such as generic, product type, and brand may convey different meanings to analysts; and (2) there are alternative product-market levels.

The term *generic* product-market designates a broad group of products that satisfy a general, yet similar need. For example, several types of products can be combined to form a generic product-market for home entertainment. Stereos, radios, TVs, and various other types of products fall into this generic category. Note that the term *generic* is also used to designate nonbranded versions of a specific product like aspirin. There are also differences in the use of product-market identification according to brands of products. Some analysts use the term *product-market* to designate brands competing for a specific set of needs. Using this frame of reference, Godiva luxury chocolates compete in a different product-market from those in which Whitman and other less expensive chocolates compete. This product-market definition assumes that there is one product-market level comprised of brands that directly compete with each other.

The definitional differences can be resolved by recognizing that there are different levels of product-markets.

Generic Product-Market. This level includes all products or services that can satisfy a generic need such as housing. Since people with the same need may not satisfy the need in the same manner, generic product-markets are often heterogeneous, that is, comprised of different end-user groups. The generic product-market can be designated as a group of types of products that satisfy a set of generic needs. Included in the housing generic product-market are apartments, single-family homes, condominiums, and other types of housing.

Product Type Product-Market. This level represents all brands of a particular product such as apartments. Since all of the brands in a specific product category may not compete with each other, this level also often contains user groups with dissimilar needs (e.g., people who want luxury apartments and those who desire economy apartments).

Product Variants. Differences in products within a product type may exist, creating subcategories.[6] Cereal (a type of product), for example, has several product variations, including natural, nutritional, pre-sweetened, and regular cereals. Variants of coffee include ground and instant coffee, with caffeine-containing and decaffeinated varieties for each. The product variant distinction is important as a level of analysis, providing there is limited substitution of variants by the end user.

Brand Product-Market. The various brands that compete on a direct basis form a brand product-market. It is often comprised of a subset of brands from the same type of product-market that can satisfy the needs of people who make up a particular segment of the market. In some instances the brands may come from more than one type or variant of the product, such as single-family houses and condominiums.[7]

Some analysts use the term *product-market* to refer to only the brand level.[8] If all relevant brands are included at the brand level, the multilevel and the single-level designations should be equivalent at the brand level. As is discussed later, there are some advantages to the multilevel product-market definition.

Determining Product-Market Structure

One important issue is determining how broad the generic category should be. This is because ultimately all products and services fit into a generic product-market concerned with meeting human needs. Such a huge category is obviously of no value in market analysis and strategy development. At the other extreme, if we define the relevant product-

---

EXHIBIT 5-1   Some Illustrative Product-Markets

Generic Level	Product Type Level	Brand Level*
Agricultural equipment to meet the needs of farmers in the production of crops.	Tractors Combines Plows Mowers Corn pickers Hay handlers Others	Allis-Chalmers Deere & Company Hesston Corp. Case New Holland Yarity Others
Financial services to meet the needs of individual investors.	Life insurance Commodities Savings accounts Bonds Stocks Money market funds Real estate Others	Merrill Lynch Citicorp Travelers Aetna Chase Manhattan E. F. Hutton Golden West Others
Products to meet peoples' needs for eating away from home.	Fast-food restaurants Nightclubs Cafeterias Family restaurants Others	McDonald's Red Lobster Morrisons Cafeterias Local restaurants Others

*These brands do not compete in all of the product type product-markets shown.

---

market as the market served by a specific product such as microwave ovens, we exclude potentially useful information about how kitchen appliances correspond to an overall generic need for cooking food.

Judgment is often involved in establishing product-market boundaries. A study of industry practices, management experience, and a thoughtful analysis of product uses will assist us in defining a logical generic product-market. It is often easier to define industrial and other organizational product-markets than to define consumer product-markets. In both industrial and consumer markets, our focus should be on the end-user of the product or service—the person or organization that consumes the product. For example, if a firm makes haystack loaders, the end-user is the farmer rather than the distributor or dealer.

Product-market levels provide a useful framework for guiding customer definition and building user profiles. They also help us in making an analysis of the industry and key competitors, in targeting and positioning guidelines, and in forecasting demand. Exhibit 5-1 shows some illustrations of product-market levels. Since the choice of the product-market boundaries is arbitrary, we may need considerable insight and analysis in a given situation to arrive at an operationally useful definition.

An examination of the eating-away-from-home product-market highlights some of the definitional issues we encounter when trying to

EXHIBIT 5-2 Characteristics of People's Generic Needs for Food and Beverages

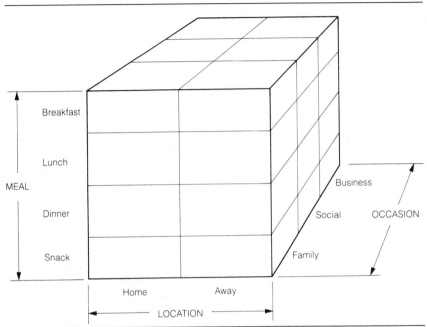

establish product-market boundaries. Exhibit 5-1 uses the eating-away-from-home situation to define the generic product-market. (Only food is included—not food and beverages.) There are several ways a generic classification could have been formed, as shown in Exhibit 5-2. Other alternatives for establishing generic boundaries exist by using one or a combination of the categories shown in Exhibit 5-2. The important consideration is to avoid a generic definition that is either too narrow or too broad. For most purposes the entire block shown in Exhibit 5-2 is too broad, whereas one cell may be too restrictive if by using it, we exclude competing products and brands.

Industry categories are often concentrated at the product type product-market level and thus are too restrictive for use in generic definition. For example, if we define product-market structure by starting with candy, frozen foods, or dairy products, this would eliminate from consideration many competing and complementary products. Because of the interrelationships of people's needs and wants, competing products and services do not always fall into well-defined categories. An illustrative product-market structure for cereals is shown in Exhibit 5-3.

EXHIBIT 5-3   Illustrative Product-Market Structure

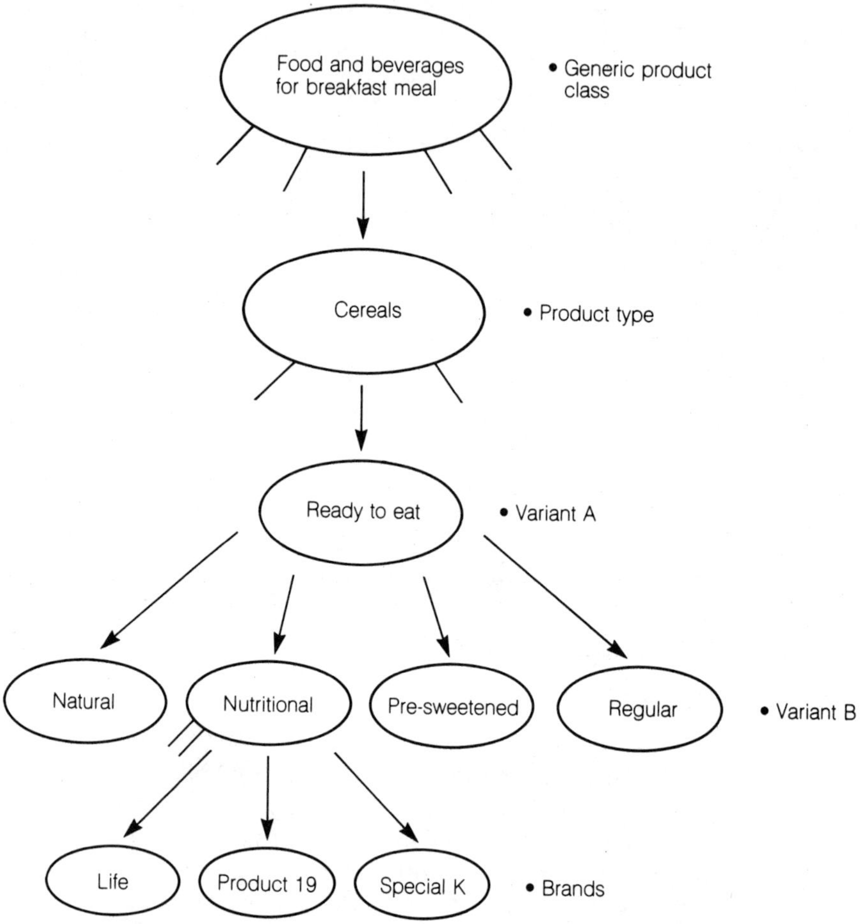

```
        ┌─────────────────────┐
        │  Food and beverages │      • Generic product
        │  for breakfast meal │        class
        └─────────────────────┘
                  │
                  ▼
            ┌───────────┐
            │  Cereals  │            • Product type
            └───────────┘
                  │
                  ▼
          ┌──────────────┐
          │ Ready to eat │          • Variant A
          └──────────────┘
```

| Natural | Nutritional | Pre-sweetened | Regular | • Variant B |

| Life | Product 19 | Special K | • Brands |

Considerations in Forming Product-Markets

Three factors may affect the formation of product-markets:

1. The number of distinct uses or applications for a specific product.
2. The number of usage situations encountered by each user.
3. The number of alternatives in the users' consideration set.[9]

Product uses relate to the functions provided by the product. For example, steel can be used in many ways, while a surgical skin stapler performs the single function of stapling skin together after surgery. The usage situation refers to the various situations in which the product may be used, such as the consumption situations of food and beverage shown in Exhibit 5-2. Finally, a buyer typically considers only a limited set of product (brand) alternatives when making a purchase decision. Consider, for example, the different men's suit brands offered by Hartmarx. Few, if any, buyers include all these brands in their consideration set.

When there are many uses or applications, many usage situations by each user, and many alternatives to be considered, the resulting product-market structure can become quite complex. At the other end of the spectrum, the task of product-market definition is more straightforward. To gain a better perspective of the task, we need to examine some of the considerations involved in forming product-market boundaries.

Aggregating versus Disaggregating. Should we start with an SBU and attempt to break it down into specific product-markets? Or, instead, should we try to build a market structure that considers applications, use situations, and product alternatives? A third possibility is to start by defining a generic product-market and then determining the specific product-market categories that are competitive with each other. It may, in fact, be appropriate for us to give consideration to all these viewpoints, depending upon the purpose of our product-market analysis.

While one should not allow existing market or industry classification schemes alone to determine how product-market boundaries are established, we should consider existing schemes. Many of these market definition approaches are based upon industry guidelines and thus may not sufficiently consider types of needs and alternative ways of meeting the needs. They typically focus upon product categories rather than user needs. Since industry groups, government agencies, and other organizations generate a great deal of information about products and markets, we should attempt to utilize this information. An example of the industry market classification approach is shown in Exhibit 5-4. While the information is not broken out according to product-market categories, an analysis involving household furniture could certainly be drawn from the data. For instance, we could estimate annual growth rates for each product type such as bedding. The SIC (Standard Industrial Code) numbers (e.g., SIC 2515) are Standard Industrial Classification code designations of industry and product groups. One problem is that competing brand alternatives may fall into different SIC categories.

Purpose of Analysis. Another consideration is the purpose of the product-market analysis. If management is deciding whether or not to exit from an SBU, primary emphasis may be on financial performance and competitive position. Detailed analysis of product-market structure may not be necessary. Alternatively, if the firm is trying to find an

EXHIBIT 5-4   Recent Performance and Forecast: Household Furniture (SIC 251)
(in millions of dollars except as noted)

Item	Amount				Percent Change		
	1982	1983	1984	1985	83/82	84/83	85/84
Industry Data							
Value of industry shipments							
Household furniture (SIC 251)	12,769	14,608	16,346	—	14.4	11.9	—
Wood (SIC 2511)	5,078	5,819	6,593	—	14.6	13.3	—
Upholstered (SIC 2512)	3,552	4,156	4,667	—	17.0	12.3	—
Metal (SIC 2514)	1,573	1,746	1,868	—	11.0	7.0	—
Bedding (SIC 2515)	1,930	2,156	2,404	—	11.7	11.5	—
Value of industry shipments (1972$)							
Household furniture	6,599	7,384	8,012	8,332	11.9	8.5	4.0
Wood	2,448	2,717	2,948	3,066	11.0	8.5	4.0
Upholstered	1,978	2,263	2,485	2,584	14.4	9.8	4.0
Metal	814	899	971	998	10.5	8.0	2.7
Bedding	1,044	1,158	1,233	1,271	10.9	6.5	3.1
Total employment (000)	262	271	288	—	3.4	6.5	—
Production workers (000)	220	228	242	—	3.6	6.3	—
Average hourly earnings of production workers	5.74	6.02	6.24	—	4.9	3.7	—
Product Data							
Value of product shipments							
Household furniture	12,310	14,079	15,758	—	14.4	11.9	—
Wood	4,867	5,579	6,321	—	14.6	13.3	—
Upholstered	3,355	3,927	4,411	—	17.0	12.3	—
Metal	1,463	1,624	1,737	—	11.0	7.0	—
Bedding	2,040	2,278	2,540	—	11.7	11.5	—
Value of product shipments (1972$)							
Household furniture	6,364	7,124	7,729	8,038	11.9	8.5	4.0
Wood	2,347	2,606	2,828	2,941	11.0	8.5	4.0
Upholstered	1,868	2,137	2,346	2,440	14.4	9.8	4.0
Metal	757	836	903	927	10.5	8.0	2.7
Bedding	1,103	1,215	1,294	1,334	10.9	6.5	3.1
Product price index (1972 = 100)							
Household furniture	194.7	199.5	205.7	—	2.5	3.1	—
Wood	208.2	217.0	226.5	—	4.2	4.4	—
Upholstered	179.6	184.0	188.2	—	2.2	2.3	—
Metal	193.3	194.1	195.0	—	0.5	0.0	—
Bedding	185.1	183.4	192.0	—	−0.9	4.7	—
Trade data							
Value of exports (ITA)	239	204	195	—	−14.6	−4.4	—
Value of imports (ITA)	1,079	1,434	2,048	—	32.9	42.8	—
Export/shipment ratio	0.02	0.01	0.01	—	—	—	—
Import/new supply ratio	0.08	0.09	0.12	—	—	—	—

SOURCE: U.S. Department of Commerce, Bureau of Industrial Economics *1985 U.S. Industrial Outlook* (Washington, D.C.: U.S. Government Printing Office, 1985), 47–4.

attractive niche to serve in a product-market, the depth of analysis may need to be much greater than for an SBU. For example, when different products can satisfy the same need, the product-market boundaries of brand levels should contain all relevant products.

Boundary Shifts.   Finally, changes in product-market boundaries may occur as new technologies become available and competitive structures are altered as a result of new entrants. Consider, for example, the major changes that occurred in the mid-1980s in such deregulated industries as financial services, transportation, and communications. New service alternatives modified the sets of competing firms. Bankers became brokers, and retailers offered financial services. Consumers were offered many new service alternatives that were previously not available because of regulation.

These guidelines for establishing product-market boundaries serve various purposes. Product and markets can be linked together in various ways when we recognize that in all cases *needs* must be matched with *products* that can satisfy the needs. Product-market boundaries should be formed in a manner that will be of strategic value to the enterprise, allowing management to capitalize upon existing and potential opportunities and to help avoid possible threats.

ANALYZING PRODUCT MARKETS

A complete solution to determining product-market structure should establish definitional boundaries for product-markets, their size and composition, and the brand and/or product categories competing for the needs and wants of specific end-user groups. Suppose the management of a firm is interested in expanding its mix of products, and that the present line of products meets a generic need for such household cleaning functions as laundry and dishes. A logical expansion would be to move into a closely related generic product-market, thus gaining possible advantages through common distribution channels, manufacturing, advertising, and research and development. The Maytag Co. fits this situation with its line of washers, dryers, and dishwashers. In 1980 Maytag acquired the Hardwick Stove Co., a maker of gas and electric ranges and microwave ovens. In 1982 Jenn Air Corp., a premium-priced specialty electric range manufacturer, was purchased. As shown in Exhibit 5–5, it is possible to define a product-market structure for use in evaluating possible opportunities in the food-heating generic product-market. By breaking out the product-market boundaries, management can analyze the various specific product-markets and the different brand product-markets.

Guide to Analysis

A guide to product-market analysis is shown in Exhibit 5–6, which indicates the types of information relevant at each level of the analysis. First, it is important to know as much as possible about the people/ organizations that are the end users in the product-market at each level. These market profiles of customers are useful in evaluating opportunities and guiding our strategies in market targeting and positioning.

EXHIBIT 5–5 Breaking Out Product-Market Boundaries

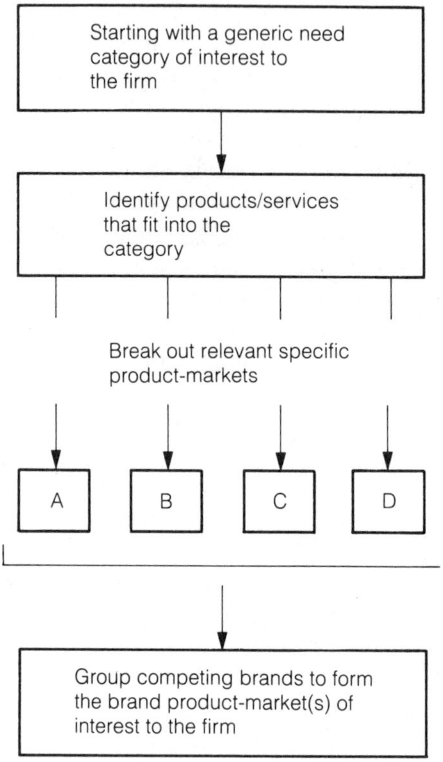

```
┌──────────────────────────────┐
│  Starting with a generic need │
│  category of interest to      │
│  the firm                     │
└──────────────────────────────┘
              │
              ▼
┌──────────────────────────────┐
│  Identify products/services   │
│  that fit into the            │
│  category                     │
└──────────────────────────────┘

        Break out relevant specific
        product-markets

     ▼       ▼        ▼        ▼
   ┌───┐   ┌───┐    ┌───┐    ┌───┐
   │ A │   │ B │    │ C │    │ D │
   └───┘   └───┘    └───┘    └───┘

              ▼
┌──────────────────────────────┐
│  Group competing brands to form│
│  the brand product-market(s) of│
│  interest to the firm          │
└──────────────────────────────┘
```

Second, identification and analysis of firms that offer products and services at each product-market level are essential to strategy development, including both similar types of firms (e.g., manufacturers) and those functioning at different levels in channels of distribution (e.g., distributors, retailers). Third, a comprehensive assessment of major competitors is essential to guiding marketing strategy decisions. Fourth, the analysis should help management decide what target market strategy to adopt and the product or brand positioning strategy to follow. Finally, management is interested in the size of each product-market and estimates of future growth. Forecasts are needed one to three years in the future for detailed business planning, and longer-term projections are required in strategic analysis and planning.

Developing Customer Profiles

Since the objective of the enterprise is to meet customers' needs and wants, it is essential to learn as much about our customers as possible.

EXHIBIT 5-6   Guide to Product-Market Analysis

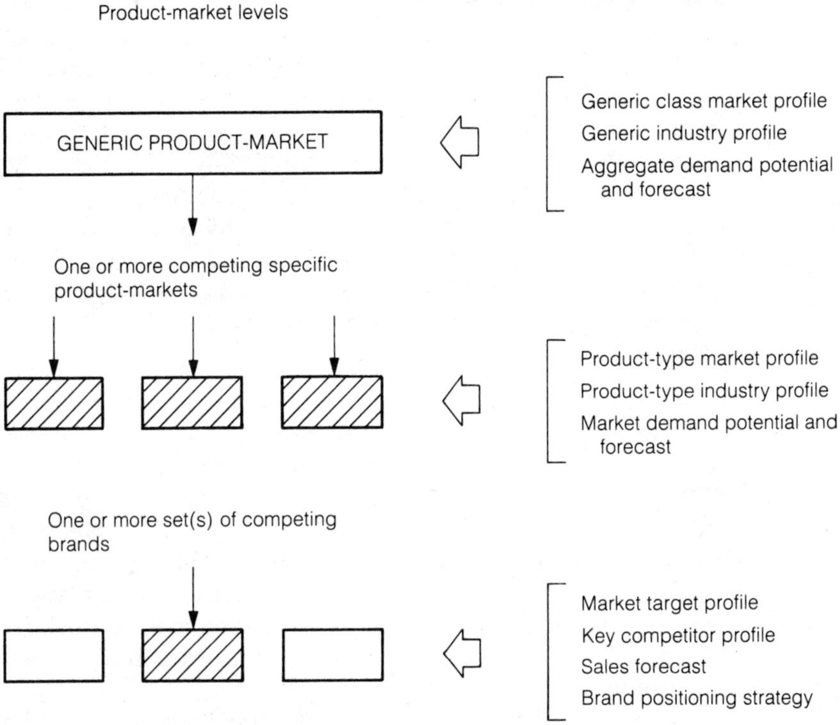

Product-market levels

Generic class market profile
Generic industry profile
Aggregate demand potential
   and forecast

GENERIC PRODUCT-MARKET

One or more competing specific
product-markets

Product-type market profile
Product-type industry profile
Market demand potential and
   forecast

One or more set(s) of competing
brands

Market target profile
Key competitor profile
Sales forecast
Brand positioning strategy

SOURCE: Adapted from David W. Cravens, Gerald E. Hills, and Robert B. Woodruff, *Marketing Decision Making: Concepts and Strategy,* rev. ed. (Homewood, Ill.: Richard D. Irwin, 1980), 120.

Answers to the following four questions will supply important information for constructing profiles of customers:

1. Who are the existing/potential customers?
2. What are the characteristics of the customers?
3. How do the customers decide what to buy?
4. What factors, other than customer characteristics and company marketing efforts, influence buying?[10]

Identifying and Describing Buyers.   Typically, demographic and socioeconomic characteristics are used to identify potential users in generic, type of product, product variant, and brand product-markets. Various characteristics, such as family size, age, income, geographical location, sex, and occupation, are often useful in identifying buyers in consumer markets. Illustrative factors used to identify end users in industrial markets are type of industry, size, location, and product application. Many published sources of information are available for use in identifying and describing customers. Some examples include U.S.

Census data, trade association publications, and studies by advertising media (TV, radio, magazines). The important task is to find the characteristics that will identify potential customers. When experience and existing information do not clearly identify buyers, research studies may be necessary to locate and describe customers and prospects.

Descriptive profile information on buyers should become increasingly specific, moving from the generic to brand levels. An important issue is determining the extent to which buyer's needs vary at each product-market level. For example, demographics may provide useful general profiles of voters yet not indicate why certain voters prefer one candidate over another. Often, simply describing buyers does not provide sufficient information for targeting and positioning decisions. Determining *why* people buy offers important insights for marketing strategy.

Identifying Buyer Decision Criteria. In learning how customers decide what to buy, it is useful to analyze how people move through the sequence of steps leading to a decision to purchase a particular brand. Buyers normally follow a decision process: they begin by recognizing a need; next, they seek information; third, they identify and evaluate alternative products; and finally, they choose a brand. This process varies by product and situation since some decisions that are repetitive and for which a buyer has past experience tend to be routine. One essential aspect of studying buyer decision processes is finding out what criteria people use in making decisions.

Consider Exhibit 5–7, which illustrates an architectural firm's efforts to determine the criteria that commercial building developers use in selecting their architects.[11] A sample of decision makers in 80 developer firms identified and rated the importance of 21 factors considered in making such a selection. Surprisingly, the national prestige of an architectural firm is not considered very important. Analysis of buyer behavior is an essential part of product-market analysis. A more comprehensive discussion of why and how people buy is included in Chapter 6.

Environmental Influences. The final step in building customer profiles is to identify external factors that may influence buyers. Environmental influences include the government, social change, economic shifts, technology, and other macroenvironmental factors that alter buyers' needs and wants. Typically, these factors cannot be controlled by the buyer or the firms that market the product. Yet substantial changes in these uncontrollable influences can have a major impact on customers. Therefore, we need to identify the relevant external factors for a product-market and estimate their future impact. Over the past decade various shifts in market opportunities have occurred as a result of environmental factors. Illustrations include the effect of gasoline prices upon the demand for automobiles and services related to oil fields.

EXHIBIT 5-7   Average Ratings in Ranked Order of Importance of Factors
Considered in Architect Selection

Factor	Average Rating
1. Responsiveness	9.2
2. Competent staff	9.2
3. Experience with project like mine	9.1
4. Meets deadlines	9.1
5. Working relationship	9.0
6. Understands my needs	9.0
7. Quality of design documents	8.8
8. Stays within budget	8.7
9. Design creativity/capabilities	8.4
10. Ongoing participation of principals	8.1
11. Economic feasibility know-how	7.6
12. Engineering know-how	7.4
13. Personal references	7.2
14. Construction supervision	6.9
15. Used architect before	6.8
16. Competitive fees	6.7
17. Proximity of architect to the project	6.7
18. Presentations by architect	6.6
19. Postconstruction follow-up	6.2
20. National prestige of the firm	5.5
21. Full range of services	5.3

One of the more controversial marketing strategy debates of the mid-1980s concerned the extent to which consumers around the world have the same needs and wants. Some marketing experts have argued that consumers are becoming more alike throughout the world, and thus global marketing strategies are appropriate. Nevertheless, caution is necessary in attempting to apply the same marketing strategy in two different countries. In a study of the pros and cons of global versus multinational strategies, 70 of 120 senior marketing executives named computer hardware as the appropriate category among more than 20 product categories for global marketing.[12] In general, these executives indicated that global strategies are limited to only a few product types.

Industry and Distribution Analyses

We need to identify and analyze the ways in which products and services reach end users. Normally an analysis is conducted from the point of view of a particular firm. For example, a department store chain such as Dayton-Hudson would include other retailers in its industry analysis. This analysis would include two kinds of information: (1) a study of the industry of which the company of interest is a part, and (2) an analysis of the distribution channels that link together the various organizations serving end users' needs and wants. The former consists of a horizontal analysis covering similar types of firms (e.g., steel producers), whereas the latter analysis focuses on the vertical network of firms operating within a distribution channel.

Industry Analysis. The information needed by management for an industry analysis includes: (1) industry characteristics and trends, such as sales, number of firms, and growth rates, and (2) operating practices of the firms in the industry, including product mix, service provided, barriers to entry, and related information.[13]

The first step in an industry analysis is to determine the composition of the industry. This includes identifying the companies that comprise the industry and developing descriptive information on the industry and its members. As an illustration of an abbreviated industry analysis, consider the catfish product-market.[14] In 1985 Church's Fried Chicken, Inc. began to offer catfish in 1,235 of its restaurants, creating a new stage of growth for the industry. The 1985 catfish forecast was 185 million pounds, nearly four times higher than the 1980 production, and a ninefold increase over the past decade. Freshwater catfish has gained a price advantage over ocean fish such as perch because of reductions in supply as a result of overfishing the oceans. U.S. catfish producers are concentrated in Mississippi, Alabama, and Arkansas. The fish are produced in artificial ponds by using production techniques that generate a quality product very efficiently. Many of the producers are farmers who sell their fish to major processors. Cotton fields of the south are being converted into catfish farms. Anticipating further expansion of the market, large processors invested heavily on new forms of plant and equipment between 1983 and 1985. For example, Farm Fresh Catfish Co. opened a new plant in Arkansas in 1984 at a cost of over $16 million.

Analysis of Distribution Channels. In addition to the industry analysis, a study of distribution channels is important in understanding and serving product-markets. While in some instances producers go directly to their end users, many work with other organizations through distribution channels. The extent of vertical integration by competitors backward (supply) and forward toward end-users is also useful information. An example of distribution channels used in the carpet industry is shown in Exhibit 5–8. Suppose that you are the marketing manager for a fiber producer and are selling to carpet makers (tufters) through manufacturers' agents. By looking at other distribution approaches, we can identify important patterns and trends in serving end users. Distribution analysis can also uncover new market opportunities that are not covered via present channels of distribution. Finally, by obtaining information from various distribution levels, we can find help in forecasting the end-user demand. For example, by contacting retailers and contractors (as shown in Exhibit 5–8), a carpet fiber pro-

EXHIBIT 5-8   Illustrative Distribution Channels in the Carpet Industry

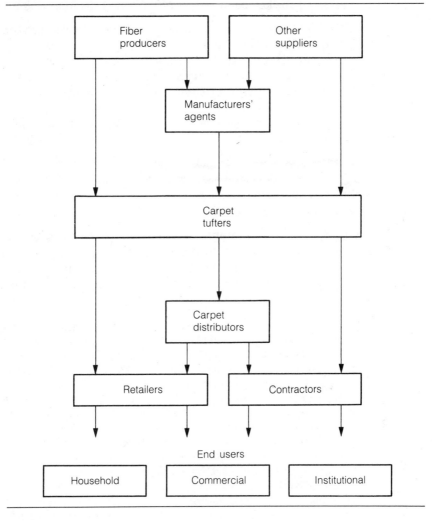

ducer can gain important insights as to end users' needs and wants
(e.g., shifts in color preferences).

Analysis of the Key Competitors

Since a company does not normally compete on a direct basis with all
firms in an industry, it is necessary for us to find out which firms are
our key competitors. Also, if specific customer needs can be satisfied
by product types from other industries, these potential competitors

should be included in our analysis. Information that is obtained from an analysis of the key competitors often covers the following areas:

Estimated overall business strength of each key competitor.
Present market share and past trends.
Financial strengths and performance.
Management capabilities (and limitations).
Technical and operating advantages (e.g., patents, low-production costs, new products).
Description and assessment of strengths and limitations of marketing strategy.

Keeping up with what the competition is doing is one of management's most important responsibilities. The above information should be obtained and studied on a regular basis. A step-by-step approach to the analysis of competitors is presented in Chapter 7.

Targeting and Positioning Guidelines. Finally, product-market analyses supply information that is needed in developing marketing strategy. For example, Kikkoman International's management identified and analyzed potential customers and competition for its soy sauce in the United States as follows:

Twenty years ago, when Kikkoman was first entering the U.S. market, the company's promotional efforts at home were largely confined to splashing its name on posters and flashing it out in neon lights. The company also provided free soy sauce to the huge cooking classes attended by young Japanese women about to be married (and it still does so).

This low-key approach was a far cry from the mass marketing of food products in the United States. So before setting up an American subsidiary, Kikkoman took a close look at how goods are sold here. "Kikkoman studied, studied, studied marketing, marketing, marketing." says Yukio Ike, senior vice president of Yamaichi International (America) Inc., the New York subsidiary of the Japanese brokerage house.

One of Kikkoman's studies found that Japanese-Americans had become so westernized in their eating habits that they no longer constituted a growing market. Therefore, the study concluded, the marketing target would have to be the American population as a whole.

Another study focused on the competition. The U.S. soy sauce market, then only $1 million a year, was dominated by two brands, Chung King (now owned by R. J. Reynolds Industries Inc.) and LaChoy (now belonging to Beatrice Foods Co.). Both companies had lines of Chinese foods, which also have long employed soy sauce, and neither promoted soy sauce as anything other than a condiment for the food products. Therefore, the relatively few Americans who knew about soy sauce generally thought of it only in terms of Oriental cookery.

So Kikkoman concluded that to gain a foothold—much less expand—in the United States, would entail educating Americans about soy sauce and emphasizing its versatility. Earlier, in Japan, Kikkoman officials already had noticed that American occupation troops sprinkled soy sauce on everything from hamburgers to pork chops. And the executives' hunches were backed up by the American advertising agency that they had retained when they first decided to try cracking the U.S. market.[15]

By early 1978 Kikkoman soy sauce was the leading brand in the $20 million-a-year U.S. market. The company had been instrumental in expanding the market to its present level. It was apparent from the consumer studies that in order to gain a profitable market position for its soy sauce, people must be educated about the product and its variety of uses. This information led to the following promotional strategy:

> Kikkoman decided to rely heavily on television advertising. Only in this way, the company believed, could its educational programs succeed. "We had to explain what soy sauce was and how to use it, and what the difference is between our soy sauce and what is made in this country and called soy sauce," Mr. Suzuki says, adding: "What goes under the name soy sauce here would never be called that in Japan."
>
> Therefore, the TV ads emphasized how Kikkoman soy sauce is specially brewed and aged, like beer; the American brands, the ads noted correctly, are made chemically. "Add Quality; Add Kikkoman" was the slogan.
>
> Getting these points across nationwide was Kikkoman's ultimate aim. However, because of the size of the United States, the company decided to start out regionally. Its first target was San Francisco, where it based its U.S. subsidiary.
>
> In a sense, San Francisco was an easy target. Its large Japanese-American population knew about soy sauce and the Kikkoman brand. But this time, of course, the company was trying to tell not only Japanese-Americans but the rest of the population as well that soy sauce *wasn't* strictly Japanese and that Kikkoman was the premium product. (The latter claim was buttressed by a decision to price Kikkoman a few cents higher than competing brands.)
>
> While it was all a new idea for Americans, it was equally new for Kikkoman. The company, after all, was used to consumers who took its product—and its preeminence—for granted. But the Americans caught on, and so did the subsidiary. By 1959, it was ready to tackle Los Angeles. Over the next 10 years, Kikkoman expanded very gradually on a region-by-region basis. In all cases, the company used food brokers, on the ground that maintaining its own sales force would cost too much; and it still uses them.[16]

Strategy guidelines obtained from market analyses include market target alternatives, product requirements, pricing practices, distribution options, communications needs, and various other inputs to selecting target markets and developing positioning strategies of the marketing program.

FORECASTING

Forecasts represent the last category of information needed to complete the product-market analysis (see Exhibit 5–6). Two kinds of size estimates are used in product-market analysis. One is a measure of the market potential that exists. This estimate provides a measure of the opportunity in the product-market. Since, in most instances, this opportunity is never fully realized by the firms serving the product-market, a second measure is needed. This is a forecast of what is likely to occur for the time period under consideration. Thus potential represents an upper limit while the forecast is normally something less than the total potential. In addition to size estimates, expected growth rates over the planning period are very useful in strategic planning. Recall, for example, their use in measuring product-market attractiveness for portfolio and grid analysis as discussed in Chapter 3.

The following forecasts are often used in product-market analysis:

Market potential represents the total sales that *could* be realized in a geographical area and time period if the industry were capable of fully developing all demand for a specific product or service.

The *market forecast* is an estimate of the extent to which all firms in the industry can achieve the market potential that exists. The forecast is typically less than the potential because of the inability of the firms serving the product-market to take advantage of the potential. This gap may be the result of out-of-stocks, ineffective marketing practices, strikes, and other factors.

The *market share* forecast is an estimate of the percent of the market forecast that the firm's brand will capture.

The *sales forecast* is the amount of the market forecast that a firm's brand is expected to achieve.[17]

Estimates of expected growth rates are often included with the above forecasts. One of the most important factors in preparing forecasts is to specify exactly what is being forecasted (defined product-markets), the time period involved, and the geographical area. Otherwise, comparisons of sales and market share with that of competing firms will not be meaningful. Several operational problems may occur in forecasting as a result of differences in measures of sales (e.g., dollars versus units), problems in defining the relevant market, leads and lags in distribution channels, promotional pricing practices, and the handling of intracompany transfers.[18]

The Forecasting Management Task[19]

To develop a sales forecasting approach we must (1) define the forecasting problem, (2) identify appropriate forecasting techniques, (3) evaluate and select a technique, and (4) implement the forecasting system as

EXHIBIT 5-9 The Forecasting Management Task

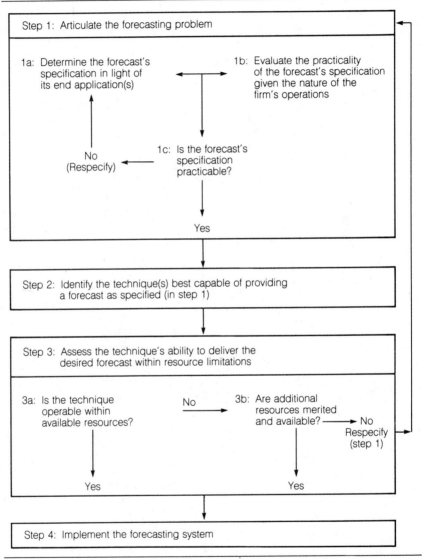

SOURCE: Lawrence R. Small, *Sales Forecasting in Canada* (Ottawa: The Conference Board of Canada, 1980), 4.

shown in Exhibit 5-9. A brief review of each step indicates important issues and considerations.

Defining the Forecasting Problem. Several questions must be answered in establishing the nature and scope of the forecasting task. This involves deciding what characteristics the forecasting method should display and what output is required. Important factors to be determined in defining the forecasting application include the time horizon, level of accuracy desired, the uses to be made of the forecast results, and the degree of disaggregation, including product/market detail, units of measurement, and time increments to be covered.

Identify, Evaluate, and Select Forecasting Technique(s). Since several forecasting methods are available, each with certain features and limitations, we need to match company needs, resources, and data with the appropriate techniques. Often companies use combination approaches that incorporate two or more techniques into the forecasting process. Typically, one technique is used as the primary basis of forecasting whereas the other techniques are used to check the validity of the primary forecasting method. Also, techniques offer different outputs. Some are effective in obtaining aggregate forecasts, and others are used to estimate sales for disaggregated units of analysis (e.g., products). An overview of the major forecasting techniques is provided in the next section.

Implementation. In most companies a forecasting approach evolves over several years. Many firms begin with very informal approaches that primarily use projections of past experience coupled with a subjective assessment of the future market environment. As companies grow and their forecasting needs increase in nature and scope, more formalized forecasting methods are developed. Factors that often affect the choice of a forecasting system include the type of corporate planning process used, the volatility and complexity of markets, the number of products and markets, and the organizational units that have forecasting needs.

Forecasting Techniques

A complete examination of forecasting techniques is beyond the scope of this book. Instead, the major approaches used in forecasting are briefly described. Forecasting techniques generally follow two basic avenues. The first involves making *direct* estimates of brand sales; the second forecasts brand sales as a product of several *components* (e.g., industry sales and market share).[20] Often two or more forecasts are prepared independently and then compared. The various methods used for forecasting sales are described below:

Judgmental Forecasting A common approach relies on a jury of executive opinion to obtain sounder forecasts than might be made by a single estimator. To put the results in better perspective, the jury members are usually given background information on past sales; and their estimates are sometimes weighted in proportion to their convictions about the likelihood of specific sales levels being realized.

Sales Force Estimates   The sales personnel of some firms—field representatives, managers, or distributors—are considered better positioned than anyone else to estimate the short-term outlook for sales in their assigned areas.

Users' Expectations   Although the dispersion of product users in many markets—or the cost of reaching them—would make such an approach impractical, some manufacturers serving industrial markets find it possible to poll product users about their future plans, and then use this information in developing their own forecasts.

Traditional Time-Series Analysis   In a familiar approach the historical sales series may be broken down into its components—trends and cyclical and seasonal variations, including irregular variations—which are then projected.

Time-series analysis has the advantage of being easy to understand and apply. But there is a danger in relying on strictly mechanized projections of previously identified patterns.

Advanced Time-Series Analysis   For short-term forecasting purposes, several advanced time-series methods have been generating new interest and acceptance. Most rely on a moving average of the data series as their starting point; and requisite computer software facilitates their use. The methods include variants of exponential smoothing, adaptive filtering, Box Jenkins models, and the state-space technique. All assume that future movements of a sales series can be determined solely from the study of its past movements. However, certain of these methods have the alternative advantage of being able to take into account external variables as well.

A great deal of experimentation often precedes the adoption of these advanced methods, which clearly are best suited for experienced forecasters who are able to judge their strengths and limitations in a particular forecasting situation.

Econometric Methods   The econometric approach provides a mathematical simplification or "model" of measurable relationships between changes in the series being forecast and changes in other related factors. Such models are employed most often in the prediction of overall market demand, thus requiring a separate estimate of a company's own share. Increased interest in this approach reflects a growing concern over macroeconomic events, as well as a preference for spelling out assumptions that underlie forecasts.

Input-Output Analysis   When developing forecasts for intermediate or commodity products, some firms are finding it advantageous to employ input-output measures within comprehensive forecasting systems that begin with macroeconomic considerations and end with estimates of industry sales. Still other methodologies must be employed in such systems; and specialists are required for the correct application and interpretation of input-output analysis.

New Product Forecasting New products pose special problems that are hard for the forecaster to circumvent. A sales forecast for a new product may rest upon any of several bases, including results of marketing research investigations; assumptions about analogous situations in the past; or assumptions about the rate at which users of such products or services will substitute the new item for ones they are presently buying.[21]

On the basis of a survey of Canadian companies, only 13 percent of the firms doing regular sales forecasting use only one technique.[22] The two most popular methods are the sales force composite and the jury of executive opinion. Statistical models such as regression analysis are not used by many of the companies surveyed. Over half the companies indicated that they are highly satisfied with the performance of their forecasting systems.

METHODS FOR ANALYZING COMPLEX PRODUCT-MARKET STRUCTURES

Special research methods may be required when several alternative product types can satisfy a particular need and when other variations complicate defining product-market boundaries. Product-market definition is based primarily upon customers' needs and requirements. The underlying premise of these approaches is as follows:

> People want the benefits that products provide rather than the products per se. Specific products or brands represent the available combinations of benefits and costs.
>
> Consumers consider the available alternatives from the vantage point of the usage contexts with which they have experience or the specific applications they are considering.[23]

Various research methods are included in the consumer-oriented approaches to building product-market boundaries and analyzing complex product-market structures.

Overview of Research Methods

Consumer-based research approaches have gained considerable attention in recent years as a result, in part, of the inadequacy of judgment, experience, and available information in revealing complex product-market structures. As shown in Exhibit 5-10, the various research

---

EXHIBIT 5-10   Research Methods for Customer-Oriented
Product-Market Definitions

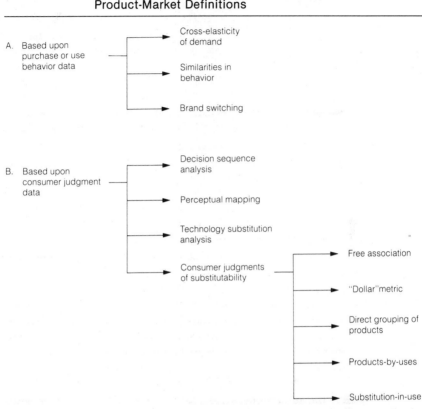

A. Based upon
purchase or use
behavior data

- Cross-elasticity of demand
- Similarities in behavior
- Brand switching

B. Based upon
consumer judgment
data

- Decision sequence analysis
- Perceptual mapping
- Technology substitution analysis
- Consumer judgments of substitutability
  - Free association
  - "Dollar" metric
  - Direct grouping of products
  - Products-by-uses
  - Substitution-in-use

SOURCE: Adapted from George S. Day, Allan D. Shocker, and Rajendra K. Srivastava, "Customer-Oriented Approaches to Identifying Product-Markets," *Journal of Marketing* 43 (Fall 1979), 11, published by the American Marketing Association.

methods fall into two broad categories: those that use *behavioral* data (purchase or use behavior), and those based upon *consumer judgment* data. Since an excellent assessment of the various methods has been made by Day, Shocker, and Srivastava, we shall concentrate here upon the general characteristics of the methods. Afterward, we examine an application of substitution-in-use analysis, one of the more promising methods.[24]

Purchase or Use Data.   These methods of product-market definition create boundaries based upon the present situation or upon the historical record. They do not take into account the possible use of substitute products. The use of behavioral data may fail to include relevant products or brands. Studies of the cross-elasticity of demand have typically considered two specific product categories (rather than brands). Their objective has been to determine the extent to which one product can be substituted for another. In practical situations various factors may affect demand and should be accounted for in measuring cross-elasticity of demand, although they have normally not been considered. This method is of limited usefulness for product-market definition because of its restrictive nature (e.g., the limited number of products) and its unrealistic assumptions. In fact, it seems to presume a definition on *a priori* basis.

The study of similarities in customer usage behavior seeks to identify various specific product categories that meet the same customer need. Through customer research we can determine by monitoring usage practices the extent to which products have been used as substitutes. A customer panel, which is used to track usage over time, involves collecting information at repeated time intervals from a sample of consumers. The approach appears potentially useful in studying usage behavior.

Brand switching studies can be used when the set of competing products is known. These studies attempt to measure probabilities of purchase of brands. Brand switching analysis requires the use of a customer panel and starts with a set of specific brands. Thus it appears more useful in examining interbrand relationships than in defining product-markets. Also, brand switching analysis is primarily applicable to frequently purchased items. This technique has been used largely for forecasts of sales and market share rather than for product-market definition.

Consumer Judgment Methods. These methods can reveal new uses for existing products and identify which products and brands are regarded as potential or actual substitutes, and why. More flexible than the behavioral methods, the consumer judgment methods tend to establish wider product-market boundaries in instances where a variety of products may satisfy various use situations. *Decision sequence analysis* attempts to track the processes of consumer buying decisions for products and brands, and it can be used to measure the extent of competition among brands. People are asked to describe what they think about in making purchase decisions during a shopping trip. This is part of an attempt to determine how criteria are used in making buying decisions. This research technique for product-market definition can help us gain insights into product relationships and competitive patterns from the consumers' point of view. This is because "it is important to know whether buyers first decide on the type of vegetable (corn, beans, peas, etc.) or the form (fresh, frozen, or canned)."[25] Using this method is complicated for the following reasons: (1) it requires interviewing skills; (2) the respondents have problems in describing their thought processes; (3) we cannot always be sure that the responses are truly representative; and (4) the costs of data collection and analysis are fairly high. Therefore, the use of the technique is likely to be very selective.

Perceptual mapping includes several techniques that generate a graphic representation of customers' perceptions of the characteristics of products or brands comprising a previously defined product-market. The map provides a picture of how a sample of people perceives competing products relative to each other or compared to an ideal product. These methods have become very popular over the past decade because of their potential use in analyses of market segmentation, brand positioning, and new product planning. Use of mapping techniques requires the analyst to have technical skills and an awareness of the technique's limitations. The maps are deceptively simple in that several evaluative factors are synthesized into two or more composite dimensions. The user must be able to evaluate and interpret the results. We discuss perceptual mapping further in Chapter 8.

Technology substitution analysis has as its objective the forecasting of what will happen when one material, process, or product is substituted for another. Curve-fitting methods and historical data are used to develop forecasts of substitutability. The method is potentially useful in certain situations where past data are available and actual relationships can be described by using curve-fitting techniques. It seems most useful as a partial aid to product-market definition, particularly in quantitatively estimating the interrelationships between products or processes.

Consumer judgments of substitutability seek to obtain information on product and brand substitution from samples of customers. As shown in Exhibit 5-10, there are at least five ways of obtaining this information. Each is briefly described:

Free Association   People are asked to free-associate the names of similar or substitute brands. The results indicate frequency of mention and rank-order of brand substitutes.

Dollar Metric Approach   Respondents work with exhaustive combinations of pairs of brands, indicating for each which would be purchased in a forced choice purchase (regular prices are shown for each brand). Then they indicate at what price increase they would switch to the other brand, thus measuring preference by price increment.

Direct Grouping into Product Categories   The method starts with related sets of brands. Respondents are asked to divide the brands into groups, to indicate the bases of grouping, and to judge intragroup similarity. Statistical analysis is then used to determine groupings.

Products-by-Uses Analysis   Large lists of products/brands and potential uses are generated by respondents. Then another sample of people determines the appropriateness of the lists. The underlying logic of the method is clear; the data analysis requirements are massive.

Substitution-in-Use Analysis   Similar to the products-by-uses method, this approach extends the former by incorporating some additional steps regarding the usage situation and the degree of substitutability.[26]

Most of the research-based methods shown in Exhibit 5–10 have not been used extensively for product-market definition. They represent potential candidates rather than providing operational, well-developed tools for the task; an exception to this is perceptual mapping. Since the substitution-in-use way of obtaining consumer judgments of substitutability is one of the more promising research methods for defining product-market structure, it will serve as an illustration of how these methods are applied.

Substitution-in-Use Application

As shown in Exhibit 5–11, this method begins by asking a sample of consumers to indicate possible uses for a target product or service.[27] In the Srivastava and Shocker study, respondents were asked to suggest as many uses as possible for bank credit cards (the target service), and then to indicate additional services appropriate to the same users. Restrictions as to the extent of applicability of one service versus another were also identified. The long lists of services and uses that were generated were classified:

> Similar services offered by different financial institutions were combined into a more generic type of service, using management's insights and information gained from interviews. This resulted in 46 service alternatives.
>
> Usages were classified to reduce the number of situational descriptions from 300 to 56. This was done by applying a systematic, yet subjective procedure which identified the usage characteristics that appeared to influence the choice between pairs of services.
>
> A team of bank managers rated the appropriateness of the 46 services for the 56 situations, and this effort resulted in the identification of three major, overlapping submarkets. The one containing the target service was selected for further research (services and situations were reduced to 27 each).

Next, a convenience sample of people rated the appropriateness of each service for use in each situation. Statistical analysis was then used to construct a first stage (tentative) situational taxonomy. The following

---

EXHIBIT 5–11   Steps in Substitution-in-Use Research

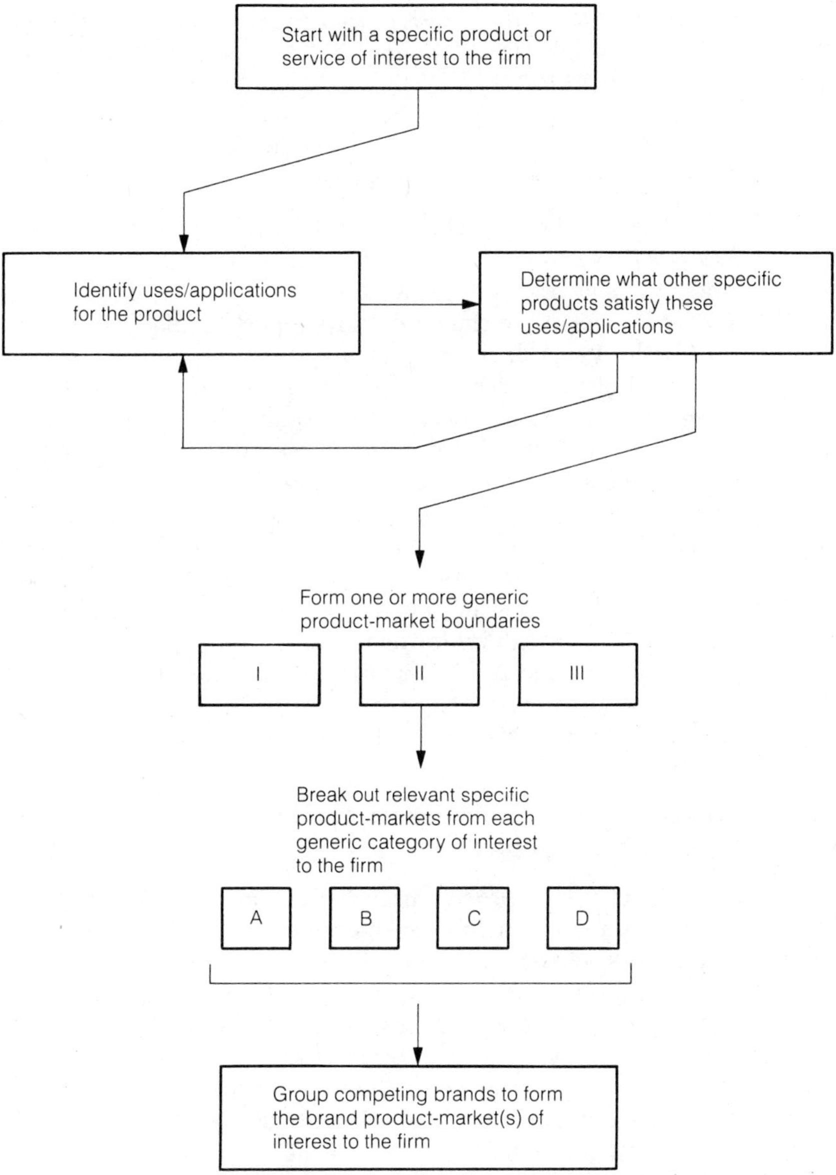

```
              ┌──────────────────────────────┐
              │ Start with a specific product │
              │ or service of interest to the │
              │ firm                          │
              └──────────────────────────────┘
```

```
┌──────────────────────────┐       ┌──────────────────────────┐
│ Identify uses/applications│  →    │ Determine what other      │
│ for the product           │       │ specific products satisfy │
│                           │       │ these uses/applications   │
└──────────────────────────┘       └──────────────────────────┘
```

Form one or more generic
product-market boundaries

```
┌────────┐   ┌────────┐   ┌────────┐
│   I    │   │   II   │   │  III   │
└────────┘   └────────┘   └────────┘
```

Break out relevant specific
product-markets from each
generic category of interest
to the firm

```
┌────┐  ┌────┐  ┌────┐  ┌────┐
│ A  │  │ B  │  │ C  │  │ D  │
└────┘  └────┘  └────┘  └────┘
```

```
┌──────────────────────────────┐
│ Group competing brands to form│
│ the brand product-market(s) of│
│ interest to the firm          │
└──────────────────────────────┘
```

situational characteristics accounted for most of the variance in the appropriateness of services:

1. *The dollar amount required* for payment (subsequent analyses revealed three ranges as relevant: $50–$399, $400–$999, $1,000–$2,000).
2. *Location* (local versus out of town).
3. *Retail credit availability* (Was the purchase being made in an establishment offering purchase credit?).[28]

The second step in the study attempted to verify the tentative situational taxonomy. This step included a second data collection effort and extensive tests designed to verify the results of the first stage. The reader is referred to the study for supporting discussion and technical details. In general, the results were promising, suggesting the future potential of this method for use in product-market definition. Consistent with prior research, the study found a high degree of homogeneity in the respondents' perceptions of product-usage associations and an ability to account for a substantial variance in these perceptions by a small number of interpretable dimensions.

This method offers some exciting possibilities for determining product-market structure, particularly when multiple-use products and multiple-need situations together create complex situations. The discussion also highlights the research requirements that underlie the use of the method. While Srivastava and Shocker obtained promising results by using relatively small sample sizes, the data requirements and technical expertise needed in using this method are significant.

Analyzing Product-Markets by Using Research-Based Approaches

The structured approach discussed earlier in the chapter (see Exhibit 5–6) attempts to define product-market levels within a hierarchical framework whereas the research methods, like the substitution in use method, are trying to form arenas of competing products and brands from a pool of many products and uses. The two approaches seem best viewed as complementary rather than as substitutes. They both start from a large generic product-market category, although the research methods may generate products and uses that conceivably could form more than one generic product-market. Each approach defines the set of brands that is competing for a particular set of customer needs. The structured approach draws upon management judgment and experience and available information on products and markets. Of course, customer participation research (and other research approaches) can be used with the structured approach. In fact, research should be used when attempting to define complex product-market situations that use the structured guidelines.

One of the real strengths of the structured approach is that it links families of product-markets into a hierarchy that can be systematically examined at increasingly more specific levels. The premise underlying the method is that the generic product-market will be defined so that it contains all competing specific product-market categories. If only management judgment and experience are used to define the generic level, the structured approach may fail to identify a relevant product category, particularly in a complex or changing product-market situation. Thus, if not used with care, the approach may be too rigid in some instances.

Using the structured method of product-market definition, the analyst can draw from common types of information regardless of the product-market under study. Moreover, this information will be needed for guiding strategic marketing decisions. In a new product-market the end user may be unable to answer the questions that are necessary in research analysis. Finally, there are many product-market definitional situations that do not require extensive consumer research. Field research is costly. Its costs should be compared to potential benefits.

CONCLUDING NOTE

It is essential to understand product-markets in order to make sound corporate and market strategy decisions. Defining and analyzing product-markets are probably more central to making sound strategic planning decisions than are any other activities in the enterprise. The uses of product-market analyses are many and varied. One of the more important aspects of market definition and analysis is moving beyond a product focus by incorporating market needs into the analysts' viewpoint.

In this chapter we examined the important concept of a product-market. Various considerations in forming product-markets were described. By using different levels of aggregation (generic, product type, product variant, and brand), we can position products and brands within more aggregate categories, thus aiding in the analysis of customers, product interrelationships, industry structure, distribution approaches, and key competitors. The approach to product-market analysis presented in the chapter offers a consistent guide to needed information, regardless of the type of product-market being analyzed. The approach encourages the use of various kinds of information, including management judgment and experience, published data, and special research studies. Perhaps most significant is the fact that the approach does not require consumer research studies in order to define and analyze product-markets, although research can be incorporated into the analysis, when needed.

The potential user should be alert to some limitations of the approach. Because it is highly dependent upon how the generic product-market is defined, it may generate so much information that analysis and interpretation will be difficult if the definition is too broad. Excess information can be as dangerous as not enough. At the other extreme, very narrow product-market boundaries can result in excluding relevant competing product categories. The analysis approach, by its very nature, may create a myopic (nearsighted) tendency on the part of management. For example, even if competing product categories are included when we establish generic product-market boundaries, the approach tends to focus attention within a specific product category. Finally, this approach may encourage a product or supply orientation, and therefore it may fail to give adequate attention to customers' needs.

An important part of product-market analysis is forecasting sales. The forecasts often used in product-market analysis include estimates of market potential, the market forecast, market share forecast, and the sales forecast. This information is needed for various purposes and is prepared for different units of analysis, such as type of product, brands, and geographical areas. The forecasting approach and techniques should be matched to the organization's needs.

Some promising research methods for analyzing complex product-markets are available. They seem best viewed as complementary approaches to the hierarchical approach to market analysis rather than as alternatives. The substitution-in-use method is particularly promising. The framework provided by the multilevel approach is useful, regardless of whether or not one of the consumer-oriented research methods is used.

NOTES

1. Snap-on Tools Corporation 1984, *Annual Report,* 1–6.
2. The following discussion is based upon suggestions provided by Professor Robert B. Woodruff of the University of Tennessee, Knoxville.
3. George S. Day, Allan D. Shocker, and Rajendra K. Srivastava, "Customer-Oriented Approaches to Identifying Product-Markets," *Journal of Marketing* 43 (Fall 1979): 10, published by the American Marketing Association.
4. The following discussion is based upon suggestions provided by Professor Allan D. Shocker, University of Washington.
5. "Staving off Oblivion," *Forbes,* September 4, 1978, 94.
6. George S. Day, *Strategic Marketing Planning,* St. Paul, Minn.: West Publishing, 1984, 75.

7. For an expanded discussion of product-market levels, see Chapter 5 of David W. Cravens, Gerald E. Hills, and Robert B. Woodruff, *Marketing Decision Making: Concepts and Strategy*, rev. ed. (Homewood, Ill.: Richard D. Irwin, 1980).

8. Rajendra K. Srivastava and Allan D. Shocker, "The Validity and Reliability of a Method for Developing Product-Specific Usage—Situational Taxonomies: Implications for Marketing Research" (Working Paper No. 372, Graduate School of Business, University of Pittsburgh, 1980).

9. The three factors are suggested by George S. Day, "Strategic Market Analysis: A Contingency Perspective" (Working Paper, University of Toronto, July 1979).

10. Cravens, Hills, and Woodruff, *Marketing Decision Making*, 111–13.

11. David W. Cravens, Terry Dielman, and Kent Harrington, "Using Buyers' Perceptions of Service Quality to Guide Strategy Development," *1985 AMA Educators' Proceedings*, Series No. 51, 291–301.

12. Nancy Gieges, "Executives Say Global Strategies Are Limited," *Advertising Age*, June 3, 1985, 56. See also Edward H. Mayer, "Consumers around the World: Do They Have the Same Wants and Needs?" *Management Review*, January 1985, 26–29.

13. Robert B. Woodruff, "A Systematic Approach to Market Opportunity Analyses," *Business Horizons*, August 1976, 59.

14. John Valentine, "Catfish Demand Explodes since Fillets Reached Church's

Fried Chicken Menu," *The Wall Street Journal*, July 8, 1985, 20.

15. John E. Cooney, "Selling American: Top Soy Sauce Brewer in Japan Shows how to Crack U.S. Market," *The Wall Street Journal*, December 16, 1977, 29.

16. Cooney, "Selling American," 29.

17. Woodruff, "A Systematic Approach," 61–62.

18. Bernard Catry and Michel Chevalier, "Market Share Strategy and the Product Life Cycle," *Journal of Marketing*, October 1974, 29, published by the American Marketing Association.

19. The following discussion is based on Lawrence R. Small, *Sales Forecasting in Canada* (Ottawa: The Conference Board of Canada, 1980), 3–7.

20. Vithala R. Rao and James E. Cox, Jr., *Sales Forecasting Methods: A Survey of Recent Developments* (Cambridge, Mass.: Marketing Science Institute, 1978), 17.

21. David L. Hurwood, Elliott S. Grossman, and Earl L. Bailey, *Sales Forecasting* (New York: The Conference Board, 1978), i–ii.

22. Small, *Sales Forecasting in Canada*, x–xi.

23. Day, Shocker, and Srivastava, "Customer-Oriented Approaches," 10.

24. The following discussion of the methods shown in Exhibit 5–10 is drawn from Day, Shocker, and Srivastava, "Customer-Oriented Approaches," 8–19.

25. Ibid., 14.

26. Ibid., 15–17.

27. The following discussion is based on Srivastava and Shocker, "Validity and Reliability of a Method."

28. Ibid., 17.

QUESTIONS FOR REVIEW AND DISCUSSION

1. Discuss some of the issues that should be considered in defining the product-market for a totally new product.

2. Under what product and market conditions is the consumer more likely to make an important contribution to product-market definition?

3. What recommendations can you make to the management of a company like Keuffel & Esser Co. to help them identify new competitive threats early enough so that counter-strategies can be developed?

4. There are some dangers in concentrating product-market analysis only upon a firm's specific brand and those brands that compete directly with a firm's brand. Discuss.

5. Using the approach to product-market definition and analysis discussed in the chapter, select a brand and describe the generic, product type, and brand product-markets of which the brand is a part.

6. For the brand selected in Question 5, indicate the kinds of information needed in order to conduct a complete product-market analysis. Suggest sources for obtaining each type of information.

7. Discuss the conditions that might favor the use of one of the research methods for product-market definition.

8. In what ways are the consumer judgments of substitutability methods more useful than other research methods for defining product-markets?

9. Many of the more popular forecasting techniques draw substantially upon past experience and historical data. Discuss some of the more important problems that may occur in using these methods.

STRATEGIC APPLICATION 5-1

ROLLS-ROYCE MOTORS INC.

Tokyo—Rolls-Royce Motors Ltd. is looking for Japanese with 35 million yen to spare.

The British luxury-car company thinks there are scores of drivers here who will be willing to part with that amount of money for the 2.5-ton, 6,700cc Bentley Turbo R "sports car" it has just brought to Japan.

Shunsuke Ihara may be one such buyer. His 1964 Rolls-Royce Silver Cloud is getting on in years. And he isn't sure whether the 25-million-yen ($116,200) Ferrari he bought earlier this year is altogether right for him.

"This is the perfect car for me," croons the 35-year-old trading company co-owner, eyeing a deep-green Bentley parked in the garden of a Tokyo hotel. "It doesn't have the vulgar nouveau-riche air of a Rolls. Instead, it has a sort of subdued elegance."

Disdain for Ostentation

Rolls-Royce sees a future in young but well-heeled Japanese car lovers such as Mr. Ihara who disdain the ostentatious image the company's flagship cars have here. And as newly affluent Japanese increasingly trade in their Toyotas for BMWs and Mercedes-Benzes, the prestigious British maker wants to cater to even wealthier drivers who wish to go one better with a Bentley.

The Bentley is for "the guy whose mother-in-law will no longer fit in the back of his Ferrari," says Peter Ward, managing director of marketing at Rolls-Royce. "We're looking forward to a few cramped grannies in Japan."

The trick is in the grille. Buyers in the U.S. and Hong Kong won't settle for a car made by Rolls-Royce unless it comes complete with the classic grille, company executives say. But they say the grille is a handicap when it comes to trying to sell the Rolls to the Ferrari-driving crowd in Japan.

Stuffy Chauffers

The conventional Rolls is viewed here as a chauffer-driven car for the elderly rich. The average Rolls owner in Japan is over 55 years old. Still worse, the car is seen as a gaudy, even garish, display of wealth. So Rolls-Royce is offering the Bentley, which has a softer grille and a sporty interior, plus a souped-up engine and suspension. (Although the Bentley name has been used in Britain for many years, this is the first time Bentleys have been officially sold in Japan.)

Potential customers who showed up for the Bentley's unveiling here are impressed. Classic Rolls "are too loud, too conspicuous," says a 48-year-old Tokyo doctor, who didn't want to be named. "But this is a different matter," he says of the Bentley he thinks would make a nice replacement for his Mercedes. His wife agrees: "It's so refined and genteel."

Rolls-Royce expects at least 20 Japanese next year will dish out 25 million to 45 million yen—the price of a modest house in a Tokyo suburb—for a Bentley. Ryo Miyama, publishing director of Motor Magazine, a Japanese auto publication, thinks Rolls-Royce won't have any trouble. "It's got the right character for the upper crust who really know their cars," he says.

Gangster Wheels

Japan is already Rolls-Royce's top Asian market. The classic Rolls is popular among film stars, tycoons and even gangsters. There are 806 registered owners of Rolls-Royce cars in Japan and the company expects to sell 76 Rolls this year and up to a hundred in 1986.

The rest of Asia hasn't been as good to Rolls-Royce. Hong Kong is famous for its 600-plus Rolls owners. But the colony's taste for the opulent auto has soured in recent years. In 1981 Hong Kong bought 50 Rolls-Royces, but only seven last year.

The only other Asian market that holds any hopes for Rolls-Royce is Taiwan, says John Craig, chairman of the Canada-based Rolls-Royce subsidiary that covers sales to Asia. Rolls-Royce set up shop this year in Taipei and sold six cars. The company hopes to sell at least 10 there next year.

Countries like Malaysia and Thailand tax the cars so heavily that only a few sultans can afford them, says Mr. Craig. The Philippines bans the car, he says. North Korea was a prospect last year when President Kim Il-Sung ordered the most expensive Rolls-Royce model, a Phantom Six limousine. But Mr. Kim canceled his order, Rolls executives say, when he found the car would take two years to make.

Japan's stable appetite for the custom-built, leather-upholstered walnut-paneled automobiles has made the country Rolls-Royce's most promising market. "The order of priority must be Japan first," says Mr. Craig.

The company is bringing in three versions of its Bentley. For those who think the price tag on the Turbo R is too steep, Rolls-Royce is offering an "affordable" version—the $116,300 Eight. The convertible Bentley Continental goes for about $210,000.

"You'll never find people beating a path to our door for cars at our price," says Mr. Ward. So Rolls-Royce is knocking on doors instead. Cornes & Co., Rolls-Royce's distributor in Japan, keeps in touch with old Rolls owners and calls on wealthy Japanese who appear on a much-publicized list of top tax payers.

One Rolls fan high on Cornes's list is Yoshiho Matsuda, a Japanese real estate magnate who owns a collection of Porsche and Bentley autos. He bought the first Bentley Turbo, the deep green one, before it left England. The second Bentley is also spoken for. Anybody wanting one here will have to wait until early next year.

Rolls-Royce thinks the time is ripe for its Bentleys. More and more Japanese are turning to high-priced European cars: Japanese have bought 7,439 Mercedes and 8,817 BMWs so far this year, up 36% and 40% from the same period last year. And with the average well-to-do person buying those cars, the especially wealthy will be more eager to buy Bentleys, says R. V. Pearce, Cornes's general manager. "BMWs are doing well, Mercedes are doing well, and that's good for us."

Noriaki Hirata, a 33-year-old hospital owner and potential Bentley buyer, agrees: "A lot of people are getting tired of their Mercedes."

SOURCE: Stephen Kreider Yoder, "Rolls-Royce Thinks Bentleys May Be a Better Bet for Japan", *The Asian Wall Street Journal Weekly,* October 28, 1985, p. 3

DISCUSSION QUESTIONS

1. Define and describe the generic, product-type, and brand product-market for the Bentley Turbo R automobile in Japan.
2. Do you agree with management's assessment of the market opportunity for the Bentley automobile in Japan? Discuss.
3. Develop a descriptive profile of potential Bentley buyers.
4. Suggest important marketing strategy guidelines for marketing the Bentley automobile in Japan.

STRATEGIC APPLICATION 5-2

MIRAFLORES DESIGNS INC.

The Gideons have known it for years, but at last the hotels themselves are catching on: If you want to get your message out, let the guests steal it.

While towels are still taboo, bathroom products such as minisoaps, shampoos and shower caps are being customized for the big hotel chains. The idea is to make these amenities so attractive they not only spruce up the hotel room, they also find their way back to the visitors' homes.

Entrepreneur Diane Sullivan is at the vanguard of this new industry. As president and founder of Miraflores Designs Inc., she designs "bathroom goodies" and their packages for the Hyatt, Sheraton, Wyndham and Intercontinental hotels, among others. With annual sales of $7 million in an industry that didn't exist five years ago, Ms. Sullivan sees bathrooms as the next frontier.

Before establishing her amenities company in 1980, Ms. Sullivan ran a fashion accessories company in Los Angeles for seven years. And before *that,* laughed the svelte velvet-shirted businesswoman, "I was a contract negotiator in the aerospace industry."

Always attracted to "designing *little* things"—jewelry and so forth—Ms. Sullivan turned to bath products as a new venture when she moved to New York in 1978. Here she hooked up with John Chapman, a soap importer, who soon became her business partner. Mr. Chapman introduced her to Cody Plott, rooms executive of the newly rebuilt Grand Hyatt Hotel on 42nd Street, formerly New York's Commodore Hotel.

The location and opulence of this Hyatt, Mr. Plott told Ms. Sullivan, cried out for art deco flourishes: What could she add? With his encouragement, Ms. Sullivan designed her first soap and shampoo packages: A set of silver and black bottles and boxes to adorn the Hyatt's bathrooms.

She was feeling pretty pleased with the results until word came from Hyatt higher-ups: No deviation from the corporate color scheme allowed. And Hyatt's colors were brown and beige.

Instead of chucking the project, a disappointed Ms. Sullivan worked up a new amenities set, this time in the "right" colors. When the Grand Hyatt bought the line, she felt satisfied, but when the Hyatt Corp. informed her they would distribute the set nationally, she felt even better.

Hyatt was among the first hotels to customize its bathroom freebies, according to Sullivan. "Before that, stuff was brand-named or mismatched. Things were not designed, they just . . . happened."

Pint-size soaps were embossed with "Ivory" or "Palmolive" instead of "Hyatt" or "Sheraton." Instead of boxed, they came wrapped in wax paper. Their colors said nothing but "Wash up and get out."

In hotel rooms today, "Soap and shampoo have become not a luxury but a necessity," says Kidder, Peabody household products analyst Jay Friedman, and he believes customizing is here to stay.

"For an incremental few pennies you can add another product in your own bottle. It's an inexpensive way to enhance the image of your room." Mr. Friedman expects the $40 million-to-$50 million customized hotel amenities market to climb to $300 million in the next few years.

Customized bathroom curios serve a double purpose. They not only brighten up a room (and, as Ms. Sullivan points out, give the guest something to play with) but they also serve as advertisements.

Within the room, bubble-bath bottles and their buddies add warmth and class. Their colors reflect the hotel's color scheme, and even the shapes and smells of the products are customized. Shera-

ton, for instance, provides a coral-colored oatmeal almond soap.

The more expensive the room, the more chock full of amenities it is—and the packaging gets more elaborate, too. For example, the basic Hyatt bathroom contains shampoo, hair conditioner, bath gel, two soaps (one for hand, one for bath), a shoe sponge—"impregnated with clear shoe polish," as Ms. Sullivan explains—and a shower cap folded in an attractive cardboard envelope. Incidentally, shower caps allow the amenities designer the most creative freedom because they can be stuffed into any kind of container.

"I never do baggies," swears Ms. Sullivan on the subject.

In addition to the above, Hyatt's vip rooms provide a bottle of 4711 cologne, a salt shaker-like cardboard tube of talcum powder, glycerine soap, hair conditioner, hand lotion, a shoe horn and a sachet of potpourri.

When conventions come to town, hotels often go one step further, says Ms. Sullivan. They'll grace each room with an extra aftershave product, or soap dish. These extras also are being customized now, as are superduper amenities, such as large shampoos or colognes, for visiting dignitaries and the like. In fact, Ms. Sullivan has just completed a catalog for Sheraton that lists all these optional products, including fabric wash and suntan lotion. Individual hotels in the chain can order these by the single case.

But why are hotels offering so many knickknacks—including, often, a choice of two or three different kinds of soaps: Standard, deodorant and glycerine? "People want luxury," declares Ms. Sullivan. "They don't want a routine bar of Safeguard."

Bath products are the perfect upscale plaything: They're fun, unfattening and make the user feel good. They're moral and legal.

It's even moral and legal to pack them and sneak them out. Hotel executives "*want* people to take them home," stresses Ms. Sullivan. The little bath gel bottle that says "Vista" reminds travelers of their holiday and its hotel when they bubble back home.

This marriage of designer goods and hotel distribution works well for both parties, claims Ms. Sullivan. Sheraton gains the panache of Cardin and Cardin gets thousands of well heeled travelers to try his products. Miraflores also has contracted with Finesse shampoo, available to hotels wishing to provide name brand hair products. The deal between supplier and hotel is very simple: Suppliers provide their products at cost, taking the sampling opportunity as profit.

Aside from name brands, Ms. Sullivan tries to bring a unique personality to the packages she designs. For the Intercontinental Hotel in Houston, for instance, she emphasized the chain's Lone Star logo. And for a hotel in Atlanta she recommended soap scented with peach.

Nail polish remover may be the next nicety hotels provide. Ms. Sullivan is developing a manicure set which will include packets of the remover, because "hotels are really interested in what they can do for women." The woman traveler is the fastest-growing segment of the hotel market, Ms. Sullivan says. "They'll be 50% by 1990 if the growth curve continues where it's going."

SOURCE: Lenore Skenazy, "Sullivan Shines for Hotel Guests," *Advertising Age*, July 11, 1985, 2.

DISCUSSION QUESTIONS

1. Define and describe the generic, product-type and brand product-markets for hotel bathroom amenities.
2. Identify and discuss the factors likely to influence the growth of this market over the next decade.
3. Describe the distribution channel for hotel amenities.
4. Prepare a five-year forecast for the hotel amenity product-type market(s).

CHAPTER 6

Analyzing Consumer and Organizational Buyers

Analyzing buyers' needs and preferences is a major part of the American Greetings Corporation's marketing strategy development.[1] The company is the world's largest publicly owned manufacturer of greeting cards and related social-expression merchandise. Women purchase over 90 percent of all greeting cards. American Greetings's consumer research indicates that women enjoy browsing and shopping for greeting cards. Thus the company concentrates on making the card shopping area large and attractive. An analysis of the buyers has also determined that a woman purchases a card only if it is appropriate. It is important that the card's verse and design combine to convey the sentiment she wishes to express. Since one of American Greetings's chief competitors is *forgetfulness,* a major promotion objective is to remind people to send cards. The company is responsive to changing lifestyles. Social trends in divorce, remarriage, working women, single parents, the graying of America, careers and business, travel, and relocation offer opportunities for new products to help people communicate.

The study of buyers is essential to making good decisions on marketing strategy. Buyer behavior analysis provides insights into *why* consumers and organizations buy goods and services, *how* their purchase decisions are made, and the factors that *influence* their decision-making processes. It goes beyond describing buyers to examine their decision-making processes and the implications of these analyses for market targeting, product planning, distribution, pricing, advertising, and personal selling strategies.

This chapter considers buyer decision making for consumer and organizational buyers, including the types of decisions that are made and the processes that are followed. Various individual and environmental influences on consumer and organizational buyers are also discussed and illustrated. The chapter concludes with an overview of how buyer behavior information is used to guide various strategic marketing decisions.

TYPES OF BUYER BEHAVIOR

Since buying decisions vary according to their importance and complexity, it is useful to classify purchase decisions to better understand their characteristics, the products to which they apply, and the marketing strategy implications of each type of buyer behavior. Henry Assael classifies buyer decisions according to the extent the buyer is involved in the decision and according to whether it is a decision-making process or an action based on habit.[2] A *high-involvement* decision may be infrequent, expensive, risky, and important to the consumer's ego and social needs. The decision situation may be simple or complex, depending upon whether multiple brands or a single brand are considered. Four types of buyer behavior are shown in Exhibit 6-1, based on the amount of involvement and the decision-making differences.

These categories are very broad in that both the involvement and decision dimensions represent a range of situations. Nevertheless, the four types of buyer behavior provide a useful basis of comparing and contrasting buying situations. Also, a situation may vary for individuals. For example, a high-involvement purchase for one person may not be such for another person. A closer look at each category highlights its features and the marketing strategy implications.

Complex Decision Making

This situation corresponds to a decision process consisting of several stages, as shown in Exhibit 6-4 in the next section. Various products and services fall into this classification, including major surgery services, financial planning, personal computers, and architectural services. These decisions are often unfamiliar ones for buyers who may seek information and evaluate alternative brands before making a purchase decision. Making a good choice is important, yet complex, because a high level of uncertainty exists and a bad decision could have serious consequences for the buyer. Buyers may find it difficult to identify the proper criteria for evaluating brand alternatives. People in this category want and need information to help them understand the nature and scope of decision making.

The model describing this type of buyer behavior is that the buyer develops certain beliefs regarding the product, evaluates it, and then

EXHIBIT 6-1 Four Types of Buyer Behavior

| | Type of Purchase Decision | |
	High-Involvement	Low-Involvement
Decision Making (information search, consideration of alternatives)	*Complex decision making* (medical services, autos, financial planning services, diamonds)	*Impulse purchasing* (cereals, snacks)
Habit (little or no information search, consideration of only one brand)	*Brand loyalty* (perfume, cigarettes, beverages)	*Inertia* (light bulbs, soaps, paper towels)

SOURCE: Adapted from Henry Assael, *Marketing Management* (Boston: Kent Publishing, 1985), 127.

acts.[3] As theoretical support for this type of buying it is suggested that cognitive learning takes place through the buyer's problem-solving efforts. Communications are important in building brand preference. In developing a marketing strategy, it is important for us to understand the buyer's sources and uses of information. Consider, the example, the favorable brand positioning Humana Inc. gained for its open-heart surgery services through the firm's highly publicized artificial heart transplants in 1985. If Humana's physicians can successfully perform artificial heart transplants, they should also represent a competent source of medical services for open-heart surgery.

Brand Loyalty

When a buyer first purchases a high-involvement product, the decision process is complex. Through the experience of the purchase and use of the product, the decision process is simplified and loyalty to a particular brand often develops. Buyers' loyalty to certain brands of cigarettes and perfumes is illustrative. Logos on clothing in the form of crocodiles, horses, and other symbols have been useful in establishing brand identity for products that are otherwise very similar. The important factor in positioning products in this category is gaining a favorable perception by potential buyers. The successful introduction of Revlon's Charlie perfume as a life-style product for liberated women is illustrative:

> But having a good fragrance is only part of the battle. The way the product is marketed is vitally important, industry executives say. As a result,

when one fragrance makes it big with a successful approach, other companies are quick to try something similar.

When Revlon Inc.'s Charlie was introduced in 1973, for example, the industry at first scoffed at the idea of a woman's fragrance with a masculine name. But Charlie was heavily promoted by Revlon as a scent for liberated, freewheeling women. "Charlie was for an outgoing person," says Paul P. Woolard, President of Revlon's domestic division. He describes the fragrance as "sensuous but not too far from innocent."

Charlie caught on immediately with American women. Sales reached $10 million the first year, putting the product solidly in the black. Other companies soon responded with similar appeals. Fabergé Inc. brought out Babe. Coty, Inc. introduced Smitty, and Max Factor came out with Call Me Maxi.

None managed to catch up to Charlie, which Revlon boasts has become the world's best-selling fragrance. Call Me Maxi, for one, foundered as a fragrance (although cosmetics under the same name did well), and soon Samuel Kalish, who had been lured from Revlon to be president of Max Factor, was out of a job. Max Factor spent $10 million in promoting Call Me Maxi. About $10 million worth was sold, but a lot was eventually returned. Buyers said it simply had an unsatisfactory scent.[4]

Impulse Purchasing

Low involvement alters the buying situation from the previous two categories. Many of the day-to-day purchases made by consumers fall into this category. Needs exist and purchases are intended to satisfy these needs. Impulse-purchasing decisions are not so important to the buyer as those reflecting a high involvement. The decision process (see Exhibit 6–4) is simplified and usually occurs during a short time span. Alternative brands are evaluated but not extensively. Also, brand loyalty may not be the dominate factor in the purchase decision. Instead buyers may be oriented toward variety. Needs exist in low-involvement situations, but they do not represent critical needs. The search for information is very limited or nonexistent. A limited evaluation usually occurs at the purchase location or during use or consumption. Many food products, for example, are impulse items. A favorable use experience with the initial purchase may lead to repurchase.

Inertia

This buying situation involves the recognition of a need and a purchase. But low involvement makes the decision relatively unimportant. Brand choice is habitual in nature and an information search does not occur. Experience may lead to repeat purchases of the same brand.[5] Nevertheless, brand loyalty does not exist. Instead, the buyer stays with a familiar brand in order to simplify the buying process. An interesting distinction between situations of low involvement and those of high involvement is that in the former the buyer makes the purchase decision, and subsequently evaluates it. In the complex decision situation, however, purchase follows evaluation.

Marketing Strategy Consequences

Type of Involvement. The marketing strategy consequences of high- and low-involvement buying situations vary substantially. In high-involvement situations the importance of the decision makes the buyer receptive to information and interested in learning about alternative brands. Marketing efforts can be directed to different stages in the buying process (see Exhibit 6–4). In fact, the marketing program can be designed to help the buyer move through the decision process. Advertising and sales promotion activities can be designed to satisfy the information needs of buyers through the various stages of complex decision making. Marketing efforts can also assist in developing and retaining brand-loyal customers.

High-involvement situations are probably more favorable for companies, particularly those that have strong brand positions. Many products represent low-involvement situations for buyers. A different marketing task occurs for products in the low-involvement category. Rather than moving through the multistage decision process, buyers typically do not spend much time and effort on low-involvement decisions. This situation makes it more difficult to target communications and other marketing activities. The focus of marketing efforts is on building an overall awareness and favorable perception of a brand. By making the purchase decision easy for the buyer, we can create an advantage for a firm. Examples include the use of trial samples, coupons, and promotional displays in retail stores. Advertising is useful in developing brand awareness. Creative advertising can be useful for increasing the probability of impulse and inertia purchases. For example, 11 fast-food restaurant chains spent a total of $664 million in 1984 on television advertising.[6] The winner—on the basis of advertising recall tests—was Wendy's "Where's the beef?" campaign.

Differences across Buyers. It is important to recognize that some buyers of a product type or variant may display high involvement and others low involvement.[7] Under these conditions the positioning strategy of the marketing program should correspond to the extent of involvement of the consumers who are targeted. It may be appropriate to have market segmentation so that our positioning strategy can be adjusted to each group of buyers. Examples of marketing strategy differences include offering brands that appeal to high- and low-involvement segments. Differences may also be appropriate in product features, distribution channels, prices, advertising, and sales promotion. Since the appropriateness of the use of involvement for market segmentation de-

---

EXHIBIT 6-2   Illustrative Marketing Strategy Variations by Extent of Involvement

---

Market Segmentation

Segments may exist in both low and high involvement situations. Rather than serving as a basis of segmentation, involvement may be a useful variable for describing buyers in segments (see Chapter 8).

Positioning Strategy

Low involvement buyers are more likely to be influenced by a simple, focused positioning strategy rather than a comprehensive strategy stressing multiple attributes of the brand that may be appropriate in a high-involvement situation.

Product Strategy

Strategies for high-involvement products depend upon the strength of position of a firm's brand and upon whether complex decision making or habit represents the purchase situation. Product features and improvements are important for complex decision-making situations. Assurance of competence is important for intangible services such as major surgery.

Low-involvement product strategy should focus on a key product feature that differentiates the item from competing brands. Product characteristics that help increase involvement may also be appropriate for low-involvement products.

Distribution Strategy

Complex decision-making products normally are not widely distributed in retail outlets. Otherwise, there are no major differences in the buying situations with respect to the distribution strategy.

Price Strategy

Price is more often an active component of marketing strategy for low-involvement products as compared to high-involvement products. Price may also be used to encourage a trial of brand-loyal products. Estée Lauder has been successful in using promotional pricing (buy this item and get these items free) to encourage a trial of the firm's line of cosmetics.

Promotion

Personal selling is often important for high-involvement products. Other differences in strategy for high- and low-involvement products consist largely of the type of message. Promotion for low-involvement products is often totally brand-oriented rather than focused on several specific attributes.

---

pends on a number of issues, we will consider further in Chapter 8 buyer behavior bases for segmentation. In addition to segmentation by extent of involvement, market segments may exist within an involvement category.

Marketing Strategy Variations.   Exhibit 6–2 shows a comparison of several marketing strategy variations between high- and low-involvement situations. These comparisons are illustrative since a marketing strategy situation depends on various factors in addition to the buyer and are discussed in Chapter 7. The purpose of Exhibit 6–2 is to show why involvement may be one relevant consideration in strategy development rather than the only basis that guides a strategy design.

Increasing Buyer Involvement.   Increasing the amount of involvement of a buyer for a product may offer a strategic advantage to a company, particularly if the involvement is brand-specific. Advertising can

EXHIBIT 6-3 Framework for Analyzing Buyer Behavior

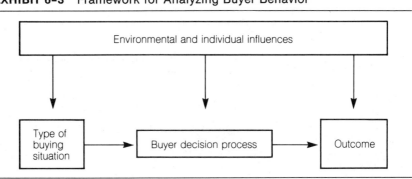

be useful in highlighting certain brand benefits that are linked to involvement. Product features may also increase involvement. Tylenol's initial linkage with physicians and dentists as a recommended pain reliever helped create a high-involvement situation for many buyers regarding this brand.

BUYER DECISION MAKING

Framework for Analysis

The analysis of buyer behavior seeks to gain an understanding of the decision-making processes that buyers move through—from the initial stimulus creating a need to purchase to the eventual response regarding this need. The nature and scope of the buying process depends, in part, on the type of buying situation, which may range from the simple to the complex. Various external and individual influences may provide the stimulus, affect the buyer's decision-making process, and influence the buyer's ultimate response. A framework for analyzing these factors is shown in Exhibit 6-3.

The buying process may vary in length and complexity, depending upon the buying situation. The process is influenced by various factors associated with the buyer and by environmental influences, such as friends, economic conditions, marketing efforts of firms, and other factors. Buying is a complex interrelationship of influencing factors that affect the buyer's decision process between the initial stimulus and the response. A buyer processes different kinds of information in moving from need recognition to decision outcome. The buyer's action may consist of decisions regarding a brand, a retail store, or other choices, including the decision to terminate the decision process without making a purchase decision.

EXHIBIT 6-4 Stages in a Buyer's Decision Process

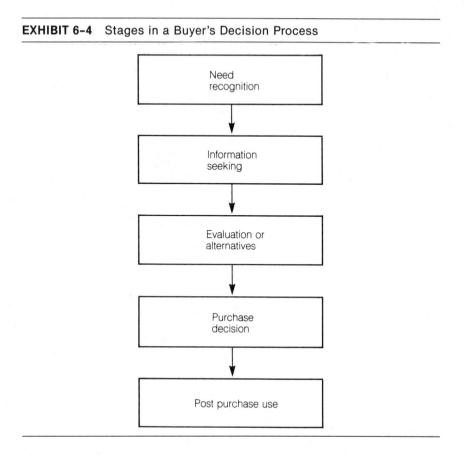

Decision Process Stages

It is useful to describe the buyer's decision process shown in Exhibit 6–3 as a sequence of steps or stages. The major steps beginning with the buyer's recognition of a need are shown in Exhibit 6–4.

Need Recognition. One or more influences may trigger a need. These influences may be the result of the marketing efforts of companies and/ or interpersonal influences, such as discussions with friends. Advertising is often used to encourage need recognition. A college graduate may realize that a new job will involve considerable travel, thus creating a need for a way to finance the travel costs. A credit card for charging food, travel, and lodging expenses would be useful. The card should be one accepted by travel agencies, airlines, hotels, restaurants, and other retailers. Other desirable features of the product may be identified at this stage.

Information Seeking. Unless the buyer is making a familiar purchase, he or she will have to obtain information about the type of product in order to learn about its features, limitations, and uses. People often turn to their friends, business associates, and publications to gain information on a type of product. For example, the new graduate might discuss various types of credit cards with parents and friends. He or she might request literature from banks and other financial institutions. American Express displays brochures at many retail locations so that people interested in obtaining a credit card can easily obtain information and an application form. After need recognition, the buyer is alert to marketing stimuli, such as advertising, during the search for information.

Evaluation of Alternatives. Unless a routine purchase is being made and/or the buyer is loyal to a particular brand because of use experience, purchase alternatives may be evaluated. The buyer must identify the brands of interest and the criteria used to compare alternatives. Some brands may be rejected at this stage. Relevant choice criteria should be apparent to the buyer, identified either at the need recognition stage or during the information seeking stage. The buyer begins to formulate a brand selection strategy by screening alternatives against factors considered important. Often this process is not highly structured but subjective in nature. Typically, the set of brands under consideration includes only a few alternatives. The buyer evaluates the brands that may display differences when they are compared to the criteria used by the buyer in his or her evaluation. For example, criteria that may be important to credit card users are the annual card charge, interest costs, charge limits, and the number and types of retailers accepting the card.

Purchase Decision. At the completion of the evaluation stage, the buyer should select the preferred brand. This purchase represents the completion of the transaction between buyer and seller. It is possible that the buyer may decide not to purchase the preferred brand. In fact, the decision process may abort at any stage in the process. Many companies try to favorably reinforce the buyer's decision to purchase during the postpurchase stage.

Postpurchase Use. It is important for the seller to make sure the buyer has a favorable use experience with the product. Many firms regard this as an important factor in the decision to repurchase the product or to recommend it to other buyers. Typically, the buyer moves into the use stage with definite expectations concerning the product; these expectations are either confirmed or proved incorrect on the basis of use experience. Companies use a variety of actions to encourage customer satisfaction with a purchase, including follow-up letters, liberal return policies, after-the-sale services, and warranties. Some automobile manufacturers distribute a magazine to all owners as a means of further promoting customer satisfaction.

The nature and extent of the buyer's decision process vary according to the product. As discussed earlier, the various types of buying situations affect the nature and scope of the decision process. In unfamiliar buying situations the process may be very extensive, particularly if the purchase is important to the buyer. In other situations buying is the result of a habit developed through experience.

INFLUENCES ON CONSUMER BUYERS

In addition to the marketing efforts of firms, various factors associated with the *buyer* and his or her *environment* may influence the buying situation and the decision process (see Exhibit 6–3).

The Buyer's Environment

Current policies in the People's Republic of China provide an interesting illustration of how the buyer's environment affects buying behavior. New economic policies are enabling buyers to purchase an expanded range of products. Clearly, a spending spree is under way in China with consumers purchasing everything from television sets to track suits:

> Outside Shanghai Far East Gold & Silver Ornament Co., 40 shoppers are tussling for position and the chance to buy gold jewelry when the shop opens in an hour. Inside Shanghai Fabric Co., an old man wearing an arm band and a no-nonsense expression is keeping the customers at the counter to four deep, holding back the rest with a long pole.
>
> In an alleyway, Huangpu District Industrial Co. is stacking its sale merchandise on wooden crates while customers surge around, snapping up cut-price T-shirts and socks. And in the basement of the No. 1 Department Store, Go Ming Mi and Wu Chian Ming, who together earn $50 a month in steel factory, are deciding on a sewing machine. They are getting married soon and already they have bought a radio, a bed, a sofa and a fan.[8]

The new policy is intended to stimulate production by offering rewards and incentives, encouraging free market trading, and allowing some private ownership. The new economic environment has had a major impact on Chinese buying behavior.

Several important environmental factors influence consumer buyers, including *culture, social class, reference group,* and *family.* A brief overview of each factor will indicate the nature and scope of its influence.

Culture. Culture normally applies to a nation. The nature and scope of the impact of a country's culture on buyer behavior can be significant in certain buying situations. "Culture refers to the learned patterns of symbolism and behavior that are passed from one generation to the next; it represents the totality of values that characterize a society."[9] Culture regulates and prescribes an individual's behavior in society, thus affecting what people buy and use. Culture is reflected by people's values, beliefs, and attitudes toward various issues. Contrast, for example, the use of mail-order purchases by people in the United States and Japan. Until recently, catalog buying had a shoddy image in Japan.[10] In 1985 catalog sales accounted for less than 1 percent of total retail sales in Japan, compared to 10 percent in the United States. Lower prices and time constraints as the result of more women entering the work force are rapidly expanding catalog sales in Japan. Also, consumers are not so particular as they were in the past about seeing products before purchasing them. The new trend in Japan clearly represents a sharp break with tradition.

A culture is comprised of various groups within the society, called *subcultures,* which include ethnic, religious, racial, and geographical groups. Needs and preferences often vary among subcultures. Moreover, tastes and preferences have been found to vary within groups. For example, in the United States, the Hispanic subculture displays a substantial amount of heterogeneity regarding buying behavior. A study of the differences between the French-Canadian and the English-Canadian subcultures in Ottawa found significant variations with respect to the consumption of food and beverages as well as with respect to store patronage behavior, exposure to newspapers and television, furniture expenditures, automobile ownership, and preferences for features offered by major appliances.[11]

Social Class.   Social stratification occurs in most societies. A social class denotes equality of its members from the point of view of the society at large. Social classes in the United States are defined by occupation, education, and type of housing, and are designated as upper, middle, and lower class with subcategories. People in these classes often display different preferences regarding products, advertising media, types of stores, and prices. The analysis of buyers from a social class perspective provides useful guidelines for the development of a marketing strategy for buying situations influenced by considerations of social class.

Reference Group.   Individuals may be influenced by various specific groups, depending upon the buying situation. People who have the same values and beliefs about how one should behave comprise a reference group. A reference group may be either one of which the buyer is a member or a group the buyer would like to join. A wide range of formal and informal reference groups includes friends, business associates, fraternity members, church members, social service groups, car or van pools, trade unions, professional associations, and many other groups. The extent of influence of the reference group varies widely by product type. Products that are "socially visible" and represent high involvement are likely to be affected by reference group(s). Reference groups are observed and interacted with on a day-to-day basis by buyers, thus representing potentially important influences on buying behavior for various products.

Opinion leaders in reference groups are the specific individuals who influence buyers through word-of-mouth communication. These influential individuals may be available in our daily contacts or they may be celebrities conveying advertising messages. For example, recall the well-known personalities whose names are frequently shown on American Express cards in advertising this popular charge card. These messages help convey a status image to having and using an American Express card. Their objective is to establish a reference association via the message.

Reference groups are used in advertising to accomplish three kinds of influences: *informational, comparative,* and *normative.*[12] The first influence seeks to supply buyers with believable information. The second is intended to enable buyers to compare their beliefs, attitudes, and behavior to those of the group. The third type of influence encourages buyers to conform to the norms of the group.

Family. The family is the most important primary, normative reference group for buyers. The family role structure is often an important determinant of buyer behavior. The relative roles of male and female heads of the household vary depending upon the product. For some purchases the husband is the primary decision maker. Examples include lawn equipment, tools, electronic equipment, and financial services. The wife is often the decision maker for appliances, home decoration items, food brands, children's clothing, and medical services. Joint decision making may occur on vacations, the choice of restaurants, and home purchase. Children also are important influences for some purchases. One study found that when shopping for clothes men are accompanied by women 50 percent of the time and women exert:

A major influence on the purchase (61 percent).
Some influence (20 percent).
No influence (19 percent).[13]

Various changes may occur in the nature and extent of family influences. One of the more important recent trends is the changing structure of roles of husbands and wives when both spouses work. In general, males are becoming more involved in shopping for food. One recent study estimated men's participation in supermarket buying decisions at 50 percent compared to 10 percent a decade earlier.[14] Other changes include altered life-styles, unmarried couples living together, and an increasing number of singles.

The family has an important influence on individual members with respect to religious beliefs, social identity, self-worth, attitudes, beliefs, and other factors. These influences may occur during the time the individual is part of the household or after the individual has left the family setting to set up his or her own household. Firms use family-centered advertising in various ways because of their recognition of the importance of family influences in buyer behavior.

The Buyer

Human behavior involves a complex set of variables, interrelationships, and processes. The factors representing the consumer include thought variables and characteristics:

> *Consumer thought variables* are the cognitive processes involved in decision making. The three types of thought variables are perceptions of a brand's characteristics, need for or benefits from the brand, and attitudes toward the brand. *Consumer characteristics* are variables used to describe consumers such as demographics, life-styles, and personality characteristics.[15]

A brief examination of these intrapersonal variables will illustrate how they influence buyer behavior.

Consumer Needs.   The driving force influencing consumer behavior are needs. Needs motivate people to act. Understanding needs and how buyers satisfy them are essential guidelines for marketing actions. Consumers attempt to match their needs with products that meet their needs. People have a variety of needs, including basic physiological needs (food, rest, and sex); the need for safety; the need for relationships with other people (friendship); and personal satisfaction needs.[16] Measurement of the nature and intensity of a need is important in: (1) determining how well a particular brand may satisfy the need; and/or (2) indicating what change in the brand may be necessary to provide a better solution to the buyer's needs.

An interesting example of meeting needs is the growing desire of consumers for food that is both good-tasting and convenient.[17] Food companies are adding value to products and making them easier to use by tailoring them to the needs of working women, smaller households, and singles. These firms are increasing their profits by helping people solve their problems of food preparation. Studies by the food industry indicate that shoppers from almost every age and income bracket are not as concerned about economizing on food as their counterparts of previous decades were. Many buyers want food that is easy and quick to prepare. Interestingly, the pride of preparation and creativity that prevailed in past decades has yielded to a desire to reduce effort while maintaining quality. Buyers are willing to pay for convenience. For example, chicken sells in the supermarket for less than $1 a pound whereas chicken Cordon Bleu, and breaded breast fillets are priced at $4 a pound or more.

Attitudes. Buyer's attitudes toward brands are important because experience and research findings indicate that such attitudes do influence behavior.[18] Attitudes are enduring systems of favorable or unfavorable evaluations about brands.[19] They reflect the buyer's overall liking or preference for a brand. Attitudes may develop from personal experience, interactions with other buyers, or by marketing efforts, such as advertising and personal selling.

Consider, for example, people's attitudes toward air travel safety. Fear of flying represents an important attitudinal barrier that air transportation firms must cope with on a continuing basis. In a *Business Week*–sponsored study in 1985, over 83 percent of respondents expressed mild to great concern about hijacking, bombs aboard the airplane, poor maintenance, and pilot error.[20] Even frequent flyers indicated concern about safety in the air. There is an apparent decline in public confidence about air safety. In a similar study conducted in 1970, 60 percent of those surveyed indicated that flying was safer compared to five years earlier. By 1985 only 16 percent of those surveyed believed that air travel was safer than in 1980.

Attitudes are important in various aspects of developing a marketing strategy. A marketing strategy may be designed either to respond to established attitudes or to attempt to change an attitude. In a given strategic situation, relevant attitudes should be identified and measured to indicate how brands compare. If the attitudes that are important influences on buyer behavior can be identified and a firm's brand measured against these attitudes, we may be able to improve our brand's position by using this information. Attitudes are often difficult to change, but firms may be able to do so through communications, particularly if buyers' perceptions about the brand are incorrect. For example, if the trade-in value of an automobile is important to a buyer and a company learns that its brand (which actually has a high trade-in value) is perceived as having a low trade-in value, advertising can communicate this information to buyers.

Perceptions. "Perception is defined as the process by which an individual selects, organizes, and interprets information inputs to create a meaningful picture of the world."[21] Perceptions are how consumers select, organize, and interpret marketing stimuli, such as advertising, personal selling, price, and the product. Perceptions form attitudes. Buyers are selective in the information they process. As an illustration of selective perception, some advertising messages may not be received by viewers because of the large number of messages vying for his or her attention. Or a salesperson's conversation may be misunderstood or not received fully because the buyer is trying to decide if the purchase is necessary while the salesperson is talking.

People often perceive things differently. Businesses are interested in how their products, salespeople, stores, and companies are perceived. Perception is important strategically in helping management to evaluate its current positioning strategy and in making changes in this positioning strategy. Perception mapping is a useful research technique for showing how brands are perceived by buyers according to various criteria (see Chapter 5). A set of attributes can be reduced through computer analyses to form two-dimensional maps based on consumer perceptions of brands. A preference map for automobile brands is shown in Chapter 7. The use of preference mapping as a method of market segmentation is discussed in Chapter 8.

Characteristics of Buyers. *Demographic* variables describe buyers according to their age, income, education, occupation, and a host of other factors. Such information is of limited value in predicting buyer behavior but is often important in describing groups of buyers. For example, demographic information can help describe groups of buyers such as heavy users of a product or brand. Demographics used in combination with other buyer behavior information are useful in segmenting markets, selecting distribution channels, and other decisions on marketing strategy. As an illustration of the role of income in describing buyers, consider the use of coupons to save on shopping bills according to household income category (see Exhibit 6–5). In 1984 shoppers saved an estimated $2 billion by using coupons, with nearly 80 percent of U.S. households clipping coupons.[22]

Life-style variables describe what people do (activities), their interests, their opinions, and their buying behavior. Called AIO variables, life-style characteristics extend beyond demographics and offer a more penetrating description of the consumer.[23] Profiles can be developed using life-style characteristics. Life-style information has been used to segment markets, position products, and guide the design of advertising messages. The use of life-style variables to segment markets is discussed in Chapter 8.

Finally, *personality* information may be of value in gaining a better understanding of buyer behavior. "Personality is more deep-seated than lifestyle since personality variables reflect consistent, enduring patterns of behavior."[24] Typically, marketing research results have shown a weak relationship between personality variables and purchase behavior. One problem is that the measures used have typically not been related to marketing. Nevertheless, some success has been achieved. For example, personality profiles of beer drinkers were developed by Anheuser-Busch Companies, Inc. in the early 1970s.[25] The research identified four types of drinkers, their demographics, personality type, and drinking patterns. On the basis of their characteristics the types were designated *reparative, social, indulgent,* and *oceanic* drinkers.

EXHIBIT 6-5 Shoppers Coupon Usage by Household Income

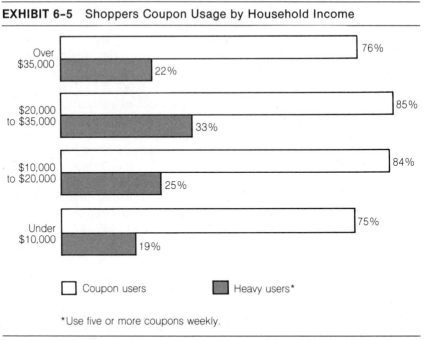

Coupon users   ▢

Heavy users*   ▨

*Use five or more coupons weekly.

SOURCE: A. C. Nielsen Co. Reprinted by permission of *The Wall Street Journal.* © Dow Jones & Company, Inc., July 18, 1985. All rights reserved.

ORGANIZATIONAL BUYER BEHAVIOR

Our discussion now shifts from consumer buyers to organizational buyers. Gaining an understanding of organizational buyers is essential in marketing strategy development. An example indicates how cultural differences affect industrial buyers. Doing business in Japan demonstrates the wide variations in organizational buying behavior that may occur between countries with very different cultures. Consider this description:

> The first difference—and the one most Westerners find hardest to grasp—is that you don't "do" business in Japan. Business is not an "activity"; it is a "commitment." The purchasing agent orders goods, to be sure. But first he commits himself to a supplier, and to a relationship that is presumed to be permanent or at least long-lasting. And until the newcomer—whether Japanese or foreign—proves itself committed in turn, the purchasing agent will not buy its wares no matter how good their quality or how cheap their price. American Hospital Supply, by now, enjoys leadership in the tightly regulated Japanese health-care market. But when it first opened in Japan, 20 years ago, the company spent five years knocking on doors before it wrote its first order. Indeed, quick results in Japan often mean ultimate failure—you are doing business with the wrong people.[26]

In addition to expecting a commitment from the supplier, after-the-sale service and brand recognition are very important to Japanese buyers. Successful entry is often accomplished by using a market segmentation strategy. For example, Millipore identified one particular market niche in water treatment and then concentrated over a long time period to attain leadership in that niche.

In marketing to Japanese organizations, one must also recognize important structural and cultural differences.[27] Rank must equal age within a given social group, such as managers in a company. Another interesting practice is that the manufacturer is expected to finance and look after the distributor. Additionally, a retired high government servant can act as an effective go-between in business relations with the government.

While there are many similarities between organizational and consumer buyer behavior, some important differences exist between the two types of buyers. The framework for analyzing buyer behavior shown in Exhibit 6-1 generally applies to organizational buyers. But organizational buying situations, influences on buyers, and certain other buying process characteristics are different from consumer buyer behavior.

How Organizational Buying Differs

People Involved. Organizational buying typically includes participants from different functional areas, since the purchase may be of interest to individuals with different responsibilities. For example, the selection of a large computer affects people in various departments. The cost is important to the chief financial executive. Performance and service are evaluated by the executive responsible for operating the system. Purchase of a large computer system may involve top management because of the significance of the purchase.

The term *buying center* is used to identify the participants in the organizational buying process. Although the participants in organizational buying vary according to the situation, they normally are from one or more of the following categories:

Purchasing Department. Purchasing personnel are responsible for negotiation with suppliers and coordination of purchasing activities within the firm.

Technical and Operating Personnel. These individuals include the users of the goods or services being purchased as well as others affected by the purchase. They often establish the specifications for the item being purchased.

Financial Executives. On purchases involving large amounts of money, financial executives may participate in the buying process by approving the purchase, arranging payment terms, and other functions.

Top Management. Purchases that require a substantial amount of money or represent an important decision for the organization may include the participation of top corporate or business unit executives.

Because of various points of influence on the organizational buying decision, personal selling is essential in order to maintain proper contact with all parties that may play a role in the purchase decision.

Buyer/Seller Relationship. Organizational buying involves long-term relationships between suppliers and buying firms. While the task of initially establishing a relationship is not as lengthy in the United States as in Japan, many buying situations are part of a long-term relationship between vendors and buyers. A supplier may have to be approved by a buying committee before a purchaser will consider the supplier as an acceptable vendor. A new supplier often finds it difficult to break into an established relationship. For example, grocery wholesalers often establish purchasing criteria that a firm with an unknown brand may find difficult to satisfy, such as national or regional advertising of the brand. A small food producer may not have the financial resources necessary for aggressive brand promotion at the retail level.

Criteria that are important to buyers include economic, performance, and service factors. Responsiveness of the supplier to the buyer's needs often represents a key consideration in the strength of the buyer/seller relationship. As an illustration, National Can Company evaluates its suppliers on the basis of competitive pricing, on-time delivery, product quality, emergency assistance, communication, technical service, cost-reduction ideas, and inventory program.

Buyers Are Professionals. The typical organizational buyer is well informed about the characteristics of products being purchased and the attributes of different brands. The purchasing staff of a firm buying complex products and services may have science and engineering degrees plus experience in using the product being purchased. Technical and operations personnel are sometimes transferred into purchasing after gaining experience about the products produced or distributed by the firm. Product knowledge is essential for the supplier's salespeople selling to the buying firm. U.S. Surgical, a leading producer of surgical staplers, puts each salesperson through a comprehensive training program:

> Proper use of the company's instruments requires detailed instruction and technical support. These functions are assigned to the company's sales force, which is given a 240-hour training program covering basic anatomy, physiology, surgical terminology, scrubbing and gowning, and operating room protocol, in addition to the operation of the company's products. Beside giving demonstrations to operating room personnel, a company salesperson often guides surgeons during initial operative procedures.[28]

EXHIBIT 6-6   Illustrative Range of Organizational Purchasing Situations

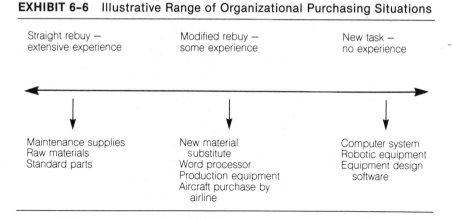

Straight rebuy —
extensive experience

Modified rebuy —
some experience

New task —
no experience

Maintenance supplies
Raw materials
Standard parts

New material
 substitute
Word processor
Production equipment
Aircraft purchase by
 airline

Computer system
Robotic equipment
Equipment design
 software

Derived Demand.   The driving force of economic activity for many kinds of business products is the consumer. Purchases of industrial supplies and equipment often depend upon consumer purchases. When people reduce their purchases of gasoline, this development impacts oil and gas production, which in turn reduces the purchases by oil companies of drilling equipment and services. Thus the demand for business and industrial products is often derived from the demand for products and services utilizing the products and services of organizational suppliers.

Types of Buying Situations

Organizational buying is normally repetitive in nature for many kinds of purchases. Rebuying is the rule rather than the exception. We can classify buying situations according to the extent to which the purchase is new to the buyer; and we can also classify them according to the extent of the buyer's familiarity with the product being purchased. Using this basis of classification, there are three types of organizational buying: a *new task,* a *modified rebuy,* and a *straight rebuy.*[29] Several examples of each situation are shown in Exhibit 6-6.

New Task.   This situation presents the buyer with a new purchasing task, a situation that corresponds to complex decision making (see Exhibit 6-1). Since the buyer has no experience with this product type, it will be necessary for him or her to obtain information, identify alternative suppliers, evaluate the alternatives, and decide which brand to purchase. The decision process shown in Exhibit 6-4 applies. Of course, we need to recognize that there may be several participants in the process, and that the environmental influences in organizational buying are different from those in consumer buying processes.

China's opening of its markets to foreign business representatives is an interesting example of a broad array of new-task buying situations.[30] Uncertainty is high for both buyer and seller, although the Chinese have done research and are familiar with international markets. China has buying corporations that negotiate for purchases on behalf of factories and other end users. Price is an important consideration for the Chinese buyer. Even communicating with the buyer is a challenge, and the negotiating process is much longer than in the West. It is important for the Chinese to show their superiors that they are effective bargainers. A long negotiation helps emphasize the buyers' involvement in the purchase decision.

Modified Rebuy. The buyer has some experience with this purchase decision. Nevertheless, it requires the purchasing organization to seek and evaluate information, and in this way to move the situation toward making a complex decision. The use of a substitute material such as plastic for steel illustrates the modified rebuy situation. The function is the same, but the two materials display different characteristics. The members of the buying center must examine the tradeoffs associated with the two materials and attempt to select the alternative that offers the better solution.

Straight Rebuy. The purchasing organization has extensive experience in this situation. Frequently purchased items fall into this category, and the purchasing process is simple and routine in nature. These purchases involve little or no information search. They correspond to habitual purchases from a preferred supplier (see Exhibit 6–1). Many industrial distributors' sales are straight rebuy situations. Examples include medical supplies, steel, paint, fasteners, and chemicals.

The Vallen Corporation is an interesting example of a distributor whose sales are comprised of a large number of straight rebuy situations. Vallen distributes a wide range of safety items to industrial buyers. Operating primarily in the Sunbelt, it had sales of $40 million in 1985. Vallen's strategy for meeting customers' supply requirements is to convince the customer to establish a systems supply agreement (also called a vendor stocking program).[31] This cost-effective solution to the straight rebuy situation reduces total costs by transferring certain responsibilities and functions from the buyer to the vendor. The program also simplifies the acquisition/possession/disbursement cycle. The advantages to the buyer include fast response, reduced paper work, elimination of inventory and backorders, reduced ordering errors, and predetermined prices.

INFLUENCES ON ORGANIZATIONAL BUYING

The major slowdown in computer purchases that occurred in 1985 provides an interesting example of the impact of various internal and external influences on the organizational buying of computers. The following factors contributed to an industrywide problem:[32]

1. A slowdown in general manufacturing activity, which led to reduced computer purchases (demand for buyers' products).
2. The decision by organizational buyers to wait for new models to become available (technology).
3. The fact that computer equipment is not user-friendly (individual influence).
4. The desire for fully integrated computer systems (technology).
5. Past purchase experience of noncompatible computers and software (buying center).
6. The decision to learn how to fully utilize existing equipment before buying more (organizational influence).

There are four major kinds of influences on organizational buying: (1) external factors, (2) the organization, (3) the buying center, and (4) individual buyer characteristics. Since these influences vary across buying situations, the objective in this brief overview is to describe the nature and scope of these influences.

External Influences

Many external influences may affect the buying process, including technology, the economy, society, government, nature, industry, the buyer's markets, and distribution channels. Consider, for example, the impact of low prices for grain and an oversupply of agricultural commodities on farmers' income in the mid-1980s. These conditions led to severe reductions in farm equipment purchases. During this period the agricultural equipment industry experienced a significant negative impact. Companies like Deere & Company and J. I. Case curtailed their purchases and others sold their businesses. Many industrial firms experienced cyclical sales that affected their buying practices.

It is important to identify the relevant external influences in a given buying situation. The influences of primary interest may cause organizational buyers to alter their purchasing patterns by buying more, less, or differently. Some influences may be favorable while others are not favorable. Our discussion of market opportunity analysis in Chapter 5 provides a framework for analyzing various influences on the buyers in a particular product-market.

Organizational Influences

An organization establishes certain buying policies and practices that may influence the buying process. These include the extent of decentralized purchasing authority, practices of vendor evaluation, criteria for selecting suppliers, and a variety of other purchasing rules and guidelines. It is critical for the seller to understand an organization's buying guidelines since two otherwise comparable firms in the same industry may have different buying policies and practices.

An organization exerts the following influence on the buying process: (1) the categories of buying situations necessary to achieve the objectives of the organization; (2) the systems of communication, authority, status, rewards, and work flow; (3) the managerial capabilities of the organization; (4) the corporate culture, a topic that is discussed in Chapter 7; and (5) the people that participate in and influence the buying process.[33] These influences vary according to the size of a firm, its stage of development, its type of business, and its managerial orientation. Small firms are likely to be informal and flexible in their purchasing practices while larger firms tend to be more formalized. The federal government probably displays the most formalized purchasing policies and practices of all organizations.

Understanding the organizational environment is essential to understanding buying processes. This is one of the reasons why personal selling is an important strategy component in business-to-business marketing. Suppliers must study the buying organization to identify its specific characteristics, opportunities, and requirements.

Buying Center

Texaco, Inc. buys about $1 billion of materials each year in order to find and produce oil, run its refineries, and bring its products to customers:

> As the sixth largest corporation in the world, Texaco must buy a tremendous variety of materials; every Texaco purchase over $1,000—and all purchases against purchasing agreements—go through the Purchasing Department. The biggest dollar volume involves three categories: *chemicals; pipe*—called "tubulars and accessories"; and *oil field equipment*—drilling equipment, and accessories for handling gas, oil, and water.
>
> On any given day the department might be processing hundreds of items ranging from a $1,200 order for chopped sirloin to a multi milliondollar heater for a new unit at the Convent, Louisiana, refinery.[34]

Professional buyers assigned to the purchasing department are an essential part of the buying centers of firms like Texaco.

In addition to professional purchasing people, the buying center includes people and departments that have a stake in a particular purchase. The composition of the buying center will vary, depending upon the item being purchased. The members of the buying center accomplish various functions, including setting specifications for items to be purchased, evaluating vendors and products, collecting operating and application information, selecting the brand to be purchased, arranging for payment and terms, and working with the supplier after the purchase transaction is completed.

The buying process involves far more than economic considerations, and the buying center members often represent a complex combination of economic, technical, political, and social interactions. For example, it is not uncommon for operating departments (e.g., manufacturing) to attempt to bypass the purchasing department in buying goods and services. Consider Texaco's argument in support of the professional buyers:

> Whether or not the buyers actually save money for Texaco is a matter intensely studied each year. The answer is that they do. "Our studies . . . show that Texaco saves a minimum of 10 percent on purchases when a department comes to us rather than doing it themselves, and that's just from routine competitive bidding. In 1982, in addition to the 10 percent, our buyers documented further savings of $18.9 million. Each buyer in this department is worth a half-million dollars a year."[35]

Individual Influences

Like consumer buyers, organizational buyers are influenced by a variety of intrapersonal factors, including needs, attitudes, perceptions, and descriptive characteristics (demographics, life-style, and personality). Intrapersonal influences may conflict with the objectives of the organizational and buying center. As a result of organizational politics, power struggles, and perceived threats, individual participants tend to make organizational buying relatively complex, particularly for important purchases.

The organizational buying process is influenced by a variety of environmental, organizational, buying center, and individual factors. Marketing strategies for organizational buyers must analyze these influences and identify those that are likely to affect the buying process in a particular situation.

STRATEGIC IMPLICATIONS OF BUYER BEHAVIOR ANALYSIS

Gaining an understanding of buyer behavior contributes to various aspects of marketing strategy. And marketing strategy itself is an important influence on buyer behavior. The discussion up to this point in the chapter provides a conceptual framework for guiding strategic analysis of buyer behavior. We have identified important variables, interrelationships, and buying processes. To complete the examination of consumer and organizational buyers, the role of buyer behavior analysis in strategy development is highlighted. The topics we shall consider include the role of marketing research in buyer analysis and the importance of buyer behavior analysis in tracking shifts in buyer's needs and wants. Also included are some brief comments on the role of buyer behavior analysis in market segmentation and the positioning strategy of the marketing program.

Role of Marketing Research

Analyzing buyers frequently requires marketing research information that is collected and analyzed on a longitudinal basis. While intuition, judgment, and experience are useful inputs to buyer analyses, they are not sufficient guidelines for marketing strategy development in many instances.

The BehaviorScan marketing research system of Information Resources Inc. (IRI) illustrates a variety of computerized information services that are being developed. Founded in 1979, IRI had grown by 1984 to $36 million in sales. Using panels of consumers in selected minimarket cities in the United States, the firm collects data on panel members' packaged food and drug purchases. The panel member inserts a plastic card into a special slot of the cash register at participating supermarkets and drugstores.[36] This causes the complete scanner cash register information to be transferred to a computer data bank. BehaviorScan incorporates UPC (Universal Product Code) scanner data, individually targetable TV advertising (via cable), and tracks individual purchases of sample households in each minimarket. BehaviorScan can be used to track market tests, pricing strategies, and promotional strategies, such as the effects of sampling and couponing. Participating clients like The Procter & Gamble Co. and General Mills, Inc. pay a base price of $150,000, which provides exclusive rights to IRI's services in two minimarkets for one product category. The firm has divided packaged consumer goods into 450 categories. A major value of BehaviorScan is the system's ability to track purchasing behavior over time under controlled conditions. An example of information provided by the BehaviorScan system is shown in Exhibit 6-7. By analyzing this information in conjunction with the characteristics of panel members, management can identify the target market(s) for the new product, test advertising and promotion strategies, and evaluate other aspects of marketing strategy.

EXHIBIT 6-7   Monitoring the Performance of a New Brand with BehaviorScan®

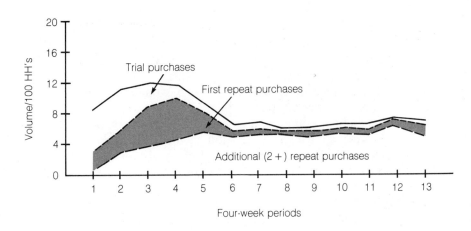

Sales per 100 households

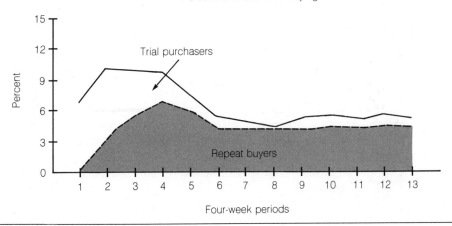

Percent of households buying

SOURCE: Information Resources, Inc., 520 N. Dearborn St., Chicago, IL 60610.

Shifts in Wants

The study of demographic data is often inadequate for identifying changes in buyers' preferences for products and brands. Buyer behavior analyses probe deeper into the decision processes of buyers, and identify and evaluate changes in buying patterns. An interesting illustration of the changes that occur in buying is the shift in male and female shopping stereotypes regarding clothing. Consider the following findings resulting from analyses of people's shopping patterns and practices:[37]

Men's shopping patterns are becoming more like women's historical practices of browsing more and showing more interest in style.

Women, nevertheless, continue to spend more than men on clothes. Experts estimate that professional women allocate 15 to 20% of their incomes on clothes.

Men make fewer shopping excursions a year than women, although women appear to be developing a distaste for shopping.

Women want better service, and many are responsive to good service by purchasing an entire wardrobe from a store that meets their needs.

Price continues to be an important factor. One study found that 38% of a working woman's wardrobe is bought at reduced prices.

Role models (president, department head, colleagues) seems to be important in influencing what men purchase.

The importance of buyer behavior analyses is clearly indicated in several of these trends in men's and women's clothing buying patterns.

Market Segmentation

The needs and wants of the buyers in a product-market are typically not the same. Buyer behavior research can uncover these differences and link them to purchasing patterns. We can facilitate market segmentation by identifying differences across buyers and by relating these differences to buyers' responsiveness to alternative marketing strategies. Chapter 8 examines how buyer behavior and other information can be used to segment and describe consumer and organizational product-markets.

An interesting study of the differences in people's life-styles was conducted by SRI International in the early 1980s. A representative sample of 2,700 individuals was asked 800 questions about values defined as "the entire constellation of a person's attitudes, beliefs, opinions, hopes, fears, prejudices, needs, desires, and aspirations."[38] Nine American life-styles were identified:

Survivors. They are hanging on the best they can, tending to be despairing, depressed, withdrawn, and poor (4 percent of the population).

Sustainers. Anxious, combative people who often feel left out (7 percent).

Belongers. These people follow the rules, leading conservative traditional lives (35 percent).

Emulators. Young and ambitious individuals comprising 10 percent of the population.

Achievers. Diverse, gifted, hardworking people comprising society's leaders and doers (23 percent).

I-Am-Me. Students and other young people that are in transitional roles (5 percent).

Experimentals and *Socially Conscious* (respectively 7 percent and 9 percent). Similar groups that view themselves as sophisticated and politically effective.

Integrateds. They have an intercompleteness, are trusted by others, and may serve as role models (2 percent).

These groups are not universal market segments, but each group displays different needs and preferences, indicating in this way the wide range of variability in the population. Moreover, life-style variation is a promising market segmentation variable for some products.

Marketing Program Positioning Strategy

Buyer behavior analysis makes an important contribution to the design of strategies on product, distribution, price, and promotion. Our earlier discussion of marketing strategy variations for high and low involvement situations (see Exhibit 6–2) provided several illustrations. Additional examples illustrate the nature and scope of buyer behavior information that is useful in developing a positioning strategy.

Product Strategy. Buyer's perceptions of products are important in their positioning of a company's brand. In developing new products and modifying existing products, a firm can benefit from an understanding of buyers' perceptions of the product. For example, Waterford, the maker of fine handmade Irish crystal, lost market position in the mid-1980s by failing to design products for affluent baby boomers—single and married, male and female—with a taste for expensive crystal.[39] During the decade ending in 1982, the company did not introduce a single new stemware pattern and was complacent in marketing its products. By not identifying the shifts in consumer tastes, Waterford failed to fully capitalize on U.S. sales of fine lead crystal which nearly tripled from 1979 to 1983. In 1985 its management began to introduce new crystal lines intended to update the Waterford image and help broaden its appeal.

Distribution and Price Strategies. One key aspect of distribution is determining which distribution channels provide the best access to buyers. The type of channel and the price strategy are often interrelated.

The cosmetics industry offers an interesting example of the changing preferences of women and the impact of these changes on where they buy their cosmetics. Working women have less time to buy makeup and are more likely to buy it when they shop at food stores and mass marketing outlets like K mart Corporation and Target Stores. Between 1980 and 1984 mass merchandisers and food stores increased their market share of cosmetics sales from 17 percent to 23 percent.[40] Companies like Maybeline and Noxell (CoverGirl) benefited by these distribution shifts with their popular-priced brands. Note also the negative impact of working women on direct sales companies like Avon Products, Inc. and Mary Kay Cosmetics Inc.

Promotion. Advertising and personal selling strategies probably gain more direction from buyer behavior information than other aspects of marketing strategy. While illustrations of applying buyer behavior information to advertising abound, none is as revealing as the insights used by DeBeers Consolidated Mines Ltd. and the diamond monopolists' advertising agency. United States sales of diamonds expanded from $23 million in 1939 to more than $2 billion in 1979. The advertising strategy was developed on the premise (supported by research findings) that the essence of the diamond transaction is a gift from a man to a woman.[41] As we move through the 1980s, it will be interesting to see how the changing role structures of career women may alter DeBeers's promotion strategy. Interestingly, part of the current promotion of diamonds includes attempts to persuade women to buy them for men as a way to help expand the market.

These brief examples are intended to indicate the importance of buyer behavior information in various aspects of marketing strategy planning rather than to provide an exhaustive discussion of the topic. In moving through the remaining chapters in the book, we will demonstrate further the key role of buyer behavior analysis in guiding marketing strategy in a variety of settings, for both consumer and industrial products.

CONCLUDING NOTE

This chapter examines an important aspect of marketing strategy: consumer buyers and organizational buyers. The analysis of buyers includes a study of the types of decisions they make, the influences affecting their decisions, and the decision processes they follow. We illustrate the contribution and relevance of buyer behavior analyses to marketing strategy in a variety of ways throughout the chapter. By integrating the buying decision process, types of buying decisions, and influences on buying, we develop a framework for buyer behavior analysis.

Consumer buying situations can be classified according to the extent of involvement of the buyer in the purchase and according to whether the purchase decision is based on a decision-making process or on habit. High-involvement decisions tend to be infrequent, expensive purchases that are both risky and important to the consumer's ego and social needs. Four broad types of buying occur: *complex decision making* and *brand loyalty* under high-involvement conditions, and *impulse purchasing* and *inertia* under low-involvement conditions. The marketing strategy consequences of high- and low-involvement buying situations vary substantially.

The nature and scope of the buying process depend mainly on the type of buying situation confronting the buyer. It is useful to describe the buyer's decision process as a sequence of steps or stages consisting of need recognition, information seeking, evaluation of alternatives, purchase decision, and postpurchase use. This process applies to complex decision-making situations. It may be altered or simplified for other types of buying situations.

The influences on consumer buyers consist of individual and environmental factors. Environmental influences include culture, social class, reference group, and family. The factors describing or affecting the consumer include thought variables and characteristics. Life-style, for example, offers a useful basis of describing consumers and their buying behavior.

While there are many similarities between consumer buyers and organizational buyers, there are also important differences between them. The framework for analyzing buyer behavior (Exhibit 6–3) generally applies to both groups. Organizational buying differs in terms of the people involved (buying center), the nature of the buyer/seller relationship, the product knowledge of the professional buyer, and dependence of demand for the organizational purchases upon the purchases of consumer products. Organizational purchasing situations can be classified as a new task, a modified rebuy and a straight rebuy. Influences on organizational buying consist of external, organizational, buying center, and individual factors.

Many strategic implications of buyer behavior analysis are discussed in the remaining chapters of the book. Marketing research is essential in studying buyers and their decision processes. Information gained from buyer behavior studies and trends is useful in spotting shifts in the preferences, market segmentation, and design of the positioning strategy for the marketing program.

NOTES

1. This illustration is based on American Greetings Corporation, *1985 Annual Report*, 6–7.

2. Henry Assael, *Marketing Management* (Boston: Kent Publishing, 1985), 126–27.

3. Henry Assael, *Consumer Behavior and Marketing Action*, 2nd ed. (Boston: Kent Publishing, 1984), 86.

4. Stanley H. Sloam, "Taking Fragrances to Market Isn't Easy; Making Them Successes Is even Harder," *The Wall Street Journal*, August 16, 1978, 46.

5. Assael, *Marketing Management*, 135.

6. Kelly Walker, "Here's the Beef," *Forbes*, August 12, 1985, 88.

7. Assael, *Marketing Management*, 137.

8. June Kronholz, "Buying Spree", *The Wall Street Journal*, October 26, 1983, 1.

9. William Lazer and James D. Culley, *Marketing Management* (Boston: Houghton Mifflin, 1983), 381.

10. Masayoshi Kanabayashi, "Busy Japanese Turning to Mail Order, Which They Once Spurned as Shoddy," *The Wall Street Journal*, June 26, 1985, 24.

11. Charles M. Schaninger, Jacques C. Bourgeois, and W. Christian Buss, "French-English Canadian Subcultural Consumption Differences," *Journal of Marketing*, Spring 1985, 82–92.

12. Assael, *Marketing Management*, 172.

13. "Apparel Approval," *The Wall Street Journal*, February 28, 1985, 31.

14. "More Men Shop for Groceries," *USA Today*, February 7, 1984, 4B.

15. Assael, *Consumer Behavior and Marketing Action*, 15.

16. A. H. Maslow, "Theory of Human Motivation," *Psychology Review*, July 1943, 43–45.

17. Betsy Morris, "How Much Will People Pay to Save a Few Minutes of Cooking? Plenty," *The Wall Street Journal*, July 25, 1985, 23.

18. See, for example, Gail Smith, "How GM Measures Ad Effectiveness," *Printers' Ink*, May 14, 1965, 25–26.

19. Assael, *Consumer Behavior and Marketing Action*, 650.

20. Stuart E. Jackson, "Americans Get Queasier about Air Travel," *Business Week*, July 15, 1985, 37.

21. Bernard Berelson and Gary A. Steiner, *Human Behavior: An Inventory of Scientific Findings* (New York: Harcourt Brace Jovanovich, 1964), 88.

22. *The Wall Street Journal*, July 18, 1984, 25.

23. Assael, *Consumer Behavior and Marketing Action*, 225.

24. Ibid., 266.

25. Russell L. Ackoff and James R. Emshoff, "Advertising Research at Anheuser-Busch (1968–1974)," *Sloan Management Review*, Spring 1975, 1–15.

26. Peter F. Drucker, "Business in Japan Isn't Just 'Done,'" *The Wall Street Journal*, July 18, 1985, 22.

27. Ibid.

28. "United States Surgical Corp.," *The Value Line OTC Special Situations Service* (New York: Arnold Bernhard & Co., April 28, 1980), A–96–7.

29. Charles W. Faris, "Market Segmentation and Industrial Buying Behavior," *Educators' Proceedings*, ed. R. Moyer and J. Vosburgh, (Chicago: American Marketing Association, 1967), pp. 108–10.

30. This illustration is based on Vigor Fung, "As Chinese Markets Open, Foreign Businessmen Learn the Special Tricks of Making a Deal There," *The Wall Street Journal*, August 1, 1985, 22.

31. Vallen Corporation, *Capabilities Unlimited*, 1985, 10–11.

32. "The Computer Slump," *Business Week*, June 24, 1985, 74–75.

33. Based, in part, on Frederick E. Webster, Jr. and Yoram Wind, *Organizational Buying Behavior* (Englewood Cliffs, N.J.: Prentice-Hall, 1972), Chapter 5.

34. "Texaco's Buyers Get Their Money's Worth," *The Texaco Star,* January 1984, 12.
35. Ibid.
36. Kevin Higgins, "High-Tech Research Firm Is Hit with Advertisers and Investors," *Marketing News,* March 2, 1984, 1 and 28.
37. Joan Kron, "Clothes-Shopping Habits Changing as Men Seek Style, Women Service," *The Wall Street Journal,* December 21, 1984, 23 and 33.
38. Andrew Hacker, "The 'Lifestyle' Approach," *Fortune,* May 2, 1983, 291–2.
39. "Waterford Learns Its Lesson: Snob Appeal Isn't Enough," *Business Week,* December 24, 1984, 63–4.
40. "How Cosmetics Makers Are Touching Up Their Strategies," *Business Week,* September 23, 1985, 66.
41. "How N. W. Ayer Manipulated American Attitudes Toward Diamonds," *Adweek,* June 28, 1982, 80 and 82.

QUESTIONS FOR REVIEW AND DISCUSSION

1. Does open heart surgery represent a complex buying behavior situation? Discuss.

2. How may a framework for analyzing buyer behavior contribute to the design of marketing strategy?

3. What reference group(s) might be important in analyzing behavior for a product like Lenox china?

4. How and to what extent are buyers' attitudes useful in the development of marketing strategy?

5. What are the advertising strategy implications in cases of joint decision making (male and female head of household) for product purchases in the household?

6. Discuss the important distinctions between consumer and industrial buying behavior.

7. Describe the stages in the decision process of the purchase of an automobile by a middle-income household in which the head of the household falls into the *belonger* category discussed in the text.

8. Discuss the features and limitations of demographic data in buyer behavior analyses.

STRATEGIC APPLICATION 6-1

COCA-COLA

Atlanta—In a stuffy hotel meeting room here last Monday, Brian Dyson, the president of Coca-Cola Co.'s domestic soft-drink operation, listened patiently as a group of company bottlers voiced their frustrations.

One told how his deliverymen were being harassed by grocery shoppers who disliked the "new" Coke. Another said he had become too embarrassed to tell people what he did for a living. Still another declared, "We've got to cut our losses."

Top executives of Coca-Cola had pretty much decided on their course of action by that time, but the bottlers' solidarity clinched matters.

A Public Apology

On Wednesday, as everyone in America must know by now, the soda-pop giant made its startling announcement. In one of the most stunning flip-flops in marketing annals, Coke publicly apologized for scrapping a 99-year-old product that had perhaps become more American than apple pie. Henceforth, it said, the old Coca-Cola would be revived as Coca-Cola Classic and would be sold right alongside the sweeter, reformulated new Coke introduced in April.

Thus, in one stroke, Coke largely undid what 4½ years of elaborate planning and market research had dictated was the right move. The abrupt decision, without any detailed marketing and advertising plans, surprised industry analysts and Coke's competitors alike. Coke executives, in fact, were still huddling Friday to try to settle such basic issues as whether its advertising agency should handle the two Cokes as one account or two.

The company felt it had little choice in its action. After the initial success of the reformulated Coke, company executives suddenly sensed that the expected howls of diehard old-Coke drinkers were possibly being adopted by the public at large. Coca-Cola's own weekly surveys showed that a major swing in consumer sentiment had begun on Memorial Day. By early July, antagonism toward the new Coke was so great that it was losing heavily in the Thursday-night surveys not only to old Coke but to Pepsi as well.

The company's quick decision to cut its losses drew immediate praise from many quarters. But Coke's troubles are far from over. Besides the blow to the company's reputation as one of the nation's premier marketing machines, Coca-Cola still faces the difficulty of making its new two-cola strategy work.

Not a Panacea

"We know we can't treat this as the silver bullet that solves all our problems," concedes Sergio Zyman, the senior vice president for marketing at Coke's domestic soft-drink arm. "We have a major job ahead of us."

The marketing of two versions of Coke, for example, raises far different problems than the 1982 decision to market Diet Coke, the first product to borrow the prized Coke trademark. Diet Coke quickly became the nation's No. 3 soft drink.

One danger repeatedly mentioned in the company's own discussions is the prospect that the return of original Coke might irreparably discredit the newer version. The company wants the improved product as its flagship, but there already are signs that some bottlers will fight to give old Coke the main prominence. Meanwhile, Pepsi officials can laughingly gloat that the actions show that Coke obviously has doubts about both products.

Coke's most optimistic view is that having two colas with its famous trademark will allow it to capture more customers than it could with just one. At the same time, though, it also recognizes that it now is a long way from the strategy it laid out for itself only a few months ago. Says Ira Herbert, Coke's executive vice president for marketing: "There are a lot of questions we have to talk our way through."

Coke's original plan, hatched only after one of the most exhaustive research projects ever for a consumer-goods company, was intended to break what for several years has been Pepsi's biggest advantage in the market: its ability to win taste tests against Coke consistently. "The idea," says one of Coke's top ad strategists, "was to take all the positive qualities associated with the current product, its heritage and so on, and transfer that to an improved tasting product."

Misjudging the Public

What Coke misjudged, however, was the willingness of consumers to go along with that concept. The company's change of heart wasn't just an attempt to satisfy a few disgruntled loyalists; Coke's research and sales figures suggested a far more broad-based rejection of its strategy. In some important markets, shipments fell as much as 15% in June. And when company researchers two weeks ago asked 900 consumers which Coke they liked better, 60% said "old" and only 30% "new."

Toward the end of June and in the first week of July, the company gradually began to feel it was losing control of how the public perceived its product. As the numbers in the weekly surveys grew worse, Roy Stout, the head of Coke's market-research department, began giving regular briefings to the company's top management. During one, the company president, Donald Keough, wondered whether a broader study might show a different trend. The following week the company surveyed 5,000 consumers, but the results only further confirmed the bad news.

Coke officials put some of the blame on the press for fanning public discontent. After an Atlanta newspaper quoted him as critical of new Coke, Franklin Garrett, a retired Coke public-relations executive, received an angry call from Robert Goizueta, Coke's chairman.

Until the end of May, however, Mr. Goizueta had little reason to be upset. In the first month after its introduction, new Coke showed every sign of fulfilling the chairman's declaration that the decision was "one of the easiest we ever made." Shipments to Coke bottlers during the month rose by the highest percentage in five years. New Coke was tried by a record number of people for any product, and more than three-quarters of those who tried it indicated they would eagerly buy it again.

But suddenly the mood of consumers changed. "It started all at once," says Mr. Stout. "At one point we were ahead of schedule with all of our targets. Then, it went completely the other way."

Bottlers, who are Coke's front-line contact with consumers, were the first to feel the heat. At a regional convention in Dallas June 18, a petition was circulated demanding the return of the old formula. F. M. Bellingrath, a Pine Bluff, Ark., bottler, took the message to Coke's chairman.

Meanwhile, top Coca-Cola executives in Atlanta considered alternatives, including changing the new Coke. Mr. Zyman, the marketing executive, ordered all members of his staff to monitor telephone calls coming in from consumers, to look for ideas on how the company might counter the trend.

The Customers Speak

Mr. Zyman also watched through one-way mirrors as Coke researchers interviewed focus groups of consumers about why they didn't like new Coke. After one such session in New Jersey, he decided to ask what Coke could do to get consumers to be happy with the new product. "All they could say was to bring back old Coke," Mr. Zyman says.

Coke's agonizing neared a peak just before Thursday, July 4. On Wednesday, the company's top executives met privately with the five bottlers who represent the company's largest markets. All worried that the company was confronted with a potentially dangerous situation: If the sales slide accelerated, the company might not be able to reverse the trend.

Resting at home on Thursday, says Mr. Keough, the Coke president, he decided that regardless of what embarrassment it might cause, the company had to bring back its old formula. On Friday, he began ordering departments of the company to prepare for a relaunch of the product as though a final decision had already been made.

In market research, Mr. Stout began testing alternative names for the product. Among the suggestions: Original Coke, Coke 100, Coke 1886, Old Coke and Coke 1. Several dummy commercials also were filmed announcing the move, one featuring Mr. Keough and two featuring professional actors.

Calling In the Admen

Unlike its elaborate preparations for the introduction of reformulated Coke, the company didn't include outside consultants or ad agencies in its decision making until the last minute. As a result, when the company filmed the ads, it asked McCann Erickson to send a video crew to Atlanta without explaining why.

The design of the Coke Classic package wasn't begun until two days before the announcement, requiring the company to create a phony paper label for the can it used in the commercial.

Having told Mr. Keough that he would submit his final recommendation on what the company should do last Monday, Mr. Dyson, the president of Coca-Cola U.S.A., waited until the weekend of July 6 and 7 to decide. While training for a triathalon under the Confederate monuments at Stone Mountain, Ga., he decided that the return of old Coke was the company's best option.

Last Monday, some Coke executives still wanted to wait and see whether the hostile feelings toward the company would die down. One argument held that the furor would subside once the company proceeded with plans to remove the word "new" from the label on the Coke can.

"In some ways, I think the sentiment already had begun to turn (for the better)," says Mr. Stout, the Coke market researcher. "But there also was a feeling the experience might leave deep scars."

Loss of Faith?

Another potential problem was a loss of faith, mainly among the company's bottlers, in Coke's research. At the bottler meeting with Mr. Dyson on Monday, a number of those present said they were tired of hearing the company's projections. It was shortly after that meeting that Mr. Dyson relayed his final recommendation to Mr. Keough.

Coca-Cola was forced to announce its plans on Wednesday, a day sooner than it wanted to, because of leaks on Wall Street. But even as they finished plans for a formal news conference last Thursday, Coke executives were just beginning to look at some important aspects of how they could make the new strategy work.

It wasn't clear whether the company would want to keep its current "Coke is It" advertising campaign or to what extent the company would run ads broadcasting the reappearance of old Coke.

Over the past weekend, Mr. Stout began an elaborate research effort to determine how the announcement has affected the company's reputation, its products and its credibility with consumers.

"This company is exposed in a way that it never has been before," one of the company's top ad officials says. "There's a good reason, though, why we earned a reputation as smart marketers. If any company can work its way out of this mess, we can."

SOURCE: John Koten and Scott Kilman, "How Coke's Decision to Offer 2 Colas Undid 4½ Years of Planning." Reprinted by permission of *The Wall Street Journal.* © Dow Jones & Company, Inc., July 15, 1985. All rights reserved.

DISCUSSION QUESTIONS

1. Assuming Coca-Cola's top management considered Pepsi's erosion of Coke's market share a major threat, identify and discuss Coke's strategic alternatives for countering the threat.
2. Discuss the advantages and limitations of the introduction of New Coke.
3. Critique Coca-Cola's buyer research, indicating changes or additional research that could have helped management more fully evaluate the proposed New Coke introduction.
4. Discuss the marketing implications of reintroducing Coca-Cola Classic.

STRATEGIC APPLICATION 6-2

K MART APPAREL BUYERS

Masan, South Korea—Back home in New Jersey, Joseph Antonini wouldn't rate more than a glance and a smile of greeting while on a factory tour. So Mr. Antonini is clearly embarrassed by what is happening here.

As he rides up to the Hanil Synthetic Fiber Industrial Co. plant, security guards straighten and bark a word that sounds like "choof." Workers spring to open Mr. Antonini's door, and dozens of applauding Hanil office workers crowd around, hailing the startled visitor. Mr. Antonini and his associate, Ronald L. Buch, are handed large floral displays.

"Can you beat that?" asks Mr. Antonini, the president of K mart Apparel Corp.

Gulping Potent Liquor

Lots of people are trying. A few days earlier, Mr. Antonini survived a 21-course banquet in his honor at a Chinese clothing factory. Then there was the *mao-tai* party, an affair of fortitude at which toasts were continually exchanged in gulped servings of the potent Chinese liquor. "I tasted that for days," Mr. Antonini says.

This is an Asian buying trip. It sounds like great fun, but it is serious business for the 30 or so buyers of K mart Apparel, the clothing arm of the U.S. discount chain. The buyers, often with their bosses in tow, scour a dozen Asian nations for 1985 fall merchandise worth hundreds of millions of dollars. They look for bargains, but they also use the trip to make contacts for new sources of supply and to learn what the competition is doing.

It is a demanding, ritualized process of negotiating to the third decimal point by day, cementing deals, and then renewing good will at night in an atmosphere of luxury, power, and privilege.

All for "The Pencil"

"It can go to your head," notes Mr. Antonini, a 20-year K mart veteran who remembers living in one-room apartments as a young store manager. Now he and his buyers fly first-class, stay only in luxury hotels and drive around Hong Kong in Mercedes-Benz limousines. In Hong Kong a merchandise source treats Mr. Antonini to a $400 bottle of wine at dinner. And in Japan, a source serves him rich meals of Kobe beef at $200 a plate.

Indeed, those with "the pencil"—the buyers' term for the authority to order merchandise—are treated royally. "But once you lose the pencil, it's over," says the wife of one K mart executive. "You've got to understand it's for the pencil, not you."

Those pencils are busiest through late fall when hundreds of apparel retailers and importers descend on Asian capitals to compete for the best values and the vendors' production time. "It's like a convention of old buddies from Seventh Avenue," says a buyer, referring to the New York City street at the center of the garment industry.

The lure is quality, often superior to that of U.S. products at prices held down by low Asian pay scales. Japan, Hong Kong, Taiwan and South Korea—the Big Four of Asian countries from which the U.S. imports consumer goods—produce some of the world's best merchandise, from fabrics to electronic goods.

Adding Quality

Even developing nations, such as Bangladesh, Mauritius, and Indonesia, find it relatively easy to produce apparel that appeals to the U.S. market. "You can add a dollar's worth of quality for 10 cents of cost," says Gil Waschman, senior vice president for non-apparel goods at Target Stores, a Dayton-Hudson Corp. unit.

But Asian buying is fraught with difficulties. Travel can be arduous. Communication can be sticky. "Our buyers learned that the Japanese say yes often," says Michael Rouleau, a former Target executive vice president. "But it's 'Yes, we can,' or 'Yes, we can't.' You have to learn which yes it is."

A tricky problem is dealing with the quotas. The U.S. limits apparel and textile imports through a combination of treaties and unilateral embargoes. Each nation has its own system for allocating its quota. That confusing system bedevils buyers trying to secure sources of supply. Target bought wool sweaters from China for several years, but because of pricing and quota limits, China refused to make any more for 1984. Wal-Mart Stores Inc.'s shirt importer had to scramble last fall when Indonesian production was unexpectedly embargoed by the U.S., for a time trapping 480,000 dress shirts. "You don't control your own destiny in these places," says a spokesman for the importer.

After months of planning, K mart begins a part of its Asian buying trip in Europe. As part of its goal to offer more upscale merchandise, K mart sends Mr. Buch and several others to gather sweater designs from London, Paris and other European fashion capitals. They buy 80 examples of the latest in "leading edge" fashions, including sweaters with harsh geometric patterns, clashing colors or unusual features, such as ribbed shoulders or quilted yokes. K mart intends to sell acrylic and wool-blend versions of the sweaters in its stores in about a year. (The company says it isn't doing anything illegal because fashion designs aren't protected by the law and because K mart is "emulating" or improving, not copying, the designs.)

K mart knows that nine out of 10 of its customers will be attracted to the flashy look but will take the basic cardigan and pullover anyway. "You must have both," says Mr. Buch, vice president and general merchandise manager. "We spend more time working on 2,000-dozen fashion sweaters than we do on 20,000-dozen basics," he says.

The buyers' next stop is Korea. They want to compare the sweater-maker Hanil's ability to make complicated sweaters with that of a competing factory in Taiwan that has done superior work with difficult designs. K mart also needs to review Hanil's progress on many of the retailer's basic sweaters.

But there is a catch. The Korean government requires its manufacturers to negotiate prices higher than a national-average benchmark price for their goods each year. Hanil made about three million sweaters for K mart last year, but the Korean government said it must cut production by 120,000 sweaters because last year it negotiated prices that were too low.

K mart makes Hanil strut its stuff. In an office crammed with thousands of sweaters, Gary Kovie, a senior buyer, compares each original with Hanil's copies. The manufacturer hasn't done well on every complicated, high-fashion design. He examines an original Claude Montana ski sweater, with bold X's and O's marching across the chest. Hanil's sample is short several characters, and those that are there are the wrong size.

But the Korean company does well on the more-basic patterns. Mr. Kovie makes changes nonetheless. He snips a yarn from one sweater and asks that it be used in another. Styles are rebuilt; crew-neck sweaters become V-necks, sleeveless sweaters sprout sleeves. He holds up a ski sweater with a snowflake design on the chest and shoulders. Picking up yarns of blue, white, navy and gray, he decides which could substitute for the colors in the patterns. "The white might show through too much," offers a K mart staffer. Mr. Kovie announces gray, blue and natural as his choices, and the Hanil man across the table scribbles the order furiously.

Sometimes Mr. Buch, the boss, intervenes. "Don't get too wild now," he tells Mr. Kovie, who is looking at a striped sweater. "Black and gray is more salable than black and red," he says. Mr. Kovie changes the color combination.

Reproducing a Crack

Like other companies, K mart takes an active role in the manufacturing process. Failure to be specific can produce startling results. One year, a gift-ware buyer was horrified when an Asian factory, faithful to a demitasse sample damaged during shipment from Europe, reproduced thousands with a tiny crack down the side. And Target was astonished when the maker of an inflatable rubber boat put it in a box with a Chinese sampan on the cover.

The laborious sweater-ordering process goes on for days, punctuated only by breaks for Cokes or coffee—the Americans won't drink the water because they fear they will get sick—or glances at a ball game on television.

Throughout the process, prices are negotiated. K mart can win low prices because its immense orders keep the knitting machines running longer and more efficiently. It also takes delivery of merchandise earlier, helping factories through slack periods. The formula works with Hanil. In the first step of negotiations, Hanil accepts K mart's first price without the usual haggling, Mr. Antonini says. By the time the process ends in early January, Hanil has won half of K mart's imported-sweater production, including four of 12 contested fashion designs.

Evenings are often a welcome respite. Daewoo Corp., a large Korean industrial concern that makes shirts for K mart sponsors the first formal dinner, at the Seoul Hilton, where a three-foot carved ice tower supports the K mart corporate symbol. The buyers and executives are served from a French menu that includes frog-leg consommé, and fish and scallop with watercress sauce. Toasts and testimonials are mixed in with small talk. Mr. Buch raises his glass and toasts "the good times, when prices could have risen but didn't, and the bad times, when we both took risks to help each other." The buyers say the evening was comparatively tame. Last year, Kim Woo Chong, Daewoo's chairman, entertained K mart in his hotel penthouse with South Korea's finest opera singer.

Socializing Required

Business is rarely discussed at the dinners—similar ones are given in Taiwan, Hong Kong and Japan. Rather, buyers say they go not to make deals but because attendance is expected. "The socializing is part of the process," says Mr. Buch. "If we didn't go to dinner, it would be an insult."

Two K mart and Daewoo incidents illustrate how the Asian trade is built on business and personal relationships. K mart helped Daewoo get its start in the apparel business with a pattern of early and steady orders. This paid off for K mart in 1983, when Daewoo initially said it couldn't meet the retailer's shirt-production needs. But Mr. Buch was able to obtain the needed additional shirts by personally intervening with Daewoo's chairman in a half-hour meeting in which they relived old times.

Daewoo has reciprocated with small favors of its own. When Norman Milley, the president of K mart stores, complained that the company's shirts wouldn't fit his 15-inch neck and 44-inch waist, Daewoo made up a special batch of shirts with a 15-inch neck, medium yoke and extra-large body.

The Korean buying trip also gives the K mart buyers a chance to see what competitors are doing. On a courtesy tour of a Daewoo shirt plant, Mr. Buch admires a crisply packaged K mart Ketch brand shirt. He also examines a shirt made by Daewoo under the Oleg Cassini label that can sell in department stores for twice the price of the Ketch shirt. Mr. Buch tells the Daewoo executive that the shirts are of nearly equal quality, and the executives agree. "This is why I'll have an 8% market share in dress shirts in three years," he says.

("Our shirt is better made, has a better finish, than the K mart shirt," asserts George W. Camacho, vice president and sales manager of Burma Bibas Inc., the holder of the Oleg Cassini dress-shirt license. "They may be made in the same factory, but our construction is different.")

In Hong Kong, the K mart shirt buyers keep busy. K mart wants Smart Shirts Ltd., a unit of St. Louis-based Kellwood Co., to make some of its sport shirts. Smart Shirts asks whether K mart needs all of its previously committed production time, an indication that Smart Shirts wants to make expensive shirts for others. (R. H. Macy Co.; Saks Fifth Avenue, a unit of B. A. T. Industries PLC; and Lands' End are among its customers.) But K mart says it does need the production time, and Smart Shirts agrees to honor its commitment.

K mart quickly agrees to Smart Shirts' price of about $5 a long-sleeve shirt, even though it is higher than it would like. K mart gets the concession that the pattern on the pockets, flaps and seams will match the pattern on each shirt, a feature that normally costs 12½ cents a shirt more. Usually, protracted discussions on prices are the rule. Haggling over details as small as a dyed snap can be important. For instance, a retailer can save three cents a garment, or $36,000 on a typical order, by insisting that the snap be part of the deal, not an extra.

Why a Shirt Costs $20

Retailers enjoy a handsome profit by buying shirts in Asia. T. F. Ying, the president of Smart Shirts, says the average polyester shirt takes about $1.50 of material. Fine cotton would cost between $4 and $6. Special features raise the cost: 20 cents a shirt extra for single-needle tailoring or 30 cents a shirt extra for 16 to 18 stitches an inch instead of 12. Thus, a chiefly cotton dress shirt selling for more than $20 in a U.S. department store can cost as little as $5 to buy from an Asian manufacturer.

On the Japanese leg of the trip, K mart executives visit several Osaka-area trading companies. Labor costs in Japan are about 25% higher than in Taiwan or Korea, some manufacturers say. K mart deals with trading companies that contract orders out to neighboring nations, often at lower prices than what K mart could negotiate by itself. But this year, prices are higher than usual at some suppliers, and the trip hasn't been fruitful quickly.

A courtesy call at Hamamatsu Chuo Orimono K. K., a trading house known more simply by Westerners as Rainbow, helps K mart's score. The sales manager, during an otherwise dull showing of basic corduroy merchandise, holds up a pair of pants that he says Rainbow obtained for Lane Bryant, a unit of Limited Inc. and a major U.S. chain specializing in quality clothes for large women.

"You make that to Lane Bryant specification?" asks Mr. Antonini. Rainbow does. K mart has accidentally found a supply of pants that match Lane Bryant stock and that it could sell at discount prices. "Would you make the same thing for us?" Mr. Antonini asks. The sales manager agrees, and Mr. Antonini later sends a buyer to Rainbow to clinch the deal. "You never know what you'll find," he says.

Bargain Basement Prices

Buyers find bargains for themselves, too. One brings home a fur coat from Seoul, which he says he got for a bargain-basement price. Another traveler gets pearls in Hong Kong and a $500 watch he says would cost twice that in the U.S. The buyers wear trophies from past overseas trips, like custom-made suits and gold Rolex watches.

By late December, almost all of K mart's commitments for fall 1985 are made. Imports make up two-thirds of its sweater line; 100% of the dress shirts are from Asia and Mauritius. (About 10% of all merchandise is imported.) All the buyers were able to find supplies, and prices ranged from 2% below last year's to 5% above. "It was a good trip," Mr. Antonini says.

But next fall's selling season remains uncertain. No one knows whether consumers will be in the buying mood. K mart's more affluent customers might be turned off by the washable-blend sweaters demanded by its low-income and moderate-income shoppers. And lower-income customers might not like the designer knock-offs. Success is selling 80% of any style at its normal price. "Anything less than that can chip at profitability," says Mr. Buch.

"There's been a lot written about the uncertainties of 1985," says Mr. Buch.

"Buying isn't a science. It's a crapshoot. You can never be sure you're right."

SOURCE: Steve Weiner, "Asian Bargains: K mart Apparel Buyers Hopscotch the Orient to Find Quality Goods." Reprinted by permission of *The Wall Street Journal.* © Dow Jones & Company, Inc., March 19, 1985. All rights reserved.

DISCUSSION QUESTIONS

1. What are some of the important differences in buying apparel in Asia compared to the United States?
2. How likely is bribery of the organizational buyer to be part of the apparel buying process? What strategies can management use to eliminate opportunities for bribery?
3. Considering the various influences on organizational buying, which factors are particularly important in K Mart's apparel buying situations?
4. Does the buyer or seller control the buying process for imported apparel?

CHAPTER 7

Analyzing the Strategic Situation and Competition

Cie, Generale des Ets. Michelin is the world's second-largest tire maker. This company's strategic responses to competitive threats during the last decade provide an interesting look at competition in action.[1] Until the start of the 1980s, Michelin held the lead position in the radial tire market. The French tire maker's product differentiation strategy proved to be so successful that other major competitors around the world were forced to develop radial tires. By 1980 the Goodyear Tire & Rubber Company and others offered high performance tires through strong distribution channels. In 1985 Michelin's top management was revamping the firm's marketing strategy in an attempt to be a survivor in the shakeout occurring in the mature global tire industry. Michelin entered the United States market with a proven radial tire, spending over $3 billion from 1978 to 1982 for five plants and a test center. During this huge expansion the recession flattened the tire market. The market domination approach used by Michelin was too ambitious and poorly timed. Other strategic errors were made, including an attempt to obtain a higher price than U.S. brands because of the Michelin name and reputation for quality. The European tire maker irritated the tire dealer network by its take-it-or-leave-it approach. In 1985 the results of Michelin's revamped marketing strategy began to appear in the marketplace. In an attempt to catch up with the competition that had developed innovative tire designs much earlier than Michelin, management introduced an all-weather tire against competitors' third-generation competing tires. Michelin's marketing efforts were increased and refocused on consumer needs and wants. Management also expanded research and development efforts to strengthen its 18 percent share of the world tire market—second to Goodyear Tire &

EXHIBIT 7-1 Determinants of Marketing Strategy Situation

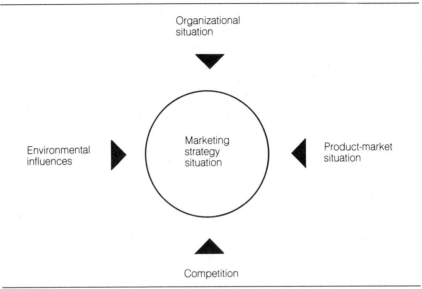

Organizational
situation

Environmental
influences

Marketing
strategy
situation

Product-market
situation

Competition

Rubber. Michelin was also encountering strong competition from Japanese tire makers such as Bridgestone Corp., which was challenging Michelin's market position.

In developing a marketing strategy, the essential starting point should be to understand the strategic situation that confronts an organization. Michelin's experience shows the importance of evaluating the customer, understanding buyer preferences, and monitoring environmental threats as one formulates a marketing strategy.

As shown in Exhibit 7-1, the strategic factors that determine the strategic situation consist of (1) the organizational situation, (2) the product-market situation, (3) the competition, and (4) environmental influences. An examination of the nature and scope of each determinant provides important insights as to how it may impact a firm's strategic marketing situation. A diversified corporation that is active in various markets and product categories should consider the marketing strategy situation for each product-market in its corporate or SBU portfolio.

Strategic marketing decisions regarding the selection of market targets and the positioning strategy (product, distribution, price, and promotion) should be guided by the existing strategic situation and estimated future trends. The relationship between strategic situation and marketing strategy selection is shown in Exhibit 7-2. Various fac-

---

EXHIBIT 7-2 Marketing Strategy Process

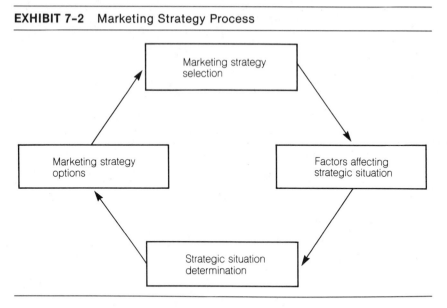

---

tors may affect the strategic situation. Typically, a limited set of action alternatives is feasible for a given situation. We should select the appropriate marketing strategy from the available strategies. The marketing strategy process in Exhibit 7-2 is continuous; it emphasizes that strategic situations change over time and should be regularly assessed by management.

In this chapter we first consider the factors that determine the strategic marketing situation faced by a company. The organizational situation, product-market situation, competition, and environmental influences are examined. A step-by-step approach to analyzing the strategic situation follows. Next, we consider the marketing strategy options appropriate for various situations. Finally, we present and illustrate an approach to conducting a competitor analysis.

ORGANIZATIONAL SITUATION

An assessment of the organizational situation should include a consideration of the stage of corporate development, the corporate culture, the size of firm, and the market position. The organizational situation summary should indicate the firm's strength and weaknesses.

Stage of Corporate Development

Chapter 2 considers the stages of corporate development. We now reintroduce and expand this discussion because it provides a useful start-

---

EXHIBIT 7-3 Companies at Various Stages of Corporate Development

Stage	Company
Entrepreneurial	California Closets—home remodeling services to make closets more efficient.
Growth	Guest Supply—supplier of customized personal care amenities to the hotel and lodging industry.
Maturity	Pier One—specialty retailer of imported gifts and home furnishings.
Diversification	The Limited—women's apparel retailer serving various segments including The Limited Stores, Lane Bryant, and Victoria's Secret.
Retrenchment	General Mills—diversified from the food processing core business into restaurants, toys, and speciality retailing. In 1985 plans were announced to sell the toy business and certain specialty retailing units.

---

ing point for assessing a marketing strategy situation. The directions of development beyond the core business include expansion into new markets and/or products and diversification. Examples of companies at various stages of development are shown in Exhibit 7-3. The present discussion centers on the marketing strategy implications of the corporate development stage.

Entrepreneurial Stage.   A new company starts with one or more entrepreneurs. For example, in some industries, such as electronics, employees may leave the firm and start a new company. The marketing characteristics of newly formed firms are entrepreneurial in nature.[2] Founders rely upon prior business and personal relationships to obtain sales. Often products are custom-designed. After a few years management may decide to move toward a larger customer base by using a more standardized product offering.

California Closets, one of a number of companies that has recently carved out a market niche in the home-remodeling market by making closets more efficient, provides an interesting profile of business development.[3] Neil Balter started California Closets as a part-time business while attending Pierce Community College in Los Angeles. He expanded the business from sales of $50,000 in 1979 to a $6 million business in 1984 with 24 franchises across the country.

> Franchisees pay $45,000 for a package that includes vans, equipment and inventory. The company gets 5% of their revenue. Franchisees agree to spend another 5% of their revenue on local advertising, or pay that amount to the parent company. The entire company spent about $600,000 last year on advertising, which Mr. Balter believes is crucial to its success. "We literally have to go out and educate the public," he says. "They've never heard about redecorating a closet before."[4]

Growth. In moving beyond the entrepreneurial stage, there are three possible avenues for growth:

1. *Increasing the customer base by expanding market coverage.* California Closets utilized franchising to add to its geographical market coverage.
2. *Expanding the product line and/or mix of lines.* California Closets has added accessories (hangers and tie racks) to its core service.
3. *Moving into new markets with existing products.* California Closets is also planning to use this avenue for growth by developing and marketing a do-it-yourself closet kit.

During the corporate growth stage, marketing activities normally become more formalized, although the sales function represents the primary marketing activity. Coordination of marketing program components, such as product planning, distribution, pricing, advertising, personal selling, and marketing research, is fragmented and incomplete. And the orientation of the marketing function has a narrow tactical focus. Top management often maintains responsibility for product planning and pricing during the growth stage.[5]

Maturity. When a company reaches maturity, it has developed expertise in the areas of technology (e.g., electronics), manufacturing or distribution, accounting and finance, and marketing. A successful company should have accumulated substantial financial resources at this stage in corporate development. Mature companies may not have strengths in all business functions. Recall, for example, our earlier discussion of the flaws in Michelin's marketing strategy.

Diversification. Hershey Foods Corporation lost the No. 1 position in the candy market to Mars Inc. in the 1970s. Interestingly, until 1969 Hershey spent no money on consumer advertising. Since that time Hershey has become an aggressive and highly successful marketer. New products, extensive advertising, and diversification into food-related businesses such as the Friendly chain of about 700 retail restaurants are major components of Hershey's marketing strategy:

> Under Hershey, Friendly has become "much more marketing and new-product-oriented," says Carl DeBiase, president of Restaurant Trends, an industry newsletter. It has tripled its promotional spending, opened about 75 new units, and remodeled existing outlets. Along with new entrees, such as fried scallops and spaghetti, the chain has launched a bevy of new ice cream products, many using Hershey ingredients. Says Chairman Dearden: "Friendly seems to be a real growth vehicle on a real roll now."[6]

Expansion into new business areas increases the marketing strategy needs of a firm. Typically, each business unit and each market target require a separate and distinct marketing strategy, although some aspects of strategy may benefit from the firm's experience in the core business. For example, Dayton Hudson's retailing expertise and knowledge of consumer markets were beneficial in its diversification into the Target, Mervyn's, and B. Dalton retail businesses.

Divestment. After trying diversification some corporations may decide to eliminate business units or market segments. Examples include General Mills, Inc.'s divestment of specialty retailing units and Exxon's exit from the office equipment business. A divestment situation tends to hold marketing strategy at its current level until divestment is complete. Loss of key management personnel may occur because of the future uncertainty of the business.

Corporate Culture, Size of Firm, and Market Position

Corporate culture also affects an organization's marketing strategy situation. Organizational culture is a complex combination of the business environment, its values (basic concepts and beliefs of an organization), its heroes or role models, its rites and rituals, and its cultural network or informal communications.[7] Although a corporate culture is difficult to quantify or even to describe, it is clear that companies have cultures, and that there is a linkage between culture and performance:

> Every business—in fact every organization—has a culture. Sometimes it is fragmented and difficult to read from the outside—some people are loyal to their bosses, others are loyal to the union, still others care only about their colleagues who work in the sales territories of the Northeast. If you ask employees why they work, they will answer "because we need the money." On the other hand, sometimes the culture of an organization is very strong and cohesive; everyone knows the goals of the corporation, and they are working for them. Whether weak or strong, culture has a powerful influence throughout an organization; it affects practically everything—from who gets promoted and what decisions are made, to how employees dress and what sports they play. Because of this impact, we think that culture also has a major effect on the success of the business.[8]

Using size of firm and market position, Philip Kotler identifies the types of firms that exist in a variety of industries:[9]

> *Market-Leader:* This firm has the largest market share in the industry and often is the leader in strategic actions such as introducing new products, pricing, and aggressive promotion. Examples include Goodyear in tires, IBM in computers, and Acme in brick.
>
> *Market-Challenger:* Some industries contains one or more firms that are attempting to gain market leadership through aggressive marketing efforts. American Airlines in the air transportation industry is illustrative.

Market-Follower: This category contains firms that are willing to follow the actions of leaders regarding new products, pricing, distribution, and other marketing actions. The higher performing firms in this category typically possess one or more advantage over the market leaders such as geographical concentration, lower wage rates, etc. TWA, Northwest, and Delta airlines are illustrative market-followers.[10]

Market-Nicher: Concentrating on one or more segments of the market is often an effective strategy for small firms. Differential advantage over competing firms may be achieved through specialization, product features, special expertise, or other strengths. Examples include Estée Lauder in cosmetics, Nucor in steel, and Tootsie Roll in candy.

This classification scheme is useful for placing industry members into categories by size and market position.

Organizational Situation Summary

An assessment of the organization's *strengths* and *weaknesses* relative to the product-market under consideration is essential to gauging the strategic situation. We can use the following information to summarize the firm's strengths and weaknesses in each product-market of interest:

- Business scope and objectives
- Market position
- Market target(s) and customer base
- Marketing program positioning strategy
- Financial, technical, and operating capabilities
- Management experience and capabilities
- Special capabilities (e.g., access to resources, patents)

PRODUCT-MARKET SITUATION

The *product life cycle* and the *product-market characteristics and structure* also offer useful insights into the nature and scope of the marketing strategy situation confronting a particular firm.

Product Life Cycle

Products, like people, move through life cycles. The life cycle of a typical product is shown in Exhibit 7–4. Sales begin at the time of introduction and increase over the pattern shown. Profits initially lag sales since expenses often exceed sales during the initial stage of the product life cycle (PLC) as a result of heavy introductory expenses. Industry

EXHIBIT 7-4 Life Cycle of a Typical Product

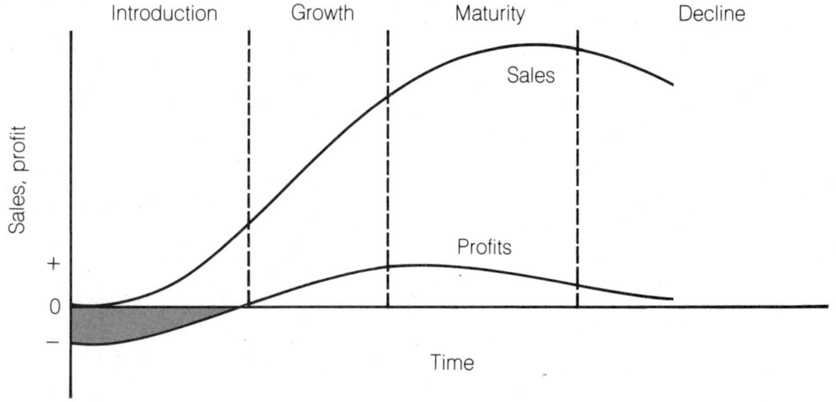

sales and profits decline after the product reaches the maturity stage. Often profits fall off before sales. A closer look at each PLC stage will provide important insights into the nature of competition over the life cycle of a product. We also examine the PLC in Chapters 10 and 11 as we discuss guidelines for positioning strategy and for product strategy.

Introduction. Following a successful introduction, sales increase as people recognize the benefit offered by the product. Normally only a single firm has the product. As buyer interest expands because of the firm's promotional efforts and informal communications among people, market penetration continues. Although the firm that first enters the market with a new product holds a monopoly position, this situation often changes rapidly unless there are substantial market entry barriers, such as high research and development costs, technical expertise, and patents.

If the sales and profit experience of the first firm to enter the market is favorable, competition is likely to follow. Consider, for example, the filmless camera planned for introduction in late 1985 by the Japanese electronics manufacturer, Hitachi.[11] The camera, which sold initially at $2,000, records images on a tiny magnetic disc. Pictures can be viewed on a television screen or printed out as color snapshots on a printer. While the initial picture quality was not up to par with color photos made from film, the innovation was a potential threat to conventional camera and film makers such as Polaroid Corporation and Eastman Kodak Company. Not surprisingly, both firms began expanding their electronic imaging research. Reducing price and improving picture quality will be important factors to the success of filmless photography.

Growth. As a product moves into this stage, both sales and profits increase rapidly. Industry profits peak and may start to decline near the end of the stage. New competitors will be attracted if sales opportunities are favorable and a profit potential exists. The firm that first introduced the product is faced with rapidly developing competition. For example, before Hitachi had even introduced its filmless camera in 1985, Canon, Sony, Minolta, Panasonic, and Copal were expected to market their versions of the camera in 1986.[12] And several other Japanese companies were in the final stages of developing similar products.

If a product follows a typical PLC, recognizing when it is nearing the end of the growth stage is an important strategic consideration. Aggressive competition is on the horizon and will demand that successful firms plan and implement effective marketing strategies. Achieving cost, marketing, and other advantages will help firms to be successful against weaker competitors.

Maturity. Sales continue to expand as the industry moves into the maturity stage of the PLC. Competition is normally very intense as market demand begins to level off. Interestingly, the conventional camera and film market was at this stage at the time the filmless camera was introduced. If successful, the new method of photography could have serious impact upon a variety of firms, such as film makers, film processors, and chemical producers.

The number of competitors will typically be greatest at the maturity stage. Prices may decline rapidly during maturity, although firms may try to differentiate themselves from competing firms in order to obtain price advantages. The use of price competition during 1985 in the airline industry was illustrative of competitor actions in a mature market, where differentiation is difficult. Note that new competitors may enter the industry during maturity. Although successful entry at this stage is possible, unless the new entrant has an important advantage over existing firms, success is doubtful.

Decline. Some products remain in the maturity stage for a long period while others reach maturity in a short time. Decline is the stage where industry sales move below the peak level. In some markets the decline may be substantial. The number of competitors often decreases during this stage, although those remaining are firms with strong marketing capabilities, cost advantages, and experience with the product. Products in this stage may face competitive threats from new products if customer needs continue to exist. Consider, for example, the decline in purchases of manual typewriters because buyers have decided to purchase electronic typewriters and word processors.

EXHIBIT 7-5 Portions of the Product Life Cycles for Home Electronic Components

	Factory Sales to Dealers (in millions of units)				
	1981	*1982*	*1983*	*1984*	*1985**
Color TVs	11	11	14	16	16
VCRs	1	2	4	8	11
Audio systems	3	3	3	3	3
Compact-disk players	—	—	.035	.208	.6
Home computers	†	2	5	5	4
Home-computer software	†	†	35	40	45
Video-game cartridges	30	60	75	54	20

*Projected †No figures available

SOURCE: Electronic Industries Association, John Marcom, Jr., "Movie-Like Realism in Computers Could Put Sizzle in Home Market." Reprinted by permission of *The Wall Street Journal.*

PLC Characteristics

Examples of products at different stages in their life cycle are shown in Exhibit 7-5. While the table does not provide complete PLC data, we can make an approximate determination of the PLC stage in 1985. For example, compact-disk players appear to be moving into the growth stage while video-game cartridges are at the decline stage. VCRs seem to be somewhere between growth and early maturity.

Some products die quickly in the introduction stage while others take a long time to reach the growth stage. Products that do succeed may be difficult to track through the various PLC stages, since product life cycles vary a great deal in length. In general, PLCs are getting shorter as a result of rapid development of new technology, aggressive marketing, and the willingness of buyers to try new products. The marketing efforts of industry members may alter the shape of the PLC through product modification, market development, and other activities. Environmental forces may also affect the PLC.

It is important to recognize that the PLC is not a theory. Instead, it is a general pattern of sales and profits that various products seem to follow over time. The concept applies to an industry rather than to a single firm.

Product-Market Characteristics and Structure

The discussion of product-market structure in Chapter 5 is useful in determining alternative types of competition, as shown in Exhibit 7-6.

EXHIBIT 7-6 Competition at Different Product-Market Levels

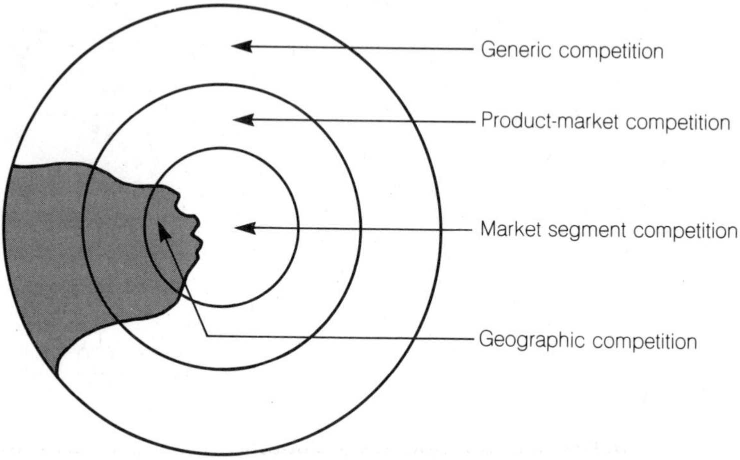

- Generic competition
- Product-market competition
- Market segment competition
- Geographic competition

These include generic, product-market, market segment, and geographic levels of competition.

Generic Competition. Generic competition exists among suppliers of products that satisfy a similar set of generic needs such as photography. The electronic imaging camera first introduced in 1985 by Hitachi competes with various conventional forms of photographic equipment, supplies, and services. The new camera offers a substitution threat to existing camera producers.

Product-Market Competition. Firms competing within the same product-market represent competition within an industry. An example is the U.S. airline industry in which major commercial airlines compete against each other in a deregulated market. Unless all user needs within the product-market are very similar and no major differences exist among brands, it is unlikely that all brands in an industry are directly competing with each other. Instead, competition within segments of the product-market is more likely.

Market Segment Competition. The firms at this level are competing for customers in a segment of the product-market. In contrast to the general competition that occurs within an industry, market segment competitors are called key competitors, each competing with specific brands. Coca-Cola, for example, is competing with Pepsi-Cola. Another example is the medium- to high-price quality hotels that are targeting business travelers. On a national basis, Marriott, Hyatt, and similar hotels fall into this set of key competitors.

Geographic Competition. This type of competition may occur at any of the above three product-market levels. While geography is a basis for segmenting a market, it is also useful to consider the firms competing in a particular geographical area within a segment, product-market, or generic market. Geographical competition may occur on a global basis, in areas of the world, in specific countries, in regions within countries, and in metropolitan areas.

Competition over the PLC

The nature and scope of competition vary substantially during the life cycle stages of products. By considering the characteristics of each PLC stage in combination with the types of competition that occur at different product market levels, we can gain useful insights regarding competition, as shown in Exhibit 7-7.

At the introduction stage competition is primarily from alternate product forms that meet the same generic needs. The exact nature of competition will depend upon the life cycle stage of the products competing with the new product. Consider, for example, the filmless camera and its acknowledged picture quality limitations compared to conventional snapshots. Initial market entry opportunities appear to exist in newspaper photography and business applications:

> If today's electronic cameras can't compete with Kodachrome, they can take pictures suitable for reproduction in newspapers. News photographers, along with commercial and industrial applications, are the first targets for the filmless cameras. During the Los Angeles Olympic Summer Games, prototype cameras from Sony and Canon were used by photographers from the Japanese newspapers *Asahi Shimbun* and *Yomiuri Shimbun,* respectively, who relayed their photos by phone to Japan in time to make the morning editions.[13]

Competition is primarily focused on product features for products at the growth stage, with many of the firms in the industry competing on a direct basis. As the product moves into maturity, market segmentation is often used; this results in subsets of competitors going after specific market segments. The wise choice of segments may enable firms with a small market share to compete with giants of the industry. Finally, in the decline stage competition may vary from market segmentation to generic, depending upon the particular characteristics of the situation. If decline is rapid and there are few firms remaining in the industry, the major competitive threat may be outside the industry. A more gradual decline could lead to a concentration of the competition with specific segments.

An important factor in gaining a strategic advantage through segmentation is the extent to which differentiation in products and/or

---

EXHIBIT 7-7 Competition over the Product Life Cycle

Product Life Cycle Stage	Type of Competition
Introduction	Generic
Growth	Product-market
Maturity	Market segment
Decline	Market segment/generic

---

markets exist. In a situation involving a commodity product where there are no differences between brands and where buyers' needs are similar, it will be difficult to achieve differentiation.

COMPETITIVE SITUATION

The examination of competition during the product life cycle and at different product-market levels provides insights into different types and intensities of competition. In gaining further understanding of the competitive situation, it is useful to consider the industry environment and important forces that affect competition.

Industry Environment

A logical starting point in examining the structure of an industry is to consider the number and size of competing firms. Another structural characteristic is the degree of differentiation that exists among competitors on the basis of the market served and the positioning strategy of each firm. The former refers to market segmentation and the latter may include product differentiation as well as differentiation of other components of the marketing mix.

Michael E. Porter suggests that an industry environment is influenced by the extent of concentration of its firms, the stage of its maturity, and its exposure to international competition. Five illustrative generic environments indicate the range of industry structures:[14]

> *Emerging.* These industries are newly formed or reformed, created by various factors such as a new technology, the changing needs of buyers, and the identification of unmet needs by suppliers.
> *Fragmented.* In this type of industry, no company has a strong position regarding market share or influence. Typically, a large number of relatively small firms comprise the industry. There are many fragmented industries in the United States.
> *Transitional.* These industries are shifting from rapid growth to maturity, as represented by the product life cycle. The personal

computer industry is probably currently at the transitional
stage.

Declining. In this type of industry, real sales are declining. Producers of movie cameras are illustrative of a declining industry. Note
that this industry category is not cyclical such as the sales of machine tools. Rather, a declining industry is actually fading away
instead of experiencing a temporary decline.

Global. Firms in this category compete on a global basis. The earlier
tire industry illustration involving Michelin represents a global
industry.

The five industry categories are neither exhaustive nor mutually
exclusive. Moreover, changing environmental and industry conditions
may alter the industry classification. Porter provides several supporting analyses for the above classifications, using market share data and
other comparisons. The implications of the strategy situation vary
substantially by type of industry.

Competitive Forces

The traditional view of competition can be expanded by recognizing
five competitive forces that determine industry performance:

1. Rivalry among existing firms.
2. Threat of new entrants.
3. Threat of substitute products.
4. Bargaining power of suppliers.
5. Bargaining power of buyers.[15]

The first force recognizes that active competition among firms
helps determine industry performance. The second force recognizes
that the possibility of new competitors entering the market may affect
the existing competitive situation. Existing firms may attempt to discourage new competition through aggressive expansion and other
types of entry barriers. The third force acknowledges the potential impact of substitutes, such as the filmless camera. The fourth force is concerned with the power of suppliers upon firms in an industry. For example, the high costs of labor have had a major impact on the airline
industry. Finally, buyers may exert power upon suppliers. Sears Roebuck & Co., for example, has a significant influence upon suppliers of
its various lines of products. The intensity of each force is influenced by
industry structure. A major consequence of this view of competition is
that the competitive arena may be altered as a result of the impact of
the five forces upon the industry. For example, in the case of diamonds,
all five forces are at low or negligible levels of intensity because of De-
Beers's global control of diamond distribution. In contrast, where low

barriers of entry exist, the number of firms tends to increase, leading to greater rivalry among competitors. Strategies of individual firms can also influence the five forces.

The five competitive forces also highlight the existence of vertical and horizontal types of competition. Horizontal competition consists of rivalry among firms in the same industry, such as personal computer producers. Vertical competition involves rivalry among and within distribution channels. The intensity of vertical competition is related, in part, to the bargaining power of suppliers and buyers. The location (level) of an organization in its distribution channel and the extent of its control over the channel may affect the marketing strategy situation. For example, the marketing strategy for an Ethan Allen furniture dealer consists essentially of implementing the producer's strategy. Individual members of corporate-owned or corporate-controlled channels have limited control over marketing strategy formulation. Thus an important strategic issue is whether or not a firm controls its channel of distribution.

ENVIRONMENTAL INFLUENCES

Economic, social, technological, governmental, and natural influences may affect a marketing strategy situation in various ways, often impacting the market opportunity and competitive structure. Environmental influences fall into two categories: (1) an *industrywide influence* that may be long-term in nature and may possibly represent a permanent alteration in the strategic situation confronting a firm, and (2) *a company-specific influence* that may be either a temporary or permanent alteration in the strategic situation. The essential difference between the two influences is that the industry situation calls upon us to adjust our marketing strategy on the assumption that the situation will prevail for an extended period in the future and will affect all firms in the industry.

Industrywide Influence

The deregulation of transportation services illustrates this type of influence. While reregulation may occur in the future, the managements of firms in this industry are generally assuming that a new era of unregulated competition is under way. For example, the railroads are moving aggressively into intermodal services that combine rail and truck services. Burlington Northern Railroad has been an innovative leader in this area. The marketing strategy implications of deregulation include opportunities to target new markets, expansion into multimodal services, flexibility in price strategy, the development of global distribution networks, and a wide range of new competition.

Company-Specific Influence

These influences may temporarily alter a strategic situation. Instead of calling for a permanent change in marketing strategy, this situation requires actions to cope with a short-term influence that may be favorable or unfavorable. Environmental influences may affect buyers, a company, and/or its products. Interest rate fluctuations affect buyers of products such as homes. Adverse publicity may affect a company and faulty products may result in recalls. The 1982 deaths apparently due to the substitution of cyanide for Tylenol are illustrative of this situation. Before the deaths, Tylenol was generating more than $400 million in sales and $70 million in profits in 1981.[16] Management's strategy for countering the impact of the strategic situation included three components: (1) an immediate and massive effort to remove all Tylenol capsules from retail stores and all other points in the distribution network; (2) package designers launched a crash program to develop tamper-resistant containers; and (3) an extensive (and expensive) marketing effort was planned and implemented to restore the trust of doctors and buyers in the Tylenol brand. The strategy was effective in moving Tylenol rapidly back to its leading market position, an accomplishment that many industry experts doubted could be accomplished. Another tampering incident in 1986 caused Tylenol's management to permanently withdraw capsules from the market.

STRATEGIC SITUATION ASSESSMENT

Management should evaluate the strategic situation confronting a firm, business unit, or specific market target to determine the feasible marketing strategies available to the firm. An examination of the nature and scope of the organizational situation, product-market situation, competition situation, and environmental influences provides important insights as to how these factors may affect a firm's strategic marketing situation. A diversified corporation that is active in various markets and product categories must consider a situation assessment for each product-market in its corporate portfolio.

Illustrative Strategic Situations

A classification scheme offers a useful basis for identifying strategic situations. In classifying strategic situations, one of our major considerations should be to create enough schemes to portray the range of situations while avoiding the creation of too many situations. Exhibit 7-8 shows four illustrative situations based on type of industry and a firm's competitive position. The names are illustrative. Note that we do not consider explicitly additional strategic variables, such as the product-

EXHIBIT 7-8 Illustrative Strategic Situations*

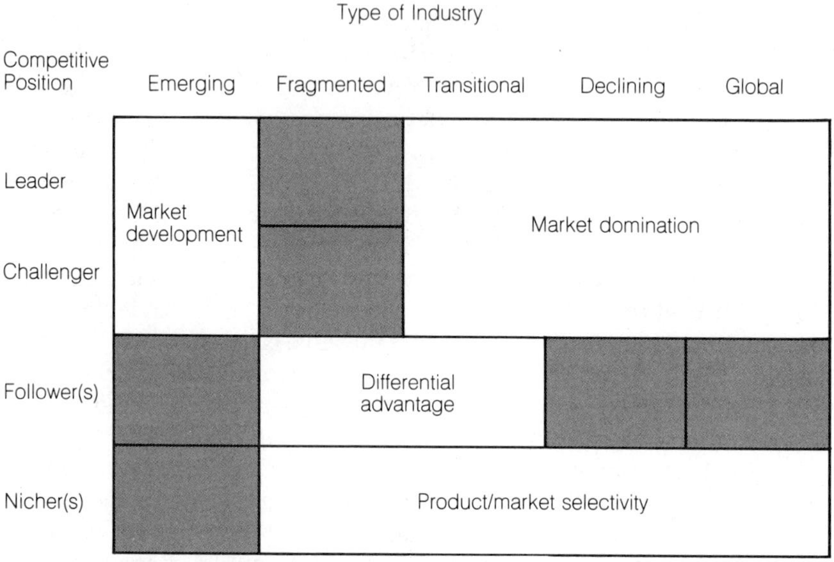

Type of Industry

Competitive Position	Emerging	Fragmented	Transitional	Declining	Global
Leader	Market development		Market domination		
Challenger	Market development		Market domination		
Follower(s)		Differential advantage			
Nicher(s)		Product/market selectivity			

*Grid dimensions are based on Philip Kotler, *Marketing Management: Analysis, Planning and Control*, 5th ed. (Englewood Cliffs, N.J.: Prentice-Hall, 1984), chapter 12; and Michael E. Porter, *Competitive Strategy* (New York: Free Press, 1980), chapter 9.

market situation, in Exhibit 7-8. These factors are integrated into the strategic situation analysis later in the discussion.

We need to recognize several implications of the four basic (preliminary) strategic situations shown in Exhibit 7-8:

The situations portray strategic *zones* rather than specific positions. Consideration of additional strategic factors may create more specific situations.

The empty cells are assumed to be empty or to represent a harvest/divest situation for a particular firm.

It is important to note that the four situations provide an *initial* basis for assessing the nature and scope of the relevant strategic variables (organization, product-market, competition, and environmental situation).

The grid shown in Exhibit 7-8 represents a snapshot at one point in time. Strategic situation analysis should be considered in a dynamic rather than static setting.

A closer look at each of the four situations will provide greater insights into their features, characteristics, and strategy implications.

Market Development. This situation is favorable in terms of both market opportunity and competitive strength. Building market position is important. It is appropriate to concentrate our efforts on major customer groups within the product-market in establishing a basis for market domination, should the market-opportunity become less favorable in the future and should competition expand. Examples include Guest Supply (hotel amenities), ChemLawn (lawn care), and U.S. Surgical (surgical staplers). This situation involves potential competitive threats from new entries unless substantial entry barriers exist.

Differential Advantage. Survival may be a key consideration in this situation. A firm with special capabilities may be able to establish a differential advantage over key competitors. Small firms are likely to be more successful when both differentiated customer needs and differentiated products exist. Nucor, the relatively small speciality steel producer, has been successful through its geographical concentration (the Sunbelt), product specialization (steel joists), and high productivity.

Product/Market Selectivity. A firm in this situation may encounter favorable market opportunities, but may not be strong enough to be a major competitor. An analysis of the firm's strategic advantages should identify one or a few customer groups in which the firm has (or can develop) a favorable market position. Differences in products offered and customer needs should generally be favorable to smaller firms. Examples include small retailers serving special market niches. Tootsie Roll Industries is also illustrative.

Market Domination. This situation may involve a favorable or unfavorable market opportunity. A firm with a strong position should concentrate on holding its sales and profit position. Major market segments present the best opportunities to the market leader and other larger competitors if differentiated needs exist. Multiple segment strategy is appropriate. Examples include Deere in agricultural equipment, Kodak in photography supplies, and General Motors in automobiles.

It is possible that a firm may be in a situation of *no advantage*. If so, none of the four situational categories explains the firm's strategic situation.

Incorporating Additional Strategic Variables

Strategic variables, in addition to the type of industry and competitive position, are essential in describing a strategic situation. Exhibit 7–9 shows the variables that are often useful in refining the basic strategic situations shown earlier in Exhibit 7–8. The stage of corporate develop-

---

EXHIBIT 7-9   Incorporating Additional Strategic Variables into the Strategic Situation

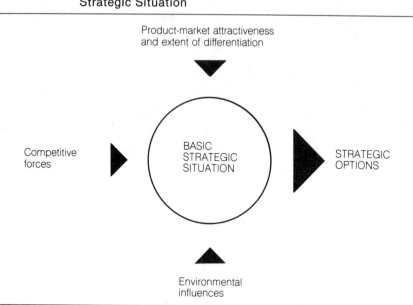

Product-market attractiveness
and extent of differentiation

Competitive
forces

BASIC
STRATEGIC
SITUATION

STRATEGIC
OPTIONS

Environmental
influences

---

ment is not included since this factor is related to the competitive position. Nevertheless, it should be incorporated into the situation analysis when appropriate.

Product-Market Situation.   In general, product-market attractiveness *decreases* and product-market differentiation *increases* as we move from left to right on the grid shown in Exhibit 7–8. High attractiveness occurs typically in an emerging industry and can also be present in a fragmented industry. Attractive market segments may exist, regardless of the life cycle stage of the product type or product variant product-market.

The extent of product and market differentiation varies widely among industries and markets, although the differentiation is likely to be more prevalent in mature product-markets, as opposed to emerging industries. In a specific situation we need to make an analysis in order to determine the nature and scope of differentiation that exists.

Competitive Forces.   The competitive situation may change at any time as a result of the five competitive forces (rivalry, new entrant threats, substitute threats, and the bargaining power of suppliers). For example, in 1986 the composition of the airline industry in the United States was in a state of flux.[17] Texas Air's takeover of troubled Eastern Airlines would make the new combination the largest airline. Weak airlines were being acquired by market leaders. The restructuring of the industry was expected to continue because of the deregulation and intense competition among air carriers.

Environmental Influences.   Economic, social, technological, governmental, and natural influences affect a marketing strategy situation in various ways; they often impact the market opportunity and competitive structure. It is important to identify the specific environmental factors that may affect a particular strategic situation. The impact of these factors may be favorable or unfavorable depending upon circumstances. Regular monitoring of key environmental factors should be part of management's strategic analysis activities.

MARKETING STRATEGY OPTIONS

A brief examination of marketing strategy options, strategy selection, and implementation will complete our discussion of the strategic situation analysis.

Marketing Strategy Options

Many possible strategies may be appropriate for various strategic situations. Six strategy categories are used to represent the range of possibilities: (1) multiple targeting, (2) selective targeting, (3) differential advantage, (4) acquisition/merger/joint venture, (5) diversification, and (6) harvest/divest. These strategy alternatives are not necessarily exhaustive, and should be considered illustrative rather than all-encompassing. Many specific strategies exist within each category. Also, a combination of strategies may be used such as multiple targeting and differential advantage.

Multiple Targeting.   Targeting several segments within a product-market is an appropriate strategy for a market development or domination situation. This strategy seeks to build or protect market position by the leader or a challenger. The objective in a market development situation is to expand the market by increasing the number of users. The pioneering firm in a new market may initially target only one broad group of buyers. Yet segmentation may be feasible at an early stage of market entry. Segments may be identified by using fairly broad categories such as large, medium, and small organizational buyers. This strategy can be effective when a sizable market potential exists as compared to existing industry sales.

An effective strategy for market domination is to target all or most of the segments in a mature market. By expanding into several segments, a firm can gain or expand its dominance. Typically, mature markets contain buyers with differentiated needs, and thus segmentation is necessary and appropriate. A strategy of multiple segment targeting using several brands of beer has proved very effective for Anheuser-Busch Companies, Inc. in the United States beer market.

Selective Targeting. Market niching is often essential for small firms in mature product-markets, providing that real differences in buyer needs exist. For example, Snap-on-Tools's success in targeting professional mechanics for its line of tools has been impressive. Selective targeting is an appropriate option for either the situation of the differential advantage or the situation of product/market selectivity.

Differential Advantage Strategy. Various actions may be effective when seeking to obtain a marketing program positioning leverage, depending upon the strategic situation. The following positioning actions may be useful in creating an advantage over the competition:

Product Differentiation Perceived product quality and service-free performance are key strengths of Maytag in the competitive kitchen appliance market. Positioning leverage is achieved by gaining a strong brand preference, particularly in the replacement market.

Product Specialization Some firms are able to gain a strong position over competition by specializing on a product category. Ethan Allen, for example, dominates the traditional American furniture market.

Cost Advantages Low-cost producers have major price and profit advantages over competing firms. The new wave of deep discount warehouse retailers, such as The Price Club that operates 20 warehouse, membership-only stores, illustrates the use of narrow margins and low costs in retailing. Entering the market in 1979, Price increased its sales to $2 billion in 1985.

Distribution Strengths Well-developed distribution channels are key advantages in providing services to customers in many industries. Examples include Tandy in consumer electronics and Ethan Allen in furniture.

Advertising and Personal Selling Capabilities The establishment of a strong customer franchise through advertising and sales promotion offers a strong competitive advantage. Favorable relationships with customers and marketing channel organizations resulting from personal selling efforts are important strengths over the competition.

Acquisition/Merger/Joint Venture Strategies. These strategies have been very popular in recent years as a result of slow growth, intensive competition, attractive value/cost ratios, and other factors. The joint venture strategy is used to spread the risks of a market development situation over to one or more venture partner firms.

Since targeting and positioning strategies are closely related, the selection of a marketing strategy must incorporate both targeting and positioning actions, even though the differential advantage may only be due to a single factor, such as a low cost, a protected niche, or a powerful distribution network.

Diversification.   As discussed in Chapter 2, moving away from the core business may be a sound strategy for certain strategic situations. It is particularly appropriate when opportunities in the existing product-market are limited by the growth potential and/or an already dominant position by a firm. Diversification offers the advantage of spreading risks over two or more business areas.

Harvest/Divest Strategy.   In strategic situations where a firm is unable to gain a differential advantage or where product/market selectivity is not feasible, harvest or divestment strategies may be the only feasible options. Alternatively, even though other strategies may be feasible, management may be unwilling to commit additional resources to the task.

Exhibit 7–10 provides an illustrative matching of the six strategic options to the four basic strategic situations shown in Exhibit 7–8. Several examples of firms occupying the various cell positions are also shown. Note that these illustrations are for a particular point in time (1985). These grid positions are likely to change over time as a consequence of shifts in the strategic situation and alterations in the business and marketing strategies.

Strategy Selection, Implementation, and Results

As shown in Exhibit 7–10, more than a single strategy is often feasible for a given situation. Note also that some options are not applicable for certain situations. Deciding how to implement the strategy (e.g., selective targeting) requires a penetrating analysis of the situation. In selecting a strategy, we have to consider the results desired by management.

Typically, corporate, business unit, and marketing strategies are concerned with achieving one or more of the following outcomes:[18]

Increasing sales volume;
Increasing profitability through improved productivity or margins;
Harvesting or divestment; and
Turnaround.

The volume and profitability objectives correspond to the strategies of market domination, market development, and product/market selectivity. Harvesting or divestment may become necessary if the sales and profit performance does not reach acceptable levels for firms in the dif-

EXHIBIT 7-10 Illustrative Matching of Strategic Options to the Strategic Situation

Strategic Situation	Strategic Options					
	Multiple Targeting	Selective Targeting	Differential Advantage*	Acquisition Merger/Joint Venture	Diversification	Harvest/Divest
Market development	Guest Supply (personal care amenities for hotels)	N/A	U.S. Surgical (surgical staplers)	Communications Satellite (satellite communications)	N/A	N/A
Differential advantage	N/A	Snap-on-Tools (mechanics tools)	Komatsy (low cost producer)	Mergers of small regional banks	N/A	Amfac (hotel SBU)
Product/market selectivity	N/A	The Limited (women's apparel retailer)	Ethan Allen (traditional American furniture)	Public accounting firms	N/A	Sperry (sale of Remington razor unit)
Market domination	Seiko (time instruments)	N/A	Schlumberger (wireline services for oil well drilling)	Texas Air	Singer (sewing machines)	N/A

N/A = Not applicable.

*Low cost, differentiated marketing mix, product specialization.

ferential advantage strategic situation. Turnaround strategies may correspond to various strategic situations whenever performance has declined to unacceptable levels and pressures for improvement exist.

Determining the strategic situation helps us to identify possible marketing strategy options and guides our strategy selection. Since marketing strategy consists of decisions on the market target and positioning, our strategy options consist of feasible targeting and positioning decisions.

Application Illustration

Two firms in the food-processing industry provide an interesting example of strategic situation analysis and strategy selection. In the mid-1970s the industry was experiencing a slow growth. Both General Mills and Pillsbury held strong positions in the markets served by their brands, and more cash was being generated than was needed to support their food-processing operations. General Mills diversified into several areas, including speciality retailing, toys, and restaurants. In contrast, Pillsbury followed a concentrated diversification strategy of becoming a leading multichain restaurant company. Pillsbury initially tried nonfood diversification but sold or closed down those units in 1973.

By 1985 Pillsbury was pulling ahead of its Minneapolis rival General Mills, indicating the success of concentrating on the restaurant business.[19] Pillsbury has six distinct chains of restaurants: Burger King, Bennigan's, Steak & Ale, J. J. Muggs, Quik Wok, and Bay Street. These chains serve 40 million meals each week and generate sales of $4.6 billion. Pillsbury has also used acquisitions to move into selected food-processing areas with promising growth potential. This strategy enabled the company to expand its consumer foods business by 35 percent from 1980 to 1985, even though the overall industry was barely growing.

Thus two companies faced with similar strategic situations selected somewhat different strategies. General Mills apparently tried to move into too many diversified areas. Pillsbury's more concentrated strategy enabled management to focus its efforts in one new market area.

ANALYSIS OF COMPETITION

Our discussion so far has centered on defining the competitive arena for a particular firm and describing the strategic situation of such a firm. Further discussion of competition is appropriate because of the central role competition assessment plays in strategy analysis and formulation. The major steps in competitor analysis are: (1) definition of the competitive arena, (2) description of the competing firms, (3) evalu-

EXHIBIT 7-11 Steps in Analyzing the Competition

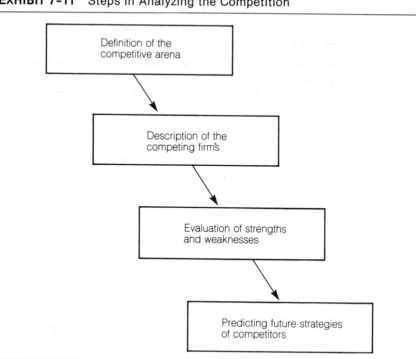

ation of the strengths and weaknesses of each firm, and (4) predicting the future strategies of our key competitors. These steps are shown in Exhibit 7-11. We will describe and illustrate each step to indicate the nature and scope of competitor analysis.

Defining the Competitive Arena

In defining the competitive arena, we should first center on identifying the complete set of industry participants. Additionally, the subset of firms with which a company is competing on a direct basis represents the key competitors. Since the types of information needed for industry and key competitor analyses are similar, the step-by-step approach described in Exhibit 7-11 can be used for either purpose. The major distinction between industry and key competitor analysis is that an industry analysis does not examine each firm in depth. The industry analysis provides background information for a comprehensive evaluation of key competitors.* The following discussion is concerned with conducting a key competitor analysis.

---

*An excellent guide to preparing an industry analysis is contained in Appendix B of Michael E. Porter, *Competitive Strategy* (New York: Free Press, 1980).

EXHIBIT 7-12 Information Needed for Describing Key Competitors

---

- Business scope and objectives
- Market position
- Market targets(s) and customer base
- Marketing program positioning strategy
- Financial, technical, and operating capabilities
- Management experience and capabilities
- Special capabilities (e.g., access to resources, patents)

A *key competitor* is a firm going after the same market target as the firm conducting the analysis. Typically, the competitor's product is the same product type or a substitute that meets the same need. For example, when U.S. Surgical Corp. entered the market for surgical skin closure with its line of surgical stapling equipment in the early 1970s, the new product type represented a competitive threat to needle and suture suppliers. There were no other surgical stapler manufacturers at that time.

Strategic group identification is useful in identifying key competitors. The differences among the firms that comprise an industry can be used to determine strategic groups. Business definition provides a basis for group identification.[20] Typically, the performance of firms in an industry varies. Analysis of strategic groups is useful in determining the differences in strategies among competitors that contribute to performance variations.

Description of the Competition

A summary of the types of information useful in preparing a descriptive profile of key competitors is shown in Exhibit 7-12. Both published and unpublished information should be incorporated into the analysis. Illustrative information sources include annual reports, industry studies by government and private organizations, magazines and newspapers, company reports by financial analysts (e.g., *Value Line Investment Survey*), standardized data services (e.g., MRCA and Nielsen), suppliers, customers, and salespeople. Financial analysts' research reports can be very useful as a first step in competitor description. Consider the following excerpt from a report for U.S. Surgical Corp. prepared by an investment research firm:

> Ethicon out-marketed USSC by focusing on operating room supervisors, who control non-critical purchasing—into which category skin products fall. USSC salesmen, by contrast, were focusing on surgeons, who alone control purchase of the less competitive internal stapling products. USSC's preoccupation was understandable, since its backorder problems in skin products made it more productive to concentrate on internals.[21]

EXHIBIT 7-13   Areas of Evaluation of the Competition

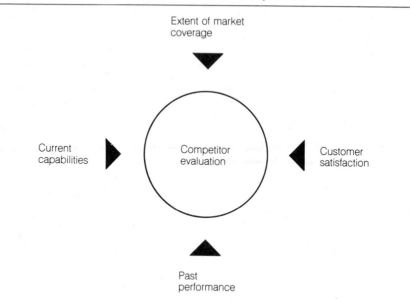

A descriptive profile of a competitor should provide a historical picture of the marketing decisions made by management. Past decisions show the pattern of changes in marketing strategy and tactics as management responded to changing market conditions. Analysis of the decisions should attempt to match them with specific changes taking place in markets or with competition. An experienced marketer can then develop a feel for the management style of a key competitor by looking for patterns or consistencies in these decisions.

We can usually obtain adequate information on key competitors, although the time and effort necessary to locate and study the information may be substantial. Thus management must evaluate the costs and benefits of obtaining additional information. The challenge to the analyst is to assemble a penetrating and objective description of each competitor of interest.

Evaluation of the Competition

While the description and evaluation of the competition are interrelated, it is useful to separate the two activities. The overall objective of evaluation is to determine the strengths and weaknesses of each competitor for the areas shown in Exhibit 7-13. When we evaluate the extent of market coverage, customer satisfaction, past performance, and current capabilities, a basis is provided for estimating future actions of the competitor.

EXHIBIT 7-14   Analyzing Market Coverage for Automobile Brands

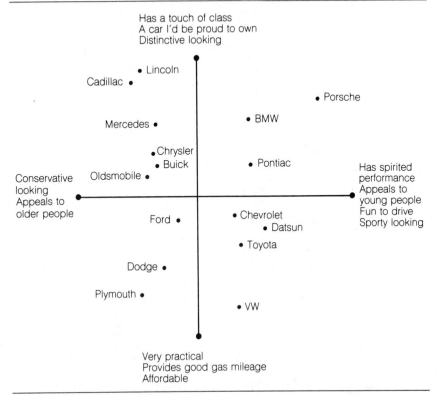

Extent of Market Coverage.   This evaluation should focus on which market target(s) segments the competitor is going after and the competitor's actual and relative market share position. Relative market position can be measured in reference to the share of the firm with the highest market share in the segment. It is important to consider all segments in the product market that could be targeted by the firm conducting the competitor evaluation. Consider, for example, the brand positioning map shown in Exhibit 7-14, which is used by Chrysler Corporation to evaluate possible positioning opportunities. The upper-right quadrant offers a possible position for Chrysler and other U.S. automobile manufacturers. This analysis suggests segments where competitors are not providing market coverage.

There are sometimes very favorable market opportunities in targeting small niches or segments of a product-market. One example is Playbill Inc., the small but highly profitable company that produces, prints, and distributes *Playbill.*[22] This handout is given to people at-

EXHIBIT 7-15   Illustrative Comparison of Two Architects by a Sample of Commercial Building Developers

Factor	Architect Rating*		A Compared to B
	A	B	
Responsiveness	8.5	7.4	Better
Understands my needs	8.0	8.0	Same
Engineering knowhow	8.0	9.5	Weak
Competitive fees	8.2	7.3	Better
National prestige of the firm	6.0	8.0	Weak

*1 to 10 scale with 10 being the highest rating.

tending Broadway shows. A companion publication, *Showbill*, is distributed to off-Broadway theatergoers. The company has the exclusive right to sell advertising in 100 theaters that generated sales of $11 million in 1984 and before-tax net profits of 30 percent on the sales dollar. Playbill Inc. holds a near monopoly position in this very specialized niche of publishing. The publication is required by the actors' union to assure that the audience knows the names of the players. Additionally, Playbill Inc.'s management has developed a strong relationship with the theater owners. The publisher pays for the printing and sells advertising in the programs. Nearly a million *Playbill*s are distributed to Broadway theaters each month. One page of color advertising in the program costs an advertiser $24,000.

Customer Satisfaction.   This aspect of competitor evaluation is concerned with gauging the extent to which competitors are meeting customer needs. The starting point in this assessment is determining the criteria buyers use to evaluate suppliers, followed by an evaluation of each supplier. Two aspects of customer satisfaction are important. First, buyers have ideal preferences as to various attributes of a supplier or product. For example, a consumer may have an ideal amount of chocolate in ice cream. Second, customers have preferences concerning alternative suppliers or brands. The amount of chocolate in brand A is preferred to the amount in brand B.

Exhibit 7–15 shows how two architects compare on the basis of developers' ratings of criteria used in architect selection. The information shown is illustrative. A complete assessment would include the determination of all relevant factors in client evaluation of architects, the determination of the relative importance of each factor, and the rating of key competitors.

Past Performance.   An analysis of each key competitor's past sales and financial performance provides a useful assessment of how well the competitor has performed on a historical basis. A typical period of anal-

EXHIBIT 7-16 *Deposit* Market Share Comparison for Key Competitors (1974-1982)

Bank	1974	1976	1978	1980	1982
A	26.2	25.5	23.43	23.8	23.5
B	24.4	23.3	21.8	19.9	15.9
C	10.1	8.9	8.9	9.4	9.1
D	1.1	1.1	1.6	2.1	2.4
E	2.6	2.4	2.3	2.2	2.3
F	1.8	1.9	1.9	1.9	2.0
G	1.8	1.9	1.8	1.6	1.6
H	0.8	0.9	0.9	0.9	0.8
I	—	—	—	0.3	0.4
J	0.2	0.2	0.4	0.4	0.4
K	—	—	0.1	0.3	0.4
L	0.1	0.2	0.3	0.3	0.3

ysis is five to 10 years. Performance information may include sales, market share, net profit, net profit margin, cash flow, and debt. Additionally, for specific types of businesses other performance information may be appropriate. For example, deposit market share trends are important performance gauges in banking. Note in Exhibit 7-16 the substantial decline in Bank B's deposit market share from 1974 to 1982. The analysis also indicates that several new competitors have entered the market.

Current Capabilities. Analyses of the extent of market coverage and customer satisfaction and the assessment of past performance provide us with useful information. On the basis of this information, we can develop an overall evaluation of the key competitor's strengths and weaknesses. Additionally, we should incorporate information on the competitor's management capabilities and limitations, technical and operating advantages/weaknesses, marketing strategy, and other key strengths and limitations into our current capabilities analysis. Since competitors often display differences in strengths and weaknesses, it is important for us to highlight these differences. An illustrative analysis of competitor capabilities is shown in Exhibit 7-17.

Anticipating Actions by Competitors

The final step in our analysis is trying to determine what each key competitor will do in the future. It is also important to identify new competitors that may enter the market. The competitor evaluation analyses are helpful in estimating future trends. We will find an analysis of industry structure and competitive forces useful in identifying potential competitors.

EXHIBIT 7-17   Illustrative Analysis of Competitor Strengths and Weaknesses

Competition Indicators	Major Competitors				Business Area
	A	B	C	D	E
Market position	Vulnerable	Prevalent	Strong	Vulnerable	Attackable
General trend in market position	Steady	Steady	Up	Down	Down
Profitability (low, average, high)	Low	Average	Average	Average	Low
Financial strength (low, average, high)	Low	High	Unknown	Low	Low
Product mix (broad, narrow)	Narrow	Broad	Narrow	Narrow	Extensive
Technological capability (strong, weak, average)	Average	Strong	Average	Weak	Average
Cost outlook (favorable, unfavorable)	Unfavorable	Favorable	Favorable	Unfavorable	Unfavorable
Quality (good, satisfactory, minimum)	Minimum	Good	Satisfactory	Minimum	Satisfactory
Product development	Minimum	Good	Satisfactory	Satisfactory	Good

SOURCE: Reprinted by permission of the publisher from Darryl J. Ellis and Peter P. Pekar, Jr. "Linking Resources to Strategic Marketing Plans," *Industrial Marketing Management* 6, 1977, 5. Copyright 1977 by Elsevier Science Publishing Co., Inc.

In some situations the entry of new competitors can be predicted with a reasonable degree of certainty. We illustrate this situation by examining a completely new product and an established product.

Surgical Staplers.   By the late 1970s U.S. Surgical Corp. had reached $50 million in sales and accounted for about 10 percent of the total wound-closure market.[23] In view of the firm's rapid growth, lack of direct competitors, and the potential opportunity for surgical stapling to capture a substantial portion of the market, it was not surprising to see Johnson & Johnson's Ethicon subsidiary enter the market with a disposable stapler in 1978. The disposable option became very attractive for certain types of surgery, and Ethicon captured a substantial portion of U.S. Surgical's skin suture market share. This caused U.S. Surgical to initiate a major catch-up program that cost $100 million over a four-year period.

Tylenol.   As of the mid-1970s Tylenol held most of the nonaspirin pain relief market. Tylenol's profit margins were extremely large and marketing costs were relatively low for a consumer product. No consumer advertising had been used to promote Tylenol. Instead, promotion efforts had been concentrated in medical and dental professional publications and direct selling contacts. When we consider the large market opportunity, the attractive profit margins, the market dominance by one firm, and the ease of product duplication, the entry of a new competitor was predictable. Datril entered the market with an aggressive advertising campaign and prices substantially below Tylenol's. Interestingly, a decade later Tylenol continued to dominate the market. Even the cyanide deaths in 1983, which were attributed to tampering with Tylenol packages, failed to topple Tylenol from its strong market position.

Companies are increasingly developing intelligence systems on the competition to help monitor existing competitors and spot emerging competitors. Various techniques are used, including accessing large computer data bases, customer surveys, interviews with suppliers and other marketing channel participants, hiring competitors' personnel, and studying competitors' products. The data bases available for competitor analysis are impressive:

> Obtaining competitive information is getting easier these days. Electronic data bases, which store information to be retrieved by computer, are proliferating. Some 2,000 are now available. One, called Economic Information Systems, published by a subsidiary of Control Data Corp., lists the names and locations of industrial facilities along with estimates of each plant's dollar volume of output, number of employees, and the share of market that its production represents. Another data base, called Investext, published by Business Research Corp. of Brighton, Massachusetts, gives subscribers the full text of research reports on companies by security analysts and investment bankers.[24]

There are also instances of illegal corporate espionage, although such occurrences are apparently not extensive. An expanded discussion of these intelligence systems is provided in Chapter 18.

CONCLUDING NOTE

By analyzing the strategic forces that affect marketing strategy, we obtain essential guidelines for determining the strategic situation confronting a firm. Normally these forces impact a firm in its markets, creating both opportunities and threats. The primary objectives of this chapter are to develop approaches for analyzing the strategic marketing situation and analyzing the competition. These topics are closely related since competition is an important aspect of the strategic situation.

The starting point in the chapter is an examination of the major determinants of a strategic situation. These include the organizational situation, product-market situation, competition situation, and environmental influences. The organizational situation assessment includes a consideration of the corporate development stage, the corporate culture, and the organization's strengths and weaknesses. The analysis of the product-market situation includes a description of the product life cycle (PLC) and the nature and scope of the competition over the PLC. We consider the competition also at the generic, specific, and market segment levels of a product-market. The analysis of the structure of competition examines the various structural characteristics of industries, the competitive forces that affect the performance of firms in an industry, and illustrative types of industry structure. Emphasis is given to how we can define and analyze the structure of the competition. Environmental influences may be industry-wide or company-specific.

Determining the strategic situation begins with the assessment of the organizational situation of the firm conducting the analysis. We then identify and describe other key determinants of the strategic situation. The summary of the strategic situation completes the process. In summarizing the strategic situation that exists, we identify four illustrative strategic situations on the basis of the market opportunity and competitive situation. These situations are designated as product/market selectivity, differential advantage, market domination, and market development. Next, we discuss and illustrate a brief overview of the alternative marketing strategy options available to cope with various strategic situations. These include market building, domination, selective targeting, differential advantage, harvest/divest, and merger or joint venture strategies.

Finally, the steps in analyzing key competitors are outlined and illustrated. The analysis process includes the identification, description, and evaluation of competitors as well as an estimate of their actions. Techniques for obtaining competitor intelligence are also overviewed.

This chapter provides an important foundation for marketing strategy development and strategic marketing programming—topics that are discussed in Parts 3 and 4.

NOTES

1. This illustration is based upon Thomas Kamm, "Michelin Is Revamping Its Strategy in Bid to Inflate Its Position in the Tire Industry", *The Wall Street Journal*, December 12, 1984, 30.

2. T. Tyebjee Tyzoon, Albert V. Bruno, and Shelby H. McIntyre, "Growing Ventures Can Anticipate Marketing Stages," *Harvard Business Review*, January–February 1983, 62, 64, and 66.

3. Jennifer Bingham Hull, "California Closets Find Niche in Remodeling Storage Space," *The Wall Street Journal*, March 19, 1984, 29.

4. Ibid.

5. Tyebjee et al., "Growing Ventures," 64.

6. "Hershey: A Hefty Ad Budget Has Profits Flying High," *Business Week*, February 13, 1984, 88.

7. Terrence E. Deal and Allan A. Kennedy, *Corporate Cultures* (Reading,

Mass.: Addison-Wesley Publishing, 1982), 13–15.

8. Ibid, 4.

9. Philip Kotler, *Marketing Management: Analysis, Planning and Control*, 5th ed. (Englewood Cliffs, N.J.: Prentice-Hall, 1984), Chapter 12.

10. Kenneth Labich, "Why Bigger Is Better in the Airline Wars," *Fortune*, March 31, 1986, 55.

11. "The Filmless Camera Is Here, but Will It Sell?" *Business Week*, April 15, 1985, 151 and 154.

12. Ibid., 151.

13. Ibid., 154.

14. Michael E. Porter, *Competitive Strategy* (New York: Free Press, 1980), chapter 9.

15. Michael E. Porter, *Competitive Advantage* (New York: Free Press, 1985), 5.

16. Michael Waldholz, "Johnson & Johnson Plans to Reintroduce Tylenol Capsules in more Secure Package," *The Wall Street Journal*, November 12, 1982, 3.

17. *Business Week*, "Airlines in Flux: And Then There Were Five?," March 10, 1986, 107, 110, and 112.

18. George S. Day, *Strategic Market Planning*, St. Paul, Minn.: West Publishing, 1984, 102.

19. Subrata N. Chakravarty, "Pizzas, Anyone? Hamburgers? Trout Almandine?," *Forbes*, September 9, 1985, 74–75.

20. Gary L. Frazier and Roy D. Howell, "Business Definition and Performance," *Journal of Marketing*, Spring 1983, 59–67; and Day, Strategic Market Planning, 95–96.

21. Kenneth S. Abramowitz, *United States Surgical Corporation* (New York: Sanford C. Bernstein & Co., 1980), 5.

22. Maria Fisher, "Joe Schumpeter Meet Art Birsh", *Forbes*, April 8, 1985, 116–17.

23. Robert Teitelman, "Case Study," *Forbes*, May 7, 1984, 142 and 144.

24. Steven Flax, "How to Snoop on Your Competitors," *Fortune*, May 14, 1984, 30.

QUESTIONS FOR REVIEW AND DISCUSSION

1. In the mid-1980s fast-food industry experts were predicting a shakeout of small firms. Identify several key strategic factors affecting the marketing strategy situation of a small fast-food chain.

2. Select an industry and describe its characteristics, participants, and structure.

3. What are some of the limitations in using the product life cycle as a basis for determining a strategic situation?

4. Select a company or business unit and prepare an evaluation of its strategic marketing situation. Indicate the marketing strategy options that appear feasible for the firm.

5. Identify several important environmental influences that should be monitored by an airline such as Delta Air Lines, Inc. or American Airlines, Inc.

6. Outline an approach to competitor evaluation, assuming you are preparing the analysis for a regional bank holding company.

STRATEGIC APPLICATION 7-1

DRESSER INDUSTRIES INC.

Dallas—The field is littered with big-name casualties like International Harvester Co. and IBH Holding Inc., the failed West German concern. Caterpillar Tractor Co. is bleeding, and General Motors Corp. has fled.

Welcome to the moribund business of making mammoth machines for huge construction and mining projects. In its third year of recession, the $17 billion industry world-wide posted combined losses of more than $500 million last year. The Japanese are invading the U.S. market, and an impending shakeout is expected to winnow today's dozen major players to just three or four by 1995.

Nonetheless, Dresser Industries Inc. has decided it is a good time to try to become a heavyweight in heavy equipment.

Dresser's annual revenue—which was $3.73 billion in its fiscal year ended Oct. 31, 1984—comes primarily from its oil and gas equipment business. But now it is acquiring construction and mining equipment plants in the economically unfashionable Frost Belt. It is negotiating behind closed doors in West Germany to expand its product line. And its chairman is trotting the globe, peddling gear ranging from desk-size pneumatic compressors to trucks that are as big as a house.

Opportunity in Slump

Is Dresser dreaming? Dresser officials and some industry experts don't think so. They reason that Dresser can take advantage of the industry slump by buying high-quality plants from competitors that are hard-pressed for cash. That is exactly what happened when Dresser bought International Harvester's Libertyville, Ill., plant for $82 million, or 25% of book value. Dresser got a

similarly deep discount on a Peoria, Ill., truck plant it bought from American Standard Inc. for $66 million. Under Dresser, the two plants were among the few U.S. construction and mining equipment operations to post a profit last year.

"Dresser just may have the wherewithal to pick the plums from the people who've been racked by the recession," says William Goessel, president of Harnischfeger Corp., a Milwaukee-based heavy equipment concern.

Dresser has another inducement to expand. To compete effectively with giants like Caterpillar and Japan's Komatsu Ltd., a company has to offer a full range of products. In fact, some independent dealers say that is just what they have been telling Dresser for years. A wide product line helps win important customers, like foreign governments and huge corporations, because they can buy all of their construction and mining equipment from one maker.

"Dresser either had to sell what equipment operations they had or buy more to make it as a world-class competitor," says Frank Manfredi, head of a Los Altos, Calif., marketing firm that specializes in heavy equipment.

Plunging headlong into heavy equipment is risky, but Dresser officials believe that the industry will turn around. "I think as long as we've got some kind of civilization on this earth, we're bound to have additional major mining and construction projects," says John J. Murphy, Dresser's cigar-smoking, 54-year-old chairman. "It's human nature. It's just the way it's going to be."

In addition, Dresser feels comfortable with highly engineered products, whether they are oil rigs and drill bits or bulldoz-

Dresser Industries' Revenue and Profit (Year ended October 31, 1984)

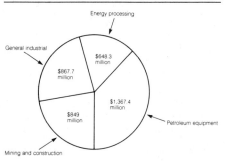

General industrial

Energy processing

$648.3 million

$867.7 million

$1,367.4 million

$849 million

Petroleum equipment

Mining and construction

Revenue	$3.73 billion
Net income	$96.7 million
Per-share earnings	$1.24
Total assets	$3.32 billion
Current liabilities	$879.3 million
Long-term debt	$410.6 million

ers and road graders. And many of Dresser's big energy-products customers also are shopping for heavy equipment. Dresser sees particularly big markets for both petroleum and construction gear in the Soviet Union and China. As long as Dresser is making a pitch for energy equipment, the thinking goes, why not try at the same time to peddle a few giant Wabco trucks?

Selling for more than $1 million each, Dresser's Wabcos—with tires 12 feet high and dumpers big enough to hold four stretched Cadillac limousines—are used to haul ore out of surface mines in 250-ton loads. Its Marion power shovel, a mammoth version of the old steam shovel, can cost as much as $30 million. The biggest ones scoop up 25 cubic yards at a time, enough to fill the average bedroom.

But the market for such machines has crumbled over the past five years because of the recession in the industry and the Third World debt crisis. In a struggle to avoid bankruptcy, International Harvester shed most of its heavy-equipment operations. GM, concentrating on sav-

ing its auto business, unloaded its Terex heavy-equipment unit. And IBH, the West German concern that acquired Terex, went bankrupt.

Caterpillar, the industry leader with 35% of the market world-wide, is still posting losses. About 35% of the industry's capacity stands idle. A wave of consolidations continues, such as Clark Equipment Co.'s purchase of Euclid Inc. and its subsequent merger of construction-equipment operations with those of Sweden's AB Volvo. Meanwhile, Japan's Komatsu, a low-cost producer, has snared 20% of the market world-wide, making it No. 2.

Into this world of struggling behemoths marches Dresser, a heavyweight that has had its own problems in the gritty oil-and-gas equipment business. When Mr. Murphy, an engineer who had recently completed a master's degree in business administration, took over as Dresser's chairman in 1983, the company had just reported its first quarterly loss in 37 years, sales were off 15% from a 1981 peak of $4.6 billion and the outlook for energy was grim.

Mr. Murphy quickly embarked on a program to turn the company around, reducing its work force, selling marginal operations and moving to make Dresser a world-class player in the businesses it kept. That is where the construction and mining equipment maneuvers fit in.

Besides buying plants on the cheap, Dresser's mining and construction gear division has cut labor costs through automation, increased spending on product development and begun to explore joint ventures to expand its product line further.

One cost-cutting tactic calls for foreign plants to make simple, labor-intensive parts, while Dresser's U.S. operations concentrate on more complex, highly engineered parts and assemble the product. This technique has been used for years by the electronics and auto industries, and now Dresser believes it is time for heavy equipment to follow suit. Already, Dresser has cut the cost of its bulldozer blades 30% by making them in South Korea in a joint venture with Samsung Group Ltd. Other parts are being made in Brazil.

Dresser is going out of its way to avoid militant unions and high labor costs. In acquiring the Libertyville plant, Dresser insisted that International Harvester complete a plan to consolidate with it operations from a plant in Melrose Park, Ill., that had a reputation for violent labor relations.

Conservatively run Dresser has low debt. It has available cash of about $250 million and seems willing to spend it, too. After acquiring the Libertyville truck plant, Dresser installed computerized manufacturing systems that cut operating costs 30%.

George DiPrima, the Libertyville plant manager, had to scrape for every penny he got for engineering and product development under International Harvester's ownership. After submitting his first budget to Dresser, he got a telephone call from Mr. Murphy, the Dresser chairman. Rather than suggesting more cuts, Mr. Murphy offered Mr. DiPrima an even fatter budget for engineering and development.

Global Marketing Strategy

Mr. Murphy, youthful in appearance and gregarious, has scored major successes in pushing the company's global marketing strategy. On overseas trips in recent months, he helped to snare an $85 million contract to sell heavy trucks to China and a $10 million agreement to sell front-end loaders to the Soviet Union.

In addition, Dresser is trying to negotiate some sort of arrangement with Orenstein & Koppel, a West German equipment maker, that might add lighter construction machinery to Dresser's line. Industry sources suggest a joint venture agreement could be in the offing; Dresser declines to comment.

So far, Dresser's big gamble seems to be paying off. The company has increased its share of the mining and construction market to about 5% from 4.5%. The division had a $25.5 million profit in the fiscal year ended Oct. 31, up from $7.4 million a year earlier. Sales in the current year are expected to rise 17% to $1 billion, making Dresser No. 3 or No. 4 in the industry world-wide.

Success isn't guaranteed, though. Dresser's heavy-equipment profit last year partly reflected low plant-acquisition costs, and those advantages won't last, says Andrew Silver, an analyst with Donaldson Lufkin & Jenrette Securities Corp., New York. He says Dresser doesn't have plants as sophisticated or a product line as broad as Caterpillar or Komatsu.

Dresser has distribution problems, too. The company's 230 dealers match Caterpillar's and exceed Komatsu's 178, but Dresser's dealer network is a hodgepodge with many overlapping territories and geographical gaps. Until recently, for example, Dresser had three dealers in the Phoenix, Ariz., area who were selling different parts of its product line. Moreover, Dresser markets gear under more than a half-dozen brand names, a marketing problem the company says it intends to solve by gradually moving toward a single brand name.

DISCUSSION QUESTIONS

1. Prepare an industry analysis for the mining and construction equipment industry.

2. What strategic forces are important to Dresser Industries Inc. in the mining and construction heavy equipment industry?
3. Prepare a detailed summary of Dress-er's strategic marketing situation in the industry.
4. Evaluate Dresser's global marketing strategy. What changes do you recommend?

STRATEGIC APPLICATION 7-2

BMW

Munich, West Germany—Eberhard von Kuenheim, for 15 years the keeper of the BMW mystique, is a mystified man.

The auto-making factories of Bayerische Motoren Werke AG are running flat-out. Every car produced is being sold as fast as it rolls off the assembly line. World-wide sales are up, just as they have been for each of the past 10 years. The wrappers have just been removed from four new model versions.

Still, the critics persist with a vexing question: What have you done lately?

"What more can we do?" asks—beseeches—Mr. von Kuenheim, sitting in the chairman's suite atop the cylindrical BMW tower. "What more can we do?"

In years past, BMW always seemed to have a ready answer. After all, the BMW mystique dictates dynamism, agressiveness, mobility, technology, innovation. The three initials are more than a car, they are an image, a way of life.

Lately, though, BMW is groping for new directions. The auto maker's breakneck growth of the past two decades is slowing. Its share of the German market slipped in the first several months of the year, before recovering some. Auto analysts and industry press are calling the existing models "outdated" and "boring." Technical and service problems are arising. And BMW's mid-size luxury car niche is under invasion from all sides.

What's more, BMW still hasn't come out with a convincing answer to the Mercedes-Benz 190, the hot-selling "Baby Benz," that sped into BMW's terrain nearly three years ago. In fact, the two German auto makers seem to have switched images: Mercedes, maker of the establishment car, is being seen as the innovative one and BMW as the conservative one.

The BMW veneer has been further scratched by an unusual crush of bad press. "The three initials BMW are no longer enough, particularly against aggressive competition, to hold the attention of the public," writes *Auto Motor and Sport,* the West German car industry magazine.

And industry analysts, who have come to expect more than just profits from BMW, have been voicing disappointment. Says one European auto analyst: "How long can you live off your current image without doing something bold?"

Mr. von Kuenheim, who is one of the longest-serving chairmen at a major auto maker, cooly brushes aside such criticism. "When you are out in front of a certain area for 20 or 25 years," he says, "it is no disgrace to pause a short while to catch your breath for a new leap forward."

But, he concedes, "Through success one produces problems." And BMW has a special problem: Much of the appeal of the auto is the image. The car is expensive, but in many ways the image is more valuable.

Thus, preserving the BMW mystique, and living up to it, is presenting the 56-year-old chairman with perhaps his biggest challenge since taking over the wheel of BMW in 1970. Mr. von Kuenheim, a soft-spoken Prussian-Bavarian, finds himself fighting the image battle on three fronts. He is trying to maintain BMW's aura of exclusivity while selling half of a million cars around the world, a large number and big market for a specialty car maker. He is wrestling to retain the market mystique by elbowing competitors—Mercedes, Audi, Volvo, Saab, Mazda, Ford, among others—away from BMW's customer group. And he is struggling to keep the upwardly mobile look while steering the company through a period of slower growth.

In 1970, the Bavarian auto maker produced about 160,000 cars and posted earnings equivalent to about $12 million on sales of $600 million. Last year, the company turned out more than 430,000 cars and record profits of $116 million on sales of $4.5 billion. Mr. von Kuenheim boasts that over the past two decades BMW has grown faster than any other auto maker outside of Japan, and faster than the average of the Japanese auto industry.

Now, he concedes, the impressive increases of the past will be hard to repeat, although the company is expecting its 1985 numbers to be well above last year's strike-reduced results.

"Growth is not a corporate goal for us. We don't want to be a mass producer," the chairman says. "We will be somewhat bigger, but we won't grow in the same percent numbers as in past years." He smiles and adds, "We can live well with smaller growth."

But can the image survive? Mr. von Kuenheim is trying to assure that it does by promising "something new, every half year." He won't give specifics, but BMW engineers are working on giving a more sporty look to the smaller models—the three-series cars that are BMW's "bread and butter"—and sprucing up the styling and technology on the larger five-series and seven-series models. The company will open up a new production plant in the fall of 1986, giving it added capacity and flexibility.

But as production rises, the task of squaring BMW's "world car" billing with its "only-one-in-the-neighborhood" exclusiveness becomes ever harder. Thus, the auto maker is setting sales limits for its two largest markets, West Germany and the U.S.

In Germany, BMW has about 6.5% of the market. "But," says Mr. von Kuenheim, "if we had 10% of the German market, it might give us some concern." And in the U.S., the current level of 80,000 cars, or 18% of BMW's production, is "a point where one should say we shouldn't let this climb too much," the chairman notes.

As a result, he says, "We must look at the world market. We must consider that our auto is for Singapore and Saudi Arabia. That it is not only for California, but also for Kansas City. For Japan and for Germany. It should be fast, but not too fast. And it should be comfortable, but not too expensive."

SOURCE: Roger Thurow, "BMW's Plight: Success Is not Enough." Reprinted by permission of *The Wall Street Journal.* © Dow Jones & Company, Inc., August 12, 1985. All rights reserved.

DISCUSSION QUESTIONS

1. Prepare an analysis of the strategic situation confronting BMW.
2. What strategic options are appropriate for BMW?
3. Which strategy do you recommend, and why?
4. Prepare a brief analysis of BMW's key competitors. Who are some potential future competitors?

PART 3

Marketing Strategy Development

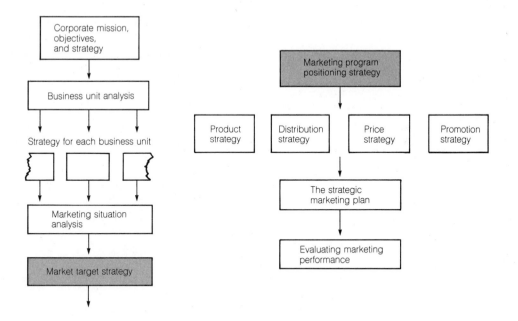

CHAPTER 8

Market Target Strategy

Spiegel Inc., the Chicago-based fashion catalog retailer of women's apparel and home furnishings, wants to reach $1 billion in sales by 1988.[1] By the end of 1984, about 70 percent of the 1988 sales objective had been achieved. An important part of Spiegel's marketing strategy is targeting career women 21 to 54 years old with household incomes of $25,000 and above. These working women are looking for ways to save time, but are also interested in fashion and quality. They represent 26 million of the nation's 88 million households. A decade ago Spiegel had a blue-collar image. Today the firm is battling for a large piece of the highly competitive mail-order market. The market segment targeted by Spiegel is large and growing, but many other retailers are also after career women. Spiegel doubled its 1984 advertising budget to $4 million in an attempt to increase its awareness by women in the target group. In 1983, 33 percent of the women surveyed knew Spiegel as it wants to be known.

The *market target* decision is the choice of the people or organizations in a product-market that an organization will target with its positioning strategy. Selecting a market target strategy is one of management's most demanding challenges. Should a firm attempt to serve all people who are willing and able to buy? Or should it selectively focus on one or more subgroups? We must gain an understanding of a product-market, buyers, and competition in order to make the market target decision.

In analyzing the corporate and marketing strategies of successful companies, one feature stands out. Each has a market target strategy that has proved to be a major factor in gaining a strong market position for the firm. This is the case even though the strategies used by the different companies are often quite different. It is interesting to note that this characteristic cuts across firms in all kinds of businesses, including those providing industrial and consumer products. In this chapter we first consider the strategic options available to a firm in selecting a market target. Next, we take up the bases for segmenting a market. A discussion follows of methods for forming segments and developing descriptive profiles. Finally, guidelines for analyzing market segments are presented and the important issues in selecting market targets are examined.

MARKET TARGETING OPTIONS

The possibilities for selecting the firm's target group of customers in a product-market range from attempting to appeal to most people in the market (a mass market approach) to going after one or more market segments (subgroups) within the market:

Mass market target strategy. All potential customers in a product-market are assumed to be sufficiently similar in their responsiveness to a marketing program positioning strategy.[2] Note that *mass* refers not to absolute size but instead to the fact that the firm is aiming one marketing program at all of the people or organizations rather than going after one or more subgroups within the product-market by using a different marketing program for each subgroup.

Segmentation market target strategy. Using this strategy, one assumes that the people or organizations within a product-market will vary as to their responsiveness to any marketing program positioning strategy. The objective is to establish two or more subgroups within the product-market so that the people or organizations comprising each subgroup will respond similarly to a marketing offer designed to meet their particular needs and wants. A segmenting strategy can be implemented by going after a single segment or by using a different marketing program for each segment that is targeted.

Different terms are sometimes used. *Market niche* and *market segment* are often used to describe a market target strategy that is intended to focus on subgroups within a product-market. In this book they are used interchangeably. The term *vertical market* is sometimes used by marketing executives. Vertical markets are segments according to an industry basis of classification. An example of a vertical segment is the banking industry. Several illustrative market target strategies are shown in Exhibit 8–1. We will examine mass and segment targeting alternatives in order to find out more about their features and limitations.

EXHIBIT 8-1 Illustrative Market Target Strategies

Targeting Strategy	Consumer Products	Industrial Products
Mass	Kikkoman International Inc. (soy sauce)	U.S. Surgical Corp. (surgical staplers)
Single segment	Godiva Chocolatier, Inc. (luxury chocolates) Payless Cashways, Inc. (do-it-yourself home improvement)	Snap-on-Tools (mechanics' hand tools) *Oil & Gas Journal* (magazine)
Multiple segments	Hartmarx Corp. (men's clothing) Anheuser-Busch (beer)	Guest Supply Inc. (hotel bathroom amenties) IBM (computers)

Mass Strategy

The founder of Federal Express Corporation, Frederick W. Smith, created a new service-market in 1971 by offering an overnight pickup and delivery service for small high-value packages. There was no reason to look for a segment. The entire service-market contained a small, but rapidly growing, group of people and organizations with a specific need for fast delivery of valuable merchandise (e.g., documents, drawings, photographs) at acceptable prices. The weight of items transported is normally under 70 pounds. Federal's fastest growing service is the Courier-Pak, which handles up to two pounds for under $25. The company has experienced an explosive growth, with sales in 1986 likely to move above $2.5 billion. Federal's newest service, Zap Mail, an electronic facsimile transmission service, offers a promising market opportunity.

There was a variety of potential users for Federal's small package service. Their needs until 1971 had not been met with existing services, such as the U.S. Postal Service. During the last decade several firms entered this service-market, including Emery Air Freight Corporation, Airborne Freight Corporation, the U.S. Postal Service's Priority Mail, and some airlines. As this service-market gains maturity and as special needs develop for subgroups within the market, segmenting strategies are occurring. For example, the U.S. Postal Service is offering a substantially lower-priced service than Federal Express for customers wanting fast delivery (two- to three-day small package delivery) but not requiring overnight service. This maturing market is beginning to provide opportunities for segmentation.

The Federal Express illustration highlights several conditions that often favor use of a mass market target strategy. New product-markets typically contain buyers with similar needs whereas a mature product-market is likely to be larger and its buyers' needs to be more complex. There are few competitors in a new product-market and sometimes none. The costs of serving new product-markets are also relevant. Federal decided to get into business on a scale suitable for offering services throughout the United States. This made a lot more sense than starting on a city-by-city basis since it would be difficult to control the customer's shipping destination. In most new product-markets as well as some that have reached maturity, it may not be feasible to identify niches that can be served by a firm. In these instances, a mass approach may be the most appropriate market target strategy.

Segmentation Strategy

A *segmentation strategy* consists of: (1) identifying segments within a product-market, (2) deciding which segment(s) to target, and (3) designing and implementing a marketing program positioning strategy for each targeted segment. Thus segmentation extends beyond subgroup identification. It is a type of marketing strategy.

Companies typically appeal to only a portion of the people or organizations in a product-market, regardless of the market target strategy that is used. Management may identify one or more specific segments for its firm to serve. Alternatively, although no specific segment strategy has been formulated, the marketing program selected by the firm will position it in a product-market in such a way that the firm will appeal to a particular subgroup within the market. The former situation is obviously preferred. Finding a segment by chance does not provide management the opportunity of evaluating different niches in terms of the revenue, cost, and profit implications associated with each. At the other extreme, the task of selecting the very best market target is often impossible as a result of the product-market complexity, research and analysis costs, and the difficulty of estimating the market segment response to a marketing effort. When a segmentation strategy is employed, it should be by design and the underlying analyses should lead to the selection of at least a promising target opportunity.

The market segmentation strategy used by the Hartmarx Corporation, a leading diversified manufacturer and retailer of men's and women's apparel, provides an interesting illustration of market targeting. The various segments served by the company's brands are shown in Exhibit 8–2. Note the use of price and style as bases for segmenting the men's apparel market. The buyers in these segments have been identified and described by Hartmarx. For example, the new Henry Grethel line focuses on a younger, more contemporary customer who is interested in forward fashion and is responsive to a retail price range of $255–375 for a suit of clothing.[3] Marketing research findings identified "The Right Suit," a national advertising campaign in 1984–85 that proved to be right on target in reaching executive buyers of the Hart Schaffner & Marx label, one the firm's best-performing brands. Hartmarx is also moving aggressively into the market for women's suits.

EXHIBIT 8-2 Market Segments Targeted by Hartmarx Corp. (men's suits, by retail price and style)

Retail Price	Contemporary	Designer/Personality	Traditional	Forward Fashion
$525+	Hickey-Freeman—Walter Morton			
$450–$500	Jaeger	Christian Dior Grand Luxe		Walter Holmes—Society Brand
$325–$450	Hart Schaffner & Marx		Graham & Gunn	
$255–$375		Christian Dior Monsieur Pierre Cardin	Austin Reed of Regent Street	Henry Grethel
$215–$275		Nino Cerruti	Racquet	
$170–$245	Jaymar Allyn St. George	Johnny Carson		
$120–$180	Kuppenheimer			

SOURCE: Hartmarx 1984 Annual Report, 17.

Considerations in Strategy Selection

Several of the same variables that lead to the choice of a mass market strategy may, depending upon their values, suggest a segmentation strategy. For example, if the competitive intensity in a product-market is high instead of low, this may indicate that a segmenting strategy should be considered. Likewise, if buyers' needs and wants in a particular product-market are quite different, a niche strategy may be appropriate. When the various factors affecting the targeting decision suggest a mass strategy, they often do not favor a niche strategy and vice versa. This is admittedly an oversimplification. More specific guidelines for selecting a market target strategy are presented later in the chapter.

When following a segmentation strategy, a company may decide to serve more than a single segment. It may select a few segments or it may seek intensive coverage of the product-market by targeting all or most of the segments. No matter how many segments are targeted, the objective is to aim a specific marketing effort at each segment that management may choose to serve. Anheuser-Busch Companies, Inc., the leading U.S. brewer, with its multiple-brand offering is going after several major population groups within the total product-market. Some of the groups are quite large, and there are undoubtedly people who buy more than one of the Anheuser-Busch brands. Acknowledging some overlap in population groups, the firm's market target strategy is more of a segmentation approach than a mass strategy since different brands, prices, distribution, and promotional programs are involved.

In some large product-markets the companies have selected market target strategies that offer buyers a *variety* of products. On the surface this appears to be a niche strategy, with each product offering a different appeal. Yet these strategies are the result of giving buyers brand alternatives. When a buyer desires a brand change, a switch can be made to another brand or product version offered by the same firm. Sometimes, without conducting consumer research studies, it may be difficult to distinguish whether a firm is using a segmentation or a variety strategy, and there may be some elements of both strategies present. For example, the firm may offer variety to buyers in a particular market segment. Offering customers different flavors or varieties of food products are illustrations of variety strategies. The strategy is similar to a mass approach in which the variety of products is intended to offer a broad appeal. Mars, Inc.'s wide variety of candy bars is illustrative of this strategy. The variety strategy seems most popular in food and beverage product markets.

EXHIBIT 8-3   Steps in Selecting a Market Targeting Strategy

---

1. Identify basis of segmentation
2. Form segments
3. Profile segments
4. Analyze segments
5. Select market target(s)
6. Design and implement positioning strategy for each market target

---

Steps in Selecting a Market Targeting Strategy

In view of the rapid adoption of segmentation strategies by companies, it is assumed that management will consider a segmentation strategy in evaluating alternative market targeting options. There are six major steps in selecting a market targeting strategy as shown in Exhibit 8-3. *Step 1* consists of selecting one or more variables to use in identifying market segments. In *Step 2* the segments are formed by using one or more segmentation methods. In *Step 3* the buyers that comprise each segment of interest to the firm are profiled to describe their characteristics and other buying information. *Step 4* consists of analyzing each segment to determine the opportunity it offers, the segment's marketing requirements, and other strategy considerations. In *Step 5* one or more market targets is selected. *Step 6* involves designing and implementing an appropriate positioning strategy for each market target. Steps 1 through 5 are examined and illustrated in this chapter. The marketing program positioning strategy is considered in Chapter 9.

Segmentation may enable a company to gain worthwhile advantages compared to using a mass approach. These advantages may include a higher profitability and greater strength over the competition through a more effective use of the firm's capabilities and resources. By selecting segments each of which contains people or organizations that exhibit some degree of similarity, management can gain greater customer responsiveness from the effort expended than if the firm were to direct the same marketing effort to all people or organizations in the product-market. Management must somehow identify possible segments and then, for each one that is of interest, determine which positioning strategy will obtain the most favorable profit contribution, net of marketing costs. Since there are many ways to divide a product-market and several marketing program combinations that might be used for each segment, it is probably impossible to find the very best (optimal) market target and marketing program positioning strategy. One should first decide whether moving away from a mass strategy is advisable, and, if so, determine what market target alternative looks attractive to management.

IDENTIFY THE BASIS OF SEGMENTATION

Certain requirements must be satisfied by the segments that are identified. First we examine these requirements, and then discuss the role of the segmentation variables. Finally, the types of variables that can be used to divide product-markets into segments are examined.

Requirements for Segmentation

An important question is whether or not it is worthwhile to segment a product-market. Guidelines are needed for evaluating the worth of a particular segmentation scheme. Since there are many ways to form product-market niches, how does the marketing strategist make the choice? Five criteria are useful for this purpose.[4]

Response Differences.   Identifying the responsiveness of people in the product-market to marketing program efforts is central to segment identification. Suppose the people in a product-market are divided into four groups, each a potential segment. If each group responds (e.g., amount or frequency of purchase) in the same way as all other groups to any given marketing program strategy, then the groupings are *not* market segments. If four (or any) segments actually exist in this illustration, a different marketing program strategy will work best for each group. Management may simply feel—on the basis of their experience and judgment—that response differences exist, and that the basis used for dividing the market (e.g., age, income, industry-type) will separate people or organizations into similar response categories. Nevertheless, to substantiate the existence of real segments requires supporting evidence of actual response differences. After meeting the first condition, the other requirements come into play.

Identifiable Segments.   It must be feasible to identify the two or more customer groups that actually display response differences. Finding the correct groups may be difficult because it is not apparent which variable(s) is/are appropriate for dividing the market into segments. Unfortunately, it is easy to find differences among the buyers in a product-market. The key issue is whether these variations are related to response differences.

Actionable Segments.   A firm must be able to aim a marketing program strategy at each target market. As an illustration, demographics may not be helpful in such an effort.[5] Suppose the target segment is middle-class families, with an average of 2.2 children, living in a city of 50,000 population. This description does not provide much direction as to how to reach these people with a marketing program. Product or use situation factors are generally more effective bases of segmentation.

Cost/Benefits of Segmentation.   In terms of revenues generated and costs incurred, segmentation must be worth doing. Frederick W. Winter comments on this requirement:

> Market segmentation is the recognition that groups or subsegments differ with respect to properties which suggest that different marketing mixes might be used to appeal to the different groups. These subsegments may then be aggregated if the reduction in cost exceeds the reduction in benefits (revenues). This aggregation is based on the fact that both subsegments respond most to the same marketing mix.[6]

Stability over Time.   Finally, the segments must exhibit adequate stability over time so that the firm's efforts via segmentation will have enough time to reach the desired levels of performance. If buyers' needs are changing rapidly, a group with similar response patterns at one point in time could display quite different patterns several months later. The time period may be too short to justify using a segmentation strategy.

If a firm is unable to meet the five above-listed criteria, the use of a segmentation strategy is questionable. For example, if a segment formation scheme does not identify different groups, each of which exhibits a similar responsiveness within and a variation among groups, then dividing the product-market is of doubtful value. The ultimate criterion, of course, is performance. If a niche scheme leads to improved performance (profitability) in a product-market, then it is worthwhile.

Role of Segmentation Variables

Segmentation variables perform two important functions. The *basis* variable is the criterion used to divide a product-market into segments. The *descriptor* variable discriminates among segments of the product-market along the criterion (basis) of interest.[7] In practice, the distinction between bases and descriptors is often not apparent since the same variable may be used for both purposes and the two types of variables may be interrelated.

In forming market segments, the basis should clearly identify segments that satisfy the requirements discussed earlier. Finding differences within product-markets is not difficult. Importantly, the differences must be relevant to the segmentation objective. An interesting example comparing useful and irrelevant segmentation descriptors is shown in Exhibit 8–4. The solar water heater product-market is the seg-

EXHIBIT 8-4 Relevant and Irrelevant Segment Descriptors

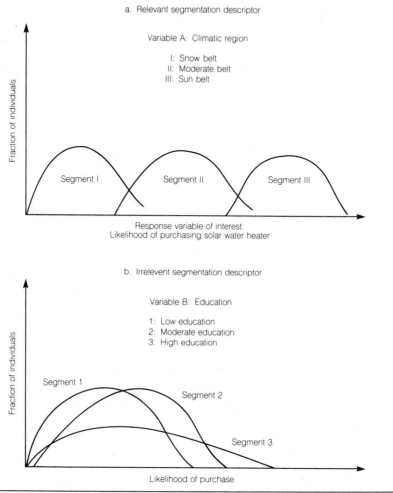

a. Relevant segmentation descriptor

Variable A: Climatic region

I: Snow belt
II: Moderate belt
III: Sun belt

Fraction of individuals

Segment I   Segment II   Segment III

Response variable of interest:
Likelihood of purchasing solar water heater

b. Irrelevent segmentation descriptor

Variable B: Education

1: Low education
2: Moderate education
3: High education

Fraction of individuals

Segment 1
Segment 2
Segment 3

Likelihood of purchase

SOURCE: Gary L. Lilien and Philip Kotler, *Marketing Decision Making* (New York: Harper & Row, 1983), 292.

mentation objective. The response (basis) variable is the likelihood of the purchase of a solar water heater. In Exhibit 8–4a three segments are identified by using the relevant descriptor, climatic region. In contrast, the use of education (Exhibit 8–4b) does not discriminate among segments, since Segments 1, 2, and 3 consist of substantially the same people.

The four categories of variables shown in Exhibit 8–5 indicate the wide range of segment bases and descriptors. Demographic and psychographic (life-style and personality) characteristics of consumers

EXHIBIT 8-5 Variables for Dividing Product-Markets into Segments

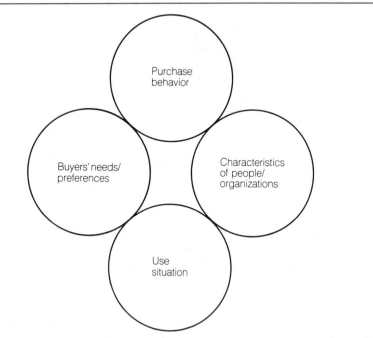

and various characteristics of organizational buyers are of interest since several of these variables are available from the U.S. Census reports and other published sources. The use situation refers to how the buyer uses the product, such as purchasing a meal away-from-home for the purpose of entertainment. Variables measuring buyers' needs and preferences include attitudes, brand awareness, and brand preference. Purchase behavior variables focus on various aspects of brand-use and consumption. A closer examination of each type of variable will highlight its uses, features, and other considerations important in segmentation. Since several of these variables are described in Chapter 6, the discussion here will be brief.

Characteristics of People/Organizations

These variables fall into two major categories: (1) geographic and demographic, and (2) psychographic (life-style and personality). Demographics have not been found very useful in segmenting consumer markets. Nevertheless, these variables are popular because available data often relate demographics to the other segmentation variables shown in Exhibit 8–5. Geographic location is useful for segmenting certain

---

EXHIBIT 8-6 Popular Vehicles by State

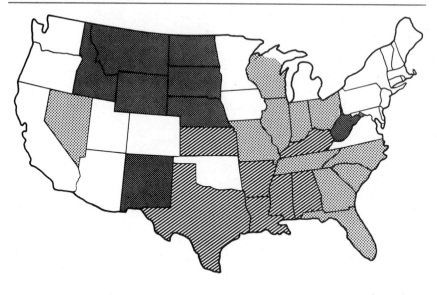

■ Ford F150 pickup

▨ Chevrolet C10 pickup

▦ Oldsmobile Cutlass

SOURCE: Eugene Carlson, "Personality of Area's Drivers Offers Key to Auto's Success." Reprinted by permission of *The Wall Street Journal*. © Dow Jones & Company, Inc., December 13, 1983. All rights reserved.

---

kinds of product-markets. Note, for example, the regional differences in the popularity of transportation vehicles in various states, as shown in Exhibit 8–6. Interestingly, in fifteen states the most popular vehicle is a pickup truck. The "truck belt" runs from the upper Midwest south through Texas and the Gulf states. Ford is dominant in the northern half of the truck belt and Chevrolet leads in the southern half.

Segmentation using life-style variables has proven useful in identifying differences within particular demographic categories. Life-style may be relevant in segmenting markets for high-involvement products, as we learned in Chapter 6. Revlon's success in the 1970s with its Charlie perfume was due, in part, to management's recognition of the importance of life-style as a basis for determining Charlie's market segment.

Organizational characteristics are useful in segmenting business markets. The type of industry (vertical market) is related to purchase behavior for certain types of products. Industry segmentation enables suppliers to specialize their efforts and satisfy customer needs. For various reasons industry types are often geographically concentrated. For example, petrochemical processing is heavily concentrated along the Gulf coast. Concentration may be due to the availability of labor and material supplies, transportation costs, and other factors.

Use Situation

Markets can be segmented by the usage situation. As an illustration, several marketing efforts have been launched in recent years to encourage people to use foods for different occasions. The advertising campaign, "Orange juice isn't just for breakfast anymore," is illustrative. Peter R. Dickson identifies several other applications:

> Many other examples of situation segmentation can be found in the design of furniture, appliances, china, bicycles, motorcycles, automobiles and camping equipment. Some lounge suites are designed for small apartments, others for beach side holiday homes and yet others for executive suites and lounge bars. Color TVs are designed as feature furniture pieces for family rooms and as robust portables for trailers and bedrooms. Special refrigerators are designed for trailers and basement bars. Expensive china is designed for entertaining guests, while cheap, robust Corelle dinnerware is designed for everyday family use. There are commuting motorcycles, dirt motorcycles, farm motorcycles and highway cruisers. Pick-ups and four-wheel drive station wagons are primarily designed for different usage situations than a VW Rabbit or Rolls Royce. Camping gear is designed to be adaptable, but specialist equipment is designed for use in tropical and/ or very cold climates and situations where space and weight are at a premium. The clothing and footwear market has long been person-situation segmented to accommodate not only differing sex and size but also differing weather conditions, physical activities and social role playing.[8]

The use of a person-situation and product benefit as a segmentation technique is discussed later in the chapter.

Buyers' Needs/Preferences

Many factors are specific to products and brands and can be used as segmentation bases and descriptors. Illustrative variables include brand loyalty status, benefits sought, and proneness to make a deal. Buyers sometimes are attracted to different brands on the basis of matching the benefits they want from a product with the benefits offered by a particular brand. For example, Jerome Schulman, a chemist, developed Shane toothpaste to meet the needs of people with bleeding gums and sensitive teeth.[9] The brand sells for $5.95 for a 6.4 ounce tube. Mr. Schulman is a one-person enterprise. Shane does not have a multimillion-dollar advertising budget or the endorsement of the

EXHIBIT 8-7   Illustrative Segmentation Bases and Descriptors

	Consumer Markets	Industrial/Organizational Markets
Characteristics of people/organizations	Age, gender, race Income Family size Life-cycle stage Geographical location Life-style	Type of industry Size Geographical location Corporate culture Stage of development Producer/intermediary
Use situation	Occasion Importance of purchase Prior experience with product User status	Application Purchasing procedure New task, modified rebuy, straight rebuy
Buyers' needs/preferences	Brand loyalty status Brand preference Benefits sought Quality Proneness to make a deal	Performance requirements Brand preferences Desired features Service requirements
Purchase behavior	Size of purchase Frequency of purchase	Volume Frequency of purchase

American Dental Association. Initially concentrating in the Chicago area, Mr. Schulman sold 150,000 tubes in a few months to drug and food chains.

Purchase Behavior

Consumption variables such as the size and frequency of a purchase may be useful in segmenting consumer and business markets. Marketers of various industrial products often classify customers and prospects into categories on the basis of the volume of the purchase. A speciality chemical producer concentrates its marketing efforts on chemical users that purchase at least $50,000 of chemicals each year. The firm further segments the market on the basis of the use situation.

Exhibit 8-7 shows several segmentation bases and descriptors for consumer and organizational markets. An examination of the methods of segment formation will further demonstrate the role of segmentation variables in the segment determination and analysis.

FORM AND PROFILE SEGMENTS

In deciding how to form market segments several considerations are important:

1. Selecting the segmentation basis variables to be used. The options include buyer characteristics, use situation, buyer needs/preferences, and purchase behavior.
2. Determining the type of information to be used in the analysis (experience and available information versus research studies).
3. Deciding the segment formation approach. Should the segments be formed by an aggregation of the buyers or by breaking out segments from a product-market?
4. Selecting the method of analyzing segment information. The alternatives range from cross-classification tables to various multivariate statistical techniques.

The following examination of methods of forming segments is divided into segment breakout and aggregation methods. Keep in mind that the segments formed should generally satisfy the five requirements discussed earlier in the chapter.

Segment Breakout

The use of a disaggregation approach requries a clearly defined product-market structure. After a product-market has been defined, it may be possible to analyze the resulting structure to identify population groups that offer promising segments for consideration by a company. This can be done by using management judgment in combination with the available information and/or marketing research data.

In segment breakout, management selects one or more variables as the basis of segmentation. These segments are substantiated either through management judgment and experience or by supporting statistical analyses. Examples of each approach are presented to show how segments can be determined.

Experience and Available Information. There are many product-markets where management's knowledge of customer needs is a useful guide to segmentation. Experience and analysis of published information are particularly useful in segmenting business markets. Consider, for example, Guest Supply, a leading firm in a new industry that supplies personal-care bathroom amenities to the hotel and lodging industry.[10] The company's line of products includes soap, shampoo, shower caps, shoe-shine cloths, mouthwash, and other personal-care products using popular brand names such as Vidal, Sassoon, and Roger & Gallet. These amenities are designed to make the hotel guest's stay more pleasant, while promoting the hotel and the brand. Guests are encouraged to take the unused items with them. Guest Supply has segmented the hotel amenities market using the bases of size, room price, and chain affiliation. The top 25 chains in the United States represent

EXHIBIT 8-8 Guest Supply Inc.'s Target Segments

Marketing Approach	Market Segment
Customized-Strategy: National brand-name products and customized initial consulting, design, presentation, execution, and delivery and services. Analyses of customer needs establish a hotel's profile, guiding the recommendation of an amenity program that corresponds to its image.	**Segment A:** Major hotel chains with large properties (over 300 rooms) in the medium- to upper-price range.
Standardized-Strategy: High-quality products offered in attractive, low-cost standardized packages. A computer-assisted telemarketing team supports the outside sales force to reduce the time and cost of personal sales visits.	**Segment B:** Smaller chains and independent establishments in the medium size and price range that cannot justify the cost of customization.

SOURCE: Guest Supply Inc., *1984 Annual Report.*

about 30 percent of the 2.7 million rooms that are available. Guest Supply sells to nine of the top 25 major chains. It supplies Holiday Inns, Inc. with a complete line of 20, custom-designed guest amenities. This contract represented an estimated $8 million in sales over a two-year period. Guest Supply has targeted two major market segments, as shown in Exhibit 8-8. In addition to direct selling and telemarketing, Guest Supply promotes its services through a newsletter, "Guest Impressions," and through brochures, descriptive information, and a calendar showing events for the worldwide hospitality industry. It offers various amenity packages such as luxury, deluxe, standard, and economy programs.

Cross Classification Analyses. A study of industry publications and other published information may identify ways to break up a product-market into segments. Consider, for example, the illustrative demographic comparison of users of two beer brands shown in Exhibit 8-9. For each characteristic notice the differences in the percentage of people that are Budweiser versus Heineken drinkers. Such consumer panel data provide a wide range of consumer characteristics, advertising media usage, and other information analyzed by product and brand usage. Panel data are generated from a large sample of households through the United States.

A note of caution is in order. A wide array of information is available for use in forming population subgroups within product-markets. We can use many sources, such as the information shown in Exhibit 8-9, as well as management's insights and hunches regarding the market. The key, of course, is whether a segmentation scheme establishes groups that possess different product and brand responsiveness. The

---

EXHIBIT 8-9 Illustrative Characteristics of Budweiser and Heineken Beer Users

	Percent	
Characteristic	*Budweiser*	*Heineken*
Age 18–54	54	69
Mid-Atlantic	26	39
Graduated college	20	29
Income $25,000 or more	20	33

SOURCE: *Target Group Index 77,* vol. P-9 (New York: Axiom Market Research Bureau, 1977), 60–61, 68–69.

---

more evidence of meaningful differences, the better support we have that useful segments exist. As Exhibit 8-9 indicates, the differences in people's responsiveness to Budweiser and Heineken beers may not be captured by age, region, education, and income. Despite these limitations of product-market analysis, cross classification does have some real advantages in terms of cost and ease of use. And, in particular situations, there may be a strong basis for choosing a niche scheme that uses this approach. This is probably more often the case in business and organizational markets in which a firm typically has a good knowledge of user needs because there are fewer users than there are in consumer product-markets. Alternatively, the analysis may be a first step leading to a more comprehensive type of analysis.

Multivariate Analysis. A typical approach to segmentation analysis has been for us to select a dependent variable as a basis for our segmentation. In this way we can attempt to find a relationship with the basis variable by using one or more predictors. Various measures of market response are used as basis variables, including usage rates (e.g., heavy, medium, or light usage), size of purchase, and user categories. As shown in Exhibit 8-5, several demographic, psychographic, use situation, and buyers' needs/preferences variables have served as descriptive predictor variables. Our objective is to distinguish buyers in different basis categories by using the predictor variables. Analysis techniques may include automatic interaction detection (AID), multiple regression, and discriminate analysis.[11] An AID application illustrates how such analyses help identify and describe market segments.

AID Analysis. This technique divides a sample of data into categories. It determines groupings using variables (e.g., income) that achieve the largest discrimination for the basis variable (e.g., usage rate). By analyzing a sample of buyers from a product-market, we can determine potential segments. Use of AID analysis to identify segments in the long-distance telephone market is shown in Exhibit 8-10A. A sample

EXHIBIT 8-10   Illustrative Segmentation for Long-Distance
Telephone Service

A

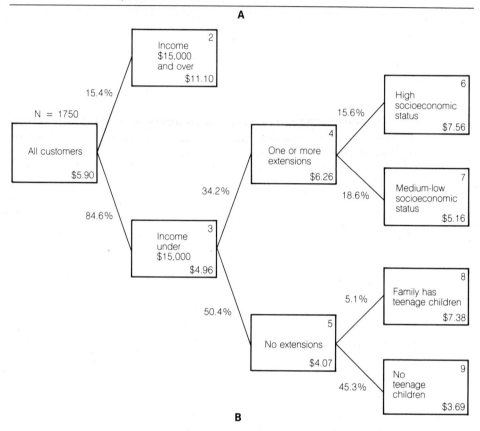

B

Five Segments Produced by the Final Output
of the AID Analysis

Segment Profile	Average Long-Distance Bill	Percent of Sample	Percent of Total Long-Distance Billing Accounted for by Segment
1. Income $15,000 & Over.	$11.10	15.4%	29.0%
2. Income less than $15,000, one or more extensions, higher socio-economic status based on education and occupation.	7.56	15.6	20.1
3. Same as #2, but medium-to-low socioeconomic status.	5.16	18.6	16.2
4. Income under $15,000, no extensions, and family has teenage children.	7.38	5.1	6.4
5. Same as #4, but no teenage children.	3.69	45.3	28.3

SOURCE: Henry Assel and A. Marvin Roscoe Jr., "Approaches to Market Segmentation Analysis," *Journal of Marketing,* October 1976, 70.

of 1,750 consumers was analyzed by AT&T to identify heavy and light long-distance callers.[12] Exhibit 8-10B shows the five segments identified in the AID analysis, including a descriptive profile and purchase data. Demographic and use situation (type of equipment) data identified the segments. Interestingly, while the heavy user segment (#1) accounted for 29 percent of the $ billing on calls, it comprised only 15 percent of the sample.

The intuitive logic underlying these methods is appealing. By selecting a segmentation basis that corresponds to customer responsiveness to a marketing mix such as usage rate, we can preestablish promising niches. If the analysis indicates homogeneity of users within a niche and differences between niches, then we have identified promising segments. Unfortunately, strong and distinct differences have not often been found through predetermined niche analysis. Rather, the differences identified in many instances have been weak and inconclusive. Nevertheless, in large, mature product-markets there has been some success in establishing user profiles on the basis of brand preference. We should also consider that many of the more apparent segment formations have probably been achieved without extensive customer research. Instead, they have been achieved through the product-market analysis approach guided by experience that we discussed earlier. Two other possibilities may explain why segments have not been identified. In some product-markets useful segments may simply not exist. In others, the segment interrelationships may be so complex that an analysis of predetermined groupings will not identify useful segments.

Segment Aggregation

An alternative to using a predetermined segmentation approach is to aggregate buyers by using one or more bases to form the segments. Using an aggregation model incorporating market-potential assessment, we show four microsegments in the potential market for industrial solar air conditioning in Exhibit 8-11.[13] The analysis indicates the sizes of the segments, decision participants, extent of satisfaction with the existing cooling system, and other useful buyer profile information. This approach is useful for segmenting markets for both new and existing products. The calculation of expected market response is based on estimates of segment size, buyer awareness of solar cooling, feasibility, and conditional probability of a group choice, given the feasibility. This same modeling approach has been applied in segmenting markets for computer terminals, copiers, solar panels, photovoltaic cells, airline meals, and industrial heating equipment.

Segment aggregation approaches draw more extensively from buyer behavior information than the predetermined segment techniques discussed earlier. Note, for example, the information on the buying center,

EXHIBIT 8–11 Microsegments of Organizations in the Potential Market for Solar Air Conditioning

Item	Segment 1	Segment 2	Segment 3	Segment 4
Microsegment size in potential market	12%	31%	32%	25%
Major decision participants in a/c equipment-selection decision (frequencies of involvement)	Plant managers (1.00) HVAC consultants (0.38)	Production engineers (0.94) Plant managers (0.70)	Production engineers (0.97) HVAC consultants (0.60)	Top management (0.85) HVAC consultants (0.67)
Satisfaction with current a/c system	Medium High	Low	Medium Low	High
Consequence if new a/c less economical than projected	Medium High	Low	Medium Low	High
Consequence if new a/c less reliable than projected	Medium High	Low	High	Medium Low
Company size	Medium	Large	Large	Small
Percentage of plant area requiring a/c	Medium Large	Small	Large	Medium
Number of separate plants	Medium Large	Small	Large	Medium Small

Note: Abbreviation a/c means air conditioning and HVAC means heating, ventilating, and air conditioning.
SOURCE: Gary L. Lilien and Philip Kotler, *Marketing Decision Making* (New York: Harper & Row, 1983), 283.

decision participants, extent of satisfaction, and use situation for the solar air conditioning segmentation analysis (Exhibit 8–11). We will examine two additional applications to more fully explore the potential of segment aggregation approaches.

Cluster Analysis. This technique groups people according to the similarity of their answers to questions such as brand preferences on product attributes. The objective of cluster analysis is to identify groupings in which the similarity within a group is high and the variation among groups is as great as possible. Each represents a potential segment. A life-style segmentation study of the snack foods market illustrates how cluster analysis is used.[14] Using a sample of 1,500 snack food users, information on various life-style characteristics and benefits sought in snack foods was collected and analyzed. A summary of the results of the study is shown in Exhibit 8–12. Six potential segments emerged from the analysis. Comparisons of the groups indicate several differences useful in market targeting and marketing program development. Note the variation in the type of snacks usually eaten by the members of each segment. Also there is substantial variation in demographic characteristics across segments.

Perceptual Maps. Another promising research technique uses consumer research data to construct perceptual maps for products and brands. Recall, for example, the discussion in Chapter 7 of the automobile brand preference map (Exhibit 7–14). Such positioning studies represent an active marketing research area. The analyses are useful in selecting market target strategies and in deciding how to position a product or brand to serve the chosen market target. Various other techniques are available, including several of the customer-oriented methods for establishing product-market boundaries discussed in Chapter 5.

While the end result of positioning research is simple to understand, its execution is demanding in terms of research skills. Although there are variations in approach, the following steps are typically included:

1. Selection of the product-market area to be examined.
2. Determination of the brands that fall into the product-market.[15]
3. Collection of consumer perception data for available brands (and an ideal brand) obtained from a sample of people.
4. Analysis of data to form one, two, or more composite attribute dimensions, each independent of the other.
5. Preparation of a map (two-dimensional X and Y grid) of attributes on which are positioned consumer perceptions of competing brands.
6. Plotting of consumers with similar ideal preferences to see if subgroups will form.

EXHIBIT 8–12 Life-Style Segmentation of the Snack Food Market

	Nutritional Snackers	Weight Watchers	Guilty Snackers	Party Snackers	Indiscriminate Snackers	Economical Snackers
Percentage of snackers	22%	14%	9%	15%	15%	18%
Life-Style characteristics	Self-assured Controlled	Outdoor types Influential Venturesome	High anxiety Isolate	Sociable	Hedonistic	Self-assured Price oriented
Benefits sought	Nutritious No artificial ingredients Natural snack	Low calorie Quick energy	Low calorie Good tasting	Good to serve guests Proud to serve Goes well with beverage	Good tasting Satisfies hunger	Low price Best value
Consumption level of snacks	Light	Light	Heavy	Average	Heavy	Average
Type of snacks usually eaten	Fruits Vegetables Cheese	Yogurt Vegetables	Yogurt Cookies Crackers Candy	Nuts Potato Chips Crackers Pretzels	Candy Ice cream Cookies Potato chips Pretzels Popcorn	No specific products
Demographics	Better educated Have younger children	Younger Single	Younger or older Females Lower socioeconomic group	Middle-aged Nonurban	Teens	Larger families Better educated

SOURCE: Henry Assael, *Consumer Behavior and Marketing Action*, 2nd ed. (Boston: Kent Publishing, 1984), 262.

EXHIBIT 8-13   An Illustrative Consumer Perception Map

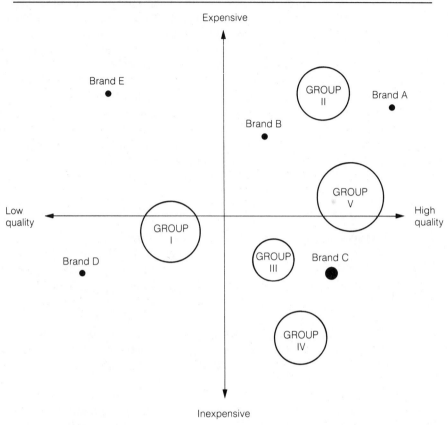

7. Evaluation of how well the solution corresponds to the data that are analyzed.
8. Interpretation of the results as to market target and product positioning strategies.

An illustrative end result of a perceptual mapping application is shown in Exhibit 8-13. The obvious appeal of this research method should be clear after one studies the illustration. Because of the technical requirements for applying the research approach, marketing research skills and experience are essential. Nevertheless, the potential value of a properly designed and executed study can be significant.

Suppose that the underlying analysis for Exhibit 8-13 strongly supports the mapping as indicated. If your brand is C, what are the strategic implications of the analysis? Segment V is a logical market target for your firm, and III may represent a secondary market target. To appeal most effectively to group V, you will probably need to change somewhat group V consumers' price perceptions of brand C. Offering another brand less expensive than C to appeal to group IV is another possible action. Of course, management should study the research results in much greater depth than we have in this brief examination of Exhibit 8-13. The objective is to show how the results might be used. Perceptual mapping, like many of the research methods used for segment identification, is expensive and represents a technical challenge. When used and interpreted properly, these methods offer powerful tools for management in analyzing product-market structure to identify possible market target niches. There are many issues that must be considered in specific applications such as the choice of attributes, identification of relevant products and brands, sampling design, and evaluating the strength of results.[16]

Application Illustration

Person-situation segmentation offers a promising framework for segment identification and strategic analysis.[17] The procedure is outlined in Exhibit 8-14. This method of segmentation provides a general set of guidelines that can be adapted to a particular application situation, utilizing management judgment as well as research data. Note that it is not necessary to identify and describe every possible usage situation. The matrix (Step 3) is useful in identifying key differences among particular groups of consumers in specific usage situations. Dickson comments on the illustrative matrix shown in Exhibit 8-15:

> Many more distinct groups of people and situations could be included. Some of the special benefits or features desired in the particular usage situations or sought by the particular groups of users are listed in the row and column margins (some of these are purely speculative). To serve the needs of a particular person-situation submarket, the product should meet the needs listed at the end of the row and the bottom of the column. This demand can result in both person and situation segmentation. Some person-situation cells have unique needs that should be noted in the individual cells (e.g., a winter scented lotion for female skiers). Each cell should also contain an assessment of the size of the market and a list of the company and competitive brands that are designed to meet the specific needs of this market.[18]

The person-situation segmentation matrix can contribute to strategy analysis in several ways. It offers useful information for market opportunity analysis, targeting, and positioning. A firm's products can be placed on the matrix along with competing brands. Key competitors can be positioned and market gaps can be identified.

EXHIBIT 8-14   Person-Situation Segmentation Procedure

Step 1   Use observational studies, focus group discussions, and secondary data to discover whether different usage situations exist and whether they are determinant, in the sense that they appear to affect the importance of various product characteristics.

Step 2   If Step 1 produces promising results, undertake a benefit, product perception and reported market behavior segmentation survey of consumers. Measure benefits and perceptions by usage situation as well as by individual difference characteristics. Assess situation usage frequency by recall estimates or usage situation diaries.

Step 3   Construct a person-situation segmentation matrix. The rows are the major usage situations and the columns are groups of users identified by a single characteristic or combination of characteristics.

Step 4   Rank the cells in the matrix in terms of their submarket sales volume. The situation-person combination that results in the greatest consumption of the generic product would be ranked first.

Step 5   State the major benefits sought, important product dimensions, and unique market behavior for each nonempty cell of the matrix (some person types will never consume the product in certain usage situations).

Step 6   Position your competitors' offerings within the matrix. The person-situation segments they currently serve can be determined by the product feature they promote and other marketing strategy.

Step 7   Position your offering within the matrix on the same criteria.

Step 8   Assess how well your current offering and marketing strategy meet the needs of the submarkets, compared to the competition.

Step 9   Identify market opportunities based on submarket size, needs, and competitive advantage.

SOURCE: Peter R. Dickson, "Person-Situation: Segmentation's Missing Link," *Journal of Marketing* (Fall 1982), 61.

Selecting a Segmentation Method

Choosing a method to use for forming segments in a product-market often is situation-specific. The choice of method depends on such factors as the complexity of product-market structure, the competitive situation, and other considerations. A general approach is presented in Exhibit 8-16, starting with management's knowledge and experience in the product-market. As we move through the stages shown, the costs of segment identification increase, reaching the highest level when consumer research studies are involved. We should make maximum use of

EXHIBIT 8–15 Speculative Person-Situation Segmentation Matrix for Suntan Lotion

Persons → Situations ↓	Young Children Fair Skin	Young Children Dark Skin	Teenagers Fair Skin	Teenagers Dark Skin	Adult Women Fair Skin	Adult Women Dark Skin	Adult Men Fair Skin	Adult Men Dark Skin	Situation Benefits/Features
Beach/boat sunbathing	Combined insect repellent				Summer perfume				a. Windburn protection b. Formula and container can stand heat c. Container floats and is distinctive (not easily lost)
Home-poolside sunbathing					Combined moisturizer				a. Large pump dispenser b. Won't stain wood, concrete, or furnishings
Sunlamp bathing					Combined moisturizer and massage oil				a. Designed specifically for type of lamp b. Artificial tanning ingredient
Snow skiing					Winter perfume				a. Special protection from special light rays and weather b. Antifreeze formula
Person benefit/features	Special protection a. Protection critical b. Nonpoisonous		Special protection a. Fit in jean pocket b. Used by opinion leaders		Special protection Female perfume		Special protection Male perfume		

SOURCE: Peter R. Dickson, "Person-Situation: Segmentation's Missing Link," *Journal of Marketing*, Fall 1982, 62.

EXHIBIT 8-16 How to Identify Product-Market Niches

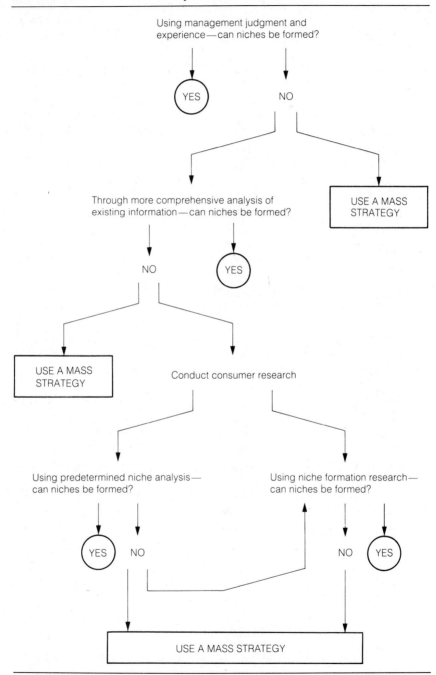

management's knowledge about the product-market in combination with the analysis of available information. In some instances this will provide a sufficient basis for niche formation. If not, experience and existing information are often helpful in guiding the design of consumer research studies.

How does one decide when a segmentation scheme is acceptable? What criteria should be used to determine if useful niches have been formed? For this purpose we can use the five-market segmentation criteria discussed earlier, after first determining if response differences exist among niches. Deciding if the criteria are sufficiently satisfied rests with management. Management should select a segmentation strategy that satisfies the responsiveness criterion plus the other four criteria (end users identifiable, accessible via marketing program, niche(s) economically viable, and niche stability over time). After implementation of the scheme, we should continue to evaluate the segmentation approach. Improvements in segment identification may be possible as the firm gains experience.

Consideration should be made of the trade-off between the costs of developing a better segmentation scheme and the benefits gained. For example, instead of using one variable to segment, we might use a combination of two or three variables. The costs of a more insightful segmentation scheme include the analysis time and the complexity of strategy development. The benefits could include better determination of response differences, thus enabling the design of more effective marketing mix strategies.

Developing Segment Profiles

In the process of forming niches, it is important to find out as much as possible about the people or organizations that occupy each segment. Recall that the segmentation examples discussed earlier in the chapter also included descriptive profile information.

Factors such as those used in dividing product-markets into segments are also helpful in describing the people in the niches. The discussion of product-market analysis in Chapter 5 indicated that the following information is needed to profile a product-market:

Market profile of customers.
Size and growth estimates.
Distribution channels.
Analysis of key competitors.
Product or brand positioning strategy.

This same information will provide a profile for each segment of interest to the firm. The more management can learn about the people in each niche, the better it can evaluate the potential value of the segment opportunity to the firm.

The failure of Polaroid's instant movie camera provides an interesting example of the importance of identifying and analyzing market segments in advance of introducing new products. Management assumed that a segment existed in the product-market for moving pictures, and that the people in the segment wanted instant movies as had been the case with instant still photography. Yet there were several flaws in this line of reasoning. Unlike instant still photographs, giving people their pictures did not have the same on-the-spot effect as using an instant movie cassette. This problem, in combination with the product's high cost, low quality (compared to conventional movies), and the unnecessary use of time provided to the user, resulted in a small demand for the product.[19] The one advantage—on-the-spot filming and developing—was not enough to convince people to buy the product. Would some consumer research have given management enough information to question the economic feasibility of the product? Considering the large investment that was made in the venture, extensive marketing research studies would appear essential. Several key product-market analysis questions should have been answered, including the attractiveness of the home movie market, threats from videotape systems, and consumers' perceived benefits versus the costs of instant movies. Such analyses would likely have shown that there was not a sufficient number of people with special needs or preferences for instant movies. Although Polaroid's management apparently assumed such a segment existed, sufficient demand for the product did not materialize when the product was introduced.

After an acceptable segmentation scheme is adopted and the people in each niche are described, an evaluation of each niche of interest to the firm should follow.

ANALYZE SEGMENTING ALTERNATIVES

Market target alternatives are shown in Exhibit 8–17. The possibilities range from a mass strategy to one, more than one, several, or all niches. When serving multiple segments, the positioning strategy used for each segment may be totally different from those used in other segments, or each marketing program may overlap to some extent with the programs used in other niches. Thus a firm may have a unique combination of the product offering, distribution approach, price, advertising, and personal selling to serve each segment, or instead some of the marketing mix components may be similar (overlapping) for different segments. For example, the same airline services are used to appeal to

EXHIBIT 8-17 Alternative Target Market and Positioning Strategies

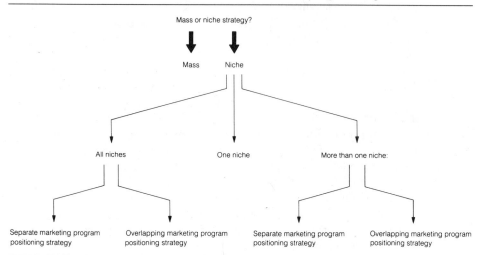

business, special travel groups, and pleasure travelers, although different advertising and sales efforts are aimed at each niche and fare prices may vary across segments.

Once segments are formed, each one of interest to the firm should be evaluated to accomplish three purposes:

1. Since there is often more than one promising positioning strategy that can be used for a given segment, a selection of the best alternative is necessary for each segment candidate.
2. After our evaluation is complete, those segments that still look attractive as market target candidates should be ranked as to their attractiveness.
3. Finally, management must decide if a segmentation strategy is better than a mass market approach.

We will consider each kind of evaluation in the following discussion, which establishes several guidelines for making the market target decision.

Evaluating Targeting Alternatives

Positioning Strategy Options for a Segment.   Although developing a positioning strategy for each of the firm's market targets is covered in Chapter 9, it is important for us to briefly examine this decision now since the evaluation of alternative market target strategies requires management to make some preliminary choices as to what positioning

EXHIBIT 8–18 Selecting a Marketing Program Positioning Strategy for a Product-Market Niche

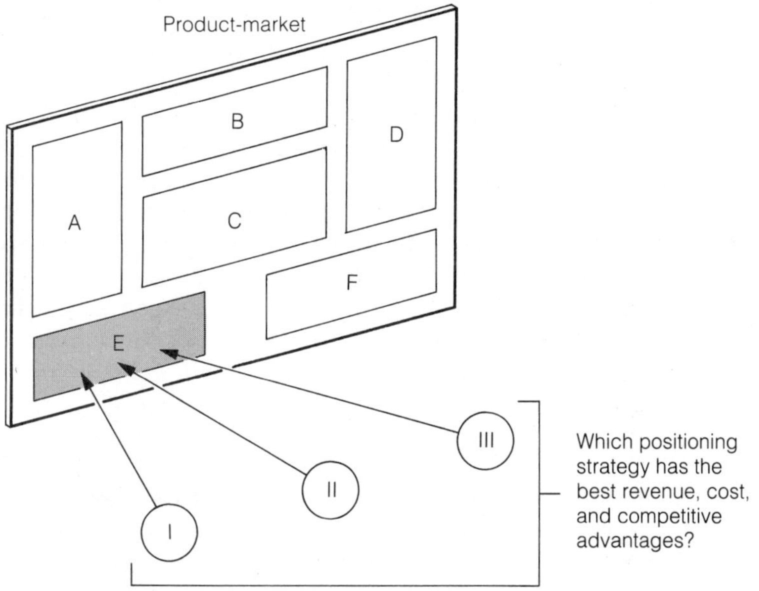

strategy to use for each market target alternative. One objective of product-market analysis is to obtain guidelines for developing a positioning strategy.

A firm has some flexibility in deciding what marketing program strategy to use in positioning the firm against its competition in a segment. As shown in Exhibit 8–18, the positioning decision typically involves evaluating a few of the most promising strategies as to the product, distribution, pricing, advertising, and personal selling. In this illustration, management has identified three possible marketing program strategies—I, II, and III—for use on market target E. We need to evaluate each positioning strategy as to *revenue, costs, competition,* and the best alternative selected.

Segment Evaluation.   In evaluating a segment, two kinds of assessments are necessary. As we learned in the discussion of strategic business unit screening in Chapter 3, we can make an assessment as to *segment attractiveness* and *business strength* for each segment. This will provide an evaluation relative to the market and competition. Note that the basis of evaluation is the segment rather than the entire product-market. The second assessment consists of revenue, cost, and segment profit contribution projections over management's planning horizon.

Since screening is examined in Chapter 3, our present discussion concentrates only upon the financial analysis of a segment.

The purpose of financial analysis is to estimate sales and costs for each segment of interest. By using this information, management can determine the segment's estimated profit contribution. One key consideration is deciding how far into the future we should attempt to estimate sales and costs. Management is typically interested in a comparison of market target opportunities over some planning horizon. Since accurate forecasting is difficult if the projections are too far into the future, management may find it most effective to develop detailed projections two to five years ahead. Then by using the segment position evaluation plus the financial forecasts, we can consider both these factors in comparing the opportunities of alternative segments. In all instances the risks and returns associated with serving a particular niche should be considered.

Illustration of a Segment Evaluation

An illustrative segment evaluation analysis is shown in Exhibit 8–19. A two-year period has been used for estimating sales, costs, contribution margin, and market share. Depending upon the forecasting difficulty, estimates for a longer time period may be feasible. When appropriate, estimates can be expressed as present values of future revenues and costs. Business strength in Exhibit 8–19 refers to the present position. Alternatively, it can be expressed as the present position and an estimated future position, based upon plans for increasing business strength. Attractiveness is typically evaluated for some future time period. In the illustration we have assumed a five-year projection.

While there should be more detailed information to support the analysis shown in Exhibit 8–19, such as assessments of key competitors, it illustrates how segment opportunities can be ranked according to their overall attractiveness. This is admittedly a subjective process since decision makers will vary in their weighing of estimated financial position, business strength, and niche attractiveness. Using the information in Exhibit 8–19, how would you rank niches X, Y, and Z as to their importance for a firm? Unless management is ready to allocate a major chunk of resources to niche Z to build business strength, it appears to be a candidate for the last-place position. Yet Z has some attractive characteristics. It has the most favorable market attractiveness of the three, and its estimated total niche sales are nearly equal to Y for the next two years. The big problem with Z is its business strength. The key question is whether Z's market share can be increased. If not, X looks like a good prospect for top rating, followed next by Y, and by Z in third position. Of course, management may decide to go after all three segments.

EXHIBIT 8-19   Illustrative Segment Evaluation

Estimated	Segment		
($ millions)	X	Y	Z
Sales*	10	16	5
Variable costs*	4	9	3
Contribution margin*	6	7	2
Market share†	60%	30%	10%
Total segment sales	17	53	50
Segment position:			
Business strength	High	Medium	Low
Attractiveness‡	Medium	Low	High

*For a two-year period.
†Percent of total sales in the segment.
‡Based upon a five-year projection.

SELECTING A MARKET TARGET STRATEGY

Daimler-Benz, the German automobile manufacturer, has one of the more successful (and envied) strategies in the automobile industry. The strong performance of this luxury car manufacturer is impressive. The company's sales position is admittedly small in comparison to that of General Motors. Nevertheless, Daimler-Benz has successfully targeted upon a high-price, high-quality niche. Interestingly, the firm uses different marketing strategies for different product lines, as for example in heavy trucks where it has a strong worldwide market position. Daimler-Benz is a tough, innovative competitor in a highly competitive industry. The chairman of the firm describes its passenger car market target strategy:

> "We have a special segment of passenger car production, and we are not interested in leaving it. We know it's a limited sector. We are in the *Spitzengruppe*—at the top level—with a special category of customers." He explains, with an implied sideswipe at BMW and Porsche: "Not the unreliable people: one day this car and another day a Lamborghini or whatever." Among Mercedes' most reliable customers are taxi drivers: some 75 percent of German taxis are Mercedes. In many parts of the world, the Mercedes has become the ultimate status symbol.[20]

How does a firm like Daimler-Benz decide what market target strategy to follow? We turn now to establishing some guidelines for making this decision.

Assuming that niches can be identified in a product-market, management has the option of selecting one or more niches as a market target or, instead, the option of using a mass strategy. The following factors often affect this decision:

Stage product life cycle;
Extent of buyer differentiation;
Company position in the product-market;
Structure of competition;
Corporate resources and capabilities;
Economy of scale considerations.

An examination of each factor will provide a better understanding of its influence upon the market target decision. It is unlikely that all of the relevant factors in a given situation will point in the same direction (e.g., toward a mass strategy). And some factors may not be important in a particular situation. The relative importance of each factor will often vary by company situation. The objective is to highlight how each factor is useful in guiding the decision as to the market target strategy. Thus we should apply these factors by taking into account the particular characteristics of the situation for which they are being used. Since the nature and scope of several of these factors are described in Chapter 7, this discussion highlights market targeting considerations.

Stage of the Product Life Cycle

Market segmentation strategies are more likely to occur during the maturity stage of the product life cycle (PLC), although segmentation may be appropriate at any stage. At the introductory stage there are few if any product-type competitors; competition may occur among alternative product types. If product-type substitutability exists, such as between a filmless electronic camera and a conventional 35 mm camera, the new entry may benefit from targeting one or more segments in the existing product-market. For example, the electronic filmless camera will be targeted initially to newspaper photographers and other business use situations.

If there are no product-type substitutes, a mass strategy may be appropriate at the introductory stage of the PLC. As the product moves toward maturity, the opportunity (and need) for segmentation typically increases. The nature and intensity of competition that occur at each PLC stage are important in guiding market-targeting decisions. Segmentation strategies are often essential at the maturity stage, particularly for small firms in industries dominated by a few large competitors.

Extent of Buyer Differentiation

The particular product-market that a firm decides to target has a strong influence upon the choice of a market target strategy. When buyers' needs and wants are similar across the product-market, there is no real basis for establishing niches. A product-market made up of a relatively small number of end users also argues in favor of a mass strategy, particularly if dollar purchases per buyer are small. The amount of complexity present in the product-market structure is another key consideration, overlapping to some extent the other factors. The more complex the structure as to competing firms, variety of product offerings, variation in user needs and wants, and other factors that contribute to complexity, the more likely is it that a useful niche scheme can be found. Consider the U.S. Surgical Corporation. When the firm entered the new product-market for surgical staplers, the use of a mass market target strategy was a logical decision in view of the users' needs and the size and lack of complexity of the market. There was no apparent way to distinguish among surgeons' needs; the number of users was small in any particular location; and U.S. Surgical had no direct competitors other than the companies supplying needles and thread.

Market Position

In an existing product-market a firm's market share is an important factor in deciding what market target strategy to use. Low-market share firms can often strengthen their position against the competition by finding a niche where they have (or can achieve) a differential advantage. Strategy guidelines for low market share firms are described below:

> A low share company must compete in the segments where its own strengths will be most highly valued and where its large competitors will be most unlikely to compete. Whether that strength is in the type and range of products offered, the method by which the product is produced, the cost and speed of distribution, or the credit and service arrangements is irrelevant. The important thing is that management spend its time identifying and exploiting unique segments rather than making broad assaults on entire industries.[21]

An interesting illustration of how a small firm in a very competitive market can gain a strategic marketing edge through effective market targeting is provided by Pasquale Food Co. Management has repositioned the troubled old pizza chain into a new market segment in which the firm performs a new role in the distribution channel.[22] Pasquale sells tomato sauce, pizza crust, and sausage meat to deli sections of 5,000 supermarkets, including Kroger and Safeway. Through creative market targeting management has avoided the intensive competition of brands in the supermarket freezer section by using a new marketing strategy. Pasquale's staff trains supermarket personnel to make and sell fresh pizza. The firm's sales increased from $11 million to $65 million in the five years ending in 1985.

Structure and Intensity of Competition

The more firms there are serving an industry, the more likely it is that segmentation will be an appropriate market target strategy. Segmentation may be essential for small firms in fragmented, transitional, and global industries, as we learned in Chapter 7. Large firms also may find segmentation profitable, as illustrated by Anheuser Busch, the industry giant. As shown in Exhibit 8-20, the firm uses a multiple-niche strategy, offering a wide range of price, quality, and flavor alternatives, each of which is aimed at a group of target customers. Notice that the differences in the preferences of beer consumers, the company, and the competitive situation in this mature and highly competitive product-market strongly indicate a segmentation strategy.

Other Considerations

The availability of resources may create an opportunity for firms to consider various market target alternatives. In contrast, limited resources may force a company to adopt the only feasible target option, such as a single segment. Market analysis capabilities may also offer advantages to particular firms, particularly when the segmentation task is complex. Both resources and capabilities offer important flexibilities in choosing market targets to firms that have these advantages.

Finally, production and marketing scale economies may influence management in choosing a strategy. For example, the production process may require a large-scale output to achieve necessary cost advantages. The same may be true for marketing and distribution programs. If so, a mass strategy may be necessary in order to gain the sales volume necessary to support large-volume production and distribution.

CONCLUDING NOTE

Choosing the right market target strategy for each product-market is a most important decision that affects the total enterprise. This decision is central to properly positioning a firm in the marketplace. Sometimes a single target cannot be selected for an entire strategic business unit when the SBU contains different product-markets. Moreover, locating the firm's best differential advantage may first require a detailed analysis of several segments. Market target decisions integrate strategic planning and marketing strategy. Targeting decisions establish key guidelines for strategic planning and decisions about the positioning strategy of the marketing program. When segmenting is feasible, man-

---

EXHIBIT 8-20   Anheuser-Busch's Target Market Niches

Brand	Illustrative Target Customers
Budweiser	Heavy beer-using blue-collar males in the 20–34 age range desiring a premium-priced beer
Michelob	Socially conscious drinker, older, desiring a special taste, high-priced quality beer
Michelob Light	Calorie-conscious drinkers that desire an expensive, high-quality beer
Natural Light	Heavy beer using drinkers that are both taste conscious and are calorie conscious and want a beer with popular appeal.
Busch	A popular-priced beer for people interested in a special taste appeal.
Classic Dark	People desiring the special taste of a dark beer.
Würzburger (import)	White-collar (e.g., professional, managerial) people who want the flavor and status of a European imported beer.

---

agement should form segments, evaluate them, and then choose between niche and mass strategies.

Segmentation of a product-market requires that response differences exist between segments, and that the segments be identifiable, and stable over time. Also the benefits of segmentation should exceed the costs. The steps in selecting a market target strategy consist of identifying the basis of segmentation, forming segments, describing each segment, analyzing and evaluating the segment(s) of interest, selecting the market target(s), and designing and implementing a positioning strategy for each market target. The types of variables useful as bases for forming and describing segments include the characteristics of people/organizations, use situation, buyers' needs/preferences, and purchase behavior. The two approaches available for forming segments are segment breakout (disaggregation) and segment aggregation.

Segment analysis and evaluation should identify the segments available to a particular firm and their strengths and limitations. We can follow several guidelines to assist management in evaluating segmentation opportunities and risks. The choice of a mass strategy or a segmentation strategy should consider product the life cycle stage, the extent of buyer differentiation, the company market position, competition, corporate resources and capabilities, and the economy of scale. Market target selection provides important guidelines for the positioning strategy.

NOTES

1. Frank E. James, "Spiegel Employs New Tactics to Fight Its Blue-Collar Past," *The Wall Street Journal*, March 29, 1984, 27.
2. David W. Cravens, Gerald E. Hills, and Robert B. Woodruff, *Marketing Decision Making: Concepts and Strategy* (Homewood, Ill.: Richard D. Irwin, 1980), 171. ©1980 by Richard D. Irwin, Inc.
3. Hartmarx, *1984 Annual Report*, 7.
4. Cravens, Hills, and Woodruff, *Marketing Decision Making*, 171.
5. Frederick W. Winter, "Market Segmentation: A Tactical Approach," *Business Horizons*, January–February 1984, 59.
6. Frederick W. Winter, "A Cost-Benefit Approach to Market Segmentation," *Journal of Marketing*, Fall 1979, 103–11.
7. Gary L. Lilien and Philip Kotler, *Marketing Decision Making* (New York: Harper & Row, 1983), 291.
8. Peter R. Dickson, "Person-Situation: Segmentation's Missing Link," *Journal of Marketing*, Fall 1982, 57.
9. Bill Abrams, "A New Toothpaste Takes off, Promoted by Single Employee," *The Wall Street Journal*, May 26, 1983, 29.
10. This illustration is based on Guest Supply, *1984 Annual Report.*
11. For a complete discussion of segmentation analysis using these techniques, see Ronald E. Frank, W. F. Massy, and Y. Wind, *Market Segmentation* (Englewood Cliffs, N.J.: Prentice-Hall, 1972).
12. Henry Assel and A. Marvin Roscoe Jr., "Approaches to Market Segmentation Analysis," *Journal of Marketing*, October 1976, 67–76.
13. Lilien and Kotler, *Marketing Decision Making*, 282–85.
14. Henry Assael, *Consumer Behavior and Marketing Action*, 2nd ed. (Boston: Kent Publishing, 1984), 261–62.
15. Brand may refer to a product or service or to an entire company, such as a restaurant, department store, or bank.
16. Several research techniques for market segment identification are discussed in Paul E. Green and Donald S. Tull, *Research for Marketing Decisions*, 4th ed. (Englewood Cliffs, N.J.: Prentice-Hall, 1978), Chapter 16.
17. Dickson, "Person-Situation," 56–64.
18. Ibid, 63.
19. Mitchell C. Lynch, "Instant Movies Falter: Is Polaroid's Chairman Wrong for a Change?" *The Wall Street Journal*, August 9, 1979, 1, 29.
20. Barbara Ellis, "Stupid We Are not," *Forbes*, September 3, 1979, 65–66.
21. R. G. Hammermesh, M. J. Anderson, Jr., and J. E. Harris, "Strategies for Low Market Share Businesses," *Harvard Business Review*, May–June 1978, 98.
22. Toni Mack, "Pizza Power," *Forbes*, September 23, 1985, 106–7.

QUESTIONS FOR REVIEW AND DISCUSSION

1. Discuss some of the reasons why a mass target market strategy is appropriate for U.S. Surgical Corporation, and is not a good strategy for Hartmarx.

2. In terms of guiding marketing strategies, why are there advantages in using demographic characteristics to break out product-markets into segments?

3. The real test of whether a segment formation scheme is a good one occurs after it has been tried and the results evaluated. Are there ways to evaluate alternative niche schemes without actually trying them?

4. Suggest ways of obtaining the information needed to conduct a market segment evaluation like that shown in Exhibit 8-19.

5. Why may it become necessary for companies to alter their target market strategies over time?

6. "Market segmentation is a strategy that is primarily suitable for use in U.S. markets." Discuss.

7. What exactly is the distinction between a *separate* and an *overlapping* positioning strategy of the marketing program? Under what conditions is each appropriate?

8. Under what circumstances may it *not* be possible to break up a product-market into segments? What are the dangers of using an incorrect segment formation scheme?

STRATEGIC APPLICATION 8-1

MARRIOTT CORP.

In early 1982, Marriott Corp. started building the prototype of a new mid-priced hotel chain, something more modest than its usual hotels. Sample rooms with movable walls were assembled and furnished in the company's Gaithersburg, Md., hotel. Hammers and calculators labored in unison as Marriott executives slid walls back and forth, settling on three possible room shapes.

Then, over several weeks, hundreds of prospective customers were herded through the test rooms and quizzed. They howled at the idea of a room a foot shy on width, but they made nary a peep when length was trimmed 18 inches.

That little discovery should save Marriott more than $80,000 on each hotel property, or at least $24 million over the life of the project. It also says a lot about the changing nature of the hotel industry. In the late 1970s, market research wasn't in such vogue. Marriott, like most hoteliers, had grown easily with one sort of hotel that it duplicated again and again.

But a building boom has left several cities and some market segments saturated. And many hotel companies have spent the last few years researching and retooling in order to develop new growth strategies that are just now becoming clear. The new hotels themselves—and the development of the new systems needed to operate them—portend vast changes for this $33 billion industry.

Competing in New Markets

Holiday Corp., for example, is entering three new market segments. Hyatt Corp., Ramada Inns Inc., Imperial Group PLC's Howard Johnson Co., and Manor Care Inc.'s Quality Inns International have all targeted new groups of customers. "What all of us are trying to do," says Darryl Hartley-Leonard, the executive vice president of Hyatt, "is steal some market share."

No lodging company is more ambitious than Marriott. The Bethesda, Md., company, which also owns contract food-service businesses and owns and franchises Big Boy and Roy Rogers restaurants, plans to build 300 "Courtyard by Marriott" hotels by the early 1990s in a bid to take market share away from mid-priced mainstays, Holiday Inns and Ramada Inns.

Marriott Corp.—1984	
Sales	$3.5 billion
Net income	$139.8 million
Employees	140,000
1984 lodging revenue	$1.6 billion
Resort hotels	21
Convention hotels	12
Other hotels	114
Rooms	65,279

In addition, Marriott is expanding its downtown convention network, launching a line of suites-only hotels and testing the time-share condominium market. Still on the drawing board: a retirement-community business that would incorporate the features of a nursing home, and a scaled-down model of its regular, full-service hotel aimed at smaller markets.

The stakes are high. The outcome of this segmentation movement could dramatically affect the makeup of this industry for the next decade and beyond. Some chains, such as Howard Johnson and Ramada, have already gone through hard times. Independent operators, who provide about half the hotel rooms in the country, also are feeling the heat as industry giants fight it out. "Some old-line chains will gradually lose market share, and some newer, more aggressive chains are going to gain market share," says J. W. Marriott Jr., the company's president and chief executive officer. "The question for us is: How successful will we be with these new products?"

The biggest question for Marriott is Courtyard, a two-story, 150-room suburban hotel aimed at the $45- to $65-a-night market. (A traditional Marriott hotel room rents for $65 to $100 a night.) Analysts say many properties in the midpriced sector are old and could be vulnerable to a new competitor, and success here would vastly broaden Marriott's customer base.

But such an ambitious invasion of new turf has its risks. Marriott is com-

mitting more than $2 billion over the next several years to build Courtyard. What's more, Marriott is entering a market with different pricing and marketing strategies, different service levels, and a different clientele.

The company hasn't taken the move lightly. It spent about three years researching Courtyard before a test model was built. "I must have slept in a couple hundred midpriced facilities," says Donald A. Washburn, the vice president for market development.

Marriott's research indicates that room quality and outdoor surroundings matter most to a would-be guest. So Marriott is trying to keep Courtyard's rooms as close as possible in quality to its full-service rooms, while throwing in a landscaped courtyard with serpentine walkways and, of course, a swimming pool.

Most of the cost cutting has come out of public space and service. A Courtyard hotel has a tiny lobby and lounge, just one restaurant, a couple of small meeting-rooms, and no doorman, bellman or room service. Marriott now has six test-Courtyards in Georgia and boasts of an average occupancy rate of 90%. "You get a room that's worth more than you're paying for it," says John J. Rohs, a vice president for research at Wertheim & Co. Adds an executive at a competing chain, "If Bill Marriott builds 300 of those, he could hurt a lot of people."

Marriott spent many years in the highly competitive, low-profit-margin family restaurant business before building its first hotel in 1957. And its aggressive interest in market segmentation stems in part from an intense desire to set itself apart from the rest of the hotel industry. While most hotel chains grow primarily through franchising, Marriott likes to keep to itself by designing, building, financing and managing (but not owning) its hotels. The hotels usually are sold to limited partnerships or institutions and managed by Marriott. It rarely uses outside consultants, and it doesn't like to hire general managers from competing hotels.

Unions are grudgingly tolerated at most companies, but Marriott fights them on every front. Its only unionized hotel, at San Francisco's Fisherman's Wharf, is neither owned nor managed by Marriott. (It is one of the few hotels Marriott has franchised.) Many chains publicly release occupancy rates; Marriott generally won't, though Courtyard has been an exception. "It's a competitive world we live in," says Mr. Marriott.

Such attitudes have led to allegations of arrogance and union busting, but few disparage Marriott's achievement. The hotel division, which accounted for about half of Marriott's $327.7 million pretax operating profit last year, has increased both revenue and profit at an annual rate of 20% for the past 20 years.

Since 1980, the hotel chain has more than doubled in size to 147 properties. More important, it has become the largest single operator of hotel rooms in the U.S., and its lucrative management contracts have made Marriott one of the industry's most profitable companies. "Right now," says a rival executive, "they're the darlings of the industry."

The source of drive for the company has always been a workaholic member of the Marriott family. The first was J. Willard Sr., a devout member of the Church of Jesus Christ of Latter-day Saints, who founded the company as a root-beer stand in 1927 and who died last month at age 84. Also, a Mormon, Mr. Marriott's eldest son—known as Bill—became chief executive in 1972. He remembers spending the vacations of his youth with his father in California visiting several family restaurants a day in search of ideas to take back to the East Coast.

Now Bill Marriott, aged 53, emulates his father's practice, visiting about 100 Marriott hotels a year and about that number of competitors' hostelries. (Mr. Marriott at the moment is recovering at

home from burns of his hands and legs sustained when his motorboat caught fire near his New Hampshire summer home Aug. 24. He was hospitalized for two weeks after the accident.) While the younger Mr. Marriott is expanding the chain at a much faster pace, the hotels are still run in the same old way: rigidly centralized and with great attention to the bottom line.

Mr. Marriott recalls a visit to a small luxury chain earlier this year. Despite its 10% occupancy, the hotel insisted on putting fresh flowers in every room. "The only person who saw [most of] them was the maid who took out the dead ones and put in the fresh ones," he says. "This happens more than you think in this industry."

But it couldn't happen at a Marriott. Marriott hotels are "run by the book, and the book is controlled by central people," says Gary L. Wilson, who recently left his post as Marriott's chief financial officer for a similar job at Walt Disney Productions. "The book" is in fact a dozen or so encyclopedia-like tomes detailing, among other operations, how to remove hair from bathroom sinks. The "central people" are numerous. Hyatt, traditionally Marriott's most direct competitor, estimates that for every two hotel executives it employs, Marriott has seven. No ingredient in hotel food may be changed without the explicit approval of headquarters. "We test our recipes," says Mr. Marriott. "We know what they cost. We won't let anyone mess with the food specs."

While concentrating on operations, however, Marriott, like most of its competitors, historically did little else. Consumer research and extensive marketing were rare. Room decor was chosen according to the personal taste of Marriott's decorators, and with a nod from Bill Marriott. The company got quite a jolt in the early 1980s, when its first forays into consumer research showed those decor decisions weren't going over with guests. Marriott's trademark reds and loud patterns were thereupon scrapped in favor of subtle shades of rust and beige.

Undirected Growth

"You might say the hotel industry grew inspite of itself," says Mark V. Lomanno, the associate director of research at Laventhol & Horwath, the consulting and accounting firm.

That changed with the onset of the 1980s, however, when many lodging companies began forecasting tough times. Tax incentives, in the form of investment tax credits and accelerated depreciation, lured scores of investors into hotel construction, often in areas where it wasn't needed. Marriott was running out of places to put its standard hotel, a 300- to 400-room, full-service facility located near an airport or a large suburban population center. In search of new markets, "we had to make the shift from a purely operations-driven company to a marketing-oriented company," says Frederic V. Malek, the executive vice president for hotels who had been a White House aide in the Nixon administration.

For Marriott, the move has meant bolstering the marketing staff, altering promotion paths and compensation scales to keep its best people selling, and starting a frequent-guest bonus program that costs $16 million a year to operate, according to a study done by a competing chain. It has also meant automating its hotel operations to allow more efficient tracking of guests, and attempts at jazzing up Marriott's rather staid image.

The company's internally designed hotels, for example, had a reputation for efficiency and consistency, but not for style or chic. So Marriott has been acquiring and building more resort properties, and it has turned to outside architects. John C. Portman Jr., known for his cavernous atriums, glass elevators and other extravagances, designed the new Marriott Marquis hotels in Atlanta and New York.

The Price of Chic

Fashion, however, has its price. The Times Square property, which opened this month, cost $400 million and thus is one of the most expensive hotels ever.

But the key change, and the most difficult, has been the development of new operating cultures needed to succeed in new markets. When the first Courtyard was built, for example, Marriott moved the Courtyard management team from the hotel division and put it in a division that includes the company's fast-food chains, hoping to foster more creativity. "We make some decisions without all our flanks covered," says A. Bradford Bryan Jr., the Marriott vice president in charge of Courtyard. He concedes that such a statement would be heresy in the hotel division.

In fact, none of the hotel division's traditions seems sacred at Courtyard. All-cotton towels, a hallmark of Marriott's hotel chain, have given way at Courtyard to cheaper fabric. Even a biography of the company founder, free for the taking in other Marriott hotel rooms (right beside the Bible), is sold at Courtyard vending machines, for 75 cents.

The hard part for Courtyard executives, however, is just beginning. Marriott plans to open 30 Courtyards in 1986 and about one a week thereafter, for the next several years.

Of course, competitors aren't taking this frontal assault lightly. Holiday Corp. is refurbishing some of its older properties, building about 50 Holiday Inns a year and throwing out an equal number of marginal properties. Says Richard Gonzalez, Holiday's director of new-business planning: "Marriott may find that there's some very, very strong competition in the midscale market."

Some of Marriott's stiffest challenges may be internal. There are some thorny marketing issues. To consumers, "the Marriott name may just mean expensive," says Daniel R. Lee, a senior analyst at Drexel Burnham Lambert Inc.

Francis W. Cash, a Marriott executive vice president, acknowledges that the company must condition potential guests to expect fewer frills and less service with Courtyard. "If you think [Courtyard] is the little Marriott," he says, "you're going to be disappointed."

The company is attempting to run the smaller, less complicated hotels with managers who have much less experience than its traditional general managers. And it plans to deviate from tradition by hiring managers from competing chains.

As the time to begin "mass production" approaches, Courtyard executives continue to tinker with the "product." For example, a fully equipped office for guest rental has failed and will be replaced, probably by an exercise room. And a large game room, designed to create a "home away from home" atmosphere, has been shrunk to the size of an extra-large closet. Marriott found that

Courtyard guests didn't go for pingpong and pool, so a few video games should do nicely.

SOURCE: Steve Swartz, "Basic Bedrooms: How Marriott Changes Hotel Design to Tap Mid-priced Market." Reprinted by permission of *The Wall Street Journal.* © Dow Jones & Company, Inc., September 18, 1985. All rights reserved.

DISCUSSION QUESTIONS

1. Describe the market segments and Marriott's market target strategy in the lodging product-market.
2. Critically evaluate Marriott's Courtyard venture in terms of market opportunity.
3. Identify and evaluate the key competitors of the Courtyard chain.
4. What strategy options are appropriate for marketing the Courtyard chain? Which do you recommend and why?

STRATEGIC APPLICATION 8-2

1988 OLYMPIC GAMES

New York—"There are only four elements that really travel across borders: sports, music, violence and sex," says Jurgen Lenz as he tries to sell the Olympics to multinational corporations. "It's difficult to sponsor violence and sex."

Though the Games are more than two and a half years away, the race for corporate backing and advertising dollars has begun. TV networks are trying to sell $1 billion of commercial time while Mr. Lenz and his associates are attempting to raise $300 million from corporate sponsors that want to link their products to the world's top amateur sporting event.

Most companies, however, have yet to show the enthusiasm for the 1988 Games that they displayed in Los Angeles last year. Because of the high costs to busi-

nesses and other factors, the marketability of the Olympics may have peaked. A company that wants an Olympics marketing program with all the trimmings—TV advertising, special promotions and the use of the Olympic rings on packages and ads—could face an expenditure of $50 million or more.

"That's not advertising, that's a capital expenditure," says Steve Leff, chief media buyer for Backer & Spielvogel Inc., a New York ad agency whose clients include Miller Brewing Co. "You could build a factory for $50 million."

The stakes are high for all the participants. American Broadcasting Cos., which will televise the Winter Games from Calgary, Canada, and National Broadcasting Co., which will show the

Summer Olympics from Seoul, South Korea, need to sell a total of $1 billion of commercials to break even on their investments.

Meanwhile, Mr. Lenz and others at ISL Marketing, a Swiss company, have been retained by the International Olympics Committee and national Olympic committees to find some 20 corporate sponsors for the 1988 Games. ISL, which is controlled by the German family that owns the Adidas shoe and sporting-goods company, wants to raise $300 million from those sponsors. The money would be divided among the two hosts of the 1988 Games; the International Olympic Committee, which will distribute much of it to Olympic committees in poorer countries; and the U.S. Olympic Committee.

Hosting an Olympics is expensive. Organizers of the Calgary Games estimate their cost at $818 million, though $348 million of that will go for facilities that will be reused for years. The Seoul Olympics is expected to cost more than $1 billion.

But last year's Summer Games, which ended with a $215 million surplus, proved a well-run Olympics can turn a profit. Although TV fees of $225 million were a major revenue source, Los Angeles also attracted $180 million of corporate sponsorships.

Compared with 1984, marketing of the 1988 Games is off to a tardy start. ABC has just begun approaching advertisers for Calgary, and the network's pricing reflects its cautious attitude. A prime-time 30-second ad will sell for about $320,000, only a 5% annual increase from the $260,000 ABC asked for the 1984 Winter Games.

NBC, which obtained the rights less than a month ago after bidding was delayed for more than a year, hasn't started visiting advertisers.

The choice of Seoul as the site of the Summer Games also complicates selling

1984 Summer Olympics Top Network Advertisers	
McDonald's	$30 million
Coca-Cola	26 million
Sears	20 million
Anheuser-Busch	20 million
Miller Brewing	20 million

SOURCE: Broadcast industry estimates.

that meet. The 14-hour time difference between Korea and the eastern U.S. will reduce the number of events televised during prime-time evening hours, and audience ratings may be hurt. Moreover, Seoul won't be able to draw on the patriotism that motivated some corporate commitments to the Los Angeles Olympics.

Skepticism about TV ad sales is common this far before an Olympics. Some executives at other networks estimate that ABC, which will pay $309 million for the rights to broadcast the Calgary Games, could lose more than $50 million. ABC officials, however, say they expect their broadcasts to be profitable. NBC, which will have nearly twice as many hours of advertising for virtually the same rights payment—$300 million— also expects a profit. Even many of the advertising executives who now express skepticism acknowledge that past sponsors usually won't abandon established links between their brand and the Olympics.

Meanwhile, sports officials and corporate marketers are watching ISL in its Olympic trial. The company's mission is to find about 20 corporate sponsors for 44 internationally marketed product categories, such as computers, cameras, credit cards, financial services and gasoline. The ISL is also supposed to simplify the complex process of signing such sponsors. In the past, a multinational company had to sign separate agreements with the hosts of the Summer and Winter Games and, because every country controls the use of the Olympic logo inside its borders, with numerous national Olympic committees.

In 1984, for example, Coca-Cola Co. signed more than three dozen agreements to tie its product to a world-wide Olympics marketing program. By representing the International Olympic Committee, Seoul, Calgary and nearly every national Olympic committee, ISL now provides one-stop shopping for multinational companies.

While that might make things easier for companies, U.S. athletes could be shortchanged. Of the total money collected from sponsors—nearly all of which are U.S. companies—the U.S. Olympic Committee gets only 10%.

By not selling the marketing rights itself the U.S. "gave up quite a bit to be nice guys," says Gen. George D. Miller, executive director of the USOC, which now has a deficit of more than $5 million. "The Olympics movement has to sustain itself somehow, but the money is coming from the U.S."

But Richard Kline, general counsel of the USOC, says the committee "has retained total control of our destiny." The USOC, he says, can veto any ISL contract with a U.S. sponsor that the committee thinks is too low. Next spring, he adds, the U.S. committee has the right to regain control over any product category that ISL hasn't sold. The USOC has also retained marketing rights for some other products.

ISL's Mr. Lenz acknowledges that the company is off to a sluggish start. Of 51 companies it has contacted, only two—Coca-Cola Co. and Eastman Kodak Co.—are signed. At this stage before the Los Angeles Games, a dozen companies had already agreed to be sponsors. Thirteen other companies are in "advanced negotiations," Mr. Lenz says.

Some are balking at ISL's asking price; Coke is believed to be paying $10 million, but the company won't comment. "Most major advertisers are considering long and hard before making that kind of money investment," say Michael Kirby, director of advertising and promotion for Xerox Corp., a former Olympics sponsor.

The idea for ISL was conceived by Adidas Chairman Horst Dassler, whose financial backing for amateur athletic events and teams has made him an important behind-the-scenes power in international Olympics politics. Though Mr. Lenz says ISL doesn't expect to make a profit on the 1988 Games, the company could end up with a virtual lock on future Olympics sponsorships. That could mean substantial profits for Mr. Dassler. He and his four sisters—who also own all of Adidas—own 51% of ISL. The rest is owned by Dentsu, the largest ad agency in Japan.

SOURCE: Bill Abrams, "Marketing the Olympics: As Race Begins, Firms Are Wary of Costs." Reprinted by permission of *The Wall Street Journal.* ©Dow Jones & Company, Inc., October 31, 1985. All rights reserved.

DISCUSSION QUESTIONS

1. What is the product being marketed for the 1988 Olympic Games?
2. Analyze the marketing strategy situation for the 1988 Olympics.
3. Identify and describe the market target(s) for the 1988 Olympics.
4. Identify the important issues to be considered in developing a positioning strategy for the games.

CHAPTER 9

Marketing Program Positioning Strategy

Tupperware International is a unit of Dart & Kraft, Inc., with sales of nearly $800 million (8 percent of Dart & Kraft sales). In early 1985 Tupperware's management initiated a series of strategic actions designed to reposition the company and increase sales and profits, which had been declining since 1981.[1] A marketing situation analysis identified several strengths of the Tupperware system, including informative product demonstration (Tupperware parties), superior-quality products, fast distribution, personal service, and a strong consumer franchise of the Tupperware brand name. The study also identified some important strategic issues. Altered life-styles of working women are placing new time pressures on Tupperware customers. Younger working women are being targeted as well as former partygoers. The traditional party format would need to be more flexible, including one-hour, lunch-hour meetings, and rush hour gatherings at places like health clubs and offices. Individualized custom-kitchen parties were also being tested, where the available kitchen space is reorganized using Tupperware containers for expanded storage, efficiency, and convenience. Other marketing strategy actions include large increases in mass-media advertising to stimulate product sales as an alternative to recruiting salespeople; new and meaningful incentives for hostesses, dealers, and managers; and expanded dealer and manager training programs. Capping off Tupperware's updated marketing program repositioning strategy is the new Ultra 21 ovenware line, a proprietary plastic product that can withstand conventional oven temperatures over 500 degrees, and is also effective for microwave, freezer, dishwasher, and serving uses. The company spent over $70 million developing the Ultra 21 line. Management hopes this new line will give the company an edge over Rubbermaid and other competitors. Ultra 21 was launched with a $10 million advertising campaign. Tupperware established a new department in 1985 staffed by marketing research, planning, and marketing personnel to concentrate on an accelerated development of new products.

Marketing program positioning consists of integrating strategies for products, distribution, price, and promotion. The term *position* designates how a company's marketing program is perceived by the buyer in relation to the programs of key competitors; in other words, how a firm's brand is positioned against its competition with respect to the product offering, distribution approach, prices, advertising, and personal selling. All elements of the marketing program can potentially affect the position.[2] Thus the positioning strategy should provide a focus for the marketing program. A clearly defined positioning strategy helps to combine program elements in such a way that they will be consistent and supportive.

The key issue in developing and implementing a positioning strategy is how it is perceived by the people in a target market. If a marketing program is considered identical to a competitor's, then the two firms would have the same positioning strategy. Distinctions in the minds of consumers always exist among competitive offerings. Typically, the product becomes the focal point of a positioning strategy since distribution, prices, advertising, and personal selling all are working toward positioning the product in the eyes of the buyer. Thus the designation *product positioning strategy* is often used. Since position can be achieved by using a combination of marketing program components, product positioning is the result of more than just the product.

In this chapter we will first relate the positioning strategy to strategic planning for the enterprise. This strategy linkage provides essential direction for setting marketing objectives. A discussion of critical issues in choosing a positioning strategy follows. Next, we will consider strategic position analysis and the role of marketing program components. Finally, several positioning strategy guidelines are presented. This chapter provides a foundation for shaping the strategy of each marketing program component.

SETTING MARKETING OBJECTIVES

Corporate and business unit strategies provide important strategic guidelines for the marketing strategy (Chapters 2 and 3). These interrelationships are shown in Exhibit 9-1. The selection of the market target strategy (Chapter 8) sets the stage for determining objectives and developing a positioning strategy.

EXHIBIT 9-1   Integrating Corporate and Marketing Strategies

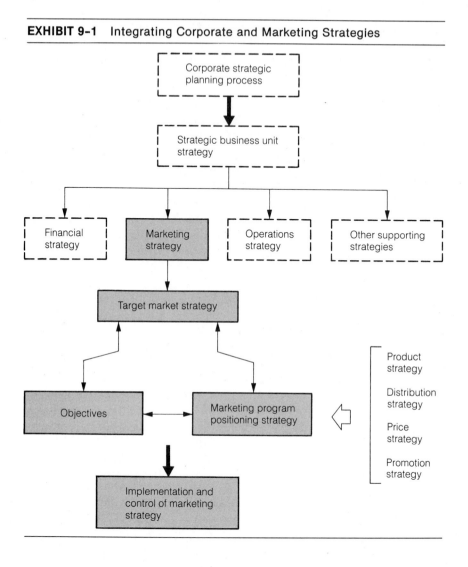

Strategic Importance of Objectives

The need for setting objectives is so obvious that it is surprising how little attention is often given to this important management activity. Even when objectives are specified, they often do not provide a basis for tracking actual performance. An illustration will demonstrate several of the characteristics that useful objectives should have. As one of its marketing objectives, the management of a savings and loan association stated, "Our objective is to strengthen the association's image as a family financial center." While the value of achieving this objective seems clear, the statement has several defects. Will reaching this objective contribute to the objectives of corporate performance? For example, what will happen to the savings inflow, loans closed, and profit contribution if the association's image is strengthened? Toward what target customer group will the effort to strengthen the firm's image be directed? What exactly does it mean to strengthen the association's image? Will this objective be accomplished by attracting more savers, more dollars of savings and loans, greater awareness of the association by consumers, increased usage of services, or what? Assuming a way of measuring image can be specified, what level of results will be considered successful, and over what time period will the objective apply? Finally, who will be responsible for meeting the objective? This illustration highlights several important criteria that should be satisfied if the objectives are to provide useful guides to marketing actions and standards for gauging performance. We examine and illustrate each of these criteria.

In this book no distinction is made between a *goal* and an *objective.* Either term identifies something to be achieved by an organization or individual during a specific time period. The purpose of an objective is to indicate *what* is to be accomplished, not *how* to do it. The attainment of objectives is achieved through those strategic and tactical actions designed to accomplish desired results.

Relevant and Consistent Objectives

The marketing function contributes to the bottom-line performance of corporate and business units by generating sales and by consuming resources such as advertising media expenditures. Marketing objectives should, when accomplished, meet the sales results desired by management while keeping resource consumption at levels that yield favorable contributions to profits. In linking the marketing function to corporate and business unit operations, it is essential that the objectives at various levels in the organization be *relevant* and *consistent.* Relevancy refers to whether accomplishing a particular objective, such as increasing consumer awareness of a brand, will contribute to organizational performance. Consistency is concerned with establishing marketing objectives that are consistent in their interrelationships with higher-level objectives and with other objectives at the same level. For example, suppose marketing management wishes to increase sales by eliminating customers with a low purchasing potential and instead decides to identify and develop a small number of customers with a high purchasing power. Next, suppose that a salesperson sets as one objective, increasing his/her number of accounts 20 percent by the end of 18 months. The salesperson's objective is not consistent with the higher-

EXHIBIT 9–2 Illustrative Objectives at Different Organizational Levels

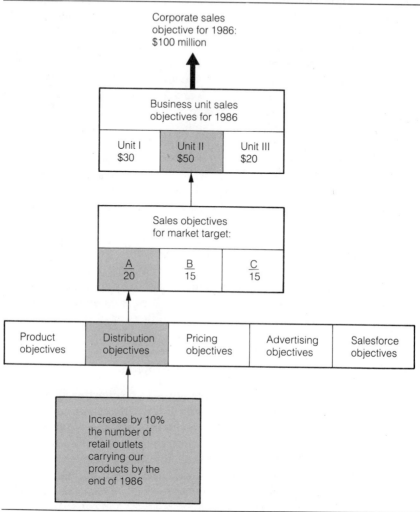

Corporate sales
objective for 1986:
$100 million

Business unit sales
objectives for 1986

| Unit I $30 | Unit II $50 | Unit III $20 |

Sales objectives
for market target:

| A 20 | B 15 | C 15 |

| Product objectives | Distribution objectives | Pricing objectives | Advertising objectives | Salesforce objectives |

Increase by 10%
the number of
retail outlets
carrying our
products by the
end of 1986

level objective, which is aimed at selectivity rather than at expanding the number of customers.

Selecting objectives that are relevant to overall performance and also consistent among the different organizational levels is a challenging task. An illustration will be helpful in showing the hierarchical nature of objectives. Look at Exhibit 9–2. Suppose that one channel of distribution objective is to increase by 10 percent the number of retail outlets carrying the products offered to market target A in business unit II. This objective should contribute to meeting the sales objectives at the different levels shown in Exhibit 9–2. Yet it is entirely possible that adding more retailers will not contribute as much to sales as increasing the assistance and support provided to the firm's existing retailers. Also, a particular objective should not work against other objectives. Suppose, for example, that the 10 percent increase in the number of retailers will help to meet the $20 million sales objective for market target A. But the effort needed to find, screen, and assist the new retailers will consume more in resources than will be gained in revenues over a time period considered acceptable by management.

Marketing objectives must also be consistent with the objectives of other functional units, such as finance, operations, and research and development. Suppose one of the marketing manager's distribution objectives is to reduce the percent of stock-outs (product not available to fill an order) to retailers from 15 percent (based on invoiced amounts in dollars) to 5 percent. Operations has set an objective to reduce finished goods inventory for all products by 15 percent at the end of 12 months. The two objectives may be in conflict unless the reductions are made in product categories that will not affect stock-outs. Alternatively, perhaps marketing's stock-out objective is too optimistic and will cost more than the benefits to be gained by meeting it. The illustration indicates the importance of coordinating objectives among functional areas.

Setting Objectives

Since each objective must be established while taking into account all other related objectives, where should the starting point be for setting objectives? Top management's objectives for the enterprise and each of the business units establish key guidelines for the objectives of marketing and other organizational units. After these guidelines are determined, objectives at various management levels can be set. One of two major approaches is typically used in establishing objectives. The first is a top-down approach where objectives at each level in the organization are determined based on the objectives at the next higher level. For example, referring back to Exhibit 9–2, the sales objective for business unit II of $50 million would be designated by top management, and then the SBU management would allocate the $50 million among market targets A, B, and C. The amount of give-and-take at each level will depend upon the extent of coordination and participation by the managers involved.

The second approach is more flexible than the first in that it specifically calls for participation and interaction among managers at all levels of the organization. Broad guidelines are indicated by top management, subject to inputs from other management levels. This approach involves far more participation than the first and, when properly implemented, it provides an effective method for setting objectives. Actually, the two approaches differ primarily according to the extent of flexibility and participation that is present. Both require top management to indicate its expectations for the enterprise.

Clear Guide to Accomplishment

An objective's value is based on how closely it shows what is expected to happen and the extent to which the objective has been achieved when compared to actual results. The components of an objective are identified in Exhibit 9-3. First, it is useful to indicate the type of objective (e.g., profitability) involved since this will help to tie the objective to others contributing to the same purpose. The major categories of organizational objectives are:

1. *Marketing*—market position, customer services, and customer relations.
2. *Innovation*—building a differential advantage over the competition.
3. *Management of human, capital, and physical resources*—procurement, deployment, and development.
4. *Productivity*—costs of operations.
5. *Social responsibility*—pollution, ethical behavior, and so on.
6. *Profitability*—profit contribution, return on sales and investment, and other financial performance objectives.

After establishing the type of objective, it is essential to indicate what is to be accomplished and the desired level of performance, as illustrated in Exhibit 9-3. Note that the objective specifies in quantitative terms what is to be done, when it is to be accomplished, and who is responsible for meeting the objective. When setting objectives, we should pay attention also to how performance will be measured. This may include regular reports and analyses prepared by the firm and, when appropriate, special research studies. Finally, it is helpful to indicate key actions that, if taken, promise to improve performance over and above the level of performance specified (e.g., increasing houseware sales to more than 30 percent of total sales).

The time frame for accomplishing an objective may range from a month or quarter up to a year or more, although objectives extending beyond three to five years are best characterized as desired events rather than as targets for specific results. Individuals, however, may set objectives for each day or week. The time span of objectives will depend upon the planning horizon utilized in a particular firm and the organizational level where the objectives are set.

Since objectives are not of equal importance, management should have a sense of priorities regarding objectives. Because a comparison

---

EXHIBIT 9-3 Components of an Objective

Type of objective:
  Profitability
Desired level of performance:
  The manager of the health and beauty aids division of XYZ Wholesale
  Products, Inc. is responsible for increasing the percent of houseware
  sales from 25 percent to 30 percent of total sales in dollars by one year
  from now (houseware products have the highest profit margin of all
  products in the product mix).
How performance will be measured:
  Sales reports, salesperson product sales reports, and customer sales
  analyses.
Actions that will improve performance:
  Expand warehouse space.
  Increase awareness of salespersons concerning the need for a higher
  proportion of houseware sales.
  Sales incentive plan.

---

of objectives is somewhat like comparing apples, tomatoes, and television, establishing the relative importance of objectives rests substantially upon management's judgment and experience. Nevertheless, an effort should be made to indicate which objectives are critical to the performance of the enterprise and which can contribute to the performance, but are not as important as those assigned a critical status. Setting priorities is one of management's most important responsibilities because of the problem of scarce resources.

The Conference Board, Inc., surveyed a broad cross section of consumer and industrial products firms to determine the specific items covered by objectives and strategies in the marketing plans of the firms. The results of those surveys are shown in Exhibit 9-4. For most of the items covered, consumer and industrial products manufacturers are quite similar. Some major differences exist in the areas of advertising and field sales.

Objectives and People

Two aspects of the human side of objectives are important. First, how realistic are the objectives that are established? Management must distinguish between hoped-for results and those that are actually achievable. Objectives should be realistic yet demanding. Managers, in their review of subordinates' objectives, must be alert to whether an objective is unrealistic, achievable, or below expectations. Established at proper levels, objectives can serve as important motivational tools, particularly when linked to incentive programs.

EXHIBIT 9–4 Areas where Companies Specify Marketing Objectives and Strategies

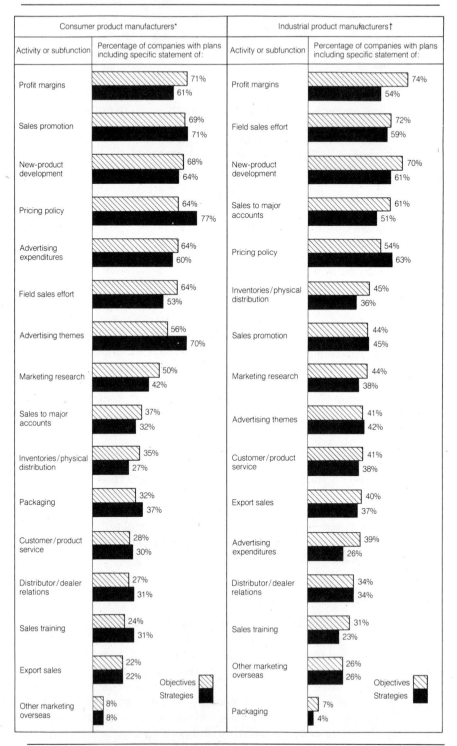

Consumer product manufacturers*		Industrial product manufacturers†	
Activity or subfunction	Percentage of companies with plans including specific statement of:	Activity or subfunction	Percentage of companies with plans including specific statement of:
Profit margins	71% / 61%	Profit margins	74% / 54%
Sales promotion	69% / 71%	Field sales effort	72% / 59%
New-product development	68% / 64%	New-product development	70% / 61%
Pricing policy	64% / 77%	Sales to major accounts	61% / 51%
Advertising expenditures	64% / 60%	Pricing policy	54% / 63%
Field sales effort	64% / 53%	Inventories/physical distribution	45% / 36%
Advertising themes	56% / 70%	Sales promotion	44% / 45%
Marketing research	50% / 42%	Marketing research	44% / 38%
Sales to major accounts	37% / 32%	Advertising themes	41% / 42%
Inventories/physical distribution	35% / 27%	Customer/product service	41% / 38%
Packaging	32% / 37%	Export sales	40% / 37%
Customer/product service	28% / 30%	Advertising expenditures	39% / 26%
Distributor/dealer relations	27% / 31%	Distributor/dealer relations	34% / 34%
Sales training	24% / 31%	Sales training	31% / 23%
Export sales	22% / 22%	Other marketing overseas	26% / 26%
Other marketing overseas	8% / 8%	Packaging	7% / 4%

Objectives / Strategies

*Based on information provided by 98 companies.
†Based on information provided by 138 companies.
SOURCE: David S. Hopkins, *The Marketing Plan* (New York: The Conference Board, 1981), 23, 24.

Second, who is to be responsible for meeting objectives? Reaching an objective often depends upon more than one person. In various instances the people involved may not be from the same organizational unit. This is a situation involving shared responsibility. Consider, for example, the director of product planning for a pharmaceutical producer. This person has responsibility for new product planning, advertising and sales promotion, and all other marketing activities except the management of the sales force. Who should be assigned the sales objective for the firm's line of products? Clearly, both the product planning director and the sales director can have an impact upon the product sales objective. The alternatives are to assign them a shared objective, to assign the objective to the person they both report to, or to assign the objective to all three individuals. Coping with these interrelationships requires close coordination among those people involved. In this example we recommend designating responsibility to all three individuals and making explicit the dependence of each director upon the other in meeting the objective. It is also important that the two directors coordinate their marketing plans.

Designating responsibility for objectives requires an understanding as to how much control a person has over the outcome of a particular objective. Even when an objective is not shared, its achievement may depend significantly upon uncontrollable external factors. These influences must be taken into account in establishing objectives and gauging results. To illustrate this point, suppose that two salespeople are judged equal in experience, competence, and motivation. The market potential in each territory is about the same. Last year's sales in the two territories were $2 million and $3.6 million. Should their sales objectives for the coming year be the same? Apparently, there are factors other than sales effort influencing sales in these territories such as the intensity of competition. Management should take into account such uncontrollable effects in setting objectives.

Setting objectives is further discussed in each of the chapters in Part 4. The above guidelines for setting objectives are useful in developing objectives for each of the marketing mix elements.

CHOOSING A POSITIONING STRATEGY

Kelly-Moore Paint Co. is a small paint producer and retailer in an industry dominated by firms like Sherwin-Williams, Glidden, and DuPont. Yet the regional firm's performance has been impressive compared to the nationals. Market targeting and positioning strategies have been instrumental in Kelly-Moore's success. Concentrating in the western part of the United States, the company sells primarily to contractors.[3] They are demanding customers who are slow to pay their bills. Kelly-

Moore's management has designed the marketing program to service contractors' needs. The high-quality paint is formulated to cover well in one coat by using more of the expensive titanium than is used by competitors. Credit approval is the responsibility of salespeople, whose bonuses are reduced if customers fail to pay their bills. Since the company stores the buyer's paint, it knows the inventory of a given buyer at any time. Inventory turnover is 12 compared an industry average of about 5 times per year. The company also caters to do-it-yourself painters. Promotion to this group is assisted by the touch-up cans left by professionals at the homes of the do-it-yourself customers.

Positioning may be an attempt to differentiate a marketing offer from a competitor's, to appear similar to a particular competitor, or to serve customers in one or more target markets. Kelly-Moore's strategy is illustrative. A positioning strategy is the design of a marketing program consisting of the following decisions:

1. The product or service offering.
2. How distribution will be accomplished.
3. Choice of a pricing strategy.
4. Selection of a promotional strategy.

These decisions represent a bundle of strategies. The objective is to form an integrated program, with each of the above components fulfilling its assigned role, in helping to position the firm in the product-markets management chooses to serve. The result often distinguishes a company, product, or brand from its competitors as a result of the customers' perceptions of the product or brand. The product, the method of distribution, the price, advertising, and personal selling all help to establish these perceptions, as do the marketing program actions of competitors plus other uncontrollable factors (e.g., government safety ratings of automobiles). When a positioning strategy is properly selected, the needs of the people or organizations that comprise the target market are satisfied. The essence of a good positioning strategy is one that will deliver customer satisfaction to the firm's target market and also meet corporate and marketing objectives.

Target market and positioning strategies are like the two sides of a coin. They are inseparable; each depends upon the other. Note how Kelly-Moore has designed its marketing program so as to give paint contractors attractive services. Working out of their homes, these buyers benefit by having the paint stored for a job at the retail location. One-coat paint also means less labor per job. The pieces all fit together into a very logical strategy that has helped to generate impressive financial performance for the firm.

Programming Decisions

Programming consists of deciding how to combine the marketing mix components into an overall positioning strategy. The strategic marketing programming decisions are: (1) determining the total amount of resources to be used for the marketing program; (2) deciding how to allocate these resources among product, distribution, price, advertising, and personal selling; and (3) choosing what to do with the resources assigned to each program component. These programming decisions have important characteristics:

> They are interrelated with the first constraining the second, and the second constraining the third.
> The decisions are both quantitative and qualitative in nature in that management must decide how much to spend and how to spend it.
> There are many strategic alternatives that can be selected, depending upon the size, deployment, and use of resources.

These characteristics add considerably to the complexity of the programming decision. How does management select an appropriate positioning strategy? Typically, it is a combination of management judgment and experience, trial and error, some experimentation (e.g., test marketing), and sometimes field research. Attempting to find the ideal positioning strategy is impossible in most situations because of the many influences that much be taken into account. Nevertheless, good strategies can be selected through sound analysis.

Factors Affecting the Positioning Strategy

The choice of a positioning strategy for the marketing program depends primarily upon the factors shown in Exhibit 9-5. The starting point is the target market that management has selected. Market opportunity analysis will supply information about the characteristics and the people/organizations in the target market. The programming task is to estimate the responsiveness of the target market to alternative positioning strategies while taking into account the competition, management's performance criteria (e.g., sales, market share, profit contribution), and available resources. As we saw in Chapter 8, these same factors are considered in making the market target decision. Marketing management is concerned with finding the best match between the market target and a positioning strategy.

What guidelines does the market target strategy provide for shaping a marketing program? First of all, the characteristics and needs of

---

EXHIBIT 9–5   Factors Influencing the Choice of a Marketing Program
Positioning Strategy

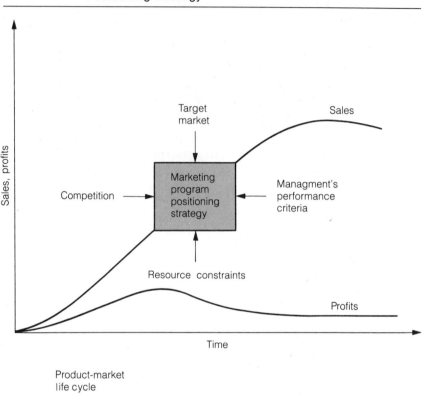

Product-market
life cycle

---

the target market will give an indication of the type of marketing program necessary to gain a favorable response from the target market. For example, if the people in the target market want a high-quality product, then meeting their needs will require a marketing mix that will be perceived as providing high quality. The market target also indicates who are our key competitors. Similarly, the choice of the market target will establish a feasible range for sales and market share. Finally, the selection of our target market should have taken into account the firm's resource capabilities for serving the target market. The objective in building the marketing program is to work within the guidelines established by the market target strategy.

The stage of the product-market life cycle may have a significant impact upon the role and importance of the different marketing program components. In moving through the introductory, growth, maturity, and decline stages, the roles of the mix elements often are adjusted to respond to changing conditions. Price, for example, typically declines over the life cycle of a product-market. Advertising, initially, is used to create awareness of a new product and to interest potential buyers in the offering. At later stages advertising may stress the advantages of one brand over competing brands.

Management's performance criteria for the market target also have a major influence upon the positioning strategy of the marketing program. Depending upon management's priorities, emphasis may be placed on expanding market share, holding position and generating profits, reducing the firm's commitment, or actually leaving the product-market. Thus positioning strategy is tied to the strategic business unit (SBU) strategy. Each alternative calls for a quite different marketing program. If marketing management is shaping a major growth program while the SBU management favors a hold position, conflict is inevitable. What top management wants to do in an SBU must correspond to the selected positioning strategy.

Consider the positioning strategy used by Maker's Mark Distillery, the producer of a premium-priced bourbon with the cap sealed by a distinguishing hand-dipped red wax.[4] The bourbon was first marketed in 1958. Management has built an impressive growth and performance record, particularly when one considers that bourbon industry sales have declined substantially in the past decade. Meeting the needs of bourbon drinkers who desire a superior product with a mellow flavor is the crux of the firm's business purpose. The distilling formula substitutes more expensive wheat for rye to give a smoother taste. The positioning strategy consists of a high-quality product with a pleasant taste placed in a distinctive package and given a prestigious brand name. Marketing takes place through distributors to retailers and is backed up by a highly effective sales effort conducted by the president and two other top executives. The firm has no field sales force. Advertising is targeted at newspapers; regional editions of magazines such as *Time, Playboy,* and *Penthouse;* and specialty publications such as *Southern Living* and *Louisville Lawyer.* The budget is small by consumer products standards. The brand commands a premium price that is over 50 percent higher than the popular-priced Jim Beam bourbon. Interestingly, some observers are convinced that management has not taken full advantage of the market opportunity for Maker's Mark. Instead, management has chosen to grow at a slow but steady rate of 8 to 10 percent per year, thus demonstrating the influence of management's performance criteria on the marketing program design.

Evaluating a Positioning Strategy

How does management know if it has developed a good positioning strategy? What criteria are used to judge the worth of a positioning strategy? Two criteria are appropriate:

1. Does the strategy yield performance results that correspond to management's expectations with regard to sales, market share, profit contribution, growth rates, and other relevant objectives?
2. To what extent does the strategy place the firm in a position that cannot be easily duplicated by the competition?

The former criterion is more quantitative in nature than the latter, which is admittedly qualitative. Gauging the effectiveness of a marketing program strategy that uses specific criteria, such as market share and profitability, is also more straightforward than evaluating the competitive advantage. Yet the development of a marketing program strategy that cannot be easily copied is an essential consideration. For example, a competitor would need considerable resources —not to mention a long time period—to duplicate the strong retail furniture dealer network developed by Ethan Allen, Inc. In contrast, an airline is able to respond immediately with a price cut to meet the price offered by a competitor. Thus a strong distribution channel is more difficult for a competitor to copy than a price cut.

Considerations about Targeting/Supporting Activities

A positioning strategy is usually developed to serve a market target with either a single product (microwave ovens) or a line of related producted (kitchen appliances). Alternative programming approaches are shown in Exhibit 9–6. It is difficult to generalize as to which approach is best since the decision is often situation-specific, depending upon such factors as the size of the product-market, characteristics of the product or service, the number of products involved, product interrelationships in the consumers' use situation, and various other considerations. For example, Procter & Gamble, Johnson & Johnson, and Chesebrough-Pond's marketing programs are oriented around particular brands whereas firms such as General Electric Company and IBM use product line or combination program approaches. In a firm that is serving several market targets, there may also be umbrella strategies developed for specific marketing program components, such as advertising and personal selling. The programming guidelines developed in this chapter can be used with any of the programming approaches shown in Exhibit 9–6.

The Positioning Statement

The positioning statement indicates the positioning strategy selected by management using some frame of reference. Often the competition

---

EXHIBIT 9-6 Alternative Marketing Programming Approaches

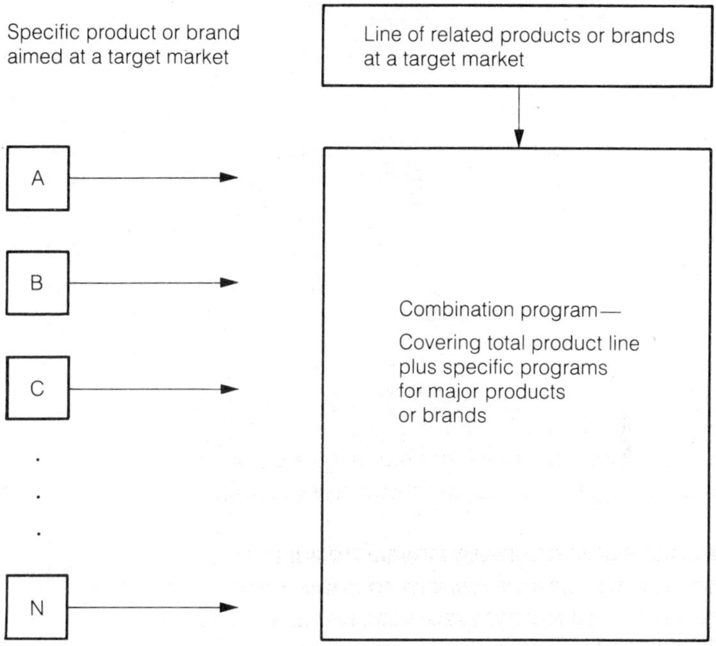

Specific product or brand
aimed at a target market

Line of related products or brands
at a target market

A →

B →

C →

.

.

.

N →

Combination program—

Covering total product line
plus specific programs
for major products
or brands

---

serves as either an explicit or implicit frame of reference. Several positioning approaches can be used.[5]

Attribute. Use of one or more attributes, product features, or customer benefits associated with the firm's product brand.

Price/Quality. Various positions on the price/quality scale may be selected depending upon management's positioning objective. Examples range from Neiman-Marcus at the high end to Toys-R-Us at the low end.

Use or Application. This strategy positions the brand according to how the product is used or applied, such as "Orange juice isn't just for breakfast anymore." Application positioning is used for various industrial products.

Product User. This type of positioning focuses on the person using the product. Revlon's Charlie cosmetic line introduced a life-style positioning strategy.

Product Class. This positioning approach involves association with a product-class, such as freeze-dried coffee compared to regular and instant coffee.

Competitor. This strategy explicitly positions a firm's brand against the competition. Datril used this approach when it entered the nonaspirin market against Tylenol.

Positioning by attribute was used for Kraft's Breyers ice cream.[6] Breyers does not contain artificial flavoring, added coloring, stabilizers, or emulsifiers. It produces better "flavor release" and distinctive "mouth-feel." Breyers was positioned as "The All-Natural Ice Cream," focusing on consumers' emerging interest in natural foods. The positioning strategy concentrated on an ingredient rather than a health or ecological appeal. The all-natural positioning strategy was very effective, with sales doubling in Breyers' traditional geographical areas three years after the new strategy was introduced.

POSITIONING COMPONENTS OF THE MARKETING PROGRAM

Within the framework of the overall positioning strategy, we must make various marketing program decisions. First, we overview these decisions, and then discuss the relationship between marketing effort and response.

Marketing Program Decisions

An illustration will highlight how the marketing program components are combined into a positioning strategy. S. C. Johnson & Son, Inc. is a successful marketer of personal care products such as Agree Creme Rinse and Agree Shampoo. Known for its waxes, polishes, and related household products, management moved into the market for personal care products in the late 1960s as a result of the rapid growth prospects in that market. One product, Edge shave cream, was an instant success. Several others failed because they did not offer any advantage over existing products and because the marketing programming used was faulty. The product development and marketing strategy for Agree Creme Rinse demonstrated management's ability to learn from its failures and to formulate and implement successful positioning strategies. Agree Creme Rinse, introduced in 1977, had by 1979 a 20 percent market share and was first on the basis of unit sales. These are the major features of the positioning strategy of the marketing program used for Agree:

A successful brand entry into the highly competitive market for personal care products must have distinct competitive advantages that can be recognized by consumers. Agree satisfied these requirements.

Marketing research is essential at various stages in product planning to help identify the opportunity, define the target market, determine program positioning strategy, and define the physical characteristics and performance attributes of the product. For example, a mail panel study of hair-care practices, using a large national probability sample of women, provided useful concept development guidelines regarding hair-care practices, characteristics of women's hair, and user and nonuser data.

Extensive testing was conducted as to product use, advertising, laboratory market tests using a simulated store, and, finally, actual market tests in Fresno, California, and South Bend, Indiana.

The product was launched nationally with a $14 million marketing effort—a sampling program that reached over 30 million women at a cost of $7 million and $7 million for TV and magazine advertising.[7]

Agree was developed and positioned to appeal to young women with oily hair. While there were many other specific activities involved in the strategic marketing planning for Agree Creme Rinse, the illustration provides an insight into the development of a positioning strategy of the marketing program.

An overview of the various decisions that must be made in developing a positioning strategy is shown in Exhibit 9–7. Since these areas are examined in depth in Part 4, our objective here is to show how they fit into the positioning strategy. The positioning strategy should indicate how (and why) the product mix, line, or brand is to be positioned to serve the target market. This statement should indicate:

An overview of product strategy including how the product(s) will be positioned against the competition in the product-market.

Distribution approach to be used.

Pricing strategy.

Advertising strategy.

Sales force strategy.

The statement should describe each marketing program component strategy, objectives, and specific programs for accomplishing the operational objectives. For example, S. C. Johnson's strategic marketing plan would logically include a complete marketing plan for each new product, such as Agree Shampoo, as well as for existing products.

Strategic marketing planning activities fall into two categories. First, it is necessary to establish the major strategy guidelines for every marketing program component. For example, what type of channel of distribution should be developed? Once these guidelines are determined, they may not be altered for several years. After Ethan Allen's management initially decided to use a vertically coordinated type of

EXHIBIT 9–7 Positioning Strategy Overview

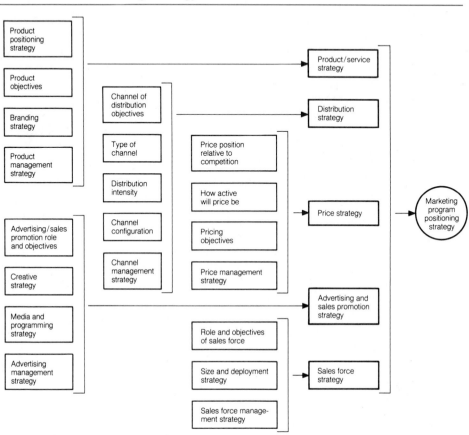

channel distribution and a selective distribution intensity, it followed these decisions for over a decade. Second, many of the ongoing, strategic plannng activities in a company consist of management strategies for each of the program components. For example, distribution management strategy in Ethan Allen's case would involve recruiting of new retailers, providing support to them, and making necessary changes in the strategy over time. Both categories of marketing planning activities emphasize the importance of first determining the various long-range strategic guidelines and then appraising them on a regular basis. Much of the actual content of the plan consists of the various management strategies.

EXHIBIT 9–8 Effort to Response Relationships for Marketing Programs A, B, and C

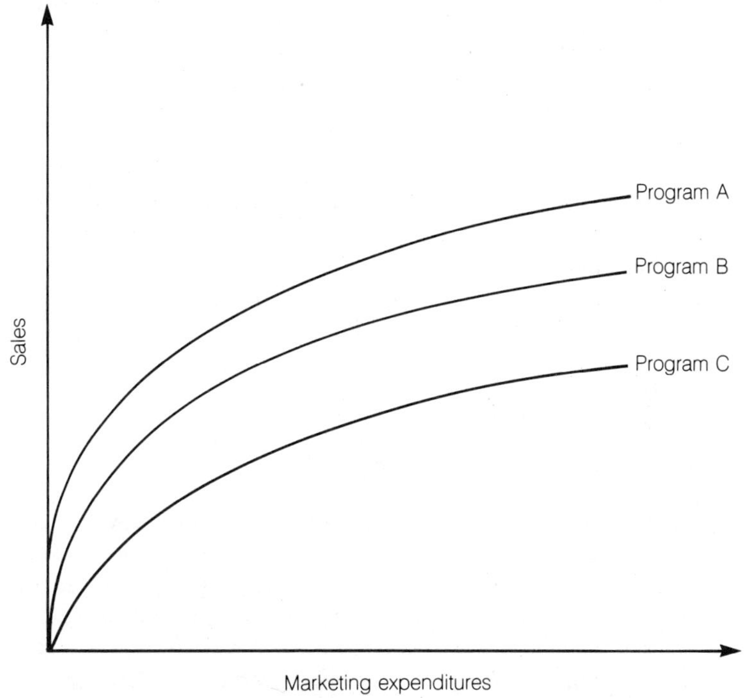

Effort to Response Relationship

A central consideration in selecting a positioning strategy is estimating how the market target responds to the marketing program used. Response is normally measured by sales. We can measure the amount of effort represented by marketing through the expenditures for the program. Assuming that the size and composition of the marketing program have an effect on sales, management needs to understand the relationship between marketing effort and sales response.

Suppose that three alternative marketing program strategies display the sales to marketing effort relationships shown in Exhibit 9–8. At any level of expenditure, Program A offers the most favorable total sales response. The choice of the specific marketing expenditure level will require an analysis of sales and costs to determine the most profitable level of expenditure. While Exhibit 9–8 is admittedly oversimplified, it demonstrates the nature of the marketing programming task.

In the next section we discuss and illustrate several methods of analyzing the relationship between effort and response.

POSITIONING ANALYSIS

The development of a positioning strategy consists of defining the existing position, and then deciding whether to maintain and strengthen the existing position or to develop and implement a repositioning strategy. Positioning analysis is concerned with identifying competitors; determining how they are perceived, evaluated, and positioned; and analyzing customer needs and preferences.[8] Several methods can be used by management to analyze marketing program positioning strategy. Illustrative techniques include customer and competitor analysis and research, market testing of proposed strategies, and the use of analytical models.

Customer/Competitor Research

Knowledge of customer needs and wants and how people in the target market will respond to alternative marketing programs enhances the development of a good positioning strategy. Research studies generate useful buyer and competitor information for designing positioning strategies. Several of the research methods discussed in Chapters 5 and 8 defining the product-market structure and identifying market segments, are also effective in guiding the development of a positioning strategy. For example, research about the product and brand positioning can be helpful in formulating a marketing program strategy by mapping customer preferences for various competing brands.

An illustration will show how customer research can yield important information for strategy development. The example involves a mature, heavy-apparatus industry in the United States with a modest growth opportunity:

> Exhibit 9-9 shows shifting market shares of competitors in this industry over nearly 30 years. In particular, it traces the entry of a new competitor in about the 19th year, who was able to expand its market share against the dominant producer while commanding a price premium that started at 3 percent and grew to 8 percent. How did the newcomer do it?
>
> The key was management's recognition that its company's products offered significantly lower fuel consumption under extended highspeed operating conditions (see Exhibit 9-10). Traditional market segmentation was in terms of the geographical location of major users. Instead, the new company segmented the market across all user areas in terms of types of applications where its products would offer significantly lower cost operation.

EXHIBIT 9-9 Changing Market Shares of Competitors in an Industry (selected years over 28-year period)

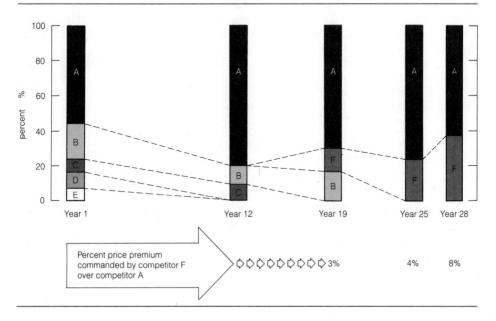

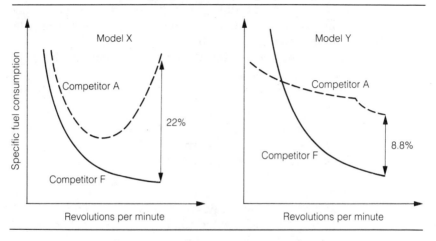

EXHIBIT 9-10 Comparison of Fuel Consumption and Speed Characteristics of Two Competitors' Products

It then concentrated its marketing efforts on helping users measure the difference.

The dominant competitor could not match this performance without abandoning its basic technical approach, and without diluting the strength of its own position in other portions of the market where it still had an advantage.

An essential aspect of the smaller competitor's strategy was recognizing that it would never "take" the dominant position, but that it could selectively capture a sizable portion of the market against the stronger competitor by concentrating on segments where measurable economic performance differences were in its favor.[9]

Note in this illustration the use of management judgment in combination with research and analysis of customer needs in finding a product-market segment and then developing a positioning strategy for serving the target market. Interestingly, company F was able to penetrate a mature market by using a premium-price strategy and building upon F's product features that could not be easily duplicated by competitor A. These positioning guidelines provided the basis for advertising and personal selling strategies.

Test Marketing

Market testing is sometimes used to generate information about the commercial feasibility of a promising new product or to try out new positioning strategies for new products. The decision to test the market depends primarily upon the following factors:

1. How much risk and investment are associated with the venture? When both are low, launching the product without a test market may be appropriate.
2. How much of a difference is there between the manufacturing investment required for the test versus the national launch? A large difference would favor a test market.
3. What are the likelihood and speed of the competitive response to the product offering?
4. How do the marketing costs and risks vary with the scale of the launch?[10]

While usually less than the costs of a national introduction, test marketing is nevertheless expensive. And the competitive risks of revealing one's plans must be weighed against the usefulness of test market information. The major returns from testing are risk reduction through better demand forecasts and the opportunity to fine-tune a marketing program strategy. Urban and Hauser indicate that "$1 million is typical for packaged goods in a one-city test market and some firms spend $1.5 million or more."[11] And more than a few strategists are admittedly uneasy about using marketing test results from only one city to project the national performance of a new product.

Test marketing can be used to generate two kinds of information: national forecasts and the effectiveness of alternative marketing program strategies. Both are highly dependent upon the extent to which results from one or a few test markets will provide accurate projections of the national market. Model-based analysis is an approach designed to help overcome problems associated with idiosyncrasies of test cities by using a detailed behavioral model of the consumer to analyze test market measurements and develop forecasts that can be made for the effect of modified marketing strategies.[12] Test marketing of new products is discussed in Chapter 11.

Positioning Models

Obtaining relevant information about customers and prospects, analyzing it, and then developing strategies based on information and upon management judgment is the crux of positioning analysis. Some promising results have been achieved by incorporating research data into formal models of decision analysis. We will review two illustrative models to indicate the nature and scope of their use. Comprehensive discussion of marketing modeling is available from other sources.[13] As indicated above, we will discuss new product planning models in Chapter 11. The more comprehensive new product models also determine several aspects of the marketing program.

The ADVISOR Models. ADVISOR is a comprehensive marketing mix budgeting model developed for industrial products.[14] We can use this model to set a marketing budget and then split it into budgets for personal and impersonal (e.g., advertising) communications. ADVISOR is a multiple regression-type model that incorporates several predictor variables, including the number of users, customer concentration, fraction of sales made to order, attitude differences, proportion of direct sales, life-cycle stage, product plans, and product complexity. The model is similar in concept and approach to the PIMS model described in Chapter 3, although ADVISOR concentrates on the marketing budget and its components rather than on offering complete strategies for business units or products.

An ADVISOR application using a sample of 131 products from 29 U.S. companies and 80 products from 55 European countries indicates that the overall relationship between strategic variables and advertising and marketing spending levels does not differ between the United States and Europe.[15] Some differences in the importance of individual strategic variables between the two regions were found. A comparison of the results is shown in Exhibit 9–11.

EXHIBIT 9-11 ADVISOR USA and Europe Norm Models for Marketing and Advertising Budgets

Independent Variable	Marketing Budget		Advertising Budget	
	U.S. Sample Regression Coefficient (+t value)	Eur. Sample Regression Coefficient (+t value)	U.S. Sample Regression Sample (+t value)	Eur. Sample Regression Coefficient (+t value)
Constant[a]	0.187	−0.469	−0.342	−1.312
Sales	0.710 (12.72)	0.681 (9.49)	0.576 (9.08)	0.528 (5.34)
Number of users	0.079 (3.00)	0.106 (2.39)	0.105 (3.95)	0.214 (3.25)
Customer concentration[a]	−1.634 (3.18)	−0.579 (0.82)	−1.650 (2.81)	−2.193 (2.15)
Fraction of sales made to order[a]	−0.997 (2.81)	−0.100 (0.26)	−1.711 (4.21)	0.213 (0.37)
Prospect-customer attitude difference[a]	−0.206 (1.11)	−0.018 (0.06)	b	b
Proportion of direct sales	0.179 (0.52)	0.166 (0.31)	b	b
Stages in life cycle[a]	−0.428 (2.07)	−0.242 (0.89)	−0.864 (3.79)	−0.805 (2.18)
Product plans[a]	0.814 (3.87)	0.526 (1.99)	1.197 (4.87)	0.511 (1.29)
Product complexity[a]	0.548 (2.64)	0.841 (3.37)	b	b
Adjusted R²	0.69	0.67	0.55	0.45
Sample size	112	75	109	75
Chow test statistic	0.847		2.046	

[a]Note that here, as in Lilien (1979), the coefficients reported for the discrete independent variables are the natural logarithms of the β's in equation 1.

[b]Variable excluded from this relationship in Lilien 1979, original ADVISOR analysis.

SOURCE: Gary L. Lilien and David Weinstein, "An International Comparison of the Determinants of Industrial Marketing Expenditures," *Journal of Marketing*, Winter 1984, 50.

Hierarchy Model of the Marketing Mix. The analytic hierarchy process (AHP) can be used to assess and allocate resources in a portfolio.[16] The decision situation is structured hierarchically, as shown in Exhibit 9-12. Using an associated measurement-and-decomposition process, we establish priorities that are consistent with our objectives. Items in the hierarchy are compared on a pairwise basis as to which item contributes to the attainment of an objective. In this application the decision problem is to select the appropriate marketing mix for a consumer service. While this use of AHP was exploratory, the results are encouraging. This pilot study will help management to generate innovative marketing mix strategies, to evaluate alternative strategies, to gain a consensus among conflicting interests, and to identify additional needs for research information.

Models like ADVISOR and AHP appear more useful in the analysis of complex decision situations than in supplying optimal solutions. The models provide management with useful comparative analyses that help to evaluate alternative strategies.

A summary of the various positioning analysis approaches and the sequence in which they would be used is shown in Exhibit 9-13. Note

EXHIBIT 9–12   Analytic Hierarchy Process Application to the Marketing Mix Decision: Benefits to the Hierarchy

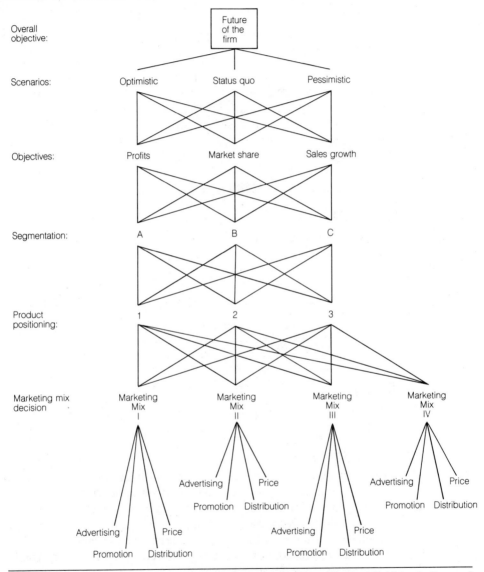

SOURCE: Yoram Wind and Thomas L. Saaty, "Marketing Applications of the Analytic Hierarchy Process," *Management Science*, July 1980, 655.

EXHIBIT 9-13 Marketing Program Positioning Analysis Approaches

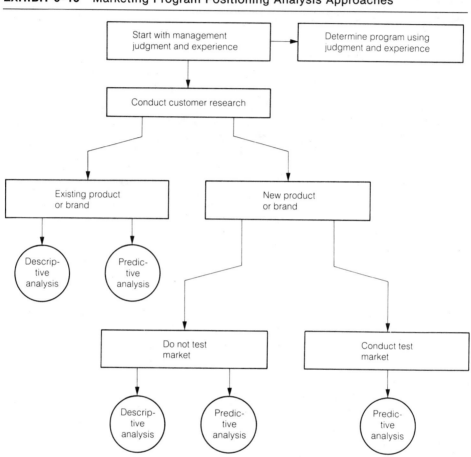

that two additional factors are incorporated into Exhibit 9-13. First, in considering position analysis, it is useful for us to distinguish between an existing product or brand and one that is being developed. Second, management should recognize the type of analysis that is being used. A research effort may result in either a *descriptive* or a *predictive* analysis. In the former case, management must correctly interpret the information for use in guiding marketing program strategy. In the latter situation, analysis provides a prediction of what will happen on the basis of the information obtained from customer research and test marketing. For example, preference mapping is descriptive in nature, although behavioral modeling approaches can be used to make predictions.

MAKING THE POSITIONING DECISION

ChemLawn Corp. uses an interesting positioning strategy that has proved effective in gaining a rapid growth in sales and profits. The focal point of ChemLawn's marketing program is the guarantee offered on all services.[17] For example, advertising of CarpetClean carries this message: "ChemLawn CarpetClean keeps working till you say it's clean or you don't pay." The guarantee is shown on all its 4,000 trucks. ChemLawn has expanded into new service areas such as carpet cleaning and indoor exterminating, building on the customer base developed in the lawn care business. ChemLawn's marketing expenditures were $25 million in 1984, increasing more than sixfold in a five-year period. Some industry observers question the logic of ChemLawn's movement into nonlandscaping markets.

Deciding when to Reposition

In an existing product-market situation management must decide whether to follow its current positioning strategy or to reposition. Companies do not alter their positioning strategies on a frequent basis, although adjustments are often made at different product life cycle stages and in response to environmental, market, and competitive forces. When a marketing mix strategy is working, it is logical to keep on using it. Consider, for example, the very successful advertising campaign for LIFE cereal using the "Mikey" series of commercials. The commercial shows an older brother commenting that his little brother (Mikey) really likes the cereal. The campaign of 2,500 network showings helped Quaker Oats Co. build an $80 million business out of LIFE cereal. After 14 years three new campaigns were being considered in 1985. Interestingly, the Mikey campaign had faced the threat of replacement for all but the first two years of its existence.[18]

Even though frequent changes are not made, a successful positioning strategy should be evaluated on a regular basis to identify shifting buyer preferences and changes in competitor strategies. We can use marketing research methods, such as consumer panels, preference maps, and image studies, to monitor positioning strategy.

Positioning and Segmentation Strategies

It is important to maintain a continual awareness of the interrelationship between market target and positioning strategies.

> Positioning usually means that an overt decision is being made to concentrate only on certain segments. Such an approach requires commitment

and discipline because it's not easy to turn your back on potential buyers. Yet, the effect of generating a distinct, meaningful position is to focus on the target segments and not be constrained by the reaction of other segments.[19]

Positioning becomes particularly challenging when management decides to target several segments. The objective is to develop an effective positioning strategy for each segment, while avoiding any adverse effect from the positioning strategy for a particular segment on other segments. The use of a different brand for each targeted segment is one means of focusing a positioning strategy.

Determining Positioning Feasibility

"It is tempting but naive—and usually fatal—to decide on a positioning strategy that exploits a market need or opportunity but assumes that your product is something it is not."[20] In selecting a positioning strategy, management must realistically evaluate the feasibility of the strategy, taking into consideration the product's strengths, the positions of competing brands, and the probable reactions of buyers to the strategy. Marketing research evaluations such as use tests can help to gauge the reaction of buyers.

Cherry Coke, which was introduced nationally in mid-1985, surprised many industry observers with its strong sales performance at the same time that New Coke and Classic Coke were in the limelight.[21] Network TV and radio spots positioned Cherry Coke as an "out and outrageous" alternative to the other cokes. The new brand was launched with a $50 million budget, which generated a surprisingly strong and fast payback. Positioning was in terms of the flavor of the soft drink, thus using an attribute strategy.

CONCLUDING NOTE

Developing a positioning strategy of the marketing program requires the blending of the product, distribution, price, advertising, and personal selling strategies that focus on a market target. The result is an integrated strategy that will achieve management's performance objectives while gaining the largest possible differential advantage over the competition. Shaping this bundle of strategies is a major challenge to marketing decision makers. This chapter highlights the issues involved in marketing programming. It shows how programming is linked to the strategic planning of the enterprise and to the other two key aspects of marketing strategy—target market selection and setting objectives.

Building on an understanding of the market target and the objectives to be accomplished by the marketing program, positioning strategy seeks to match the firms' capabilities to market target buyers' needs. Programming decisions consist of determining the amount of expenditure, deciding how to allocate these resources to the marketing program components, and making the most effective use of resources within each mix component. Several factors affect program strategy, including the market target, the competition, resource constraints, management's performance criteria, and the product life cycle. The positioning statement describes the desired positioning relative to the competition.

Central to the positioning decision is determining the relationship between the marketing effort and the market response. Positioning analysis can be useful in estimating the market response as well as in evaluating competition and buyer preferences. Analysis methods include customer/competitor research, market testing, and positioning models. Using analysis information in combination with management judgment and experience, we select a positioning strategy. The close tie between positioning and segmentation strategies make essential a close coordination of these strategies. Finally, it is important to realistically assess the feasibility of success of a positioning strategy under consideration by management.

Part 4 examines each marketing program component and considers its role and function in forming a total strategy. In moving through these chapters, we need to recognize several characteristics of the marketing mix variables. They are both supplemental and complemental in nature. Some must work together to be effective, such as the need to communicate the features and availability of a new product. Other elements can, to some extent, serve as substitutes for each other. For example, pricing can be used in a promotional role. Each mix component frequently establishes some constraining guidelines for those decisions that remain. The mix variables are placed in a sequence that begins with the product or service as the least constrained component and ends with promotion as the most constrained element. This same sequence corresponds to the time frequency of decisions, with product and distribution decisions extending over rather long time horizons compared to much shorter time spans for promotional decisions.

NOTES

1. Dart & Kraft, Inc., *1984 Annual Report,* 17–20.
2. David A. Aaker and J. Gary Shansby, "Positioning Your Products," *Business Horizons,* May-June 1982, 56.
3. The remainder of this account is based on Roger Neal, "Color It Profitable," *Forbes,* January 28, 1985, 76.
4. This illustration is based upon the article by David P. Garino, "Maker's

Mark Goes against the Grain to Make Its Mark," *The Wall Street Journal*, August 1, 1980, 1, 4.

5. Aaker and Shansby, "Positioning Your Product," 56.

6. Samuel R. Gardner, "Successful Market Positioning—One Company Example," in *Product-Line Strategies*, ed. Earl L. Bailey (New York: The Conference Board, 1982), 40–41.

7. This illustration is based upon a presentation by Frederic D. Mordeen, marketing research manager, and Neil DeClerk, associate research manager, published in *Marketing News*, January 12, 1979, 14–15, published by The American Marketing Association.

8. Aaker and Shansby, "Positioning Your Product", 60.

9. This illustration and the accompanying exhibits is reprinted from William E. Johnson, "Trade-Offs in Pricing Strategy," in *Pricing Practices and Strategies*, ed. Earl L. Bailey (New York: The Conference Board, 1978), 50–51.

10. N. D. Cadbury, "When, Where, and How to Test Market," *Harvard Business Review*, May-June 1975, 97–98.

11. Glen L. Urban and John R. Hauser, *Design and Marketing of New Prod-*ucts (Englewood Cliffs, N.J.: Prentice-Hall, 1980), 419.

12. Ibid.; see Chapter 15 for a discussion of alternative methods for analyzing test markets.

13. See, for example, Gary L. Lilien and Philip Kotler, *Marketing Decision Making* (New York: Harper & Row), 1983.

14. Gary L. Lilien, "Advisor Z: Modeling the Marketing Mix Decision for Industrial Products," *Management Science*, February 1979, 191–204.

15. Gary L. Lilien and David Weinstein, "An International Comparison of the Determinants of Industrial Marketing Expenditures," *Journal of Marketing*, Winter 1984, 46–53.

16. Yoram Wind and Thomas L. Saaty, "Marketing Applications of the Analytic Hierarchy Process," *Management Science*, July 1980, 641–58.

17. Gary Levin, "ChemLawn Branches out so Profits Grow," *Advertising Age*, June 4, 1984, 4 and 65.

18. "Reign of Quaker Oaks' Commercial is in Danger," *USA Today*, March 13, 1985, 7B.

19. Aaker and Shansby, "Positioning Your Products," 61.

20. Ibid, 62.

21. Julie Franz, "Cherry Coke Takes the Fizz out of Sister Brands," *Advertising Age*, October 28, 1985, 4.

QUESTIONS FOR REVIEW AND DISCUSSION

1. During the early 1980s generic products, such as facial tissues, canned foods, and soaps, were rapidly gaining market share in supermarkets. Discuss the type of positioning strategy that would be most effective for manufacturers of branded products, such as Procter & Gamble, General Foods, Pillsbury, and Heinz, in competing against generic products.

2. Compare and contrast the positioning strategy used by Revlon, Inc. for a brand like Charlie perfume with the strategy used by Caterpillar in marketing earth-moving equipment.

3. Suppose that you find it necessary to explain to a vice president of sales why marketing objectives should be relevant and consistent. How would you approach this task?

4. It is probably impossible to make a perfect set of decisions concerning product, distribution, price, and promotion strategies. Why?

5. Select a product and discuss how the size and composition of the marketing program might require adjustment as the product moves through its life cycle.

6. Suggest an approach that can be used by a regional family restaurant chain to determine the firm's strengths over its competitors.

7. Select and discuss a strategy that corresponds to each of these positioning approaches: attribute, price/quality, competition, application; product users, and product class.

8. Discuss some of the more important reasons why test market results may *not* be a good gauge of how well a new product will perform when it is launched in the national market.

9. "Evaluating marketing performance by using return-on-investment (ROI) measures is not appropriate because marketing is only one of several influences upon ROI." Develop an argument against this statement.

10. Two factors complicate the problem of making future projections as to the financial performance of marketing programs. First, the flow of revenues and costs is likely to be uneven over the planning horizon. Second, sales may not develop as forecasted. How should we handle these factors in financial projections?

STRATEGIC APPLICATION 9-1

PLAYBOY ENTERPRISES, INC.

Few things better evoke the male-fantasy aura of Playboy than its cotton-tailed Bunnies. Yet when Hugh Hefner officially reopens Playboy's New York club this fall, the hostesses greeting guests will be wearing long, glittering Jean Harlow-style gowns. Not only that, some of the waiters will be men.

Absent from the club will be the traditional pool table, party balloons and Leroy Neiman paintings. Instead, Playboy will offer video effects, stage acts and music by a 10-piece house orchestra.

The magazine, meanwhile, is on the stands with new graphics, new yuppie-oriented content and a new binding meant to lend it more class.

Playboy Enterprises, Inc. is trying to airbrush itself a new image. Once considered a trend setter for urban sophisticates, the adult-leisure company in recent years has increasingly found its offerings out of step with the times, from the Tiny Tim picture on menus at its Chicago club to the sometimes-stale Party Jokes in its magazine.

"The image of the playboy in a smoking jacket is obsolete," contends Barbara Ehrenreich, a writer on social issues. "People today are more interested in their cars and their careers than they are in sex."

While *that* may be open to dispute, Playboy has reason to be alarmed. The circulation of its flagship magazine has dwindled to just over four million a month from more than seven million in 1972. The number of Playboy Club key holders has fallen steadily. The cable-television Playboy Channel, once seen as crucial to the future, loses money and has yet to prove it can survive in its highly competitive field.

In just three years, Playboy's revenue has fallen by nearly 50%. It has earned a profit on operations in only one of four years since 1982, when it was forced by old legal problems to give up its lucrative casinos. The company was in the black (by $6.7 million) in the June fiscal year only because of returns on its $60 million in investments. And its auditors have qualified their opinion on the financial statement for that year because of uncertainty over whether Playboy can collect all it is owed on one casino sale.

In a sense, Playboy is a victim of the social changes it helped promote. Attitudes toward sex have evolved rapidly since the days when the magazine could shock millions by publishing two photographs of an undraped Marilyn Monroe. Today, Playboy has to compete not only with countless far-more-lurid "skin books" but also against the popular media; rock songs may have X-rated lyrics, and an episode of "Dynasty" on TV may be nearly as titillating as a centerfold.

"We no longer can contrast ourselves to a gray-flannel Eisenhower society," says Arthur Kretchmer, the magazine's associate publisher." It's now a lot more difficult for us to offer something unique."

Yet Playboy also finds itself considerably vexed these days by those who consider its businesses immoral or sexist or both. Although its cable-television fare isn't hard-core, for instance, it has repeatedly been challenged in court (so far unsuccessfully) by communities that want it banned.

After ABC recently broadcast a film based on Gloria Steinem's critical account of her 1963 stint as a Bunny, Playboy President Christie Hefner fired off a memo asking her staff to "ponder what it is Playboy and all of its resources can and should be doing to counter the . . . misimpression out there that we are not good guys."

Perhaps a tougher problem for Miss Hefner, though, is finding a clear mission

Playboy Enterprises (for year ended June 30, 1985)	
Revenue	$192.3 million
Net income	$6.7 million
Employees	895
Playboy magazine circulation	4.1 million
Subscribers to Playboy Channel	762,000
Number of owned and franchised clubs	13

for Playboy in the 1980s, one as potent as her father's former vision for the company. In an era of aggressive careerism—by both sexes—the company no longer gets much mileage out of the so-called Playboy Philosophy, Mr. Hefner's concept of the life style of a man of leisure.

Some company officials, in fact, believe that one of Playboy's biggest handicaps may be its association with the public image of its founder, now 59 years old. "Pajamas just aren't as fashionable as they used to be," one Playboy executive says.

Though still the best-selling magazine for men, Playboy has fallen far behind arch-rival Penthouse in lucrative newsstand sales. "Its market is older; their readers are passing into oblivion," says Penthouse publisher Bob Guccione, adding that Playboy "thinks of itself as hip, but they're not."

He is anything but a disinterested observer, of course, and Playboy says the readership age difference is minimal. But there are other worrisome signs. Steve Jones, a Chicago newsstand operator who has sold a lot of copies of Playboy, speaks of the typical buyer as "a guy who thinks he's up to date but isn't." One woman who posed for a pictoral was surprised, when she saw the letters the feature generated, to find that "a whole bunch of them were from guys in prison." And Lee Gotlieb, who is a former public-relations executive for Playboy, contends that the company "doesn't want to face reality—that time has passed them by."

Against this background, Playboy Enterprises is undertaking what Miss Hefner calls a "repositioning." The strategy, she says, is to go after a more upscale audience by being more in tune with current tastes and values. "I think we can be on the cutting edge," she says, "of how people who have changed their behavior to reflect a more liberal life style are going to live."

The October issue of Playboy, marked "collector's edition," begins what the company calls the magazine's next generation. This is to include greater coverage of such "life-style" subjects as personal finance and home electronics. An ad in the current issue asks, "What sort of man reads Playboy?" and offers as an example race-car driver Danny Sullivan. Posing in a black silk evening jacket, he explains that he "grew with the magazine," learning, for instance, to care about clothes. Curiously, elsewhere in the issue is a piece satirizing the consumer society.

Sensitive to criticism that it portrays women as sex objects, Playboy intends to feature some who are more mature or more accomplished, Mr. Kretchmer says. The planned lead feature in the November issue may be a nod in this direction, but it hardly seems likely to defuse the issue. Picturing members of Mensa, the club people can join only if they have high IQs, the feature is entitled "America's Smartest Girls Pose Nude."

Nevertheless, Miss Hefner says Playboy's effort to move upscale is working. As evidence, she notes that the October issue carries advertising for Campbell Soup's Le Menu frozen dinners.

Covers of the new-generation Playboy are to have a glitzier look. They are planned in long meetings by a committee of fashion and art experts who try to base their designs as much on the latest fashion as on erotic content.

The graphics also are slicker, and a different printing process binds pages with glue instead of staples, giving a more finished look. "The magazine is supposed to look a lot more like the kind of thing you'd put on a coffee table," says art director Tom Staebler. That goal may be a bit optimistic, however; newsstands say that half of the buyers of Playboy still ask for a paper bag to carry it home in.

The new magazine retains many of the standard features, like the Playboy Advisor, which intersperses advice about sex with answers to questions about stereos or turbochargers. Some editors complain about the uneven quality and occasionally questionable taste of color cartoons. Mr. Hefner himself is said to have rejected an editors' plea to eliminate the Party Jokes feature, which in the latest issue regales readers with one-liners like, "What's boffo box office among milkmaids? 'Pail Rider.'"

The "repositioning" also applies to the Playboy clubs, which haven't had a major updating since they were started a quarter-century ago. Even with a recent redecorating, the club in Chicago, with its plush red carpeting and black leather bar stools, looks a little like a museum for the jazz age. A gift shop up front peddling Playboy T-shirts, cigarette lighters and golf putters lends a touristy atmosphere to the place.

Rather than confront the deteriorating image of its big-city clubs, Playboy several years ago headed for the hinterlands, franchising clubs in places like Lansing, Mich., and Des Moines, Iowa, where they might still have novelty value. But without a strong big-city base, the whole chain lost its urban gleam. The Lansing club began resorting to such decidedly unglamorous promotions as lip-sync contests and valet parking for farm tractors.

All that is supposed to change with the reopening of the New York club. Its new look is being sculpted by Richard Melman, a Chicago restaurant entrepreneur whose Lettuce Entertain You Enterprises Inc. is noted for elaborate "concept" restaurants that are as much show-biz productions as eateries.

Mr. Melman says he selected Bunnies with talent as body-builders, astrologists and jugglers, though he won't say what he has in mind for them. Costumes will range from a sequined one called the Michael Jackson outfit, to sweater-dresses, to a takeoff of the current cottontail suit. The idea of male waiters (called rabbits) is to help women feel more comfortable in the club, which, Mr. Melman promises, "won't look like anything Playboy has ever done."

One of his ideas didn't get far, however. He wanted to drop "Playboy" from the club's name. He and company officials settled on "Playboy's Empire Club." He did win approval to play down the rabbit-head logo.

It remains to be seen how much of this will be transferred to the other 12 Playboy Clubs, 10 of which are franchised rather than company-owned. A section of the club called "Cafe Playboy" may be tested as a prototype for a chain of franchised bars open to the public. (A Playboy key still is needed for admittance to the clubs, though temporary memberships are readily available.)

Playboy's products division, too, is working to bolster the company's image, or at least stop endangering it. The division has sold countless key chains, air fresheners and the like, even though doing so risked cheapening the company's trademark. "We thought we were in the souvenir business," laments A. William Stokkan, who currently heads the division. He says Playboy is moving away from novelty items and into things like fashion apparel and branded consumer products. One success is Playboy men's underwear, the second-best-selling brand.

Playboy still has some hard thinking to do about its video operation. The division, which launched the first sex-oriented cable channel for a mass audience five years ago, had identity problems from the start. Unable to decide how racy to be, the channel wound up alienating viewers at both ends of the spectrum. "People are either outraged or bored," says one independent cable operator.

Earlier this year, for instance, the channel stopped offering erotic programming during prime time, switching to main-stream movies and quasi-journalistic specials like one entitled "Omar Sharif Hosts the Prostitutes of Paris." Viewership dropped, and Playboy soon reverted to prime-time prurience.

Partly because of its turnabouts, the Playboy Channel has had the highest disconnect rate in the industry, 13% of viewers each month. Its current level of about 762,000 subscribers isn't enough to pay for the quality programming that might attract a larger audience. At $20 million, the channel's yearly budget is less than a network might spend during a season on a single series.

As a result, Playboy is deemphasizing the channel as its main outlet for programming and will focus more on cassette sales and a recently launched pay-per-view service. It also is weighing a return to producing a late-night variety show or hour-long specials, either of which it would try to sell to one of the networks. "We'd like to do a 'Saturday Night Live' type of thing," says Miss Hefner.

Still, Playboy's video operations, like the rest of its empire, is continuing to grope for the right formula for today's audience. "We have to reflect a modern, sophisticated image," says Michael Brandman, a former Lorimar executive brought in to run the channel. "You can't survive by being an anachronism."

SOURCE: John Koten and Robert Johnson, "Fixing a Fantasy: As Men's Values Shift, Playboy Seeks a Way to Still Seem Exciting." Reprinted by permission of *The Wall Street Journal.* © Dow Jones & Company, Inc., September 12, 1985. All rights reserved.

DISCUSSION QUESTIONS

1. Identify and discuss mission alternatives that appear appropriate for Playboy Enterprises Inc.
2. Evaluate Playboy's market target strategy.
3. Discuss the appropriateness of the changes being made in Playboy's marketing mix.
4. Is Playboy's marketing strategy sound, considering the changes occurring in the marketplace and competitive threats?

STRATEGIC APPLICATION 9-2

MIAMI BEACH

Miami Beach, Fla.—This town's love affair with the elderly is over.

For years Miami Beach marketed itself aggressively as a haven for the elderly, a retirement Mecca. But now the city is courting a new crowd: yuppies.

And the old folks don't like it a bit.

Developers, merchants and the city government are falling over themselves seeking the young professional's dollar. The city plans a $350,000 privately funded advertising campaign next spring beckoning young people to Miami Beach. It's building a marina and park—with jungle gyms—to lure the younger set, and it recently rezoned the city's southern tip for a developer to build four high-rises that have health clubs, tennis courts and a disco.

"We want to give the yuppie a break," says Robert Blum, owner of two highrise apartments that offer a "young professionals rate" of 15% off the rent to people between 25 and 50. "We've been too busy trying to keep the elderly happy." Occupancy at his buildings has gone from all seniors to 30% under 50 since last May.

Meanwhile, the city recently began charging $75 for ambulance runs, and tried unsuccessfully to raise the price of seniors dances and to close a small library frequented by seniors. "This whole yuppie program is aggressive and nasty," says Barbara Capitman, an activist for the elderly who thinks Miami Beach is forsaking its old people.

To the city, it's a question of survival.

Retirees, many of them from New York, flocked to this 6.4-square-mile island after World War II. By 1980, 51.7% of residents here were more than 65 years old; the median age was 65.8 years. But about five years ago retirees virtually stopped coming—scared off by riots, crime and refugees (many from Cuba). "It got to be a slum, so no one came any more," says Celia Bloom, a silver-haired woman sitting on a bench in the city's Flamingo Park. Many affluent elderly people moved to less crime-prone retirement communities in central Florida, and elderly women who outlived their husbands headed back north.

Miami Beach turned from being a premiere vacation spot into a weathered city with slums and nursing homes. The apartment vacancy rate soared to 16.1% in 1984, and the city's tax base dropped by 3% between 1983 and 1985.

City officials say that being a retirement haven wasn't the boon they thought. Many old people came on fixed incomes or Social Security. They don't spend as freely as younger, working people, instead stashing their money away in the 36 financial institutions that have branches here, says Stuart Rogel, direc-

Miami Beach Grows Younger

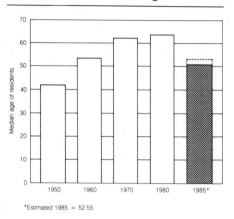

*Estimated 1985 = 52-55

SOURCE: Census Bureau; mayor's office estimate for 1985.

tor of economic development for the city. Mr. Rogel points to Lincoln Road Mall, once known as the Fifth Avenue of the South, which has turned into a row of dusty discount stores, one-fifth of them empty.

The elderly also placed demands on the city. Organized into influential political groups, they pressured government to hold low-cost dances three times a week, give free emergency medication and prosthetic devices to indigents and even has a doctor ride on every ambulance call (13,000 last year).

As the number of elderly dwindled and their demands increased, city officials say they saw only one solution: young professionals—many who work in downtown Miami, seven minutes away across a causeway. "A younger population is a working population," says Mr. Rogel. "They are more apt to spend money on goods and services."

Miami Beach beefed up police protection and will add street lights in areas where yuppies are moving, and it helped fund the South Florida Arts Center. Mr.

Blum is opening a $400,000 health club; he put a swing set on his beach and is offering a free Italian baby stroller to any tenant who gives birth. John Forte, president of the 1,339-unit Forte Towers Apartments, now allows children, and he has extended pool hours to 9 P.M. from 5 P.M. He also opened a fancy grocery store that carries $1,100 bottles of Chateau Latour Bordeaux, truffles and other foods he says young professionals like.

And three companies are refurbishing 38 of the area's more than 800 art deco buildings and breezy oceanfront hotels. The buildings' streamlined designs, glass tiles, porthole windows and pipe railings, all in sun-bathed colors of seagreen, bubble-gum pink and baby blue, appxal to the young, especially since the buildings are often featured on television's "Miami Vice." This, together with the planned opening of at least three new restaurants and several nightclubs, has lured young professionals.

"I'm getting a taste of the good life before I'm 65 and retired," says 35-year-old Alma Acevedo, sunbathing by the shimmering turquoise pool that's flanked by Mr. Blum's high-rise, the 300-foot-wide sandy beach and the emerald ocean.

Meanwhile, the young—many of them poorer Cuban families—are changing things; schools, once closing, are now overcrowded and South Beach Elementary is slated to reopen. The number of registered voters over 65 years old has dropped to 58.9% from 65.2% in 1979. Burdine's Sunshine Fashions, a large department store, recently began opening on Sundays. Its research showed the average age of its shoppers dropped to 57 from 65 between 1983 and 1984; it expects a similar decline this year.

The influx has heartened city officials and developers, but not many of the city's elderly. "They say the image of Miami Beach is of dirty old people. They say it's not their problem that they are growing older and dying off," says Mrs. Capitman, who says city officials have shown an increasing insensitivity to the elderly.

Harry Plissner, the 84-year-old chairman of Citizens Advocating Rights of the Elderly, points to a recent ordinance prohibiting adult congregate-living facilities (housing that provides seniors with food and some medical attention) on the ocean, bay or any major tourist-oriented street. "They want to keep us out of sight," says Mr. Plissner. The ordinance is being challenged in U.S. District Court in Miami.

"When this thing started they were cursing at me, spitting at me. I've been threatened," says Mr. Blum of how elderly tenants reacted to his young professionals discount. The older people's dismay grew when Mr. Blum removed the sofas from the front lobby, where they used to sit, saying he wanted to give the area a sense of motion. "People (including his elderly mother) have told me they aren't praying for my good health," he says.

Miami Beach Mayor Malcolm Fromberg insists that there's plenty of room in his city for yuppies and the elderly. But Mrs. Capitman, the activist, says that gentrification will ultimately push up rents, forcing the elderly to go elsewhere. For many of the elderly, who can barely function in familiar surroundings, "that's pretty scary," she says.

SOURCE: Sonia L. Nazario, "Miami Beach Courting Younger People as It Tries to Shed Retirement Image." Reprinted by permission of *The Wall Street Journal.* © Dow Jones & Company, Inc., October 8, 1985. All rights reserved.

DISCUSSION QUESTIONS

1. Describe the strategic marketing situation confronting Miami Beach, identifying important strategic issues.
2. Identify and analyze feasible positioning strategies that might be appropriate for Miami Beach.
3. Critique the positioning strategy implemented in 1985 by city officials and businesses.
4. Discuss the similarities and differences in developing a marketing strategy for a city, compared to a strategy for a commercial project.

PART 4

Strategic Marketing Programming

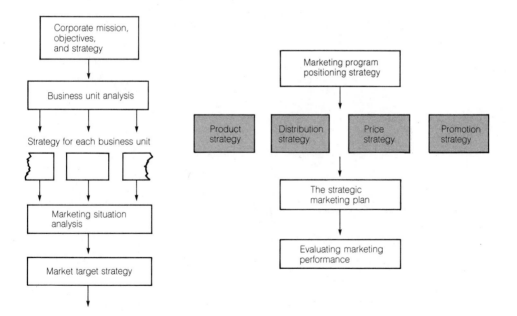

CHAPTER 10

Product Strategy

Measurex Corporation is a leading producer of computerized manufacturing process control systems. Founded in 1968, management initially targeted process control applications in the paper industry. By concentrating on a single market segment Measurex's sales and engineering personnel were able to learn the customer's business and to match the process control design to the customer's needs. Systems ranging from $0.25 to $1.0 million plus were sold on a "results-guaranteed" basis. Less than 1 percent of all systems sold by Measurex have been returned. The company is solutions-driven rather than product-driven. The paper industry accounts for about three fourths of sales. Management is moving into other user segments, such as an automobile industry venture with Ford (Motor Company) to develop software for assembly line discrete manufacturing processes. Sales in 1986 should approach $200 million. Measurex's product capabilities are communicated to the customer by the sales representative, supported by a team of technical experts. Sales calls in this high-technology company cost $1,000 per call. The company's technology capabilities include communications, data processing, computer systems, and software for providing full plantwide automation. End user solutions are the focal point of Measurex's product strategy.[1]

Measurex illustrates the close tie between product and marketing strategy. Note, for example, how the company matches its diverse system technologies to market segment needs through its salesforce. Product strategy is the core of strategic planning for the enterprise, and it plays a pivotal role in shaping marketing strategy. Management's strategic decisions about the products to be offered are among the most important of those affecting the future of a company. No other strategic decision has such widespread impact, cutting across every functional area and affecting all levels of an organization.

In this chapter we first examine the strategic role of product decisions, which is followed by a discussion of brand strategy. Next, the strategic analysis of existing products is considered. Finally, we discuss how to establish product priorities and product strategy alternatives.

THE STRATEGIC ROLE OF PRODUCT DECISIONS

Chapter 1 emphasizes the dangers of taking a product-oriented approach to business. Yet without a product or service a business does not exist. Product decisions play a key role in any enterprise. We first examine the strategic role of product decisions by defining product strategy, and then we show the interrelationship between product strategy and other strategic decisions.

Product Strategy

Recall the strategic product-market options discussed in Chapter 2, which are shown in Exhibit 10–1. Since Part 1 considers issues associated with building the corporate mission using one or more strategic business units (SBUs), it is assumed that the product strategy is being developed for a single SBU. These product strategy guidelines can also be extended to multiple SBU situations. We take a single SBU focus for the remaining chapters in the book.

A product strategy consists of:

Deciding how to position a business unit's product offering (specific product, line, or mix) to serve its target market(s).
Setting strategic objectives for the product offering.
Selecting a branding strategy.
Developing and implementing strategies for new and existing products.

There are several options as to the product composition of an SBU regarding the product mix and product line(s) and the specific product(s) that comprise the mix. Exhibit 10–2 shows that a product mix is determined by the number of product lines and specific products included in each line. The possibilities range from a single product or single line to various lines and specific product combinations. The shaded areas with Xs in Exhibit 10–2 indicate an illustrative product mix for an SBU. The product composition of an SBU should be delineated in a

---

EXHIBIT 10-1 Strategic Product-Market Options for the Enterprise

---

| | | Market | |
		Single	Multiple
Single		SBU	One or more SBUs
Product			
Mix		One or more SBUs	Multiple SBUs (related or unrelated)

---

manner similar to Exhibit 10–2 to provide a basis for product strategy development.

A product strategy begins with deciding how to position each product or combination of products against the competition. This involves selecting the quality, price, and features to be offered. The decision establishes key guidelines for new product development and product improvement activities. It is important for us to recognize how interrelated product positioning, objectives, branding, and management are in choosing a product strategy. Also, note how these decisions are interwoven with mission determination, SBU priorities, and the target market strategy.

Early in the development of a product strategy, management must determine what it expects the products to accomplish. For example, if management wants the business unit to be perceived as the most innovative firm in the product-market, then this strategic objective should be made explicit since it will influence all aspects of the product strategy. Product objectives may be used to achieve a variety of purposes for the enterprise or a business unit. Illustrations include the market penetration, profit contribution, establishing a reputation for quality, and offering a complete line to distributors. Often a combination of objectives is used.

EXHIBIT 10-2 Illustrative Product Mix for an SBU

Specific product

	1	2	3	·	·	·	n
A	X		X				
B		X	X				X
C	X	X	X				X
D	X						
·							
·							
·							
M	X	X					X

Product line

Product Success Depends on Other Decisions

Products are necessary to execute a business purpose, but they alone cannot guarantee a business success. Management must match products with market needs, and then develop corporate and marketing strategies to meet the needs that are targeted. Standard Brands management (Planters, Baby Ruth, Fleischmann's) struggled with a bold new product strategy during the last half of the 1970s that was "designed to lift the company into the front rank of the food industry's best consumer marketers such as General Mills, Beatrice, and Pillsbury by pumping life into its established brands and by moving rapidly via acquisition and new product development into the hot new segments of packaged foods."[2] Hampered by insufficient market research, strong competition, poor execution, and an antiquated marketing structure, the product strategy was not successful. This experience highlights the fact that product strategies alone cannot deliver management's performance goals, and must be matched with other key corporate and marketing strategies.

Competitive pressures and the changing needs and wants of buyers help to explain the high priority given to planning the product portfolio. Another reason for developing good product management procedures is to reduce the failure rate of new products. A 1979 Conference

EXHIBIT 10-3   Illustrative Product Decisions and the
Strategy Implications

Decision	Strategic Implications of the Decision
Coca Cola's withdrawal of Classic (old) Coke from the market in 1985.	Coca Cola's market share was threatened by Pepsi. On the basis of extensive favorable taste tests of a new sweeter formula, old Coke was replaced by new Coke. Loyal old Coke consumers revolted and management reintroduced old Coke as Classic Coke. By late 1985 the old formulation was outselling new Coke by a substantial margin.
Minolta's introduction in 1985 of the Maxxum 35 mm SLR camera	This completely automated state-of-the-art camera enabled Minolta to strengthen its market position in the highly competitive camera market, challenging Cannon, the market leader.
International Harvester's 1985 sale of its farm equipment division.	This product elimination decision was one of several strategic actions intended to keep International Harvester from financial failure. Low farm prices had caused major reductions in farm equipment purchases.
The Beef Industry Council's marketing strategy to promote beef consumption.	Responding to declining per capita consumpton of beef, advertising public relations and product development activities were launched in 1985 to increase the demand for beef.

Board, Inc., study of 148 medium- and large-sized American manufacturers that launched major new products during the last five years found a failure rate of one in three rather than the 90 percent often cited.[3] The study identified insufficient and poor market research as the major cause of new product failures, followed by technical problems and errors in timing the introduction.

Product strategies often are a major component in top management's plans for improving the performance of a business. Actions may include modifying products, introducing new products, and eliminating products. Several illustrative product decisions and their strategic implications to the organizations involved are shown in Exhibit 10–3.

Marketing's Role in Product Strategy

Marketing has three major contributions to an organization's product strategy. First, market analysis is needed at all stages of product planning; the analysis provides information for matching new product ideas with consumer needs and wants. The knowledge, experience, and marketing research methods of marketing professionals are essential in the product strategy development. Product-market analysis is needed in finding and describing unmet needs, in evaluating products as they are developed and introduced, and in evaluating the performance of existing products. Various methods of product evaluation and testing are available in the marketing professional's portfolio of techniques. Several of these methods are discussed in this and the following chapter.

Marketing's second contribution concerns product specifications. Increasingly, top management is looking to marketing for the establishment of characteristics and performance features for new products. Information about customers' needs and wants must be translated into specifications for the product. For example, at General Electric Company, marketing is responsible for determining these specifications. Research and development people need direction as to where their efforts should be concentrated. Consider the high-performance paper towel, Bolt, introduced by American Can in 1976, that "looks and performs like cloth."[4] Industry experts question the need for the performance specifications of the towel, particularly in view of the fact that its price is double that of popular-priced brands. The issue, of course, is whether Bolt offers more quality than consumers want and are willing to pay for.

The third contribution of marketing to product strategy is the selection of target market and program positioning strategies. Marketing management must select the best strategy for targeting and marketing the product. This positioning of product attributes to the buyers' needs is often critical to the success of both new and existing products. Since the choice of product specifications and positioning are very much interrelated, marketing strategists must incorporate an analysis of product positioning alternatives early into the marketing planning process. Positioning decisions may involve a single product or brand, a line of products, or a mix of product lines within a strategic business unit.

Product decisions are also important for marketing intermediaries, such as wholesalers, distributors, and retailers. Like manufacturers, marketing intermediaries are vitally concerned with new product decisions, such as deciding when to expand into new product areas and identifying products that should be eliminated. While many of these decisions involve the evaluation, selection, and dropping of products that are developed by manufacturers, intermediaries may develop their own new products and services. For example, financial institutions are more like intermediaries than producers. Yet many service innovations have been developed, tested, and offered commercially during the past several years—money market funds being a case in point. Product strategies are important in any kind of business or institution concerned with meeting the needs and wants of people.

BRANDING STRATEGY

Brand identification offers a company several important advantages. The name(s) that identifies a company's products can be very important in positioning the products. A brand name provides a way to distinguish a product from competitor's products. A strong brand identify offers a major competitive advantage. A familiar brand encourages repeat purchases. Consider, this assessment by a Korean executive of the importance of brand recognition in the consumer-electronics market:

> "We are producing almost the same quality as the Japanese manufacturers," says Mr. Kim, president of Gold Star Electronics International Inc., the U.S. sales subsidiary. "The only reason our products are cheaper is because the Gold Star name isn't known to the American consumer. Our main strategy is to increase our brand image and awareness among American consumers."
>
> Gold Star is discarding a long-successful strategy for selling in the U.S. in favor of one whose outcome is far from certain. It is forsaking its profitable, but low-profile, position in the lower end of the consumer-electronics market to try to capture a more visible position among the well-known brand names at the upper end.
>
> There is some doubt whether dealers will go along. "We don't want Gold Star to become a Panasonic or a Sony," says Lorin Bardele, a merchandise manager for the 34-outlet Kohl's Department Stores of Brookfield, Wis. "We need Gold Star to continue being our promotional brand. We're trying to make sure we—and they—don't price Gold Star [products] out of what I feel is their strongest niche."[5]

One of several brand strategy options may be appropriate in a given strategic situation. We first examine the nature and features of alternative strategies, and then discuss the strategic advantages that may be gained through brand identity.

Branding Strategies

The major branding strategy alternatives are shown in Exhibit 10–4. As each is examined, note that branding is appropriate for services as well as goods.

No Brand Identity. Many small and medium size manufacturers do not have an established brand identity even though the company name is printed on the package or item. The lack of financial resources and marketing capabilities make it difficult for a firm with an unknown brand to build buyer awareness in the marketplace. Major expenditures are required to introduce and promote the brand. A firm in this

EXHIBIT 10-4   Alternative Branding Strategies

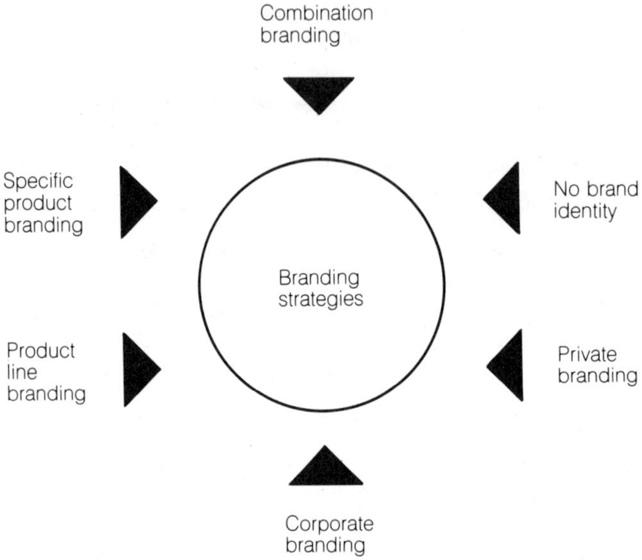

Combination
branding

Specific
product
branding

No brand
identity

Branding
strategies

Product
line
branding

Private
branding

Corporate
branding

situation often relies on marketing intermediaries to encourage buyers to purchase the unknown brand. An unknown brand is dependent on the reputation and support of marketing intermediaries such as wholesalers and retailers. The buyer's perception of an unknown brand is based upon the perception of the intermediaries. Typically, the producer with an unknown brand concentrates its marketing efforts on wholesalers and retailers rather than end users. Unknown products may develop consumer loyalty if users' experience with the product is favorable, and if it is purchased frequently. Thus through extended use the brand may develop customer loyalty.

Even if a firm does not have the resources to promote a brand, management should consider assigning it a name, particularly if the item is repurchased on a continuing basis. Favorable use experience and word-of-mouth promotion with friends can help to build the brand's reputation with buyers.

A firm may decide not to designate a brand name on a product in order to offer a generic option to buyers. This strategy is used by large manufacturers and intermediaries attempting to attract buyers who seek nonbranded equivalents to brand name products, such as tissues, paper towels, and various other frequently purchased products.

Private Branding.   A manufacturer who selects this strategy places the brand name of a retailer or other intermediary on the products. For example, Sears Roebuck & Co.'s products are produced under private branding arrangements with various manufacturers. Retailers with established brand names, such as Sears, K mart, Target, and Wal-Mart Stores, Inc. typically contract with producers to have the retailers' brands placed on the products manufactured. A major advantage to the producer is eliminating the need for expending marketing efforts on end users. The primary consequence of a private label arrangement is the dependence of the manufacturer on the buyer. Producing private label merchandise for one intermediary is risky. Nevertheless, a mutually satisfactory private branding arrangement can yield benefits to both the supplier and intermediary. Sales volume of the producer can be expanded rapidly. The retailer can use its private brand to build store loyalty since the private brand is only available in the retailer's stores.

Corporate Branding. This strategy places primary emphasis on building brand identity using the corporate name. The name of the company provides an umbrella identity to the firm's entire product offering. Examples include IBM in computers, AT&T in communications, and Cummins in diesel truck engines. Corporate branding offers the advantage of using advertising and sales promotion to support all of the firm's products. An established corporate identity also facilitates the promotion of new products. The shortcomings of the strategy include a lack of focus on specific products and possible adverse affects on the entire product mix if the corporate name encounters negative publicity. Corporate branding as a primary branding strategy is appropriate when it is not feasible to establish specific brand identity and when the product offering is relatively narrow.

Product Line Branding. This strategy establishes brand identification for a line of related products. Examples include Sears's Kenmore and Craftsman brands. Hartmarx's various brands of men's suits is also illustrative of product line branding. Product line branding provides more of a product focus than corporate branding, while gaining the advantage of economies of promoting an entire line rather than a specific product. This branding strategy is effective when a firm has one or more lines, each of which represents an interrelated offering of items. London Fog outerwear, for example, can be more effectively marketed as a line of apparel rather than by attempting to establish a brand identity for each item in the line.

Specific Product Branding. The strategy of assigning brand names to specific products is used by various producers of frequently purchased items, such as Procter & Gamble's Crest toothpaste, Pampers diapers, and Ivory soap. The advantage of an individual brand on a product is its unique identification in the marketplace. A successful brand can gain a strong buyer loyalty over time. Products that repre-

---

EXHIBIT 10-5 Annual Advertising Expenditures for Various Brands ($ millions)

Duncan Hines	$45.1
Ivory Products	42.6
Folgers	34.7
7UP/Diet 7UP	35.6
Marlboro	55.3
Milk Bone	4.9
Del Monte	21.0

SOURCE: "The Mighty Urge to Merge," *Advertising Age*, October 28, 1985, 38, 40, and 44.

---

sent low-involvement purchases benefit from a popular brand name. The major limitation of brand names on individual products is the high expense of building and supporting a brand through advertising and sales promotion. One danger is that the brand name may become so popular that it becomes a generic term for the product type. Companies work aggressively to avoid this and other misuses of popular brand names. Annual advertising expenditures for several brands are shown in Exhibit 10-5. Building a new brand name through advertising can cost over $50 million plus the additional expense of maintaining brand identity in the market place.

Combination Branding. It is not uncommon for a company to use a combination of the branding strategies shown in Exhibit 10-4. Sears, for example, uses both product line and corporate branding. An interesting illustration of a combination branding strategy is Beatrice Companies, Inc.'s expenditure of $23 million in 1984 to inform buyers that the company sells everything from Stiffel lamps to Martha White grits, using the following promotional approach:

> "You've known us all along," a typical commercial breezes through a litany of 14 products and drops the Beatrice name 18 times. The rationale is similar to Nabisco's, but Beatrice started cold with virtually no name recognition and a much greater hodgepodge of products than Nabisco. Says Nabisco's Mr. Abbott: "There's a significant question as to whether consumers who like Samsonite luggage will find that reason enough to also buy Beatrice food products."[6]

Some industry experts question the effectiveness of corporate advertising like that used by Beatrice for inexpensive frequently purchased consumer brands. For example, companies like Proctor & Gamble, Chesebrough-Ponds (Vaseline, Q-Tips, and Bass) do not actively promote the corporate identity.

Gaining Strategic Advantage through Brand Identity

Established brands may be useful to introduce other products in addition to supporting the brand itself. A brand name that is familiar to many buyers can be used for other noncompeting products. The primary advantage is immediate name recognition for the new product. Exhibit 10-6 describes how Hartmarx is developing new strategies, using the advantage of its strong brand identity in men's suits. Two popular methods of capitalizing upon existing brand identity are brand extension and licensing.

Brand Extension. This strategy uses the identity and consumer franchise of an existing brand name to launch a new product line of a different product type. The new line may or may not be closely related to the brand from which it is being extended. Examples of related extensions include Ivory shampoo and conditioner, Hershey chocolate milk, and Hart, Schaffner & Marx women's suits. Examples of extensions that are not closely related are ChemLawn's CarpetCare service and Black & Decker personal-care products.

Critics of brand and line extensions such as Al Ries, an advertising agency executive, indicate that they often do not succeed and may damage the mother product.[7] Ries argues that a brand name is weakened when it stands for two things. Some observers have questioned Procter & Gamble's use of the Duncan Hines brand image to launch its bagged cookies because some ads encourage using bake mixes while others promote purchase of ready-made cookies.

Licensing. The sale of a firm's brand name to another company for use on a noncompeting product represents a major business activity. One authority predicts total retail sales of licensed products will reach $75 billion by 1990.[8] Apparel and accessories accounted for 38 percent of licensed products in 1984 followed by 19 percent of toys/games, 12 percent of publishing/stationery, and 11 percent of gifts/novelties. The advantage of licensing to the firm granting the license is additional revenue with only limited costs. The creator also gains free publicity for the brand name. This is also a potential limitation since the licensee may create an unfavorable image for the brand. Licensing may be used for corporate, product line, or specific brands. Anheuser-Busch Companies, Inc. (Budweiser beer) is one of the largest corporate licensers.

THE STRATEGIC ANALYSIS OF EXISTING PRODUCTS

Evaluating the performance of existing products provides management with diagnostic information to guide its strategies for new products, product modification, and product elimination. Strategic analysis of existing products is essential to selecting future product strategies. Consider, for example, the marketing battle underway for the leading position in the $1 billion U.S. toothpaste market. Procter & Gamble's Crest brand, the market leader, was attacked beginning in 1980 with sweet-tasting gels and pump dispensers.[9] Crest's share declined from

---

EXHIBIT 10-6 Gaining Strategic Advantage from Established Brands

---

Chicago—For years, Hartmarx Corp. has been content to jealously guard its good names—high-quality men's clothing labels such as Hart, Schaffner & Marx and Hickey-Freeman.

But the clothing maker and retailer is stepping out, in much the same way that Coca-Cola Co. has put its highly prized Coke trademark on a variety of products. In fall of 1986, Hartmarx plans to introduce a line of pricey women's suits under the Hart, Schaffner & Marx label. The company also indicated it may put others of its labels, including Hart Schaffner, Hickey-Freeman, Austin Reed, on new lines of better-quality men's ties, shirts, belts and other accessories. And Hartmarx is pondering other uses for its brands: shoes, sportswear, raincoats and other merchandise.

The moves appear to continue a search by Hartmarx for new strategies to improve sales in the firecely competitive garment industry. Back in January, the company said it would start a mail-order business to sell its higher-priced shirts, ties and sportswear.

"We're going to exploit our brand names, and we're evaluating the possibilities now," Richard P. Hamilton, Hartmarx's chairman, president and chief executive officer, said. "Hart, Schaffner & Marx is the strongest name in quality men's clothing. In surveys, people already sometimes say they prefer Hart Schaffner shirts, and there aren't any yet."

Hartmarx's new-found aggressiveness comes at a time when the company's earnings have been hurt by promotional price cutting. Also painful, according to Mr. Hamilton, have been the costs of an accelerated program to consolidate some operations at the company's various stores and of repositioning the Kuppenheimer store division, which sells moderately priced merchandise. . . .

There are risks to the new strategy, of course. Other companies that exploited their brand-name recognition have found that the brands lost their exclusivity as merchandise has shown up on the shelves of off-price retailers. Hartmarx hopes to avoid this problem by maintaining its traditional tight control over distribution.

The new line of Hart Schaffner women's suits, priced at about $350 each, will feature the same fabrics and tailoring as the corresponding lines of men's tailored suits. Hartmarx officials said that classic styles are more important than fashion in professional clothing, and that Hartmarx "feels comfortable" in that market.

The company is mailing a catalog of professional women's clothing. It hopes to build the mail-order business to annual volume of $30 million to $50 million in the next five years.

Hartmarx said it has several offers for its 26-store Chas. A. Stevens women's wear chain in the Chicago area. John R. Meinert, vice chairman and chief financial and administrative officer, said, "We're receptive to more offers." In the past year, the chain's results have been hurt by fierce competition in the area.

Mr. Hamilton said that the new men's furnishings business, to be built initially by acquisition of "small core companies," should produce sales to department and specialty stores of $50 million to $60 million annually in three or four years.

The program to consolidate distribution, credit, accounting and buying operations at 23 store divisions began earlier this year and will cost about $10 million by the time it is completed next June. But Mr. Hamilton said it should save $10 million to $12 million a year and permit Hartmarx to be operated as one company with lower costs.

Kuppenheimer, acquired in December 1982, expanded too rapidly to 127 stores from about 40, Mr. Hamilton said. During the next year, the stores and merchandise will be improved. The pilot store opened in Kansas City, Mo., last week, and all stores will be remodeled in the next year, he said. "We expect to position Kuppenheimer as the top-value men's clothier in America," he said.

EXHIBIT 10-7   Tracking Product Performance

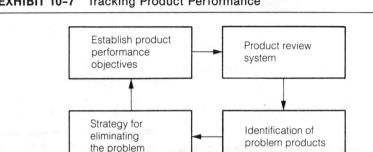

double Colgate's size in 1980 to a 31 percent share in 1985 compared to Colgate's 28 percent. Colgate's strategy is to overtake Crest with Dentagard, which was launched in 1985 with a $30 million marketing budget. Colgate's earlier introduction of a gel form of toothpaste, ahead of P&G, also helped narrow the share gap between the two brands. Critics of P&G's strategy indicate that the firm should have reacted earlier to competitive threats from gels and pumps.

The strategic analysis of existing products requires tracking the performance of the products in the portfolio, as shown in Exhibit 10-7. Management must first establish the criteria and levels of performance for gauging product performance. These may include both financial and nonfinancial factors. Because of the various demand and cost interrelationships among products, management needs a good information system to establish how well a particular product is doing. The objective of a tracking system is to establish and maintain a product review system that will spot problem products so that management can select a strategy for eliminating the problem.

Several methods are available for the strategic analysis of existing products. We examine the product life cycle analysis, the product portfolio analysis, and the positioning analysis to demonstrate the kinds of information that can be used in diagnosing product performance and identifying product strategy options.

Product Life Cycle Analysis

In Chapter 7 we examine the basic characteristics of the product life cycle (PLC). Recall that the major stages of the PLC are the introduction, growth, maturity, and decline. Building on this discussion, the important strategic issues related to PLC analysis are the following:

1. Determining the length and rate of change of the product life cycle.

2. Identifying the current stage of the product life cycle and selecting the product strategy that corresponds to that stage.
3. Anticipating strategic threats and finding opportunities for altering and extending the PLC.

Rate of Change. The length of product life cycles is becoming shorter for many products. Consider, for example, the analysis shown in Exhibit 10–8. This study of consumer durable goods found that the introduction period was substantially shorter from 1965 to 1969 compared to the 1922–42 time period. There are, of course, wide variations in the length of PLC stages for particular products. The rate of change of the PLC is strategically important because management must adjust its marketing strategy to correspond to the situation. A short and rapidly changing PLC requires modifying marketing strategy under dynamic conditions. The short PLC of the personal computer is illustrative; in a few years the product moved from its introduction into the growth stage, and it is now rapidly moving toward maturity. Fast movement through the PLC also highlights the need for attempting to alter the pattern of the cycle and/or introducing new products.

Stage and Strategy Identification. The product's position on the PLC has important implications regarding all aspects of targeting and positioning. Four strategy zones are encountered in moving through the PLC, as shown in Exhibit 10–9. While the strategy guidelines are illustrative, they indicate the changing focus of marketing strategy over the PLC.

It is not always clear as to the PLC stage occupied by a product at a specific point in time. Analysis of the growth rate, sales trends, time since introduction, intensity of competition, pricing practices, and competitor entry/exit information are useful in stage analysis. Identifying when the product has moved from growth to maturity is more difficult than determining other stage positions. Analysis of industry structure and competition (see Chapter 7) is probably the most useful basis of estimating when a product has reached its maturity.

Strategic Opportunity/Threat Analysis. By predicting the path of a PLC, a firm wins a strategic advantage in avoiding threats and capitalizing upon opportunities. Some progress has been made in predicting the sales volume of a product class and identifying the factors that influence the shape and amplitude of the volume projections.[10] A PLC model has been developed for short- and long-range planning for housewares and businesses involved with electronics consumer goods. While the model was designed for evaluating projects concerned with new product development, a similar approach appears feasible for pre-

EXHIBIT 10-8 Product Life Cycle: Shortening over Time

Time Period	Introductory (years)	Growth (years)
1922–42		
1. Clothes washers	12	37
2. Total coffeemakers	18	40
3. Hotplates	6	23
4. Gas ranges	7	14
5. Electric ranges	15	40
6. Refrigerators	7	44
7. Irons	13	28
8. Toasters	15	43
9. Vacuum cleaners	18	40
10. Waffle irons	9	18
11. Heating pads	15	37
12. Portable electric heaters	15	42
Mean	12.5	33.8
1945–69		
13. Air conditioners	16	19
14. Bed coverings	8	9
15. Broilers	6	20
16. Can openers	0	12
17. Gas clothes dryer	5	21
18. Electric clothes dryer	5	22
19. Corn poppers	4	22
20. Dishwashers	11	16
21. Disposers	8	24
22. Home freezers	3	26
23. Fry pan skillets	0	21
24. Food mixers	13	28
25. Gas water heaters	9	18
26. Electric water heaters	11	24
27. Blenders	10	13
28. B/W TV	3	17
Mean	7.0	19.5
1965–79		
29. Calculators	2	6
30. ADC coffeemakers	1	6
31. Curling irons	0	7
32. Digital watches	0	7
33. Hand-held hair dryers	3	6
34. Hair setters	0	4
35. Electric knives	1	3
36. Slow cookers	0	7
37. Color TV	11	15
Mean	2.0	6.8

SOURCE: William Qualls, Richard W. Olshavsky, and Ronald E. Michaels, "Shortening of the PLC—An Empirical Test," *Journal of Marketing*, Fall 1981, 77.

EXHIBIT 10-9 Illustrative Product Strategy at Each PLC Stage

Marketing Strategy Considerations

Types of Brand Strategies

Type	Brand development	Brand reinforcement	Brand repositioning	Brand modification
Objectives	Establish market position	Expand target market	Seek new market segments	Prepare for re-entry
Product strategy	Assure high quality	Identify weaknesses	Adjust size, color, package	Modify features
Advertising objectives	Build brand awareness	Provide information	Use imagery to differentiate from competitors	Educate on changes
Distribution	Build distribution network	Solidify distribution relationships	Maintain distribution	Re-establish and deliver new version
Price	Skimming or penetration strategy	Meet competition	Use price deals	Maintain price

| Phase in Life Cycle | Introduction | Growth | Maturity | Decline |

SOURCE: Adapted from Ben M. Enis, Raymond La Grace, and Arthur E. Prell, "Extending the Product Life Cycle," *Business Horizons* 20 (June 1977), 53. Copyright 1977 by the Foundation for the School of Business at Indiana University. Reprinted by permission.

dicting the PLC of an existing product that occupies an intermediate point in the PLC. The prediction of the timing and magnitude of turning points of a successful product introduction is an illustrative application of the model.

The PLC model determines sales volume by combining estimates of original purchases and replacements.[11] Original purchases are forecasted using three predictor variables: (1) consumer need/want, (2) number of competitors, and (3) amount of advertising and promotional effort (industy total). Replacement estimates are a function of the product's useful life, the percent of owners who will replace it, the tradeoff of repair versus replacement, and the level of the initial purchases. Validity tests of model predictions against actual PLCs indicate a close correspondence between PLC shapes.

Product Portfolio Analysis

The strategic analysis of products seeks to determine if each product is measuring up to management's minimum performance criteria, in combination with an assessment of the relative strengths and weaknesses of the product portfolio. We can facilitate a comparative analysis of products by using the grid methods for SBU diagnosis discussed in Chapter 3.

An example of a product portfolio analysis by a medium-size farm and industrial equipment manufacturer is shown in Exhibit 10–10. The product names have been removed to avoid revealing confidential information. Note the heavy concentration of products in the low/intense category. One or more of the products F through J may be candidates for product elimination. The analysis also indicates that the firm needs some new products to strengthen the portfolio, unless products A and B are contributing substantially to sales and profits. Even if A and B are strong contributors, life cycle changes will require new products to enter the portfolio in the future. Management must make important resource allocations for the entire product portfolio. While further analysis is necessary, it appears that resource allocations to products F through J should be held to the minimum. It is doubtful that improvement can be made in the relative portfolio position of these products.

Portfolio grids are useful in highlighting differences among products. After identifying the relative attractiveness and business strength of the products in the portfolio, a more comprehensive analysis of specific situational factors may be appropriate. The following factors are useful in product evaluation:

- Profit contribution.
- Barriers to entry.
- Sales fluctuations.
- Extent of capacity utilization.
- Responsiveness of sales to prices, promotional activities, service levels, and other influences.
- The nature of technology (maturity, volatility, and complexity).
- Alternative production and process opportunities.
- Environmental considerations.[12]

Certain of these factors may be included in the grid analysis if we use composite grid dimensions.

The grid analysis can also be used to compare competing brands with a particular product. This type of analysis may be useful when brands are targeting different market segments. Otherwise, the market attractiveness dimensions of the grid will be constant across all brands targeting the market.

EXHIBIT 10-10   Illustrative Product Portfolio Analysis

Competitor status

	Light	Moderate	Intense
Dynamic	Product A		
Average	Product B		Product D Product E
Low		Product C	Product F Product G Product H Product I Product J

(left axis label: Industry potential)

Competition equals anything the customer is likely to buy in place of our product.
Industry potential equals environmental forces influencing the entire industry.

Positioning Analysis

Perceptual maps are potentially powerful analysis tools for assessing products. The position analysis for segment identification is discussed in Chapter 8. Recall that such a map is developed by obtaining preference information on a set of competitors from a sample of buyers. Various product attributes are used, and the results are summarized into a two-dimensional preference map.

Mapping analysis offers various guidelines to strategic product positioning. The analyses can relate buyer preferences to various brands and suggest possible brand repositioning options. New product opportunities may also be identified through the analysis of preference maps. Longitudinal studies can identify the impact of repositioning strategies.

The use of factor analysis to map consumer perceptions of financial services is shown in Exhibit 10–11. A six-cluster solution was obtained

EXHIBIT 10-11   Financial Services Market Structure (overlapping clusters)

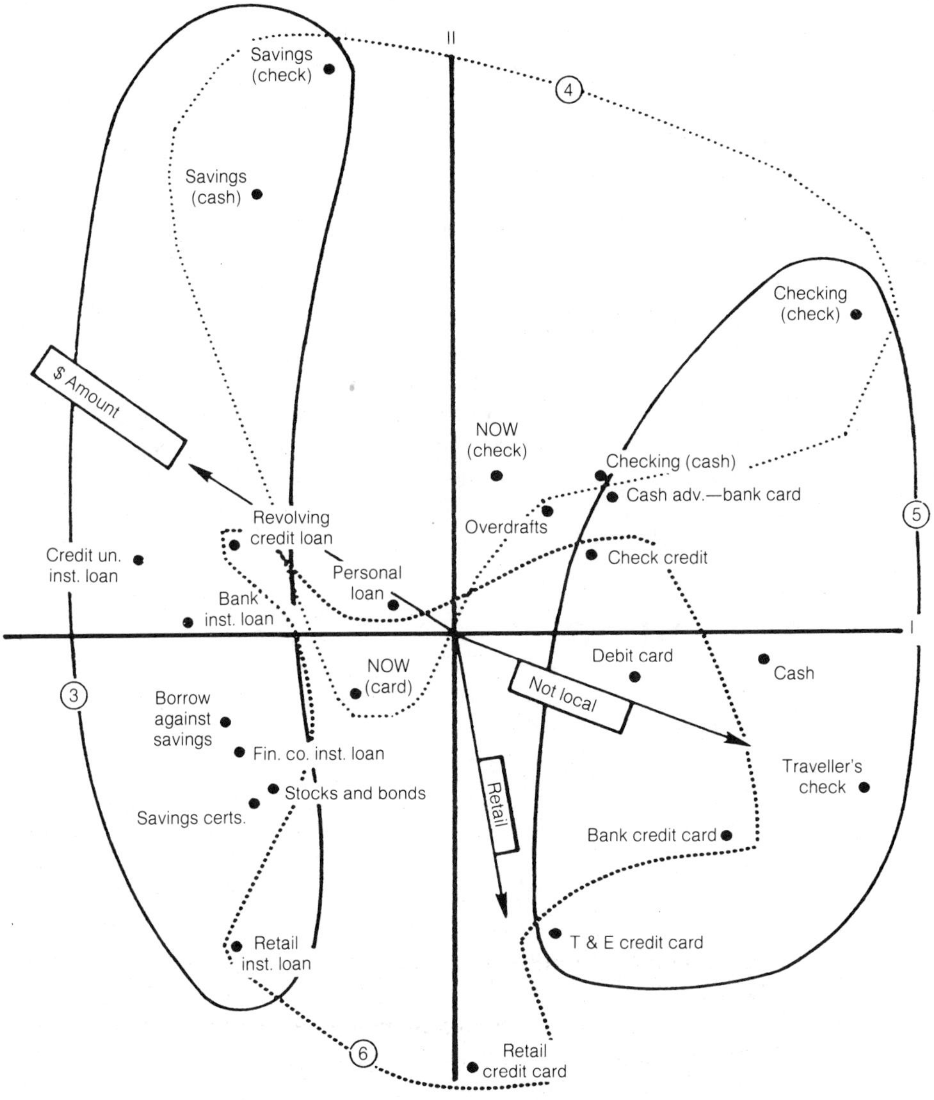

SOURCE: Rajendra K. Srivastava, Mark I. Alpert, and Allan D. Shocker, "A Customer-Oriented Approach for Determining Market Structures," *Journal of Marketing,* Spring 1984, 41.

on the basis of a similarity in the appropriateness for use of products across situations. Clusters 3 through 6 are enclosed by contours on a multidimensional representation of products. The axes represent factors I and II. Factor scores indicate the degree to which financial services were considered suitable for use situations that were highly correlated with that factor. Note the high positive correlation of "not local" to factor 1. Consider, for example, cluster 5. It contains services that are likely to be used when low/medium amounts of money are required in out-of-town settings. In contrast, cluster 3 contains financial services involving large amounts of money for use in retail (local use) settings.

Other Product Analysis Methods

Other analysis methods are available in addition to product life cycle, portfolio, and positioning analysis. Many of the techniques of financial analysis discussed in Chapter 4 are essential in the strategic analysis of existing products. Research studies that identify the relative importance of product selection criteria to buyers and rate brands against these criteria are useful in indicating brand strengths and weaknesses. The comparison of the two architects discussed in Chapter 7 (see Exhibit 7–15) is illustrative. Many of the standardized information services provided by marketing research firms, such as Information Resources Inc. and A. C. Nielson Co., are also useful in monitoring the performance of existing products.

PRODUCT STRATEGIES

Cadillac's market share of the U.S. luxury car market declined from 28.5 percent in 1980 to 22.6 percent in 1985.[13] The brand is losing old customers and failing to attract younger new customers. European imports like Mercedez-Benz, BMW, Audi, and Volvo are attracting Cadillac's prospects. The Cadillac Cimarron was intended to compete with the luxury imports, but Cimarron's sales have been disappointing. When Cadillac began downsizing its cars, the Lincoln Town Car started to post record gains. Cadillac's front-drive cars look very similar to Buick and Oldsmobile models. The new 1986 Eldorado and Seville were restyled to help differentiate Cadillac from other General Motors cars. The 1987 Allante, the $50,000 two-seat luxury coupé, is intended to help provide a new image for Cadillac. Dealers are adjusting their hiring practices to add more salespeople with characteristics similar to those of buyers of European cars.

The Cadillac illustration shows how important product strategy is in business performance. Management is implementing strategies to stop the loss of its market share. The array of product strategies includes strategies for the existing product, the new product, and the product mix modification, as shown in Exhibit 10–12. An examination of each strategy will highlight the nature and scope of the decisions that are involved.

EXHIBIT 10-12   Product Strategies

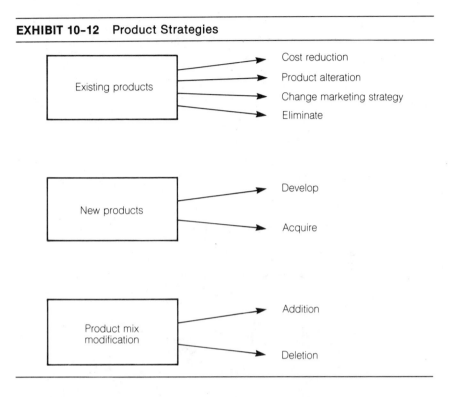

Establishing Priorities

The first step in product strategy development is to assign priorities as to the importance of each product. Since individual products and product lines are not equally important to the future of a given firm, management should establish the strategic importance of each product and/or line. In carrying out strategic planning for the enterprise—a topic discussed in Chapter 3—management should have made such a determination for each SBU. In instances where multiple products or lines comprise an SBU, management should also indicate its strategic priorities for all product categories within the SBU. These priorities are needed to guide product planning activities for the SBU. They are useful in showing where to allocate resources for product development and improvement.

Exhibit 10-13 indicates how the management of an industrial equipment SBU has positioned each product line according to business strength (internal) and market (external) factors. The factors evaluated to obtain the positioning shown in Exhibit 10-13 included competition, required resources, profit contribution, company strengths, industry potential, and other factors. The positioning represents a composite of these factors. Note the higher resource priorities established for prod-

EXHIBIT 10-13 Establishing Product Line Priorities and Strategic Guides for an Industrial Equipment SBU

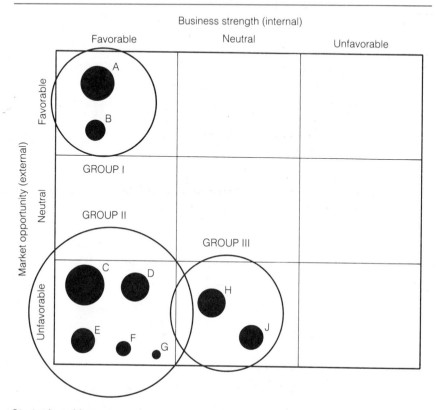

Strategic guides:
Group I: Increase product development/improvement and sales development effort to expand market share.
Group II: Increase profit contribution by reducing costs and selective sales development.
Group III: Reduce assets and reduce costs.
Product Lines A, B, C, D, and E to receive 80 percent of SBU effort.

Note: Diameters of circles indicate relative size of product line based on sales in dollars.

uct lines A–E and the strategic guidelines indicated for each product group. Exhibit 10–13 illustrates how management can indicate where resources are to be deployed among various products in the mix. These decisions then guide specific product planning activities for new and existing products.

Product strategy decisions guide new and existing product planning activities. These decisions, along with the priorities management assigns to each product group, line, and specific product, indicate the new product areas of interest to the firm and how resources for product development and improvements will be deployed.

Strategies for Existing Products

Once the need for a strategy change for an existing product is identified, management has several options for responding to the situation as shown in Exhibit 10-12. These include cost reduction, product alteration, product style, marketing strategy alteration, and product elimination. The choice of a strategy is primarily influenced by the nature of the problem associated with the product. Each strategy is examined to indicate the issues and scope of the action.

Cost Reduction.   Low costs offer a company a major advantage over the competition. As an illustration, Nabisco's Ritz Cracker was introduced in 1934 and is the best-selling cracker in the world.[14] Nearly 16 billion crackers are sold each year, generating $150 million in sales. The basic ingredients have remained essentially the same during the half-century the brand has been available. In addition to a flavor that has wide appeal, Ritz's low price compared to other types of crackers gives it a major competitive advantage. Ritz's high volume contributes to keeping costs low.

Costs can be reduced by changes in the engineering design, manufacturing improvements, and increases in marketing productivity. After the right cost reduction strategy is selected, it is essential to develop and implement a specific plan. The product analysis and planning form used by the Eltra Corporation (shown in Exhibit 10-14) highlights several key aspects of good planning for a problem product. Included are financial analyses and projections, the basic corrective strategy to be used, major activities, and scheduled completion dates. This same approach to planning and implementing cost strategies can be used for other existing product strategies.

Product Alteration.   Products can be improved by changing their features, quality, and styling. Automobile features and styles are modified on a continuing basis. Procter & Gamble is attempting to regain its market position for Pampers diapers using a product alteration strategy. P&G introduced Blue Ribbon Pampers in 1985, a thicker, fully shaped diaper.[15] At the same time a thinner, superabsorbent Pampers was being market tested. In this $2.8 billion market Kimberly Clark's Huggies had a 32 percent share, followed by P&Gs Pampers at 30 percent and Luvs at 16 percent.

Features provide a way of differentiating a brand against competition. The Hewlett-Packard Company Series 10 line of hand-held calculators is targeted to professionals in science and engineering and finan-

EXHIBIT 10-14 Product Analysis Form by the Eltra Corporation

ELTRA

_____ DIVISION

LOW PROFIT PRODUCT PROJECT

(000)

Product _____   Market(s) _____

	Actual		Estimated	Plan Year	Forecast		
	19___	19___	19___	19___	19___	19___	19___
Sales							
Gross Profit							
Gross Profit %							

Project Schedule

Basic Strategy	Major Steps	Scheduled Completion Date
Price Increase ☐	_____	_____
Cost Reduction:	_____	_____
Engineering ☐	_____	_____
Manufacturing ☐		
Marketing ☐	_____	_____
Volume Increase ☐	_____	_____
	_____	_____
	_____	_____

SOURCE: David S. Hopkins, *Business Strategies for Problem Products* (New York: The Conference Board, 1977), 24.

cial services. Special programmed features simplify calculations such as present value determination. Another option is to provide the buyer a choice regarding features. Optional features offer the buyer more flexibility in selecting within a brand category, a strategy used by many automobile manufacturers.

Quality may be improved or altered as a strategy. J. C. Penny's upgrading of its image in the early 1980s included the offering of higher quality merchandise than in the past. A 1984 survey of consumers indicated the following as the most important determinants of merchandise value:[16]

Workmanship	23%
Price	21
Materials	14
Looks	13

These findings suggest that quality may be more important than style in the customers' selection of merchandise.

Product Style. Despite the probable greater importance of product quality, style may offer an important competitive edge for certain types of product. Moreover, style may serve as a proxy for quality in certain product categories. Seiko has very effectively used style (and other features) to make its watches attractive to buyers. Because many different styles are offered, consumers are allowed a wide range of choice. There are many other examples of product style strategies, including Ethan Allen in furniture, Mercedes in automobiles, and Hartmarx in men's clothing. Ethan Allen offers traditional American-styled furniture. Mercedes has created a strong customer preference for its boxlike body design with the large grill. Hartmarx offers a variety of suit styles and prices to appeal to various market segments.

Marketing Strategy Alteration. There are various ways of repositioning a product by using marketing mix components. Adjustments in market targeting and positioning are often necessary as a product moves through its life cycle. Problems or opportunities may indicate the need to adjust marketing strategy during a particular PLC stage. Consider, for example, New England Apple Products Co. Inc., a small wholesaler selling juice-products under private labels to stores and supermarkets.[17] A new logo and new packaging transformed a commodity product into a marketing success. By adopting a branding strategy, the firm was able to establish its brand identity in a market comprised of two giant brands—Tree Top and Mott's—and many small firms. The label was developed by a design firm. It shows a partially eaten apple in red and green colors and the brand name, Very Fine. The wraparound foam label helps insulate the 10 ounce, single-serving bottle. New England drinks are distributed in 35 states. The company has expanded its juice offering to include several other fruit drinks. Interestingly, New England Apple's marketing strategy changes benefitted from the natural food trend that expanded rapidly in the early 1980s. Sales increased nearly 40 percent from 1984 to $75 million in 1985, with pretax profits reaching $3.8 million.

Product Elimination. A product may eventually need to be dropped from a company's offering. Elimination is the most drastic action that can be made for existing products. This decision for a problem product is normally considered when cost reduction, product improvement, or marketing mix alteration strategies are not feasible. In deciding to drop a product, management will want to take into account a variety of performance criteria in addition to the product's sales and profit contribution. Elimination may occur at any PLC stage although it is more likely to be considered during the introduction and decline stages.

Management may decide to halt production and sell off its existing inventory, or to try to sell the product(s) to another company. Various divestment sales of entire lines to other companies have occurred during the last several years, including Black & Decker's purchase of General Electric's small household appliance lines. Leveraged buyouts have also been popular in recent years, such as Sperry Corporation's sale of the Remington Shaver unit.

The remarketing of unsuccessful new products is a successful business for Tradewell Industries, Inc. and provides a way for producers to reduce the risks of introducing new products.[18] Before introduction, Tradewell establishes with management's approval a fixed purchase price of unsold inventory up to a maximum of $10 million. This option can be exercised any time within 12 months of the introduction. Tradewell then remarkets the products under guidelines established by management. Tradewell's 1985 sales exceeded $100 million. The company remarkets products to new markets and through different distribution channels. For example, products are sold as premiums for companies' promotional programs. Products marketed by Tradewell include small appliances and other consumer items.

New Product Planning

New products are important components of the product strategies of most companies. New product development ranges from modest to huge expenditures. For example, the Northrop Corp. spent nearly $1 billion through 1985 to develop and test its F-20 Tigershark fighter jet.[19] The plane was developed without U.S. Government funding support. Competing against General Dynamics's F-16, the F-20 faced a doubtful future because of political forces, budgetary cuts, competitor price reductions, and poor timing. In late 1985 Congress was in the final stages of funding $200 million for conducting a competition between the F-20 and F-16 planes. Each plane has certain capabilities that the other does not. The F-20 is more maneuverable and has lower operating costs. The F-16 has a longer flying range and can carry certain missiles that the F-20 cannot carry. One analyst estimated that Northrop's F-20 project was reducing company profits by about $60 million a quarter. The Pentagon will select one of the two planes as a result of the planned $200 million competition. The F-16 appears to have the edge.

Booz, Allen & Hamilton, a leading management consultant firm, has conducted various research studies on the management of new products. The research contains important findings concerning new product management in the 1980s. New product introductions can be classified according to the following factors: (1) newness to the market; and (2) newness to the company. Six categories of new products are defined as follows:

1. *New-to-the-world products:* new products that create an entirely new market (10 percent of total new introductions).
2. *New product lines:* new products that, for the first time, allow a company to enter an established market (20 percent of total).
3. *Additions to existing product lines:* new products that supplement a company's established product lines (26 percent of total).
4. *Improvements in/revisions to existing products:* new products that provide improved performance or greater perceived value, and replace existing products (26 percent of total).
5. *Repositionings:* existing products that are targeted to new markets or market segments (7 percent of total).
6. *Cost reductions:* new products that provide similar performance at lower cost (11 percent of total).[20]

Typically a company's new product program includes items in all or most of the six categories. Totally new products account for 10 percent of all new product introductions. Note that improvements, repositionings, and cost reductions were included in the earlier discussion of strategies for existing products. New product planning is considered in depth in Chapter 11.

Product Mix Modifications

The modification of a company's product mix is a major product strategy change. Among the reasons for expanding the product mix are the following:

Increasing the growth rate of the business.
Offering a complete range of products to wholesalers and retailers.
Gaining marketing strength and economies in distribution, advertising, and personal selling.
Capitalizing on an existing brand position.
Diversifying to avoid dependence on one product area.

Several examples of product mix modification strategies are shown in Exhibit 10-15. We can add to the product mix through internal development or by purchase of an entire company or a line of products. Purchase has been a popular option in the 1980s as a result of low market prices compared to the costs of internal development. Acquisition offers a faster means of expanding the product mix.

Product Management Responsibility

Responsibility for the product strategy extends to several organizational levels. Three management levels often exist in companies that have strategic business units, different product lines, and specific brands within lines.

EXHIBIT 10-15 Illustrative Product Mix Modifications

Company	Product Line(s)	Strategic Purpose
ChemLawn	Carpet cleaning and insect control	Increase growth opportunities, capitalizing on the existing lawn care brand position.
IBM	Acquisition of Rolm Corp. (office phone switching equipment)	Expand into integrated communications systems
Limited Inc.	Acquisition of Lane Bryant	Appeal to fast-growing middle-age market
Maytag	Acquisition of Magic Chef	Expand kitchen appliance product mix
Philip Morris Incorporated	General Foods complete brand portfolio	Diversification away from tobacco business
Ralston Purina Company	Purchase of ITT's Continental Baking Division	Expand the grocery products business

Product/Brand Management. This activity consists of planning, managing, and coordinating strategy for a specific product or brand. Responsibilities at this management level may include market analysis, targeting, positioning strategy, product analysis and strategy, identification of new product needs, and management and coordination of product/brand marketing activities. Marketing plans for specific products or brands are often prepared at this level. Product or brand managers typically do not have authority over all product management activities. These managers are sponsors or advocates of their products, negotiating with other managers for the sales force, research and development, marketing research, and advertising support.

Product Group/Marketing Management. A business with several products/brands may assign responsibility for managing the product or brand managers to a product director, group manager, or marketing manager. This person is responsible for a group of product or brand managers, coordinating their activities and approving their recommendations. The nature and scope of responsibilities are similar to those of product/brand managers. Additionally, the product group manager coordinates product management activities and decisions with the corporate or SBU management.

Product Mix Management. This responsibility is normally assigned the chief executive at the SBU or corporate level of an organization. Responsibilities include decisions on product acquisitions, research and development priorities, new product decisions, and resource allocation. Evaluation of product portfolio performance is also centered at this level. In a multi-SBU corporation a fourth level of product management responsibilities may exist. Top management may coordinate and establish product management guidelines for the SBU management.

Since the responsibility for product management includes new product planning, further discussion of organizational approaches is included in Chapter 11. The organization of all aspects of marketing activities is considered in Chapter 17.

CONCLUDING NOTE

Product strategy, which sets the stage for selecting strategies for each of the remaining components of the marketing program, forms the leading edge of a positioning strategy. A product strategy alone is incomplete and must be matched to the right distribution, pricing, and promotion strategies. Product decisions are central to shaping both the corporate and the marketing strategy, and should be made within the guidelines of the corporate mission and objectives. Key product decisions for a strategic business unit include selecting the mix of products to be offered, deciding how to position an SBU's product offering, setting product strategy objectives, choice of a branding strategy, and developing and implementing strategies for new and existing products. An important product decision is establishing priorities for each product in the portfolio.

Branding strategy involves selecting a strategy from several options that include no brand identity, private branding, corporate branding, product line branding, specific product branding, and combination branding. Brand identification in the market place offers a firm an opportunity to gain a strategic advantage through brand extension and licensing.

A strategic analysis of existing products helps to establish priorities and guidelines for managing the product portfolio. Analysis methods include the analysis of the product life cycle, portfolio screening, positioning analysis, financial analysis, and various other techniques.

Three major decisions must be made for a specific product: (1) Should a new product be developed to replace or compliment the product? (2) Should the product be improved (and, if so, how?) and (3) Should the product be eliminated? These decisions and the activities necessary to carry them out form the core of product planning in the enterprise. Product strategy alternatives for existing products include cost reduction, product alteration, marketing strategy changes, and product elimination. New products are developed or acquired. Product mix modification may also be part of a firm's product strategy.

Most successful corporations have found that some individual or organizational unit should be assigned responsibility for product planning. Approaches that are used range from a committee to a product planning department. Planning for new products is both exciting and risky, but it is an essential activity in most firms.

NOTES

1. This illustration is based upon "Measurex: The Results Company," *Business Marketing,* November 1985, 64 and 66; and *The Value Line Investment Survey,* Edition 7, November 8, 1985, 1024.

2. "When a New Product Strategy Wasn't Enough," *Business Week,* February 18, 1980, 142.

3. *Marketing News,* February 8, 1980, 1.

4. Bill Abrams, "What Happens if the Product Offers More than Users Need?" *The Wall Street Journal,* Stepptember 25, 1980, 35.

5. Steven P. Galante, "Korea's Gold Star Is Banking on Quality to Build an Image in the U.S. TV Market," *The Asian Wall Street Journal,* November 26, 1984, 12.

6. Ronald Alsop, "More Firms Try to Associate Corporate Names with Brands," *The Wall Street Journal,* September 6, 1984, 29.

7. Ronald Alsop, "Firms Unveil more Products Associated with Brand Names," *The Wall Street Journal,* December 13, 1984, 31.

8. Joanne Y. Cleaver, "Licensing: Starring on Marketing Team," *Advertising Age,* June 6, 1985, 15–16.

9. Kathleen Deveny, "Colgate Puts the Squeeze on Crest," *Business Week,* August 19, 1985, 40 and 41.

10. Steven G. Harrell and Elmer D. Taylor, "Modeling the Product Life Cycle for Consumer Durables," *Journal of Marketing,* Fall 1981, 68–75.

11. Ibid., 70–71.

12. George S. Day, "Diagnosing the Product Portfolio," *Journal of Marketing,* April 1977, 37.

13. Paul Ingrassia, "Cadillac Wants to Attract Younger Buyers but Its 'Old Man' Image Gets in the Way," *The Wall Street Journal,* November 18, 1985, 33.

14. "If It's Not Broken, Don't Fix It," *Forbes,* May 7, 1984, 132.

15. Laurie Freeman, "P&G Tries to Shore up Struggling Brands," *Advertising Age,* June 24, 1985, 6.

16. "Product Value," *The Wall Street Journal,* October 4, 1984, 23.

17. Jeffrey A. Trachtenberg, "Small Is Beautiful," *Forbes,* December 31, 1984, 112–13.

18. Tradewell Industries, Inc., 845 Third Avenue, New York, N.Y. 10022.

19. Tim Carrington and Roy J. Harris, Jr., "Northrop's Tigershark Continues Uphill Fight," *The Wall Street Journal,* November 7, 1985, 6.

20. *New Products Management for the 1980s,* Booz, Allen & Hamilton, Inc., 1982, 8.

QUESTIONS FOR REVIEW AND DISCUSSION

1. Eli Lilly & Company manufactures a broad line of pharmaceuticals with strong brand positions in the marketplace. Yet by 1981 Lilly was also the leading manufacturer of generic drug products. Is this combination branding strategy a logical one; if so, why?

2. Discuss the advantages and limitations of following a branding strategy of using brand names for specific products.

3. In 1985 Philip Morris Incorporated acquired General Foods Co. Discuss the advantages and limitations of acquiring a company in order to obtain its established brand names.

4. To what extent are the SBU strategy and the product strategy interrelated?

5. Referring to Exhibit 10–13, do you see any benefit in separately analyzing the specific products within each of the product lines A–J?

6. Suppose that a top administrator of a university wants to establish a product management function covering both new and existing services. Develop a plan for establishing a product planning program.

7. Many products reach maturity like Jell-O. Discuss several ways that mature products can be given new vigor. How can management determine whether it is worthwhile to attempt to salvage products that are performing poorly?

8. In addition to the information shown on the Eltra Corporation product analysis form (Exhibit 10–14), what other information would be useful in evaluating product performance and designing a corrective strategy?

STRATEGIC APPLICATION 10-1

BLACK & DECKER CORP.

Black & Decker Corp.
($ figures = 000,000)

Worldwide	1984	1983	% chg.
Sales	1,532.9	1,167.8	31.3
Net income	95.4	44.2	115.8
U.S.			
Sales	870.2	536.9	62.1
Operating			
profits	87.8	50.9	72.5
Advertising	29.5	12.5	136.2
Division sales			
Power tools	479.0	443.5	8.0
Accessories	151.1	155.5	−3.0
Outdoor tools	133.0	120.9	10.0
Home			
appliances	461.0	165.5	178.0
Professional			
tools	246.0	203.3	21.0
Service	93.0	87.7	6.0

Like a powerlifter preparing for a big heft, Black & Decker Corp. is positioning itself for growth by using its muscle and strategy.

The Towson, Md., company had impressive returns in 1984, accompanied by measured advertising spending of $29.5 million in 1984, ranking it the 138th largest national advertiser. Measured spending was up 136.2% over 1983.

Net earnings for the year leaped 116% to $95.4 million, following an almost $77 million loss for 1982. Total revenues rose 31%, to more than $1.5 billion in 1984. And for the first six months ended March 31, 1985, of the current fiscal year, revenues were up 34% to $906 million, although earnings fell 12% to $43.8 million.

Strategy at Black & Decker includes two main steps: Acquisition and innovation.

The company began its move in 1982 to concentrate on electrical appliances with the sale of its McCulloch chain saw business, a division in which losses had been mounting—after-tax losses in 1981 were $6.2 million, and in 1982, $23.3 million. By 1983, most of the assets of McCulloch had been sold.

During 1983, Black & Decker completed a worldwide corporate restructuring plan. Included were manufacturing reorganization (mostly in Europe), internal finance changes and management restructuring. In April, 1984, the company took a giant step forward by acquiring the General Electric housewares division for about $300 million. Included in this product group are toasters, ovens and appliances for beverage-making, food processing, personal care and garment care.

Other recent acquisitions also are expected to strengthen Black & Decker, each in a specific area:

Zenses, a German company acquired in 1983, produces power tool accessories that Black & Decker can use to broaden its markets. The purchase of Bayerisch Boherwerke (BBW) now allows Black & Decker to manufacture drill bits. Wanting to enter the fast-growing hobby tool market (20% to 30% annual growth rate), it purchased in 1984 the German Minicraft company, a hobby and precision-tool maker.

Buying some assets of Elu, a Swiss maker of quality power tools for the professional, Black & Decker can market routers and stationary miter saws, formerly a gap in the Black & Decker product line.

Most recently, the company made a strategic move in buying the assets of two "down under" appliance makers, Rank Electric Housewares Pty Ltd., Australia, and Rank Appliances New Zealand Ltd., both owned by Britain's Rank Organisation PLC. The new companies will give Black & Decker experience in manufacturing 240–volt. electrical goods, because that is the standard service voltage in Australia and New Zealand. It is also standard in Europe, where Black & Decker plans major marketing.

Innovation is making the heart of this company beat faster today. Even without counting the former GE appliances, about one-third of 1984 sales came from products developed since 1979. Innovation is creating new products, reducing costs *and* producing profits.

Examples of Black & Decker innovation are the new lighter, smaller M47 tools and the cordless appliances. The tools' motor is only 1¾ ins. in diameter—25% smaller than standard, but delivering comparable power.

Cordless design, Black & Decker says, is an evolving technology. The company is working with battery makers toward improved designs. The goal is to produce and market tools and appliances that can be used widely by the homeowner and hobbyist, but also by the professional.

To support these production and marketing programs for its bigger household product line, Black & Decker entered fiscal 1985 saying it would launch "an unprecedented national advertising program" using print advertising to reach virtually every American household.

One source puts the total at $50 million. The stakes are high enough to warrant the cost. In 1983, GE estimated the year's total sales at $470 million for the housewares being sold to Black & Decker. And the Rank purchase may add $50 million to B&D houseware revenues.

Black & Decker wants its logo squarely on the new products it is promoting. By 1987, it will have replaced GE's monogram with its newly redesigned orange hexagonal logo, and the same changes will occur on other newly acquired product lines, although probably not on the Swiss Elu tools. Much of Elu's value to Black & Decker depends on its reputation in Europe.

To highlight the changes in its business, the company is dropping the "Manufacturing" tag in its name for a more streamlined corporate title—Black & Decker Corp.

Black & Decker operates in six product groups: consumer power tools, consumer accessories, outdoor, household, professional and service. The first four, grouped under the heading consumer products, make up 78% of Black & Decker's sales. Professional products account for 16%, and service (repair and maintenance of B&D products) accounts for 6%.

Advertising Expenditures ($000)		
	1984	1983
Magazines	8,221.0	1,579.6
Network cable	391.9	157.7
Spot TV	4,912.0	3,721.0
Network TV	15,454.6	7,047.6
Network radio	542.3	0.0
Outdoor	11.9	0.0
Total measured	29,533.7	12,505.9

SOURCE: *Advertising Age*, June 30, 1985, 20.

DISCUSSION QUESTIONS

1. Critically evaluate Black & Decker's product strategy.
2. Discuss the strategic fit of the acquisition of the General Electric housewares division with Black & Decker's existing products.
3. Is the use of a global marketing strategy appropriate for Black & Decker? Discuss.
4. How do new products fit into the company's product strategy?

STRATEGIC APPLICATION 10-2

L'OREAL

Chevilly-Larue, France—In a sprawling research complex here, a technician makes a plastic mold of the wrinkles around a woman's eyes. Soon, a computer prints out a graph of the hapless woman's crow's feet and calculates the patch of skin's "wrinkle coefficient."

Nearby, a computer screen displays a blowup of skin wrinkles and calculates the amount of shadow they cast—an approach inspired by a method sometimes used to measure craters on the moon. Armed with such data, scientists at L'Oreal S.A. measure the effect of potential wrinkle remedies.

As populations age around the world, the big French cosmetics concern thinks aging skin provides one of its hottest market opportunities. It says at least 50 of its scientists in this Paris suburb and elsewhere now devote full time to the wrinkle challenge.

Bypassing Some Rivals

This marriage of intensive research with marketing opportunity has helped L'Oreal prosper while its biggest American rivals, Avon Products Inc. and Revlon Inc., have slipped. Between 1979 and 1984, L'Oreal's earnings soared 120%, while Avon's declined 28% and Revlon's declined 27%. In the past three years, L'Oreal has bypassed Revlon and Japan's Shiseido to become the world's second largest cosmetics concern, outranked only by Avon. Revlon is engaged in an intense takeover defense against Pantry Pride Inc.'s $1.83 billion offer by attempting a leveraged buyout through Forstmann Little & Co., which plans to split the company.

American companies will be seeing more of L'Oreal. "In the next five years, the United States will probably be the country of greatest growth for us," says Charles Zviak, L'Oreal's chairman.

Once known mostly for hair-care products, L'Oreal has turned into one of France's hottest glamour companies. In the past five years, its stock has more than tripled in value, giving L'Oreal one of the five highest stock market capitalizations of all French corporations. The company's largest shareholder, Liliane Bettencourt, is reportedly the richest woman in France. L'Oreal's recently retired long-term chairman, François Dalle, is one of President François Mitterrand's oldest friends.

Patina of Science

L'Oreal, according to industry sources, spends about twice as much on cosmetics research as Avon and Revlon. A chemist who concocted France's first chemical hair dye in his kitchen sink and peddled it around Paris on a tricycle founded L'Oreal nearly 80 years ago. A chemical engineer—Mr. Zviak—runs the company today. L'Oreal says it employs 1,000 people in cosmetics research. It makes the investment pay by applying their talent to everyday products that it thinks the market wants.

A research staff of 40 toiled eight years to give the world Preference, a hair-coloring product, says Mr. Zviak. Though costlier than rivals, Preference quickly captured about 30% of the U.S. hair-coloring market. Free Hold, a brisk-selling no-rinse foam that holds hair in place without the sticky rigidity of a spray took five years to develop, Mr. Zviak says. The patent for this everyday product ran to 139 pages.

The company also has at least 20 people toiling on the lipstick challenge. "Lipsticks are a perpetual problem," says Jean-Paul Boelle, an official at the laboratory here. If they are easy to apply, they tend to melt. If they shine nicely but aren't formulated just right, they tend to spread messily beyond the lips.

Besides pushing research, the company also has developed a reputation for marketing and market timing. It introduced the hugely successful Ambre Solaire suntan lotion in the 1930s—just before the government gave in to workers' angry demands for mandatory paid vacations.

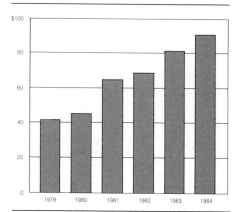

L'Oreal Earnings (in millions of dollars, converted at current rate)

Figures exclude investment reserves and capital gains and losses on disposal of fixed assets.

SOURCE: L'Oreal annual report.

Target: French Hair

After World War II, the company decided to talk the French into using a shampoo, instead of the traditional bar of soap, on their hair. "After the war, people started to see what went on in the United States, and we could see that the time was ripe," Mr. Zviak says. To make the French shampoo-conscious, L'Oreal even sponsored children's shampoo contests in local circuses, which played a big role in French life before television. The tyke who worked up the biggest lather in his hair—with L'Oreal's Dop shampoo—won a prize.

As it became dominant in French cosmetics, L'Oreal started hitting international markets. These markets accounted for about 60% of last year's sales of $1.95 billion. "There are very few French companies that are so well implanted in foreign markets," says Henri Sainte Opportune, an analyst with the Paris securities firm of Oddo Desache & Cie.

In the U.S., L'Oreal operates through Cosmair, an agency owned by the biggest L'Oreal shareholders as well as the

French company itself. Two years ago, Cosmair bought the cosmetics business of Warner Communications for $146 million. This added the Ralph Lauren, Polo and Gloria Vanderbilt fragrances to L'Oreal's U.S. product line, which also includes Lancome, L'Oreal brand cosmetics, Anais Anais perfume and other products. The acquisition also helped boost Cosmair's U.S. sales to $700 million last year, nearly double the figure three years earlier, Mr. Zviak says.

The U.S. operation helped L'Oreal benefit from the dollar's rise in recent years. But, as the company has expenses as well as sales in dollars, the recent decline of the American currency "isn't a big problem if the dollar stays around eight francs," Mr. Zviak says.

Nestlé's Stake

The company acquired a big foreign shareholder in 1974 when Mrs. Bettencourt, daughter of L'Oreal's founder, Eugene Schueller, sold nearly half of her L'Oreal stock to Nestlé, S.A., the Swiss food giant. Today, she holds 51% of a holding company that owns 58% of L'Oreal's stock. Nestle owns the rest of the holding company. With about 5% of Nestlé's stock, Mrs. Bettencourt is also Nestlé's biggest shareholder.

For all of its success, L'Oreal has its share of problems and flops. A perfume named for designer Ted Lapidus fizzled and was withdrawn from the market. More significantly, a pharmaceutical operation has proved slow to develop. Its operating profit declined 12% last year to $9.5 million.

But Mr. Zviak says heavy research spending on pharmaceuticals should start paying off in two or three years. Overall, L'Oreal's earnings advanced 12% in the 1985 first half to $50 million from $44.8 million in the year-earlier period. Revenue for the half advanced 10% to $1.1 billion from $1 billion. Mr. Zviak predicts full-year sales and earnings will advance about 13% from last year.

SOURCE: Roger Ricklefs, "France's L'Oreal, Now No. 2 in Cosmetics, Targets Lucrative U.S. Market for Growth." Reprinted by permission of *The Wall Street Journal.* © Dow Jones & Company, Inc., October 25, 1985. All rights reserved.

DISCUSSION QUESTIONS

1. Contrast and compare L'Oreal's product strategy with those of its competitors.
2. Discuss the advantages and risks associated with L'Oreal's targeting the market for aging-skin cosmetics.
3. Describe and evaluate L'Oreal's positioning strategy.

CHAPTER 11

New Product Planning

Polaroid Corp.'s top management has been fighting for nearly a decade to halt the decline in sales of instant cameras and film. Camera sales fell from 9.4 million units in 1978 to an estimated 3.4 million units in 1985. Patents on instant cameras had closed out competition for several years. In 1977 Dr. Land, the founder, introduced an instant movie system, Polavision, which did not attract enough sales to be profitable. It was withdrawn in 1979, accompanied by a $70 million writeoff. Other new product ventures included industrial applications of proprietary technologies (such as very thin batteries) and special photography applications. Nevertheless 60 percent of Polaroid's business comes from instant photography sales to amateurs. The company introduced a new Series 7000 camera in 1986, targeting younger, more affluent consumers who consider Polaroid as old-hat. Also helping to strengthen Polaroid's market position is a federal court ruling enjoining Kodak from selling any instant cameras or films after January 9, 1986. Inexpensive and high picture quality 35-mm cameras have considerably reduced the advantage of Polaroid's film. Some industry observers question whether the new Spectra camera will offer enough advantages over existing models to help the company regain its former market position in instant photography.[1]

New products are critically important to the survival and prosperity of Polaroid Corp. The company probably relied too heavily on its dominant position in instant photography. If Kodak had not been prevented from selling instant films and cameras in early 1986, Polaroid would have faced severe competitive pressures. In any event Polaroid's future depends largely on the success of its new products, since the instant photography market appears to be in the decline stage of the product life cycle.

The importance Polaroid's management assigns to new products is not unique. New products are the center of attention in most companies because of their obvious contribution to the survival and prosperity of the enterprise. Planning for new products is an essential and demanding strategic activity. New products, when matched to customer needs, offer opportunities for a firm to strengthen its position in existing product-markets, and move into new product-markets.

This chapter examines the process of planning new products, beginning with several issues important to the process. Next, the steps involved in new product planning are discussed, including generating ideas, screening and evaluating ideas, business analysis, development and testing, developing a marketing strategy, market testing, and new product introduction.

CONSIDERATIONS IN NEW PRODUCT PLANNING

Chapter 10 identifies six categories of new products, ranging from completely new products to modifications of existing products and new targeting and positioning of existing products. A *new product* is a good or service that is new to a particular company. Thus, new-to-the-world products and new product lines both represent new products. The planning process presented in this chapter is appropriate for new and improved products.

New Products and Business Performance

"The development and introduction of new products to the marketplace are vital to corporate profitability and growth."[2] In one major study, managers predicted that the contribution of new products to sales growth would increase by one third and the contribution to profits would expand by 40 percent in the 1981–86 period, compared to the 1976–81 period. During this five-year span (1981–86) companies forecast a doubling in the number of new products introduced compared to the previous five-year period.[3]

Polaroid illustrates the relationship between new products and business performance. The company has not had a strong new instant camera entry for a decade,[4] and sales and profits have declined since 1978. Instead of product improvements, Polaroid apparently needs some new products, yet the new Series 7000 represents an improvement or modification rather than a new product. Management's success in developing new products is likely to have a critical influence on Polaroid's future performance. But it is important to keep in mind that

---

EXHIBIT 11-1   Factors Contributing to the Success of New Products

---

Percentage of responses

	0	10	20	30	40	50	60	70	80	90	100

Product fit with
market needs

Product fit with internal
functional strengths

Technological superiority
of product

Top management
support

Use of new
product process

Favorable competitive
environment

Structure of new
product organization

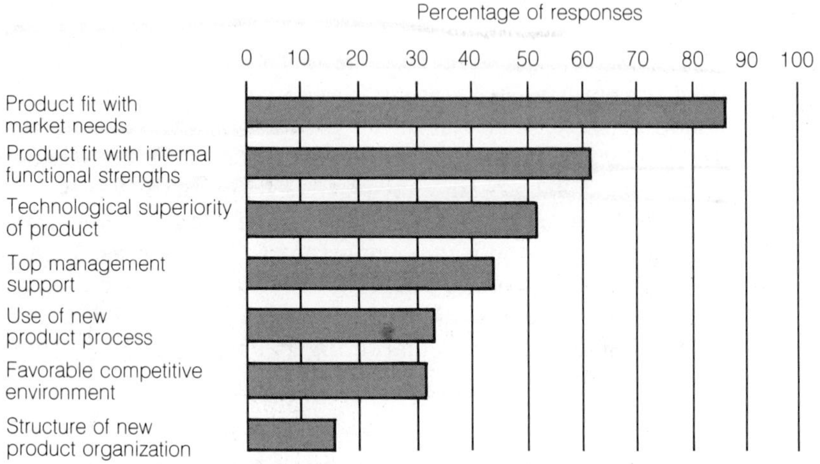

SOURCE: *New Products Management for the 1980s* (New York: Booz, Allen & Hamilton, 1982), 16.

bringing new products from the idea stage to commercialization often requires several years.

Success Criteria

Exhibit 11–1 indicates the factors that contribute to the success of new products, based on responses obtained from more than 700 U.S. manufacturers of over 13,000 new products introduced over the past five years. The study detected some differences between industrial and consumer products firms, as well as across different industries. Technological superiority is considered more important by industrial products firms, while top management support is a bigger concern for consumer durable and nondurable companies. The study also found that the importance of these factors varies by the type of new product being developed.

The Booz, Allen & Hamilton study compared companies that had successfully launched new products to those who had been unsuccessful. Successful companies displayed the following characteristics:[5]

Operating Philosophy.   These companies are committed to growth through internally developed new products and follow a formal new product planning process. Tight idea-screening practices are used.

Organization Structures.   The formal new product planning structure is located in the research and development or engineering functional area but provides for close cooperation between marketing and R&D functions.

The Experience Effect. With increased new product experience, such companies improve new product profitability by reducing the cost per introduction.

Management Styles. There is an effective matching of management style to immediate new product development needs. Management is willing to adjust its style to keep up with changing conditions.

STEPS IN NEW PRODUCT PLANNING

A new product does not have to be a high-technology breakthrough to be successful. Post-It Notes have become a big winner for Minnesota Mining & Manufacturing Co. The note paper pads come in various sizes. Each page has a thin strip of adhesive on the back and can be attached to reports, telephones, walls, and other places. Sales in 1983 were over $40 million and increasing.[6] The idea came from a 3M employee (he had used slips of paper to mark songs in his hymn book but the paper kept falling out). Interestingly, office-supply vendors questioned the need for the sticky-back note paper. But because 3M used extensive sampling as a part of its marketing program, office workers discovered how useful the pads were. Using the name of the 3M chairman's secretary, samples were sent to executive secretaries at all Fortune 500 companies. After using the supply of samples, they wanted more.

Successful new products, such as 3M Post-It Notes, require a systematic planning program. The major stages in such a program are shown in Exhibit 11–2. We will examine each of the new product planning stages to see how they depend on each other, and to demonstrate the importance of a coordinated program of new product planning. There are two key considerations in new product planning: (1) generating a stream of new product ideas that will satisfy management's requirements for new products; and (2) establishing procedures and methods for evaluating new product ideas as they move through the planning stages.[7]

Developing a New Product Strategy

Since strategies for new and existing products are discussed in Chapter 10, only a brief comment is appropriate here to link new product strategy to the planning process shown in Exhibit 11–2. The purpose of this step in the process is to determine the strategic business requirements to which new products should correspond.[8] New products provide an important strategic capability for achieving corporate and business unit objectives. Thus, it is important that businesses formulate guidelines for new product strategy planning. The discussion of strategic situations presented in Chapter 7 describes several important consider-

EXHIBIT 11-2 New Product Planning Process

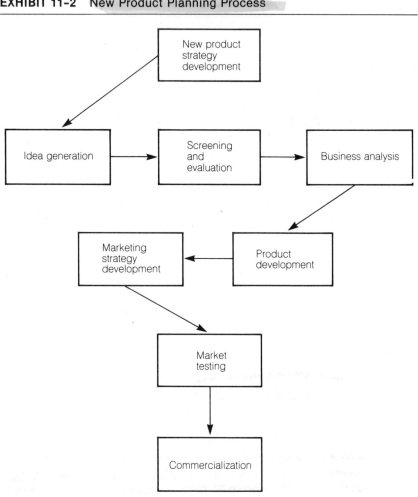

ations in strategy development. New product strategy represents one way of responding to a strategic situation.

Consider Procter & Gamble's strategy for introducing its next wave of products.[9] New products and new profit opportunities are clearly high priority targets. The company's dominance in the detergent and disposable diaper markets eroded in the early 1980s. To counter these trends, P&G introduced Duncan Hines cookies, Citrus Hill orange juice, Always sanitary napkins, Encaprin pain reliever, and Ivory shampoo and conditioner. These new products helped P&G move into markets representing 16 percent of supermarket and drug-store sales in 1984, compared to 9 percent of such sales a few years earlier. The company has registered the brand name, "Home Fresh," indicating a possible entry in the margarine market. A decade ago P&G developed a noncaloric substance that tastes like fat but cuts blood cholesterol levels 20 percent. It would be used in the new product.

Organizing for New Product Planning

New product planning requires the involvement of various business functions and executives. Thus, companies often use some organizational form to manage the planning process. How to organize for new product planning has been widely debated for several decades. Various kinds of product management systems have been developed and implemented. All have deficiencies, yet there is common agreement among managers from successful firms that new product planning requires some type of formalized approach. The objective is planning and coordinating new product opportunities. Important concerns include where to place responsibility and how to organize for new products. The prevailing alternatives are: (1) committee, (2) venture team, (3) new product/brand manager, and (4) new product department.

New Products Committee. This organizational form is widely used because it facilitates the involvement of the various functional interests in new product planning without creating an organizational unit.[10] Such an approach is quite flexible and can be used either as a coordinating mechanism for a particular project or on a continuing basis. Committees may be formed at the top management level for decision-making purposes or at operating levels for coordination or special-purpose assignments, such as screening new product proposals.

By using the committee system, companies avoid establishing a permanent, full-time organizational unit—a major advantage. Limitations of the committee system may include lack of authority, coordination difficulties, and lack of full-time monitoring. A key factor in the success of a new product committee is the chairperson. This person must be effective in moving the committee toward its assigned objectives. The selection of committee members is also important; those chosen should be able to successfully interact in and contribute to a group situation.

Venture Team. This approach requires the creation of an organizational unit to perform some or all of the new product planning functions. The group may serve as a task force, project team, or venture team:

> It is a group of people who are actually doing the work, know what is going on, and whose support is critical. These people will expedite the project or

stall it; they will achieve the necessary creative breakthroughs, or fail to. They are neither functional heads nor perfunctory representatives.[11]

Signode Industries Inc., a major producer of steel and plastic strapping systems and other industrial product lines, uses four- to six-member venture teams to generate new product ideas.[12] When 4 to 10 acceptable ideas have been screened and evaluated, the team is disbanded and the ideas are moved to the business analysis stage. One or two team members stay with the product into commercialization. Using people from operating divisions as team members encourages the support of operating management. And participants gain valuable experience in other business functions from their venture team participation.

Venture teams offer many of the advantages of committees while eliminating the disadvantages. They provide functional involvement and full-time commitment, and they can be disbanded when appropriate. Team members may be motivated to participate on a project that offers possible job advancement opportunities.

New Product/Brand Manager. As discussed in Chapter 10 this organizational form consists of an individual, sometimes assisted by one or a few additional people. The manager is responsible for planning and coordinating various business functions for the new product. In most instances the product manager is a staff person. He or she does not have authority over all product planning activities, but may coordinate activities at various stages in the planning process. A product manager usually has background and experience in research and development, engineering, or marketing and is normally assigned to one of these departments. The product manager of a major new product may report to an SBU manager or corporate executive. It is important to note that product managers' titles and range of responsibilities vary widely across companies.

New Product Department. This organizational form places new product planning responsibility in a formal department. Two versions may be found: (1) a separate department to give new products attention, push, focus, and drive, as would occur if the chief operating executive were managing the product; and (2) the product manager cluster, which consists of a manager responsible for two or more product managers.[13] The departmental approach provides a strong base of support for new product planning, but a separate department may also create internal frictions with other functional areas.

Selecting the type of organization that is the most appropriate must take into account the characteristics and needs of a specific firm. One study of 267 firms found the new product department to be the most popular organizational form, followed by the brand manager, and the new product committee.[14] Since there are so many factors involved, it is impossible to generalize about new product organizational structure other than to underscore the need for some type of organizational mechanism. Wherever responsibility is placed, new product planning, strategic planning, and marketing strategy should be closely coordinated.

IDEA GENERATION

Finding promising new ideas is the starting point in the new product development process. Executives of Minnetonka Inc., of Chaska, Minnesota, found the idea for toothpaste pump dispensers while browsing through a West German supermarket.[15] They worked out an arrangement with the manufacturer of the pump and introduced Check-Up toothpaste in pump form in the United States in 1984, ahead of Colgate, Crest, and other major brands.

Sources of Ideas

New product ideas come from many sources. Limiting the search for new product ideas to internal research and development activities is far too narrow an approach for most firms. Sources of new product ideas are shown in Exhibit 11–3. Both solicited and spontaneous ideas may emerge from these sources, and some even occur by accident. (Procter & Gamble's Ivory soap, for example, was the result of an accident; over-mixing in the manufacturing process created air bubbles in the soap, causing it to float.) The essential issue that must be faced by management is how to establish an idea generation and evaluation program that will meet the needs of the enterprise. Several questions must be answered in developing an idea generation program:

> Should idea search activities be targeted or open ended? Should the search for new product ideas be restricted to those ideas that correspond to mission, business segment, and SBU strategies?
>
> How extensive and aggressive should the firm's idea search activities be? Should search be an active or passive function within the firm?
>
> What specific sources are best for generating a regular flow of new product ideas?
>
> Where will responsibility for new product idea search be placed? How will new product planning activities be directed and coordinated?

EXHIBIT 11–3 Sources of New Product Ideas

Internal	External
Research and development	Customers
Sales people	Competition
Employee suggestions	Inventors and patents
Idea teams	Acquisition
Marketing research	Channel members

For most firms, the idea search program should probably be targeted within a range of product and market involvement that is consistent with corporate mission and objectives and business unit strategy. While some far-out new product idea may occasionally change the future of a company, more often open-ended idea search dissipates resources and misdirects efforts.

It is impossible to generalize about the other three questions since they depend on many such factors as size and type of firm, technologies involved, new product needs, resources, management's preferences, and corporate capabilities. The important consideration is that management should answer these questions and develop a plan for idea generation that will satisfy the firm's requirements.

Many new product ideas originate with customers, particularly ideas for industrial products. In an extensive analysis of the origins of successful new products, one researcher found "strong support for the hypothesis that manufacturers of new products and processes often initiate work in response to explicit customer requests for the innovation."[16] Both industrial and consumer buyers are useful sources of new product ideas.

Methods of Generating Ideas

Several alternatives for generating ideas are shown in Exhibit 11–4. Typically, a company uses more than one of these options.

Search. Systematic monitoring of various information sources may be helpful in identifying new product ideas. New product idea publications are available from companies who wish to sell or license ideas they do not wish to commercialize. New technology information is available through computerized search services such as the Aerospace Research Applications Center at Indiana University. The mission of this research center is to help transfer federal government research and development results into commercial applications. News sources may also yield information about the new product activities of competitors. Many trade publications contain new product announcements. Management must identify the relevant search areas and assign responsibility for search to an individual or group.

EXHIBIT 11–4 Methods of Generating New Product Ideas

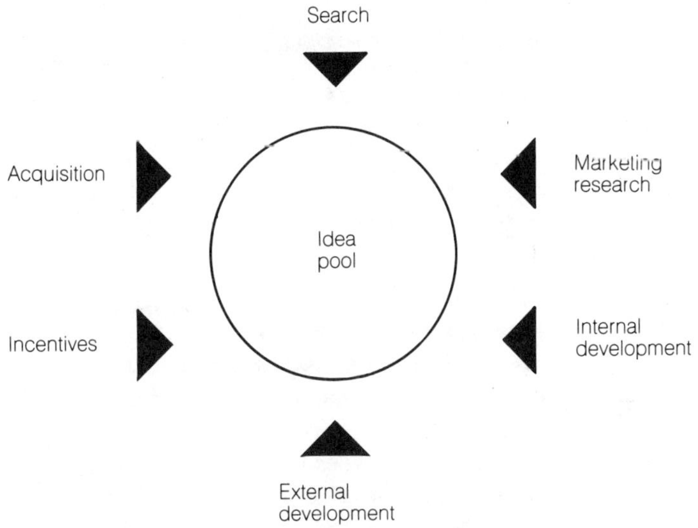

Marketing Research. Surveys of product end users can be useful in identifying needs that can be satisfied by new products. One particularly useful technique to identify and evaluate new product concepts is the focus group, which can be used for both consumer and industrial products. A small group of 8 to 12 people is invited to meet with an experienced moderator to discuss new product ideas. Idea generation might start with a discussion of product requirements for some product use situation. Subsequent focus group sessions can be used to evaluate product concepts formulated to satisfy the needs identified in the initial session. More than one focus group can be used at each stage in the process. Focus groups can be conducted using channel members and company personnel as well as customers.

Another consumer research technique that may be useful in generating new product ideas is the advisory panel. These groups are selected to represent the target market of the firm. For example, a producer of mechanics' hand tools would include mechanics on the panel.

Internal and External Development. Companies' research and development laboratories generate many new product ideas. AT&T's Bell Laboratories has a world-renowned reputation for state-of-the-art technology.[17] As a result of deregulation, AT&T is placing more emphasis on identifying new product ideas with commercial potential. A vice president who heads a management group at Bell Laboratories called Venture Technologies is responsible for identifying and evaluating ideas. When the group was first formed, letters were sent to 150 laboratory directors asking for promising ideas outside of AT&T's traditional telephone markets. The directors responded with 800 proposals for new products.

New product ideas may also originate from development efforts outside the firm. Sources include inventors, private laboratories, and small high-technology firms. For example Odetics Inc. received a contract to develop a next-generation mobile robot for RCA because of Odetics' 14 years of experience in robotics.[18] RCA planned to add electronic sensors to the robot, targeting the military as a potential customer. Odetics obtained both financial assistance and market access from RCA.

Other Idea Generation Methods. Incentives may be useful to glean new product ideas from employees, marketing middlemen, and customers. The amount of the incentive should be high enough to encourage submission. Firms should also guard against employees leaving the company and developing a promising idea elsewhere. For this reason many firms require employees to sign secrecy agreements.

Consumer-product funds are an interesting concept for generating new products, developing them, and moving the ideas into commercialization. Consider this scenario:

> Glacial Confections Inc. has a product, five employees and a chief executive officer. That's all. No factory, no distribution network, no sales, and certainly no profits. Yet this 10-month-old company, which plans to launch a line of premium frozen desserts soon, already has caught the eye of big H. J. Heinz Co.
>
> To Heinz, Glacial Confections' product may be a chance to complement its successful line of Weight Watcher frozen desserts. So it would be willing to underwrite Glacial Confections' marketing costs and let the Westport, Conn., company utilize its frozen food distribution network in exchange for an option to buy it in the future. Glacial Confections has decided to go it alone for now, but, says Walter G. Schmid, Heinz's director of corporate planning, "that's not to say we won't be talking to them again in three months."
>
> How did Heinz spot this tiny company amid the mass of start-ups? It invested in a new type of venture capital fund—one that is interested in putting its money into, say, a chocolate-chip cookie maker rather than a high-tech computer-chip concern. Among the backers of these consumer-oriented funds: major corporations seeking new products.[19]

While the objective of consumer product funds is to provide a return to investors, corporate participants may gain access to new products without the high costs of internal development. Critics of the funds argue that small venture firms do not have the experience to successfully plan and introduce new products. There is also the possibility that two or more corporate investors will try to compete for a promising new product or perhaps the entire company.

Finally, acquiring another firm offers a way to obtain new product ideas. This strategy may be more cost-effective than internal development and can substantially reduce the lead time required for new product planning. IBM's acquisition of Rohm (telecommunications) and General Motors' acquisition of Electronic Data Systems (computer systems) are examples.

Idea generation should lead to one or more product concepts to be screened and evaluated. An idea for a new product must be transformed into a defined *product concept.* A complete product concept is:

> A statement about selected anticipated product attributes that shows how they will yield selected benefits relative to other products or problem solutions already available.[20]

For example, the pump toothpaste dispenser (attribute) offers a simple and quick alternative (benefit) to the traditional tube.

SCREENING, EVALUATING, AND BUSINESS ANALYSIS

Evaluating new ideas is an essential activity in new product planning. Assume that a successful new product is one that will satisfy management's specified criteria for commercial success (e.g., sales, profit contribution, market share). Two risks are involved in evaluation, as shown in Exhibit 11-5. If the risk of rejecting a good product is set too low, then ideas will be developed that eventually must be rejected later in the process. Moving too many ideas too far into development and testing is an expensive mistake. Management must establish a screening and evaluation procedure that will kill unpromising ideas as soon as possible while keeping the risks of rejecting good ideas at acceptable levels. Expenditures build up from the idea stage to the commercialization stage, whereas the risks of developing a bad new product decline as more and more information is obtained about the product and the market. Thus, the best screening procedure is one that is not too tight. The objective is to eliminate the least promising ideas before too much time and money are invested in them. The tighter the screening procedure, the higher the risk of rejecting a good idea. Based on the specific factors involved, management should establish a level of risk appropriate for the situation.

Evaluation should occur regularly as an idea moves through the new product planning stages. Ideas may be rejected at any stage even though the objective is to eliminate the poor risks relatively early in the planning process. A useful overview of new product evaluation is shown in Exhibit 11-6. The evaluation techniques appropriate at each stage in the planning process are matched to the evaluation task.

EXHIBIT 11-5 Balancing New Product Planning Risks

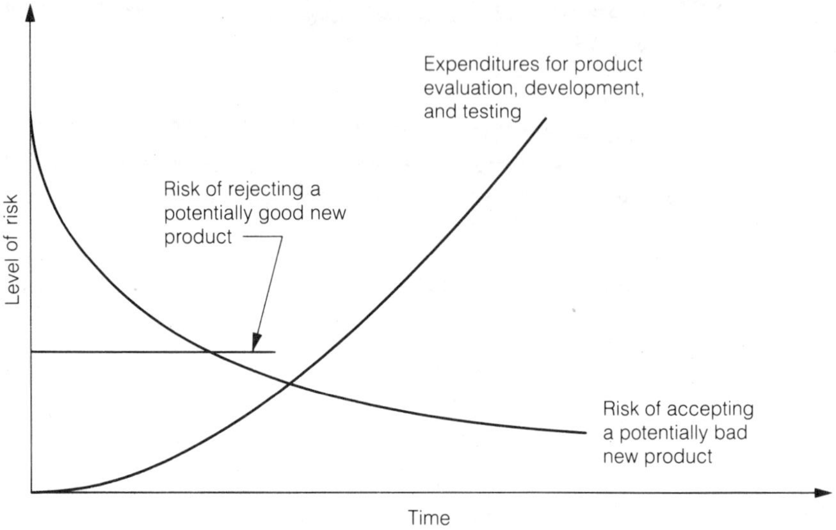

Screening

An idea for a new product should receive an initial screening to determine its strategic fit in the company or business unit. Two important dimensions should be evaluated: (1) the strategic compatibility of the idea, and (2) the commercial feasibility of the venture. Several specific factors in each category are shown in Exhibit 11-7.[21]

The purpose of screening is to eliminate ideas that are not compatible or feasible for the business. These assessments are somewhat subjective since management must establish how narrow or wide the screening boundaries should be. For example, the managements of two otherwise similar firms might have very different missions and objectives. Thus, an idea that involves a new product-market area could be strategically compatible in one firm and not in another: "The dimensions on which management evaluates ideas/concepts/products encompass all key management areas and in particular should reflect the corporate idiosyncrasies and unique situational factors."[22]

Some firms develop screening procedures using various scoring and rating techniques for the factors shown in Exhibit 11-7. The result is a score for each idea being screened. Management can set ranges for passing and rejecting. The effectiveness of these methods is highly dependent on gaining agreement on the relative importance of the screening factors from the managers involved.

EXHIBIT 11-6   New Product Evaluation Tasks and Techniques

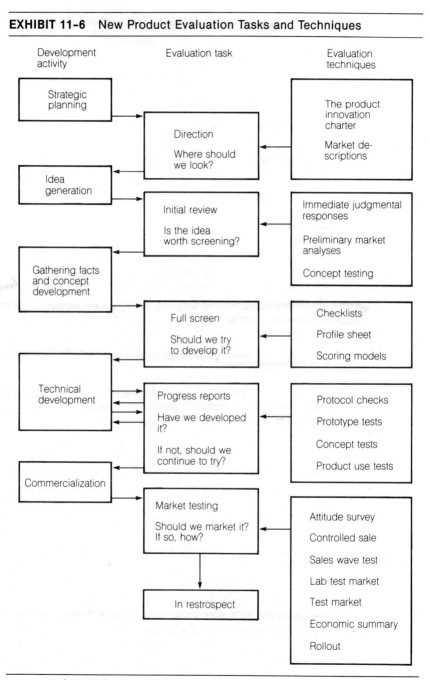

SOURCE: C. Merle Crawford, *New Products Management* (Homewood, Ill.: Richard D. Irwin, 1983), 328.

IBIT 11-7   New Product Idea Screening Factors

Strategic Compatibility:
Mission/objectives fit?
Corporate capabilities (production, marketing, distribution)
Expected proprietary status
Financial requirements
Strategic contribution/need

Commercial Feasibility:
Market size and attractiveness
Technical feasibility (technology state-of-the art?)
Social/legal/environment considerations

Evaluation

The boundaries between idea screening, evaluation, and business analysis are not clearly drawn. Some firms combine two of the evaluation stages. Nevertheless, the distinction seems appropriate. After completing initial screening, the ideas that survive are subjected to more comprehensive evaluation. Several of the factors shown in Exhibit 11-7 may be evaluated in greater depth, including buyers' reactions to the proposed concept. Concept tests are useful in evaluation and refinement of new product ideas.

Concept Testing.   The objective of concept testing is to obtain a reaction to the concept from a sample of potential buyers, before the product is developed. The product's concept may be presented to the test participants in various forms, such as a written description, a drawing, a model, or a package.[23] Typically, a statement of the concept is part of the testing procedure. The statement should be brief, consisting of one or two paragraphs. Bias must be avoided in wording of the statement.

When properly designed and implemented, the concept test offers a very useful means of evaluating a product idea very early in the development process. The costs of concept tests are reasonable, given the information that can be obtained. There are some important cautions. The test, at best, is a very rough gauge of commercial success. Since an actual product and a commercial setting are not present, the test is somewhat artificial. The test clearly has subjective dimensions.

The concept test is probably most useful in signaling very favorable or unfavorable product concepts. It also offers a basis on which two or more concepts can be comparatively evaluated. An important requirement of concept testing is that the product can be expressed as a concept and that the participant has the experience and capability to evaluate the proposed product.

Concept Selection.   The completion of the evaluation stage should yield one or more concepts for business analysis. An interesting com-

EXHIBIT 11-8   Mortality of New Product Ideas

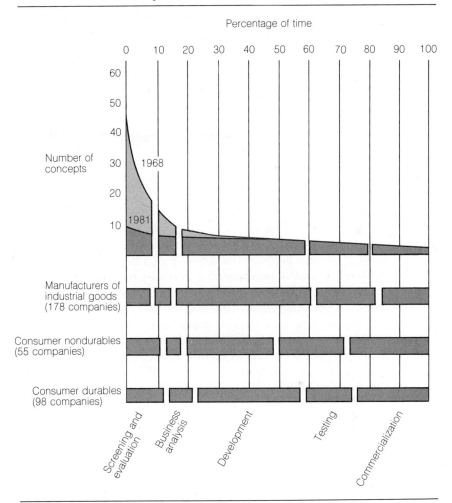

SOURCE: *New Products Management for the 1980s* (New York: Booz, Allen & Hamilton, 1982), 14.

parison of the mortality of new product ideas is shown in Exhibit 11–8. The mortality results for 1968 indicate that 58 new product ideas were considered for every successful new product, compared to 7 ideas required to generate a successful product in 1981. Also indicated in Exhibit 11–8 is the percentage of time devoted to each stage in the new product planning process by industrial goods, consumer nondurables, and consumer durables companies. In general consumer products firms spend a higher percentage of time on screening and evaluation of ideas than industrial products firms. The percentage of time devoted to development is greater for industrial goods companies than for consumer goods firms.

Business Analysis

Business analysis is concerned with estimating the commercial performance of the proposed product. Obtaining an accurate financial projection depends on the quality of the revenue and cost forecasts. Business analysis is normally accomplished at several stages in the planning process. The first assessment is conducted before the product concept moves into the development stage. Financial projections are refined at subsequent stages.

Revenue Forecasting. The newness of the product, the size of the market, and the competing products all influence the accuracy of revenue projections. In the case of an established market such as soft drinks, estimations of total market size can usually be obtained from industry information. Several industry associations publish industry forecasts. The more difficult task is estimating the market share that might be feasible for a new product entry. For example, the size of the ready-to-eat (RTE) cereal market can be projected accurately but estimating the market share of a new cereal brand is far more difficult. A range of feasible share positions can be indicated at the concept stage and used as a basis for preliminary financial projections. Established markets also may have success norms—1 percent is considered a successful entry for a new RTE cereal, for instance. A norm provides a basis for estimating the possibility of reaching a successful level of sales. Accurate forecasts of market acceptance require some type of acceptance test such as a market test.

Sales of new-to-the-world products are very difficult to forecast. One approach is to identify the potential size of the end-user market and then estimate the new product's rate of market penetration. For example, sales forecasts for an electronic filmless camera could be based on the percentage of penetration in the conventional 35-mm camera market over a specified time period.

Cost Estimation. Several types of costs are encountered in the planning and commercialization of new products. An appropriate way to categorize the costs is to estimate them for each step in the new product planning process (Exhibit 11–2). The costs increase rapidly as the product concept moves through the process. Costs for each planning stage can be further divided into functional categories (e.g., marketing, research and development, and manufacturing). An organization experienced in new product planning should be able to generate reasonable cost estimates.

Profit Projections. Several types of profit projections can be used to gauge a new product's financial performance. Various financial analysis techniques are examined in Chapter 4. Those appropriate for new product business analysis include break-even computation, cash flow, return on investment, and profit contribution. Break-even analysis is particularly useful to show how many units of the new product must be sold before it begins to make a profit.

Management must determine the appropriate length of time for projecting sales, costs, and profits. Policy guidelines may be specified; for instance, the product may be required to recoup all costs within a certain time period. Business analysis estimates should take into consideration the estimated flow of revenues and costs over the time span used in the analysis. Typically, new products incur heavy costs before they start to generate revenues.

Other Considerations. Some important issues must be considered in business analysis of a proposed product concept. First, management should formulate guidelines for the financial performance of new products. These can be used to accept, reject, or further analyze the product concept. Another issue involves assessing the amount of risk in the proposed venture. Two product proposals with comparable financial projections might have substantially different levels of risk. This factor should be included either in those projections or as an additional consideration beyond the financial estimates. Finally, the possible cannibalization of sales from existing products should be estimated. New products that are substitutes for existing products often cannibalize sales.

Application Illustration

These are the screening and evaluation steps used by the Ralston Purina Company for new consumer product proposals:

Step A—Judgmental Screening
   The first step in the screening process is the responsibility of the new products department of the company's consumer products group. The department's staff, consisting of marketing research specialists and venture directors, makes an initial rough screening of the several hundred new product ideas proposed each year. From these it selects the 25 or 30 that seem most promising and worthy of further consideration.

Step B—Preliminary Consumer Reaction Tests
   These superior ideas are then subjected to a consumer reaction check that is both quick and inexpensive. Usually, this consists of exposing selected consumers to a short statement, consisting of a paragraph of no more than 30 or 40 words, which describes a product idea. The consumers are asked to rank the various concepts so described in the order of interest to them. The consumers participating in these checks are usually procured through outside suppliers of central location testing services.

Step C—Preliminary Marketing Criteria Evaluation
   Next, the appropriate venture director—the one assigned to the product unit that would market the proposed product—receives information

assistance from his counterpart in marketing research. Each worthwhile idea identified in the preliminary consumer reaction tests is now evaluated on the basis of the following criteria: probable sales volume, concept uniqueness, incremental value, life cycle, competition, and the purchase situation and consumer appeal within the relevant market.

Step D—Preliminary Feasibility Evaluation

The best surviving prospects from Step C are then submitted to a research and development team which examines the feasibility of their manufacture. The team checks possible conflicts with competitive patents, potential technical difficulties in developing a product, and the amount of money that may be required to produce it. The team also tries to determine whether the product is unique enough to provide the company with a proprietary advantage, and the existence of any industry or regulatory standards that might pose problems with it. At this stage, manufacturing executives may also be consulted more closely regarding capital investment and production equipment requirements, including the possible use of present facilities for the new product.

Step E—Preliminary Concept Test

An outside marketing research agency is now engaged to find out how well several alternative concept statements for Step D communicate the concept to various consumer groups. The agency attempts to discover, for example, whether consumers will translate a concept statement accurately and thus recognize the advantages the product has to offer. The agency works with a focus group, consisting of six to eight individuals who have some demonstrated familiarity with the type of product in question.

Step F—Final Concept Test

It now becomes necessary to identify those classes of consumers—i.e., the target groups in the market—who will have the greatest interest in the product. A broad sample of consumers is approached and a determination made of the interest level within each of various subsections of the overall market.

Step G—Final Marketing Potential and Feasibility Evaluation

There is one last step, as a spokesman explains, "before turning the R&D people loose on the project." Once a proposal gets this far and is approved, it becomes an active laboratory project. (Ordinarily, the research and development staff is allowed to spend up to 200 hours of development time on a project without formal clearance.)

The main consideration at this late point is whether the proposed project appears in all respects to be a valid business proposition, in terms of Ralston's standards. The decision to go ahead with final development now requires more highly refined estimates as to probable sales volume, pricing, costs, profits, capital investment, market timing, and competitive factors. If all of these look favorable, the research and development department is authorized to proceed with a product's development, including preparation of test formulas and prototypes for use during the field-test marketing stage still to come.[24]

DEVELOPMENT AND TESTING

The product concept that successfully completes the business analysis stage of product planning moves next to development and testing. During this stage the concept is transformed into one or more prototypes. The prototype is the actual product, produced by research and development (R&D) rather than by an established manufacturing process. The development and testing stage includes manufacturing development as well as product development.

Product Development

An overview of product, package, and service design is shown in Exhibit 11–9. It indicates the constraints and guidelines that affect product design. Note also the decisions that are necessary. Since product development is largely a technical activity, our discussion will focus on the input information to R&D and the output of development and testing.

Product Specifications.   R&D must be provided with guidelines in order to develop the product. Consider this description for a contact lens cleaning machine:

> The machine described by the attributes below is designed for use by wearers of contact lenses. The principal purpose is to eliminate the need for tedious and time-consuming cleaning of the lenses prior to storage. The lenses need only be placed into the machine and the start button activated to effect a thorough cleansing, rinsing, and disinfecting process.
>
> The machine will:
> 1. Be compact and light enough to be carried in an overnight bag.
> 2. Be powered by standardized means (120 VAC house current and/or readily available flashlight-type batteries).
> 3. Require no operator interaction once the cleaning process has begun, and disable itself after completion.
> 4. Cleanse lenses to a degree judged acceptable by general optometric standards, including disinfection of soft lenses.
> 5. Not be detrimental to the contact lenses, even if the lenses should be inadvertently left in the machine for an extended period.
> 6. Have provisions to easily fill and drain the cleansing/rinsing/storage solution(s), and be readily cleanable both internally and externally.
> 7. Be safe to operate.
> 8. Be simple to operate and to maintain, and require only that the operator load the lenses, add solution(s), if necessary, and activate the machine.
> 9. Be aesthetically pleasing in appearance.
> 10. Be economical to own and operate, including the cost of solution(s) necessary for proper cleaning.[25]

EXHIBIT 11-9 Product, Package, and Service Design and Its Determinants

Corporate/marketing objectives regarding product design	Corporate constraints	Environmental constraints	Consumer profiles regarding
• Support positioning - prestige - low cost • Fit corporate image • Fit product line • Fit target product/ market portfolio	• Production facilities • Financial • Time • R & D expertise • Marketing strengths and weaknesses	• Legal • Distribution outlets • Technological	• Demographic • Psychographic • Consumption system

The actors

| R & D |
| Marketing research |
| Marketing |
| Legal |
| Finance |
| Manufacturing |

Product design decisions

Product:
 • Functional characteristics
 • Structural characteristics (size, shape, form, material, etc.)
 • Aesthetic characteristics (style, color, etc.)

Packaging:
 • Functional characteristics
 • Structural characteristics
 • Aesthetic characteristics
 • Identifiable characteristics (logo)

Branding:
 • Private versus national
 • Family branding

Other services:
 • Warranties
 • Financing
 • Installation
 • Usage instructions
 • After purchase services

Psychophysical transformation

Perception of product by consumers and other stakeholders

Preference and likely purchase behavior

SOURCE: Yoram J. Wind, *Product Policy: Concepts, Methods, and Strategy* (Reading, Mass.: Addison-Wesley, 1982), 340.

This statement concentrates on what the product will do rather than how should be designed. The statement clearly indicates the benefits that the cleaning machine should provide but it has one deficiency. It does not indicate performance standards. Product specifications should indicate product planners' expectations regarding benefits, including essential physical and operating characteristics.[26] This allows R&D to determine the best physical structure for delivering the benefits.

Prototype. R&D then uses the product specifications to create one or more physical products. At this stage the product is called a prototype since it is not ready for commercial production and marketing. It is a custom version of the product, differing in various ways from the commercial version. Many of the parts may be custom built, and materials, packaging, and other details may differ. Nevertheless, the prototype

---

EXHIBIT 11-10   Decisions that Define Produce Use Tests

---

1. Source of product
   Batch, pilot plant, final production
2. Identity disclosure
   Branded versus blind
3. Singularity
   Monadic, paired comparison, trio
4. Duration of use
   Single use, week, extended
5. Normality of use
   Normal, abnormal
6. Product form variants
   Size, color, shape, etc.
7. Degree of control over use
   Total control, supervised, unsupervised
8. Handling nondiscriminators
   Repeat, identify nondiscriminators
9. Communication to users
   No comment, explanations, commercial
10. User groups
    Labs, experts, employees, market users, miscellaneous
11. Mode of recording reaction
    Like/dislike, preference, descriptive
12. Mode of contact
    Mail versus personal
    Individual versus group
    Point of use versus central location
13. Research service
    Within versus outside
14. Source of norms
    Previous studies versus judgment

SOURCE: C. Merle Crawford, *New Products Management* (Homewood, Ill.: Richard D. Irwin, 1983), 397.

should be capable of delivering the benefits spelled out in the specifications.

Use Tests.   The prototype may be tested in a use situation. If use testing is feasible, the firm can obtain important feedback from users concerning how well the product meets the needs included in the product specifications. A standard approach to use testing is to distribute the product to a sample of users, asking them to try the product. Follow-up occurs after the test participant has had sufficient time to evaluate the product.

Companies must make important decisions in designing, implementing, and evaluating use tests, several of which are shown in Exhibit 11-10. Note the different options available. All of the decisions should be clear except possibly the handling of nondiscriminators (#8). This issue concerns whether or not use tests will be repeated with the same users. Often, internal testing is included as part of the use test procedure.

Manufacturing Development. A company must next develop a process for producing the product in commercial quantities, an important part of the development process for many types of products. Manufacturing the product at an acceptable cost is a critical determinant of profitability. A promising product may be feasible to produce in the laboratory but not in a manufacturing plant, due to costs, production rates, and other considerations. Initial production delays can also jeopardize the success of a new product.

MARKETING STRATEGY DEVELOPMENT AND MARKET TESTING

Guidelines for marketing strategy depend largely on what type of new product is being developed. A totally new product will require a complete targeting and positioning strategy. A product modification may only require a revised communications strategy to convey to target buyers information on the benefits offered by the improved product. Regardless of how new the product actually is, a review and assessment of the product's entire marketing strategy can help avoid problems and identify opportunities.

Strategy Decisions

Use tests and product evaluation efforts conducted before product development often provide important imformation for the development of a new product marketing strategy. Examples include potential user characteristics, product features, advantages over competing products, use situations, feasible price range, and communications needs.

It is important to begin developing a marketing strategy as soon as possible in the process of new product planning since several activities must be completed. Marketing strategy analyses and planning should be initiated during product development if feasible. Coordination activities such as packaging, product information, colors, materials, and product safety must also be completed between engineering and marketing.

Market Targeting. Selection of the market target(s) for the new product may range from offering a new product to an existing target to identifying an entirely new group of potential users. A totally new product requires a new targeting strategy (see Chapter 8). Review of all prior marketing research for the new product may yield useful insights as to targeting opportunities. It may also be necessary to test market the product before finalizing the market targeting strategy.

Positioning Strategy. Various aspects of positioning must be resolved during the marketing strategy development stage. Product strategy regarding packaging, name selection, sizes, and other aspects of the product must be decided on. If new channels of distribution are to be used, the firm must develop channel strategy. It must also formulate a price strategy; research on price may be necessary to gain feedback on buyer responsiveness to alternative price levels. The company needs to develop an advertising and sales promotion strategy; testing of advertisements may occur at this stage. Finally, the firm must come up with a personal selling strategy including necessary sales force training.

Market Testing Options

Market testing can be considered after the product is fully developed, provided that the product is appropriate for market testing. Market tests often gauge buyer response to the new product and test one or more positioning strategies. Test marketing is popular for many consumer nondurable products such as foods and health and beauty aids. In addition to conventional test marketing, less expensive alternatives are available.

Simulated Test Marketing. Marketing analysts can implement this test method by recruiting shoppers at shopping center.[27] The consumer is asked to read an advertisement for the new product and gets a sample to take home. Follow-up telephone interviews evaluate the consumer's experience with the new product. Tests conducted over a 90-day period cost about $40,000 and can be quite useful in weeding out failures, but they are less useful in predicting market success. Simulated test marketing can be conducted much faster than conventional test marketing, is far less expensive, and is not as visible to competition. The product is not advertised and is not available in stores.

Simulated test marketing typically includes the following steps:

- Recruiting participants for the test—either a general audience or a more specific group of respondents.
- Securing background information—usually awareness, usage, attitudinal, and demographic data.
- Exposing test participants to information regarding the new product; attempting to create interest in the product by presenting its primary selling proposition.
- Determining the reactions to the test product before use; assessing the deterrents, if any, to trial.
- Determining the reactions to the test product after use; assessing the deterrents, if any, to repurchase.[28]

Scanner Based Test Marketing. This test method is less artificial than simulated testing and is substantially less expensive than conventional tests. Information Resources Inc.'s BehaviorScan system pioneered the use of cable television and a computerized data base to track new products. The system uses information and responses from 2,500 panel members in each test city. The participant receives an identification card to show to participating store cashiers. Purchases are electronically recorded and transmitted to a central data bank. Cable television enables this system to use controlled advertisement testing.

Firms can use scanner testing to evaluate various aspects of marketing strategy, including what kind of advertising attracts different people. BehaviorScan was useful in determining that the audience for TV's "General Hospital" buys 25 percent more granola bars than the average viewer.[29] BehaviorScan tests take about 12 months and cost around $250,000.

The rapidly expanding popularity of electronic market testing is indicated by the explosive growth of Information Resources, Inc., which in 1985, only a few years after its founding, could boast sales in the $50 million range. A. C. Nielsen, the world's largest marketing research firm, entered the scanner test market in 1985 as a late entrant in a growing field. The firm invested $20 million in developing its information system.[30] Nielsen's clients for the new system include Gillette, Procter & Gamble, and General Mills.

Conventional Test Marketing.   This form of testing puts the product under actual market conditions in one or more test cities. It uses a complete marketing program including advertising and personal selling. Product sampling is often an important factor in launching the new product in the test market. The product is marketed on a commercial basis in the test cities, and test results are then projected to the national or regional target market. Because of its high cost, conventional test marketing represents the final evaluation before full-scale market introduction. Tests typically cost more than $1 million. Firms sometimes decide not to test market in order to avoid competitor awareness, eliminate testing costs, and accelerate introduction.

Testing Industrial Products.   Market testing is appropriate for various industrial products. Selection of test sites may need to extend beyond one or two cities to include sufficient market coverage. The test firm has substantial control of an industrial products test since it can use direct mail and personal selling. The relatively small number of customers also facilitates targeting of marketing efforts. The product should exhibit the characteristics necessary for testing, such as being producible in test quantities, relatively inexpensive, and not subject to extensive buying center influences (Chapter 6).

Factors in Test Marketing

The basic purpose of test marketing is to predict how the new product will perform during full-scale commercialization. Many factors are important in testing, such as selecting good test sites, determining the length of the test, controlling for external influences on the test (such as competition), and interpreting results. A. C. Nielsen's experience indicates that about 75 percent of products that are test marketed are successful, compared to an 80 percent failure rate for new products that are not fully tested.[31]

Selecting Test Sites.   Test sites should exhibit the market and environmental characteristics of the commercial market taraget. Since no site is perfect, the objective is to find a reasonable match between the test and commercial market. Each test city should be isolated from other cities, contain people generally comparable to market target profile, have a representative media mix, offer research and audit services, provide a diversified socioeconomic cross-section of people, and exhibit no unusual environmental characteristics.[32]

Length of the Test.   The length of the test is important in obtaining valid test results. A. C. Nielsen's analyses of more than 100 market tests of new brand introductions indicate that the predictability of national results from test market data increases significantly with time.[33] After 4 months of testing, 37 percent of the predictions were correct; after 18 months the figure was 100 percent. Manufacturers need 10 months to be reasonably sure that market share data are representative. Market tests of more than a year are common.

External Influences.   Probably the most troublesome external factor that may affect test market results is competition that does not operate on a normal basis. Competitors may attempt to drive test market results awry by increasing or decreasing their marketing efforts and making other changes in their marketing actions. It is also important to monitor the test market environment to identify other unusual influences that may occur during the test period. Unusual economic conditions may affect test results for some products.

Interpreting Results.   Various considerations are important in interpreting test results. We have discussed the length of tests and external factors. In addition, the nature and composition of results should be analyzed. Determining the characteristics of the buyers provides important information for targeting. Repeat purchase data are essential to determine whether the product will be repurchased. Several new product models are useful in analyzing test market data and predicting commercial market success.

New Product Models

Some useful models have been developed for predicting sales and market share from test market data. Some of the newer models also consider the effects of marketing mix components. The dimensions of product newness and repurchasability provide a basis for classifying available models.[34] The models fall into two categories: (1) first-purchase models designed to predict the cumulative number of new product triers over time, and (2) models designed to predict the repeat purchase rate of those buyers that have tried the product. The latter type combines an appropriate first-purchase model with a repeat-purchase model. A brief overview of the consumer adoption process for new products sets the stage for an examination of the two types of models.

Consumer Adoption Process.   Research concerning the adoption of innovations indicates that (1) new product adopters follow a sequence of stages in their adoption process; (2) their characteristics vary according to how soon they adopt the product after introduction; and (3) adoption findings may be of value in new product planning. The adoption stages are awareness, interest, evaluation, trial, and adoption.[35] Note the similarity of these stages with the buyer decision process discussed in Chapter 6. By identifying and targeting such "early adopters," firms may be able to accelerate a new product's adoption. Rogers has found early adopters to be younger, of generally higher socioeconomic status, and more in contact with impersonal and cosmopolitan sources of information than later adopters.[36] The early adopter also tends to draw from a variety of information sources and is more cosmopolitan than the later adopters.

Understanding buyers' adoption process may be useful in selecting media and messages for new product introduction. The trial stage of this process suggests the potential value of extensively sampling new consumer products, and other methods of encouraging consumers to try new products. If businesses can identify early adopters of their new product, they can focus initial marketing efforts on these people.

First-Purchase Models.   The concept underlying these models is the diffusion of the new product into the market. The models generate a life-cycle sales curve using a mathematical model that contains a small number of parameters.[37] We can estimate the parameters based on the experiences of similar products, consumer pretests, or early sales results. The range of models extends from simple exponential curve fitting using market potential and rate of penetration as parameters, to more complex, multistage models. Mahajan and Peterson have developed a comprehensive critique and comparative assessment of first-purchase diffusion models of new product acceptance.[38]

Repeat Purchase Models.   A wide variety of consumer and industrial new products are nondurables that are repurchased on a regular basis. Several repeat purchase models have been developed for projecting sales of these products and for evaluating marketing program positioning strategy combinations. The ASSESSOR model illustrates this class of models.[39] The purpose of the model is to evaluate the new product before test marketing but after decisions have been made regarding positioning strategy. We can use this information, in combination with direct behavior and attitude data obtained from laboratory and usage tests, to generate market share predictions and diagnostic information. Trial/repeat and attitude models are built into the structure of ASSESSOR. The model uses two approaches (trial/repeat and preference models) to estimate the brand's market share. This is a key feature. The use of a laboratory facility and a simulated shopping experiment is also innovative. Applications have typically utilized samples of 300 people.

New product models such as ASSESSOR are very data-dependent and complex. Their validity has not been fully tested, although for certain kinds of applications the results have been promising. Strengths of such models include their capacity to analyze interrelationships among several variables and to generate outputs based on input data. Applications appear most appropriate for frequently purchased non-durable products that are not totally new, in that some experience exists about the product category. Model applications like ASSESSOR are expensive, but they cost a small fraction of a market test or full-scale commercialization. Urban and Hauser, for example, estimated in 1980 that, "$50,000 to $75,000 is an attainable cost for pretest market analysis."[40] Considering the stakes involved in the introduction of new products, the use of modeling to reduce risks is likely to expand in the future.

Selecting a Model. The choice of a test market model should be matched to the specific new product planning situation. Possibilities range from sales prediction to marketing mix variable analysis. Narasimhan and Sen have prepared a very useful critical review of nine models that use test market data to evaluate the performance of a new brand in an inexpensive, frequently purchased product category. Their classification of the models is shown in Exhibit 11–11. Several details about each model are shown in Exhibit 11–12. Narasimhan and Sen recommend the Parfitt/Collins model if sales prediction is the primary objective. If management wants to evaluate the new product's marketing mix as well as a sales forecast, they suggest the TRACKER and NEWS models.

COMMERCIALIZATION

S. C. Johnson and Sons follows a systematic process for new product planning. The firm's consumer products group keeps as many as 20 new products in various stages of development.[41] Management prefers to introduce its products one at a time to assure complete attention to and control over the introduction. Introducing new products requires a coordinated sequence of decisions including a complete marketing

EXHIBIT 11–11 Classification of Test Market Models

		Modeling Aspects				
Model	Model Objective	Level of Model Complexity	Quality of Modeling	Type of Sales Data Required	Diagnostics	Degree of Commercial Acceptance
Fourt and Woodlock (1960)	sales	low	unsatisfactory	panel	low	low
Parfitt and Collins (1968)	brand share	low	unsatisfactory	panel	low	high
STEAM (Massy 1969)	sales	high	unsatisfactory	panel	low	low
SPRINTER (Urban 1970)	sales	high	good	panel, store audit	high	medium
Eskin (1973)	sales	medium	unsatisfactory	panel	low	medium
Nakanishi (1973)	sales	high	unsatisfactory	panel	medium	low
NEWPROD (Assmus 1975)	brand share	medium	satisfactory	survey	medium	low
TRACKER (Blattberg and Golanty 1978)	sales	medium	good	survey	high	high
NEWS (Pringle, Wilson and Brody 1982)	sales	medium	good	survey	high	high

SOURCE: Chakravarthi Narasimhan and Subrata Sen, "New Product Models for Test Market Data," *Journal of Marketing*, Winter 1983, 13.

EXHIBIT 11-12 Test Market Model Characteristics

Model	Stages Modeled	Details Regarding Each Stage				Mathematical Models for Each Stage			Estimation Issues	
		Awareness		Trial	Repeat					
		Different Ways of Becoming Aware and Trial Probability	Time of Becoming Aware and Trial Probability	Time of Becoming a Trier and Repeat Purchase Probability	Depth of Repeat and Repeat Purchase Probability	Report of Specific Models	Marketing Mix Variables Considered	Inclusion of Appropriate Marketing Mix Variables	Report of Estimation Methods	Report of Parameter Estimates
Fourt and Woodlock (1960)	trial, repeat	—*	—	no	yes	yes	none	—	no	no
Parfitt and Collins (1968)	trial, repeat	—	—	yes	no	partial	none	—	partial	no
STEAM (Massy 1969)	trial, repeat	—	—	yes	yes	yes	none	—	yes	no
SPRINTER (Urban 1970)	awareness, trial, repeat	yes	yes	no	yes	yes	advertising, price, promotion, distribution	yes	yes	no
Eskin (1973)	trial, repeat	—	—	yes	yes	yes	none	—	yes	yes
Nakanishi (1973)	trial, repeat	—	—	yes	no	yes	advertising, promotion	no	yes	yes
NEWPROD (Assmus 1975)	awareness, trial, repeat	yes	yes	no	no	partial	advertising, promotion	no	no	no
TRACKER (Blattberg and Golanty 1978)	awareness, trial, repeat	no	yes	no	yes	yes	advertising, price	yes	yes	yes
NEWS (Pringle, Wilson and Brody 1982)	awareness, trial, repeat	yes	yes	yes	yes	yes	advertising, promotion, distribution	no	yes	yes

*Dash indicates that the particular column detail is inappropriate to the model. For example, since the Fourt and Woodlock model does not consider the awareness stage, one cannot comment on the details regarding the awareness stage for this model.

SOURCE: Chakravarthi Narasimhan and Subrata Sen, "New Product Models for Test Market Data," *Journal of Marketing*, Winter 1983, 15.

plan, coordinated introduction activities of all business functions, and monitoring and control over the product launch.

Marketing Plan

The commercialization stage requires a complete marketing strategy. The strategy should indicate actions, responsibilities, and deadlines. It should be discussed with the various people responsible for the introduction, including salespeople, sales managers, and managers in other functional areas such as production, distribution, finance, and human resources. Planning and implementing marketing strategy are considered in some detail in Chapters 16 and 17.

An important decision in new product introduction is the timing and geographical scope of the launch. The options range from a national market introduction to an area-by-area rollout. The national introduction is a major endeavor, requiring a comprehensive implementation effort. Some firms prefer to introduce the product on a stage-by-stage basis. This reduces the scope of the introduction and enables management to adjust marketing strategy based on experience gained in the early stages of the launch. One limitation of the rollout approach is that it allows competition more time to develop and introduce competing products.

Monitoring and Control

Real-time tracking of new product performance at the commercialization stage is extremely important. Standardized information services are available for monitoring sales of products such as foods, health and beauty aids, and prescription drugs. Information is collected through store audits, consumer diary panels, and scanner services. Special monitoring studies may be necessary for products that are not included in standardized information services.

Management should include product performance standards in the new product plan to evaluate how well the product is performing. Performance targets often include profit contribution, sales, market share, and return on investment objectives—including the time horizon for reaching objectives. It is also important to establish values for objectives that indicate unacceptable performance. Management can designate zones for new product performance, such as above expectations, acceptable, below expectations, and unacceptable. An organization must be prepared to drop a new product if it is apparent that unacceptable performance will continue.

Application Illustration[42]

By examining a new product venture that experienced problems during commercialization, we can see how a carefully designed introduction plan may suffer from faulty implementation. In 1984 Fisher-Price Toys introduced a line of preschool playwear backed by its famous name in toys and some extensive research on users' needs. Focus group interviews and other research highlighted parents' complaints about zippers, buckles, buttons, and snaps on kids' clothing. Management was convinced that the Fisher-Price name in combination with a unique design would gain the firm a profitable segment in the highly competitive children's apparel market.

The new product offered several new features including Velcro fasteners, padded knees and elbows, extra-long shirttails, cuffs that could be unfurled as children grew, and big neck openings to accommodate large heads. Some industry observers questioned the emphasis on durability in a market where style is often a major choice criterion. The market is huge; an estimated 8 million babies will be crawling about by 1990, many representing first births. Advertising featured the Fisher-Price name and the fact that mothers had helped design the clothing. Fisher-Price toys are in 99 percent of all homes with a child under the age of six. Fisher-Price contracted production and distribution of the apparel to a girls dressmaker.

By the end of 1984, the new venture was encountering serious problems. The playwear line flopped because of faulty distribution. A strike and other product snags at a Jamaican plant caused delays in shipments to retailers. Some orders never arrived. Questions concerning quality were raised by some retailers. Management acted quickly to overcome the implementation problems by dropping the original production and distribution partner and contracting with two new companies. The spring fashion season was skipped but a 1985 fall line was planned. It was unclear how responsive retailers would be to the Fisher-Price apparel line. The firm's unfortunate experience demonstrates the critical importance of implementation in new product planning.

CONCLUDING NOTE

New product planning is a vital strategic activity in virtually all companies:

> It is a rare company that can escape the effects of today's rapidly changing markets and technology. Existing products will, in time, be preempted by new or improved products or degenerate into profitless price competition.

Only through the creation of new products in demand in the marketplace can most manufacturing companies sustain their growth and profitability in the long term.[43]

Companies that are successful in new product planning follow a formal process of new product planning guided by effective organization structures for managing new products. Experience helps them to improve product planning over time. Their management styles are responsive to new product planning needs.

Steps in new product planning include strategy development, idea generation, screening and evaluation, business analysis, product development, marketing strategy development, market testing, and commercialization. The major organization options for managing new product planning are the new products committee, the venture team, the new product/brand manager, and the new product department.

Idea generation triggers planning for a new product. The idea is evaluated as it moves through the process, and new product planning expenses accumulate. There are various internal and external sources of new product ideas. Ideas can be generated by information search, marketing research, research and development, incentives, and acquisition. Screening, evaluation, and business analysis determine if a new product concept is sufficiently attractive to justify proceeding with development.

Development and testing change the product from a concept to a prototype. Product development transforms the concept into one or more prototypes. Use testing gains user reaction to the prototype. Manufacturing development determines how to produce the product in commercial quantities. Marketing strategy development begins during or at the completion of the product development stage. A complete marketing strategy must be formulated for a totally new product. Product line additions, modifications, and other changes require a less extensive development of marketing strategy.

Completion of product and marketing strategy development moves the process to the market testing stage. At this point management often obtains some form of user reaction to the new product, providing market testing is feasible. Testing options include simulated test marketing, scanner-based test marketing, and conventional test marketing. Testing of industrial products is less extensive than testing of consumer products, although frequently purchased nondurables can be tested. Commercialization completes the planning process, moving the product toward sales and profit performance objectives. But a successful product may fail due to faulty implementation.

NOTES

1. Bob Davis, "Polaroid Seeks to Revive Instant Photography," *The Wall Street Journal*, November 11, 1985, 6.
2. *New Products Management for the 1980s* (New York: Booz, Allen & Hamilton, 1982), 1.
3. Ibid., 4.
4. Davis, "Polaroid Seeks to Revive Instant Photography," 6.
5. *New Products Management for the 1980s*, 17–18.
6. Lawrence Ingrassia, "By Improving Scratch Paper, 3M Gets New-Product Winner," *The Wall Street Journal*, March 31, 1983, 27.
7. *New Products Management for the 1980s*, 11.
8. Ibid., 11–12.
9. John Bussey, "Procter & Gamble Is Laying Groundwork to Introduce Its Next Wave of Products," *The Wall Street Journal*, December 11, 1984, 31.
10. C. Merle Crawford, *New Products Management* (Homewood, Ill.: Richard D. Irwin, 1983), 169–70.
11. Ibid., 170.
12. "Signode Rates Venture Team Method a Success," *Marketing News*, November 22, 1985, 24–25.
13. Crawford, *New Products Management*, 174–175.
14. George Benson and Joseph Chasin, *The Structure of New Product Organization* (New York: AMACOM, 1976), 21.
15. Ronald Alsop, "U.S. Concerns Seek Inspiration For Products From Overseas," *The Wall Street Journal*, January 3, 1985, 17.
16. Eric von Hippel, "Successful Industrial Products from Customer Ideas," *Journal of Marketing*, January 1978, 41.
17. Janet Guyon and Charles W. Stevens, "AT&T's Bell Labs Adjusts to Competitive Era," *The Wall Street Journal*, August 13, 1985, 6.
18. "Acquiring the Expertise But Not the Company," *Business Week*, June 25, 1984, 142B and 142F.
19. Lynn Asinof, "Consumer-Product Funds Give Giants Early Look at New Items," *The Wall Street Journal*, August 15, 1985, 27.
20. Crawford, *New Products Management*, 352–353.
21. Several of these factors are cited in E. Patrick McGuire, *Evaluating New-Product Proposals* (New York: The Conference Board, 1973), 6.
22. Yoram J. Wind, *Product Policy: Concepts, Methods, and Strategy* (Reading, Mass.: Addison-Wesley, 1982), 303–304.
23. McGuire, *Evaluating New-Product Proposals*, 34–35.
24. Ibid., 61–62.
25. Crawford, *New Products Management*, 384.
26. Ibid., 384–85.
27. Eleanor Johnson Tracy, "Testing Time for Test Marketing," *Fortune*, October 29, 1984, 75–76.
28. Herbert P. Hupfer, "Simulated Test Marketing," in *The New Products Handbook*, ed. Larry Wizenberg (Homewood, Ill.: Dow Jones-Irwin, 1986), 139–149.
29. Tracy, "Testing Time for Test Marketing," 76.
30. "Big Brother in Springfield," *Forbes*, December 2, 1985, 210–211.
31. Lee Adler, "Test Marketing—And Its Pitfalls," *Sales and Marketing Management*, March 15, 1982, 78.
32. "S&MM's Special Test Marketing Section," *Sales & Marketing Management*, March 15, 1982, 76.

33. "The True Test of Test Marketing Is Time," *Sales & Marketing Management*, March 15, 1983, 74.

34. Gary L. Lilien and Philip Kotler, *Marketing Decision Making* (New York: Harper & Row, 1983), Chapter 19.

35. Everett M. Rogers, *Diffusion of Innovations* (New York: Free Press, 1962).

36. Ibid., 192.

37. Lilien and Kotler, *Marketing Decision Making,* 706.

38. Vijay Mahajan and Robert A. Peterson, "First-Purchase Diffusion Models of New-Product Acceptance," *Technological Forecasting and Social Change* 15 (1979), 127–146.

39. Glen L. Urban and John R. Hauser, *Design and Marketing of New Products* (Englewood Cliffs, N.J.: Prentice-Hall, 1980), 397–405.

40. Ibid., 387.

41. Laurie Freeman, "S. C. Johnson Shines With New Products," *Advertising Age,* June 10, 1985, 4 and 96.

42. The illustration is based on Ronald Alsop, "Fisher-Price Banks on Name, Design in Foray Into Playwear," *The Wall Street Journal,* August 2, 1984, 27; and "From Playwear to Zapping Ads: Updating Some Topics of 1984," *The Wall Street Journal,* December 27, 1984, 13.

43. *New Products Management for the 1980s,* 24.

QUESTIONS FOR REVIEW AND DISCUSSION

1. In many consumer products companies, marketing executives seem to play the lead role in new product planning, whereas research and development executives occupy this position in firms with very complex products such as electronics. Why do these differences exist? Do you agree that such differences should occur?

2. Discuss the features and limitations of focus group interviews for use in new product planning.

3. Analyze the demographic and socioeconomic trends in the United States from 1985–90, as they relate to Fisher-Price's children's playwear line. Are the trends favorable?

4. Identify and discuss the important issues in selecting an organizational approach for new product planning.

5. Discuss the issues and tradeoffs of using tight evaluation versus loose evaluation procedures as a product concept moves through the planning process to the commercialization stage.

6. What factors affect the length of the new product planning process?

7. Compare and contrast the use of scanner tests and conventional market tests.

8. Is the use of a single city test market appropriate? Discuss.

9. What is the relationship of new product strategy to corporate and marketing strategies?

10. Do you believe the strategic importance of new products will increase or decrease during the next decade? Support your argument.

STRATEGIC APPLICATION 11-1

APEX CHEMICAL COMPANY

The Executive Committee of Apex Chemical Company—a medium-sized chemical manufacturer with annual sales of $60 million—is trying to determine which of two new compounds the company should market. The two products were expected to have the same gross margin percentage. The following conversation takes place among the vice president for research, Ralph Rogovin; the vice president for marketing, Miles Mumford; and the president, Paul Prendigast.

VP-Research: Compound A-115, a new electrolysis agent, is the one; there just isn't any doubt about it. Why, for precipitating a synergistic reaction in silver electrolysis, it has a distinct advantage over anything now on the market.

President: That makes sense, Ralph. Apex has always tried to avoid "me too" products, and if this one is that much better . . . what do you think, Miles?

VP-Marketing: Well, I favor the idea of Compound B-227, the plastic oxidizer. We have some reputation in that field; we're already known for our plastic oxidizers.

VP-Research: Yes, Miles, but this one isn't really better than the ones we already have. It belongs to the beta-prednigone group, and they just aren't as good as the stigones are. We *do* have the best stigone in the field.

President: Just the same, Ralph, the beta-prednigones are cutting into our stigone sales. The board of directors has been giving me a going over on that one.

VP-Marketing: Yes, Ralph, maybe they're not as good scientists as we are—or think we are—but the buyers in the market seem to insist on buying beta-prednigones. How do you explain that? The betas have 60 percent of the market now.

VP-Research: That's your job, not mine, Miles, If we can't sell the best product—and I can prove it *is* the best, as you've seen from my data and computations—then there's something wrong with Apex's marketing effort.

President: What do you say to that, Miles? What *is* the explanation?

VP-Marketing: Well, it's a very tricky field—the process in which these compounds are used is always touch-and-go; everyone is always trying something new.

VP-Research: All the more reason to put our effort behind Compound A-115, in the electrolysis field. Here we know that we have a real technical breakthrough. I agree with Paul that that's our strength.

President: What about that, Miles? Why not stay out of the dogfight represented by Compound B-227, if the plastic oxidizer market is as tricky as you say?

VP-Marketing: I don't feel just right about it, Paul. I understand that the electrolysis market is pretty satisfied with the present products. We did a survey, and 95 percent said they were satisfied with the Hamfield Company's product.

President: It's a big market, too, isn't it, Miles?

VP-Marketing: Yes, about $10 million a year total.

President: And only one strongly entrenched company—Hamfield?

VP–Marketing: Yes, I must admit it's not like the plastic oxidizer situation—where there are three strong competitors and about a half-dozen who are selling off-brands. On the other hand, oxidizers are a $40 million market—four times as big.

President: That's true, Ralph. Furthermore our oxidizer sales represent 25 percent of our total sales.

VP–Research: But we've been losing ground the past year. Our oxidizer sales dropped 10 percent, didn't they, Ralph? While the total oxidizer market was growing, didn't you say?

VP–Marketing: Well, the electrolysis field is certainly more stable. Total sales are holding level, and as I said before, Hamfield's share is pretty constant, too.

President: What about the technical requirements in the electrolysis field? With a really improved product we ought to be able . . .

VP–Marketing: Well, to tell you the truth, I don't know very much about the kind of people who use it and how they . . . you see, it's really a different industry.

President: What about it, Ralph?

VP–Research: It's almost a different branch of chemistry too. But I have plenty of confidence in our laboratory men. I can't see any reason why we should run into trouble. . . . It really does have a plus-three-point superiority on a scale of 100—here, the chart shows it crystal clear, Miles.

VP–Marketing: But aren't we spreading ourselves pretty thin—instead, of concentrating where our greatest know-how . . . you've always said, Paul, that . . .

President: Yes, I know, but maybe we ought to diversify, too. You know, all our eggs in one basket.

VP–Marketing: But if it's a good basket . . .

VP–Research: Nonsense, Miles, it's the kind of eggs you've got in the basket that counts—and Compound A–115, the electrolysis agent, is scientifically the better one.

VP–Marketing: Yes, but what about taking the eggs to the market? Maybe people don't want to buy that particular egg from us, but they would buy Compound B–227—the plastic oxidizer.

President: Eggs, eggs, eggs—I'm saying to both of you, let's just be sure we don't lay any!

SOURCE: Edward C. Bursk and Stephen A. Greyser, *Cases in Marketing Management*, 2d ed., 1975, pp. 204–7, 208–10. Reprinted by permission of Prentice-Hall, Inc., Englewood Cliffs, N.J.

DISCUSSION QUESTIONS

1. If you had to choose one of these two products, which would it be?
2. What criteria (and what ranking on each criterion) would you use in making this decision?
3. Could you, on the basis of this brief glimpse of Apex, give it any guidelines for product strategy that would help it to do more effective developmental or pure research?

STRATEGIC APPLICATION 11–2

MINOLTA CORP.

In 1976, Canon Inc. jolted the camera industry. By heavily promoting its new, sophisticated AE-1, the company was able to turn a once-intimidating product—the single-lens reflex camera—into a mass-market item.

"They opened our eyes," says James DeMerlier, marketing director of rival Minolta Corp.

Now, Minolta has an eye-opener of its own.

The company's new Maxxum, introduced in January, has shattered sales records in the U.S. and Japan. Like Canon, Minolta packaged new technology—in this case, automatic focusing—with splashy ads aimed at young, convenience-minded adults. The result: Minolta is challenging Canon for industry leadership.

In one sense, the Maxxum is just the latest instance of technological one-upmanship in a decade-long effort by the camera industry to automate and simplify single-lens reflex cameras, or SLRs. (The name comes from the "reflex," or reflected image, seen through the camera's single lens.) Canon showed how extensive marketing, long ignored by Japanese camera makers, could broaden the appeal of the sophisticated 35-mm products—as long as they were easy to use. Now, Minolta, by being the first to offer automatic focusing, may be building a commanding lead over its competitors.

Rivals' Moves

"All the companies are going to have to come up with the same camera if they're going to compete with Minolta," says Joe Graham, marketing director of Pentax Corp., another Japanese camera maker.

But the Maxxum may also be the *last* major advance in traditional chemical-based still photography. The drive toward automation has been fueled by stagnant sales, a demand for convenience by baby-boomers and the threat of competition from video photography. Now that SLRs are highly automated, however, the next generation of photographic equipment will probably marry video technology with current 35-mm technology. The gap is already narrowing.

Camera Imports (Japanese SLR cameras shipped to North America, in millions)

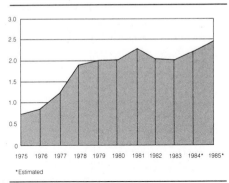

*Estimated

SOURCES: Dean Witter Reynolds Inc., Nomura Securities International Inc. Photo Marketing Assoc.

Last month, for instance, Eastman Kodak Co. disclosed plans to begin consumer testing of a still video system that will enable users to display photographs on their television screens and to print photos of TV images, such as a frame from a videotape. By the year 2000, a filmless electronic still camera could be on the market; photographers will simply transfer a disk from their cameras to a device on their televisions, eliminating film development.

Until the mid-1970s, most Americans viewed SLRs as intricate photographic gadgets that could only be mastered by perseverence and professional skill. Consequently, most consumers opted for lower-quality but easy-to-use cartridge-loading cameras, such as Kodak's Instamatic.

Then, in 1976, Canon introduced the AE-1, the first popular SLR to set a camera's lens opening and shutter speed automatically. To trumpet the AE-1, the company's marketing staff launched a massive advertising campaign with the theme: "So advanced, it's simple." Using television for the first time to advertise a 35-mm camera, Canon saturated the media with spots featuring tennis star John Newcombe and other sports celebrities.

Photography Boom

By making the difficult easier, Canon touched off a photography boom that quadrupled SLR sales within four years. Sophisticated Japanese cameras soon became a fixture among U.S. camera buyers.

In the early 1980s, however, the growth in sales leveled off, and Minolta and other camera makers became convinced that only another heavily promoted technical innovation could stimulate the market. The race toward automatic focusing, achieved first in compact 35-mm cameras, began in earnest.

A corps of 240 engineers toiled four years in secrecy to design the Maxxum. When Minolta unveiled the camera in January, the company's marketers had already been at work for 10 months. Minolta increased its advertising budget by 50% to $15 million to push the Maxxum's own high-tech slogan: "Only the human eye focuses faster." Minolta also introduced the camera in the seasonal lull after Christmas, just as Canon had with the AE-1, assuring itself of considerable attention because of the dearth of new products.

The computerized Maxxum frees the user of tasks that intimidate many casual photographers. Outfitted with two eight-bit microprocessors, the camera automatically focuses, sets shutter speed and exposure and advances and rewinds the film. The Maxxum is also an "auto-load" camera; the film advances to the first frame as soon as a film roll is loaded.

But the camera's chief lure is the automatic-focusing feature. Fuzzy objects are typically brought into focus in less than a second—as fast as a professional photographer can focus manually. "It's the simplest camera I've ever used," says Robert Curtis, an Atlanta resident who owns four other SLRs.

In spite of technical acclaim, the Maxxum's popularity is as much a marketing coup as a triumph of technology. Minolta's designers grafted the latest advances and time-saving features from other cameras, such as automatic loading and automatic advance, into a single design that included auto-focusing.

"What Minolta has done is to put it all together" in one package, says Herbert Keppler, publisher of Modern Photography magazine.

A Commanding Lead

Competitors are scrambling to catch up. But if the AE-1's success is a harbinger, Minolta will probably have taken a commanding lead by the time similar cameras hit the market. And Minolta isn't standing still. Just as Canon built an entire series of cameras with varying features around the AE-1, Minolta last month introduced a professional version of the Maxxum.

Innovation carries some risks. Polaroid Corp., for example, introduced an instant movie camera in 1977 that was instantly made obsolete by videocassette recorders. The Nimslo 3-D camera, which produced three-dimensional color prints, was a technical success and a marketing bust. Ironically, the highly automated Maxxum may show that 35-mm technology has reached its limits and thus hasten the arrival of electronic still photography.

"I try to think of what I want a 35-mm camera to do that it doesn't already do, and I really can't think of anything," says Eugene Glazer, an analyst at Dean Witter Reynolds Inc.

Many industry executives consider Kodak's venture to be the most ambitious effort yet at fusing video and still photography. "A mother who wants a picture of her son playing Little League baseball can print a photo instantly from a videotape," says Daniel A. Carp, Kodak's vice president for consumer electronics.

Kodak's color printer, though intended mainly for business, will be available by Christmas in specialty photo shops for about $700. The printer will compete with a similar system announced earlier this year by Polaroid. In Japan, Fuji Photo Film Co. already sells a playback device that allows consumers to view their photos on their televisions.

SOURCE: Ernest Beazley, "Minolta's New Camera Rattles Industry, Marks Era of Transition in Photography." Reprinted by permission of *The Wall Street Journal.* © Dow Jones & Company, Inc., October 3, 1985, p. 35. All rights reserved.

DISCUSSION QUESTIONS

1. Why is Minolta's Maxxum as much a marketing coup as a triumph of technology?
2. What future research and development strategy do you recommend for Minolta, given industry trends?
3. Identify and evaluate the product and marketing strategy alternatives available to Minolta's competitors.
4. Evaluate the potential impact of video technology on the 35-mm camera market. What strategy do you recommend to Minolta's management for coping with this potential threat?

CHAPTER 12

Distribution Strategy

Distribution is Wetterau Incorporated's mission. The company is the country's third largest voluntary food wholesaler, serving over 1,700 retailers in 24 states.[1] Wetterau also owns and operates supermarkets, department stores, and drugstores. Sales for the year ending March 30, 1985, were $3.1 billion and net earnings were $26.6 million. Management has identified and detailed five basic strategies designed to guide the company through a changing and challenging business climate: (1) aggressively campaigning to attract regional chain accounts; (2) acquiring compatible businesses that fit well with the company's current operations and plans for the future; (3) continually strengthening the support services offered to Wetterau's customers; (4) expanding and modernizing facilities; and (5) increasing productivity through computer-based warehouse mechanization systems and other improvement programs. These strategies are positioning the company to take full advantage of the dynamics of the rapidly changing food distribution industry.

While some manufacturers distribute directly to end users, many use marketing intermediaries like Wetterau Incorporated to make contact with the people or organizations in their market targets. An effective distribution strategy requires a penetrating analysis of the available alternatives in order to select the most appropriate channel network. If a business chooses intermediaries or suppliers in a helter-skelter way, distribution strategy becomes a fragmented series of decisions. Management often considers any firms that purchase its products as customers—be they distributors, dealers, or other manufacturers. Similarly, firms that call on a buying company are considered suppliers, regardless of whether they are manufacturers, distributors, or other kind of intermediaries. Thus many companies participate in distribution channels comprised of various organizations. How a firm is positioned in the distribution network should be a major strategic decision for its management.

Distribution strategy cannot be left to chance, but selecting the best strategy to fit the firm's opportunities and constraints is not easy. Management may need to alter an established distribution strategy to respond to changing conditions. For this reason, distribution strategy should be a continuing concern.

We first examine the role of distribution in marketing strategy and then discuss the issues management must consider in choosing a distribution strategy. Next we look at the factors that affect a channel of distribution strategy. Finally, we discuss the selection of a channel strategy and consider several important strategic trends in distribution.

STRATEGIC ROLE OF DISTRIBUTION

Ethan Allen, Inc. (furniture), Deere and Co. (farm equipment), and Snap-On Tools, Inc. (mechanics' hand tools) have one common feature in their marketing strategies. Each has a strong distribution channel that is a major contributing factor to the firm's performance. Ethan Allen uses a carefully selected network of independent retail dealers. Deere has a powerful worldwide network of farm equipment dealers. Snap-On Tools' independent dealers in a van provide a close link with customers, supply feedback to guide product improvement, assist customers in tool selection, and establish record sales every year.

Reaching Market Targets

Distribution strategy is important in deciding how to reach market targets and how to perform various distribution functions.

First we consider distribution strategy from a manufacturer's point of view. Although most of the strategic issues apply to firms at any level in the distribution channel—wholesale or retail—manufacturers are unique because they have the option of going direct to end users or serving them through marketing intermediaries. The factors that influence this decision are shown in Exhibit 12-1. Manufacturers have three distribution alternatives: (1) direct distribution; (2) use of intermediaries; or (3) situations in which either may be feasible.

Buyer Considerations. Customer characteristics influence the decision of whether to use a direct distribution approach. Manufacturers must consider the amount and frequency of purchase, as well as mar-

EXHIBIT 12-1   Factors Affecting Distribution Strategy

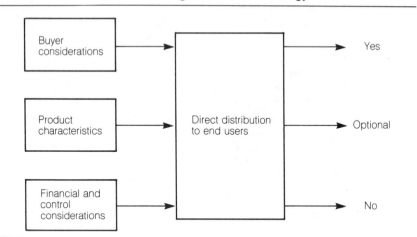

gins over manufacturing costs available to pay for direct selling costs. Customers' geographical locations are also important in evaluating the economics of direct selling. Customers' needs for product information and applications assistance must be considered to determine whether the manufacturer or a marketing intermediary can best satisfy these needs.

The personal computer (PC) industry provides an interesting illustration of the role of distribution in gaining access to end users. Tandy's Radio Shack retail chain and distribution network gave the firm a competitive edge when the market was developing. Access to consumers and small business users required retail outlets. IBM had to develop a distribution network for its highly successful PC line, introduced in 1981. The industry shakeout began in early 1984, when IBM's production of PCs caught up with demand and the company started broadening its distribution channels.[2] IBM also uses its 20,000 salespeople to push the computers through channels and to make direct contact with large corporate buyers. Several new chains, including ComputerLand Corp., developed to meet the distribution needs of PC producers. By late 1985 competition was strong at both the manufacturing and retail levels of the channel. Consumers had slowed down their buying, although sales of PCs for office use were up an estimated 40 percent over 1984. Retailers were going after business buyers in order to survive. This required developing sales forces to make calls on business firms. The nation's 4,400 computer stores were expected to make about half of their estimated $14 billion in sales to business firms in 1985. One industry expert expected half of the 4,400 computer stores to go out of the business by 1987.

The personal computer illustration indicates that channel strategy is as important to small firms with limited resources as it is to large corporations.

Product Characteristics. Complex products and services often require close contact between customers and the producer, who may have to provide application assistance, service, and other supporting activities. Chemical processing equipment, larger computer systems, pollution control equipment, and engineering design services are products and services that manufacturers often market directly to end users via their own sales forces. Another factor is the mix of products offered by the manufacturer. A complete line may make direct contact economically feasible, whereas the cost of direct sales for a single product may be prohibitive unless the item represents a major purchase. Companies whose products are frequently improved as a result of rapidly changing technology often adopt direct sales approaches. And qualified marketing intermediaries may not be available, given the characteristics of the product and the requirements of the customer. Direct contact with end users facilitates feedback to the manufacturer as to new product needs, problem areas, and other concerns. Thus, manufacturers must consider product characteristics in deciding whether to use a direct or distribution channel strategy. In some instances the decision is clear. At other times either alternative may be feasible.

Financial and Control Considerations. Some firms do not have the necessary financial resources to serve their end users. Others are unwilling to make large investments in field sales and service facilities. Management must decide if resources are available and, if they are, whether direct sales to end users represents the best use of the resources. Costs and benefits must be estimated. Direct distribution gives the manufacturer more control over distribution, since independent organizations cannot be managed in the same manner as employees.

Control of intermediaries may be an important factor to the manufacturer. Facilitated by favorable court decisions, the growth of automobile megadealers has reduced U.S. car makers' control over their dealer networks.[3] Today's 25,000 dealers represent only half the number operating in 1950, and the trend toward multiple-franchise dealers is continuing. In addition to shifting more channel power to megadealers, the trend is bringing other changes to auto distribution, including lower distribution and marketing costs (which comprise about 30 percent of a car's retail price). One New York dealer has $700 million in annual sales and accounts for 3 percent of the GM's Cadillac division sales. Territorial boundaries are also disappearing. Multifranchises are becoming common. A San Francisco dealer sells Chrysler, Toyota, Nissan, Mazda, Saab, Isuzu, Alfa Romeo, and Porsche autos in a building that was previously a department store. Manufacturers also are explor-

EXHIBIT 12-2   Factors Favoring Direct Distribution and Use
of Intermediaries

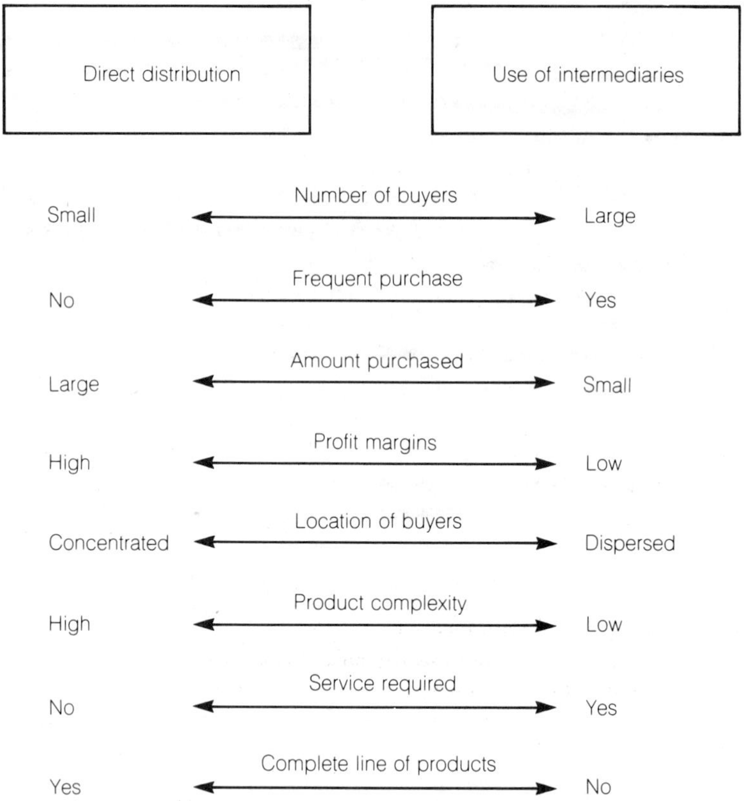

Direct distribution	Use of intermediaries

Small	Number of buyers ← →	Large
No	Frequent purchase ← →	Yes
Large	Amount purchased ← →	Small
High	Profit margins ← →	Low
Concentrated	Location of buyers ← →	Dispersed
High	Product complexity ← →	Low
No	Service required ← →	Yes
Yes	Complete line of products ← →	No

ing alternative distribution concepts, such as satellite service centers and selling cars in retail stores.

Exhibit 12–2 lists various factors that influence the distribution decision. A firm's financial resources and capabilities may also be important considerations. The comparisons in Exhibit 12–2 are general guidelines; there are exceptions. Due to end user considerations, product characteristics, and financial and control considerations, producers of industrial products are more likely than producers of consumer products to utilize direct distribution to end users. The rest of the chapter assumes that management plans to use one or more distribution channels to reach end users.

Distribution Functions

A *channel of distribution* is a network of organizations and functions that connects the producer to the end users. Importantly, the distribu-

---

EXHIBIT 12-3 Basic Channels of Distribution

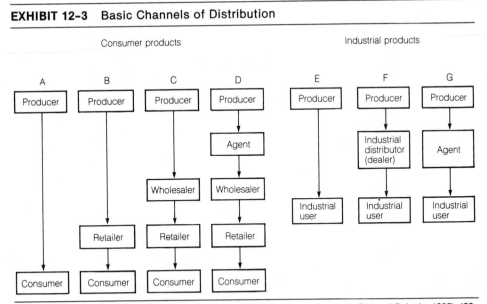

SOURCE: Paul S. Busch and Michael J. Houston, *Marketing* (Homewood, Ill.: Richard D. Irwin, 1985), 458–459.

tion channel consists of *interdependent* and *interrelated* institutions and agencies, functioning as a system or network,[4] who cooperate in their efforts to produce and distribute to end users. The basic channels of distribution for consumer and industrial products are shown in Exhibit 12-3. In addition to the primary types of middlemen or intermediaries shown, various facilitating organizations function as channel specialists. Included in this category are financial institutions, transportation firms, advertising agencies, insurance firms, and other entities. An example of distribution channels for appliances in Japan is shown in Exhibit 12-4. Note the differences in channel arrangements for domestic and imported refrigerators.

Several activities take place in a marketing channel to move the product from producer to end user. Transactions and other communications between buyers and sellers and other channel organizations (e.g., advertising agencies) trigger a number of activities, including information flows, processing and storage, transportation, financial flows, and the transfer of ownership and risk. The real issue involves deciding which organization will be responsible for each activity and selecting the level of service to be provided. Intermediaries offer substantial transactional efficiencies when distribution functions are allocated to appropriate specialists. Consider, for example, the inefficiencies that would occur if an automobile parts manufacturer with a limited line attempted to supply to automobile repair shops directly. A parts distributor can purchase parts from various suppliers and make the items

EXHIBIT 12-4 Distribution Channels for Appliances in Japan

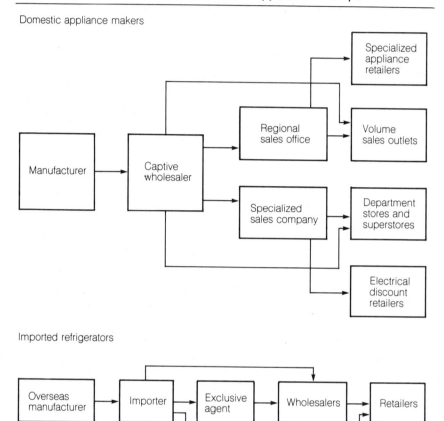

Domestic appliance makers

Imported refrigerators

SOURCE: *Planning for Distribution in Japan* (Tokyo: Japan External Trade Organization, 1982), 37.

available to repair shops and to retailers serving do-it-yourself mechanics.

Once the channel of distribution design is complete and responsibilities for various marketing functions assigned, channel strategy decisions establish guidelines for pricing, advertising, and personal selling strategies. For example, pricing decisions must take into account the requirements and functions of middlemen as well as prevailing practices in the channel. Likewise promotional efforts must be matched to the various channel participants' requirements and capabilities. Consumer products manufacturers often direct advertising to consumers to help *pull* products through distribution channels. Alter-

EXHIBIT 12-5 Components of Physical Distribution Management

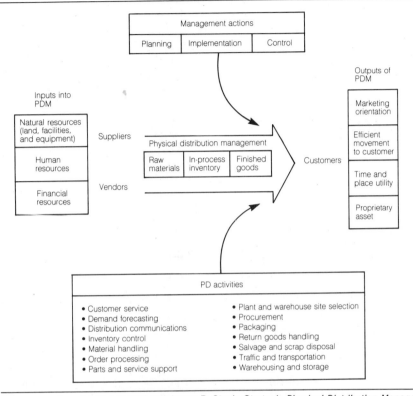

SOURCE: Douglas M. Lambert and James R. Stock, *Strategic Physical Distribution Management* (Homewood, Ill.: Richard D. Irwin, 1982), 10.

natively, promotion may be concentrated on middlemen to help *push* the product through the channel. Intermediaries may also need help in planning their marketing efforts and other supporting activities.

Physical distribution strategy has received considerable attention in recent years from logistics, marketing, operations, and transportation professionals.[5] The focus of concern has been managing the physical distribution of supplies, goods in process, and finished products (see Exhibit 12-5). Whether physical distribution should be integrated with other channel functions or managed as separately is a question that should be examined in the context of each situation, because there are instances where either separate or integrated management approaches may be appropriate. Physical distribution is a key channel function and thus an important part of channel strategy and management. Management should first select the appropriate channel strategy considering the physical distribution function and other essential

EXHIBIT 12-6   Channel of Distribution Strategy

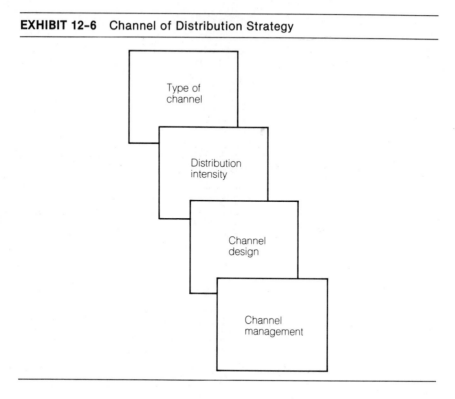

channel activities. Once a strategy is selected, evaluation of physical distribution management alternatives can be done for the channel network. Physical distribution must be accomplished in both direct distribution and channels.

STRATEGIC ALTERNATIVES

Channel strategy consists of interrelated decisions in four areas as shown in Exhibit 12-6. These decisions include selecting the type of channel arrangement, determining the desired intensity of distribution, designing the channel configuration, and managing the channel on an ongoing basis.

Type of Channel Arrangement

In the past, the typical distribution arrangement was a conventional channel:

Goods and services in the American economy have historically been distributed through highly fragmented networks in which *loosely* aligned manufacturers, wholesalers, and retailers have bargained with each other at arm's length, negotiated aggressively over terms of sale, and otherwise behaved autonomously. For the most part, the firms participating in the provisional coalitions have traditionally operated on a small scale and performed a conventionally defined set of marketing functions.[6]

The *conventional channel* is a group of independent organizations, each trying to look out for itself, with little concern for the total performance of the channel.

Managers in an increasing number of firms have realized the advantages to be gained by managing the channel as a coordinated or programmed system of participating organizations. These vertical marketing systems (VMS) dominate the retailing sector today and are significant factors in the industrial products sector. Vertical marketing systems are:

> ... professionally managed and centrally programmed networks preengineered to achieve operating economies and maximum market impact. Stated alternatively ... vertical marketing systems are rationalized and capital intensive networks designed to achieve technological, managerial, and promotional economies through the integration, coordination, and synchronization of marketing flows from points of production to points of ultimate use.[7]

The characteristics of a VMS include:

Management (or coordination) of the entire channel by a particular firm.
Programming and coordination of channel activities and functions.
Participating organizations linked together through ownership, contractual arrangement, or administrative relationship.
Prescribed rules and operating guidelines for all members concerning the functions and responsibilities of each participant.
Management assistance and services given to participants by the firm that is the channel leader.

There are three types of vertical marketing systems: ownership, contractual, and administered. In an ownership arrangement, a single firm in the channel owns all of the participating organizations. A contractual VMS establishes contractual arrangements between participants. In an administered channel, one firm manages the channel through power and influence instead of ownership or contractual ties. Often the administrator is the producer whose product line(s) represents only a portion of the products moving through intermediaries. Proctor & Gamble is the channel administrator for its brands.

Examples of firms utilizing vertical marketing systems are given in Exhibit 12–7. Note that the firm managing the channel is not always a manufacturer. A company may also utilize a combination arrange-

EXHIBIT 12-7 Illustrative Vertical Marketing Systems*

	Product/Service	
	Consumer	Industrial
Ownership	Sherwin-Williams (paint) Sears, Roebuck and Co. (retailing)	W. W. Grainger, Inc. (electric motors and equipment)
Contractual	Ethan Allen, Inc. (furniture) Wendy's International, Inc. (fast foods)	Snap-On Tools, Inc. (mechanics' tools) Deere and Company (farm equipment)
Administered	Lenox Inc. (fine china) Hartmarx Corp. (men's suits)	Butler Manufacturing Co. (metal buildings) Locktite Corp. (industrial adhesives)

*Several of the companies fall into more than one of the categories below.

ment (e.g., ownership and contractual). Distinguishing an administered channel is difficult because there is often no formal way to identify the administered relationship. The difference between it and a conventional channel is more one of degree than of kind.

Some assume that in a vertically coordinated channel, the total system and each participant perform better than in a conventional channel arrangement. This is probably a correct assumption for the managing firm, but it is not clear that each participating firm will also be as well off. The economic returns in vertical marketing systems should be higher than those in conventional channels if the system is properly designed and managed. Yet a coordinated approach forces certain firms in the channel to make certain concessions. There are rules to be followed, control is exercised in various ways, and generally there is less flexibility. Also, some of the requirements of the total system may not be in the best interests of particular participants. Recall the earlier discussion of the development of car megadealers and manufacturers' resulting loss of control of the channel. On the other hand, consider entering a conventional distribution channel with your own hamburger store. Without some special advantage, the competition would be fierce and your financial performance would no doubt fall far short of what it would be if you were a McDonald's franchisee.

Distribution Intensity

We can think of distribution intensity in reference to a geographical area such as a trading area. If management chooses to distribute its product in all or most of the retail outlets in a trading area that might normally carry such a product, it is using an *intensive* distribution approach. In contrast, if only one dealer in the trading area is selected to

---

EXHIBIT 12-8   Distribution Intensity Illustrations

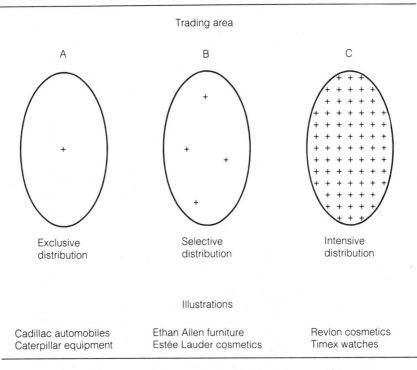

Trading area

A	B	C
Exclusive distribution	Selective distribution	Intensive distribution

Illustrations

Cadillac automobiles	Ethan Allen furniture	Revlon cosmetics
Caterpillar equipment	Estée Lauder cosmetics	Timex watches

---

distribute the product, then management is following an *exclusive* distribution strategy. Thus, a range of distribution intensities is available. *Selective* distribution falls between the two extremes, as shown in Exhibit 12-8, which gives examples of firms using different distribution intensities.

Distribution intensity depends on several factors, some the result of management's preferences, some determined by uncontrollable influences. The major steps in making the decision are:

Identifying the range of feasible distribution intensities taking into account the size and characteristics of the market target, the product, and the requirements likely to be imposed by prospective intermediaries (e.g., they may want exclusive sales territories).

Selection of the alternatives that correspond with the proposed market target and marketing program positioning strategy.

Choice of the alternative that: (1) provides the best strategic fit; (2) meets management's financial performance expectations; and (3) will be sufficiently attractive to intermediaries so that they will properly perform assigned functions.

The type of product and the market target to be served often determine distribution intensity. For example, expensive products, such as a Mercedes automobile, do not require intensive distribution to make contact with able and willing buyers. Moreover, it is unlikely that several dealers in a trading area could survive due to the car's limited sales potential. Ethan Allen's management, in choosing to serve the middle to upper price-quality niche of the market with American traditional furniture, essentially preempted consideration of an intensive distribution strategy.

Firms should adopt a distribution intensity that will match the marketing strategy selected by management. For example, Estée Lauder distributes cosmetics through selected department stores that carry quality products. The firm's management decided not to meet Revlon head-on in the marketplace, and instead concentrated its efforts on a small number of retail outlets. Thus, Estée Lauder avoids huge national advertising expenditures and uses a promotional pricing scheme to help attract customers to retail outlets.

Strategic requirements, preferences, and constraints must be evaluated to determine which intensity level provides the best strategic fit and performance potential. The requirements of intermediaries must also be considered, along with management's desire to control and motivate them. For example, exclusive distribution offers a powerful incentive to intermediaries and also simplifies management and control for the channel leader. But if the exclusive agent is unable (or unwilling) to fully serve the needs of target customers, the manufacturer will not achieve the sales results that could be obtained by using more intermediaries.

Channel Configuration Decision

The next step in selecting a distribution strategy is deciding the number of levels in the channel and the types of intermediaries to be utilized. Alternative distribution networks are shown in Exhibit 12–9, which includes suppliers of manufacturers as well as end users. The channel arrangement and distribution intensity selected provide guidelines for the configuration decision. Several factors influence the channel design decision, including:

1. Customer considerations.
2. Product characteristics.
3. Capabilities and resources of the manufacturer.
4. Functions to be performed.
5. Availability and capabilities of intermediaries.

EXHIBIT 12-9   Distribution Network from a Manufacturer's Point of View

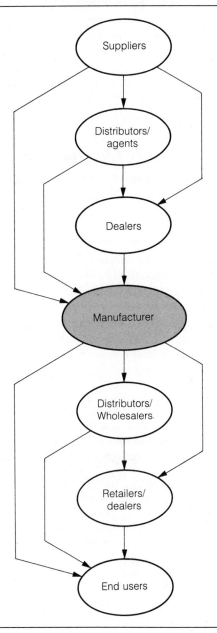

Simplicity is a virtue in channel design. A channel with only one level between the producer and end user simplifies coordination and management. The more complex the channel network, the more challenging it is to accomplish various distribution functions. Nevertheless, the allocation of functions to various channel specialists (e.g., brokers, wholesalers, dealers, financial institutions, transporters) may offer substantial economies of scale. The final choice of a channel design should occur only after management has resolved several important trade-offs.

Channel Management Decisions

After deciding on channel design, specific middlemen must be identified, evaluated, and recruited. Good intermediaries are critical to the implementation of channel strategy. The choice of channel type, distribution intensity, and channel configuration set the stage for many specific channel management activities.

Channel management decisions include the extent and type of support provided to intermediaries, development of operating policies, incentives, choice of promotional programs, and evaluation of results. Once management implements a channel strategy, the ongoing operations of the channel consume most of management's time, since channel structure is not modified frequently. When changes are necessary, they may have serious consequences for some members. For example, in 1984 Sanyo Electric Inc. restructured its distribution network:

> Many longtime Sanyo distributors have been cut off this year, the victims of the company's recent campaign to bolster its already strong position in the audio and visual equipment business. Sanyo's sales rose 70 percent in the first six months of this year, compared with a less than 20 percent gain for the consumer electronics market as a whole, according to a Sanyo spokesman.
>
> A major part of its strategy is to improve its distribution system, which company officials considered cumbersome and disorganized. While many distributors used to sell less than $1 million of Sanyo products a year, they now are expected to sell at least $5 million. Also, for the first time, distributors have exclusive territories. The results: 20 distributors today cover the ground that 90 did a year ago.
>
> Such consolidation isn't unusual; it is one of the hazards distributors face even when they get in on the ground floor with a product line that's bound for success. "The trend among companies is to seek greater control as they grow larger in size," notes a recent study on retail electronics by Venture Development Corp., a Wellesley, Mass., market-research firm.
>
> "When you start to grow, you want total concentration," says Edward W. Adis, a senior vice president of Sony Consumer Products Co., a division of Sony Corp. of America, which reorganized its distribution system 11 years ago, phasing out its independent sales representatives.[8]

Discontinued distributors that are very dependent on a manufacturer's line may have difficulty replacing it with a new line, since most companies already have distribution networks. And remaining distributors may benefit from the granting of exclusive territories and greater sales volume.

Achieving leadership and control in the channel is an important strategic issue. Some form of interorganization management is needed to assure that the channel maintains or achieves satisfactory performance as a competitive entity.[9] One firm may gain power over channel organizations because of specific characteristics (e.g. size), experience, and environmental factors, and its ability to capitalize on such factors. Thus, the channel leader's power depends on the characteristics of the firm and its environment.[10]

SELECTING A CHANNEL STRATEGY

Exhibit 12-10 summarizes the steps in selecting a channel strategy. Management: (1) chooses the channel arrangement to be used, (2) determines the desired intensity of distribution, and (3) decides on channel configuration. One of the first issues in selecting a channel strategy is deciding whether to try managing the channel or to assume a participant role. This choice often depends on how much influence and power a company has. In other words, how much bargaining power can management exert in negotiating with other organizations in the channel system? Management may decide to manage or coordinate operations in the channel of distribution, become a member of a vertically coordinated channel, or become a member of a conventional channel system. Regardless of which position it chooses, management should understand the various factors that affect the channel strategy decision. To gain these insights it must analyze and evaluate the strategic alternatives.

Strategic Analysis

Selecting a channel strategy involves evaluating alternatives at each of the steps shown in Exhibit 12-10. Analysis is complex and situation specific. We will examine the key factors that affect the channel strategy decision, illustrating how they are used in strategy analysis.

Access to Market Target. Management's choice of a market target must be closely coordinated with channel strategy since the channel is the link between suppliers and end users. The market target decision cannot actually be finalized until channel strategy is also established. Information about customers in the market target can guide management in screening out unsuitable channel strategy alternatives.

EXHIBIT 12-10   Steps in Channel Strategy Selection

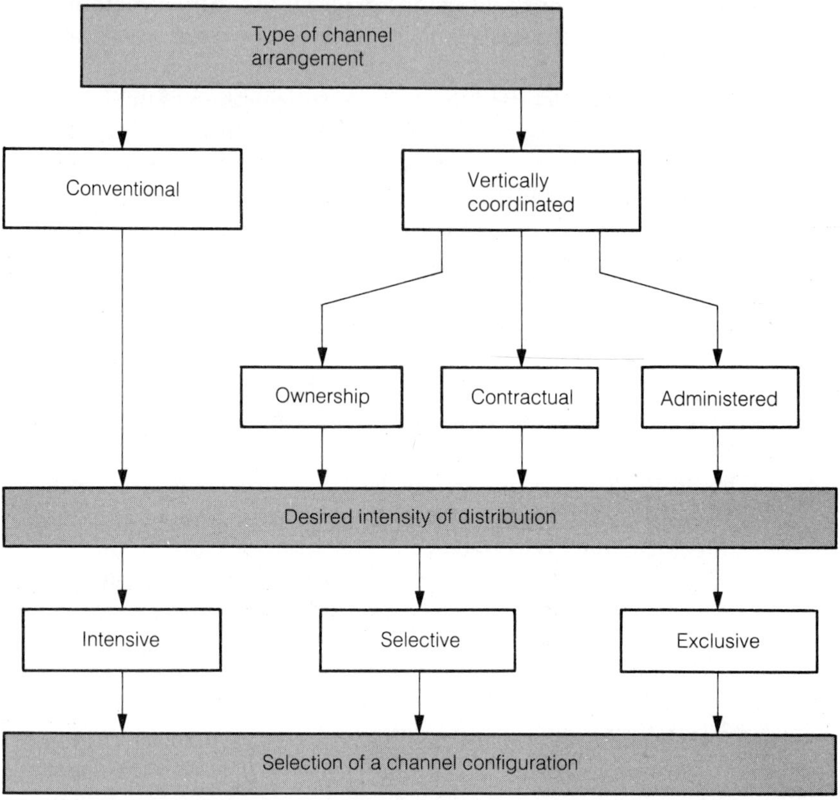

Channel Functions.   Several functions are performed in moving products from producers to end users. These include:

Buying and selling
Transportation
Financing
Processing and storage
Advertising and sales promotion
Pricing
Risk-bearing
Information flows
Servicing and repair

Buying and selling activities by marketing intermediaries are necessary to reduce the number of transactions for producers and end users. Transportation eliminates the locational gap between buyers and sellers, accomplishing the physical distribution function. Financing facilitates the exchange function. Processing and storage of goods involves breaking large quantities into individual orders, maintaining inventory, and assembling orders for shipment. Advertising and sales promotion communicate product availability, location, and features. Pricing provides the basis of exchange between buyer and seller. Reduction of risk is accomplished through mechanisms such as insurance, return policies, and futures trading. Communications between buyers and sellers include personal selling contacts, written orders and confirmations, and other information flows. Finally, servicing and repairs are essential for many types of products.

The functions needed and the organizations to be responsible for each function are major factors in channel strategy. Steel service centers illustrate functional specialization.[11] These firms buy steel coil or bar in bulk from steel producers. They cut and shape the steel at lower costs than the producers and the centers can react quicker than steel mills to customer needs. This responsiveness helps reduce the buyer's inventory. Steel service centers are performing very well compared to the steel producers. These cost-effective middlemen are expected to continue to take over more processing from the producers.

Financial Considerations. Two financial questions affect channel strategy. First, are resources available for launching management's preferred strategy? A small producer may not have the money to build a distribution network. Second, the firm must estimate the revenue-cost impact of alternative channel strategies. This task grows more complex as the channel network expands to include several levels and types of organizations. Exhibit 12–11 illustrates how revenues and costs vary among channel organizations and provides a comparative financial analysis for a fast-food wholesaler (Golden State Foods Corporation) and a full-line food service wholesaler (S. E. Rykoff & Company). Most of Golden State's revenues are from McDonald's restaurants. Firms should estimate the impact of channel strategy alternatives on their financial performance. Typically analyses include cash flow, income, return on investment, and operating capital requirements (Chapter 4).

Other Considerations. Additional factors may influence the channel strategy decision. Management should consider its desire for flexibility (for example, ease of change) in channel design and the extent of control it would like over other channel participants. A conventional channel provides little opportunity for control by a particular firm yet flexibility in channel relationships.

Legal and regulatory constraints also may affect channel strategies in such areas as pricing, exclusive dealing, and division of markets.[12]

EXHIBIT 12-11 Comparative Financial Analysis, 1978: Golden State Foods Corporation and S. E. Rykoff & Company

Component	Golden State Foods Corporation	S. E. Rykoff & Company
Current size ($ millions)		
Net sales	$272.4	$241.7
Net profit	2.5	3.4
Total assets	34.6	68.9
Employees	649	1,670
Balance sheet composition		
Current assets		
Cash	10.1%	1.7%
Accounts receivables	25.6	44.9
Inventory	26.2	37.5
All other	2.4	3.3
Total	64.3	87.4
Fixed assets	35.4	12.6
All other assets	0.3	0.0
Total assets	100.0%	100.0%
Total asset size	$34,632,000	$68,979,000
Current liabilities		
Notes payable	1.4%	12.5%
Accounts payable	41.1	16.0
All other	0.5	8.8
Total	43.0	37.3
Long-term liabilities	16.3	13.6
Net worth	38.8	48.1
Total liabilities and net worth	100.0%	100.0%
Liquidity profile		
Current assets/current liabilities (times)	1.5×	2.3×
Current assets (minus inventory)/current liabilities (times)	0.9×	1.3×
Cash/current liabilities (percent)	23.6%	4.5%
Net profits (before interest and taxes)/ interest (times)	8.8×	5.7×
Growth potential profile		
Net profits (after dividends)/net working capital (percent)	34.5%	6.4%
Net profits (after dividends)/net worth (percent)	12.8%	6.7%
Net profits (before interest and taxes)/total assets (percent)	15.0%	11.1%
Accounts payable/inventory	157.0%	42.8%

SOURCE: Reprinted by permission from J. Robert Foster, "Supplying the Eating Out Revolution: Strategic Trends in Food Service Wholesaling," in *Contemporary Issues in Marketing Channels,* ed. R. F. Lusch and P. H. Zinszer (Norman: University of Oklahoma, 1979), p. 150. Data are from Company annual reports and J. R. Foster's calculations.

Strategy at Different Channel Levels

Until now our discussion of channel strategy has focused largely on the producer's viewpoint. Distributors like steel service centers are also concerned with channel strategies, and in some instances they may exercise primary control over channel operations. Sears is a powerful force in its channels. Large food wholesalers like Wetterau are major factors in their channels of distribution. Moreover, decisions by wholesalers, distributors, brokers, retailers, and other intermediaries about what manufacturers' products to carry often affect the performance of all channel participants.

Channel strategy can be examined from any level in the distribution network. The major distinction lies in the point of view (retailer, wholesaler, producer) used in developing the strategy. Intermediaries may have fewer alternatives to consider than producers, and thus less flexibility in channel strategy. Nevertheless, they should look at channel strategy on an active rather than passive basis.

STRATEGIC TRENDS IN DISTRIBUTION

Several important trends are occurring in distribution channels, creating opportunities and threats for channel participants. Both institutions and patterns of distribution are experiencing shorter and shorter life cycles. The fast-food industry reached maturity in less than a decade. Management must appraise channel strategy regularly to maintain desired performance levels and to avoid problems caused by changing external conditions.

Emergence of New Distribution Concepts

Several new distribution concepts emerged in the 1980s including superstores, warehouse buying clubs, and various specialty retailers. The retailers listed in Exhibit 12–12 are relative newcomers to the retail sector, and their financial performance is far above most traditional retailers. Many of these aggressive new retailers pose major threats for established firms.

The success of warehouse buying clubs that cater to small businesses and job-related groups (e.g., government employees) demonstrates how new distribution concepts can affect existing channels. The Price Company, which was founded in 1976, is now the leading firm in this new type of distribution, with fiscal 1985 sales of $1.8 billion. The Price Club's explosive growth in sales and profits has attracted a dozen competitors including Zayre, Wal-Mart, and Pay 'n Save.[13]

EXHIBIT 12-12 Performance Profile of a New Wave Retailer (1982)

Type of Retailer	Strategic Profit Model Ratios				
	Net Profits / Net Sales (percent)	Net Sales / Total Assets (times)	Net Profits / Total Assets (percent)	Total Assets / Net Worth (times)	Net Profits / Net Worth (percent)
Hobby and craft centers	7.2%	2.2×	15.8%	1.8×	28.5%
Home decorating specialty stores	7.0	1.8	12.6	2.1	26.5
Paint and home decorating supermarkets	7.4	1.8	13.3	1.8	24.0
Super hardware stores	5.8	2.7	15.7	1.6	25.1
Super drugstores	3.6	4.0	14.4	1.8	25.9
Combination stores	2.5	5.1	12.8	2.1	26.8
Upscale discounters	3.2	4.1	13.1	2.0	26.2

SOURCE: Distribution Research Program, University of Oklahoma.

Buying clubs can be found in about half of the 100 largest markets in the United States. The typical Price Club store has 100,000 square feet and stocks 4,000 items—one tenth the items in a K mart store. Limited selection, low overhead, and $25 membership fees enable the warehouse clubs to operate on 10 percent gross margins. Business customers typically comprise 10 percent of a club's membership but represent half of total purchases.

Vertical marketing systems for services is another new distribution concept. Moving into previously fragmented industries, corporate and contractual chains have emerged in medical and dental services, lawn care (ChemLawn), travel services (American Express), real estate brokerage, and book distribution (B. Dalton Booksellers). These strong and efficient vertical marketing systems are pressuring small independent retailers. Similar consolidation trends have occurred in public accounting, where the major "big eight" CPA firms dominate the industry.

Expanding Importance of Channel Power

Gillette is one of several companies using channel-driven product strategies. These firms are developing and acquiring products that can be marketed through their existing channels. In 1984 Gillette paid $190 million in cash to acquire toothbrush maker Oral-B Laboratories from Cooper Laboratories.[14] Oral-B is the market leader in the United States and is also strong overseas. This product line addition indicates Gillette's continuing interest in expanding its mix of consumer nondurables that can be distributed through its current channels to mass merchants and food and drug retailers. Blades and razors continue to be the primary thrust of Gillette's product strategy, accounting for one third of 1984 revenues and two thirds of operating profits. The company has also eliminated from its product mix unprofitable lines such as its Cricket disposable lighter business, which was sold to Swedish Match AB in 1985. Toiletries and cosmetics represent Gillette's second largest segment. National distribution of White Rain Shampoo began in 1985, and a line of 10 unisex toiletries, under the brand name Good News, was being test marketed in Seattle.

Channel-Driven Product Strategies. Consumer products firms' corporate and marketing decisions are influenced by distribution channel considerations for several reasons. A wider range of products moving through the same channel network enhances bargaining power with middlemen. Operating efficiencies can be gained in sales and distribution costs. Market trends are easier to spot. And channels that are moving a wide range of successful existing products also facilitate new product introductions.

Multiplex Distribution.   Another important trend in distribution is the use of multiple channels to gain access to end user consumers. Dayton Hudson in retailing and Hartmarx in apparel manufacturing are good examples. Dayton Hudson markets through its traditional department stores, through its discount retailers (Target and Mervyn's), and through specialty stores such as B. Dalton. The unifying component of Dayton Hudson's strategy is merchandising and the merchant orientation of top management.[15] In the mid-1960s, Dayton Hudson recognized the mass merchandising trend and moved into discount retailing through Target and more recently Mervyn's to promote the latest fashion and the best deal.

Power May Create Conflict.   When one firm holds the balance of power in a channel, conflicts and risks may develop for other channel members. The problem is illustrated by Haagen-Dazs ice cream distributors. In 1985 Haagen-Dazs, a Pillsbury subsidiary, began buying some of its independent distributors in southern California because they were not performing up to corporate expectations.[16] One distributor in San Diego was forced to sell his business at a price lower than he considered acceptable because the company had the right to take over the business of his major customer. Haagen-Dazs has great control over its 275 distributors. Thus, the channel leader has power that sometimes results in conflicts and the exit of participants, regardless of the good intentions of channel members. Haagen-Dazs, for example, does not want its distributors carrying another super-premium ice cream brand and will cut its ties with distributors who do so. (One such distributor filed a restraint of trade suit.)

Direct Marketing

The explosive growth of direct marketing during the last decade represents an important trend in distribution. Customer contact is made by mail or phone. These channels include catalog retailers such as Spiegel and L. L. Bean, phone and media retailers, and electronic shopping. These direct marketing methods attract business away from conventional retailers. Convenience buying has been stimulated by today's lifestyles (two-income families, limited leisure time, high incomes), the ease of shopping via catalogs and toll-free phone numbers, and effective marketing by the firms involved.

Direct marketing which now accounts for 14 percent of all retail transactions, should account for 20 percent of sales by 1990. A wide variety of firms serve this market. Sears is the market leader, followed by J. C. Penney. Many small firms target special segments. Targeting is essential in building a profitable business. Consider this strategy:

Selling sports-car ski racks in Minnesota? Match the list of motorists who own cars that will accommodate ski racks (readily available from the state's department of motor vehicles) with the list of ZIP Codes for relatively affluent areas (from the Census Bureau) with the list of *Ski Magazine* subscribers. All this may cost as much as 15 cents per name, but you buy darn good prospects.[17]

Using an existing customer list facilitates entry into direct marketing. (American Express has been very successful in using its credit card membership list), but the existing customer base must be willing to purchase by mail. Pier 1, the speciality import retailer, found that many of its existing customers did not use catalogs to purchase products. Unable to build a profitable catalog business, Pier 1 terminated its direct mail venture in 1985, two years after it was launched. If management had conducted more extensive customer and prospect research before launching the catalog venture, Pier 1 might not have moved into the direct mail market.

Distribution Productivity

Marketing intermediaries are developing a strategic advantage by improving distribution productivity. Recall in the chapter-opening illustration that two of Wetterau's five basic strategies for the future are facility improvement and increasing productivity. American Airlines' Saber reservation and information system has given the air carrier an important advantage over competing airlines. The firm's data bank can track reservations to analyze load factors and other areas important in improving distribution productivity.

Durr-Fillauer Medical, Inc., a medium-sized drug wholesaler, is concentrating on improving operating efficiencies.[18] The wholesale drug division distribute products to 2,000 independent and chain drugstores and hospital pharmacies in the southeast. In 1984, 96 percent of the division's orders were received electronically, and selling, general, and administrative expenses declined to 4.6 percent of sales compared to 5.1 in 1983. Other efforts to increase channel efficiency and customer satisfaction include the Priceguard™ total marketing program, which provides merchandising assistance and advertising support to independent drugstores and smaller chains. Interestingly, wholesalers accounted for 65 percent of all pharmaceuticals distributed for human consumption in 1983, an 8 percent rise since 1980.

Monitoring changes taking place in distribution, and incorporating distribution strategy considerations into the strategic planning process are essential strategic marketing activities.

CONCLUDING NOTE

The channel of distribution is comprised of the network of organizations that connect the producer with the end users of the firm's goods or services. A strong distribution channel provides a company with an important strategic edge over competition. Distribution strategy represents a crucial step in deciding how to reach market targets. The choice between direct distribution to end users and the use of intermediaries is guided by end user needs and characteristics, product characteristics, and financial and control considerations.

To distribute through middlemen, firms must select the type of channel to be used, determine distribution intensity, design the channel configuration, and manage various aspects of channel operations. Channels are either conventional or vertical marketing systems (VMS). VMS is the dominant channel for consumer products. In a VMS, one firm owns all organizations in the channel, a contractual arrangement exists between organizations, or one channel member is in charge channel administration. Firms must also decide on intensity of distribution and channel configuration design. Channel management includes implementing the channel strategy and coordinating channel operations.

Selecting a channel strategy begins when management decides whether to try managing the channel or assume a participant role. It must use strategic analysis to identify and evaluate strategy alternatives. Several factors should be evaluated, including access to the market target, channel functions to be performed, financial considerations, and legal and control constraints. The channel strategy adopted establishes several guidelines for price and promotion strategies.

Several important strategic trends are occurring in distribution channels, creating both opportunities and threats for participants. These include the emergence of new distribution concepts, the expanding importance of channel power, the explosive growth of direct marketing channels, and increased emphasis on distribution productivity.

NOTES

1. Wetterau Incorporated, *1985 Annual Report*, 4–5.
2. John Marcom Jr., "Consumers Are Taking a Back Seat As Computer Stores Court Business," *The Wall Street Journal*, July 26, 1985, 21.
3. Amal Nag, "Car Megadealers Loosen Detroit's Tight Rein," *The Wall Street Journal*, July 1, 1985, 6.
4. Louis W. Stern and Adel I. El-Ansary, *Marketing Channels*, 2nd ed.
   (Englewood Cliffs, N.J.: Prentice-Hall, 1982), 3–4.
5. See, for example, Douglas M. Lambert and James R. Stock, *Strategic Physical Distribution Management* (Homewood, Ill.: Richard D. Irwin, 1982).
6. Bert C. McCammon, Jr., "Perspectives for Distribution Programming," in *Vertical Marketing Systems*, ed. Louis P. Bucklin (Glenview, Ill.: Scott, Foresman, 1970), 43.

7. Ibid., 43.
8. Jacob M. Schlesinger, "Sanyo Sales Strategy Illustrates Problems of Little Distributors," *The Wall Street Journal,* September 10, 1984, 31.
9. For a complete discussion of channel management see Stern and El-Ansary, *Marketing Channels,* Chapter 9.
10. Michael Etgar, "Channel Environment and Channel Leadership," *Journal of Marketing Research,* February 1977, 70.
11. Elizabeth Sangler, "Proving Their Mettle," *Barron's,* July 9, 1984, 13 and 20.
12. See Chapter 8 of Stern and El-Ansary, *Marketing Channels.*
13. "Boom Times In a Bargain-Hunter's Paradise," *Business Week,* March 11, 1985, 116 and 120.
14. Frank Campanella, "Looking Sharp," *Barron's,* April 29, 1985, 41–42.
15. M. Howard Gelfand, "Dayton Hudson Keeps its Vision," *Advertising Age,* July 9, 1984, 4, 46–47.
16. Sanford L. Jacobs, "Haagan-Dazs Distributors Find Big Profits, but Little Security," *The Wall Street Journal,* November 18, 1985, 33.
17. Richard Greene, "A Boutique in Your Living Room," *Forbes,* May 7, 1984, 91.
18. Durr-Fillauer Medical, Inc., *1984 Annual Report,* 6–7.

QUESTIONS FOR REVIEW AND DISCUSSION

1. Using the examples of Tandy Corp. (Radio Shack) and IBM in personal computers, discuss why and how product branding and distribution strategies are closely related.

2. Distribution analysts indicate that break-even on sales for supermarkets is about 98 percent. What influence does this high break-even level have on supermarkets' diversification into delis, cheese shops, seafood shops, and nonfood areas?

3. Why do some large, financially strong manufacturers choose not to own their dealers, and, instead, establish contractual relationships with them?

4. What are the advantages and limitations of the use of multiple channels of distribution by a manufacturer?

5. Discuss some likely trends in the distribution of automobiles during the 1980s, including the possibility of a shift away from exclusive distribution arrangements.

6. During the early 1980s, Radio Shack began opening retail computer stores rather than depending on existing electronics stores to serve the small computer market. Discuss the logic of this strategy, pointing out its strengths and shortcomings.

7. Identify and discuss some of the factors that should increase the trend toward vertical marketing systems.

8. Why might a manufacturer choose to enter a conventional channel of distribution?

9. Suppose the management of a raw material supplier is interested in performing a financial analysis of a distribution channel comprised of manufacturers, distributors, and retailers. Outline an approach for doing the analysis.

10. Discuss some of the important strategic issues facing a drug manufacturer in deciding whether to distribute veterinary prescriptions and over-the-counter products through veterinarians or distributors.

STRATEGIC APPLICATION 12-1

APPLE COMPUTER INC.

Apple Computer Inc. is putting into place marketing programs aimed at recharging its stalled business.

The actions follow by two months a sweeping corporate reorganization and come on the heels of Apple's first quarterly loss as a public company.

Computer retailers say that Apple, the nation's second-largest computer maker, last week quietly introduced a series of incentives apparently aimed at encouraging dealers to push its machines more aggressively in the critical back-to-school season.

The sales incentives, though likely to put some pressure on Apple's profit, could ease long-strained relations between the company and some of its bigger dealers. Dealers had complained that profit margins on Apple machines were too tight. According to Future Computing Inc., a market research concern, the number of dealers considering dropping Apple products has risen since January.

New Bulk Discounts

In Cupertino, Calif., Apple declined to comment on the new incentives, but dealers say they have been told of new wholesale discounts of about 4% on bulk orders of certain Apple products. In addition, the company will contribute $1,500 to marketing programs for dealers who order six or more of its Macintosh computers.

The incentive programs would primarily benefit such large computer-store chains as Computerland Corp. and Computercraft Corp. A number of smaller dealers fear the incentives would hurt them by giving an edge to their larger competitors.

"There are only about a half-dozen big dealers who are going to get anything out of the program," said John Vito, owner of a five-store chain, Computer Stores Northwest, based in Corvallis, Ore. "The rest of the industry desperately needs some encouragement to move Apple's machines."

However, dealers are still awaiting word of Apple's plans to promote sales during the Christmas season. That consumer spending spree is the most important sales period for the personal computer industry.

InfoCorp, a market research concern, estimates that 40% of the industry's $39 billion in annual sales are made in that period. With so much at stake, dealers like to start planning for the Christmas rush as early as July. Their plans—such as picking a computer for a display window or designing an advertising campaign—can play an important part in boosting a computer maker's sales.

"Every dealer is trying to put his finger on which computer is going to be *the* product this Christmas," said Rick Inatome, president and chief executive officer of Inacomp Computers Inc., a Troy, Mich.-based chain of 53 stores. "Our marketing department is meeting three times a week to figure out which product to push."

But some dealers privately worry that management turmoil within Apple in recent months, as well as the company's subsequent restructuring and the dismissal of 1,200 workers in a cost-cutting campaign, could be hampering its ability to form a marketing strategy. "Frankly, I don't know who is left at Apple to call," said one dealer.

In remarks to securities analysts last week, John Sculley, president and chief executive, indicated that Apple expects a poorer Christmas season this year because of the current industrywide slump. He said the company wouldn't undertake advertising as extravagant as last year's Christmas blitz, which cost an estimated $17 million. The ad cutback further worries some dealers.

"Cutting back advertising is a smart move when your back is against the wall, and, in the short run, Apple probably won't be hurt too much," said Jeffrey McKeever, president and chief executive of MicroAge Computer Stores, a 151-outlet chain based in Tempe, Ariz. "But in the long run, if money isn't restored, Apple will lose market share."

Apple's Software Links

In other developments, Apple has moved to strengthen ties with companies that produce software and computer accessories, as it promised it would.

"In the past, there would be technical changes in (Apple) products, and Apple wouldn't get around to telling you for awhile," said Grant Jasmin, president of Advanced Logic Systems Inc., a Sunnyvale, Calif., software and hardware developer. "Now, Apple is getting a lot more concerned about communications."

For a time, Apple had shunned some software companies, and many turned to producing programs for machines made by International Business Machines Corp., the largest personal computer maker. The subsequent flood of accessories and software helped propel IBM sales.

Even now, some of these outside companies say Apple's efforts to improve relations have fallen short. Stephen Beck, president of Bech-Tech Corp., a Berkeley, Calif., concern that makes an accessory that increases the memory of the Macintosh, complains that even as Apple's marketing managers entertain suggestions of cooperation, Apple's legal department warns that installing the accessory violates the computer's warranty.

Apple still may be feeling aftereffects of its recent reorganization. In June, the company announced a restructuring that resulted in the closure of three

plants and the dismissal of one-fifth of its work force. Last month, it posted a $17.2 million quarterly loss, reflecting a $40.3 million one-time charge for the restructuring. The company had its first public stock offering in 1980.

The reorganization restored some stability and direction to Apple, which had suffered from bitter infighting. And it apparently dispelled a debilitating rivalry between the two divisions responsible for manufacturing and marketing the Macintosh and the company's other main product line, the Apple II computer.

Still, sources close to Apple say engineering efforts on a computer due out next year have run into snags, in part because of a lack of direction and, as one former manager put it, "the new bunker mentality" among employees who survived the layoffs.

In particular, there have been hitches in work to put the final touches on Project Phoenix—the code name for the new Apple II computer—because of committee indecision over such issues as the design of the computer's plastic case, these sources say. Most of the important design decisions have been made, however, and not all engineers are frustrated by the design process.

More than two dozen top engineers have left Apple this year, some complaining that their projects were being ignored. And the company has been without a engineering director for months. "There is no strong hand to guide development," said one engineer who recently left for another company.

Sources familiar with the new Apple II say it will have a 16-bit microprocessor as its heart, increasing the computer's speed. The current Apple II has an 8-bit processor. The new machine will have a 3.5-inch disk drive with 800,000 characters of storage, more than a fivefold increase. The added storage and speed will encourage software developers to write more business programs for the machine.

Meanwhile, work continues on Project Jonathan, the next-generation Macintosh. Sources say engineers are designing a machine capable of color graphics and equipped with a modem allowing the computer to transmit data over telephone lines.

Analysts said they don't expect Mr. Jobs's sale to erode investor confidence in Apple. "If a chairman of a company who played a key operating role started selling stock, that would signal that something's going on ... but I don't think this sale reflects anything about Apple's prospects," said Michele Preston, a computer analyst at L. F. Rothschild, Unterberg, Towbin.

Two other Apple insiders recently sold big chunks of the company's stock. Vice Chairman A. C. Markkula Jr., the company's second-largest inside holder, sold 500,000 shares in January for $30.125 a share, or $15.1 million. The sale brought Mr. Markkula's stake down to slightly less than five million shares, or about 8% of the company's common shares outstanding. In late 1984, Steve Wozniak, who founded Apple with Mr. Jobs and for years was the company's third-largest inside holder, sold more than three million shares, nearly all his Apple stake, for $70 million. Mr. Wozniak left the company in February.

Separately, Apple said it named Peter Lycurgus, 30 years old, a manager. The company said he will have responsibility for developing strategies for sales programs with dealers and for analyzing geographic issues. He is the former manager of business planning and development of Pepsi U.S.A., a division of PepsiCo Inc.

Mr. Lycurgus is the second Pepsi executive to join Apple since John Sculley, former president of PepsiCo.'s Pepsi-Cola Co. unit, was named Apple president and chief executive officer in 1983.

SOURCE: Patricia A. Bellew, "Apple Computer Intensifies Marketing." Reprinted by permission of *The Wall Street Journal.* © Dow Jones & Company, Inc., August 2, 1985, 4. All rights reserved.

DISCUSSION QUESTIONS

1. Identify and discuss the important issues concerning channels of distribution in the marketing of personal computers.
2. Critically evaluate Apple's distribution strategy. Compare it with IBM, Commodore, Tandy, and other key competitors.
3. What suggestions can you make to Apple's management to help avoid conflicts with their retailers?
4. Recommend a distribution strategy for Apple, including the type of channel system, the distributor intensity, and other distribution strategy guidelines.

STRATEGIC APPLICATION 12-2

FACELIFTERS FRANCHISE SYSTEM

A kitchen remodeling company has begun franchising nationwide to capture a larger share of the booming $5.7 billion kitchen rehab market.

Facelifters Franchise System, an International Cabinet Co. subsidiary that has operated 30 national dealerships since 1978, started franchising in January to create a national kitchen remodeling network. Elk Grove Village, Ill.-based Facelifters so far has opened a franchise in Detroit, two in Chicago and one in Baton Rouge, La. Another in Mount Vernon, N.Y., is expected to open this month.

The company, which is negotiating to go public, hopes to raise $3 million to $5 million to carry out its program, which includes opening two types of franchises and investing about $1 million in advertising and marketing.

As opposed to dealerships, franchises give the company more control and guarantee that kitchen remodeling is the primary business, said Michael Busch, International Cabinet vice president, Facelifters' chief operating officer.

Mr. Busch is a franchise specialist who founded Medicine Shoppe International, a 500-store pharmacy franchise.

To reach possible franchisees, *Facelifters* advertises in *The Wall Street Journal* and *USA Today* and is considering running TV ads next year.

This year, $120,000 was budgeted to attract franchisees and that figure is expected to increase to $200,000 in 1986.

For consumer advertising, Facelifters' service centers, which are located in major markets to service area franchises, will handle print in-house. Seeger & Associates, Pittsburgh, handles broadcast.

TV, radio and print ads list a toll-free number, which can be dialed to set up a Facelifters' appointment or receive a brochure.

Mr. Busch says by pooling its resources in advertising, each franchise gets more exposure—which is imperative since franchises depend on scheduled appointments, rather than walk-ins.

Facelifters specializes in quick-service remodeling and charges between $1,500 and $20,000 for each remodeling project, which is generally completed in two days. Franchises offer about 250 different types and styles of counter laminates and kitchen cabinets, which are made by International Cabinet Co.'s Brooklyn plant.

The company intends to open two types of franchises. The traditional franchise will require a $25,000 franchise fee, plus $25,000 to $75,000 to open a facility and hire installers.

The second type requires about $20,000 less capital because the franchisee opens only a showroom and receives all his services, from telemarketing to ordering to installing a showroom, from Facelifters service center.

The company now is converting its Elk Grove Village prototype store into a service center and expects to open about eight Facelifters franchises in the area. Within the next six months, the company intends to open three more service centers in markets with a population of two million or more.

Facelifters views its only national competitor as Sears, which has offered kitchen remodeling services within its home remodeling department since 1950. Sears kitchen remodeling, however, represents only a small portion of the mass merchandiser's marketing effort, and a spokeswoman said the chain has only about a 3% market share.

The rest of the market is divided among small contractors, a few local franchises and kitchen specialty stores, said a spokeswoman for the National Assn. of the Remodeling Industry, Arlington, Va.

Facelifters plans to open 60 to 80 franchises within the next three years, bringing the company's total retail revenues to $40 million to $50 million, said Mr. Busch. The company projects $15 million in retail revenues for 1985.

If industry projections are correct, International Cabinet Co.'s Facelifters has a good chance of capturing territory that has yet to be tapped by other large corporations, such as K mart Corp or J. C. Penney Co.

Industry projections are that, by 1989, kitchen remodeling will represent a $17.6 billion industry.

NARI said the professional kitchen remodeling industry has been growing by about 12% to 17% annually, and should reach $6.9 billion by yearend.

"The industry is growing at a phenomenal rate," said the NARI spokeswoman.

"With the high cost of housing and more baby-boomers having kids, people are thinking twice about moving if they don't like a feature of their home. Now they tend to remodel."

SOURCE: Pat Winters, "Facelifters Opens Eyes to Franchises", *Advertising Age,* September 16, 1985, 108S.

DISCUSSION QUESTIONS

1. What criteria do buyers use to select a kitchen remodeling service?

2. What marketing capabilities are likely to be important to Facelifters in gaining a profitable position in the kitchen remodeling market?

3. What advantages can Facelifters offer buyers, compared to local independents and contractors?

4. Critically evaluate the two types of franchises that the company intends to open.

5. Discuss several of the important issues in building a successful franchise system.

CHAPTER 13

Price Strategy

The pricing of goods and services is playing an increasingly important strategic role in many firms as a consequence of deregulation, intense competition, slow growth, and the opportunity for firms to strengthen market position. The aggressive pricing strategies of air passenger carriers is illustrative. Most visible are the tactical actions of price cuts and special promotions. Underlying the maze of discounts offered by competing carriers are price strategies guided by computers that track travel patterns.[1] This increasing sophistication is allowing airline price strategists to confine new bargain rates to selected cities, seats, and shorter time periods. For example, fares to two cities the same distance away on the same airline under the same travel restrictions may differ by as much as 200 to 300 percent! One analyst uses the analogy that in the past airlines used an ax to cut fares whereas today they use a scalpel. The effectiveness of price strategies will have an important effect on the financial performance of airlines. The rate of growth in air travel has slowed. Information technology is enabling carriers to keep fare wars out of many cities, although in places like Denver, Dallas, Hawaii, Newark, and Washington heavy discounting persists. In 1985, American Airlines offered huge discounts of up to 85 percent for traveling on Thanksgiving Day and returning the next Saturday.

This chapter considers the factors involved in developing a price strategy. Pricing decisions can have explosive and far-reaching consequences. Once implemented, it may be difficult to alter a price strategy—particularly if the change calls for a significant increase. And, improper pricing actions can land executives in jail. Price has many possible uses as a strategic instrument in corporate and marketing strategy. During the last decade, price gained a much more active role in strategy. This revolution in pricing practices has led to more flexible price strategies and tactics, as illustrated by air carriers' use of price in the mid-1980s. The underlying forces contributing to this departure from a gradually and predictably changing price structure were correctly forecast a decade ago by the editors of *Business Week* magazine:

> . . . two recessions in five years, price controls introduced by a Republican administration, and double-digit inflation have undermined the predictability and stability of growth as planning assumptions. And the restrictive policy reaction to inflationary forces—particularly in oil prices in 1974—sealed the doom of the old price strategy, by producing slow growth and excess industrial capacity around the world.[2]

In early 1986 the world-wide oil glut led to major declines in oil prices, creating new pressures on pricing strategies. Some of the consequences were favorable, while others created new threats for the firms affected by oil prices. Pricing policies and structure must be developed to properly establish the role of price in marketing strategy, while retaining enough flexibility to respond to changing conditions.

First we examine the strategic role of price in marketing program positioning strategy and discuss several key influences on price strategy. Next an approach to strategic situation analysis for pricing decisions is presented, and several applications are provided to illustrate the nature and scope of analysis activities. A discussion of selecting a price strategy follows. Finally, guidelines for establishing pricing policies and structure are considered.

STRATEGIC ROLE OF PRICE

Companies use price in many different ways in their marketing strategies:

> Until the early 1980s Caterpillar, the giant construction equipment maker, was able to price at a 10 percent to 20 percent premium over competition in the United States and throughout the world.[3] Foreign competition, a slowdown in construction, and a strong U.S. dollar drastically altered the situation. Komatsu Ltd. began to gain market share with lower prices, quality equipment, and a strong commitment to customer service. Caterpillar responded with competitive prices and aggressive marketing, and by slashing expenses and negotiating with labor to lower costs.
>
> DeBeers comes close to monopolizing the world diamond market . . . Why should a monopolist worry when prices are rising? For two reasons: (1) By breaking the old pattern of steady appreciation, the recent price explosion may have prepared the way for the first bust in diamond prices in modern history, and (2) it has weakened DeBeers' control of the market— DeBeers is run for long-term prosperity, not short-term profits.[4] (DeBeers,

---

EXHIBIT 13-1   How Price Fits into Marketing Program
Positioning Strategy

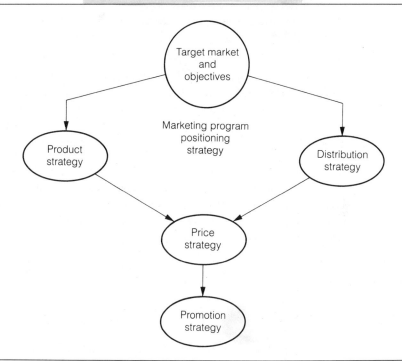

---

for many years, has used regular and controlled price increases to offer consumers price appreciation potential and to assure high profits for the company.) An excess supply of diamonds in the early 1980s weakened De-Beers' control over prices.

A designer wool coat will more than triple in price between the runway and sales floor. Designer royalties average 7 percent of manufacturer's price, $407; customs duties add another 30 percent. The store's share of the $1,345 retail price is 59 percent.[5]

As shown in Exhibit 13–1, how price fits into marketing strategy depends on the target market, the product, and the distribution strategies management selects. These strategic choices set important guidelines for both price and promotion strategies.

Guide to Strategic Price Planning

Developing a price strategy consists of:

Analyzing the strategic situation.
Setting the specific objectives to be accomplished by the price strategy.

Deciding how to position price within the range of feasible prices.
Establishing whether price will be used as an active or passive element in the marketing program.
Developing policies and structure for guiding pricing decisions.
Implementing and managing the strategy.

These decisions are part of several price planning activities, as shown in Exhibit 13-2. Price strategy is influenced by the requirements and constraints imposed by product and distribution strategies (Step 1). Situation analysis (Steps 2 and 3) of the product-market, costs, competition, and legal and ethical factors provides a basis for estimating how much flexibility exists in price strategy. These steps lead to setting price objectives (Step 4) and identifying and evaluating alternative price positions (Step 5). The selection of a price positioning strategy is followed by choosing how active or passive price will be in the marketing program (Step 6). The last step in strategy formulation is developing the policies and structure (Step 7) for setting specific prices for the products in the mix. Finally, the strategy must be implemented and managed to deliver the results expected from the strategy (Step 8). Each of the steps shown in Exhibit 13-2 is examined in the remainder of the chapter.

Responsibility for price strategy varies between organizations—it is not always assigned to the chief marketing executive. But there is some danger that marketing strategy will be fragmented if pricing is not part of the chief marketing executive's responsibilities. Price decisions must be coordinated with other decisions in marketing program positioning. Operations, financial, and other executives should, of course, participate in strategic pricing decisions, regardless of where responsibility is assigned. Coordination of strategic and tactical pricing decisions with other aspects of marketing strategy is critical because of the interrelationships involved.

Product and Distribution Strategies

Product and distribution strategies selected by management often set the framework for a price strategy. Such factors as product quality and features, type of distribution channel, end users served, and intermediaries functions all tend to establish a price range. Of course, if direct distribution is used, then the channel distribution considerations are not an issue in pricing strategy. The major influences on pricing decisions due to product and distribution strategies are shown in Exhibit 13-3. Each influence is considered briefly since the discussion in Chapters 10, 11, and 12 provides considerable insight into how these factors establish guidelines for pricing strategy.

EXHIBIT 13-2 Steps in Strategic Price Planning

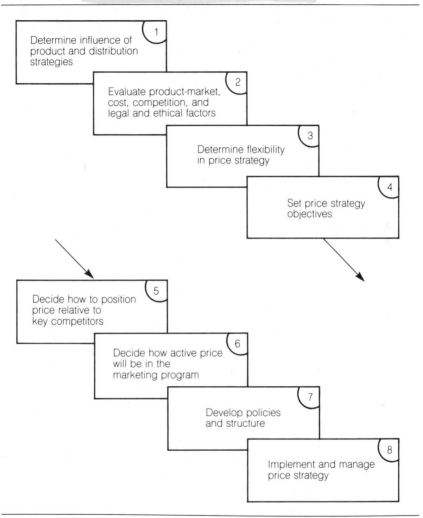

1 Determine influence of product and distribution strategies

2 Evaluate product-market, cost, competition, and legal and ethical factors

3 Determine flexibility in price strategy

4 Set price strategy objectives

5 Decide how to position price relative to key competitors

6 Decide how active price will be in the marketing program

7 Develop policies and structure

8 Implement and manage price strategy

Product Strategy. When a single product is involved, the price decision is simplified. Yet in many instances a line or mix of products must be priced. Consider a situation involving a product and consumable supplies for the product. One popular strategy is to price the product at competitive levels and set more attractive margins for supplies. Examples include film for cameras, parts for automobiles, and refills for pens. Prices for products in a line do not necessarily correspond to costs. Prices in supermarkets are based on a total mix strategy rather than in-

EXHIBIT 13-3 Influence of Product and Distribution* Strategies on Price Strategy

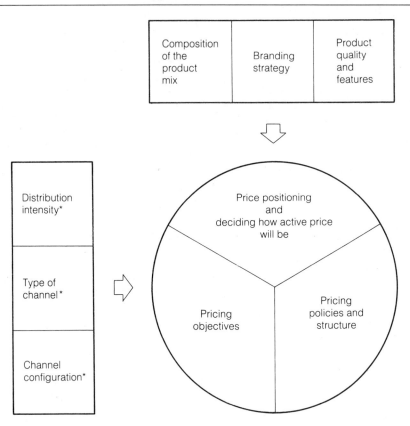

*These influences are eliminated if distribution is direct to end users.

dividual item pricing. Understanding the composition of the mix and the interrelationships among products is important in determining pricing strategy, particularly when the branding strategy is built around a line or mix of products rather than on a brand-by-brand basis. Product quality and features affect price strategy. A high-quality product may require a high price to help establish a prestige position in the marketplace and to satisfy management's profit performance requirements. Alternatively, a manufacturer supplying private branded products to a retailer like Sears must price competitively in order to obtain sales. Firms should analyze product mix, branding strategy, and product quality and features to determine the effects of these factors on price strategy. The product provides the central focus in the discussion of price strategy throughout this chapter.

Distribution Strategy. Type of channel, distribution intensity, and channel configuration also influence price strategy. The needs and motivation of intermediaries should be considered in setting prices. Firms must provide margins to pay for middleman functions and to offer sufficient incentives to obtain their cooperation. Pricing in vertically coordinated channels reflects total channel considerations more so than in conventional channels. Intensive distribution is likely to call for more competitive pricing than selective or exclusive distribution. Analysis of pricing strategy should consider channels of distribution.

An important consideration in pricing strategy is determining the role and influence of various channel members. A particular firm may be very active or passive depending on its role and power in the channel network. A firm that manages the channel usually plays an active role in pricing for the entire channel, subject to legal constraints and restrictions.

ANALYZING THE PRICING SITUATION

Analyzing the pricing situation—the second step in price planning—provides guidelines for strategy development. The need for a strategy is obvious in the case of a new product or new venture. Pricing analysis is important in evaluating new product ideas, in test marketing, and in selecting a national introduction strategy. Analysis also is necessary for existing products because of changes in the market and competitive environment, unsatisfactory performance of products, and modifications in marketing strategy over the product's life cycle. Recall, for example, the earlier discussion of Caterpillar's price strategy to combat international competition in slow-growth markets. Regular surveillance of a price strategy's performance is essential. Flexibility in selecting a price strategy is determined by: (1) product-market characteristics; (2) product costs; (3) competition; and (4) legal and ethical factors.

Product-Market Characteristics

Understanding the characteristics of the product market is a critical aspect of price strategy. One of the challenges of pricing in a new industry is estimating how buyers will respond to alternative prices. The pricing of software for personal computers illustrates this situation. Buyers have difficulty evaluating the applicability and cost benefits of these products. Several thousand new programs were introduced in 1984.[6] One software manufacturer offered a new program at $395 and supported it with an aggressive advertising campaign. Designed to compete with Lotus' Symphony and Ashton-Tate's Framework, both listing at $695, the program did not move off the shelves. Experimenting with alternative prices and no advertising, management selected a price of $89.95 after encountering buyer resistance above $100. Since software is apparently sold on the basis of features and performance, management may have relied too much on price (low price may convey an inferior image to buyers).

Product-market analysis with respect to price should yield answers to the following questions:

1. How large is the product-market in terms of buying potential? $1 million? $10 million?
2. What market target strategy is to be used?
3. How sensitive is demand to changes in price?
4. How important are nonprice factors, such as features and performance?
5. What are the sales forecasts at different price levels?

Since estimation of product-market size and target market strategy are considered in Part 2, the following discussion centers on the final three questions.

Price Elasticity. Price elasticity is the percentage change in the quantity demanded when price changes, divided by the percentage change in price. Note that elasticity corresponds to changes in price from some reference price level and is not necessarily constant over the range of prices under consideration. Surprisingly, research indicates that people will buy more of some products at *higher* prices, thus following a price-quantity relationship that slopes upward to the right. In these instances, people seem to be using price as a measure of quality. Estimating the exact shape of the demand curve (price-quantity relationship) is probably impossible in most instances. Even so, there are ways to estimate how sensitive sales are to price. Test marketing is sometimes used for this purpose. Analysis of historical price and quantity data may be helpful. End-user research studies, such as consumer evaluations of price, are also used. These approaches, coupled with management judgment, can provide an estimate of the sensitivity of sales to price. It is important to estimate how responsive buyers will be to price changes in the range under consideration.

The following observations concerning price elasticity by the president of a marketing research firm are based on research findings for several consumer product categories:

Research confirms that demand elasticity varies from brand to brand within a product category. In one product category brand elasticity ranged from 0.84 to 4.56!

EXHIBIT 13-4 Demand Curves with Differing Price Elasticity

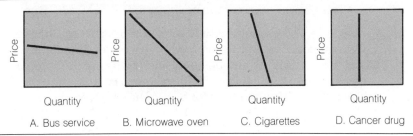

| A. Bus service | B. Microwave oven | C. Cigarettes | D. Cancer drug |

SOURCE: David W. Cravens and Robert B. Woodruff, *Marketing* (Reading, Mass.: Addison-Wesley Publishing Company, 1986), 443.

Demand elasticity for a brand varies from market to market and from segment to segment.

Demand elasticity is independent of share of market but not independent of price level. Elasticities have been found to be higher for those brands whose prices are nearer to the average for the category.

Upside (above present price) demand elasticity and downside demand elasticity can differ.

Elasticity is influenced by many variables, such as product design, promotion, and distribution.

Brand-to-brand price elasticities usually are higher between brands in the same price class.

Two brands with equal market shares will differ in demand elasticity when one has a higher repeat purchase rate (it will have a lower downside demand elasticity).[7]

These findings are illustrative rather than applicable to a broad range of product categories. Nevertheless, the results demonstrate the usefulness of pricing research. Demand curves for a range of products are shown in Exhibit 13-4. Elasticity varies across products because buyers' responsiveness to price changes differs from one product to another.

Nonprice Factors. Nonprice factors may be important in analyzing many buying situations. Buyers may be willing to pay a premium price to gain other advantages or to forgo certain advantages for lower prices. E. I. du Pont de Nemours & Company marketing research has obtained measures of nonprice factors:

> . . . it is the buyer's perception of the total relative value of the offerings that will result in a willingness to pay a premium price for one offering as compared with another, or consistently to choose one offering over another at the same price. . . . In the face of a perceived need, the buyer is aware of,

or acquires awareness of, alternative means of satisfying that need. Prior knowledge, combined with communications from sellers and others, results in perceptions of the attributes of the seller's offerings.[8]

The price of a product with in-kind competition can be separated into two components: (1) the commodity price that fluctuates with the ebbs and flows of supply and demand; and (2) the premium price differential that one or more firms may achieve due to customers' perceived values. The differential advantage for one of Du Pont's products is:[9]

	Du Pont Advantage
Quality	$1.70
Innovation	2.00
System	0.80
Service	0.25
Delivery	0.15
Retraining	0.40
	$5.30
Base Price: $100	

Forecasts. The final step in product-market analysis for pricing decisions is to forecast sales for the range of prices that management is considering, given the results of demand analysis. These forecasts, when combined with cost estimates, enable management to examine the financial impact of different price strategies. The objective is to estimate sales in units for each product (or brand) at the prices under consideration.

Assuming all other marketing program variables remain constant, elasticity estimates can be used to develop sales projections. Look at the example in Exhibit 13–5. The parity price (Step 1) corresponds to an index value of 100. This indicates that the firm's price is equal to the average for the product category in which it competes. Then in Steps 2 and 3, the effects of price changes are estimated. Using these relative measures of elasticity, forecasts can be made from test market data, or historical sales data in the case of existing products. Other methods of forecasting are discussed in Chapter 5.

Cost Analysis

An understanding of product costs is an essential input to the selection of a price strategy. A guide to cost analysis is shown in Exhibit 13–6. First, firms should determine the structure of the cost of producing and distributing the product. This involves determining fixed and variable components of cost. They should also determine the portion of product cost accounted for by purchases from suppliers. For intermediaries this will be a large part of the total cost. It is useful to separate cost compo-

EXHIBIT 13-5   Demand Elasticity to Price Change

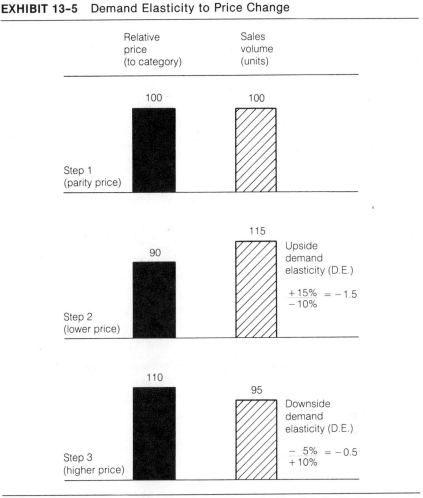

SOURCE: Earl L. Bailey, ed., *Pricing Practices and Strategies* (New York: The Conference Board, 1978), 8.

nents into labor, materials, and capital categories in studying cost structure.

Next, companies examine cost and volume relationships. How are costs expected to vary at different levels of production or quantities purchased? To what extent can economies of scale be gained over the volume range that is under consideration, given the target market and intended program positioning strategy? At what volumes are significant cost reductions possible? The main task in this part of the analysis is to determine the extent to which the volume produced or distributed should be taken into account in selecting a price strategy.

EXHIBIT 13-6 Guide to Cost Analysis

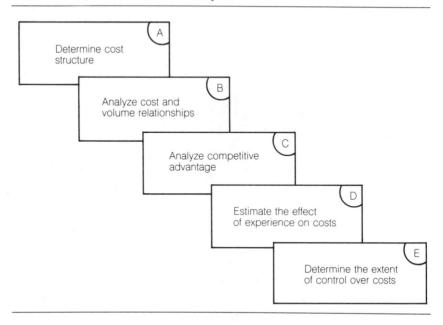

Comparing key competitors costs is often valuable. Are their costs higher, lower, or about the same? Although such information is sometimes difficult to obtain, experienced managers and analysts often make estimates. The important consideration is placing key competitors into relative product cost categories. In some situations analysts can estimate competitive cost information from a knowledge of wage rates, material costs, production facilities, and related information. Exhibit 13-7 illustrates competitive cost advantage. The basis of comparison is the power output of the product, a commercial equipment item. Notice how competitive advantage changes at different power outputs for companies X and Y. Company X, which is smaller than Y, the industry leader, has some important cost advantages over Y in two zones of power output due to technical differences in their products. Thus, cost advantages depend on the power output required by buyers. X has an advantage in some applications, Y in others.

The next aspect of cost analysis is estimating the effect of experience on costs. Experience or learning curve analysis (using historical data) indicates that costs and prices for various products decline by a given amount each time the number of units doubles. Price declines may be uneven due to competitive influences. When unit costs (vertical axis) are plotted against total accumulated volume (horizontal axis), costs decline with volume. The underlying logic supporting these stud-

---

EXHIBIT 13-7 Zones of Competitive Advantage for Competing Products

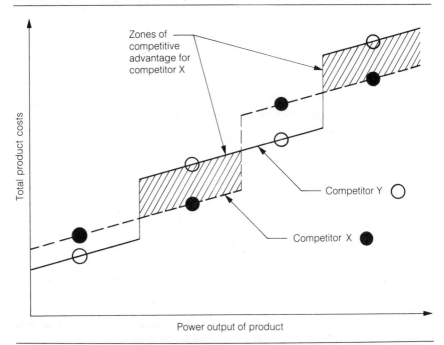

SOURCE: Earl L. Bailey, ed., *Pricing Practices and Strategies* (New York: The Conference Board, 1978), 52.

---

ies is that experience increases the efficiency of production operations. As discussed in Chapter 3, experience curve analysis is used in strategic planning. The extent of the experience curve effect should be examined on an industry and company basis since the effect is not the same across all product categories. There are several issues to be evaluated in experience curve estimation including aggregation of data, errors in variables, functional form, and measurement.[10] The experience curve can be estimated using the total direct costs required to complete the first unit (or a later unit) and the improvement rate due to experience.[11] Cumulative total direct cost at any point will be equal to cost of the first unit times the number of units raised to the power equal to 1 minus the improvement rate. The improvement rate ranges between 0 and 1, and the equation for cumulative cost is:

$$(\text{Unit 1 cost}) \, (\text{Number of units})^{1 \,-\, \text{Improvement rate}}$$

Finally, management should determine how much influence or control the firm may have over costs in the future. To what extent can research and development, bargaining power over suppliers, innovation, and other factors be expected to reduce costs over the planning horizon? These considerations are interrelated with experience curve analysis, yet may operate over a shorter time range. Bargaining power in channels of distribution, for example, can have a major effect on costs, and the effects can be immediate.

Competitor Analysis

Management should evaluate each competitor's price strategy in addition to studying the competitor costs, to determine:

> How competing firms are strategically positioned on a relative price basis and the extent to which price is used as an active part of their marketing strategies.
>
> Which firms represent the most direct competition (actual and potential) for the market target under consideration.
>
> How successful each firm's price strategy has been.
>
> What key competitors' probable responses to alternative price strategies will be.

The most difficult of these questions is the last one—predicting what key competitors will do in response to alternative price strategies. No changes are likely unless one firm's price strategy is viewed as threatening (low) or greedy (high). Competitive pressures, actual and potential, often narrow the range of feasible price strategies and rule out the use of extremely high or low prices relative to competition. In new product-markets, competitive factors may be insignificant except for the fact that very high prices may attract potential competitors. For example, Tylenol's high profit margin was a major reason for Datril's entry into the nonaspirin market in 1975. Yet Bristol-Myers lost $10 million in its attack on Tylenol, whose responsive price strategy matched Datril's market entry price.[12] In early 1983 Bristol-Myers tried again with Datril 500 and spent $3 million on advertising during the first six weeks. The ads stated that Extra-Strength Tylenol was priced 25 to 45 percent more than Extra-Strength Datril, based on a national survey. Management indicated that achieving a 2 to 3 percent market share for Datril would be considered strong performance. Datril had obtained about a 1 percent market share a year after introduction.

Legal and Ethical Considerations

The last activity in strategic analysis is identifying legal and ethical factors that may affect the choice of a price strategy. Consider the following description of what happened when several companies in the art supply industry including Binney & Smith (Crayola brand) were involved in price-fixing lawsuits:

Seven plaintiffs representing as many as 1,000 buyers filed the lawsuit, following formal charges of price fixing filed by the Federal Trade Commission and the Justice Department in 1979 and 1980. Binney & Smith in 1980 agreed to pay $1 million to settle the FTC charges without admitting guilt, which reduced earnings $540,000, or 16 cents a share, according to the company's annual report. In February 1982, Binney & Smith paid an additional $350,000 fine and pleaded no contest after a federal grand jury in Toledo indicted it and three other companies on price-fixing charges.

The $5 million settlement announced Friday could reduce Binney & Smith's earnings by about 72 cents a share, observers said. The company earned $10.2 million, or $2.86 a share, in 1982. It earned $315,000, or nine cents a share, in the first quarter.

The federal charges alleged that executives of Binney & Smith and three other companies met on at least 17 occasions between 1964 and 1976—including gatherings at an airport lounge in New York and at a trade show in the Bahamas—to conspire to fix prices of crayons, chalk, and other products, according to Wayne Thomas, a lawyer for Cumberland Farms Inc., one of the private plaintiffs.

The other defendants were Milton Bradley Co., Joseph Dixon Crucible Co.'s American Art Crayon Co. unit, and American Art Clay Co. All four manufacturers were named in the FTC and Justice Department charges and in the private litigation. They remain defendants in suits filed by 14 state and county agencies alleging the same charges.[13]

Pricing practices that have received the most attention from government are:

Price fixing—price collusion between competitors such as the art supply industry illustration. Conditions involving narrow profit margins are more likely to lead to price fixing.

Price discrimination—charging different customers different prices without an underlying cost basis for discrimination.

Price fixing in channels of distribution—specifying the prices of distributors.

Price information—violating requirements concerning the form and the availability of price information for consumers. Unit pricing and consumer credit requirements are examples.[14]

Ethical issues in pricing are far more subjective. For example, consider the price strategy used by AT&T for its Picturephone.[15] Satellite Business Systems (SBS) argued that AT&T Picturephone rates were artificially low, subsidized, in effect, by AT&T's monopoly telephone services. (Such a claim may seem surprising since the rate ranged from $150 to $395 an hour!) Yet there appeared to be a developing market for Picturephone for use in holding remote video business meetings to counter high travel and lodging costs. Anticipating this opportunity in teleconferencing services, SBS could not compete at AT&T's current rates. AT&T argued that while the rates were not "cost justified," they were not harmful to competition. This illustration points out the difficulty in determining what is unethical. Firms typically adopt a price strategy in their own best interests, regardless of the effect on competition.

How Much Flexibility Exists?

Demand and cost factors determine the extent of price flexibility. Within these upper and lower boundaries, competition and legal and ethical considerations may influence the choice of a specific price strategy. Exhibit 13–8 illustrates how these factors determine flexibility. The feasibility range for price between demand and cost may be narrow or wide. A narrow gap simplifies the decision; a wide gap suggests a greater range of feasible strategies.

Choice of a price strategy within the gap is influenced by competitive strategies, present and future, and by legal and ethical considerations. Management must determine how high or low to price within the gap shown in Exhibit 13–8. In competitive markets the feasibility range may be very narrow. New markets or market segments in mature markets may allow a firm substantial flexibility in strategy selection.

The concept of a *price band* indicates that the amount of flexibility in pricing compared to competition is a function of (1) competitive intensity, and (2) the value of the brand as perceived by buyers.[16] Consider the illustration of price brands for different segments in the ice cream market shown in Exhibit 13–9. Note the differences in the width of the price band. In situations where price competition is not strong and buyers seek high quality, the price brand is relatively wide. In contrast commodity-type brands have a narrow price band.

SELECTION OF A PRICE STRATEGY

Pricing Objectives

Companies set their price strategies to achieve several objectives. They may price for results (sales, market share, profit), for market penetration or position, for certain functions (e.g., promotional pricing), or to avoid government intervention. Normally, more than one objective will be involved, and some objectives may conflict with each other. If so, limits may need to be imposed on one of the conflicting objectives. For example, if one pricing objective is to increase market share by 20 percent while another is to price to break even on sales, management should determine if both objectives are feasible. If not, one must be adjusted. Objectives establish essential guidelines for price strategy.

EXHIBIT 13-8   How Much Flexibility in Price Strategy?

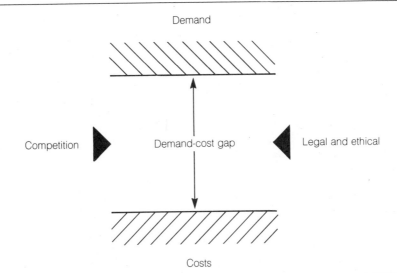

Demand

Competition   Demand-cost gap   Legal and ethical

Costs

Price As an Instrument of Strategy

At this stage in price planning, firm selects a price strategy. Product and distribution strategies, in combination with analyses of factors affecting price, may indicate a particular price strategy. Price objectives spell out price's role in marketing strategy. Referring back to Exhibit 13-2, price strategy is guided by deciding how to position price and choosing how active price will be in the marketing program.

Two factors establish the arena for price strategy: deciding how a firm's prices are to be positioned relative to competing firms in a product-market, and whether management chooses to use price as an active or passive instrument of strategy. Under pure competition a single firm has no control over the situation whereas a monopolist or a cartel has a substantial influence on prices, particularly when there is no government regulation, as in some international commodity situations (e.g., oil and diamonds). When pricing a mix of products and specific products within each line, establishing a pricing structure becomes more challenging. Management must decide how to use price as an instrument of strategy. Price can be used in various ways in program positioning strategy—as a signal to the buyer, an instrument of competition, a means to achieve financial performance, and a way to perform other marketing mix functions.

Signal to the Buyer.   Price offers an immediate means of communicating with the buyer. Maker's Mark, a producer of expensive whiskey, refers to price in its promotional efforts: "It tastes expensive and is."

EXHIBIT 13-9   Price Flexibility for Ice Cream Brands

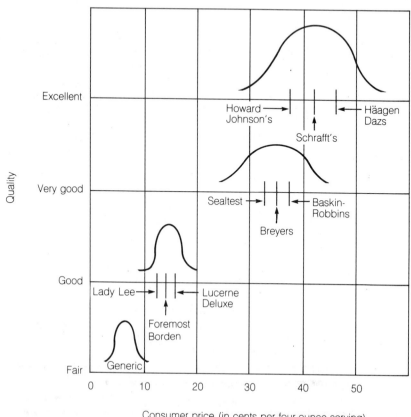

Consumer price (in cents per four-ounce serving)

SOURCE: Reprinted by permission of the *Harvard Business Review.* An exhibit from "Making Money with Productive Pricing" by Elliott B. Ross (November/December 1984). Copyright © 1984 by the President and Fellows of Harvard College; all rights reserved.

Maker's Mark uses a high price relative to competition, and it uses price as an active, visible element in its marketing program. When the product cannot be evaluated, price may serve as a proxy for value.

Instrument of Competition.   Price offers a way to immediately attack competitors, or, alternatively, to position a firm away from direct competition. Catalog showroom retailers such as Service Merchandise have successfully used a low-price strategy against discount chains and other retailers. Price strategy is always connected to competition whether firms use a higher, lower, or equal price.

Analysis of the retailing price war that was widespread in 1985 suggests that intense retail competition will prevail in the future.[17] Excess inventories, markets overcrowded with competitors, and aggressive price cutting created a "get on the band wagon" effect for many retailers. Consumers are increasingly following a "wait until the sale" strategy. This trend has serious implications for retailers. Strategic alternatives to a low-price strategy include positioning, salesmanship and service, convenience, and sensory retailing. The latter strategy focuses on making the shopping experience exciting and entertaining.

Achieving Financial Performance. Price and costs determine financial performance. Price strategies should be assessed as to their estimated impact on the firm's financial statements, both in the short and long run. Historically, financial considerations have been major factors in the pricing strategies of large firms in mature industries such as oil, steel, rubber, automobiles, and chemicals. In fact, these industries have historically used target return methods for pricing, that is, they set a desired profit return and then compute the price necessary to achieve this return. International competition in the late 1970s forced a growing number of firms to consider pricing approaches that are more demand oriented. The earlier discussion of Caterpillar's pricing strategy is a good example. Financial objectives may include pricing for short-term recovery of investment, long-term profitability, or market penetration on a break-even basis. The issue is the nature and extent to which a firm will use financial considerations to establish the role of price.

Marketing Mix Considerations. Price may serve as a substitute for selling effort, advertising, and product quality. Alternatively, price may be used to reinforce other activities in the marketing program. The role of price often depends on how other variables in the marketing mix are used. For example, price can be used as an incentive to intermediaries and company salespeople, as the focus of promotional strategy, and as a signal of value. Determining the role of price in marketing strategy requires that management evaluate the importance of price to competitive positioning, the buyer, financial requirements, and interrelationships in the marketing mix.

Selecting a Strategy

The choice of a price strategy depends on how management has decided to price its good or service relative to competition, and whether price will have an active or passive role in the marketing program. The use of price as an active or passive factor refers to how actively price is used in advertising, personal selling, and other promotional efforts. The strategies shown in Exhibit 13–10 demonstrate the range of price strategies that companies can use. Moreover, many firms choose to price at or near the prices of key competitors, and instead they emphasize nonprice factors in their marketing strategies.

EXHIBIT 13-10 Illustrative Price Strategies

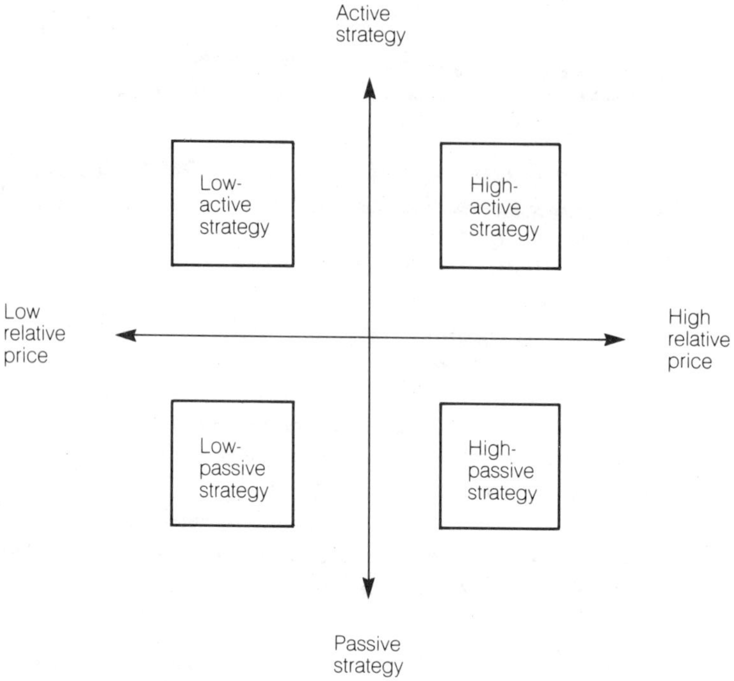

High-Active Strategy.   There are certain conditions where this strategy may be appropriate. When the buyer cannot easily evaluate the quality of a product, price can serve as a signal of value. This helps to explain the active use of price in promoting Maker's Mark whiskey. High prices may be essential to gain the margins necessary to serve small target markets, produce high-quality products, or pay for the development of new products. While high price is more frequently used as a passive factor in a marketing program, making price visible and active can appeal to buyers' perceptions of quality, image, and dependability of products and services. A firm using a high price strategy is also less subject to retaliation by competitors, particularly if its product can be differentiated.

High-Passive Strategy.   Management may choose to concentrate on nonprice factors. Product features and performance can be stressed when the people in the target market are concerned with product quality and performance. The Maytag Co., which charges higher prices than its competitors, stresses dependability and durability instead of price:

> Maytag's margins are the envy of the industry. The company has the best manufacturing margins in the appliance industry, mostly because it is able to charge premium prices for the *Maytag* brand name. This year the company's emphasis on the higher end of the market should pay off in a big way.[18]

Maytag has consistently outperformed other appliance manufacturers on the basis of net profits to sales and its products are strongly preferred by consumers. Maytag's product mix includes automatic washers and gas and electric dryers for home and commercial use, dishwashers, ranges, microwave ovens, and food waste disposals.

Low-Active Strategy. Many retailers use this strategy, including Home Depot (home improvement), Dollar General Stores (apparel), Toys R Us (toys), and Pic 'N Pay Shoe Stores (family shoes). When price is an important factor in the buyer's decision, a low-active price strategy can be very effective. However, this strategy may start a price war, and it is a more attractive when the competition for the market target is not heavy or when a company has cost advantages and a strong position in the product-market.

Low-Passive Strategy. This is not a widely adopted strategy although it is used by some small manufacturers with lower quality products than their key competitors. By not emphasizing low price there is less danger that potential buyers will link price with quality. Some firms participating in conventional channels may not spend much on marketing their products and thus may use low prices because of lower costs. Not-for-profit government organizations such as the Tennessee Valley Authority price at cost and yet do not aggressively market their services.

The marketing objectives that are assigned to price have a direct bearing on the choice of how price will be positioned against competition and how active price will be in the marketing program. Because of this, objectives guide the choice of a price strategy.

ESTABLISHING POLICIES AND STRUCTURE

Setting price objectives, positioning price against competition, and deciding how active a component it will be in the marketing program do not establish the operational guidelines necessary for implementing a price strategy. In the final step before implementation, management must determine policies and price structure (Exhibit 13–2).

Toys R Us is an exciting example of the success of specialty retailing in the 1970s. It is the largest retailer of toys in the United States, and company sales were $2 billion in 1985, compared to $1 billion in

1982. With over 200 stores, Toys R Us' rapid growth should continue into the 1990s. The firm is unique in that its stores handle only toys in large barnlike outlets averaging 43,000 square feet. The major elements of the company's strategy:[19]

> Low prices are the keystone of the firm's corporate and marketing strategies, with additional volume generated by aggressive expansion of stores.
>
> A tight rein is kept on inventories using a computer control system.
>
> Management prides itself on never running a sale, and to keep customers coming back, it prices its goods accordingly.
>
> Stores are adding employees to provide fast service and keep customers happy.

Price forms the cutting edge of this firm's marketing strategy. Growth and financial performance of the firm have been impressive. Notice how the price strategy is clearly established and how objectives (e.g., profit performance) depend significantly on the success of the strategy. Considering the range of toy prices and the variety of playthings from dolls to electronic games, the need for pricing policies and structure is clear.

Product Relationships and Price Structure

Any time more than one product is involved, a firm must determine product mix and line interrelationships in order to establish price structure. For example, Toys R Us' strategy of low prices does not automatically provide management with specific prices for each item offered by the firm. And, when more than one market target is involved, what relationships exist between the products offered in each? Assuming differences in products, should price be based on cost, demand, or competition?

Price structure concerns how individual items in the line are priced in relation to one another. The items may be aimed at the same market target or different end-user groups. For example, department stores often offer economy and premium product categories. In the case of a single product-market, price differences among products typically reflect more than variations in costs. Large supermarket chains price for total profitability of the product offering rather than for performance of individual items. These retailers have developed computer analysis and pricing procedures to achieve sales, market share, and profit objectives.

Once product relationships are established, some basis of determining price structure must be selected. Many firms base price structure on market and competitive factors as well as differences in the costs of producing each item. Some use multiple criteria for determining price structure and have sophisticated computer models to examine alternate pricing schemes. Others use rules of thumb developed from experience. Correct pricing of a product line should reflect the following guidelines:

1. Price each product in relation to all others; noticeable differences in products should be equivalent to perceived value differences.
2. The top and bottom prices in the line should be priced so as to facilitate desired buyer perceptions.
3. Price differences between products should become larger as price increases over the line.[20]

Most approaches include not only cost considerations, but also demand and competitive concerns. For example, industrial equipment manufacturers sometimes price certain products at or close to cost and depend on sales of high-margin items such as supplies, parts, and replacement items to generate profits. The important consideration in any firm is to price the entire mix and line of products to achieve price objectives.

Special Considerations

Beyond product relationships and price structure, several other price considerations often require management's special attention. Three often encountered price considerations are new product pricing, determining price flexibility, and product life cycle pricing.

New Product Pricing.   A key policy concern is establishing the basis for pricing a new product. A range of possibilities exists. Firms can charge a relatively low entry price with the objective of building volume and market position, or they can set a high price to generate large margins. Lack of previous market response to the product complicates the pricing decision. Several factors may affect the choice of a pricing approach for a new product: cost, the estimated life span of the product, the estimated responsiveness of buyers to alternative prices, and assessment of competitive reaction. The major difference between pricing new products and pricing existing products is the uncertainty involved. The guide to strategic price planning shown in Exhibit 13–2 can be used to select a price for a new product.

Price Flexibility.   Another policy consideration is how flexible prices will be. Will prices be firm, or will they be negotiated between buyer and seller? Toys R Us uses low yet firm prices and avoids special sales, but it does adjust prices over time (in 1985 it lowered the prices of many toys). Perhaps most important, firms should make price flexibility a policy decision rather than a tactical response. Some companies' price lists are very rigid while others have list prices that give no indication of actual selling prices. It is also important to recognize the legal issues in pricing products when using flexible pricing policies.

Life Cycle Pricing. Some firms have policies to guide pricing decisions over the life cycle of the product. Depending on its stage in the product life cycle, the price of a particular product, or an entire line, may be based on market share, profitability, cash flow, or other objectives. Because of life cycle considerations, different objectives and policies may apply to particular products within a mix or line. For many products, price becomes a more active element of strategy as they move through the life cycle and competitive pressures build, costs decline, and volume increases. Life cycle pricing should correspond to the overall marketing program positioning strategy used.

Determining Specific Prices

Finally, price planning reaches the stage where it is necessary to either assign a specific price to each product item or to provide a method for computing price for a particular buyer-seller transaction. Many methods and techniques are available for calculating price.

Price determination is based on cost, demand, competition or a combination of these factors. *Cost*-oriented methods use the cost of producing and marketing the product as the basis for determining price. *Demand*-oriented pricing methods consider estimated market response to alternative prices. *Competition*-oriented methods use competitors' prices as a reference point. The price selected may be above, below, or equal to competitors'. Typically, one method (cost, demand, or competition) provides the basis for pricing, although the others may have some influence.

Break-even pricing is a cost-oriented approach. The basic computation is as follows:

$$\text{Break-even}_{\text{(units)}} = \frac{\text{Total fixed costs}}{\text{Unit price} - \text{Unit variable cost}}$$

To use this method price analysts select a price and then compute the number of units that must be sold at that price to cover all fixed and variable costs. Next, they assess the feasibility of exceeding break-even and thus generating a profit. One or more prices may be evaluated in the analysis. Break-even analysis is not a complete basis for determining price since both demand and competition are important considerations in the pricing decision. Using break-even price as a frame of reference, demand and competition can be evaluated. The price selected may be higher or lower than the break-even price depending on the influence of the other factors.

There are many pricing methods in use, so it is important to select specific prices within the guidelines provided by price strategy and to incorporate demand, cost, and competition considerations.[21]

CONCLUDING NOTE

Price strategy gains considerable direction from the decisions management makes about the product mix, branding strategy, and product quality. Distribution strategy also influences the choice of how price will work in combination with advertising and sales force strategies. Price, like other marketing program components, is a means of generating market response.

Looking ahead to 1990, two important trends are apparent in the use of price as a strategic variable. First, companies are designing far more flexibility into their strategies in order to cope with the rapid changes and uncertainties in the strategic environment. Second, price is more often used as an active, rather than passive element of corporate and marketing strategies. This trend is particularly apparent in the retail sector where aggressive low-price strategies are used by firms such as Toys R Us and Dollar General Stores. Assigning an active role to price does not necessarily lead to low prices relative to competition—companies may use relatively high prices.

Our look at the strategic importance of price demonstrates how product, distribution, price, and promotion strategies must fit together into an integrated strategy of program positioning. The guide to strategic price planning shows the major stages that lead to selection of a price strategy. Any firm can use this planning guide to develop a price strategy for a mix or line of products, or to select a price strategy for a new product or brand. Much of the chapter is devoted to discussing the stages shown in Exhibit 13-2. Underlying strategy formulation are several important strategic activities, including analyses of the product-market, cost, competition, and legal and ethical considerations. These analyses indicate the extent of price flexibility. This is followed by the setting of price objectives. Price strategies can be classified according to the firm's price relative to the competition and how active promotion of price will be in the marketing program. The next step examines price positioning alternatives and the extent to which price may be used as an active element in the marketing program. Finally price policies and price structures were discussed. These policy guidelines and price relationships establish the basis for implementing and managing price strategy.

NOTES

1. This illustration is based on Jonathan Dahl, "Airlines Use a Scalpel to Cut Fares in the Latest Round of Price Wars," *The Wall Street Journal,* November 26, 1985, 31.
2. "Flexible Pricing," *Business Week,* December 12, 1977, 78–79.
3. Harlan S. Byrne, "Caterpillar, Facing Japanese Competition in Earth-Movers, Tries to Regain Footing," *The Wall Street Journal,* December 9, 1983, 52.
4. Paul Gibson, "De Beers: Can a Cartel Be Forever," *Forbes,* May 28, 1979, 45.
5. Marcia Berss, "Paris, When It Sizzles," *Forbes,* April 23, 1984, 48.
6. "Software Economics 101," *Forbes,* January 28, 1985, 88.
7. William T. Moran, "Insights from Pricing Research," in *Pricing Practices and Strategies,* ed. E. L. Bailey (New York: The Conference Board, 1978), 9–12.
8. Irwin Gross, "Insights from Pricing Research," in *Pricing Practices and Strategies,* ed. E. L. Bailey (New York: The Conference Board, 1978), 35.
9. Ibid, 39.
10. David B. Montgomery and George S. Day, "Experience Curves: Evidence, Empirical Issues, and Applications," in *Strategic Marketing and Management,* ed. H. Thomas and D. Gardner (Chichester, U.K.: John Wiley & Sons, 1985), 213–238.
11. A guide to determining experience curves is provided in Kent B. Monroe, *Pricing: Making Profitable Decisions* (New York: McGraw-Hill, 1979), 115–119.
12. "Datril Again Tries Price Vs. Tylenol," *Advertising Age,* March 21, 1983, 2 and 52.
13. "Binney & Smith to Pay $5 Million to Settle Price-Fixing Lawsuit," *The Wall Street Journal,* June 27, 1983, 20.
14. These and other aspects of marketing and the law are discussed in David W. Cravens, Gerald E. Hills, and Robert B. Woodruff, *Marketing Decision Making: Concepts and Strategy* (Homewood, Ill.: Richard D. Irwin, 1980), Chapter 21.
15. Jeffrey A. Tannenbaum, "Picturephone Pricing Riles AT&T Rival," *The Wall Street Journal,* August 28, 1980, 21.
16. Elliot B. Ross, "Making Money with Proactive Pricing," *Harvard Business Review,* November/December 1984, 145–155.
17. Leonard L. Berry, "Reflections on Retailing's Price War," *Zale Retailing Issues Letter* 1, no. 1, Zale Corporation, 1985.
18. *The Value Line Investment Survey, Ratings and Reports* (New York: Value Line, 1985), 142.
19. "Up and Down Wall Street," *Barron's,* October 27, 1980, 1 and 35.
20. For an excellent examination of product line pricing, see Monroe, *Pricing* chap. 10.
21. See Monroe, *Pricing,* for a complete discussion of all aspects of pricing.

QUESTIONS FOR REVIEW AND DISCUSSION

1. Discuss the role of price in the marketing strategy for Rolex watches. Contrast Timex's price strategy with Rolex's strategy.

2. In 1981, General Motors introduced three new automobiles—its J series—designed to compete with Audi, BMW, and other imports. All

were basically the same except that the Cadillac Cimmaron sold for about $4,000 more than its Chevy and Pontiac counterparts. Discuss the features and limitations of this price strategy.

3. Indicate how a fast-food chain could estimate the price elasticity of a proposed new product such as a chicken sandwich.

4. Real estate brokers typically charge a fixed percentage of a home's sales price. Advertising agencies follow a similar practice. Discuss why this may be sound price strategy. What are the arguments against it from the buyer's point of view?

5. In what businesses is the experience curve effect not applicable? What influence may this have on price determination?

6. In some industries prices are set low, subsidies are provided, and other price-reducing mechanisms are used to establish a long-term relationship with the buyer. Utilities, for example, sometimes use incentives to encourage contractors to install electric- or gas-powered appliances. Manufacturers may price equipment low, and then depend on service and parts for profit contribution. What are the advantages and limitations of this price strategy?

7. Some private clubs exclude prices from their menus. Analyze this price strategy using Exhibit 13-2 as a guide to your discussion.

8. Discuss some of the ways that estimates of the costs of competitors' products can be determined.

9. Discuss how the strategic price planning guide (Exhibit 13-2) could be used by a new firm to price its business analysis software line.

10. Suppose a firm is considering changing from a low-active price strategy to a high-active strategy. Discuss the implications of this proposed change.

STRATEGIC APPLICATION 13-1

B. DALTON BOOKSELLER

Dayton Hudson Corp. announced an intensified discounting program at its B. Dalton Bookseller chain, signaling a price war in the $11 billion-a-year business that could further undermine the weak financial condition of many independent bookstores.

Boake A. Sells, president, said that to retain market share and respond to surging new discounter competition, B. Dalton has begun discounting books that appear on the New York Times hardcover best-seller list by 25% to 35% off the cover price. The 746-store chain has scheduled nine nationally advertised book sales a year, is broadening its bargain book offering and, in California, is testing 25% discounts on as many as two dozen backlist titles, said Sherman A. Swenson, B. Dalton chairman.

B. Dalton's chief rival, the 932-store Waldenbooks unit of K mart Corp., said it now is offering 25% discounts on bestsellers nationally and, as of about 10 days ago, 35% discounts in 13 highly competitive markets.

"The book business is in for a tough time," said Harry Hoffman, president and chief executive officer of Waldenbooks. "When we begin to sell on price, they begin to sell on price, and everyone else follows. The industry has been laid back for too long."

Many independent booksellers, already buffeted by the rapid growth of the chains, may not survive this latest challenge, industry executives said. "I think this is terrible," said Carl A. Kroch, owner of the 17-store Kroch's and Brentano's chain in Chicago. "It's going to be awfully tough on stores without a big stock or long history."

Andrew H. Ross, a board member of the American Booksellers Association and owner of Cody's Books, Berkeley, Calif., said: "Walden and Dalton may already have 50% of the general retail book business. They skim the cream, taking away sales we need of the highly commercial books. It's bad news for us."

It also is potentially bad news for discounters like Barnes & Noble Bookstores Inc. in New York; Philadelphia's Encore Books Inc., a unit of Rite-Aid Corp.; and Crown Books Corp., the 187-store discount chain started just eight years ago, which has been responsible for much of the book price pressure. But Robert M. Haft, Crown president and chief executive officer, said he believes he will retain his customers.

"Every day, every book in all of our stores is discounted, not just the best-sellers or selected titles for short times," said Mr. Haft. "The avid book buyer knows the difference—it's a philosophy of operating, not just a few lower prices."

Mr. Sells said Dayton Hudson has stopped expansion of its 38-store Pickwick discount book chain because of the new B. Dalton strategy and the need to evaluate whether Pickwick's low-service, small-store format can be consistently profitable. Results so far have been mixed, Mr. Sells said. Similarly, Walden-books said it won't expand its five-store Reader's Market discount chain.

Neither B. Dalton nor Waldenbooks plans to reduce service because of the intensified discounting, both companies said. Mr. Hoffman said Waldenbooks re-lies increasingly on returns from audio-cassette, videocassette and game sales. Mr. Sells said Dalton is trying to develop new store strategies that will enable it to grow outside of its usual shopping-mall environment; it also is testing computer software "stores within a store" at more than 30 locations, with plans to expand to 100.

At a meeting for securities analysts, Dayton Hudson said it plans to open 150 more B. Dalton stores during the five-year period running through 1990. A previous plan called for the company to open 200 such stores in the five-year period ending in 1989.

Overall, the Minneapolis-based retailer said it plans to spend $4 billion on new store expansion during the five-year period; the previous plan called for spending of $3.2 billion. The 226-store Target discount chain will open 117 stores during the period; 72 openings were included in the previous plan; Mervyn's, the 147-store chain selling clothing, accessories and household soft goods, plans to open 160 new stores; 140 were in the previous plan.

Dayton Hudson plans no new department stores but will add 13 Lechmere stores—which sell appliances, housewares and electronic goods—to the 10 now in place, and three more R. G. Branden's home-furnishings stores. Branden's, begun in March, now has five stores.

The company said working capital to support sales in the new stores will total about $700 million during the five-year period. The company will need about $200 million to $300 million in external financing annually to pay for the stores, it said.

DISCUSSION QUESTIONS

1. Describe the role of price in B. Dalton's marketing strategy.
2. Why was Pickwick's pricing strategy not successful?

3. What are the possible risks associated with B. Dalton's pricing strategy?
4. What was the interrelationship of Pickwick and B. Dalton stores?

STRATEGIC APPLICATION 13-2

J. C. PENNEY CO.

J. C. Penney Co.'s transformation into an upscale merchandiser so far hasn't worked precisely according to plan.

In 1983, the company unveiled a plan designed to turn itself from a drab, middle-market retailer into a chain where shoppers would feel comfortable buying more expensive, department store-type merchandise. In the process, it discarded such products as big appliances and bargain-basement garments, remodeled its stores, added expensive designer clothes, and stocked more name brands.

The changes, officials said, eventually would make New York-based Penney a nationwide department store, much like merchants such as R. H. Macy Co.

But Penney's earnings declined for four of the last five quarters. And sales, excluding new stores, dropped slightly through the company's current fiscal first half ended July 27. Moreover, some company officials are worried that sales from longtime Penney customers have been lost amid their dogged pursuit of more affluent consumers—shoppers who generally have resisted the new Penney allure. "In the beginning (Penney management) thought it was going to be easy," says a supplier who asked not to be identified because of a business relationship with the company. "They figured they were already getting the woman who was buying socks and underwear.

They thought by upgrading womenswear, they'd get her to buy both."

Penney Isn't Discouraged

William R. Howell, Penney's chairman and chief executive officer, said in an interview that he wasn't pleased with the company's performance but that it will continue its redirection plan with some adjustments. "We acknowledge the fact we've been somewhat disappointed," he said. "But I use the word disappointment specifically rather than discouragement."

Penney's program has been plagued by a generally lackluster, yet extremely competitive, retail environment. Severe price-cutting triggered by a slowdown in consumer spending have eroded the big chains' profits since early last year. And even Penney's critics concede that such a massive turnaround plan will take years to complete.

But there also are signs of success. Mr. Howell said that sales of women's and juniors' apparel rose 17% in fiscal 1984 and accounted for $3 billion of $12.37 billion in store and catalog sales. In addition, 14 million more adults shopped Penney stores last year he said.

The company, however, is concerned that its plan hasn't progressed more quickly. "It's traumatic for them," says a source close to the company. "They're trying to decide whether they're doing the right thing or (whether) they've gone too far."

Penney also is facing heat from Wall Street. Some retail analysts contend the company's plan is facing a crucial test as it begins the important fiscal second half, which usually accounts for about 70% of Penney's annual earnings. "After all this rehearsal, they've got to prove they can put on a good show," says Bernard Sosnick, an analyst with L. F. Rothschild, Unterberg, Towbin.

The company also is grappling with its old image as a moderately priced mass merchant. "It's taken much longer for the (new) image to take hold among consumers because Penney still doesn't have the names a department store has, doesn't have the excitement of department stores, and isn't as aggressive as off-price retailers that feature the same name brands," explains Morgan Stanley & Co. analyst Walter Loeb, who figures it takes retailers as long as seven years to change consumer perceptions of them.

Penney's problems are apparent in an early-year survey conducted by Leo Shapiro & Associates, a Chicago research firm, and Chain Store Age, a trade magazine. In Atlanta, where in 1982 the chain remodeled and upscaled merchandise in three stores, Penney finished a distant third when consumers were asked to name the store that has "the fashion and the looks I want."

But Penney officials also admit that certain merchandise lines and customers have been ignored at the expense of the program. "In our enthusiasm for fashion and nicer stores, we may have forgotten our regular customer," a Penney executive said. "We have to get back to that customer." For example, in one Midwest department store, a brand-name dress shirt was on sale for $15.95. But at a nearby Penney store, the lowest priced shirt, a private-label brand, was $18. "There's no reason why we can't be fashionable and still have shirts for $13.95, the kind our customers have come to expect," the Penney official said.

Penney Earnings (change from prior year by quarter)

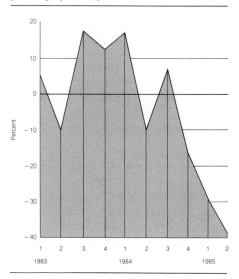

Problem Pricing

Pricing has been one of Penney's biggest problems, competitors and analysts contend. "They've adopted a strategy that requires wide gross (profit) margins for success at a time when margins are continuing to be under pressure," says an executive of a big department store concern.

Adds Edward Weller, an analyst with E. F. Hutton & Co., "Penney is providing higher-end merchandise at a day-in-day-out price, but the hitch is that the department store at the other end of the mall has that item on sale."

For example, Mr. Weller says Penney tries to sell Levi's 501 jeans nationally for $21.99, often several dollars too high because department stores generally make jeans a sale item.

But Mr. Howell insisted the company's pricing strategy is sound. In fact, he contended, some department stores are cutting prices because Penney is gaining market share. "Somebody is going to feel the sting when J. C. Penney picks up more than a billion dollars in sales," he said.

Despite the recent earnings and sales declines, Mr. Howell expects business to improve in the second half. He wouldn't project earnings, but he said sales should increase 5% to 6% in the final two quarters. In addition, he expects Penney's redirection program to begin bearing fruit in the first half of next year when Penney will have more than 100, high-volume stores completely remodeled.

"It was a real gutsy move" to change the chain's direction, said Harvey Weinberg, chairman of Chicago-based Hartmarx Corp.'s specialty stores group. "They have to ride out the bumps and look to long-term viability, not quarterly results."

The financial community may not wait that long, however. "Penney cites surveys that show their customers like it," says E. F. Hutton's Mr. Weller, who hasn't recommended Penney's stock for a year. "But the shareholders can't eat surveys. They have to get something on the bottom line."

SOURCE: Hank Gilman and Steve Weiner, "Penney's Plan to Tap Upscale Market So Far Is Failing to Improve Earnings." Reprinted by permission of *The Wall Street Journal.* © Dow Jones & Company, Inc., August 28, 1985, 6. All rights reserved.

DISCUSSION QUESTIONS

1. Discuss Penney's target market and the importance of price to the buyers in their market segment.
2. Critically evaluate Penney's price strategy.
3. How should Penney's management use other elements of the marketing mix in combination with price in order to favorably position the retailer with its target market?
4. Why is Penney seeking a repositioning strategy?

CHAPTER 14

Promotion and Advertising Strategies

J. Walter Thompson, the seventh largest advertising agency in the United States, tied with Ogilvy & Mather Worldwide as the nation's best ad agency in 1985, based on *Advertising Age*'s surveys of corporate advertising directors.[1] In each of the past four years viewers indicated that Thompson had created more memorable ads than other agencies, including the "battle of the burgers" campaign for Burger King and ads for other clients such as Ford and Eastman Kodak. The company is successfully turning around its stodgy image with a new surge of creativity. New business is being obtained from the Miller High Life account at an estimated $75 million budget and Sears' new Discover credit card at $45 million. The holding company, JWT Group, has various operating divisions, including Thompson (for international general advertising); Simmons Market Research Bureau, Inc. (demographics, marketing systems, and audience measurement); Thompson Recruitment Advertising (executive recruitment); Hispania Advertising Inc. (marketing to Hispanics); Deltakos Advertising (medical and pharmaceutical marketing); and a direct marketing unit.

Advertising agencies play a vital role in the promotion strategies of companies like Miller and Sears. Advertising is one of several forms of communication used to inform and persuade people in a firm's market targets, channel organizations, and the public at large. The promotion mix consists of advertising, personal selling, public relations, and sales promotion activities. Increasingly, marketing management is finding it profitable to combine these components into an integrated strategy for communicating with buyers and others involved in making purchasing decisions. Since each component has strengths and shortcomings, the promotion strategy adopted should capitalize on their advantages to devise a cost-effective promotion mix.

This chapter begins with a discussion of the marketing communications process and an overview of the promotion mix. Next it examines several considerations in selecting a promotion strategy and considers the major decisions involved in choosing an advertising strategy and the factors affecting these decisions. Finally, the development of public relations strategy is discussed. Selling and sales promotion strategies are examined in Chapter 15.

THE COMMUNICATIONS PROCESS

Understanding how communications occur is essential in designing an effective promotion strategy. Communication is a process linking a source and a receiver, as shown in Exhibit 14-1.[2]

The Communications System

The components shown in Exhibit 14-1 form the total communications system. In order for communication to occur between a source and a receiver, each component must fulfill its role.

Source. Communications sources include a company's promotional activities, such as advertising and personal selling, personal word-of-mouth sources such as friends and relatives, and other communications such as newspaper articles and television shows. The process is initiated by the sender, who has one or more communications objectives. For example, a manufacturer may be interested in making buyers aware of a new product.

Receiver. The person on the receiving end of the process attempts to decode the contents of the message and determine their meaning. Consumers watching a TV commercial are decoding. How they respond depends on how they perceive the message.

Message. The source constructs a message that may inform, create awareness, and/or encourage action. Encoding is expressing concepts and ideas using written words, pictures and symbols, and sounds. A television commercial is a message, as is a salesperson's verbal presentation to a potential buyer.

Communications Interference. The communications process may be adversely influenced by various distractions (noise) so the receiver either fails to notice or misinterprets a message. In addition some messages don't reach the intended audience.

EXHIBIT 14-1 The Communications Process

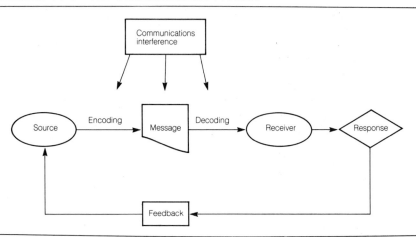

Response. The goal of marketing communications is to obtain some response from the receiver—awareness of or interest in a product, desire to purchase a product, or actual purchase. *Feedback* indicates the receiver's response to the communication and provides a basis for evaluating the message's effectiveness.

PROMOTION COMPONENTS

Marketing management should develop an integrated promotion strategy as shown in Exhibit 14–2, coordinating the roles of the promotion components, and selecting strategies for advertising, personal selling, sales promotion, and public relations. The marketing strategist has little or no control over word-of-mouth communications or the communications of other organizations. Nevertheless these communications may influence a firm's target audience.

Advertising

"Advertising is any paid form of nonpersonal presentation and promotion of ideas, goods, or services by an identified sponsor."[3] Advertising expenditures in the United States are expected to exceed $100 billion in 1986, compared to $85 billion in 1984. Major advertising expenditures are necessary to launch and maintain consumer products. In 1985, Burger King spent $30 million in just eight weeks to announce a 6-ounce increase in the size of its Whopper sandwich.[4] (The campaign was not particularly effective in increasing consumer awareness of

---

EXHIBIT 14-2   Components of an Integrated Promotion Strategy

---

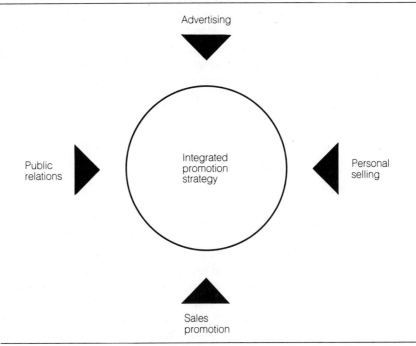

Advertising

Public
relations

Integrated
promotion
strategy

Personal
selling

Sales
promotion

Burger King, perhaps because consumers thought the message was not very significant.) The same year, Procter & Gamble and Colgate-Palmolive each spent over $10 million promoting the new Crest Tartar Control Formula and the new Dentagard plaque-remover toothpastes, respectively.

The high costs of advertising require effective strategy formulation and implementation. Among the advantages of using advertising to communicate with buyers are its low cost per exposure, the variety of media (newspapers, magazines, television, radio, direct mail, and outdoor advertising), control of exposure, consistent message content, and the opportunity for creative message design. In addition, appeal and message can be adjusted to respond to new communications objectives. However, advertising has some disadvantages. Advertising cannot interact with the buyer and may not be able to hold viewers' attention. Morever, the message is fixed for the duration of an exposure.

Personal Selling

"Personal selling is the oral presentation in a conversation with one or more prospective purchasers for the purpose of making a sale."[5] Annual

expenditures on personal selling are substantially larger than advertising, perhaps twice as much. However, both share some common features, including creating awareness of the product, transmitting information, and persuading. Personal selling is expensive. Cost per sales call exceeds $200 for industrial products compared to less than $10 per 1,000 exposures for national television advertising. Personal selling has several unique strengths: salespeople can interact with buyers to answer questions and overcome objections, they can target buyers, and they have the capacity to accumulate market knowledge and provide feedback.

Sales Promotion

Sales promotion consists of various promotional activities including trade shows, contests, samples, point-of-purchase displays, and coupons. Annual expenditures are high, exceeding the amount spent on advertising. This portfolio of special communications techniques and incentives offers several advantages: promotion can be used to target buyers, respond to special occasions, and create an incentive for purchase. The Coupon Counter is a new sales promotion technique that dispenses manufacturer coupons at the point of purchase and generates valuable marketing research information for participating firms.[6] Shoppers need a special card to access the machine. The bar code on each card identifies who receives what coupons and a random number of coupons are issued to each shopper.

Publicity

"Publicity is nonpersonal stimulation of demand for a product, service, or idea by means of commercially significant news planted in the mass media and not paid for directly by a sponsor."[7] Publicity or public relations can make an important contribution to promotion strategy if the activity is planned and implemented to achieve specific promotion objectives. (Public relations can also be used for other organizational purposes.) Publicity can be negative as well as positive, and cannot be controlled to the same extent as other promotion components. Since media coverage is not purchased, publicity is a cost-effective method of communication. The media are usually willing to provide coverage if the topic is of public interest.

PROMOTION STRATEGY

The Canadian government developed an effective promotional program to counter a decline in U.S. tourism.[8] Marketing research studies identified two major reasons why people want to visit Canada: (1) the beautiful outdoor scenery and wildlife; and (2) the country's fascinating culture. Characteristics of people interested in the outdoors were found to be quite different from those of culture enthusiasts. A promotion strategy was designed to appeal to both targeted groups:

> The promotion budget was just about doubled to $20 million. A promotion strategy emphasizing the dual benefits of visiting Canada—outdoor beauty and culture—was created. Target audiences included both the trade (tour operators, travel agencies, and conference planners) and American tourists. And a promotion mix was developed that relied heavily on advertising, publicity, and sales promotion activities. For instance, two message themes were created for advertising: "Come to Canada, the endless surprise," and "America borders on the magnificent—Canada." Advertising media were switched from a concentration in the northern United States to nationwide. Trade shows, dinners, and meetings were held for the trade to win their support. In addition, the arts were promoted by taking Canadian actors, ballet dancers, jazz musicians, and opera singers on tour of U.S. cities, getting wide press coverage at every stop.[9]

The strategy was successful in increasing tourism.

Promotion strategy includes deciding on communications objectives, a promotion budget, and the role various components in the promotion mix, and selecting strategies for advertising, personal selling, sales promotion, and public relations (see Exhibit 14-3).

Market Targets and Positioning Strategy

Market targets, as well as product, distribution, and price decisions, help to establish: (1) the role of promotion strategy in the total marketing program; and (2) the specific communications tasks to be accomplished by promotion activities. One important question is deciding whether promotion will play a primary or supporting role in marketing strategy. Typically, advertising, personal selling, or a combination of the two forms a major part of a firm's marketing strategy. The roles of sales promotion and public relations vary considerably among firms. When promotion is not an important part of the marketing program, it is usually handled by other firms in the distribution channel. For example, producers of private label brands depend on retailers for promotion activities.

Public accounting firms have been aggressive in segmenting and studying markets, developing new products, and marketing them.[10] A 1978 decision by the accounting professional organization lifted a ban on advertising. CPA firms now use customer research to uncover needs and communicate with customers and prospects using advertising, personal selling, and direct mail. Personal selling is likely to prove to be

EXHIBIT 14-3   Developing a Promotion Strategy

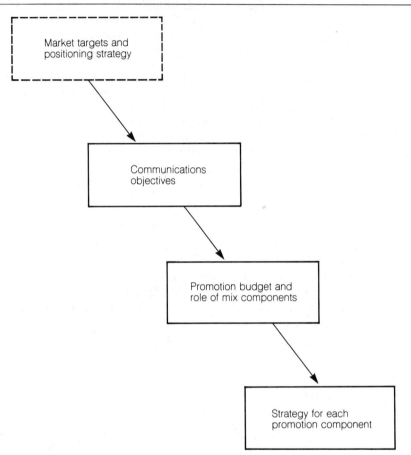

a key promotional component for CPA firms, as it is for other professional services such as architecture, law, and management consulting.

Communications Objectives

Communications objectives provide the basis for selecting how advertising, personal selling, and sales promotion will be used in the marketing program. The stages of a buyer's decision process discussed in
Chapter 6 are useful to indicate the range of communications objectives possible.

Need Recognition.   One communications objective, typical for new
product introductions, is to trigger a need. However, need recognition
may also be important for existing products and services, particularly

those the buyer can postpone purchasing or choose not to purchase (life insurance is a good example).

Gathering Information. Promotional efforts can aid a buyer's search for information. Often, one of the objectives of new product promotional activities is to help buyers learn about the product. Prescription drug companies now advertise to the public to make people aware of diseases and brand names;[11] in the past, they targeted doctors through ads in medical journals and contacts by salespeople. A U.S. Food and Drug Administration market research study found that consumers want more information on prescription drugs, and drug companies are finding that advertising is an effective way to provide it. Advertising is often a more cost effective way to disseminate information than personal selling, particularly when the information can be supplied by electronic or printed media.

Evaluation of Alternatives. Promotional communications can be used to help buyers choose among alternative products or brands. Both comparative advertising and personal selling can be effective in demonstrating a brand's strengths over competing brands. Drackett Co., a business unit of Bristol-Myers and the maker of Vanish toilet bowl cleaners, launched a multimillion dollar campaign against some of its competitors, alleging that their products may be unsafe.[12] Drackett attacked automatic toilet cleaners that used the chemical hypochlorate, arguing that these cleaners could destroy plastic, rubber, and even metal plumbing fixtures if toilets were not flushed regularly.

Decision to Purchase. Firms often use personal selling for consumer durables and industrial products. Door-to-door selling organizations such as Avon use a highly programmed selling approach to encourage buyers to purchase their products. Point-of-purchase sales promotion such as displays in retail stores are intended to encourage the purchase decision as are samples and coupons. One of the advantages of personal selling over advertising is its flexibility in responding to the buyer's objectives and questions at the time the decision to purchase is being made.

Product use. Companies are finding that communicating with buyers *after purchase* is an important promotional activity. Follow-up by salespeople, advertisements stressing a firm's service capabilities, and toll-free numbers placed on packages to encourage users to report problems are some illustrations of post-purchase communications.

Various objectives may be assigned to promotion strategy. The uses of promotion vary according to the stage of the buyer's decision process, the maturity of the product-market, the role of promotion in the marketing program, and various other factors. Communications models have been developed to guide management in formulating promotion objectives and strategies. Two examples are the AIDA model (attention, interest, desire, action) and the hierarchy-of-effects model. The steps in both models move from awareness to action.[13]

BUDGETING AND MIX STRATEGIES

Several strategic decisions must be made in developing a promotion strategy. Management must set a promotion budget, establish the role of the communications mix, and formulate and implement a strategy for each promotion component. Adjustments are often necessary as products move through their life cycles.

Budgeting Approaches

The optimal promotion budget is one in which marginal or incremental increases in sales are just equal to the marginal expenditures on advertising. However, this concept is difficult to apply because factors other than promotion also influence sales. Thus, one of the more feasible methods of budget determination is normally used in practice. They are: (1) objective and task; (2) percent of sales; (3) competitive parity; and (4) budgeting models. Similar approaches are also used to determine an advertising budget.

Objective and Task. This logical and cost-effective method is probably the most widely used and appropriate budgeting approach. Management sets communications objectives, determines the tasks necessary to achieve the objectives, and adds up costs. This method also establishes the mix of promotion components by selecting the component(s) appropriate for each objective. Marketing management must carefully evaluate how the promotion objectives are to be achieved and choose the most cost-effective components. The effectiveness of the objective and task method depends on the judgment and experience of the chief marketing executive and staff.

Percent of Sales. This method calculates the budget as a percent of sales and is therefore quite arbitrary. The percentage figure is often based on past expenditure patterns. The fundamental problem with the method is that it fails to recognize the relationship between promotion efforts and results. Moreover, it can lead to too much spending on promotion when sales are high and too little when sales are low. In a cyclical industry a countercyclical strategy of promotion expenditure might be more appropriate.

Competitive Parity. Budgets using this method take the lead from competitors. Promotion expenditures are guided by how much competitors spend. However, differences in marketing strategy between firms may require different promotion strategies. Revlon uses a mass distribution strategy, while Estée Lauder targets buyers by distributing through select department stores.

Budgeting Models. This method determines the budget using a mathematical model, often developed from analysis of historical data. The basic concern in using a model for budget determination is establishing the validity of the model and its stability over time. Advisor 2, a comprehensive model for marketing mix budgeting that was developed for industrial products, can be used to set a marketing budget and can then be split into budgets for personal and impersonal (e.g., advertising) communications.[14] Advisor is a multiple regression-type model that incorporates several predictor variables, including number of users, customer concentration, fraction of sales made to order, attitude difference, proportion of direct sales, life cycle stage, product plans, and product complexity. The model is similar in concept and approach to the Profit Impact of Marketing Strategy (PIMS) model, although Advisor concentrates on the marketing budget and its components, rather than offering complete strategies for business units or products.

Role of Mix Components

Several factors may affect a firm's promotion strategy (see Exhibit 14–4). For strategic situations between the two extremes, a more balanced mix strategy may be appropriate. Note that both personal selling and advertising are included in most promotion strategies.

Zales, the Dallas jewelry unit of Zales Corp., and Boeing Co., the aircraft manufacturer, illustrate advertising-dominant and personal selling-dominant promotion strategies. Zales' promotion strategy favors advertising because of the large number of jewelry buyers, their information needs (anxiety about purchasing jewelry), the company's ability to launch a national advertising campaign, and advertising's ability to communicate cost-effectively with the target market. By contrast, Boeing uses high-level, executive selling to promote its commercial aircraft. In Boeing's market, there are only a few customers (commercial airlines); orders are huge ($3 billion from Delta Air Lines for the 757 jet); and the product is so complex that communications must be tailored to individual customers. And personal selling is more cost-effective than advertising for Boeing.

Integrating Promotion Strategies

Developing integrated promotion mixes is a major challenge today. Advertising, publicity, personal selling, and sales promotion strategies

EXHIBIT 14-4 Illustrative Factors Affecting Promotion Strategy

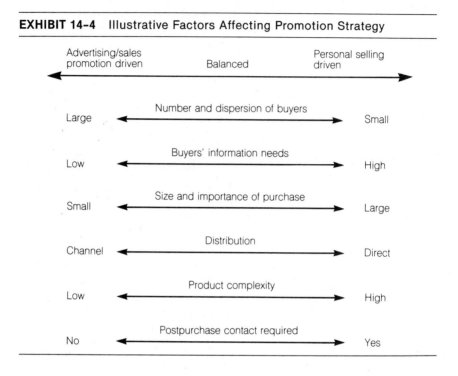

are often fragmented due to divided organizational responsibilities, differences in priorities, and the complexity of evaluating productivity. The lack of coordination between selling and advertising is particularly apparent in firms marketing to industrial buyers. These firms tend to follow personal selling driven promotion strategies. The same separation of selling and advertising strategies prevails in a variety of consumer products firms, particularly retailers.

Integrated marketing communications (IMC) strategies are beginning to replace fragmented advertising, publicity, and sales programs.[15] These strategies differ from traditional promotion strategies in several ways:

1. IMC programs are *comprehensive.* Advertising, personal selling, retail atmospherics, behavioral modification programs, public relations, investor relations programs, employee communications and other forms are all considered in the planning of an IMC.
2. IMC programs are *unified.* The messages delivered by all media, including such diverse influences as employee recruiting and the atmospherics of retailers upon which the marketer primarily relies, are the same or supportive of a unified theme.

3. IMC programs are *targeted*. The public relations program, advertising programs and dealer/distributor programs all have the same or related target markets.
4. IMC programs have *coordinated execution* of all the communications components of the organization.
5. IMC programs emphasize *productivity* in reaching the designated targets when selecting communication channels and allocating resources to marketing media.[16]

The Limited, the women's apparel retailer, has been unusually successful in implementing an integrated marketing communications program, and Byerly's in Minneapolis uses atmospherics to communicate that the supermarket is the place to be seen by trendy people.[17]

Adjusting Promotion Strategy

Both the communications mix and specific promotion activities should be evaluated continuously; they may require adjustment due to external influences, competitive pressures, costs of promotion, and other factors. By adjusting promotion strategy, firms may also be able to reposition products to appeal to different or broader markets.

Pfizer Inc.'s promotion strategy for its Ben-Gay pain remedy illustrates how adjustments are made as a brand moves through its life cycle.[18] Ben-Gay, which has been on the market for nearly 100 years, has been repositioned from a very old product for very old people to a fitness aid for athletes. In 1981 the company obtained technical data supporting the value of Ben-Gay as a warm-up preparation. The following year, Pfizer launched a "sports-active," $6.3 million promotion campaign primarily on network television (double the 1981 budget). The ads featured sports celebrities such as basketball's Larry Bird. Daytime advertising in the winter still targets the arthritic market. Aggressive competitors such as Aspercreme and Sportscreme are also going after the pain relief and sports markets, but Ben-Gay continues to be the market leader in the topical and analgesic category.

ADVERTISING STRATEGY

Advertising expenditures for Federal Express Corporation are shown in Exhibit 14–5 (sales in 1984 were $1.435 billion). Note the various media included in the advertising program. Network TV accounts for two thirds of advertising expenditures. The company's new electronic facsimile transmission service, Zap Mail, was introduced in 1984, and consumed over 40 percent of the 1984 budget. New products often require major promotional support.

EXHIBIT 14-5 Federal Express Corp. Advertising Media Expenditures ($000)

	1984	1983
Magazines	3,152	1,430
Network cable	711	1
Spot TV	6,959	2,766
Network TV	23,675	20,005
Spot radio	488	42
Outdoor	22	32
Total	34,867	24,276

SOURCE: *Advertising Age,* June 13, 1985, 37.

The steps in developing an advertising strategy are shown in Exhibit 14-6. The starting point in strategy development is identifying and describing the target audience. Business firms and other organizations were the major targets for Zap Mail so the advertising program was designed to communicate with this audience. Next, firms should establish the role and scope of advertising, decide on an advertising budget and set specific objectives. The creative strategy represents how the objectives will be accomplished, while the media and programming schedules are used to implement the creative strategy. The final step is implementation and evaluation of the advertising program.

Advertising is not always directed to the end user. For example, Johnson & Johnson, the maker of Tylenol, did not advertise to consumers until Datril entered the market in the mid-1970s. For several years Tylenol had been promoted in printed media for physicians and dentists. When designing an advertising strategy, management also needs to identify the individuals and organizations that may influence sales to end users.

Advertising's Role in Promotion Strategy

Estimating advertising's impact on buyers is the basis for deciding the advertising's role and scope in the marketing program and for choosing specific objectives. Management's perception of what advertising can do also weigh heavily on the size the advertising budget.

One study used the PIMS (profit impact of marketing strategy) data bank to identify factors that underly advertising's role in marketing strategy. This study also provides research support for several of the factors shown in Exhibit 14-4. Using a sample of 789 businesses that spent at least 0.01 percent of sales on advertising and promotion, Farris and Buzzell found the following characteristics in firms with higher ratios of advertising and promotion to sales.

EXHIBIT 14-6   Steps in Developing an Advertising Strategy

---

1. Identify and describe the target audience.
2. Determine the role of advertising in the promotional mix.
3. Indicate advertising objectives and decide on the size of the advertising budget.
4. Select the creative strategy to be used.
5. Determine media and programming schedule.
6. Implement the advertising program and measure effectiveness.

Standardized products.
Many end users.
Typical purchase amount is small.
Auxiliary services important.
Sales through channel organizations.
Premium-priced product.
Manufacturer's contribution margin is high.
Relatively small market share and/or surplus production capacity.
High proportion of sales from new products.[19]

Although the Farris and Buzzell analysis, using multiple regression, describes existing relationships rather than indicating what they should be, it represents a large cross section of firms. The factors found to be linked to high advertising and promotion expenditures offer useful guides for examining the role and scope of advertising—more so than the approach, so often recommended, that emphasizes the distinction between consumer and industrial products.

Setting Objectives and Budgeting

Advertising Objectives.   Exhibit 14–7 shows alternative levels for setting advertising objectives. In moving from the lowest level (exposure) toward the highest level (profit contribution) the objectives are increasingly closer to the purchase decision. For example, knowing that advertising has caused a measurable increase in sales is much more useful to the decision maker than saying that advertising exposed a specific number of people to an advertising message. The important question, of course, is the extent to which the objectives at the lower levels in Exhibit 14–7 are linked to purchase behavior. For example, will people that are more aware of a brand be more likely to purchase it? Achievement of lower and midlevel objectives often can be measured whereas those at the top of Exhibit 14–7 often cannot be.

Research indicates that brand awareness leads to increased market share and in turn to greater profits. The results of a study conducted by

EXHIBIT 14-7   Alternative Levels for Setting Advertising Objectives

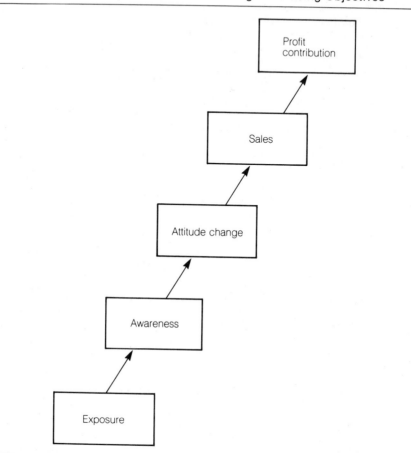

the Strategic Planning Institute involving 73 industrial products businesses supports the idea of a link between brand awareness, sales, and profits.[20] Exposure measures of advertising effectiveness are subject to much more debate and are more useful in guiding media allocation decisions than in gauging the value of advertising to a firm.

Budget Determination.   The PIMS program of the Strategic Planning Institute offers useful guidelines for budgeting. The earlier discussion of the Farris and Buzzell research identified characteristics of firms whose advertising and promotion expenditures as a percentage of sales are higher than other firms. Additionally, these factors are related to advertising and sales promotion expenditures:[21]

Market share
New products
Market growth
Utilization of plant capacity
Unit price of product
Product purchases as a percentage of total purchases
Product pricing
Product quality
Breadth of product line
Standard versus custom (made-to-order) products.

Specific relationships for four of the factors are shown in Exhibit 14–8. The Cahners Publishing Company and the Strategic Planning Institute have developed a guide for estimating an advertising budget.[22] For example, the estimate for a media advertising budget based on a firm's market share of 12 percent and annual sales of $100 million is:

$$0.7 \times \frac{100,000,000}{1,000} = \$70,000$$

If this same computation is repeated for each factor, the results can be averaged to provide a budget estimate. Factors can also be weighted to take into account their importance in a particular firm or industry.

The PIMS budgeting approach is a useful diagnostic tool for comparing a firm's current advertising budget with the PIMS guidelines. When used in conjunction with management's experience, the guide can indicate that a budget may be too high or too low compared to PIMS norms.

Creative Strategy. A strategy must be formulated to guide the advertising campaign. Two considerations affect the strategy selection: (1) whether the campaign is intended to maintain or to change market conditions, and (2) whether the campaign is meant to communicate information or imagery and symbolism.[23] Maintenance and reinforcement strategies are used to support an established brand. A strategy to change market conditions might attempt to reposition a brand, expand the market for a brand, or launch a new product. Informational messages communicate product benefits whereas image messages seek to either reinforce or create change using symbolism and imagery.

The advertising strategy used for Alka-Seltzer is an interesting example of a maintenance strategy using an informational message execution. In an attempt to stop a steady drop in sales, the strategy emphasizes heartburn and humor, a return to the advertising approach that was very successful two decades ago.[24] The 1984 campaign promoting the brand as a remedy for stress in the executive suite did not turn sales around with the loyal, but aging customer base. Miles Labo-

EXHIBIT 14-8 Guidelines for Advertising and Sales Promotion Expenditure

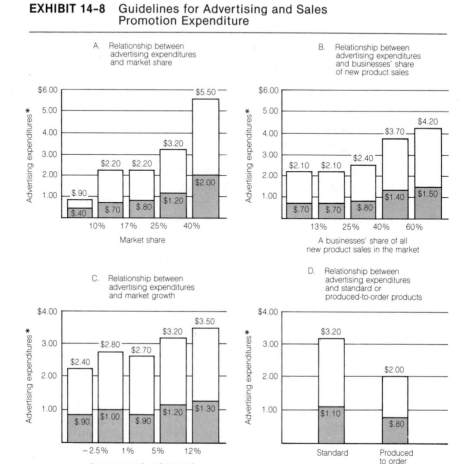

A. Relationship between advertising expenditures and market share

B. Relationship between advertising expenditures and businesses' share of new product sales

C. Relationship between advertising expenditures and market growth

D. Relationship between advertising expenditures and standard or produced-to-order products

☐ Media advertising and sales promotion

▨ Media advertising only

Advertising expenditures: media advertising and sales promotion expenditures per $1000 market sales.

SOURCE: Valerie Kijewski, "Advertising and Promotion: How Much Should You Spend," Pamphlet prepared by The Strategic Planning Institute, June 1983, 4, 5, 6, and 11.

ratories is now trying to attract young people with a new lemon-lime Alka-Seltzer. Because of slow growth in the antacid market, competitors have started promoting attributes unrelated to indigestion; Di-Gel touts its calcium content to target women worried about osteoporosis.

Creativity can substantially enhance the effectiveness of advertising expenditures by binding together the various parts of an advertising campaign. Agencies, who receive 15 percent of gross billings, are experts in designing creative strategies. They may copy the competition or design unique themes to position a product or firm in some particular way. The choice of a creative strategy can spell success or failure for an advertising agency. Choosing the right theme for the marketing situation can make a major contribution to the success of a program. While tests can be used to evaluate creative approaches, the task is more of an art than a science.

Media/Programming Strategy

A company's advertising agency should guide media and programming decisions. The agency has the necessary experience and technical ability to match media and programming to the target audience specified by the firm; marketing management often does not. Consider the media/programming strategy of Tootsie Roll Industries:

> During 1980 we had the most extensive advertising program we have had in our history. Television advertising accounted for the largest part of this advertising program. We have been increasing our advertising on national television since 1952. During 1980, we attained the heaviest TV coverage in our history. Tootsie Roll commercials appeared on television every week of the year.
> Our programming is directed at a wide range of consumers and appeared on many types of television shows. We included in our programming variety shows, musicals, news, movies, sporting events, daytime and game shows.
> During 1980, we used several different commercials for our television programs. We aired such commercials as: "Cow Fable" for Tootsie Pops; "Jingle" for Tootsie Rolls; "You're a Cool One" for Tootsie Mason Mints and "Bird" for Tootsie Pop Drops. We also introduced our newest commercial "Give Your Tootsie a Tootsie" which was written to sell the "Tootsie Family Candy Store" program, a rack display promoting a variety of our Tootsie Roll products.
> In addition to our TV commercials, we continued our successful program of offering cents-off coupons on Tootsie Roll products. An increasing number of coupons were distributed during this past year due to the fact that price-conscious consumers are redeeming more coupons.[25]

Note the varied use of advertising media, types of shows, programming decisions, and the commercials themselves. Tootsie Roll also included sales promotion methods such as rack displays and coupons in the promotion program. The company's aggressive advertising, expanded distribution, and new products helped increase sales from $72 million in 1980 to more than $108 million in 1985. During the same period earnings per share of stock increased nearly 400 percent!

The choice of media, timing, and programming are influenced largely by two factors: (1) access to the target audience(s) and (2) costs of alternative ways of reaching target groups. Suppose management is interested in reaching business executives through printed media. Possible publications and approximate costs for one page, four-color advertisements are:

U.S. News & World Report (weekly)	$55,300
Fortune (monthly)	33,940
Harvard Business Review (6 per year)	8,500

SOURCE: *Standard Rates and Data Service,* December 27, 1985.

The cost differences are based upon circulation levels and type of publication. In deciding which medium to use, firms should evaluate the cost per exposure and the characteristics of subscribers.

In recent years television has become a popular and effective means to promote Broadway stage shows. Budgeting for a typical musical is as follows:

> Mr. LeDonne recommends that his clients set aside $250,000 for pre-opening night publicity and $15,000 to $30,000 a week after the show opens. Commercials cost between $50,000 and $125,000 to produce including talent fees, and often take the biggest chunk of preopening night publicity.
>
> After the initial campaign in which the commercial might be on the air 30 times a week, at a cost of between $10,000 and $25,000 for local network time, the frequency slows and the time spots can be reduced to as little as 10 seconds.[26]

Television campaigns are normally used to promote musicals since they have larger budgets than other shows. News programs are favored for running the commercials because the programs are watched by Broadway show market targets.

Implementing the Strategy and Measuring Its Effectiveness

Before an advertising strategy is implemented it is important to establish criteria for measuring its effectiveness. Advertising expenditures can be wasted if firms spend too much or allocate expenditures improperly. Measuring effectiveness may help to reduce these problems. And the *quality* of advertising can be as instrumental in getting results as is the *quantity* of advertising.

Tracking Advertising Performance. Gauging advertising's impact on sales is difficult because other factors also influence sales. Most efforts to measure effectiveness focus on alternative objectives such as attitude change, awareness, or exposure (Exhibit 14–7). Comparing objectives and results helps firms decide when to stop or alter advertising campaigns. For example, a key objective in test marketing Procter & Gamble's Pert shampoo, introduced in Nashville and Milwaukee, was to familiarize women with the Pert benefit—"bouncin' and behavin' " hair.[27] Starting when the initial commercials aired, women were surveyed to see if they could identify a shampoo that claimed to leave hair "bouncin' and behavin'." When the level of brand recall peaked, the advertising had completed its objective.

Methods of Measuring Effectiveness. Several methods can be used to evaluate advertising results. *Historical data methods* identify a relationship between advertising expenditures and sales using statistical techniques such as regression analysis. *Recall tests* measure the awareness of specific ads and campaigns by asking questions to determine if a sample of people saw an ad. *Longitudinal studies* attempt to track advertising expenditures and sales results before, during, and after an advertising campaign. *Controlled tests* are a form of longitudinal study in which extraneous effects are measured and/or controlled during the test. Test marketing or some type of simulated testing can be used to evaluate advertising effectiveness. *Effort/results models* use empirical data to build a mathematical relationship between sales and advertising effort.

A particularly promising method for measuring advertising effectiveness is the use of consumer panels in cities with cable TV and cash register scanning of purchases. Samples of consumers can be split into groups—exposed or not exposed to advertising on cable television. Using equivalent samples, outside influences on sales can be controlled. The difference in sales between the control and the experimental (exposed) groups over the test period measures the effect of advertising. This technique is appropriate for certain types of frequently purchased consumer products such as food items and health and beauty aids.

Advertising research is not restricted to measuring the effectiveness of advertising. Research can be used for various activities in advertising strategy development including generating and evaluating creative ideas and concepts, and pretesting concepts, ideas, and specific ads.

Application Illustration. The approach that IBM uses to assess its business-to-business advertising is shown in Exhibit 14–9. Because of the difficulty in evaluating an individual ad's effectiveness, management concentrates on assessing campaigns in particular business areas such as the typewriter industry.[28] The model is implemented at the beginning of the creative development process. Effectiveness research involves pretesting and post-introduction tests, standardized information services, tracking studies, impression studies, and focus groups. Note the early determination of the campaign tracking benchmark and

EXHIBIT 14-9 IBM's Advertising Campaign Research Measurement Model

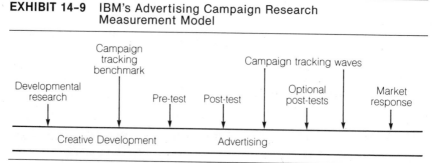

SOURCE: Byron G. Quann, "How IBM Assesses Its Business-to-Business Advertising," *Business Marketing,* January 1985, 108.

the pretesting of advertising concepts. The IBM approach utilizes evaluations and adjustments before and during the campaign.

Setting objectives is critical to determine the effect of advertising and to decide when to stop or alter a campaign. As illustrated by the Pert shampoo example, management should follow through by tracking results to measure effectiveness. Advertising strategy is rarely constant over time and should be adjusted to changing conditions.

Advertising Agency Selection

Typically, firms that advertise use one or more advertising agencies, although a firm with a very small budget may work directly with such media as local newspapers. Companies with budgets of several thousand dollars or more use an agency to develop their advertising and place it in the media. Agencies develop creative strategies, design ads, select media in which to place the ads, and evaluate ads' effects. Large full-service agencies like J. Walter Thompson, offer various marketing services.

The selection of an agency often depends on many factors. In an *Advertising Age* poll, 300 ad directors of companies with sales of over $25 million identified creative talent, knowledge of the client's business, and quality of the agency's employees as the most important agency strengths. Not surprisingly, ad directors cited lack of knowledge of the client's business as the greatest weakness among agencies. Some companies do not work with the same agency on a continuing basis. Other companies operate an in-house agency. A client seeking an agency usually selects a set of candidates and asks each to prepare a written and/or face-to-face proposal. Some clients change agencies frequently.

The 15 percent commission on advertising is the typical method of agency compensation. A 1983 study indicated that 71 percent of advertisers use the commission basis of payment and 29 percent use fee compensation, compared to 17 percent in 1976.[29] Thus, there is an apparent trend toward the use of more flexible compensation arrangements. The design of commercials, payment of celebrities shown in ads, and other selected activities normally are not included in the commission payment.

PUBLIC RELATIONS STRATEGY

Many people may have thought it was a generous, humanitarian gesture for Humana, to provide 100 artificial heart transplants, and it may have been. At an average cost of $250,000, this was a $25,000,000 humanitarian action. From the perspective of integrated marketing communications, it is important to note that the market potential for future sales of artificial hearts is estimated to be $1.25 billion. Of more immediate importance to Humana's marketing communications programs is the effect of the artificial heart program on its other businesses. Without considering the overall image that may benefit its hospital, urgent care, and group health products, the market for other open heart procedures is $7.6 billion domestically based on 241,000 annual procedures at an average price of $31,500 per procedure. Worldwide, the market potential is 365,000 annual procedures worth $11 billion. Prior to the artificial heart transplants, Humana performed 3,300 procedures annually or 1.4 percent of the domestic market in its 10 hospitals performing open heart procedures. At an estimated 55 percent gross profit rate, Humana does not have to add many points of market share to make the investment worthwhile. According to one report, Humana was on network television four out of seven days in the first five months of 1985. It is doubtful that a similar investment in media advertisement would have produced similar effects.[30]

Marketing strategists have not taken full advantage of publicity's huge potential in an integrated communications strategy. Several aspects of public relations are similar to planning and implementing advertising campaigns. Nevertheless there are important differences regarding strategy design and forms of publicity.

Strategy Considerations

Target Audience.   Like advertising, publicity should be targeted, although the audience may not have to be as specific because of the ability of public relations media to access particular groups of buyers. By sponsoring the New York City Marathon, Manufacturers Hanover Trust builds goodwill with a sizable number of runners—many potential business and professional customers—and exposes its name to the public before, during, and several weeks after the race through articles and photographs in newspapers and magazines.[31] Manufacturers Hanover research indicates that people who take to running, jogging, and physical fitness are generally successful in their jobs—just the segments the bank wants to attract. The bank spends about $300,000 to sponsor the race.

Reactive versus Proactive Strategies.   Publicity can be negative as well as positive. In some instances a firm must be ready to counteract adverse publicity during and after unfavorable events. Johnson & Johnson has had to deal with Tylenol tampering incidents, and Procter & Gamble had to launch a major public relations campaign to deal with rumors about its corporate man-in-the-moon logo. Procter & Gamble launched major public relations campaigns in 1982 and 1984 to dispel the logo rumor.[32]

A proactive public relations strategy is more appropriate as an ongoing component of the marketing communications program. Firms set objectives for publicity and design action programs to achieve the desired results. The planning process for these programs is similar to the planning process for advertising. Budgeting consists of covering the costs of personnel, materials, and a public relations agency.

Organizational Responsibility.   A company that has a public relations department may perform a variety of activities, only some of which correspond to marketing communications. Often, public relations personnel are not part of the marketing organization. Thus, coordinating marketing-related publicity is important. A close working relationship between marketing and public relations professionals is essential if publicity is to make a meaningful contribution to promotion strategy. The public relations department in many firms reports to top management rather than to the chief marketing executive. Thus the function is unique in comparison to the other promotion components.

Guide to Public Relations Strategy

The major forms of publicity are information (news) releases, special events, and participations. Examples of each type of activity are shown in Exhibit 14–10, which indicates the major decisions and activities of publicity program development for marketing communications. Note the relationship of publicity to the other promotion components. Following a proactive strategy for public relations begins with determining its role and objectives. Firms should evaluate costs and benefits of alternative publicity opportunities and compare them to other components of promotion that could achieve the same objectives.

CONCLUDING NOTE

Marketing communications comprise a vital part of a positioning strategy. When developing a strategy, a basic understanding of the communications process is essential. The components—advertising, sales promotion, publicity, and personal selling—offer an impressive array of

EXHIBIT 14-10 Overview of Publicity Strategy

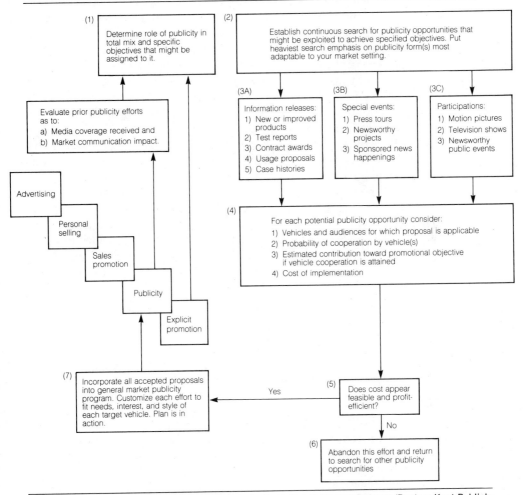

SOURCE: William P. Dommermuth, *Promotion: Analysis, Creativity, and Strategy* (Boston: Kent Publishing, 1984), 617.

capabilities for communicating with the market target and other relevant audiences. Management must decide the size of the promotion budget and allocate it to the communications components. Each type of promotion offers some unique advantages and also shares several characteristics with the other components. The major budgeting methods are objective and task, percent of sales, competitive parity and budgeting models. Several product and market factors affect whether the promotion strategy will emphasize advertising, personal selling, or a balance between the two forms of promotion. The integration of communications mixes is a major challenge for many firms today.

The steps in developing an advertising strategy consist of identifying the target audience, determining the role of advertising in the promotional mix, indicating advertising objectives and budget size, selecting the creative strategy, determining the media and programming schedule, and implementing the advertising program and measuring its effectiveness. Advertising objectives may range from audience exposure to profit contribution targets. The PIMS studies offer useful guidelines for budget analysis. Advertising agencies offer specialized services for developing creative strategies, designing messages, and developing media and programming strategies.

Public relations strategy has not been used to its full potential by many firms. Several aspects of publicity are similar to designing advertising campaigns. One important difference is that a firm does not have to pay for the use of media. Since the use of news releases and other public relations techniques is at the option of the medium, a firm has less control over the extent and timing of publicity. More control can be exercised through special events and participations than with news releases. Public relations provides a potentially useful component of promotion strategy, providing it is properly integrated with the other components.

NOTES

1. Johnnie L. Roberts, "JWT Group Recasts Its Image in Turnaround," *The Wall Street Journal*, November 27, 1985, 6.
2. James F. Engel, Martin R. Warshaw, and Thomas C. Kinnear, *Promotional Strategy*, 5th ed. (Homewood, Ill.: Richard D. Irwin, 1983), 16.
3. Committee on Definitions, *Marketing Definitions, a Glossary of Marketing Terms* (Chicago: American Marketing Association, 1960).
4. "Forecast & Review," *Advertising Age*, December 30, 1985, 14.
5. Committee on Definitions, *Marketing Definitions*.
6. Kevin Higgins, "Coupon Counter Doubles as Distribution, Research Device," *Marketing News*, April 13, 1984, 6.
7. Committee on Definitions, *Marketing Definitions*.
8. "Canadian Marketing Blitz Lures U.S. Tourists Back After Decline,"

Marketing News, August 31, 1984, 1, 6.
9. Ibid.
10. Margaret Yao, "Fierce Competition Forces Auditing Firms to Enter the Alien World of Marketing," *The Wall Street Journal*, March 18, 1981, 29.
11. "Going to the Public with Ads for Prescription Drugs," *Business Week*, May 21, 1984, 77, 81.
12. Bill Abrams, "Firm Embarks on Risky Course with Ad Attack on Competition," *The Wall Street Journal*, December 11, 1980, 29.
13. For an in-depth discussion of these models, see David A. Aaker and John G. Myers, *Advertising Management*, 2nd ed. (Englewood Cliffs, N.J.: Prentice-Hall, 1982), Chapter 4; and James F. Engel, Martin R. Warshaw, and Thomas C. Kinnear, *Promotional Strategy*, 5th ed. (Homewood, Ill.: Richard D. Irwin, 1983), Chapter 10.

14. Gary L. Lilien "Advisor 2: Modeling the Marketing Mix Decision for Industrial Products," *Management Science*, February 1979, 191–204.
15. Roger D. Blackwell, "Integrated Marketing Communications," presented at the Stellner Symposium, University of Illinois, 1985, 2–3.
16. Ibid.
17. Ibid., 9.
18. Belin Hulin-Salkin,"Pfizer's Ben-Gay Warms Up a Broader Market," *Advertising Age*, September 24, 1984, 54.
19. Paul W. Farris and Robert D. Buzzell, "Why Advertising and Promotional Costs Vary: Some Cross-Sectional Analyses," *Journal of Marketing*, Fall 1979, 120.
20. "Brand Awareness Increases Market Share, Profits: Study,"*Marketing News*, November 28, 1980, 5.
21. Valerie Kijewski, "Advertising and Promotion: How Much Should You Spend?" (Cambridge, Mass.: The Strategic Planning Institute, June 1983).
22. *Work Book For Estimating Your Advertising Budget*, (Boston: Cahners Publishing).
23. Henry Assael, *Marketing Management: Strategy and Action*, (Boston: Kent Publishing, 1985), 392.
24. Ronald Alsop, "New Alka-Seltzer Ads Revert To the Humor of Heartburn," *The Wall Street Journal*, November 7, 1985, 31.
25. Tootsie Roll Industries, Inc. *1980 Annual Report*, 4.
26. Lydia Chavez, "New Hit on Broadway: Television Advertising to Promote the Shows," *New York Times*, May 16, 1981, 31.
27. Bill Abrams, "Industry Veteran Challenges Conventional Wisdom on Ads," *The Wall Street Journal*, April 9, 1981, 31.
28. Byron G. Quann, "How IBM Assesses its Business-to-Business Advertising," *Business Marketing*, January 1985, 106, 108, 110, 112.
29. Merle Kingman, "To Fee or Not to Fee," *Advertising Age*, August 29, 1983, M-24.
30. Blackwell, "Integrated Marketing Communications," 10–11.
31. Kurt Hoffman,"Banks Earn Dividends from Special Events," *Advertising Age*, October 25, 1984, 26, 30.
32. Laurie Freeman, "Rumor Returns to Bedevil P&G," *Advertising Age*, October 22, 1984, 1, 100.

QUESTIONS FOR REVIEW AND DISCUSSION

1. Compare and contrast the role of promotion in a CPA firm such as Ernst & Whinney to its role in an airline such as American Airlines.

2. Identify and discuss the factors that are important in determining a promotion mix for the following products:
   a. Video tape recorder/player.
   b. Personal computer.
   c. Boeing 757 commercial aircraft.
   d. Residential homes.

3. Discuss the important considerations in setting communications objectives.

4. What are the important issues in determining a promotion budget?

5. Under what conditions is a firm's promotion strategy more likely to be advertising/sales promotion-driven?

6. Discuss which parts of advertising strategy development should be handled by marketing management, an

advertising agency, and jointly. When joint involvement is involved, indicate the relative responsibilities of the firm and agency.

7. Several characteristics of firms with relatively high ratios of advertising and promotion expenses to sales are discussed in this chapter. Discuss why certain factors may be more im-

portant determinants of advertising expenditures in a particular firm.

8. Discuss the advantages and limitations of using awareness as an advertising objective. When might this objective be appropriate?

9. Identify and discuss the important differences between advertising and public relations strategies in the marketing promotion strategy.

STRATEGIC APPLICATION 14-1

ADIDAS

HERZOGENAURACH, West Germany—The only tourist attraction in this remote Bavarian town of 18,125 is a one-room museum devoted to the history of sneakers. There, neatly displayed in glass cases are some 200 pairs of the most famous shoes in sports, including Jessie Owen's spiked running flats from the 1936 Olympics and Muhammad Ali's high-topped boxing shoes. A recent addition is a computerized jogging shoe that flashes a runner's time, distance and calories burned.

But the shoe museum alone doesn't explain the procession of Olympic-class athletes and sports officials who visit from all over the world. They come here to enjoy the hospitality of the Sport Hotel, a cozy 32-room inn with an indoor swimming pool, tennis courts, soccer field, saunas, coaches, trainers and a chef who would do any hotel proud. Best of all, at checkout time there is rarely a bill to be paid by the guest.

The tab is picked up by the Sport Hotel's owner: Adidas, the German shoe and sporting-goods maker. Through such largess, it wants to turn the world's top athletes into walking, running, vaulting, and kicking billboards for its logo. Adidas believes in making friends, then making deals. From the cash it once

secretly gave Olympic athletes to the free plane tickets it passes out to leaders of sports organizations, Adidas has made itself the sugar daddy of international amateur sports.

To Be Reckoned With

Marketing through patronage has helped make Adidas the largest sporting-goods company in the world and also has established Horst Dassler, its 49-year-old chairman, as one of the most important power brokers in the Olympics movement. Few who have benefited from Adidas's beneficence ignore Mr. Dassler's opinion on such issues as corporate sponsorship of athletics or whether to let professional athletes compete in the Olympics. And next October, when the International Olympic Committee selects the sites for the 1992 Winter and Summer Olympics, the winning cities may well be able to thank Mr. Dassler for his support.

"He's the real boss of sport," says Monique Berlioux, the former director of the IOC. "He wants Adidas to be the best company, but he wants to be the top man in sports. He likes the power."

Mr. Dassler's deep involvement in the politics of amateur sports has raised questions in a movement founded on the notion that amateur sports should eschew commercialism. Critics accuse him of influencing Olympic Committee votes and question why the IOC—without competitive bidding—gave a potentially lucrative contract for the 1988 Olympics to an inexperienced Swiss sports-marketing company controlled by Mr. Dassler. Though he has fostered soccer and other sports in Third World countries and helped to make the Olympics operate more efficiently, Mr. Dassler and his growing power trouble some sports leaders.

Wanting Control

"You can't run top-class competitive sports without sponsorships," says Thomas Keller, the president of the General Association of International Sports Federations, "but everyone should respect his limits. Dassler wants to control everything."

Adidas obviously isn't the only company that sees sports as an attractive marketing vehicle. Puma, the German sporting-goods maker, pays huge sums to tennis champion Boris Becker to wear its shoes; and Nike Inc., the Oregon shoemaker, finances a training facility for U.S. athletes.

What sets Adidas apart is its emphasis on amateur sports. Like its competitors, it also hires pro athletes to endorse its products—Adidas pays about $1 million a year to New York Knicks star Patrick Ewing—but Adidas has gone to unusual lengths to associate its three-stripe logo and trefoil insignia with the five interlocking rings of the Olympics.

A Lobbyist's Diligence

Besides paying more than its competitors do to outfit Olympic teams, Adidas mingles in Olympics politics with the diligence of a Washington lobbyist. An Adidas dinner or reception is commonplace at almost any IOC meeting; and an Adidas representative—usually Mr. Dassler himself—spends the day mixing with delegates.

Some Adidas practices—such as the free airplane tickets that a company-owned travel agency gives to some IOC delegates—would be frowned upon in the U.S. but not necessarily in other countries. Mr. Dassler says that he simply is trying to create a family feeling with his business contacts. Lawrence W. Hampton, an American who was an aide to Mr. Dassler from 1975 to 1980, says of Mr. Dassler's generosity: "It's a genius thing. It doesn't cost very much, and none of his competitors do it. It's not in the American mentality, but it is part of everyone's else's mentality."

Noting Adidas's failure to capitalize on the U.S. jogging boom in the 1970s, competitors wonder whether Mr. Dassler's desire for power has overtaken his drive for profits. Mr. Dassler's politicking is "a waste of time," says one of his major competitors. "We operate our company on the basis of what athletes need to run faster and jump higher."

Adds Armin Dassler, Horst Dassler's cousin and the chairman of rival Puma: "I always have refused to interfere in sports politics. You must see your limits. We are shoemakers."

Even Adidas's chairman acknowledges that, with 80% of the company's products now worn for leisure rather than for sports, its philosophy of associating its brand with champion athletes may need adjusting. One indication of that is a new, $22 million international ad campaign that begins this month. "Having the U.S. track team wear a specific suit isn't good enough anymore," says Mr. Dassler.

Nonetheless, the Adidas philosophy has paid off so far. In the four decades since Mr. Dassler's father stopped making boots for Hitler's soldiers, Adidas has become the largest sporting-goods manufacturer in the world, with 1985 sales of $1.5 billion. Its trademarks are ubiquitous at major sporting events; 89% of the countries attending the 1984

Los Angeles Olympics wore Adidas products. The brand ranks with Coca-Cola, Marlboro and Kodak as one of the most widely recognized corporate symbols in the world: Nearly eight of every 10 adults recognize the Adidas stripes and trefoil, according to a recent survey conducted in the U.S., West Germany, Portugal and Singapore.

Mr. Dassler is Adidas's undisputed chief, though he owns only 20% of Adidas directly; his four sisters have equal stakes. Including interests the family owns in the companies that market Pony shoes, Arena swimwear and LeCoq Sportif sportswear, the Dasslers control annual revenues of about $2 billion.

Adidas was founded by Mr. Dassler's father, Adolf, in 1948. (A combination of his nickname, Adi, and the first syllable of his last name, Adidas is pronounced uh-DEED-us in the U.S. and England and AH-di-dahs everywhere else.) The company was one product of a bitter feud between Adolf and his brother, Rudolf, who had been partners in a shoe factory since 1924. The reasons for their split aren't certain, but, whatever the cause, Rudolf sold his half of the family business to Adolf in 1948 and established Puma on the opposite side of the Aurauch River in Herzogenaurach. The two brothers, now both dead, never spoke to each other again.

Horst Dassler got his start in the family business at age 20, while still a student. His mother sent him to the 1956 Melbourne Olympics to give Adidas shoes to the athletes, a novel tactic at the time. "Athletes were surprised when I came up as a young chap and offered them a pair of shoes," Mr. Dassler recalls. "It was very easy."

Cash and Merchandise

And it caught on quickly. By the 1960 Rome Olympics, athletes had become accustomed to free equipment from various sporting-goods makers, including Puma. An escalating war of freebies—

and cash—had begun for Olympic athletes. Mr. Dassler acknowledges that Adidas saw that such payments had become a competitive necessity. "We would have lost all the top athletes if we hadn't done it," he says.

By the 1968 Olympics in Mexico City, the under-the-table transactions had become a public scandal. They had grown so large—$10,000 per person in some cases—and so blatant that greedy athletes would shuttle between Adidas and Puma bargaining for top dollar. A Sports Illustrated magazine expose brought the practice into public view, where Olympic officials could no longer ignore it.

Although the IOC considered such possible actions as requiring Olympic athletes to wear all-white shoes, it eventually decided to permit national Olympic teams, instead of individuals, to sign contracts with manufacturers.

That was a pivotal moment in the shoe-makers' marketing war. In most instances, decisions about the shoes and uniforms a team would wear became the province of each country's national Olympic committee. The federations that governed each sport also became more important in choosing suppliers.

Changed Focus

Adidas thus began focusing on the administrators of important sports federations and national Olympic committees. Mr. Dassler "saw that was going to be much more important than battling it out in the locker room," says Patrick Nally, a London sports-marketing consultant and former associate of Mr. Dassler's.

Adidas and its chairman gradually have worked themselves into almost every corner of sports politics. Their main vehicle has been Adidas's contracts with national teams; last year, it gave out $30 million in cash and equipment. Adidas's support for the U.S. boxing team, for example, includes uniforms, ads in its programs and even towels at competitions.

Like the best of politicians, Mr. Dassler listens more than he speaks and asks more questions than he answers. A small army of Adidas representatives stationed in many of the 160 countries where Adidas does business helps keep him abreast of local sports politics. Adidas also employs operatives like Hassine Hamouda, a Paris-based former Tunisian military colonel who has influence with sports leaders in Arab countries and in French-speaking Africa.

Adidas representatives sit on important Olympic advisory committees; Col. Hamouda, for instance, is a member of an IOC Press Commission. Adidas recently hired Thomas Bach, a former Olympic fencer who is a member of an athletes' advisory committee to the IOC. Richard W. Pound, a Montreal lawyer who is one of Canada's two IOC delegates and a member of the IOC executive board, does legal work for Adidas. Mr. Pound denies any conflict of interest, saying that he doesn't share in his law firm's profit from the account.

Mr. Dassler acknowledges that his hospitality and other acts of friendship toward national Olympic committee and federation officials directly benefit Adidas as it competes to sponsor teams. "A lot of federations get higher offers than ours but refuse them because of what we have done over the last 10 years," he says. "If we hadn't done that, we would have paid more for less."

He says, however, that many Adidas activities don't help sales. "We equip not only the top countries but any country," he says. Nor, he says, are his friendships with the presidents of the IOC and international soccer and track federations used to gain favors. "Automatically, if I equip the Russian Olympic team, I have to meet their sports minister," he explains. "If you do this for 30 years, you get pretty close to people."

Mr. Dassler says his connections enable him to bridge political and cultural differences between East and West and

between developed and underdeveloped nations. His credibility is strong, he says, because "our interest has never been political. We have never sided anywhere; we are known as being capitalists."

Mr. Dassler's Influence

Although the IOC's secret voting makes it impossible to prove that Mr. Dassler influences Olympic decision-making, several amateur-sports officials—including some who are backed by Adidas and aren't willing to be quoted by name—say that it is risky to cross a supplier of equipment, plane tickets and hotel rooms. "Along with the ticket is the understanding of how they'll vote," says the president of a U.S. sports team. Mr. Dassler denies trying to influence IOC votes but others, including Mrs. Berlioux, the former IOC director, says his support helped elect Juan Antonio Samaranch president of the International Olympic Committee in 1980.

Mr. Dassler's Olympic connections came in handy at an IOC congress in Baden-Baden, West Germany, last May when the marketing rights to the 1988 games were awarded to ISL Marketing AG, a Swiss company run by former Adidas executives. Mr. Dassler and his four sisters own 51% of its shares; the rest are held by Dentsu, Japan's biggest advertising agency. ISL is to sign corporate sponsors for the next Olympics and thereby hopes to raise $150 million for the 1988 Games and a 10% commission for itself.

Although other sports-marketing companies in the U.S. and Europe were more experienced, ISL—then only two years old—was assigned by the IOC in 1983 to develop a marketing plan for the 1988 games. Other bidders weren't invited, thus making the final approval last May of ISL's contract a virtual certainty. And despite initial opposition from the U.S. Olympic Committee, the contract was approved by the majority of the Olympic committees of about 160 nations, including the U.S.

The Olympics agreement helps establish ISL as a major factor in sports marketing. Indeed, companies that want to tie their products to international amateur sports will encounter ISL at several pending world events. ISL, for instance, has the marketing rights to the World Cup Soccer matches in Mexico next June—an event that will reach billions of people around the world by TV.

SOURCE: Bill Abrams, "Sports Boss: Adidas Makes Friends, Then Strikes Deals That Move Sneakers." Reprinted by permission of *The Wall Street Journal.* © Dow Jones & Company, Inc., January 23, 1986, 116. All rights reserved.

DISCUSSION QUESTIONS

1. Identify and describe Adidas' market target(s) and target audiences for its communications strategy.
2. Describe and evaluate Adidas' promotion strategy, indicating the role and strategy for each promotion component.
3. Discuss the possible implications if a U.S. company attempted to compete against Adidas' marketing-through-patronage strategy.
4. Should Adidas' management revise its marketing strategy in the future?

STRATEGIC APPLICATION 14-2

CORDIS CORP.

Last November, with Cordis Corp. fighting a widening storm over a Food and Drug Administration inquiry of its heart pacemakers, an outside director called top management on the carpet.

At a tense meeting in the company's boardroom, Patricia Kelsh Woolf, a Cordis director who also is a research sociologist studying ethics and science at Princeton University, went around the room and bluntly lectured each executive.

"Basically, her message was stop protesting your innocence and start cleaning up the problem," recalls Norman Weldon, president and chief executive officer of the medical-devices company. "If I had to pick a moment of truth, it was Pat Woolf's speech to the management team."

Cordis's "problem" stemmed mainly from a nearly two-year-old FDA inquiry that began as a routine inspection into a battery problem but widened into a far-

ranging investigation when it was learned that a company executive had submitted an altered document to the agency.

Picking Up the Pieces

The soul-searching November meeting helped spur a new strategy that Cordis, the world's third-largest pacemaker company, hopes will bring it out of a morass that has sullied its once-spotless reputation and caused widespread concern by the users of its products. These two factors helped cause its pacemaker sales to slip for the first time ever.

Whether the strategy succeeds or not, the episode already is an instructive management tale. By mishandling the FDA inquiry, which was serious but not unusual in an industry plagued with difficulties ranging from product recalls to allegations of unnecessary pacemaker implantations and kickbacks, Cordis turned a normal business problem into a disaster. Cordis's troubles were compounded because they came at a time when the industry was in somewhat of a slump, partly because of changes in Medicare reimbursement rules.

Cordis was stung particularly hard by the negative publicity generated by the continuing FDA inquiry and two major product recalls. Many patients called Cordis or their doctors in response to a CBS broadcast in August dealing with the company's problems.

'Somewhat Arrogant'

Cordis admits that it didn't react quickly or effectively to the situation. "We were somewhat arrogant in that we didn't pay enough attention to the FDA," says Richard Spencer, president of Cordis's marketing division.

Cordis's recovery strategy includes new products and new research approaches, but its emphasis is on winning back patients, doctors and—more important—the FDA, which tightly regulates the pacemaker business. To prosper, the company must somehow regain the agency's trust.

"We've started rebuilding our relationship with the investment community," says the 51-year-old Mr. Weldon. "It will take a longer time with physicians. It will take the longest time with the FDA."

Things seem to be improving. The FDA in July said Cordis could test and market certain new products—the first such approvals in 18 months. The products include a pacemaker that regulates hearts that beat too fast—those currently on the market regulate slow hearts—and a next-generation dual-chamber pacemaker.

"I see a lot of sincerity on the part of management and the board of directors in coming to grips with the problems," says John Villforth, the FDA official overseeing the almost two-year-old inquiry. The investigation still could turn

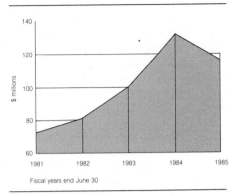

Cordis Pacemaker Sales Over a Five-Year Period

Fiscal years end June 30

up new problems but appears to be nearing completion. "Their attitude, if something's a close call, is to go ahead and do it rather than arguing."

Optimism Before the Fall

Just two years ago, the idea of Cordis needing a comeback strategy almost was unthinkable. After introducing a much-heralded pacemaker capable of sensing and stimulating cardiac activity in either or both chambers of the heart, the company's sales and profit soared. Market share world-wide rose to 18.7% in September 1983 from 15.9% in March 1983. "It looked like nothing could slow us down," Mr. Spencer says.

But on Dec. 3, 1983, the FDA began what was then a routine inspection of battery depletion problems in certain Cordis pacemakers. Four days later, the agency was provided with a company memorandum on the matter, written by John Pagones, then Cordis's vice president for corporate product assurance and its top executive in dealings with the FDA. Soon after, it was discovered that the document had been altered to delete references to eight possible problems involving the batteries in certain pacemakers.

According to Cordis, as soon as Mr. Weldon learned of the alteration, in January 1984, he ordered that the original memo be turned over to the FDA, along with an explanation of the incident. But the damage was done; the FDA began a wide-ranging inquiry into Cordis's pacemakers.

"From that day on, on reflection, it appeared that anything we said to the FDA they doubted," says Charles McDowell, vice president for corporate relations and assistant secretary.

A Hard-Line Position

Cordis didn't exactly help ease the doubts. Although it says it cooperated in resolving the altered-memo problem, its response to the inquiry in general was to stand tough against the regulators—"fighting them at every hedgerow," in Mr. Weldon's words. In hindsight, executives say that only compounded the problem.

"Cordis over the years has had the reputation for being the cleanest guy in the pacemaker industry," says Arnold Snider III, an analyst with Kidder, Peabody & Co. "It's so ironic that they were the ones that got nailed."

The FDA eventually ordered two major Cordis pacemakers recalls, one involving units with possible battery-depletion problems and the other covering models with potentially flawed printed circuit boards that could have caused the device to stop working suddenly. The agency also criticized Cordis for everything from its sterilization methods to its record-keeping procedures.

Both recalls involved models made before late 1980; the company says that even before the recalls, it had corrected the problems in newer models. It also says it is correcting the procedures cited by the agency. Cordis says that there haven't been any deaths or serious injuries attributed to defects in any of its products.

Because of the FDA inquiry, clinical testing of new products came to a halt, and for three months earlier this year sales of Cordis pacemakers were barred in Britain. For the year ended June 30, profit fell 58% and pacemaker sales fell 13%—the first sales decline since Cordis began making pacemakers in 1962. Sales for Cordis's other major division, which makes cardiac catheters, increased. However, the company's overall sales declined.

Cordis's world-wide market share in the approximately $700 million-a-year pacemaker business also was hurt. It currently stands at 16.9%, and the company says it expects that figure to decline to 16.3% by year's end before starting to rise again.

As its problems mushroomed, Cordis began seeking a way out—all the while insisting that most of the troubles weren't of its own making. Finally, at the meeting last November, Mrs. Woolf convinced management to face the facts.

For its part, Cordis's board set up a committee on quality and hired two outside quality auditors. The company also stepped up supervision of employees working on pacemakers and began keeping better records. In August, after a board-ordered investigation, Mr. Pagones and two other employees involved in the altered-document incident were fired. Mr. Pagones declined to comment.

Luring Back Customers

Cordis currently is mounting a campaign to win back the doctors who decide—or at least advise—patients on which brand of pacemaker to use. It also sent a two-page letter to all patients using its pacemakers in a bid to reassure those frightened by the negative news reports.

Whether the strategy will work isn't clear. The long FDA investigation has allowed competitors to catch up with or even gain a technological edge on Cordis. In an effort to recoup quickly, Mr. Weldon has shifted Cordis's research toward market needs rather than pure science and has focused efforts on a few of the most promising projects, including the devices recently approved by the FDA. Between August 1984 and early 1985, he reduced the total number of research projects from 96 to seven.

Still, Cordis is spending about 15% of sales on research and development—about double the industry average. Mr. Weldon says Cordis is working on several new pacemakers, an artificial artery for heart bypass operations, and a device that measures the chemical properties of blood in critically ill patients. The company, however, isn't assured of getting those products to market before competitors.

Analysts say Cordis won't really rebound until it markets new products, increases sales and trims the percentage of sales it spends on research and development.

Mr. Weldon says Cordis can't set a short-term strategy "that will erase the damage that's been done. It's going to take two or three years to rebuild it."

DISCUSSION QUESTIONS

1. What future strategic and operating guidelines do you recommend so that Cordis can avoid the problems they encountered in the mid-1980s with the FDA and with customers?
2. Critically evaluate management's new strategy to win back customers. What additional actions do you recommend?
3. How can buyer behavior analysis assist Cordis in implementing the new strategy?
4. What specific communications strategy should be used to strengthen Cordis's position with doctors?

STRATEGIC APPLICATION 14-3

HALLMARK CARDS

Hallmark Cards, Kansas City, Mo., which terms its principal field of business "social expression," ranked as the 102nd largest advertiser in 1984 with measured media spending of $40.3 million, a 91.4% increase over 1983.

Big changes at privately held Hallmark, which had total revenues of an estimated $1.5 billion in 1984, colored the company's advertising picture during 1984. In its dramatic boost of expenditures, the amount for network TV rose nearly 50% to $27.8 million; spending for print rose sharply to more than $11 million in 1984 from only $508,800 in the previous year.

In a major agency shift, Hallmark removed its more than $40 million ad account from Young & Rubicam in May, 1984, because it perceived a conflict between its own needs and those of American Telephone & Telegraph, whose $25 million account Y&R won in early 1984. Hallmark said the conflict came because it and AT&T both required "highly motivational" advertising and promoted themselves as "the best way to share love and affection." Hallmark turned over its account to Ogilvy & Mather, New York.

The company's two card brands, Hallmark and Ambassador, control 40% of the U.S. greeting card market, followed by American Greetings Corp., Cleveland, and Gibson Greeting Cards, Inc., Cincinnati, acquired by Walt Disney Productions in early 1984. Hallmark brand cards reach the public through 22,000 retail outlets, half of them gift and stationery shops, and the rest department and drugstores. About 250 of the shops are Hallmark-owned.

The Ambassador line, started in 1959, is sold through 15,000 chain groceries and other mass-market outlets. A separate staff produces and markets Ambassador cards, which Hallmark describes as the third biggest greeting card seller, with annual sales exceeding $250 million.

Hallmark's answer to this is a market-expanding multifold strategy; new licensed doll and cartoon characters, toys and gifts that can be marketed in tie-ins with cards; acquisitions of new companies, and investment in other industries.

Yet, a Hallmark spokesman stresses that the company is not veering from its main business: "A lot of media attention has focused on our acquisitions," he says, "but diversification is not where our energies are being spent. Social expression is still 90% of Hallmark."

Social expression was at the core of the company's reorganization in November, 1984, when it created a Social Expression Group to combine marketing and administration of all products in this category into one major management unit. Group vice president Robert L. Stark, promoted to senior vice president, directs the group.

Advanced card technology also shows Hallmark's continuing emphasis on its main business. A microchip gave Hallmark a new musical card in 1983. Further refinement produced a harmony musical card, first available for Christmas, 1984. In 1983, the company first used lasers to create intricate card designs, and in 1984 developed its "Perspectives" series of six cards bearing 3-D holograms.

Scheduled for completion in late 1985 is the new 170,000-sq.-ft. Technology & Innovation Center, where Hallmark plans for its artists, engineers, technicians and scientists to work together.

In content, Hallmark's cards in 1984 began reflecting sociological changes in U.S. society through its "new relationships" approach—cards for single parents, for homes with an absent father or a step-parent, a Mother's Day greeting that regards a mother not exclusively as a female parent but as someone who cares for children.

New products for 1984, created by the Hallmark Properties subsidiary, are story and doll characters Rainbow Brite and Rose-Petal Place. Mattel Inc. is licensed to make the doll versions. For 1985, there are Hugga Bunch, licensed to General Mills Toy Group, and new photo albums, paper partyware, gift wraps and fancy bags for wine, cookies or jewelry.

News of major acquisitions has come frequently the past few years from Hallmark's Crown Center headquarters, and 1984 was no exception. In March, 1984, Hallmark acquired a British maker of greeting cards and stationery, W. N. Sharpe Holdings, Bradford, England, for $52 million. In August, 1984, Hallmark bought Binney & Smith, Easton, Pa., the Crayola crayon maker, for $203 million. And Feb. 1, 1985, the company paid $50 million to take 30% equity in the textbook publisher and broadcaster SFM Cos. (formerly Scott Foresman & Co.), Glenview, Ill.

Over the years Hallmark has developed or acquired a number of companies, each with a distinctive line, including: Springbok, jigsaw puzzles (1967); Trifari, Krussman & Fishel, fashion jewelry, New York (1975); Charles D. Burnes Co., quality photo frames, Boston (1979); Litho-Krome, color printing, Columbus, Ga. (1979), and Heartline, its own designer-marketer of gifts, mostly plush toys (1983). The Hallmark International segment markets Hallmark products in 122 countries worldwide.

Hallmark employees own one-third of the company, with the remainder controlled by the Hall family. The late Joyce C. Hall at the age of 18 came to Kansas City from Nebraska 75 years ago to sell picture post cards. He stayed to found Hallmark Cards on Jan. 20, 1910. His son, Donald J. Hall, heads the company as chairman.

DISCUSSION QUESTIONS

1. Discuss the role of advertising in Hallmark's marketing strategy.
2. What should be Hallmark's advertising objectives?
3. Evaluate the logic of Hallmark's changes in the size and allocation of advertising expenditures in 1984 compared to 1983.
4. Identify and discuss various ways Hallmark can measure the effectiveness of its advertising program.

Advertising Expenditures ($000)

	1984	1983
Magazines	11,047.7	508.8
Network cable	83.2	173.0
Spot TV	1,387.6	1,381.4
Network TV	27,812.9	18,668.2
Spot radio	1.6	66.7
Network radio	0.0	276.3
Total measured	40,333.0	21,074.4

SOURCE: *Advertising Age,* June 13, 1985, 40.

CHAPTER 15

Selling and Sales Promotion Strategies

One of the more exciting challenges in selling strategy in the mid-1980s was the battle between several states to be selected as the site for General Motors' new Saturn automobile plant.[1] GM chose Tennessee, which had competed against Illinois, Ohio, Texas, and other states. The potential economic impact of the Saturn plant represented a major opportunity for the state and city selected. William Long, Commissioner of Economic and Community Development, coordinated Tennessee's selling strategy. Competing states tried various techniques and incentives: 200 Ohio school children wrote letters to GM, Illinois promised to build a $50 million recreational and childcare center for GM employees, and other states erected billboard invitations along Detroit's highways. Commissioner Long's strategy was less flamboyant. It was carefully formulated and effective; it centered on getting the right information to the right people at the right time. Tennessee officials heard rumors about the site search in late 1984, and were ready with a detailed presentation when GM made the formal announcement in early 1985. After the presentation, Mr. Long identified an executive at GM who could be contacted on a regular basis. Whenever additional information about Tennessee was requested, it was hand-delivered to General Motors headquarters. The decision by American Airlines to establish a major hub in Nashville and the upward movement of Tennessee in a national ranking of favorable manufacturing climates also contributed to Tennessee winning the site selection. Mr. Long was careful to maintain confidentiality in negotiations requested by GM. Tennessee Governor Lamar Alexander was closely involved in the selling strategy. But even though he had numerous conversations with the GM Chairman, he did not visit Detroit to promote his state as other governors did. Commissioner Long's direction of the sales campaign clearly showed what a master salesman could accomplish by planning and executing a targeted and coordinated selling strategy.

In this chapter, we consider the development of a selling strategy, followed by a discussion of the designing of the sales organization. Next, we examine recruitment, training, management, and evaluation and control of the sales force. Finally, we look at the role and scope of sales promotion strategy, and discuss sales promotion methods.

DEVELOPING A SELLING STRATEGY

The major steps in developing and implementing a selling strategy are shown in Exhibit 15-1. After understanding the selling situation, sales management must indicate what the sales force is expected to accomplish and then formulate a selling strategy designed to achieve the objectives. Next, management must determine organizational design. The recruitment, training, and management of the sales force follows. Finally, the results of the selling strategy are evaluated and adjustments are made to eliminate the gap between actual and desired results.

Analyzing the Selling Situation

In a firm's marketing program, personal selling can range from a major to minor role in marketing strategy. Salespeople may serve primarily as order takers or they may fulfill major responsibilities as consultants to customers. While management has some flexibility in choosing the role of the sales force in the marketing mix, several factors often help determine the role of selling in a firm's marketing strategy. These are shown in Exhibit 15-2.

Situation analysis should define the role of personal selling in the promotion strategy. The selling effort must be integrated into the overall communications program. It is also important that the analysis indicate the support provided to the sales force from other promotion components, such as advertising and sales promotion tools. For example, what will advertising contribute to various stages in the buyer's decision process (Chapter 6)? What sales promotion activities will be conducted during the strategy implementation period? Sales management must be aware of the plans and activities of other components.

Setting Objectives

The objectives assigned to salespeople frequently involve management's expected sales results. Sales quotas are popular means of ex-

EXHIBIT 15-1 Developing and Implementing a Selling Strategy

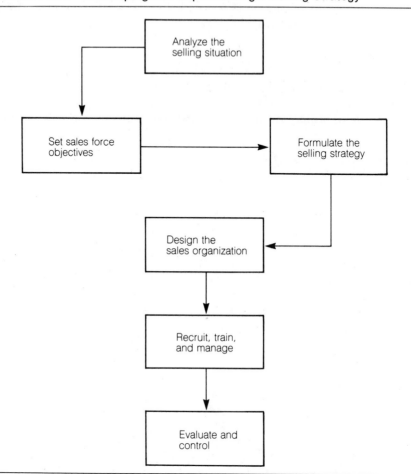

pressing these expectations, and firms often provide incentives to salespeople who achieve their quotas. Objectives other than sales are important to some organizations. Nonsales objectives may include increasing the number of new accounts, providing services to customers and channel organizations, selecting and evaluating middlemen, and obtaining market information. The objectives selected should be consistent with marketing strategy and promotion objectives, and they should be measurable so that sales performance can be evaluated.

Formulating Selling Strategy

International Business Machines revised its selling strategy in 1986 and reorganized its 10,000-member sales force.[2] IBM was acknowledg-

EXHIBIT 15-2   Factors Influencing the Role of Personal Selling in a Firm's Marketing Strategy

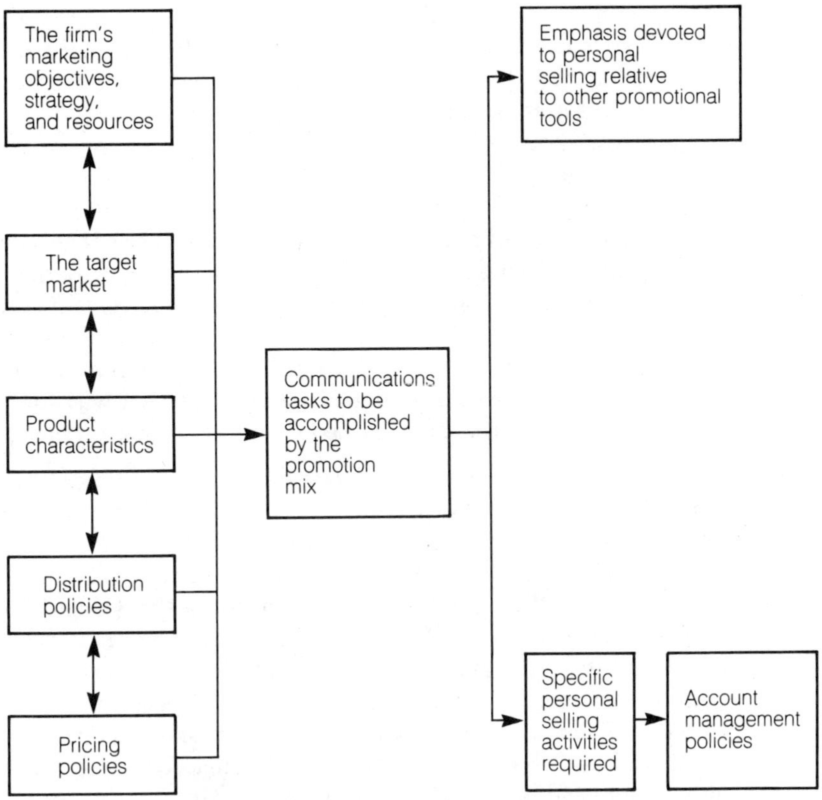

SOURCE: Gilbert A. Churchill, Jr., Neil M. Ford, and Orville C. Walker, Jr., *Sales Force Management,* 2nd ed. (Homewood, Ill.: Richard D. Irwin, 1985), 66.

ing the growing role of lower-priced computers and the expanding importance of independent dealers. Unlike mainframe computers, smaller computers lack the margins necessary to support personal selling. The costs of using a company sales force to sell intermediate-range computers were too high. Observers expected IBM to continue selling the 200 System while farming out single-system sales to agents. The company had reorganized its sales force in 1982, combining salespeople from three product divisions into two sales units of about 5,000 salespeople each, one selling to large companies and one to smaller companies. A third unit of 1,000 salespeople marketed through resellers.

New ventures require new selling strategies that must be altered to respond to changing conditions and opportunities. Selling strategy development consists of an interrelated set of decisions:

1. How can the personal selling effort best be adapted to the company's environment and integrated with the other elements of the firm's marketing strategy? In sum, what should be the firm's personal selling strategy?
2. How can various types of potential customers best be approached, persuaded, and serviced? In other words, what account management policies should be adopted?
3. How should the sales force be organized to call on and manage various types of customers as efficiently and effectively as possible?
4. What level of performance can each member of the sales force be expected to attain during the next planning period? This involves forecasting demand and setting quotas and budgets.
5. In view of the firm's account management policies and demand forecasts, how should the sales force be deployed? How should sales territories be defined? What is the best way for each salesperson's time to be allocated within his or her territory?[3]

An increasingly important consideration in selling strategy development is improving the productivity of the company sales force. Reorganizations, mergers, acquisitions, deregulation, global competition, high selling expenses, and other changes in firms' strategy situations are affecting selling productivity in various ways. Consider the analysis shown in Exhibit 15-3. In an initial reorganization, management decided that it was important to assign a salesperson to each of the 24 locations to strengthen customer relations. The productivity imbalances are clear. There are huge differences in revenue between the salespeople at the top and those at the bottom of the list. Too much effort is probably being used in territories in the bottom third of the list and perhaps not enough in the territories at the top. In early 1986 management began to revise its selling strategy to improve productivity in the low-revenue territories. Some salespeople were reassigned. Terminations and retirements allowed some shift of employees out of the low-volume locations. Management decided to convert many of these accounts to telemarketing coverage, with a few scheduled visits to the locations by personnel based elsewhere.

Illustrative Selling Strategies

Companies use a variety of selling strategies depending on the strategic factors affecting the situation and the role of selling in the promotion mix. The range of possible strategies includes new business, trade selling, missionary selling, and consultative/technical selling strategies.[4]

New Business Strategy. This selling strategy is primarily concerned with obtaining sales. Firms using this strategy are seeking new cus-

EXHIBIT 15-3 Sales Territories Analysis

Salesman	1984 Revenue ($ 10,000)	Number of Accounts	Calls per Month (in-person/phone)
1	81	20	20/15
2	69	48	55–60/80–100
3	60	60	80/250
4	48	43	48/75
5	34	40	40/*
6	24	125	50/250
7	24	56	80/85
8	22	95	48/40
9	22	67	45/*
10	17	80	40/100
11	17	45	40/100
12	16	31	28/32
13	15	35	50/200
14	13	54	75/*
15	12	45	60/250
16	10	76	100/150
17	10	66	36/150
18	6	50	60/160
19	5	25	25/300
20	4	88	160/*
21	4	40	36/40
22	2	30	60/240
23	1	30	40/80
24	.3	75	50/100

*No response

tomers who will repurchase on a continuing basis. For example, the first-time sale of sheet steel by a steel producer to a container manufacturer may lead to further purchases. Alternatively, the selling strategy may be concerned with obtaining new buyers on a continuing basis. Insurance and real estate sales firms use this strategy.

Trade Selling Strategy. This selling strategy emphasizes assisting middlemen rather than obtaining sales; this relationship is ongoing. A manufacturer marketing through wholesalers, retailers, or other middlemen may provide the intermediaries with merchandising, logistical, promotional, and product information assistance, for instance. Ethan Allen uses this selling strategy in its furniture business, and so do food processors.

Missionary Selling Strategy. A similar strategy to trade selling is missionary selling. A manufacturer's salespeople work with the customers of a channel member to encourage them to purchase the manufacturer's product from the channel member. For example, pharmaceutical sales representatives contact physicians, providing them with product information and samples and encouraging them to prescribe the producer's drugs. Also, a railroad firm offering intermodal services may encourage a shipper to use an associated trucking firm for inter-modal shipments.

Consultative/Technical Selling Strategy. Firms that use this strategy sell to an existing customer base, and provide technical and application assistance. IBM's strategy for selling direct to business customers is illustrative, as is the sale of architectural services to commercial building developers. Understanding and responding to customer needs is essential to the success of this strategy.

A company may use more than one selling strategy. For example, a transportation services company might use a new business strategy for expanding its customer base and a missionary selling strategy for servicing existing customers. Also, the characteristics necessary in a successful salesperson vary according to the selling strategy used.

DESIGNING THE SALES ORGANIZATION

Designing a sales organization requires selecting an organizational structure, and deciding how many salespeople are needed and how selling effort should be allocated.

Organizational Structure

The organizational approach adopted should depend on the firm's selling strategy. As companies adjust their selling strategies, organizational structure may also require changes.

Important influences on organizational design are the existing and potential customer base, the product, and the geographic location of buyers. Thus, organizational designs for a sales force are driven by *market, product, geography,* or a combination of these factors. Several questions should be answered in selecting an organizational design.

1. What is the selling job? What functions are to be performed by salespeople?
2. Is specialization of selling effort necessary—according to type of customer, different products, or salesperson activities (e.g., sales and service)?
3. Are channel of distribution considerations important in organizational design?
4. How many and what kinds of sales management levels are needed to provide the proper amount of supervision, assistance, and control?

The organizational design that is selected should reflect both selling strategy and other marketing mix strategies. Several types of orga-

EXHIBIT 15-4   Sales Organization Designs

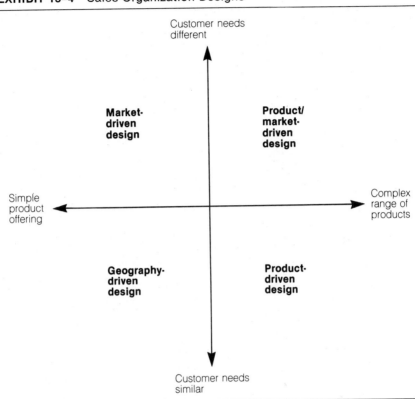

nization designs are shown in Exhibit 15-4. Whenever the customer base is widely dispersed, geography is likely to be included in the organizational design.

Sales Force Deployment

Resource allocation decisions have an important influence on the productivity of a sales organization just as equipment allocation decisions do on production operations. The operations manager must decide how many machines are needed and where each will be placed. The sales manager must decide how many salespeople are needed and how to deploy them. But there is a major distinction between the two decisions: Estimating the productivity of salespeople is far more complex than estimating the output of machines.

The problem in estimating sales force productivity is that various factors outside the salesperson's control often affect a territory's sales

EXHIBIT 15-5 Impact of Salesperson on the Results Obtained in the Work Unit

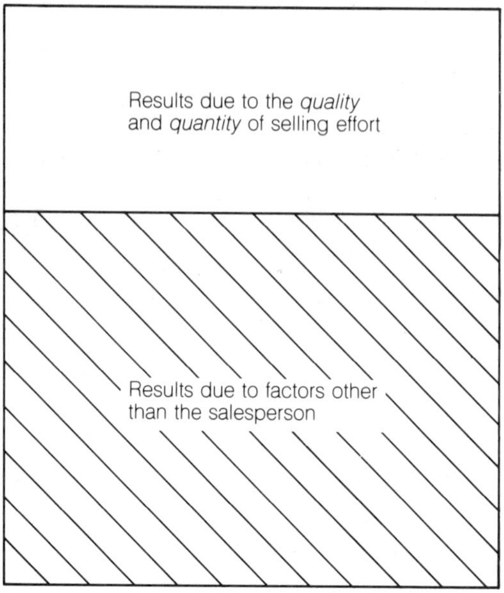

results (see in Exhibit 15-5). Such influences include market potential, number and location of customers, intensity of competition, and market position of the company. Productivity analysis should consider both salesperson factors and uncontrollable factors.

There are several methods for analyzing sales force size and deployment including: (1) revenue/cost analysis, (2) single-factor models, (3) sales and effort response models, and (4) portfolio deployment strategy models. Assume that sales and/or costs are the basis for determining sales force size and allocation.

Revenue/Cost Analysis. Most of these techniques require information on each salesperson's sales and/or costs. Two popular methods of sales force analysis are shown in Exhibit 15-6. Method A can be used to compare a sales force to an average break-even sales level, thus helping management to spot unprofitable territories. Method B examines how a deployment change will affect sales, cost, and profit contribution. It can be used to analyze the profit performance of accounts or trading areas, to estimate the profit impact of adding more salespeople, or to determine how many people a new sales organization needs.

Sales and cost analysis methods are primarily used to gauge salespeoples' existing or future productivity. If the necessary information is available, these techniques are very useful in locating high- and low-

---

EXHIBIT 15-6   Two Revenue/Cost Methods of Sales Force
Size/Deployment Analysis

A.   Break-even comparisons

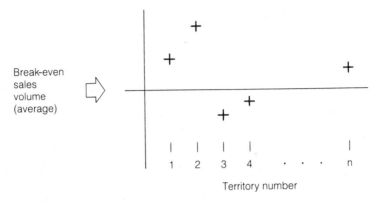

B.   Profit contribution of adding a salesperson

Estimated sales		$400,000
Contribution to overhead and profit (20%)		80,000*
Less:		
Base salary	35,000	
Incentive (2% of sales)	8,000	
Benefits	5,000	
Expenses	5,000	53,000
Net contribution after personal selling costs		27,000

---

*Before deducting direct personal selling costs.

performance territories. However, they do not indicate *why* one territory is doing better or worse than another. Management must provide this assessment using other available information plus judgment and experience.

Single-Factor Models.   These approaches share one common feature: Each assumes that size and/or deployment are determined by one factor, such as market potential, workload (e.g., number of calls required), or others whose values can be used to determine required selling effort. Suppose there are two territories, X and Y. Territory X has double the market potential (opportunity for business) of territory Y. If selling effort is deployed according to market potential, X should get double the selling effort of Y.

Single-factor models are easy to use and offer rough guides to effort allocation. Their main deficiency is that several factors may be necessary to determine the selling effort needed for a customer, product, territory, or other assigned work unit. For example, market potential by itself fails to recognize other influences on sales results, such as the intensity of competition, composition of accounts and prospects, and market position.

EXHIBIT 15-7   Sales Force Decision Model Output for Jones's and Smith's Territories

---

Trading Area†	Present Effort (percent)	Recommended Effort (percent)	Estimated Sales*	
			Present Effort	Recommended Effort
Jones:				
1	10	4	19	13
2	60	20	153	120
3	15	7	57	50
4	5	2	10	7
5	10	3	21	16
Total	100	36	260	206
Smith:				
1	18	81	370	520
2	7	21	100	130
3	5	11	55	65
4	35	35	225	225
5	5	11	60	70
6	30	77	400	500
Total	100	236	1,210	1,510

*In $000.

†Each territory is made up of several trading areas.

Sales and Effort Response Models.   There are several promising models for aiding size and deployment decisions. The starting point is a model of market (sales) response to selling effort. Two approaches have been used to build the sales response function.[5] One uses estimates from salespeople to construct sales response functions. A specific function is determined for each unit of analysis, such as customer or trading area. The other approach is based on a composite sales response function, empirically determined using multiple factors that are related to sales response. Next, the response model, used with an effort allocation model, generates recommended deployment guidelines. This can be done for an existing sales force size or for alternatives if management wants to select an optimal size.

Exhibit 15-7 gives an example of the output provided by these models. Jones's territory requires only about 0.36 percent of a person whereas Smith's territory can support about 2.36 people. These models determine allocation by increasing selling effort in high-response areas and reducing effort where sales response is low. Note that Exhibit 15-7 includes only two territories of a large sales organization. In a complete analysis of all territories, unless alternative sales force sizes are being evaluated, the sum of present selling effort must equal the sum of recommended effort.

Of all the approaches to sales force size and deployment analysis, the sales and effort response models are the most promising. Even modest allocation improvements in a sales force of 100 or more people

---

EXHIBIT 15-8 Portfolio Model Results

A. Capital equipment distributor

Strength of position

		Strong	Weak
Account opportunity	**High**	Average sales calls: 29 Average sales: $20,214 Number of accounts: 41	Average sales calls: 21 Average sales: $9,896 Number of accounts: 5
	Low	Average sales calls: 17 Average sales: $8,167 Number of accounts: 142	Average sales calls: 11 Average sales: $2,595 Number of accounts: 34

B. Grocery products marketer

Strength of position

		Strong	Weak
Account opportunity	**High**	Average sales calls: 27 Average sales: 2,438 cases Number of accounts: 97	Average sales calls: 21 Average sales: 1,248 cases Number of accounts: 15
	Low	Average sales calls: 23 Average sales: 1,017 cases Number of accounts: 26	Average sales calls: 17 Average sales: 402 cases Number of accounts: 66

The average sales calls and average sales are annual levels for the accounts in each segment of the grid.

SOURCE: Raymond W. LaForge, David W. Cravens, and Clifford E. Young, "Improving Sales-force Productivity," *Business Horizons*, September/October 1985, 56.

---

can result in substantial payoffs—payoffs that far exceed the initial costs of developing the model.

Portfolio Deployment Strategy Model. A promising approach for deployment modeling has been developed using an adapted version of the market attractiveness–business strength grid for business unit and product strategic analysis (Chapter 3). The assumption in portfolio analysis of accounts and prospects is that promising accounts should receive effort allocation based on their position on the grid.[6] An account with a high market opportunity and one for which the firm has a strong position in comparison to competition would receive a higher effort allocation. Company-specific analyses are necessary to establish guidelines for the effort allocation. Exhibit 15–8 shows the grid analy-

EXHIBIT 15-9 Management Deployment Plans

A. Capital Equipment Distributor

	Average Sales Calls for Previous Period	Average Sales Calls for New Deployment Plan	Percentage Change
Segment 1	29	32	+10.3%
Segment 2	21	24	+14.3
Segment 3	17	16	− 5.9
Segment 4	11	8	−27.3

B. Grocery Products Marketer

	Average Sales Calls for Previous Period	Average Sales Calls for New Deployment Plan	Percentage Change
Segment 1	27	36	+33.3%
Segment 2	21	24	+14.3
Segment 3	23	12	−47.8
Segment 4	17	6	−64.7

SOURCE: Raymond W. LaForge, David W. Cravens, and Clifford E. Young, "Improving Sales-force Productivity," *Business Horizons*, September/October 1985, 57.

sis of a capital equipment distributor and a grocery products marketer, while Exhibit 15-9 shows deployment guidelines based on analysis of the current allocation (Exhibit 15-8). Selling effort strategies in both firms indicate a tendency to use similar call patterns for accounts in all four segments of the grid. For example, pre-analysis call averages for the grocery products firm ranged from 17 to 27, compared to a recommended range of 6 to 36 after analysis. One major advantage of this development method is that it is easily understood by management and salespeople.

MANAGING THE SALES FORCE

Salespeople should be considered equal when making decisions as to sales force size and effort allocation. After doing so, however, management must consider the human aspects—differences in ability, motivation, and performance. Managing the sales force involves supervising, selecting, training, motivating, and evaluating. Exhibit 15-10 indicates the relationship of the environment, marketing strategy, sales management decisions, salesperson performance, outcomes, and control.[7]

Finding and Selecting Salespeople

Few sales managers agree on what criteria to use in selecting salespeople although they all want good performers. Exhibit 15-11 lists a number of characteristics that may have important ties to performance.

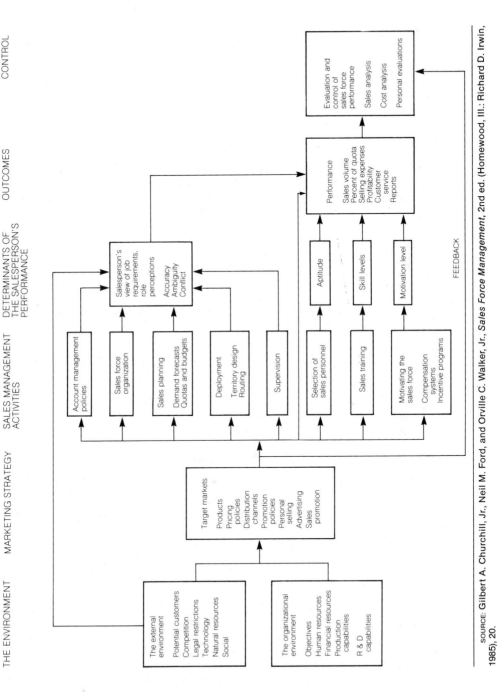

THE ENVIRONMENT   MARKETING STRATEGY   SALES MANAGEMENT ACTIVITIES   DETERMINANTS OF THE SALESPERSON'S PERFORMANCE   OUTCOMES   CONTROL

The external environment
Potential customers
Competition
Legal restrictions
Technology
Natural resources
Social

The organizational environment
Objectives
Human resources
Financial resources
Production capabilities
R & D capabilities

Target markets
Products
Pricing policies
Distribution channels
Promotion policies
Personal selling
Advertising
Sales promotion

Account management policies

Sales force organization

Sales planning
Demand forecasts
Quotas and budgets

Deployment
Territory design
Routing

Supervision

Selection of sales personnel

Sales training

Motivating the sales force
Compensation systems
Incentive programs

Salesperson's view of job requirements, role perceptions
Accuracy
Ambiguity
Conflict

Aptitude

Skill levels

Motivation level

Performance
Sales volume
Percent of quota
Selling expenses
Profitability
Customer service
Reports

Evaluation and control of sales force performance
Sales analysis
Cost analysis
Personal evaluations

FEEDBACK

SOURCE: Gilbert A. Churchill, Jr., Neil M. Ford, and Orville C. Walker, Jr., *Sales Force Management*, 2nd ed. (Homewood, Ill.: Richard D. Irwin, 1985), 20.

EXHIBIT 15-11   Characteristics Related to Sales Performance in Different Types of Sales Jobs

Type Sales Job	Characteristics that Are Relatively Important	Characteristics that Are Relatively Less Important
Trade selling	Age, maturity, empathy, knowledge of customer needs and business methods	Aggressiveness, technical ability, product knowledge, persuasiveness
Missionary selling	Youth, high energy and stamina, verbal skill, persuasiveness	Empathy, knowledge of customers, maturity, previous sales experience
Technical selling	Education, product and customer knowledge— usually gained through training, intelligence	Empathy, persuasiveness, aggressiveness, age
New business selling	Experience, age and maturity, aggressiveness, persuasiveness, persistence	Customer knowledge, product knowledge, education, empathy

SOURCE: Gilbert A. Churchill, Jr., Neil M. Ford, and Orville C. Walker, Jr., *Sales Force Management,* 2nd ed. (Homewood, Ill.: Richard D. Irwin, 1985), 354.

The characteristics vary considerably depending on the type of selling strategy, so management must first define the job that is to be performed. According to Churchill, Ford, and Walker:

> Each sales executive must try to develop his or her own specifications concerning what to look for in new sales recruits. Those specifications should be developed after careful analysis and description of the tasks and activities involved in selling the firm's products to its target market. There should also be an evaluation of the characteristics and qualifications that new salespeople must have to perform those tasks and activities.[8]

Although many hiring decisions are based on experience and judgment, managers also rely on application forms, personal interviews, rating forms, reference checks, physical examinations, and various kinds of tests. In most firms the personal interview is the most important part of the selection process.

Training

Some firms use structured programs to train their salespeople; others use informal on-the-job training. Factors that affect the type and duration of training include size of firm, type of sales job, product complexity, experience of new salespeople, and management's satisfaction with past training efforts. Training topics may include selling concepts and techniques, product knowledge, territory management, and company policies and operating procedures.

In training salespeople, companies may seek to: (1) increase productivity, (2) improve morale, (3) lower turnover, (4) improve customer relations, and (5) produce better management of time and territory.[9] Each of these objectives is concerned with increasing results from the salesperson's effort and/or reducing personal selling costs.

Sales training can be very expensive. The company is paying for the trainee and trainer's time yet neither is contributing sales. One study estimated the average annual cost of sales training per salesperson (including salary) at $16,000 for service firms, $16,600 for consumer product firms, and $24,600 for industrial product firms.[10] A sales training program needs to be evaluated regularly even though management may have difficulty gauging its impact on performance. Product knowledge training is probably more widespread than any other type of training.

Supervising and Motivating Salespeople

The sales supervisor has a key role in implementing a firm's selling strategy. He or she faces several important strategic issues. Coordinating the activities of a field sales force is difficult due to lack of regular contact. Compensation incentives are often used to encourage salespeople to sell.

In the 1980s, many firms returned to using incentives for salespeople instead of fixed salaries.[11] The favored compensation plan is a combination of salary and commission (80 percent salary and 20 percent commission is a typical arrangement). A compensation plan should be fair to all participants and create an appropriate incentive. Salespeople also respond favorably to recognition programs.

The total supervision and motivation approach should be carefully designed and implemented. Supervision and incentive compensation should function as an integrated system. Unless the basic approach to managing the sales force is sound, special motivational programs, contests, and other sales-generating techniques are not likely to be effective.

Supervision can assist and encourage salespeople, and incentives can highlight the importance of results, but the salesperson is the driving force in selling situations. Sales management must match promising selling opportunities with competent and self-motivated professional salespeople and provide the proper company environment and support. Although most sales management professionals think financial compensation is the most important motivating force, recent research suggests others: personal characteristics, environmental conditions, and company policies and procedures.[12]

EXHIBIT 15-12   Index of Personal Selling Costs and Advertising Costs
(1973 = 100)

Personal selling costs = cost of an industrial sales call

Advertising costs = cost of reaching 1,000 business paper subscribers
(based on 12X-13X One-Page B&W Rate)

SOURCE: Laboratory of Advertising Performance/McGraw-Hill Research.

SALES FORCE EVALUATION AND CONTROL

Sales management is increasingly concerned with improving the productivity of selling efforts. In recent decades, personal selling costs have risen faster than advertising costs (see Exhibit 15–12). The comparison is computed by setting the average cost of a 1973 industrial sales call of $66.68 equal to 100 and expressing subsequent years in terms of the cost ratio to 1973. For example, the 1983 call cost of $205.40 corresponds to an index of 308. The call cost information in Exhibit 15–12 was obtained from annual surveys of over 1,000 sales executives.

Considerations in Sales Force Evaluation

Evaluation of sales force performance includes analyses of sales results, costs, and salesperson performance. Several items must be considered in evaluation, including the unit(s) of analysis, measures of performance, performance standards, and adjustment for factors that the sales organization and individual salespeople cannot control.

Unit of Analysis.   Evaluation should extend beyond the salesperson to include other organizational units, such as districts and branches. Product performance evaluation by geographical area and across organization units is important in firms that produce more than one product. Sales and cost analyses are useful for customers such as national accounts and accounts assigned to salespeople.

Performance Measures.   Management needs yardsticks for measuring salesperson performance. For example, the sales force of a regional food processor that distributes through grocery wholesalers and large retail chains devotes most of its selling effort to calling on retailers. Since the firm does not have information on sales of its products by individual retail outlet, management has to base its evaluations on qualitative criteria—a highly subjective approach.

A typical firm will use both subjective and objective measures of salesperson performance. Achievement of a sales quota is a widely-used objective measure of sales performance. Profit contribution, new business generated, and other factors are also considered. Several ratios used to evaluate salespeople are shown in Exhibit 15-13. These ratios require some basis of comparison, such as prior time periods or sales force averages.

Setting Performance Standards.   Although relative comparisons of performance are frequently used, they may be misleading if the performance of the entire sales force is unacceptable. A major problem in setting sales performance standards is determining how to adjust them for factors beyond the salesperson's control; i.e., market potential, intensity of competition, differences in customer needs, and quality of supervision. A highly competent salesperson may not appear to be performing well if assigned to a poor sales territory. Management should consider these situational differences in its evaluation process since territories normally are not equal in terms of opportunity and other situational factors.

Controlling Performance

Evaluating performance is one of sales management's more difficult tasks. Typically, performance tracking involves assessing a combination of objective and subjective factors. In compensation plans other than straight commission, performance evaluation may affect the salesperson's pay.

By evaluating its personal selling strategy, management may identify various problems requiring corrective action. Problems may be

---

EXHIBIT 15-13   Common Ratios Used to Evaluate Salespeople

I. **Expense ratios**

    A. Sales expense ratio $= \dfrac{\text{Expenses}}{\text{Sales}}$

    B. Cost per call ratio $= \dfrac{\text{Total costs}}{\text{Number of calls}}$

II. **Account development and servicing ratios**

    A. Account penetration ratio $= \dfrac{\text{Accounts sold}}{\text{Total accounts available}}$

    B. New account conversion ratio $= \dfrac{\text{Number of new accounts}}{\text{Total number of accounts}}$

    C. Lost account ratio $= \dfrac{\text{Prior accounts not sold}}{\text{Total number of accounts}}$

    D. Sales per account ratio $= \dfrac{\text{Sales dollar volume}}{\text{Total number of accounts}}$

    E. Average order size ratio $= \dfrac{\text{Sales dollar volume}}{\text{Total number of orders}}$

    F. Order cancellation ratio $= \dfrac{\text{Number of cancelled orders}}{\text{Total number of orders}}$

III. **Call activity and/or productivity**

    A. Calls per day ratio $= \dfrac{\text{Number of calls}}{\text{Number of days worked}}$

    B. Calls per account ratio $= \dfrac{\text{Number of calls}}{\text{Number of accounts}}$

    C. Planned call ratio $= \dfrac{\text{Number of planned calls}}{\text{Total number of calls}}$

    D. Orders per call (hit) ratio $= \dfrac{\text{Number of orders}}{\text{Total number of calls}}$

SOURCE: Gilbert A. Churchill, Jr., Neil M. Ford, and Orville C. Walker, Jr., *Sales Force Management,* 2nd ed. (Homewood, Ill.: Richard D. Irwin, Inc. 1985), 627

---

linked to individual salespeople or to other aspects of selling strategy. A sound information system is needed to help sales management diagnose performance and take corrective action when necessary. Management must compare plans with actual results and determine if the results are on target.

SALES PROMOTION STRATEGY

The effectiveness of coupons as a promotional device is attested to by their phenomenal growth: 24 percent last year alone, to a total of 142.9 billion distributed and 5.56 billion redeemed. The coupon is even a factor in product sampling, with many manufacturers distributing free-product coupons to better target likely buyers of their products. But there are problems associated with this pervasive marketing tool, not the least of which is clutter.[13]

Coupons represent one of several methods of sales promotion that can contribute to promotion strategy. The following discussion provides a brief overview of the nature and scope of sales promotion, types of sales promotion strategies, advantages and limitations of sales promotion, and developing sales promotion strategy.

Nature and Scope of Sales Promotion

Many firms have no identifiable sales promotion strategy because they assign responsibility to different marketing functions, such as advertising, merchandising, product planning, and sales. Sales promotion strategy consists of all activities designed to promote a company and its products, exclusive of advertising, personal selling, or public relations activities. For example, a sales contest for salespeople is typically designed and administered by sales management, and the costs of the contest are included in the sales department budget. Similarly, planning and coordinating a coupon refund program may be assigned to a brand manager. Thus sales promotion activities are fragmented and often their nature and scope are not recognized.

Total expenditures for sales promotion by business and industry are estimated to be substantially larger than the total spent on advertising. One estimate of sales promotion expenditures is that they comprise about 60 percent of manufacturers' mass communications expenditures.[14] The complete scope of sales promotion is difficult to identify because its activities are included in various departments and budgets and are difficult to distinguish from advertising. There are several similarities between sales promotion and advertising and some important distinctions.

An important strategy issue is how to manage the sales promotion function. While the various activities are often used to support advertising, pricing, channel of distribution, and personal selling strategies, the size and scope of sales promotion strongly suggest that responsibility should be assigned to one executive. Some proponents argue for the establishment of a department of sales promotion. At minimum, marketing management should recognize the importance of coordinating and evaluating various sales promotion activities.

Types of Sales Promotion Strategies

A variety of methods can be used in the total promotion strategy, including trade shows, specialty advertising (e.g., imprinted calenders), contests, point-of-purchase displays, coupons, recognition programs (e.g., awards to middlemen), and free samples. Sales promotion methods typically are most effective when used as part of a total communications program, rather than when they form the primary component of promotion strategy. Nevertheless, expenditures for sales promotion may be very substantial. For example, Gaines Foods Inc. distributed more than 50 million 50-cent coupons as part of a $20 million advertis-

EXHIBIT 15–14   Sales Promotion Activities Targeted to Various Groups

Sales Promotion Activity	Targeted To:			
	Consumer Buyers	Industrial Buyers	Middlemen	Salespeople
Incentives				
Contests	X	X	X	X
Trips	X	X	X	X
Bonuses			X	X
Prizes	X	X	X	X
Advertising support			X	
Free items	X	X		
Recognition			X	X
Promotional Pricing				
Coupons	X			
Allowances		X	X	
Rebates	X	X	X	
Cash	X			
Informational Activities				
Direct mail	X	X	X	
Displays	X			
Demonstrations	X	X	X	
Selling aids			X	X
Catalogs	X	X	X	X
Speciality advertising (e.g., pens)	X	X	X	
Trade shows		X	X	

ing, trade, and consumer promotion campaign for its Gaines Burgers, Top Choice, and Puppy Choice brands.[15] At the average rate of coupon redemption of 1 in 25, about 2.2 million of the 50-cent coupons would be redeemed.

Firms may aim their sales promotion activities at consumer buyers, industrial buyers, middlemen, and salespeople, as shown in Exhibit 15–14.

Promotion to Consumer Targets.   Exhibit 15–15 demonstrates how sales promotion methods can be used for a new consumer product. Note the use of specific promotion methods directed at consumers and resellers, sales promotion to complement advertising to end users, and sales promotion in support of personal selling to middlemen. The role of each sales promotion component is targeted to a particular communication need such as visual aids to improve sales presentation. Exhibit 15–15 also emphasizes the importance of coordinating sales promotion with product, place, and price strategies.

Promotion to Industrial Targets.   While many of the sales promotion methods appropriate for consumer products are also useful for indus-

EXHIBIT 15-15 Sales Promotion Methods for a New Consumer Product

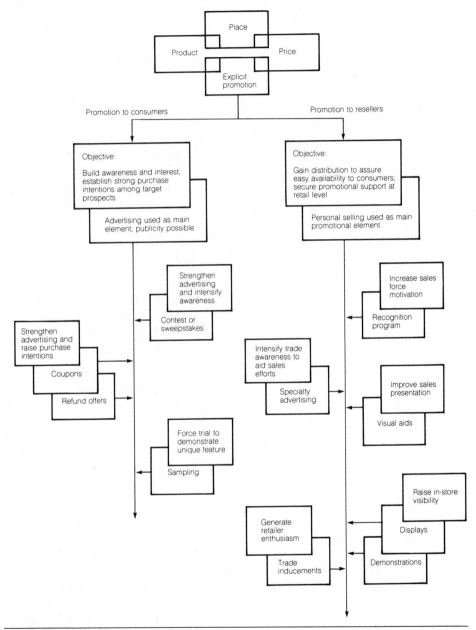

SOURCE: William P. Dommermuth, *Promotion: Analysis, Creativity, and Strategy* (Boston: Kent Publishing, 1984), 593.

trial products, the role and scope of the methods may vary. For example, trade shows are a cost-effective method of making direct contact with buyers and demonstrating equipment. Megatek, a supplier of high-performance graphics systems and software, estimates that half of its annual sales of $40 million is derived from trade shows.[16] The company allocates nearly 50 percent of its advertising and promotion budget to cover the costs of participating in 20 national, international, and local shows. A show generates about 300 leads, of which 40 are promising prospects. Eventually, about five of the trade show contacts purchase from Megatek.

Small- and medium-sized companies like Megatek can use trade shows to perform a key role in their marketing strategies. The advantage is the heavy concentration of potential buyers at one location during a very short time. The cost per contact is substantially less than calling on prospects at their offices. While people attending trade shows also spend their time viewing competitors' products, salespeople have a unique opportunity to hold prospects' attention.

Sales promotion to industrial buyers may consume a greater portion of the marketing budget than advertising. Many types of promotional activities support direct selling strategies, including catalogs, brochures, product information reports, trade shows, application guides, and promotional items such as calendars, pens, and calculators. Firms can also use incentives. The "frequent flyer" programs of the major airlines are targeted to business air travelers.

Promotion to Middlemen.   Sales promotion is an important part of manufacturers' marketing efforts to wholesalers and retailers for various products such as foods, beverages, and appliances. Catalogs and other sources of information are an essential promotional component for many lines. Promotional pricing is often used to push new products through channels of distribution. Incentives of various kinds are also popular in marketing to middlemen. Speciality advertising items are useful in maintaining buyer awareness of brands and company names.

Promotion to the Sales Force.   Incentives and informational activities are the primary forms of promotion used to assist and motivate company sales forces. Sales contests and prizes are popular. Industries such as insurance make wide use of recognition programs like the "salesperson of the year." Promotional information is vital to sales people. Presentation kits help salespeople describe new products and the features of existing products. Electronic aids such as videotapes, slides, and disk players are becoming increasingly important in helping salespeople to communicate product information. And direct mail can help salespeople find prospects.

Advantages and Limitations of Sales Promotion

Sales promotion has a wide array of incentive, pricing, and informational capabilities and thus the flexibility to contribute to various marketing objectives. Firms can target buyers, intermediaries, and salespeople, and can measure the sales response of several sales promotion activities to determine their effectiveness. For example, a company can track the success of its coupon redemption or rebates. Another advantage is that many of the incentive and price promotion techniques trigger the purchase of various products.

Sales promotion is not without its disadvantages, however. In most instances sales promotion supports other promotional efforts rather than substituting for advertising and personal selling. Pre-use analysis is essential to prevent some people from taking advantage of free offers, coupons, and other incentives. Incentives and price promotional activities must be controlled. An effective advertisement can be run thousands of times, but promotion methods are usually not reusable. Thus, the costs of development must be evaluated in advance.

Developing Sales Promotion Strategy

Exhibit 15–16 summarizes the major steps in the development of a sales promotion strategy. Marketing management should first define the communications task(s) that sales promotion is expected to accomplish.

Next, management should set specific promotion objectives regarding awareness levels and purchase intentions. The sales promotion methods selected in Exhibit 15–15 include a contest or sweepstakes, coupons, refund offers, and sampling. Management should evaluate the relative cost-effectiveness of feasible sales promotion methods and select those that offer the best results/cost combination. It is also important to integrate sales promotion into the total communications program. Both the content of the sales promotion effort and its timing should be coordinated with other promotion activities. Finally, the program is implemented and evaluated on a continuing basis. Evaluation should measure the extent to which objectives are achieved. Megatek, for example, tracked trade show results to determine how many show contacts were converted to purchases.

CONCLUDING NOTE

This chapter examines selling strategy and briefly discusses sales promotion strategy. The development of selling strategy, similar to each of

EXHIBIT 15-16   Developing a Sales Promotion Strategy

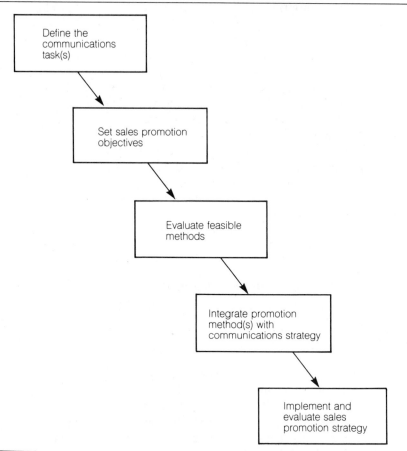

the other components of promotion, follows a logical sequence of steps. Management should begin by analyzing the selling situation, considering the firm's marketing strategy, the target market, product characteristics, distribution strategy, and pricing strategy. The situation analysis should identify the role of personal selling in the communications mix, providing the basis for sales force objectives.

The selling strategy selected should correspond to the situational factors present and the strategic role assigned to personal selling. New business, trade selling, missionary selling, and consultative/technical selling strategies illustrate the range of strategies used by various firms. The organizational design selected should correspond to the strategy situation. Decisions include the type of organizational structure to be used, the size of the sales force, and the allocation of selling effort. Organization designs may be driven by product/market, market, product, or geography factors, depending on the extent of variation in customer needs and the complexity and range of products offered. Various methods can guide decisions regarding sales force size and effort allocation.

Managing the sales force involves recruiting, training, supervising, and motivating salespeople. Evaluation and control determine the extent to which objectives are achieved and suggest adjustments in selling strategy and tactics.

The discussion of sales promotion highlighted several methods available for use in a total communications program. Typically, firms use sales promotion activities in conjunction with advertising and personal selling rather than as a primary component of promotion strategy. Sales promotion strategy should be based on the correct selection of methods to provide the best results/costs combinations for achieving the communications objectives desired.

NOTES

1. This illustration is based on Ed Bean, "William Long's Direct Style Helped Sway GM to Tennessee Site for Saturn," *The Wall Street Journal,* August 2, 1985, 22.

2. Randall Smith, "IBM Expected to Reorganize Its Sales Force," *The Wall Street Journal,* September 13, 1985, 2.

3. Gilbert A. Churchill, Jr., Neil M. Ford, and Orville C. Walker, Jr., *Sales Force Management,* 2nd ed. (Homewood, Ill.: Richard D. Irwin, 1985), 21–22.

4. Ibid., 353–56.

5. For an expanded discussion of sales force decision models, see David W. Cravens, "Sales Force Decision Models: A Comparative Assessment," in *Sales Management: New Developments from Behavioral and Decision Model Research,* ed. Richard P. Bagozzi (Cambridge, Mass.: Marketing Science Institute, 1979), 310–24.

6. Raymond W. LaForge, David W. Cravens, and Clifford E. Young, "Improving Salesforce Productivity," *Business Horizons,* September/October 1985, 50–59.

7. See, for example, Churchill, Ford, and Walker, *Sales Force Management.*

8. Ibid., 356–57.

9. Ibid., 400.

10. "Survey of Selling Costs," *Sales & Marketing Management,* February 1984.

11. John A. Byrne, "Motivating Willy Loman," *Forbes,* January 30, 1984, 91.

12. Churchill, Ford, and Walker, *Sales Force Management,* Chapter 13.

13. Kevin Higgins, "Couponing's Growth Is Easy to Understand: It Works," *Marketing News,* September 28, 1985, 12.

14. Marji Simon, "Survey Probes Strengths, Weaknesses of Promotion," *Marketing News,* June 8, 1984, 3.

15. Higgins, "Couponing's Growth," 12.

16. Liz Murphy, "Shows Mean Business for Megatek," *Sales & Marketing Management,* February 7, 1983, 64.

QUESTIONS FOR REVIEW AND DISCUSSION

1. Discuss the similarities and differences between developing and implementing selling strategies for an international public accounting firm and an electrical motor manufacturer.

2. What information does management require to develop a selling strategy?

3. Identify and discuss the major factors that have contributed to the large increase in the cost per call in industrial sales during the last several years.

4. Suppose an analysis of sales force size and deployment indicates that a company has a sales force of the right size, but that the allocation of selling effort requires substantial adjustment in several territories. How should such deployment changes be implemented?

5. What questions would you want answered if you were trying to evaluate the effectiveness of a business unit's selling strategy?

6. Discuss the relationship between size/deployment decisions and sales force management and control.

7. Discuss some of the advantages and limitations of recruiting salespeople by hiring the employees of companies with excellent training programs.

8. Is incentive compensation more important for salespeople than for product managers? Why?

9. Discuss the role of sales promotion methods in the promotion strategy of a major airline such as American or Delta.

10. Outline an approach for measuring the effectiveness of industrial trade shows for an electronic equipment manufacturer.

STRATEGIC APPLICATION 15-1

MIDWEST MEDICAL EQUIPMENT CORPORATION

Mervin Stipp, sales manager of Midwest Medical, was examining the results of an extensive data collection activity concerning Midwest's weak market position. Midwest sells in a regional market and has a market share of 8.1 percent. Midwest's products are sold primarily to hospitals and medical supply houses, which in turn sell to hospitals, clinics, doctors, convalescent centers, and other health care operations. According to the results in Exhibit 1, Midwest has 2,032 active accounts in a regional market containing 4,670 potential accounts. Stipp is concerned about an account penetration of almost 44 percent that produces only 8 percent in market share. Moreover, wide differences in market share among the sales force suggest that problems might exist concerning territory size.

Midwest sales representatives had territories composed of several counties, although two representatives, Moore and Houston, shared the Chicago metropolitan area. On the other hand, Tyler had a territory that included Dallas-Fort Worth, Houston, San Antonio, and New Orleans. Nelson's territory was the Denver area. The Detroit metropolitan area was Reitman's assignment. Minneapolis-St. Paul, Rochester, Madison, and Mil-

EXHIBIT 1 Territory Sales Analysis, 1983

Sales Representative	Territory	Sales Potential ($000)	Sales Volume ($000)	Market Share	Potential Accounts	Active Accounts	Sales Calls	Base Salary	Bonus	Sales Expenses
D. Myers	Minneapolis-St. Paul, Rochester, Madison, Milwaukee	$ 6,861	$1,036	15.1%	433	117	2,192	$ 17,500	$ 2,240	$ 4,375
J. Hester	Washington, D.C., Baltimore, Philadelphia	9,603	864	9.0	728	400	2,138	15,000	1,950	3,750
B. Moore	Chicago	11,300	893	7.9	685	343	1,855	16,250	1,825	5,125
M. Houston	Chicago	10,468	806	7.7	673	370	2,040	13,750	1,740	3,375
W. Reitman	Detroit	6,838	1,087	15.9	498	289	2,027	18,750	2,375	4,125
S. Tyler	Dallas-Ft. Worth, Houston, San Antonio, New Orleans	24,230	703	2.9	770	208	1,782	13,750	1,600	4,625
D. Nelson	Denver	6,585	1,060	16.1	428	205	2,096	15,625	2,200	3,875
T. Sikes	St. Louis, Kansas City, Tulsa, Oklahoma City	9,374	478	5.1	455	100	1,514	12,500	1,010	5,375
Totals		$85,259	$6,927	8.1%	4,670	2,032	15,644	$123,125	$14,940	$34,625

waukee comprised Myers's territory. Sikes was responsible for St. Louis, Kansas City, Omaha, Tulsa, and Oklahoma City. Finally, Hester covered Washington, D.C., Baltimore, and Philadelphia.

Each Midwest sales representative was expected to make five to 10 calls each day, although circumstances permitted considerable variation. Compensation was comprised of a base salary ranging from $12,500 to $18,750. Bonuses were paid quarterly and were based on the gross margin of each representative's sales. Gross margin was used to discourage price cutting by the sales force. Gross margin also provided an incentive for the sales force to sell more profitable products.

The sales force is expected to develop new accounts, although Stipp wonders whether the sales force has enough time. He suspects that some territories may be either too large or have too many accounts for one person to cover adequately. Realignment of territories may be a partial solution, although increasing the size of the sales force is also a possibility. Finally, Stipp feels that call patterns are not closely related to size of account. He is convinced that 20 percent of Midwest's customers provide 80 percent of the sales but that some sales representatives spend too much time calling on small accounts. He recalls reading call reports prepared by Tyler and being amazed that one customer who does an annual business of $2,500 was called on two times in one month. When questioned about this apparent misallocation of time, Tyler's response was unnerving. Tyler said, "I was in the area so I decided to drop in and see what was happening."

Analysis of account size for the active accounts produced the following breakdown:

Large 400
Medium 715
Small 917
    Total 2,032

Stipp suspected that this distribution was unlike the distribution by size for the remainder of the accounts. He was sure that the distribution among territories was not the same. Further analysis showed the following distribution by each sales representative:

Distribution of Active Accounts

	Large	Medium	Small	Total
D. Myers	40	47	30	117
J. Hester	90	130	180	400
B. Moore	53	102	188	343
M. Houston	62	105	203	370
W. Reitman	70	130	89	289
S. Tyler	17	77	114	208
D. Nelson	52	99	54	205
T. Sikes	16	25	59	100
Total	400	715	917	2,032

Further investigation by Stipp led him to believe that the following call frequencies should be adopted as guidelines:

Large accounts . . . . 24 times/year
Medium accounts . . . . 12 times/year
Small accounts . . . . 6 times/year
Prospective accounts . . . . 6 times/year

Stipp realized that not all prospective accounts should be called the same number of times a year. Some represent more substantial opportunities than others and may deserve more than six calls a year.

SOURCE: Used by permission from Gilbert A. Churchill, Jr., Neil M. Ford, and Orville C. Walker, Jr., *Sales Force Management* (Homewood, Ill.: Richard D. Irwin, 1985), 283–85.

DISCUSSION QUESTIONS

1. What evidence is there, if any, that Midwest Medical needs to realign its sales territories?
2. If the territories need realigning, how should Mervin Stipp make the adjustments?
3. Does Midwest Medical need more sales representatives? If so, how many and where are they needed?

STRATEGIC APPLICATION 15-2

NORTHROP CORP.

Six months ago Northrop Corp. set out to make its F-20 Tigershark an emblem of smart procurement of weapons. It argued that the plane would cost the Air Force millions of dollars less than the F-16 Falcon made by arch rival General Dynamics Corp.

"This is a time whose plane has come," says one executive of the Los Angeles-based aerospace concern, figuring that tighter arms budgets and more competitive procurement practices would make the Tigershark a candidate for the U.S. arsenal.

Last spring, Northrop, which developed the fighter with its own money in response to a Carter administration plan to buy a relatively inexpensive fighter for sale abroad, appeared close to winning a contract from the U.S. Air Force. But in the last few months luck and the vagaries of the budget process have turned against Northrop, and the company appears to have lost ground in its effort to sell the zippy fighter at home and use those U.S. sales to attract foreign buyers.

Leadership changes in the Air Force have delayed any decision on Northrop's low-cost offer. And just before the Paris Air Show last June, a prototype Tigershark crashed in Newfoundland, the second F-20 to go down. The first crashed during a sales demonstration in South Korea in late 1984. The company attributes both crashes to pilot error. Northrop, which only has one prototype of the F-20 left, is building another. In the meantime, its sales dogfight with General Dynamics, a St. Louis-based defense contractor, threatens to become an expensive endurance test.

Wall Street is growing impatient for Northrop to land its first F-20 sale because the company has invested nearly $1 billion in developing the fighter jet. Joseph Campbell, a defense analyst with PaineWebber Inc., says that "my confidence has eroded some." He figures that nursing the Tigershark chops Northrop's profit by about $60 million a quarter.

In Congress, where the Tigershark enjoys considerable support, representatives are pressing to end the logjam. A defense funding measure awaiting final passage earmarks $200 million for the Air Force to conduct a competition between Northrop's F-20 and General Dynamics' F-16.

Rep. Jim Courter (D, N.J.), a Tigershark supporter, agrees, however, that Northrop's campaign "appears to have lost a little bit of its momentum." He and other members of the bipartisan Military Reform Caucus—a group fighting military waste—say the F-20 battle tests the Pentagon's willingness to reward entrepreneurial defense contractors. If the F-20 flops, worries Rep. Courter, "it'll have a chilling effect" on other companies that might try to develop weapons with their own money in hopes of landing future Pentagon contracts.

Air Force rejection of the Tigershark could convince Northrop to ditch the program. Such a move would create the feeling that "we've learned our lesson," says Thomas V. Jones, Northrop's chairman. But, he notes, "profits would go up" if the company stopped pouring money into the plane.

Northrop's Healthy Earnings

As it is, Northrop's earnings are quite healthy. In the nine months, profit rose 67% to $185.2 million, or $4 a share, as sales rose 38% to $3.53 billion. The results reflect Northrop's work on the stealth bomber program for the Air Force, a big subcontracting role on the F-18 fighter for the Navy, and an array of lucrative defense-electronics systems, including the guidance system for the MX strategic missile.

Yet Northrop has a long history of losing bids for aircraft programs. Old-timers at the company bitterly recall the cancellation of Northrop's novel "flying wing" bomber after World War II.

Other times, Northrop has managed to salvage big successes after failing to win a contract. In the 1950s, after the Air Force shunned Northrop's low-cost F-5 fighter, the company sold thousands of them in 30 other countries. Even the Air Force ended up buying a trainer version of the F-5 called the T-38. Then, after the Air Force rejected Northrop's YF-17 design for a fighter program for the 1970s, the Navy picked the design for what is now the carrier-based F-18. But it named McDonnell Douglas Corp. prime contractor.

Throughout its development, the Tigershark has been whipsawed by political forces. Northrop developed the fighter in the late 1970s to meet a Carter administration request to the defense industry for low-cost, air defense planes for export. But the Reagan administration scuttled the Carter policy. An early decision denied a big F-20 order to Taiwan to avoid upsetting China. In other countries, Reaganites have encouraged exports of the hottest fighter planes in the U.S. fleet, specifically General Dynamics' F-16.

The 'Carter Plane'

Despite a personal friendship between Northrop's Mr. Jones and President Reagan, military officials seemed cool to the F-20. Some belittle it as a "Carter plane," a label Northrop rejects. Since foreign military sales are government-to-government transactions, Northrop was dependent on administration officials to pitch the Tigershark when they discussed arms sales with foreign govern-

ments. Most gave the plane short shrift. Since the Reagan administration took office, South Korea, Pakistan, Venezuela and Thailand have bought F-16s.

In the latest effort to find a U.S. market for the Tigershark, Northrop is again trying to snatch victory from the jaws of defeat. The offer to the Air Force is only for 396 planes, but Northrop figures any order that puts the jet in the U.S. arsenal would give an incentive to American allies, which like to buy what the U.S. Air Force flies.

Currently, Jordan is seeking to buy a batch of either General Dynamics' F-16s or Northrop's F-20s, whichever wins the planned Air Force competition to select a new air defense plane. The Air Force announced the competition after Northrop offered to sell the Air Force F-20s for $15 million each, well below the $19 million cost of an F-16.

But soon after Northrop's April offer General Dynamics set out to convince Congress that the F-20 is less capable than the F-16, a view Defense Secretary Caspar Weinberger has expressed as well. Then, General Dynamics stripped its F-16 of several costly features and offered the Air Force a simpler version of the plane for $13.5 million each, $1.5 million less than Northrop's F-20.

Budget Office Report

To some, the General Dynamics counterproposal confirmed the benefits of competition, but it also hurt Northrop. Making matters worse, the Congressional Budget Office reasoned in a recent report that the stripped-down F-16 would be the less expensive of the two planes.

The report also concluded that a continuous competition between the two planes would produce significant cost savings, but it didn't attempt to quantify these. Overall, says Rep. Courter, "the report hurt, there's no doubt about that."

Management changes within the Air Force also hurt. Secretary Verne Orr, a supporter of Northrop's F-20, is retiring Nov. 30. He will be succeeded by Russell Rourke, whose position on the matter isn't clear. An Air Force general who had pushed for inclusion of the F-20 in the fleet changed assignments, and another general, who supported the plane, has died.

Meanwhile, the Air Force hasn't given Northrop any official response to its proposal that it buy F-20s in lieu of some F-16s. The resulting delays don't affect the two contractors equally, since the Air Force already is buying General Dynamics' F-16s, but not Northrop's F-20s. "General Dynamics spends the government's money every day, while Northrop spends its own," notes PaineWebber's Mr. Campbell.

Winner Takes All

The Air Force plan still offers Northrop a shot at selling the F-20, but under terms the company wouldn't choose. Last May, an initial Air Force budget plan called for a continuous competition between the F-16 and the F-20, with the Air Force purchasing some of both planes each year for U.S. air defense. However, budget negotiations inside the Pentagon during the summer produced a different plan, which calls for a one-time competition between the two fighters, with the winner walking away with all the spoils.

The competition raises tricky questions. The planes differ. The F-20 scrambles into the air faster and is considered more maneuverable once it is airborne. Northrop also says the costs of maintaining its plane are much lower than those for the F-16.

General Dynamics, meanwhile, says its plane can fly longer distances without refueling and can carry certain missiles that the F-20 can't. Some congressional supporters of the F-20 worry that in setting criteria for the competition, the Air Force will put a greater emphasis on the characteristics of the F-16. "When you see the criteria, you'll know who won," says one congressional staffer.

Douglas Lee, a defense analyst with Washington Analysis Corp., a unit of First Manhattan Inc., says the Air Force probably will bias the competition toward General Dynamics' F-16. "They like the F-16 better and they always have," he says. Nonetheless, many top generals in the Air Force are talking about the need to study maintenance costs of equipment as well as the procurement costs—an approach Northrop officials say favors the Tigershark.

SOURCE: Tim Carrington and Roy J. Harris, Jr., "Northrop's Tigershark Continues Uphill Fight." Reprinted by permission of *The Wall Street Journal.* © Dow Jones & Company, Inc., November 7, 1985, 6. All rights reserved.

DISCUSSION QUESTIONS

1. Discuss the role of personal selling in Northrop's marketing strategy.
2. What similarities and differences exist between a buying center in the U.S. government and a business firm?
3. Identify the important selling strategy issues in marketing the F-20 to the U.S. government.
4. What selling strategy should Northrop use for its F-20 Tigershark in the U.S. market?

PART 5

Strategic Marketing in Action

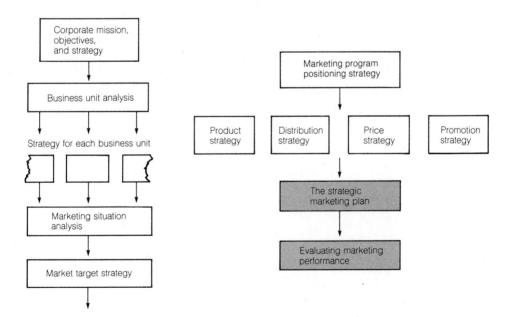

CHAPTER 16

The Strategic Marketing Plan

O. D. Schumann Inc. is a major importer of fresh Dover sole and a distributor of other delicacies, including European-grown mushrooms and vegetables, Hawaiian prawns, and Louisiana crayfish.[1] Douglas Schumann founded the business in 1978 after he discovered a market niche whose needs were not being met. On a visit back home to New Orleans, Schumann got the idea for a new business—distributing Louisiana crayfish to New York restaurants. He found a New Orleans supplier and began calling on New York chefs. They had no regular supplier and said they would buy on a regular basis from a reliable distributor. At age 61, Schumann, a textile-marketing consultant, turned a simple idea into a rapidly growing new business with 1985 sales of $3.5 million. Schumann's new venture was launched using an informal, yet effective marketing plan beginning with the targeting of New York chefs. Personal selling and fast distribution provided the major components of his positioning strategy. Schumann kept a careful control over costs and customer service. Other foods were added, including European imported Dover sole, which became the company's sales leader. The current marketing strategy includes expanding to other cities and offering a full line of gourmet products.

The marketing plan does not have to be a lengthy, detailed written document in order to be successful. Douglas Schumann correctly analyzed a market opportunity and developed a marketing strategy to take advantage of it. He was able to apply the marketing experience he gained in textiles to food distribution. The major components of his plan included targeting chefs and developing a positioning strategy to meet their needs.

EXHIBIT 16-1   Steps in Preparing and Implementing the Strategic
Marketing Plan

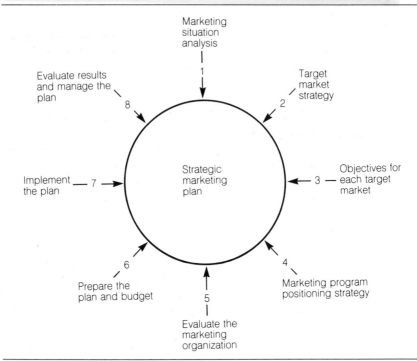

Chapters 16, 17, and 18 present and illustrate a step-by-step approach to developing, implementing, and managing the strategic marketing plan. This chapter outlines the planning approach and discusses situation analysis and strategy development.

OVERVIEW OF THE PLANNING PROCESS

Exhibit 16–1 shows the major steps in the strategic marketing planning process. Step 1, the marketing situation analysis, consists of product-market definition, customer analysis, key competitor analysis, environmental analysis, and marketing strategy assessment. Building on the findings of the situation analysis, Step 2 determines the market target strategy. Next, in Step 3 objectives for each market target are formulated. Step 4 determines the marketing program positioning strategy for each market target. Coordinated strategies are developed for product, distribution, price, and promotion. Step 5 considers the organizational design and the allocation of responsibility for the activities included in the plan. In Step 6, the plan is assembled and the supporting financial budget is prepared. The plan is put into action in Step 7. Finally, in Step 8 the plan is evaluated and adjusted. Planning process Steps 1 through 4 are examined in this chapter. Steps 5 through 8 are discussed in Chapters 17 and 18. This planning process provides a useful set of analysis and action guidelines. The preparation of the strategic marketing plan brings together the various analysis and strategy areas covered in Chapters 1 through 15.

A concise, well-executed plan is more effective than one that is elaborate and highly complex. Planning is decision making. The strategic marketing plan is a guideline for *action,* rather than an exercise in analysis and writing. The plan should be the responsibility of operating executives rather than staff planning personnel.

An Illustration

Guidelines used by Grumman Corporation illustrate the composition of an actual plan.[2] Grumman produces carrier-based aircraft, transit buses, containers, canoes, yachts, and various other products and services (see Exhibit 16-2). Note the similarity between these guidelines and the first four steps of the marketing planning process shown in Exhibit 16-1. The planning process discussed in this and the remaining two chapters of the book can be adapted to fit a particular company's needs.

The Grumman planning guide has several important features:

The planning process is concentrated on a business area.
There is a clear attempt to keep the plan as brief as possible.
Note the concern with defining the product-market (Grumman's Step 1, market definition).
A three- to five-year time horizon is used and a range of forecasts prepared.
Market segmentation is explicitly specified in the planning process.
Grumman's situation analysis (Step 2) leads logically into a statement of problems, opportunities, and contingencies (Step 3).
Objectives are specified regarding market position and financial performance (Step 4).
Finally, marketing strategy decisions are indicated and their role in business planning emphasized (Step 5).

One of the more interesting characteristics of the Grumman marketing planning guide is the fact that it serves as a kind of umbrella for technical, operations, and financial planning activities. While the guide represents one of many ways of organizing and steering the planning process, it closely follows the approach advocated in this book.

EXHIBIT 16-2 Excerpts from Marketing Planning Guidelines—
Grumman Corporation

MARKET PLANNING FOR MAJOR BUSINESS AREAS

This phase proceeds from the gathering and analysis of facts to the setting of objectives and strategy for entire business areas. There is heavy marketing emphasis, although the other business functions of technical/R&D, manufacturing/ operations, and finance are also covered. This phase sets the course for the more detailed product-oriented business planning that follows.

The steps are:

1. Market definition.
2. Situation analysis.
3. Problems and opportunities.
4. Objectives.
5. Market strategy.

The "market definition" step and the "situation analysis" step are separate items, but operate in parallel to collectively provide the total facts and information on the environment for analysis. The analysis results in a later statement of "problems and opportunities" (Step 3). The market definition is aimed at defining the broad potential marketplace for the business area. The situation analysis focuses on all aspects of our own historical performance which most probably has occurred only in a segment of the broader market definition.

A description of the requirements for each step follows:

Step 1. Market definition

The market definition addresses and examines the broad marketplace for a general line of business. Corporate goals, objectives, and guidelines should be used in determining the boundaries of these broad markets and businesses. We should be careful *not* to confine the market boundaries by our own existing or traditional product participation. The market definition analysis is purposely meant to create an outward awareness of the total surrounding market and its needs and trends that may offer opportunity or, on the other hand, challenges to our current or contemplated position.

The market definition should be approached as follows:

a. *General statement and description.* Write the statement in terms of the general categories of customers and users served and their needs. General, underlying motivations for customer and user needs should also be identified.

A second dimension that can be used in the general statement is a description of the generic family of products or services in the market served. Use of only this second dimension in the general statement is not good enough. Of the two dimensions, the customer/use oriented definition is most useful for market planning purposes.

A statement describing the relative maturity stage of the market should also be made.

Submittal Format: one page text

b. *Quantification of market size.* The market described in (a) above must be sized in total and rate of growth or decline for the past, present, and future. Both dollars and units should be identified. Domestic and foreign information should be presented if pertinent and/or appropriate. The market forecast should be for at least a three- to five-year horizon and contain ranges (minimum, maximum, most likely, etc.) where possible.

Submittal Format: one page of text/data
Chart optional

c. *Segmentation analysis.* The thought and creativity put into segmenting the market is key. There are no set categories into which the generally defined market must be segmented. However, customer and user categories are particularly important. Product characteristic categories such as price,

EXHIBIT 16-2 *(continued)*

size, weight, speed, and material are also common and useful. The segmentation may have many dimensions and combinations of dimensions. One should not retreat from trying unusual segmenting dimensions as these may reveal new insight and provide input to marketing strategy. Once the segmenting is complete, sales volumes should be identified and forecast for each segment. Needless to say, these sales forecasts are one of the most important elements in the entire business planning process.

The segmentation analysis should address the history of the market as well as the forecast.

Submittal Format: one to two pages of matrix charts
one page forecast data

Step 2. Situation analysis

The situation analysis presents the facts on "where the business has come from and where it stands." The situation analysis is necessary because it provides the basis for self-appraisal so that strengths can be built upon and weaknesses corrected. Internal performance and external impact factors are covered. The internal performance facts cover all the aspects of the business including marketing, technical/R&D, manufacturing/operations, and financial. In this sense, the situation analysis views and assesses the existing business as a whole.

The external situation analysis provides information on (1) the market segments in which we are participating, and (2) those other segments identified in the segmentation analysis where we are not presently engaged.

The information provided on the latter segments will most likely be briefer than the information provided for our own segments. However, judgment will have to be used to provide sufficient information depth to allow factual conclusions to be drawn relative to potential problems and opportunities.

Submittal Format: one half page summary text
one page competition matrix
one page trend data

Step 3. Problems and opportunities

The market definition and the situation analysis must be critically and methodically analyzed and assessed in order to identify "problems and opportunities." Each problem and opportunity should be reduced to a concise statement. Avoid the obscuring of a problem or opportunity that may be caused by combining it in the statement of another.

A checklist to assist in identifying problems and opportunities during the analysis process follows:

a. *Internal problems and opportunities*
   1. Marketing.
   2. Technical and R&D.
   3. Manufacturing/operations.
   4. Financial.
   5. Other (e.g., corporate, personnel, organization).
b. *External problems and opportunities*
   1. Market.
   2. Specific market segments.
   3. Competition.
   4. Regulation.
   5. Economic.
   6. Political.
   7. Social.
   8. International.

After the statements of problems and opportunities have been completed, they should be ranked and prioritized according to criticality to the business.

Submittal Format: one page of "one liners"

EXHIBIT 16–2 *(concluded)*

---

c. *Planning for the unexpected.* Aside from the real problems and opportunities identified and ranked above, scenarios for unexpected events and trends (sometimes called "what if's") should also be considered. Such events and trends might either have favorable or unfavorable impacts. "What if" events that are particularly pertinent to the business area should be listed in brief. Later in the business planning process, contingency plans should be formulated to deal with the eventuality of "what if" events.

Submittal Format: one page of "one-liners"

Note: Management review. At this point, a management review of the conclusions drawn in Steps 1–3 is appropriate.

Step 4. Objectives

As a result of the analysis and conclusions drawn from the market definition, situation analysis, and problems and opportunities steps, objectives for the business area are to be set. Obviously, the objectives must also be supportive and consistent with overall corporate goals, objectives, and guidelines.

Objectives should be stated concisely and precisely to "fit" the business area. They should not be lofty, generalized platitudes. Objectives might be stated in terms of any one or more of the following:

a. Market position—share, growth rate, competition, image, etc.
b. Financial rewards expected—profit, cash ROI, ROA, etc.
c. Long-term; near-term—state dates.

Whatever the description, objectives should be stated in quantifiable terms and should be measurable.

Submittal Format: one half page of "one-liners"

Step 5. Market strategy

The market strategy is the portion of the business planning process that states "how" the objectives for the business area will be met. The market strategy will govern not only the product-oriented marketing planning in this phase, but also the technical, manufacturing/operations, and financial planning functions. Market strategy is the mainstream guidance from which *all* subsequent planning functions flow. Market strategizing marks the point in the business planning process which is perhaps more pivotal to future profit success than any other phase. For this reason, strategy paths chosen must be entirely realistic with respect to resource capabilities.

The market strategy must address and describe, as appropriate, the following:

a. Market segments selected and targeted.
b. Positioning relative to competition.
c. Product-line requirements—including mix, maturity and life-cycle considerations, extensions, and protection (patents, etc.).
d. Penetration points—market segments and timing.
e. Channels of distribution—direct, distributors, dealers, reps, etc.
f. Demand creation—promotion, advertising, etc.
g. Personal selling.
h. Aftersale—warranty, service, etc.
i. Co-relationships—teaming, joint ventures, licensing, etc.

Submittal Format: two to three pages of text
(one paragraph for each
item *a* through *i*)

Note: Management Approval. At this point, management should review and approve the objectives (Step 4) and the market strategy (Step 5).

SOURCE: David S. Hopkins, *The Marketing Plan,* Report No. 801 (New York: Conference Board, 1981), 119–23.

Corporate/Business Unit Plans

Before work can start on the strategic marketing plan, top management's objectives and plans for each strategic planning unit must be clearly understood. Within the guidelines of business mission and objectives, the strategy selected for each unit of the business has an important bearing on the marketing plan as well as other functional plans. Recall the discussion in Chapter 2 and 3 concerning determination of business composition, strategic analysis of SBUs, and selection of a strategy and objectives for each unit. These three decisions establish the guidelines needed to prepare a strategic plan for each business unit. This plan includes strategic marketing, finance, operations, and other functional plans.

Top management must find answers to two major questions. First, based on an assessment of the SBU's business strength and attractiveness in each product-market, what broad strategy will the unit pursue and what financial resources will be made available to carry out the strategy? Will the unit be managed for cash flow, growth, or earnings? Second, what are the specific expectations of top management regarding sales, market share, profit contribution, and other aspects of performance? These guidelines provide the basis for developing SBU and marketing strategies. If the SBU serves two or more market targets, further strategic guidelines and priorities should be established within the SBU.

Strategic priorities for planning units should be set by the management team of each unit, working closely with the executives responsible for corporate strategic planning. For example, in determining sales and market share targets for a business unit, participation by key executives in the unit is essential. Moreover, some flexibility in the negotiations may be necessary to properly motivate managers and to give them an opportunity to execute strategies with a high probability of success.

The Limited has formulated a set of strategy guidelines designed to ensure a manageable and profitable pattern of continued growth for the highly successful retail conglomerate:

> To offer the absolute best customer shopping experience anywhere—the best store—the best merchandise—the best merchandise presentation—the best customer service—the best "everything" that a customer sees and experiences;
>
> To become the leading retailer of lifestyle fashion for women in the United States;
>
> To be known as a high quality business with an unquestioned reputation for integrity and respect for people;
>
> To maintain a revolutionary, restless, bold, and daring business spirit noted for its breakthrough, cutting-edge style;

To maintain a management style which is action oriented, always flexible and never bureaucratic;

To be tough-minded, disciplined, demanding, self-critical yet supportive of each other and our team;

To never be satisfied and to maintain a bold, aggressive and creative vision of the future.[3]

These objectives, strategies, and priorities provide important marketing planning guidelines. Note, for example, the emphasis on retailing excellence and leadership. The guidelines also express a sense of corporate culture.

SITUATION ANALYSIS

The marketing situation analysis is the first step in the marketing planning process. An important concern is deciding what unit to use as the basis for analysis and planning. Various factors affect the choice of a planning unit, including organizational structure, responsibility for planning, and the firm's areas of product and market involvement. Several guidelines are useful in making the planning unit decision.

Selecting the Planning Unit

Unless the strategic planning unit consists of a single product that meets the needs of a specific group of end users, management must choose the unit of analysis for developing the strategic marketing plan. Some firms plan and manage by individual products or brands. Others work with product lines, market targets, or specific customers. While flexibility exists in the selection of marketing planning units, several criteria should be considered in making the decision. Each planning unit should be comprised of a specific product, product line, or mix of products that:

Serves the same or a closely related market target.

Utilizes the same marketing program positioning strategy.

Shares common marketing program components, such as distribution channels, advertising, and sales force.

Is large enough to represent a meaningful unit in strategy formulation and performance evaluation.

Is small enough to facilitate analysis, planning, and management.

Consider the business composition of Magic Chef, Inc., shown in Exhibit 16–3. Clearly, the business segment "major home appliances" is too large for use in marketing planning. In fact, we could divide this segment into business units and each of *them* into marketing planning

EXHIBIT 16-3   Business Composition of Magic Chef, Inc.

Business Segments	Products	Markets	Divisions & Subsidiary
Major home appliances	Gas and electric ranges Microwave ovens Combination ranges Recreational vehicle ranges Refrigerators Freezers Dishwashers Residential laundry equipment Commercial laundry equipment Trash compactors Waste disposals Range vent hoods Dehumidifiers	Replacement Private label New homes and apartments Mobile homes Recreational vehicles	Magic Chef Division, Cleveland, Tennessee Admiral Division, Schaumburg, Illinois Gaffers & Sattler Division, Los Angeles, California Norge Division, Herrin, Illinois
Heating and air conditioning equipment	Gas, oil, and electric furnaces Central air-conditioning equipment Unit heaters Heat pumps	Replacement New homes and apartments Light commercial buildings Industrial buildings	Gaffers & Sattler Division, Los Angeles, California Johnson Corp. Division, Columbus, Ohio
Soft drink vending equipment and dispensers	Bottle and can vendors Fountain vendors Postmix vendors Postmix and premix counter units	All major bottlers including: Coca-Cola Dr. Pepper Pepsi-Cola Royal Crown Cola Seven-Up Others	Dixie-Narco, Inc., Ranson, West Virginia

Note: **Geographical Distribution.** The products of the Magic Chef, Admiral, Norge, and Johnson divisions and Dixie-Narco, Inc., are sold on a national basis. The Magic Chef and Admiral divisions have export operations for worldwide product distribution. Gaffers & Sattler Division's products are sold in the western United States.

SOURCE: *Annual Report 1980,* Magic Chef, Inc.

units. Within the segment there are at least five distinct end-user markets, as indicated in the *Markets* column in Exhibit 16-3 (replacement, private label, new homes and apartments, mobile homes, and recreational vehicles). Suppose that gas and electric ranges, microwave ovens, combination ranges, and range vent hoods are assigned to an SBU that includes the replacement, new home, and apartment markets. Assuming that the replacement and new markets are served using different distribution channels, pricing, and promotional strategies, what are possible marketing planning units? Two could be formed to concentrate planning on each market category (new and replacement). If management chooses to substantially differentiate marketing program efforts in serving the two markets, such a breakdown is appropriate. Management could consider breaking down units further in order to center planning on specific product categories, such as microwave ovens for use in existing dwellings.

Magic Chef's business composition was further altered in 1986 when the company was acquired by Maytag, resulting in the creation of a full-line household appliance corporation with strong brand positions in washers and dryers, refrigerators, stoves, microwaves, and dishwashers. These changes will require the establishment of new SBUs and marketing strategy planning units for the various product types and brands.

In addition to product-market designations, some companies may use geographical areas or functional areas (advertising, product management, sales force) as marketing planning units.

Situation Analysis

To simplify the discussion assume that the strategic planning unit consists of one specific product that meets one set of end-user needs, and that this product-market is also the marketing planning unit. To incorporate more than one product-market into the picture, it is only necessary to conduct the same kind of analysis for the other product-markets and then combine the information. Much of the situation analysis is based on the information obtained from the product-market and competitor analyses discussed in Chapters 5, 6, and 7.

As Exhibit 16–4 shows, the situation analysis should include: (1) the product-market definition, (2) customer analysis, (3) key competitor analysis, (4) environmental analysis, and (5) marketing strategy assessment.

Market Definition. The product-market, properly defined, should contain all products or services that satisfy a set of related generic needs (Chapter 5). The first task is to estimate demand, determine end-user characteristics, learn about industry practices and trends, and identify key competitors for the end-user groups being considered as possible market targets for our specific product. Some competitors may offer the same product, and others may offer a different product that will meet the same set of needs. For example, Remington electric shavers compete with brands such as Norelco, Sears, and Panasonic, as well as safety razor brands such as Gillette.

Customer Analysis. This activity consists of comprehensive analysis of who is buying and why. Chapters 5 and 6 provide important concepts and guidelines for describing buyers and analyzing their needs and wants. Estimates of demand, descriptive profiles, and criteria im-

EXHIBIT 16-4 Areas Included in the Situation Analysis

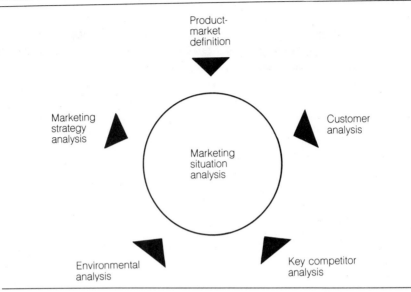

portant in the purchase decision are useful in strategy design. Firms should also include market segment identification and analysis in customer analysis.

Analysis of Key Competitors. Evaluation of competitors' strategies, strengths, limitations, and plans is a key aspect of the situation analysis. Chapter 7 outlines and illustrates an approach to competitor analysis. It is important to identify both existing and potential competitors. Typically, a subset of firms in the industry will comprise the strategic group that is the competitor set for a firm.

Environmental Analysis. This aspect of the situation assessment should identify future environmental changes that may alter market opportunity, competition, and the firm's marketing strategy. The major environmental forces that may influence market opportunities and strategies include technological advancements, demographic and social trends, governmental and political constraints, economic conditions, and the physical environment.

Marketing Strategy Analysis. An evaluation of the effectiveness of the firm's current marketing strategy should identify important strategy issues, strengths, and limitations. Management should evaluate the firm's strategic situation and the appropriateness of the marketing strategy being used for that situation. Chapter 7 considers the various determinants of the marketing strategy situation.

Exhibit 16–5, a guide to conducting the situation analysis, consists of a comprehensive assessment of end users and key competitors. The guide can be condensed or expanded to fit the needs of a particular firm. When completed, the situation analysis should summarize the opportunities and problems in the product-market. It will contain much of the information management needs to select a target market strategy (Step 2). A more extensive guide to conducting a complete strategic marketing audit is provided in Chapter 18. It is designed to guide a comprehensive assessment of marketing strategy and may suggest additional items.

EXHIBIT 16–5 Guide to Conducting a Marketing Strategy Situation Analysis

Complete the following chart for each specific product-market (e.g., microwave ovens for heating foods in the home).

Product Description
Characteristics and features
Functions
Competing substitutes

Customer Analysis	Total Product Market	Major End-User Groups	
		No. 1	No. 2 →
Estimated annual purchases (units and $)			
Projected annual growth rate (5 years)			
Number of people/organizations in the product-market			
Demographic and socioeconomic characteristics of customers			
Extent of geographical concentration			
How people decide what to buy:			
a. Reason(s) for buying (what is the need/want)			
b. Information that is needed (e.g., how to use the product)			
c. Important sources of information			
d. Criteria used to evaluate the product			
e. Purchasing practices (quantity, frequency, location, time, etc.)			
Environmental factors that should be monitored because of their influence on product purchases (e.g., interest rates)			
Key competitors serving each end-user group			

Are there other products available or under development that are or will be close substitutes for this product? If so, a situation analysis should be conducted for the product-market.

EXHIBIT 16–5 *(concluded)*

	Competitor		
Key Competitor Analysis:	A	B	C
Estimated overall business strength			
Market share (percent, rank)			
Market share trend (5 years)			
Financial strengths			
Profitability			
Management			
Technological position			
Other key nonmarketing strengths/ limitations (e.g., production cost advantages)			
Marketing strategy (description, assessment of key strengths and limitations).			
a. Market target strategy			
b. Program positioning strategy			
c. Product strategy			
d. Distribution strategy			
e. Price strategy			
f. Promotion strategy			

Summary of Opportunities and Problems in the Product-Market:
   Prepare by major end user group and for the total product-market.

Assumptions:
   Based on the situation analysis, what key assumptions regarding the next three to five years will you make in preparing the strategic plan?

Assumption:
   1.
   2.
   3.

Marketing strategy analysis:

Define the strategic situation

Effectiveness of marketing strategy:
   Market target strategy
   Positioning strategy
   a.   Product strategy
   b.   Distribution strategy
   c.   Price strategy
   d.   Promotion strategy
Summary of key strengths and weaknesses

Are strategy adjustments needed?

Contingencies:
   For each assumption what alternatives (contingencies) could possibly occur and how would the occurrence alter your situation analysis?

Contingency: *Estimated Impact on Situation Analysis*

   1a.
    b.
    c.
    .
    .
   2a.
    b.
    c.
    .
    .

Contingency Planning

Planning for contingencies involves identifying events that could happen, instead of the assumptions on which the plan is based. For example, if a bank's management is assuming that long-term interest rates for financing new retail outlets will range between 10 and 12 percent during the next three years, what effect will rates of 15 or 8 percent have on the strategic marketing plan? The last part of Exhibit 16–5 includes space for indicating key contingencies and estimating their impact on the situation analysis. Contingency analysis builds flexibility into the planning process. But every possible occurrence can't be considered, so management needs to identify one or more key contingencies that would require a major change in the strategic marketing plan. The extent of explicit planning for contingencies must be determined based on estimated probabilities of occurrence, the feasibility of implementing alternative strategies if the contingency should occur, and the costs/benefits of contingency planning. It is impossible to remove all of the risk from planning. The purpose of contingency planning is to avoid a catastrophe.

MARKET TARGETS AND OBJECTIVES

Marketing strategy development begins with Step 2, determining target market strategy. Step 1 is an important, although preliminary, aspect of strategic development.

Market Target Strategy

The market target decision is the focal point of marketing strategy; it serves as the basis for setting objectives and developing a positioning strategy. Recall that market target strategy options range from using a mass strategy to serving one or more subgroups (niches or segments) of customers within a product-market (Chapter 8). The decision to use a niche strategy is based on revenue-cost analysis and assessment of competitive position.

Once the market target decision is made, the following information is often needed in building the plan:

Size and growth rate of the market target.

Description of end users in the target group (location and characteristics).

Information about end users that will be helpful in selecting a program positioning strategy.

Guidelines for developing short-term marketing plans (e.g., media habits and preferences of end users).

As an illustration, consider a product being produced and marketed by a small electronics manufacturing firm. The product is a high-accuracy temperature measuring instrument for use in research laboratories and production operations. The instrument uses a metal probe whose electrical resistance varies according to the temperature of the surface it touches. This information from the probe is transmitted to a microprocessor, which then transmits the temperature measurement to a visual display similar to a digital clock readout. After analyzing opportunities, costs, and competitive position in several industries and for several types of temperature measurement applications (e.g., laboratory, on-line production processes, and checking and calibration of on-line measurement devices), management decided to concentrate marketing efforts in the pharmaceutical industry. A market target description is shown in Exhibit 16-6. Market target information will vary by planning situation, so the temperature measurement example is not necessarily typical.

Setting Objectives

Turning now to Step 3, management should indicate objectives for each market target. Some companies prefer to set objectives that apply to the total marketing strategy for all market targets. Importantly, overall strategy objectives represent a composite of specific objectives for each market target.

By generating sales and consuming financial resources, marketing contributes to sales, market share, and profit objectives. Firms also need various operating objectives or subobjectives to provide performance guidelines for each marketing mix component. Such operating objectives also contribute to sales, market share, and profit contribution objectives. For example, suppose that one objective of a company's advertising strategy is to increase market target customers' awareness of a particular brand by some amount during a specific time. Management believes that increasing brand awareness will have an effect on sales. In the case of operating objectives (e.g., increasing awareness), establishing a direct cause-and-effect relationship to sales is often difficult. Management may be convinced that increasing awareness will increase sales but is often unable to predict that an X percent change in awareness will cause a Y percent increase in sales. Even though this is a problem, management should still formulate operating objectives or it will have no basis to gauge progress.

Keeping the following guidelines in mind, firms can place objectives into the strategic marketing plan:

1. Indicate sales, market share, and profit contribution objectives for the total business unit and each market target. Normally

---

EXHIBIT 16-6 Market Target Description and Profile

Market target

Pharmaceutical companies in the United States with a need for moderate- to high-accuracy temperature measurement devices used in the production of intravenous or parenteral solutions which require sterilization of containers and stoppers. There are over 60 companies in this market target.

Size and growth rate

The total potential in this product-market is estimated at approximately 400 units and is estimated to grow at about a 10 percent annual rate for the next five years. At an average price of $5,000 per unit the sales potential is $2 million. Microprocessor penetration into the potential market has been minimal to date.

Description of end users

The market target firms are concentrated in the Middle Atlantic, Midwestern, and Far Western states.

The end user is an instrumentation engineer or supervisor, maintenance engineer, quality control engineer, or production manager (small plants) of market target firms.

Marketing program positioning strategy guidelines

The apparent reason for purchase of a high-accuracy instrument is to monitor the accuracy of thermocouples used in sterilizers for containers and stoppers. This need is being triggered due to a pending Good Manufacturing Practice regulation on temperature accuracy of $\pm\ 0.5°$ C. throughout the sterilizer heating cycle.

Users' needs for information on the product include demonstrations and information on product feature and performance.

Important sources of information concerning temperature measurement include quality control consultants, product brochures, and technical articles in professional journals.

Criteria used to evaluate alternative brands include accuracy, stability, service, price, ease of installation and operation, durability, mobility, and data recording capabilities.

As to purchasing practices, the end user typically determines the need and obtains approval to purchase from the plant production manager. Given approval, the user will then select the brand and type of product to be purchased.

Competitive activity in this industry has been minimal. Only one potential key competitor exists—the XYZ corporation.

Guidelines for short-term marketing plans

Direct personal selling by the manufacturer represents the most effective way of contacting end users.

Price does not appear to be a major factor in the brand decision providing there are not substantial variations in the prices of competitive units.

Advertising and sales promotion efforts should be concentrated initially upon developing product information brochures. This information can be communicated via direct mail and in conjunction with sales calls.

---

these objectives are projected into the future year by year over the period of the strategic plan (e.g., three to five years).

2. Include, as part of the marketing program positioning strategy (Step 4), operating objectives for product, distribution, price, advertising, and sales force strategies. These objectives should indicate what each mix component is expected to accomplish, and should be consistent with the objectives for other mix elements.

3. Break down business unit and operating objectives into annual objectives (Step 6).

Objectives cannot be fully determined until the company finalizes its marketing program positioning strategy (Step 4). Then the firm can make sales forecasts and estimate marketing program costs.

MARKETING PROGRAM POSITIONING STRATEGY

Selection of the positioning strategy provides the unifying concept for the role and strategy of each mix component. The positioning statement indicates how management would like the market target to view the firm's marketing mix. Positioning is typically indicated in comparison to competition. For example, People Express Airlines positioned itself as a low-fare, no-frills, passenger airline serving several heavily traveled routes.

Positioning strategy should be formulated taking into account:

1. The criteria or benefits that the buyer considers when purchasing a product, including relative importance of the criteria.
2. The extent to which, and how, the firm is differentiated from its competition.
3. The limitations of competing products regarding important buyer needs and wants.

The positioning statement (Chapter 9) is the starting point in formulating a strategy. Positioning indicates how the firm would like to be perceived in the eyes and minds of market target customers. Positioning is stated in terms of some reference basis, usually competition. The marketing mix components provide the means for positioning as shown in Exhibit 16–7. Strategy development logically begins with product strategy, followed by distribution, price, and promotion strategies. Product and distribution strategies establish important guidelines for price and promotion strategies (Chapters 10–15).

Important Considerations in Developing a Positioning Strategy

Shaping the positioning strategy using the marketing mix components is a challenging task because of the components' complex interrelationships and different roles and functions.

Matching the Market Target Needs. Positioning is ultimately determined by the buyer. The actions taken regarding the various positioning components (e.g., product quality, distribution channel(s) used, price, advertising program) in combination with the actions of competitors provide the basis for buyers' positioning of companies and their products. To develop a positioning strategy, management must under-

EXHIBIT 16–7 Positioning Strategy Development

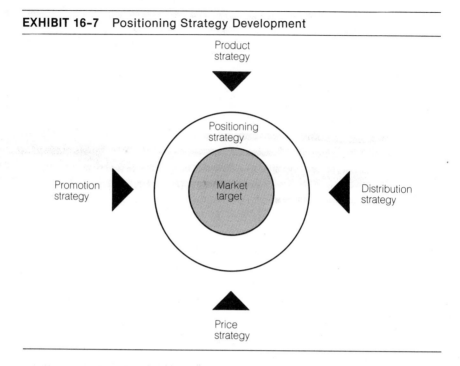

stand buyers' needs, the criteria used to evaluate purchase alternatives, brand preferences, and other positioning information. Based on this assessment management must determine how to position the product using the various mix components.

An interesting positioning strategy application is the new instant camera introduced by Polaroid in 1986, which was supported by a $40 million advertising campaign over a 12-month period.[4] The market target consists of younger, more affluent buyers, such as professionals. Polaroid's positioning strategy for the Spectra camera must convince potential buyers that it is not just another Polaroid camera and that it offers advantages over 35-mm cameras. The Spectra promotional campaign will highlight the "instant experience"—the magic of watching a photo develop. Other aspects of the positioning strategy for the product include several product features, such as improved picture quality, special technical features, and a new 10 percent larger film. The camera has an automatic focus and strobe and will be sleeker and easier to hold than Polaroid's prior models. Achieving favorable positioning with the market target will be essential to the success of Spectra.

Understanding Positioning/Market Response Relationships. The design of strategy for each mix component is based on the market's estimated responsiveness to the positioning strategy. Market response is

---

EXHIBIT 16–8   Factors Affecting Market Response

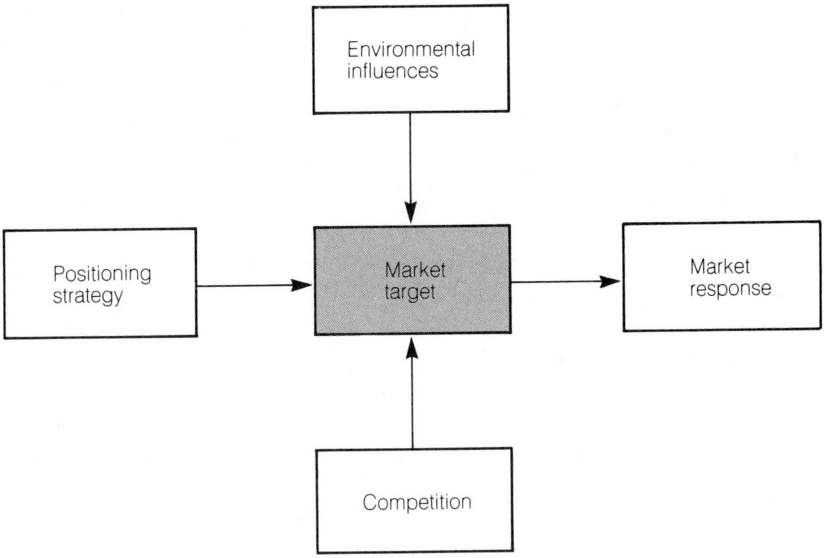

```
                    ┌──────────────┐
                    │Environmental │
                    │influences    │
                    └──────┬───────┘
                           │
                           ▼
┌──────────────┐    ┌──────────────┐    ┌──────────────┐
│Positioning   │───▶│Market        │───▶│Market        │
│strategy      │    │target        │    │response      │
└──────────────┘    └──────┬───────┘    └──────────────┘
                           ▲
                           │
                    ┌──────────────┐
                    │Competition   │
                    └──────────────┘
```

---

typically measured by sales. Selecting the appropriate mix of positioning components requires determining the total marketing budget expenditure and its product, distribution, price, and promotion allocations. As shown in Exhibit 16–8, market response is influenced by environmental factors and competition, in addition to the firm's positioning strategy.

Characteristics of the Marketing Mix.   The marketing mix components have several common features and certain unique capabilities. For example, advertising and personal selling can be used to communicate with the market target. Also mix components perform functions that other components cannot. Distribution channel functions, such as storage, assembly of orders, and physical distribution cannot be accomplished by the other mix components. Selecting an appropriate mix of components involves two kinds of decisions. First, management must determine the role of each mix component. This involves identifying the functions unique to each component as well as deciding between two mix components that can perform the same functions. The interactive effects of two or more mix components should also be evaluated. For example, advertising and personal selling combined may have a stronger effect on market response than either by itself even if expenditures are the same. These decisions determine how and to what extent each mix component is to be used in the positioning strategy. Second, management must select the most cost-effective means of performing each mix component function. Such decisions establish the composition and characteristics of the positioning strategy.

In determining the positioning strategy it is important to recognize the time period involved. The effects of some mix components, such as price, are immediate to short-term. Others, such as new product development and distribution channel development, may require several years. Once determined, certain aspects of mix component strategies remain in place for a long time. Advertising and sales promotion programs typically change more frequently than strategies for the other mix components.

Methods for Integrating Positioning Strategy Components

Achieving effective integration of the marketing mix is a complex task, but several methods can help. Most of the methods are related to the organizational design or to the management process used.

Organizational Design. The way the organization is structured and responsibilities are assigned can ease or hamper integrating the positioning strategy components. Strategy integration also is dependent on the motivation and capabilities of the people who participate. The selection of executives for positions requiring marketing program integration should include consideration of their integrating skills.

Management Processes. These processes are intended to encourage integration and coordination of strategy components. For example, the strategic marketing planning process (Exhibit 16–1) follows a step-by-step analysis and decision-making process designed to encourage and facilitate strategy development. Preparation of the plan and budget (Step 6) brings together the various components of the marketing strategy. This plan provides a basis for implementation (Step 7) and evaluating results and managing the plan (Step 8). Within the framework of the planning process, management should establish various coordination and review procedures for the organizational units and areas of responsibility within the marketing division. Business functional areas outside marketing that are involved in developing and executing marketing strategy also should be incorporated into the appropriate management processes.

Product/Service Strategy

Once determined, product positioning strategy, objectives, and branding strategy serve as the basis for developing and implementing management strategies for new and existing products (Chapters 10 and 11).

In order to formulate product strategy, management needs the following information on current and anticipated performance of the products (services) in the business unit:

1. Consumer evaluation of the company's products, particularly their strengths and weaknesses vis-a-vis competition (i.e., product positioning by market segment information).
2. "Objective" information on actual and anticipated product performance on relevant criteria such as sales, profits, and market share.[5]

These analyses assist management in formulating product management strategies for each product in the mix or line. The product typically is the focal point for positioning strategy development when companies or business units use organizational approaches emphasizing product or brand management. A product group manager may then manage lines or mixes of products. Product strategies consist of: (1) the development of plans for new products, (2) the continuation of programs for successful products, and (3) the management strategies for dealing with problem products (reduce costs, improve product). David S. Hopkins describes product management practices:

> The mix and interdependence of products comprising a line or the multiple lines of a marketing unit is a critically important element of planning. It has been traditional practice to consolidate all the plans for individual products and to relate them somehow to the overall needs, resources and capabilities of the unit (or company) that makes and sells them. If anything is seriously out of line, it then becomes a matter of "cut and fit," with support for certain products possibly reduced, new high-priority projects started, or other actions taken.[6]

Thus plans for individual products must fit into an overall product portfolio strategy. Plans for specific products should indicate actions to be taken, responsibilities, deadlines, and estimated costs.

Distribution, Price, and Promotion Strategies

One of the major dangers in building the strategic marketing plan is the fragmentation of planning efforts, which can lead to faulty or incomplete implementation. Product, distribution, price, and promotion strategies must be tied together into a coordinated plan of action. Planning matrixes or grids are proven tools for reducing this problem and have been used by marketing planners for many years. In Exhibit 16–9 advertising and personal selling are integrated into the two grids. To better see how the matrix is used, first consider the information that is placed into each of the cells in grid B. For example, look at the advertising strategy cell for Channel 1, in the wholesaler market target for plywood. For this cell and every other one in grid B, where marketing pro-

EXHIBIT 16-9 Planning Grid

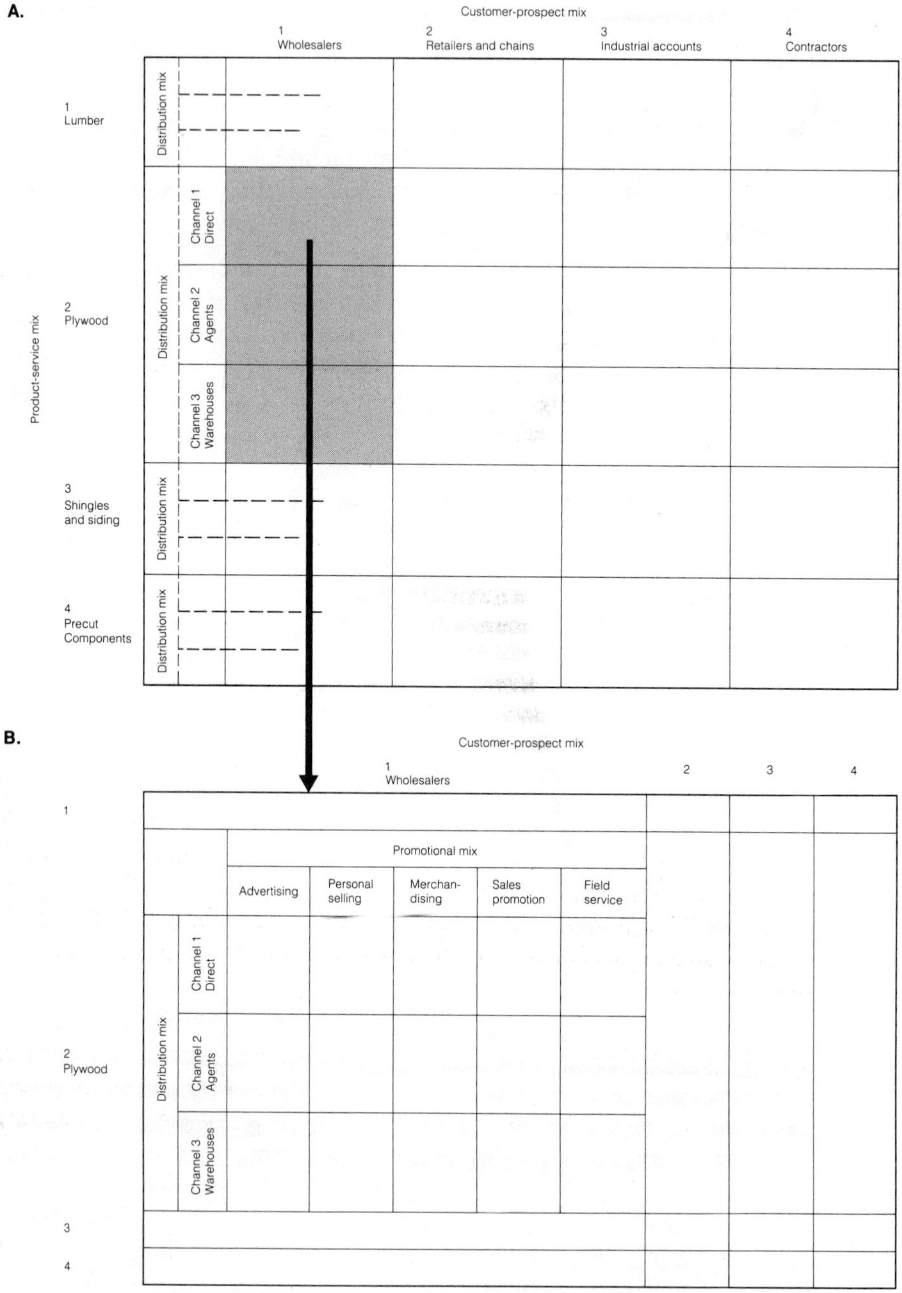

A.

Customer-prospect mix

| | 1 Wholesalers | 2 Retailers and chains | 3 Industrial accounts | 4 Contractors |

Product-service mix

- 1 Lumber — Distribution mix
- 2 Plywood — Distribution mix — Channel 1 Direct / Channel 2 Agents / Channel 3 Warehouses
- 3 Shingles and siding — Distribution mix
- 4 Precut Components — Distribution mix

B.

Customer-prospect mix

| | 1 Wholesalers | 2 | 3 | 4 |

Promotional mix

| | Advertising | Personal selling | Merchandising | Sales promotion | Field service |

- 1
- 2 Plywood — Distribution mix — Channel 1 Direct / Channel 2 Agents / Channel 3 Warehouses
- 3
- 4

SOURCE: Adapted from William J. E. Crissy and Robert M. Kaplan, "Matrix Models for Marketing Planning" *Business Topics,* Summer 1963, 64–65. Reprinted by permission of the publisher, Division of Research, Graduate School of Business Administration, Michigan State University.

gram activities are contemplated, the following information should be indicated:

Objectives.
Description of program activities.
Interrelationships with other strategy components.
Time schedules.
Responsibility for implementation.
Estimated costs.
Measurement of results.

Planning grids can be displayed on a manager's office wall, and reproduced for distribution. Too much detail is unnecessary. For example, in grid B, information should indicate who is responsible for taking the action and what they are supposed to do. The strategic plan should not include a description of specific advertisements, schedules, and related details. Such information belongs in the short-range plans of the executive responsible for advertising.

MOVING FROM PLANS TO ACTION

The development and implementation of a marketing plan highlights several important issues. One of the most satisfying experiences in business is to see the management of a company in trouble diagnose its problems, take corrective action, and achieve a turnaround. Paint manufacturer Sherwin-Williams appeared to be on the brink of disaster in 1977 after attempting unsuccessfully to launch a new strategic marketing plan. The problem was a combination of incomplete planning and faulty implementation.[7] By 1980 recovery was underway—both sales and earnings reflected impressive gains. By examining the firm's marketing strategy, its implementation, and the subsequent adjustments that were made to move the company toward profitable performance, we can see the critical link between planning and implementation:

1. *The Strategic Plan.* In the late 1960s Sherwin-Williams' management decided to shift away from contractors and professional painters and to target the do-it-yourself home decorating market. This strategy involved an ambitious and costly program of store expansion. The decision offered management an opportunity to reposition the paint segment of the business into the rapidly growing do-it-yourself market that other retail chains had found very attractive. Management reasoned that the main ingredient of the new strategy was changing their brand image in order to appeal to consumers interested in home decorating and remodeling.

2. *Implementation.* Launching the strategy involved far more than management anticipated. Many stores were in the wrong locations. All

required major—and costly—upgrading and expansion to reflect the new home decorating theme, including expanded product lines. But Sherwin-Williams had no experience in managing retail stores. Performance difficulties were compounded by the decision to pull the Sherwin-Williams paint brand out of paint and hardware stores to avoid direct competition with company stores, and to replace it with another company brand not supported by a strong national advertising effort. As a result, dealers shifted to competing brands with established brand images.

3. *Corrective action.* The company lost $8 million in 1977—its third straight year of declining earnings—and a new chairman and president, John G. Breen, was appointed. Under his leadership the company experienced an impressive turnaround. Breen shut down obsolete plants, closed more than 100 of the firm's 1,500 retail stores, and replaced half the firm's top 100 managers. (Several new executives had extensive experience in retailing.) New stores were smaller and located near suburban shopping malls. And the broad mix of decorating products was pruned. The company increased advertising expenditures dramatically and, to offer a strong brand to other retailers, acquired the Dutch Boy trademark in 1980.

Under Breen's leadership, Sherwin-Williams' profit performance continued into the mid-1980s.[8] Sherwin-Williams added 50 new paint stores in 1983 and expected to add an additional 150 in 1984. The highly competitive retail paint market forced Sherwin-Williams to adopt a discounting price strategy and to increase its 1984 advertising budget to $28 million, $8 million more than 1983.

The experience of Sherwin-Williams illustrates several important characteristics of successful strategic marketing plans. First, a strategic plan involves far more than just a good idea. A sound concept has to be translated into a cohesive and complete plan of action. Second, proper implementation is crucial. Third, few plans remain constant over time. Although the modifications made by Sherwin-Williams' management were more drastic than most, corrective action is the rule rather than the exception. Finally, the success of a strategic marketing plan must be gauged by the results it achieves, not by how elaborate and innovative it is.

CONCLUDING NOTE

Four important characteristics of the strategic marketing plan should be apparent. First, a logical process can and should be followed in developing the plan. The general approach outlined in this chapter can be implemented in any type of organization. Second, when the planning process raises relevant questions, management must supply the answers; decision makers develop strategic plans. Third, strategic marketing planning is a continuing activity that is adjusted and revised to take advantage of opportunities and threats. Finally, marketing planning forms the leading edge of planning for the entire business unit. Marketing plans must be closely coordinated with research and development, operations, financial, and other business functions. Corporate and business unit objectives and strategies provide important marketing planning guidelines.

Step 1 of the marketing planning process, the marketing situation analysis, includes defining the product market, customer analysis, key competitor analysis, environmental analysis, and marketing strategy situation determination. The target market strategy is selected in Step 2, indicating the customer group(s) to be targeted by the organization. Next, in Step 3 objectives are specified for each target market. The marketing program positioning strategy is determined in Step 4. Chapters 17 and 18 consider the remaining steps in the planning process.

NOTES

1. This illustration is based on Sanford L. Jacobs, "He Didn't Know the Business, But He Has Made It Successful," *The Wall Street Journal*, January 13, 1986, 27.

2. David S. Hopkins, *The Marketing Plan*, (New York: The Conference Board, 1981), 119–23.

3. The Limited Inc., *1984 Annual Report*, 7.

4. Lawrence Ingrassia, "Negative Images: Polaroid Faces Tough Sell with Its New Instants', *The Wall Street Journal*, March 25, 1986, 31.

5. Yoram Wind and Henry J. Claycamp, "Planning Product Line Strategy: A Matrix Approach," *Journal of Marketing*, January 1976, 2.

6. David S. Hopkins, *Business Strategies for Problem Products*, (New York: The Conference Board, 1977), 44.

7. This account is based, in part, upon Susan Wagner Leisner, "Cleaning Up: Sherwin-Williams Co. Is Recovering from Its Spill," *Barron's*, November 24, 1980, 35–36.

8. Paul Ingrassia, "Sherwin-Williams Makes Big Turnaround Under Chairman's Aggressive Leadership," *The Wall Street Journal*, December 14, 1983, 29.

QUESTIONS FOR REVIEW AND DISCUSSION

1. A financial executive questions the need for formal planning. Prepare a defense of strategic marketing planning.

2. Discuss some of the similarities and differences between the strategic marketing plan of a small savings and loan association and that of a diversified manufacturer of electronic equipment.

3. You have been assigned the top marketing post in a corporation. Although there is no specific information available on corporate mission, objectives, and strategy, you are convinced that developing and launching a strategic marketing plan is crucial to your success in your new job. What do you do?

4. Identify and discuss the kinds of problems that may occur when using a planning unit that is either too large or too small.

5. You have been asked to prepare a marketing situation analysis for a large public accounting firm. Prepare a guide detailing the areas to be examined, questions to be answered, and sources of information. (You may find it helpful to refer back to Exhibits 16–5 and 16–6.)

6. How should marketing management identify the contingencies to be incorporated into the strategic marketing plan?

7. Below are advertising awareness objectives for a retail firm operating in four market areas:

Area	Before Awareness Campaign	Awareness Objective	After Awareness Campaign
A	5%	7%	12%
B	3	4	8
C	2	4	2
D	2	3	8

Comment on the usefulness of an objective stated in this form. What improvements do you suggest?

8. Prepare a critical analysis of the Grumman Corporation marketing planning guide shown in Exhibit 16–2.

9. Are the marketing program positioning strategies of American Airlines and People Express Airlines different? Discuss.

STRATEGIC APPLICATION 16–1

THE LIMITED INC.

COLUMBUS, Ohio—When R. H. Macy & Co. announced its $3.58 billion leveraged buyout last week, the Wall Street rumor mill soon had other major retailers up for sale. High on the list of rumored acquirers is Leslie H. Wexner, chairman of Limited Inc.

Mr. Wexner, whose family controls 35.1% of Limited, won't comment, and he hasn't made any moves to satisfy the gossips. But the very appearance of his name indicates his stature and marks progress from just 18 months ago when Limited's unsuccessful bid to buy the much larger Carter Hawley Hale Stores Inc. shocked the market and triggered a wave of David and Goliath analogies.

Last week, however, the retailer capped its 2,400-plus store empire with the purchase of New York's Tony Henri Bendel shop, which Limited plans to expand internationally. That added the top layer to Limited's nationwide collection of specialty women's apparel stores,

which include large-size apparel stores, Victoria's Secret lingerie shops and the trend-setting Limited chain for the 18-to-35-year-old set. Early next month the company will open a showpiece, seven-level Manhattan store in a restored landmark building on upper Madison Avenue.

Limited's prospects appear, well, unlimited. How did the company, which started 22 years ago as a single suburban store near this midwestern city, begin to set trends for others in the fiercely competitive and fickle fashion field? And, more importantly, can it keep it up?

Mr. Wexner, the 48-year-old billionaire founder, usually gets the credit for the company's success. (He also has gotten a lot of personal publicity, including a recent cover story in New York Magazine that described his life down to the color of his maroon socks.) But behind his oft-cited retail instinct is a management team executing a series of deliberate strategies that have enabled Limited to squeeze out or buy up many competitors.

To help keep a closer eye on the industry which Limited has said repeatedly it wants to lead, the company next year will move into a newly purchased townhouse on New York's Upper East Side that will serve as its corporate offices there. "We want to tap more into world resources," says Mr. Wexner, chatting recently in the study of his suburban Columbus mansion.

He and other top officers already spend 75% of their time in makeshift quarters at the Limited divisions based in New York. But the company needs "a presence" in the city, albeit secluded and "low-profile," Mr. Wexner adds. The company will retain its extensive office and distribution facilities as its headquarters here. But the home-away-from-home also is intended to give the financial community more access to Limited.

So far, that community seems almost to worship Limited. "I'm always asking myself" where Limited could fall down, says Art Charpentier of Goldman, Sachs & Co. "It's very difficult to find any place that they seem vulnerable. What it says is that (if they trip up) it's going to be a bolt out of the blue. There'll be people who said they anticipated it."

About the only criticism competitors and other retail observers can muster suggests that Limited's corporate culture, while a strength, is so intense that it produces some management turnover. Also, the company's market domination alienates vendors who, analysts add, can't do much about it.

"Look what happened to those who tried to sue Limited" last summer when it abruptly canceled orders for its newly acquired Lerner division, says one industry executive, requesting anonymity because she is wary of Mr. Wexner's "power." Vendors backed off, she says. "They need to eat, too."

The acquisition of Lerner, which turned out to have serious inventory problems, added a note of rancor to Limited's story this year. Limited is in the early stages of a lawsuit against New York-based Rapid-American Corp., which sold the unit. The suit claims that Rapid-American failed to disclose accounting information on the inventory.

But analysts say Limited is ahead of schedule in turning Lerner around. And, despite the concern's frustrated attempt to buy Carter Hawley Hale, it rarely stumbles. Including the 751-store Lerner division, the company for the current fiscal year expects to report $2.5 billion in sales, up 87% from sales of $1.34 billion last year, on which the company earned $92.5 million, or 77 cents a share. Analysts project full-year earnings of about $1.10 to 1.15 a share.

"The only thing that worries me is Les Wexner being hit by a beer truck," says Al Pennington, president of a consulting firm bearing his name.

But Limited's success can be traced to more than Mr. Wexner's fashion eye, manic devotion to work and management touch. It also reflects, for example, Limited's intense ownership ethic (along with management, 25% of Limited employees own more than half of the company's stock) and an international manufacturing organization that, consultants say, gives Limited a critical edge over competitors in supply, pricing and timing.

Add to that Limited's willingness to leverage itself repeatedly to grab more segments of the consolidating specialty retail market, suggests Phil Barach, chairman of U.S. Shoe Corp., a competitor, who says his company moves like a "turtle," compared with Limited.

At a retail seminar earlier this year, David Kollat, a Limited executive vice president, scoffed at projections of a no-growth decade ahead for women's apparel. "We'll grow at the expense of our competitors," listeners recall him saying.

Mr. Wexner bases the company's success on its departures from "conventional wisdom." He cites its refusal to rapidly rotate buyers the way department stores do, and even the flashy, American-style interior of its offices in Hong Kong, where, he says, most Americans opt to blend in with more subtle Oriental styles.

It is not that "Limited does anything different from the rest. They just do it better," says Chris Schwartz, vice president for corporate development at Dylex Ltd., a Toronto-based specialty retailer with 2,700 stores that recently bought such Limited competitors as the Foxmoor chain.

Mast Industries

A case in point is Mast Industries, Limited's manufacturing and buying arm, whose purchase by Limited in 1978 was heavily criticized. Traditionally, says Martin Trust, who founded Mast and now heads it, many retailers have jumped into the retail supply cycle late, bought through third-party "hired guns"—often on a one-order basis—and depended on New York middleman suppliers along with the rest of the retail herd. "In the old days, it was OK to chase the market," says New York retail consultant Carol Farmer.

She says more retailers will begin to do as Mast does: Keep the retailer involved from the sewing machine on up. Mast helps Limited marketing people track and predict trends, locates countries and manufacturers, and will even set up in business a promising entrepreneur or buy machinery for a small, undercapitalized manufacturer. Full-time quota specialists try to stay ahead of the international protectionist game by buying up production "options." As a result, say industry sources, Mast has long-term relationships that speed delivery to its stores and preempt other retailers.

To illustrate Mast's power, competitors point to the "shaker" sweater, a V-necked, brightly colored, oversize garment that Limited predicted, after test marketing last year, would be a must-have item for millions of young women.

Ms. Farmer, who worked for Lerner before Limited bought it, says Limited seemed suddenly to have "jillions" of the sweaters in its stores, forcing Lerner's and others into frantic, costly catch-up efforts.

The 20% of Mast's output that goes to outsiders, including some Limited competitors, helps keep Mast up to date on the rest of the industry, says Mr. Trust. But the 25% of Limited divisions' apparel that Mast supplies is the bulk of its projected $400 million in sales this year. By contrast, Dylex's product sourcing division, which some say also is very progressive, will do only $200 million.

Mast's quick production turnarounds fit what Robert Morosky, vice chairman, describes as an important Limited strategy: flexibility. More interested in controlling budgets and employees, he says, many retailers won't allow quick reversals or unexpected budget increases. Limited gives buyers and other employees the authority to make quick decisions without layers of approvals. Accounting employees, for example, can offer suppliers prepayment in exchange for discounts, an independence other retailers wouldn't grant to mere "bookkeepers," he says.

'Entrepreneurial Zeal'

Dylex's Mr. Schwartz says the company has managed to maintain an unusual "entrepreneurial zeal." But the culture isn't for everyone. One top retail executive turned down a job with Limited, citing the company's single-mindedness, time demands and requirement that employees not stray outside Limited's very closed society. "I'm too old to join a monastery," the executive told Limited.

Whether the culture and systems can be maintained as Limited grows is an open question. "If they acquired (a big department store company) and got really lever-

Limited Inc.'s Rapid Growth Since 1981 (years ending in January)

	Net Income ($ millions)	Per Share*	Sales ($ millions)	Number of Stores
1985	$92.5	77¢	$1,343.1	1,412
1984	70.9	59¢	1,085.9	937
1983	33.6	29¢	721.4	825
1982	22.4	20¢	364.9	430
1981	13.1	12¢	295.0	352

*Restated for stock split paid in 1985.

aged, it could backfire," at least temporarily, says Mr. Pennington, the consultant.

But Mr. Morosky, the Mast vice chairman, says he is unfazed by leverage levels like the 121% of debt relative to equity that Limited recorded when it acquired Lerner. That figure is now down to 70%. And Mr. Wexner vows to get into the department-store business, either through acquisition or a joint venture.

He does concede that it is dangerous to see success as "a self-fulfilling prophecy." Goldman Sachs' Mr. Charpentier says he thinks Limited got that message back in the late 1970s when management problems hurt earnings.

SOURCE: Julie Solomon, "Limited Is a Clothing Retailer on the Move: Chairman Cites Departure From 'Conventional Wisdom'". Reprinted by permission of *The Wall Street Journal.* © Dow Jones & Company, Inc., October 31, 1985, 6. All rights reserved.

DISCUSSION QUESTIONS

1. What factors contributed to Limited Inc.'s extremely successful growth and financial performance?
2. Identify and discuss the strategic marketing opportunities and threats that Limited Inc. should consider in developing their strategic marketing plan.
3. Discuss the feasibility of Limited Inc. growing at the expense of their competitors in the no-growth decade for women's apparel expected to begin in 1985.
4. Outline a strategic marketing plan for Limited Inc. covering the period 1987–90. Make any reasonable assumptions necessary to complete your plan outline.

STRATEGIC APPLICATION 16-2

MADD

A group of scruffy toughs on motorcycles drive up to an elegant Victorian mansion. As a butler greets them, they are transformed magically into well-groomed aristocrats.

Their drink: Harley-Davidson Wine Cooler. Uncapped, it roars like a motorcycle.

Commercials such as this one, which aired recently on television in California, are splitting the ranks of the five-year-old national crusade against drunk driving. Some crusaders, health activists who say such ads perpetuate ties between drinking and driving, want to ban the ads or at least get equal time for anti-alcohol blasts. But the alcohol and broadcasting industries—with the notable support of Mothers Against Drunk Driving, or MADD—vehemently oppose those ideas.

The crusade is split on other issues as well. The health groups want to campaign against drunk driving to apply its considerable political muscle against alcohol problems broadly. Besides attacking ads, they seek health warnings on beer, wine and liquor containers. They also seek higher taxes on alcohol, and tougher licensing laws that would limit sales of alcoholic drinks at concerts and other events where drivers are deemed likely to drink.

A Softer Stance

But others take less of a hard line on drinking hard stuff. "We aren't against drinking," says Donald Schaet, the executive director of MADD, which aims to attack alcohol abuse, not alcohol itself. "We are just trying to encourage responsible behavior."

MADD and allies have prompted many states to raise their drinking age and police and courts to crack down on drunk drivers. It gets most of its funds from grass-roots contributions. But MADD money also has come from Anheuser-Busch Inc., the mother of Budweiser beer.

Alcohol producers and broadcasters, fearing the imposition of even tougher anti-alcohol policies, are lending considerable support to the softer-stance crusaders. Anheuser-Busch has given at least $70,000 to MADD. Broadcasters also have courted MADD. The National Broadcasting Co. network televised a "docudrama" about the group's founder and former head, Candy Lightner, whose daughter was killed by a drunk driver. And the National Association of Broadcasters, a major trade group, featured Mrs. Lightner in public-service announcements against drunk driving.

Industry groups have also sought to ingratiate themselves with a MADD lookalike called SADD, or Students Against Driving Drunk. Anheuser-Busch has given SADD at least $200,000, a substantial part of the group's budget. Donald Shea, the president of the U.S. Brewers Association, is one of the most active members of SADD's board.

Like MADD, SADD says it isn't battling drinking per se, and it sees no reason to refuse industry money. Says Robert Anastas, SADD's executive director: "The guy who makes beer or crushes grapes isn't the devil."

A Subtle Message?

But anti-alcohol hard-liners suggest that MADD and SADD are being co-opted. SADD's "contract," in which teenagers agree to call a parent for a ride if they get too drunk to drive, subtly supports teenage drinking, argues Allen Rice, the executive director of the Michigan Interfaith Council on Alcohol Problems, a church-financed group.

"SADD's message suggests that drinking itself is okay—a fact of life to be accepted by society," says Mr. Rice.

Especially upset about the approaches of MADD and SADD are the health lobbies, many of which have labored in obscurity for years. Says James Mosher, an associate director of the Prevention Research Center, a California think tank: "If we are to prevent (drunk driving) we must do more than threaten, cajole or persuade individuals to act more responsibly."

Infighting among these groups has always existed, but it has worsened since last year when the split over anti-alcohol ads developed. MADD has drawn new fire by declining to join a coalition that is lobbying in Congress to require the television networks to carry "counter-messages" to alcohol commercials.

Its critics say MADD's posture stems from its ties to broadcasters. "I oppose alcohol advertising, and the broadcasters won't have anything to do with me," adds Doris Aiken, the president of Remove Intoxicated Drivers, a group that says it refuses alcohol-industry money.

MADD dismisses such criticism. Says the group's Mr. Schaet: "There don't seem to be any valid studies to show that advertising contributes to drunk driving."

While refusing to join the equal-time lobby, MADD has endorsed a "public-service announcement" prepared by Joseph E. Seagram & Sons, a U.S. liquor company owned by Seagram Co. of Canada. The message: Contrary to common belief, the "typical" serving of beer (12 ounces) contains as much alcohol as the "typical" serving of wine (five ounces) or spirits (1¼ ounces).

Seagram & Sons, which boasts about MADD's support, claims its spot helps reduce drunk driving by clearing up a misconception—that drivers are less likely to get drunk on beer or wine than on liquor. But the networks have refused to run the ad, saying it violates a long-standing ban on commercials for liquor (but not beer or wine). Seagram's spot does run on cable-TV channels.

Shaun Sheehan, an official of the National Association of Broadcasters and a member of MADD's board, defends MADD's backing of Seagram. "MADD's war is with the impaired driver," he says. "It isn't with people who choose to drink, or with people who have driver's licenses."

A broader war is called for, MADD's critics insist. Anti-alcohol groups contend that booze is tied so closely with social life, and social life so closely with the automobile, that narrow attacks on just drinking and driving won't work.

Alcohol-related deaths have declined to about 23,500 last year from 28,000 in 1980 when the push for tougher laws and education programs began. But analysts think about half the decline reflects a drop in the number of teen-age drivers. According to a federal estimate cited by Laurence Ross, a University of New Mexico sociologist, eight of every 10 drunk-driving deaths involve victims who were drunk themselves or were riding in cars driven by drunks. The threat of being caught doesn't adequately deter drunk drivers, Mr. Ross says.

A Blurred Distinction

Part of the solution is to change public attitudes so that people are less likely to get drunk in the first place, regardless of whether they drive, insists George Hacker, the director of alcohol programs for the Center for Science in the Public Interest, a self-financed group concerned mostly with health and nutrition.

A first step, he suggests, would be ending ads such as those for Harley-Davidson Wine Cooler. He says the ads encourage a casual attitude toward drinking and driving, by glamorizing alcohol and blurring the distinction between alcohol and soft drinks. "Riding a motorcycle is a symbol of masculinity in our society," he says. "The ad's message is that drinking the wine cooler is part of being a man, too."

Scooter Juice Inc., the California maker of the wine cooler, believes its ads are harmless enough. The company notes that the toughs it portrays don't drink until after they park their motorcycles. Says Eldon Killian, Scooter's sales manager: "We say the time to drink is when your kickstand is down."

SOURCE: Christopher Conte, "Crusaders Against Drunk Driving Split Over Whether to Fight Alcohol Broadly." Reprinted by permission of *The Wall Street Journal.* © Dow Jones & Company, Inc., November 6, 1985, 35. All rights reserved.

DISCUSSION QUESTIONS

1. Identify the organizations and groups that MADD should include in its analysis of the market and competition.
2. What are the marketing strategy issues that MADD's management should consider in the organization's strategic marketing plan?
3. Recommend a marketing strategy for MADD, covering the next three years.

CHAPTER 17

Moving from Plans to Implementation

The Japanese have demonstrated their business talents in a variety of ways. One of their more impressive capabilities is effective implementation of marketing strategies. Consider Japan's domination of the Chinese market even though anti-Japanese sentiment is strong and widespread in China.[1] Although local reception of the Japanese traders is often unfavorable, Japan holds over twice the U.S. market share. In 1984 Japan controlled 26 percent of China's $50 billion of world trade, using an extensive network of sales offices throughout the country. The marketing strategy includes selling initially at low prices to gain market position, later raising prices and making money on spare parts and services. A Japanese trading company adds value to the trading relationship by coordinating an entire project—a feat that might take 10 or 20 American companies. Japanese traders understand and adapt to China's culture and customs, benefiting from a close location and cultural affinity. The Japanese understand and use the Chinese system called *guanxi*—a complex set of relationships whereby Chinese become obligated to each other. Gifts help Japanese traders gain access to the system. The gifts are viewed as tokens of esteem rather than bribes. Finally, the Japanese government supports trade relations with China through loans.

The Japanese are clearly skilled in moving from marketing planning to implementation. Implementation, a critical part of marketing strategy, ultimately determines the success of the strategic plan.

ORGANIZATIONAL DESIGN OPTIONS

The effectiveness of the marketing organization is considered in step 5 of the planning process (Exhibit 16–1). Functional specialization is logical for certain activities that provide services to all markets or all products, such as advertising and marketing research. Emphasis on functions may be less appropriate when trying to organize activities around market targets, products, and field sales operations. Market targets and products also influence organizational design. When two or more targets and/or a mix of products exists, companies often depart from organizational designs based on advertising, selling, research, and other supporting services. Similarly, distribution channels and sales force considerations may influence the organizational structure adopted by a firm. For example, the marketing of home entertainment products for use as employee incentives and promotional gifts might be placed in an organizational unit separate from one marketing through distributor and retail type distribution channels. Geographical factors often have a heavy influence because of the need to make the field supervisory structure correspond to sales force deployment.

Let us assume that the marketing organization is part of a business segment or business unit unless the entire firm is comprised of a single segment or unit. In this regard, two possibilities should be recognized. First, companies with multiple business activities may have corporate marketing organizations as well as business unit marketing components. Moreover, the extent of corporate involvement can range from a coordinating role to one in which the corporate staff has considerable influence on business unit marketing operations. Second, the chief marketing executive and staff may participate in varying degrees in strategic planning for the enterprise and the business unit.

First let's examine the major types of organizational approaches, including the *functional, product, market,* and *combination* or *matrix* designs. Then we will further consider the organization of corporate marketing.

Functional Design

A marketing organization developed along functional lines gives departments, groups, or individuals responsibility for specific activities, such as advertising and sales promotion, pricing, sales, marketing research, and marketing planning and services. Depending on the size and scope of its operations, a marketing organization may include some or all of these activities. The functional approach is often used when a single product or a closely related line is marketed to one market target; e.g., Snap-on-Tools' business segment that markets hand tools to professional mechanics via independent dealers in vans. Departure from a purely functional organizational structure may occur when:

The business unit serves multiple market targets and/or when the needs and requirements of the end users in the market target are different, such that the marketing activities must be varied to serve the end users.

The line or mix of products offered requires expertise due to product complexity, type of application, and other factors.

Special marketing situations call for one of the following: a concentrated marketing effort to plan for and implement a new product, entry into a new market, development of a distribution channel, or some other new project or program that does not fit logically into the existing marketing organization.

Organizational approaches have been developed to take into account these factors, recognizing that in nearly every marketing organization, functional considerations enter into the design to some degree. For example, any organization that assigns all salespeople to a single department is organizing according to the sales function regardless of how the sales force is deployed in the field.

Product Design

Several aspects of a product offering may require special consideration in organizational design. One is the planning and coordination required for new products. New products may not receive the attention they need unless someone is assigned the responsibility. This problem may also occur with existing products when a business unit offers several products and each involves technical and/or application differences. Organizational schemes can be categorized according to whether they are temporary or permanent and whether the people involved are assigned full-time or part-time.[2] Several organizational approaches for product management are shown in Exhibit 17–1.

The choice of a particular approach depends on the situation and on management's preferences. Factors that often influence the decision are the nature and scope of products offered, the rate of new product development, amount of coordination necessary among functional areas, and types of management and technical problems previously encountered with new products and existing products. For example, a firm with an existing functional organizational structure might use a temporary task force to manage and coordinate development of a major new product. Before or soon after commercial introduction, the firm would shift responsibility for the product to the functional organiza-

EXHIBIT 17-1   Organizational Approaches for Managing New and Existing Products

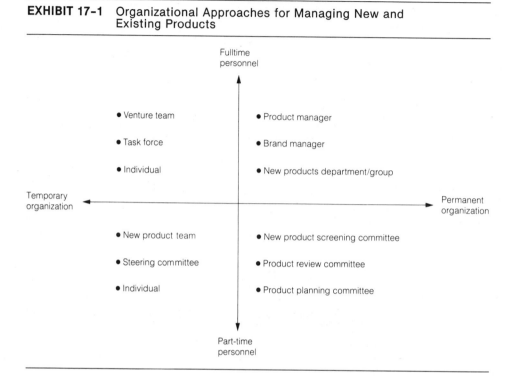

tion. The task force's purpose is to allocate enough direction and effort to the new product so that it will be properly launched.

Market Design

When a business unit serves more than one market target, customer considerations often become important in the design of the marketing organization. If this situation occurs, it is most likely to affect the structuring of the field sales organization. Some firms appoint market managers and have a field sales force that is specialized by type of customer. In these instances, the market manager operates much like a product manager, with responsibility for market planning, research, advertising, and sales force coordination.

Market-oriented field organizations may be deployed according to industry, customer size, type of application, or in various other ways to achieve specialization according to end-user groups. For decades IBM incorporated market considerations into its marketing organizational design. More recently distribution channels have influenced IBM's organizational design. Conditions that suggest a market-oriented design are:

Multiple market targets being served within a strategic business unit.

Substantial differences in needs between end users in a given target market.

Each customer or prospect purchasing the product in large volume or dollar amounts.

Choosing the appropriate design may not always be a clear-cut decision. Many organizations are influenced by a combination of functional, product, and market factors.

Combination or Matrix Design

A popular combination scheme is the matrix organization, in which a cross-classification approach is used to emphasize two different factors, such as products and marketing functions (Exhibit 17-2). Field sales coverage is determined by geography, whereas product emphasis is accomplished using product managers. In addition to working with salespeople, product managers coordinate other marketing functions for their products, such as advertising and marketing research. Other combination schemes are possible. For example, within the sales regions shown in Exhibit 17-2, salespeople could be organized by product type or customer group. Also, some of the marketing functions could be broken down by product category, such as an advertising supervisor for Product II.

Combination approaches offer a flexible response to different influences in designing the organization. The major difficulty with these designs is establishing lines of responsibility and authority. The matrix approach in particular creates overlap in responsibility and gaps in authority. Product and market managers frequently complain that they lack control over all marketing functions even though they are held accountable for results. Nevertheless matrix approaches continue to be popular, so their operational advantages must exceed their limitations.

Organizing Corporate Marketing

The marketing organization may be influenced by how the business is organized; marketing, in turn, may influence the corporate and business unit organizational structure. McGraw-Hill, the giant information and communications company, reorganized along marketing lines in 1985 to concentrate on various markets, facilitate the creation of new products, and take advantage of similarities across product lines.[3] Management used buyers' needs as the basis for organizing the company. Eleven "market-focus" units were established: computers and communications, construction, economic information services, educa-

EXHIBIT 17-2   A Marketing Organization Based on a Combination of
Functions and Products

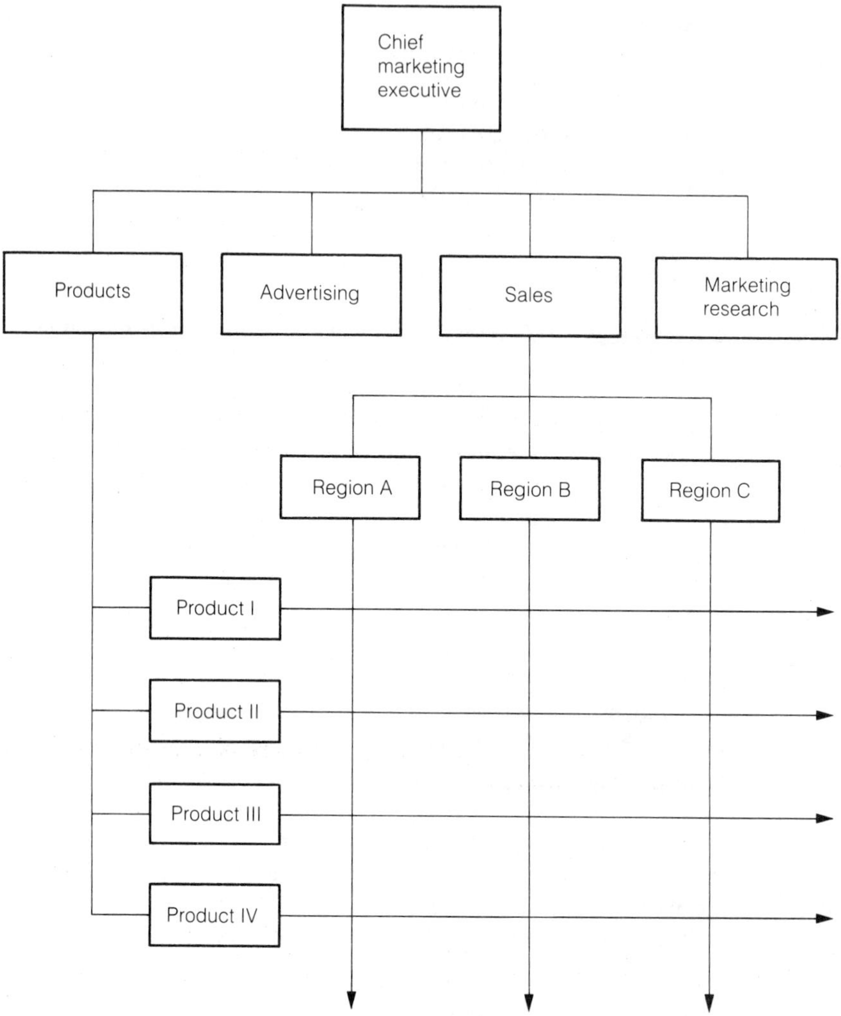

tion, energy, financial services, health care, management, manufacturing industries, process industries, and transportation. The 11 market-focus units form five new business segments. McGraw-Hill's corporate structure had traditionally been product oriented (e.g., all of the magazines in one unit). In the new organizational structure, computer and electronics magazines form part of the Information Systems Company.

Marketing's Corporate Role.   Marketing's corporate role varies among companies. An important organizational task in firms with two or more operating units is determining whether a corporate marketing function should be established, and if so, what its role and scope should be. The Conference Board, in a major study of corporate marketing organization, identifies three possible roles of marketing:

1. Performing services for the company and/or its operating units.
2. Controlling or monitoring the performance of operating unit marketing activities.
3. Providing an advisory or consulting service to corporate management and/or operating units.[4]

Services may include media purchases, marketing research, and other supporting activities. Control may cover pricing policies, new product planning, sales force compensation, and other monitoring/control actions. Advisory or consulting services provide professional marketing expertise such as market segmentation, new product planning, and marketing strategy.

Interestingly, The Conference Board found that 88 companies in its survey have a corporate chief marketing executive (CCME) whereas 206 do not. Exhibit 17–3 shows the organizational responsibility for various marketing related activities for firms that have a CCME. A comparison of the same activities for corporations without a CCME indicates substantially less corporate-level involvement for all activities, with a corresponding increase in marketing management involvement at the operating unit level.

Organizational Trends. Influenced by the trend toward decentralized management, corporations are increasingly moving to decentralize marketing functions from the corporate level to the business unit level. Decentralized marketing activities are more likely to occur:

> When senior management is moving the company toward further diversification into areas having little or no relation to its present array of businesses.
>
> When new growth leads to added organizational complexities and to a further proliferation of the company's operating components.
>
> When senior management makes no attempt to integrate newly acquired businesses into the company's existing corporate structure.
>
> When senior management tends to focus on financial results and assets management.
>
> When areas other than marketing are the principle sources of a company's strength, efficiency, and momentum.
>
> When senior management strongly prefers decentralizing as much responsibility as possible to the company's operating units.
>
> When a company has to cut corporate staff to reduce costs.[5]

EXHIBIT 17-3 Locations of Marketing-Related Activities in Companies Having a Corporate Chief Marketing Executive*

Activity	Percentage of Companies in Which Indicated Activity of Some Kind Exists at:			
	Corporate Level	Group Level	Divisional or Other Operating- unit Level	No Answer or Not Applicable
Advertising and Promotion				
Corporate or institutional advertising	83%	5%	13%	14%
Product advertising	39	22	74	1
Advertising agency policy decisions	78	13	40	5
Media selection or purchase	85	21	71	—
Sales promotion	43	16	81	1
Product publicity	50	15	72	—
Merchandising	30	16	71	12
Packaging	32	14	60	20
Sales and Distribution				
Sales to major or national accounts	35	23	82	1
Sales to other selected classes of customers	18	14	86	2
Sales to all other customers	14	11	86	—
Export sales	36	18	66	3
Other foreign marketing operations	40	18	57	14
Distributor or dealer relations	23	17	74	11
Physical distribution or traffic	48	13	67	9
Sales training	41	18	78	1
Customer service	22	16	84	1
Product service	22	15	85	2
Business Research and Analysis				
Research on markets	78	23	67	1
Research on competitors	66	26	80	—
Advertising research	63	16	49	2
Environmental scanning	55	13	35	27
Economic research	86	9	25	6
Sales analysis	50	27	83	—
Sales forecasting	50	27	84	—
Marketing information systems	69	19	64	1
Products and Planning (excluding R&D)				
Preparation of marketing plans	41	28	83	—
Product pricing	38	27	86	—
Market development	46	25	82	—
Product-line extensions	36	25	80	2
Major new products related to existing lines	53	24	77	1
Major new products not related to existing lines	76	26	49	3

*Based on information provided by 88 multibusiness manufacturing companies having a chief marketing executive at the corporate level. Percentages add across to more than 100 because of possible multiple locations for a given activity within the same company.

SOURCE: David S. Hopkins and Earl L. Bailey, *Organizing Corporate Marketing* (New York: The Conference Board, 1984), 24.

Thus the corporate role of marketing is influenced substantially by top management's approach to organizing the corporation and by the nature and complexity of business operations. Marketing strategy development should be focused at the business unit and product-market levels. A single marketing strategy for a portfolio of business units is usually inappropriate. Nevertheless, it is very important for the top management team to include strategic marketing experts. The market-driven nature of business strategy requires the active participation of a marketing professional.

Marketing may have had a less important strategic role in corporations that used to be regulated. Recall, for example, the corporate power struggles at AT&T between manufacturing and marketing, treated in Chapter 3.[6] In late 1983 manufacturing appeared to have the edge since manufacturing executives held the corporation's top positions. Considering IBM's strong marketing orientation, AT&T's deemphasis of marketing leadership may be a major disadvantage for the firm in its new deregulated environment.

ORGANIZING FOR STRATEGY IMPLEMENTATION

Several factors may influence organizational effectiveness. These influences are examined followed by a discussion of important issues in selecting an organizational design.

Factors Affecting Organizational Effectiveness

Market/Environmental Factors. Market and environmental complexity, interconnectedness, and predictability may influence an organization's effectiveness.[7] The number of product-markets in which the firm operates is a measure of the firm's *complexity. Interconnectedness* concerns the extent to which the key elements of the market and its environment are organized and interrelated. Industrial markets with a small number of buyers are highly interconnected; consumer markets are not. Finally, *predictability* is influenced by how fast the environment is changing, the extent of routinization in relationships, and the degree to which the firm is in direct contact with the environment. The use of a vertical marketing system can help increase predictability.

Characteristics of the Marketing Organization. Organizational differentiation is created by dividing decision-making authority into units with different goals, and by the number and differences between management levels.[8] Integration is the process of managing the various units that comprise an organization. Methods of integration may be conventional or nonconventional. Conventional methods include the use of plans, rules, policies, procedures, meetings, and the use of a higher level manager to resolve problems. Nonconventional mechanisms may involve the use of integrating specialists such as product managers, temporary teams assigned to a specific task, combination organizational structures such as matrix organizations, or the creation of an integrated organizational structure.

Selecting an Organizational Design

The design of the marketing organization should be influenced by market/environmental factors, the characteristics of the organization, and the marketing strategy used. A sound organizational scheme has several characteristics:

> The organization should correspond to the strategic marketing plan. For example, if the plan is structured around markets or products, then the marketing organizational structure should reflect this same emphasis.
>
> Coordination of activities is essential to successful implementation of plans, both within the marketing function and with other company and business unit functions. The more highly specialized that marketing functions become, the more likely coordination and communications will be hampered.
>
> Specialization of marketing activities will lead to greater efficiency in performing the functions. As an illustration, a central advertising department may be more cost-efficient than establishing an advertising unit for each product category. Specialization can also provide technical depth. For example, product or application specialization in a field sales force will enable salespeople to provide consultative type assistance to customers.
>
> The organization should be structured so that responsibility for results will correspond to a manager's influence on results. While this objective is often difficult to fully achieve, it should be a prime consideration in designing the marketing organization.
>
> Finally, one of the real dangers in a highly structured and complex organization is the loss of flexibility. The organization should be adaptable to changing conditions.

Some characteristics conflict with others. For example, specialization can be expensive if carried to extremes. The costs of having different sales specialists call on the same account must be weighed against the benefits obtained from the overlapping coverage. Thus, organizational design represents an assessment of priorities and a balancing of conflicting consequences.

Attempting to match the marketing organization to its markets and environment should contribute to organizational effectiveness. A framework for analyzing the structure-environment match is shown in Exhibit 17–4. It utilizes the dimensions of market/environmental com-

EXHIBIT 17-4 Structure-Environment Match of the
Marketing Organization

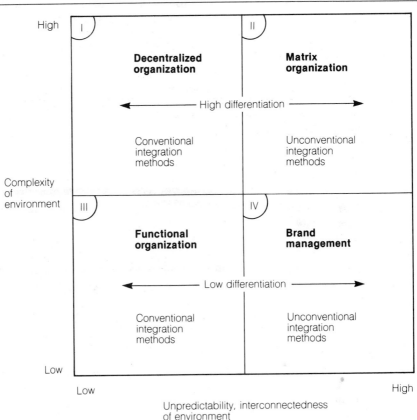

SOURCE: Barton Weitz and Erin Anderson, "Organizing the Marketing Function," in *Review of Marketing 1981,* ed. Ben M. Enis and Kenneth J. Roering (Chicago: American Marketing Association, 1981), 137.

plexity, interconnectedness, and unpredictability, and indicates organizational designs for each contingency.

In Cell I the contingency situation (high environmental complexity, predictable environment) suggests the use of a decentralized organization to gain organizational effectiveness:

> Decentralization offers many benefits for coping with a complex multi-product-market environment. The unit managers can focus their entire efforts on a specific set of products and/or markets. They are task oriented versus function oriented. All of the resources to perform the marketing function are possessed by each decentralized unit. Thus, the need to compete for shared resources is eliminated. The unit managers in a decentralized organization assume some of the decision-making and coordination

roles concentrated in the marketing manager of a functional organization. Thus, decisions are made more quickly. In effect, a complex environment has been divided up into a subset of simpler environments that can be effectively dealt with by the simple functional organizational form.

The increase in effectiveness gained through decentralization is not costless. There is duplication of functional services across units and thus these specialized services may not be used to their full capacity. This duplication and potential under-utilization may lead to a deterioration of in-depth competence. It may be difficult, for example, to attract an advertising specialist to work in a product group as opposed to an advertising department.[9]

A decentralized marketing organization reduces the problems created by a large size organization as well as environmental complexity. Management's challenge is to coordinate and integrate the activities of the units. Organizational units (e.g., market, product) that have independent marketing activities are appropriate for a decentralized organizational design.[10]

Selecting an organizational design for each of the organizational situations shown in Exhibit 17–4 represents a set of tradeoffs. An important first step in choosing an organizational structure or modifying an existing design is identifying the situation. Exhibit 17–4 provides a useful framework for organization analysis. When used in conjunction with management's assessment of other influences, such as corporate culture, available staff, and cost-benefits, it should make the selection of an effective organizational design easier.

PREPARING THE PLAN AND BUDGET

The selection of a marketing strategy and an organizational design moves the planning process to preparation of the actual plan and its supporting sales forecast and budget. Preparing the plan involves several activities and considerations, including selecting the planning cycle and frequency, deciding the nature and use the annual plan, choosing a format for the plan, and forecasting revenues and estimating expenses.

Planning Relationships and Frequency

The relationships between marketing strategy and the short-term annual plan are shown in Exhibit 17–5. The planning cycle is continuous—plans are developed, implemented, evaluated, and adjusted to keep the marketing strategy on target. Since a marketing strategy typically extends beyond one year, firms can facilitate implementation by developing an annual plan to guide short-term marketing activities.

EXHIBIT 17-5 Marketing Planning Relationships

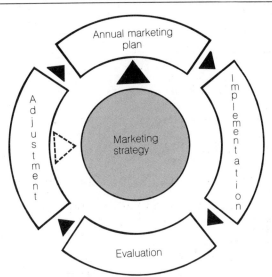

Thus the planning process can be viewed as a series of annual plans guided by marketing strategy.

Exhibit 17-6 illustrates the frequency of various activities in both strategic and short-term planning. An annual planning period is necessary, since several of the activities shown require action within 12 months or less. Longer-range strategic decisions look beyond one year.

The Annual Marketing Plan

Suppose that a new product introduction is scheduled for next year. The short-term plan for the introduction should include results, targets, actions, responsibilities, schedules, and dates. The plan should indicate details and deadlines, production plans, market introduction program, advertising and merchandising actions, employee training, and other information necessary to launching the product. The plan should answer a series of questions—what, when, where, who, how, and why—for each objective to be accomplished during the short-term planning period.

Responsibility for Preparing Plans. Normally a marketing executive is responsible for preparing the marketing plan, as shown in Exhibit 17-7. In many instances the planning process involves several people. For example, a product or market manager may prepare the formal plan for his/her area of responsibility, coordinating and receiving in-

EXHIBIT 17-6 Frequency of Planning Activities—An Example

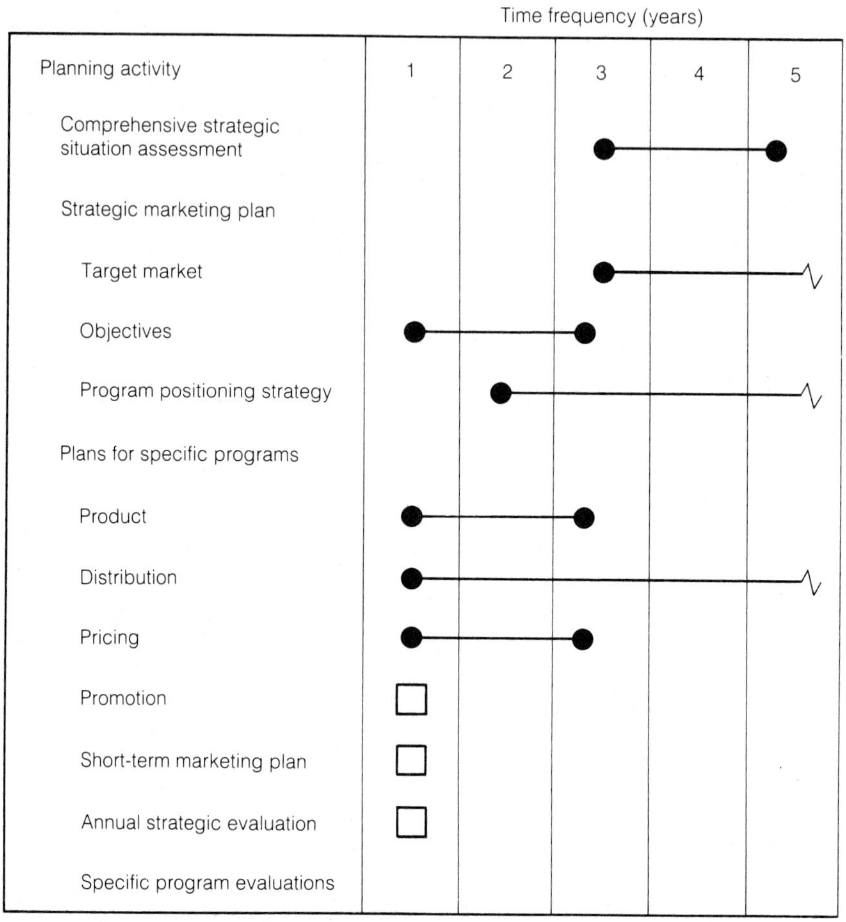

Planning activity	Time frequency (years)				
	1	2	3	4	5
Comprehensive strategic situation assessment			●————————●		
Strategic marketing plan					
Target market			●————————〜		
Objectives	●————————●				
Program positioning strategy		●————————————〜			
Plans for specific programs					
Product	●————————●				
Distribution	●————————————————〜				
Pricing	●————————●				
Promotion	☐				
Short-term marketing plan	☐				
Annual strategic evaluation	☐				
Specific program evaluations					

puts from advertising, marketing research, sales, and other marketing specialists. The product group manager will then consolidate the plans of each product manager, and the marketing director will review and consolidate the plans, creating a master plan.

Format of the Annual Plan. The Grumman example in Chapter 16 is one plan format. The Conference Board details several other examples in its report on marketing planning.[11] Formats and content depend on the size of the organization, managerial responsibility for planning, product and market scope, and other situational factors. The areas typically included in a marketing plan are shown in Exhibit 17–8. The market target provides a useful focus for preparing the marketing plan.

EXHIBIT 17-7 Responsibility for Preparing Plans

	Manufacturers of		
Title with Prime Responsibility	Industrial Products (N = 140)	Consumer Products (N = 100)	Service Firms (N = 25)
Marketing managers or directors	34%	17%	36%
Vice president–marketing or similar	25	29	12
Product managers, brand managers	15	23	—
General managers, including operating division heads	11	8	36
Sales, advertising, marketing research titles	6	9	4
Planning titles, excluding marketing planning	6	6	—
Marketing planning titles	3	7	8
Committee or team	—	1	4
	100%	100%	100%

SOURCE: David S. Hopkins, *The Marketing Plan* (New York: The Conference Board, 1981), 5.

The guide for preparing the strategic marketing audit in Chapter 18 can also be used as a checklist for the content of the marketing plan.

Because of the scope and importance of a new product, it may require a separate plan.[12] There are three reasons for this practice: (1) the approval procedure for a new product plan may differ from that for regular product plans; (2) there may be seasonal differences between the new product introduction and existing product plans; and (3) timing patterns may be different for new and existing products. The actual new product plan will often contain many of the elements that are in the plans for established products.

Forecasting and Budgeting. As we discussed in Chapter 4, marketing financial planning consists of forecasting revenues and profits, and estimating the expenses necessary to achieve the marketing plan. Individuals responsible for market target, product, geographical area, or other units may prepare the forecast. Comparative data on sales, profits, and expenses for prior years provides a useful link to previous results. If plans are developed for several similar organizational units such as products, budgets may be consolidated at a higher organization level.

IMPLEMENTING THE PLAN

Without proper implementation, plans are ineffective, so implementation represents a crucial step in strategic marketing planning. In 1985 Procter & Gamble began making changes in its long-established brand manager system so it could implement marketing strategies better and

---

EXHIBIT 17-8   Outline for Preparing an Annual Marketing Plan

---

Strategic Situation Summary
A summary of the strategic situation for the planning unit (business unit, market segment, product line, etc.).

Market Target(s) Description
Define and describe each market target, including customer profiles, customer preferences and buying habits, size and growth estimates, distribution channels, analysis of key competitors, and guidelines for positioning strategy.

Objectives for the Market Target(s)
Set objectives for the market target (such as market position, sales, and profits). Also state objectives for each component of the marketing program. Indicate how each objective will be measured.

Marketing Program Positioning Strategy
State how management wants the firm to be positioned relative to competition in the eyes and mind of the buyer.
A.   *Product Strategy*
   Set strategy for new products, product improvements, and product deletions.
B.   *Distribution Strategy*
   Indicate the strategy to be used for each distribution channel, including role of middlemen, assistance and support provided, and specific activities planned.
C.   *Price Strategy*
   Specify the role of price in the marketing strategy and the planned actions regarding price.
D.   *Promotion Strategy*
   Indicate the planned strategy and actions for advertising, publicity, personal selling, and sales promotion.
E.   *Marketing Research*
   Identify information needs and planned projects, objectives, estimated costs, and time table.
F.   *Coordination with Other Business Functions*
   Specify the responsibilities and activities of other departments that have an important influence upon the planned marketing strategy.

Forecasts and Budgets
Forecast sales and profit for the marketing plan and set the budget for accomplishing the forecast.

Contingency Plans
Indicate planned actions if events differ from those assumed in the plan.

---

shorten the time from planning to action.[13] One change is the "talk sheet," an informal memo that helps several levels of management quickly refine a proposal through conversation instead of just written communications. Top management is also beginning to delegate decision making to lower organizational levels. Interdivisional project teams are getting results, such as moving Ivory shampoo into national distribution in 4 months rather than the normal 18 months. Nevertheless this huge bureaucratic corporation faces a major challenge because many layers of organizational structure and large numbers of people complicate implementation.

EXHIBIT 17-9 The Implementation Task

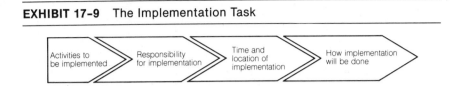

The Implementation Task

The marketing plan should address the implementation task (Exhibit 17-9), indicating what activities are to be implemented, who will be responsible for implementation, the time and location of implementation, and how implementation will be done. Consider the following excerpt from a product manager's marketing plan:

> Sales representatives should target all accounts using a competitive product. A plan should be developed to convert 5 percent of these accounts to the company brand during 1986. Account listings will be prepared and distributed by product management.

In this instance the sales force is responsible for implementing the planned action. A results target is specified but very little is provided as to *how* the accounts will be converted. The sales force plan should translate the proposed action and objective (5 percent conversion) into assigned salesperson responsibility (quotas), a timetable, and guidelines for developing a selling strategy. Training may be necessary to demonstrate the product advantages—and the competitors product limitations—that will be useful in convincing the buyer to change to the firm's brand.

Assigning Responsibility. The marketing plan should establish which organizational units and managers are responsible for implementing the various activities in the plan. Deadlines indicate the time available for implementation. In the case of the plan above, the sales manager should be the person responsible for implementation.

Roadblocks to Implementation. How marketing activities are organized clearly has an influence on implementation. Consider, for example, the four archetypal organizational forms in Exhibit 17-10. Note the usage context and performance characteristics of each structure. Since implementation may involve a usage context that combines two of the structures, tradeoffs are involved. The type of structure adopted may hinder or facilitate the implementation of certain activities and tasks. For example, the bureaucratic form should facilitate the implementation of repetitive activities such as telephone processing of air

EXHIBIT 17–10 Four Archetypal Organizational Forms

		Market versus Hierarchical Organization	
		Internal Organization of Activity	*External Organization of Activity*
	Centralized Formalized Nonspecialized	**Bureaucratic Form** *Appropriate usage context* • conditions of market failure • low environmental uncertainty • tasks which are repetitive, easily assessed, requiring specialized assets *Performance characteristics* • highly effective and efficient • less adaptive *Examples in marketing* • functional organization • company or division sales force • corporate research staffs	**Transactional Form** *Appropriate usage context* • under competitive market conditions • low environmental uncertainty • tasks which are repetitive, easily assessed, with no specialized investment *Performance characteristics* • most efficient form • highly effective for appropriate tasks • less adaptive *Examples in marketing* • contract purchase of advertising space • contract purchase of transportation of product • contract purchase of research field work
Structural Characteristics	Decentralized Nonformalized Specialized	**Organic Form** *Appropriate usage context* • conditions of market failure • high environmental uncertainty • tasks which are infrequent, difficult to assess, requiring highly specialized investment *Performance characteristics* • highly adaptive • highly effective for nonroutine, specialized tasks • less efficient *Examples in marketing* • product management organization • specialized sales force organization • research staffs organized by product groups	**Relational Form** *Appropriate usage context* • under competitive market conditions • high environmental uncertainty • tasks which are nonroutine, difficult to assess, requiring little specialized investment *Performance characteristics* • highly adaptive • highly effective for nonroutine, specialized tasks • less efficient *Examples in marketing* • long-term retainer contract with advertising agency • ongoing relationship with consulting firm

SOURCE: Robert W. Ruekert, Orville C. Walker, Jr., and Kenneth J. Roering, "The Organization of Marketing Activities: A Contingency Theory of Structure and Performance," *Journal of Marketing*, Winter 1985, 20.

travel reservations and ticketing. Once management analyzes the task(s) to be performed and the environment in which they will be done, it must determine its priorities—performance and short-run efficiency or adaptability and longer-term effectiveness:

> Activities in different categories should be structured differently whenever feasible. Some firms appear to be moving in this direction, as shown by reports of cuts in corporate staff departments, the shifting of more planning and decision-making authority to individual business unit and product-market managers, and the increased use of ad hoc task forces to deal with specific markets or problems—all of which indicate a shift toward more decentralized and flexible structures.[14]

A closely related implementation issue is the corporate culture, which may have important influence on implementation. Management should consider its own management style, accepted practices, specific performance of executives, and other unique characteristics in formulating the implementation strategy.

Facilitating Implementation

Managers are important facilitators in the implementation process, and some are more effective than others. To be effective implementors, managers need:

> The ability to understand how others feel, and good bargaining skills.
> The strength to be tough and fair in putting people and resources where they will be most effective.
> Effectiveness in focusing on the critical aspects of performance in managing marketing activities.
> The ability to create a necessary informal organization or network to match each problem with which they are confronted.[15]

In addition to people, several implementation methods may facilitate the process. These include *organizational forms, incentives,* and *communications.*

Organizational Forms. Certain organizational concepts can facilitate implementation, such as the product manager. Companies may also form implementation teams consisting of representatives from the business functions and/or marketing activities involved.

Incentives. Various rewards may help achieve successful implementation. Special incentives such as contests, recognition, and extra compensation can encourage salespeople to push a new product. However, performance standards must be fair, and incentives should encourage something more than acceptable performance.

Communications. Effective information flow, now improved by information technology, is essential to implementation. Consider, for example, the success of Videotex electronic information services in France.[16] The network is operated by the government telecommunications authority and processes 15 million calls per month. About 30 percent of the calls are from consumers to entrepreneurs and another 20 percent of the calls are business-to-business transactions. Customers can dial everything from gourmet caterers to psychiatrists.

Integrating Marketing into the Organization

Encouraging and facilitating a marketing orientation throughout all functional areas of the business is an important responsibility of marketing management. The chief executive officer of a large transportation services company states that the marketing and operations functions are the customer service components of the firm, and that the role of accounting, finance, human resources, and information systems is to support the two operating components of the business. Such supporting functions are evaluated on the basis of how effectively they meet the needs of marketing and operations. Since both areas are concerned with delivering customer satisfaction, this CEO's operating philosophy encourages (and rewards) a customer-driven approach throughout the organization.

The characteristics of an organization may have an important effect on developing a marketing orientation throughout the business. Small companies can achieve integration more easily than large, multilayered corporations. The corporate culture may facilitate or constrain marketing integration. Managers of nonmarketing functions must recognize the importance of meeting customer needs through the integrated marketing efforts of all business activities. A strong commitment and active participation by the chief executive officer are essential to integrate marketing into the thinking and actions of everyone in the firm. Lee Iacoca has played an active role in integrating marketing into all of Chrysler's organizational units.

The implementation of marketing strategy may partially depend on external organizations such as marketing research firms, marketing consultants, advertising and public relations firms, channel members, and other organizations participating in the marketing effort. These outside organizations present a major management challenge when they actively participate in marketing activities. Their efforts should be programmed into the marketing plan and their roles and responsibilities clearly established and communicated. There is a potential danger in not informing outside groups of planned actions, deadlines, and other implementation requirements. For example, the advertising agency account executive and other agency staff members should be familiar with all aspects of promotion strategy as well as the major dimensions of marketing strategy. Restricting information from participating firms can adversely affect their contributions to strategy planning and implementation.

CONCLUDING NOTE

Preparation of the strategic marketing plan is one of the most demanding management responsibilities of the chief marketing executive. It requires folding together many different information gathering and analysis activities into a comprehensive and integrated plan of action. Following a step-by-step approach in building the strategic plan is a useful way to be sure each component of the plan is covered and that important interrelationships between the components are recognized. The starting point in the planning process is understanding the corporate strategic plan since the marketing plan is one of a bundle of functional strategies that must be combined to achieve corporate and business unit objectives.

Selection of the marketing planning unit(s) provides the basis for starting the planning process. These units comprise the building blocks for the plan. The planning unit chosen may be products, lines of products, market targets, or other logical components for guiding planning activities. The situation analysis conducted in Step 1 should establish critical information about markets, competition, company strengths and limitations, and identification of key contingencies. Steps 3 and 4 determine target market strategy and objectives for each target. These steps provide guidelines for developing a marketing program positioning strategy (Step 5). Product, distribution, price, and promotion strategies must be combined into an integrated marketing program for achieving objectives in the market target.

Next, in Step 6 the marketing organization should be designed to accomplish the strategies that have been developed in Steps 1 through 5. Structuring the marketing organization should recognize important strategic and environmental factors. Long-range strategy is operationalized via the short-range marketing plan (Step 7), and then implemented, managed, and modified over a period to keep the gap between desired and actual results as small as possible (Step 8). Chapter 18 considers strategic evaluation and control of the marketing strategy that has been implemented.

NOTES

1. This account is based on Barry Kramer, "Master Merchants: Japanese Dominate the Chinese Market with Savvy Trading," *The Wall Street Journal*, November 18, 1985, 1 and 10.

2. George Benson and Joseph Chasin, *The Structure of New Product Organization* (New York: AMACOM, 1976), p. 10.

3. Stuart J. Elliott, "McGraw Rewrites the Book along Marketing Lines," *Advertising Age,* December 3, 1984, 2 and 94.

4. David S. Hopkins and Earl L. Bailey, *Organizing Corporate Marketing* (New York: The Conference Board, 1984), 23.

5. Ibid., 40.

6. Monica Langley, "AT&T Marketing Men Find Their Star Fails to Ascend as Expected," *The Wall Street Journal,* February 13, 1984, 1 and 12.

7. The following discussion is based on Barton Weitz and Erin Anderson, "Organizing the Marketing Function," in *Review of Marketing 1981,* ed. Ben M. Enis and Kenneth J. Roering (Chicago: American Marketing Association, 1981), 134–42.

8. Ibid.

9. Ibid., 138.

10. Ibid., 139.

11. David S. Hopkins, *The Marketing Plan* (New York: The Conference Board, 1981), 5.

12. Ibid., 4–5.

13. Jolie B. Solomon and John Bussey, "Cultural Change: Pressed by Its Rivals, Procter & Gamble Co. Is Altering Its Ways," *The Wall Street Journal,* May 20, 1985, 1 and 16.

14. Robert W. Ruekert, Orville C. Walker, Jr., and Kenneth J. Roering, "The Organization of Marketing Activities: A Contingency Theory of Structure and Performance," *Journal of Marketing,* Winter 1985, 23–24. See also Hopkins and Bailey, *Organizing Corporate Marketing.*

15. Thomas V. Bonoma, "Making Your Marketing Strategy Work," *Harvard Business Review,* March-April 1984, 75.

16. Thane Peterson, "Why the French Are in Love with Videotex," *Business Week,* January 20, 1986, 84–85.

QUESTIONS FOR REVIEW AND DISCUSSION

1. The chief executive of a manufacturer of fibers for use in carpets is interested in establishing a marketing organization in the firm. Sales to carpet tufters are handled by a manufacturer's agent, and advertising is planned and executed by an advertising agency. Other than the CEO, no one inside the firm is responsible for the marketing function. What factors should the CEO consider in designing a marketing organization? (See Chapter 5 for a description of distribution channels in this industry.)

2. Of the various approaches to marketing organization design, which one(s) offers the most flexibility in responding to changing conditions? Discuss.

3. Discuss the conditions where a matrix-type marketing organization would be appropriate, indicating important considerations and potential problems in using this organizational form.

4. Assume that you have been asked by the president of a major transportation services firm to recommend a marketing organizational design. What important factors should you consider in selecting the design?

5. Outline a procedure for preparing an annual marketing plan for a medium-size suburban bank with assets of $100 million.

6. Discuss the advantages and limitations of assigning a financial analyst

7. to the marketing department on a full-time basis.

7. The short-term marketing plan is an important means of implementing and managing marketing strategy. Discuss how the short-term plan should be used for this purpose.

8. Discuss some of the important issues related to integrating marketing into an organization such as a regional womens' clothing chain compared to accomplishing the same task in the Limited Inc.

STRATEGIC APPLICATION 17-1

CAMPBELL SOUP COMPANY

CAMDEN, N.J.—R. Gordon McGovern, the president and chief executive of Campbell Soup Co., was so obsessed with cooking up new products a few years ago that he sent key executives copies of "In Search of Excellence," a primer on corporate innovation. Partly as a result, the company has introduced 334 new products in the past five years—more than any other company in the hotly competitive food industry.

But now Mr. McGovern has decided that Campbell may have done too much innovating too fast. His new reading assignment has a different emphasis: This year, he sent his executives a book about how to improve product quality and production efficiency to hold down costs. "Read it carefully," Mr. McGovern wrote in an accompanying memo. Failure to control costs, he said, could leave Campbell without enough money to support its new-product strategy.

Indeed, the company's new-product recipe itself is changing. Mr. McGovern wants a more rigorous review of costly new-product ventures and a slower pace of national introductions. Herbert M. Baum, the newly installed president of Campbell's huge U.S. division, says Campbell can no longer afford to run "a new-product boutique."

When Mr. McGovern was promoted from executive vice president and chief operating officer to the Campbell presidency in 1980, his single-minded goal seemed to be turning the stodgy soup maker into a consumer-driven marketing company. In the past, Campbell had concentrated so much on production efficiency that its new products appeared to be designed on the basis of what the company could make easily, rather than what people wanted to buy. So Mr. McGovern focused on consumers by encouraging executives to visit supermarkets, restaurants and people's kitchens.

Two Superstars

To foster entrepreneurial attitudes, the new president split the company into 50 autonomous business units divided by such product categories as soup, frozen foods and beverages. Then he poured money into marketing, increasing expenditures by almost 150% between 1980 and 1985.

But the results weren't entirely satisfactory. True, the company says seven of the 10 major new brands introduced in the McGovern era have been successful, generating at least $25 million in annual sales. What's more, two new Campbell concoctions—Prego spaghetti sauces and Le Menu frozen dinners—became superstars, accounting for more than $450 million of Campbell's $4 billion in annual sales. Lately though, the company has spent heavily to promote new and existing products without reaping the expected rewards.

Some glaring examples: Juice Works, a new line of natural blends for kids, did so poorly initially that Campbell had to reformulate three flavors and revamp its advertising campaign last fall. Pepperidge Farm, a star performer in the 12 years that Mr. McGovern ran the unit, has been slow to recover from disastrous forays into new products that had little to do with the brand's premium image. After three disappointing quarters, Campbell's operating earnings in the fiscal year ended July 28 are estimated to have approximated last year's $5.93 a share—falling far short of Mr. McGovern's goal of 15% annual growth.

"I think what happened was the brand managers became so involved in looking at new products that they ignored the base businesses," says one Campbell marketing manager. Mr. McGovern himself concedes that the company has made enough mistakes for him to replace the presidents of both the U.S. division and Pepperidge Farm. But he describes his efforts to tighten control over major new-product introductions as a necessary phase of Campbell's evolution, rather than a response to soft earnings.

'Healthiest Move'

Whatever the reason, Laurel Cutler, an advertising executive who helps Campbell and other companies plot new product strategies, applauds the change. "I feel it is the healthiest possible move," says Mrs. Cutler, vice chairman of Leber Katz Partners in New York. "Nothing that important can be delegated below the most senior management."

Campbell's cost-control efforts might also protect it from the takeover fever that has swept the food industry. Certainly, Campbell's strong brands make it an attractive target. In May, Campbell stock leaped almost $8 to $76.375 a share on news that R. J. Reynolds Industries Inc. and Nabisco Brands Inc. were planning to merge. In late June, Campbell hit $79 on rumors that General Foods Corp. might be the target of a bid by Philip Morris Inc. To make Campbell stock more affordable for small investors, Campbell in June declared a two-for-one stock split that was payable last month. Yesterday, Campbell closed at $38 a share.

A Campbell merger seems unlikely any time soon. The Dorrance family owns 58% of the stock, and John T. Dorrance, Jr., who retired last fall as Campbell chairman and who is the sole beneficiary of a family trust that owns 31.5% of the stock, has said he doesn't intend to sell. But one line of speculation says the Dorrances could change their minds, especially if earnings don't improve.

Taking Risks

Despite the new emphasis on discipline, Campbell hasn't lost its penchant for taking risks. It is testing more new ideas than ever before, among them refrigerated salads, soups in microwavable containers, Pepperidge Farm ice cream and granola bread. And it is beginning an assault on the $290 million dry-soup-mix market dominated by Thomas J. Lipton Inc., a unit of the Anglo-Dutch Unilever Group. The move makes sense, Campbell officials say, because dry-soup sales in the U.S. have been growing faster than sales of canned soups.

"What we're trying to prevent is a quick trigger finger," says Mr. Baum. "We want the products that go national to be well-tested unless there is some competitive reason to go national all at once."

Lipton's aggressive response to test marketing of an early Campbell dry-soup product provided the reason to spring today's six-flavor line of soup mixes into national distribution, starting this summer, Mr. Baum says.

So Campbell committed $16 million to the launch, and Mr. Baum is watching its progress carefully. At his urging, the soup-mix team twice revised its market-

Campbell's Leading New Products
($600 million in sales for fiscal 1985)

1985 Ranking	Year Introduced
1 Le Menu Frozen Dinner	1982
2 Prego Spaghetti Sauce	1982
3 Chunky New England Clam Chowder	1984
4 Great Starts Breakfasts	1984
5 Prego Plus	1985

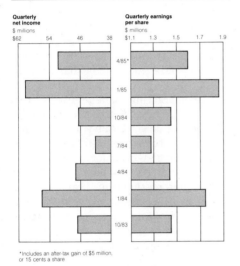

Quarterly net income
$ millions

Quarterly earnings per share
$ millions

*Includes an after-tax gain of $5 million, or 15 cents a share.

ing plan, putting more money into advertising aimed at consumers, rather than trade allowances that would lower prices.

In the past, Campbell's racing into the marketplace has produced mixed results. The strategy paid off with Le Menu, the line of premium frozen dinners that Campbell launched in the West in 1982. The company's engineers hadn't yet designed much of the production equipment needed to fill the round dinner plates automatically. So Campbell hired people to fill the plates by hand. They used ice-cream scoops to dish out rice, and they picked up meats with gloved fingers. The production line was inefficient, but demand for the dinners was strong.

Introducing Juice Works in the Northeast last fall in bottles and single-serving cans, without offering aseptic packages, turned out to be a costly error. Juice blends packed in the lightweight cardboard boxes were added to the Juice Works line in January. But because Campbell misjudged the importance of aseptic packages in the Northeast (it had tested the packages elsewhere), it initially had trouble persuading retailers to carry the products. Competition from juice blends made by Tree Top Inc., Welch Foods Inc., the Libby, McNeill & Libby unit of Nestle Enterprises Inc. and others made the task tougher.

The false starts, including ingredient problems and an advertising campaign that was scrapped when it failed to produce results, cost Campbell "several million dollars," according to Mr. Baum. In the fiscal year that just ended, Juice Works sales fell an estimated $8 million short of the $32 million Campbell had forecast.

Sales have picked up dramatically in recent months, but Mr. Baum wants to look at the results through December before taking the product national. Juice Works had been scheduled to go national last spring.

Low Morale

Pepperidge Farm suffered $9 million in losses because it rushed Star Wars cookies and apple juice into the market place in 1983. By last summer, when Richard A. Shea became the third Pepperidge Farm president in four years, morale had sunk to a low point. Press reports about the cookie and apple-juice flops—both products now are defunct—reinforced the impression that the unit had lost sight of its heritage.

Pepperidge Farm was founded in 1937 by Margaret Rudkin, who baked her first loaf of whole-wheat bread when a doctor recommended its natural ingredients as a treatment for her asthmatic son. Within a few years, Mrs. Rudkin was receiving orders from as far away as India, and the company expanded rapidly.

Campbell bought Pepperidge Farm in 1961.

To get Pepperidge Farm back on track, Mr. Shea and 50 marketing managers retreated last fall to a motel to talk about where the company was headed. They listened to presentations about consumer trends. Then they split up into small groups, first to discuss the meaning of the Pepperidge Farm brand and later to brainstorm new-product ideas. "It was amazing to me how each group kept coming up with the same . . . things," says Edith Volino Anderson, marketing manager for frozen new products. "You started to see the company take shape. You started to see a philosophy."

Among the key attributes mentioned over and over at the meeting were premium quality, natural ingredients, meeting a consumer need and an ability to build on the company's bakery heritage. But some managers were still confused about the types of products Pepperidge Farm should make, suggesting popcorn or snack cakes, for example. Mr. Shea recalls saying that Pepperidge Farm couldn't add anything to popcorn to make it a premium product and that snack cakes, as a children's product, wouldn't support a premium price.

Mr. Shea later boiled down the managers' ideas into new-product standards and priorities. He instituted monthly meetings at which once-autonomous marketing managers must compare the progress of their projects with their forecasts. He also dropped 275 products that weren't up to snuff, including several flavors of Deli's, a line of frozen, pastry-encased meat and cheese sandwiches for which Pepperidge Farm had high hopes a few years ago. The sandwiches will be phased out entirely in the fall because, despite high trial rates, most consumers didn't buy them again.

Beyond the problems of Pepperidge Farm, Mr. McGovern has the bigger picture to contend with. Now 58 years old, he is concentrating on choosing and grooming a successor to Campbell's presidency. He is expected to become chairman within a few years, and last fall, at his suggestion, the board elected William S. Cashel Jr., a retired American Telephone & Telegraph Co. executive, as a transitional chairman.

In his efforts to revitalize Campbell, Mr. McGovern must strike the right balance between disciplining the business units and leaving enough room for innovation. Some marketing managers are bound to be disappointed, since Campbell plans to undertake fewer national launches at a time when it has so many new ideas.

But marketing managers seem to be adjusting. They describe the call for discipline as a dose of reality in an environment where the sky seemed to be the limit. "The plan had been for every unit to work . . . on new products to make successes out of them all," says Patti F. Goodman, marketing manager for Juice Works. "Now we want to put our (money) behind those products that have the greatest chance of success."

SOURCE: Francine Schwadel, "Revised Recipe: Burned by Mistakes, Campbell Soup Co. Is in Throes of Change." Reprinted by permission of *The Wall Street Journal.* © Dow Jones & Company, Inc., August 14, 1985, pp. 1, 13. All rights reserved.

DISCUSSION QUESTIONS

1. Discuss some of the strategic and operating issues of coordinating corporate and business unit strategies.
2. What business unit implementation guidelines can be used to achieve proper management of existing and new products?
3. Comment on Campbell's use of 50 business units.
4. Evaluate Campbell's approach to new product planning, suggesting any improvements that are needed.

STRATEGIC APPLICATION 17-2

AT&T

NEW YORK—American Telephone & Telegraph Co., betting on a major Federal Communications Commission decision expected as early as this month, is preparing to make big changes in the way it sells products and services.

"While the scope and details still aren't known publicly, the FCC ruling sought by AT&T is widely expected to allow the company to overhaul its method of marketing communications services, phone equipment and computers—particularly to large corporations.

One result might be that business customers soon could deal with one AT&T sales representative instead of the usual two or more. More importantly, the changes would help AT&T in its battle with International Business Machines Corp. and other unregulated competitors.

"In the sense of a transition of AT&T into a business that has the freedom to compete on an equal basis, this is a very significant and important milestone for us," says Robert Casale, the executive vice president of AT&T Information Systems who is in charge of planning for the FCC's action. "From my perspective, it would be one of the most significant moves for us since divestiture."

Industry Debate

The expected changes are generating the greatest controversy in the telecommunications equipment industry since the breakup of the Bell System. The debate centers on an AT&T request that the FCC relax a ruling that since 1983 has forced the company's unregulated equipment unit, AT&T Information Systems, to operate separately from its long-distance phone service unit, AT&T Communications. The issue also is fueling rivalry within the company itself over which unit will dominate the unified marketing plan that would result from new ground rules.

The separation was aimed at preventing AT&T from subsidizing its unregulated, competitive equipment ventures through its regulated long-distance operations. Each unit is required to have its own service, marketing and other functions.

The FCC has received more than 100 comments on AT&T's request from trade groups and such companies as Tandy Corp. and Digital Equipment Corp., as well as about 90 letters from members of Congress. Most of them oppose relaxing the separation rule or urge stringent safeguards if it is relaxed. Still, a majority of the FCC's members have spoken out in favor of loosening the requirement.

"It's probably the most significant waiver of the separation rules that the commission will consider," says Albert Halprin, chief of the FCC's Common Carrier Bureau. George Kelly, a securities analyst with Morgan Stanley & Co., adds, "One way to measure the value of the regulatory relief the proposal would provide to AT&T is to look at the resistance it has prompted from the competition—it's enormous."

AT&T says the rule costs it more than $1 billion a year in duplicate staff, marketing and developing costs. Moreover, the company says, the rule prevents it from offering certain new services, confuses customers and hobbles its marketing against rivals, notably IBM, which can sell office equipment and communications services at the same time. Easing the restrictions also may spur AT&T to undertake an acquisition of a computer company or a major joint venture with one.

Rule Seen as Outdated

AT&T argues that the separation requirement, adopted in an FCC decision in 1980 called Computer Inquiry II, now is outdated. The idea behind separation was to find a way to allow the company to enter unregulated businesses without giving it an undue advantage over rivals.

The agency feared AT&T might exploit its monopoly in phone service, forcing ratepayers to subsidize its newly deregulated equipment business and allowing it to unfairly undercut competitors. Also, the commission didn't want the company to be able to discriminate against its equipment rivals by hooking up phones to the local network faster for customers who buy AT&T equipment. Separation meant AT&T equipment sales workers couldn't coordinate their efforts with the local phone company.

But AT&T notes that its monopoly in local service evaporated with the divestiture of its local operating companies in 1984. And the telecommunications giant contends that it no longer monopolizes long-distance service, either. It says that if it were to unfairly shift costs from equipment operations to long-distance operations, customers unhappy with rising rates could switch to other carriers. Meantime, IBM has bought AT&T's biggest rival in the office phone switch business, Rolm Corp., and allied itself with AT&T's biggest rival in long distance, MCI Communications Corp.

"We're looking at a market that is extremely competitive," says Mr. Casale.

Many equipment rivals, however, still worry about the subsidy issue. They say that even though the long-distance business is competitive, AT&T's huge share of the market—an estimated 85%, down from more than 95% in 1980—could be misused to subsidize its equipment business through phone rates. As safeguards, the FCC in its expected decision would continue to bar such subsidies and likely force AT&T to account separately for its unregulated ventures. But some critics say the separate subsidiary should be retained.

Competitors' Views

"Accounting just can't solve the problem that may arise," says Neal Goldberg, a Washington, D.C., attorney for Tandy, a Fort Worth, Texas, electronics concern that sells phones. "The commission staff just doesn't have enough time to do all the monitoring." IBM says it favors lifting the separation requirement, but with safeguards.

Under existing rules, sales representatives for AT&T Information Systems and AT&T Communications generally can't work together to sell communications products and services. That frustrates some large users, such as Union Carbide Corp. "Right now, we have to issue orders to Information Systems for work on a PBX (an office call-switching system) and we have to issue orders to AT&T Comunications for the line," says Thomas DiBari, who manages Union Carbide's phone network. "If we could deal with one instead of two service groups, it would help us."

AT&T wants to be able to market network services and equipment in packages, such as a private line with an office switching terminal, that can be sold by the same representative. But there's more behind the expected changes than customer convenience. AT&T wants to take advantage of its strength as a communications company to design and sell integrated communications and data systems that one day will tie together a customer's scattered offices, terminals and computers in sophisticated networks.

AT&T sees the ability to build these networks as crucial to its success in the computer and office-automation business, but says the government restrictions prevent specialists on either side of the company from working together to offer them. "Today, we can't go into a large account and offer an integrated solution," says Mr. Casale. "About the only company that can do that is IBM."

Since June, under Mr. Casale's direction, task forces throughout AT&T have been devising marketing plans the company may adopt if it wins the regulatory changes. The groups are studying how various industries move information and what kinds of systems the company could sell if the two units work together.

AT&T also is studying how to put its plans into effect. One option under review would put 10 of its approximately 500 account managers in AT&T Information Systems and AT&T Communications at the head of experimental teams, staffed by employees from both units, that would call on yet-to-be-selected national accounts, selling them equipment and long-distance services. If successful, this approach could be extended to other important accounts.

"The question is, how boldly will AT&T take advantage of the opportunity it is likely to get?" says Edward Goldstein, a former AT&T vice president of strategy and development who now is a principal at Management Analysis Center Inc., a consulting firm in Cambridge, Mass. "Painfully, AT&T has been learning the marketing game," he says. "They still have a long way to go, but if they use this opportunity right, it can help them."

Already, the Information Systems and Communications units are jockeying for position to represent the 200 national accounts they have in common. A salesman in an Information Systems office in New Jersey says the national account manager's post in his office has been left vacant until the sales forces are combined. "There's strong rumors that we'll be reporting to Communications in November," says the salesman, who asked not to be identified.

The telecommunications manager of a large industrial company says sales representatives of the two AT&T units have been sniping at one another for weeks. AT&T Information Systems is seeking an agreement allowing it to service the customer's private phone network, "but AT&T Communications is indicating

there are pitfalls" to such an arrangement, the manager says.

The anticipated FCC ruling has also revived talk of a possible AT&T computer company acquisition or joint venture. Mr. Casale acknowledges that AT&T, which has sold computers since last year, also has been looking "at a number of opportunities" with other computer makers. On Wall Street, AT&T is said to have considered acquiring computer makers ranging from Burroughs Corp. to Apple Computer Inc. AT&T has declined to comment on such reports, and none of the supposed targets has confirmed them. Although AT&T could pursue an acquisition or joint venture now, relaxing the separation rules would make such moves easier.

"The major shortcoming for AT&T in penetrating the computer market hasn't been so much the lack of expertise or product line, but its ability to convince customers that they are a viable alternative to established vendors such as IBM," says Ken Leon, a securities analyst for L. F. Rothschild, Unterberg, Towbin. "An acquisition or a joint venture will add to AT&T's credibility with customers who have been doing business with other vendors for many years."

AT&T, which asked the FCC last year to lift the separation requirement, has been chipping away at the rule through waivers. The company's recent announcement that it will eliminate 24,000 jobs by next year, for example, was in part the result of such waivers, approved by the FCC in April. The company was allowed to transfer six factories and seven management and logistics centers from another AT&T unit to Information Systems.

The company says the transfer will strengthen product development and manufacturing and save "in excess of several hundred million dollars." Mr. Casale acknowledges that further cost-cutting steps, including more employee cutbacks, are possible if the rules are relaxed further.

The expected FCC ruling could create more problems as well. The decision likely will cover only sales of computers and phone equipment. The commission has launched a separate study, known as Computer Inquiry III, of how to regulate certain advanced services such as electronic mail or data processing, which AT&T now can offer only through a separate subsidiary. If the FCC retains that requirement, while easing the separation rule for equipment, the company could be forced to change some of its plans. "It's something we don't want to have," says Mr. Casale.

SOURCE: Peter W. Barnes and Janet Guyon, "AT&T Prepares Major Changes in Marketing: An Expected U.S. Decision Would Lift Certain Restraints." Reprinted by permission of *The Wall Street Journal.* © Dow Jones & Company, Inc., September 9, 1985, p. 6. All rights reserved.

DISCUSSION QUESTIONS

1. Define and discuss the implications of the strategic marketing situation facing AT&T.
2. Outline key guidelines for an organizational design for AT&T, assuming AT&T has the freedom to compete on an equal basis with IBM.
3. Discuss some of the issues associated with implementing the organizational design.
4. What computer firm would be a promising acquisition target for AT&T?

CHAPTER 18

Strategic Evaluation and Control

The Dannon Co. waited almost too long to change its marketing strategy to respond to new competition and the changing tastes of buyers.[1] Spending for yogurt in 1985 was about $1 billion, an 11 percent increase from 1984. Dannon had a 25.5 percent market share based on dollar volume in 1984, followed by General Mills Yoplait brand with a 22.6 percent share. The Kellogg Co. is aggressively marketing its premium-priced Whitney's brand, and Dart and Kraft Inc.'s Light n' Lively has obtained a major share of the snack and lunch-box business with minipacks. Other brands such as Kraft's Breyers are using comparative advertising against Dannon. Management is attempting to reposition Dannon away from a diet emphasis to a food that "you eat to feel healthy." Advertising was increased 60 percent in 1984 and 20 percent in 1985. The company has also introduced several new flavors since 1983. Yogurt producers are trying to cultivate new users. Some 26 percent of the U.S. population eat yogurt regularly compared to 82 percent in France. Women are the heavy users. To expand the market, yogurt producers are going after men and children in their advertising. Dannon's 1985 advertising budget for network TV was $12 million.

Marketing strategy must be responsive to changing conditions. After a strategy is implemented strategic evaluation and control are essential to keep the strategy on target and to make adjustments for changing environmental, market, and competitive conditions. Dannon's management was slow to react; in a changing market, it stayed with the traditional plain and fruit-on-the-bottom yogurt.

EXHIBIT 18-1 Purposes and Areas of Strategic Evaluation

| | Purpose of Evaluation | | |
Area of Evaluation	Finding New Opportunities/ Avoiding Threats	Keeping Performance on Track	Problem Solving
Environmental scanning	X		
Product-market analysis	X	X	
Marketing program performance analysis		X	X
Effectiveness of mix components		X	X

The essence of strategic evaluation is obtaining relevant information for gauging performance, analyzing it, and then taking the actions necessary to keep performance on track. Marketing executives are continually monitoring performance and often they must revise their strategies to cope with changing conditions. Strategic evaluation, the last stage in the marketing strategy process, is really the starting point. Strategic marketing planning requires information from ongoing monitoring and performance evaluation. Discussion of strategic evaluation is delayed until now in order to first examine the strategic areas that require evaluation and to identify the kinds of information needed by the marketing strategist for assessing marketing performance in the strategic areas. Thus, the first 17 chapters establish an essential foundation for building a strategic evaluation program.

In this chapter, a step-by-step approach to monitoring and evaluating marketing performance is developed.

DEVELOPING A STRATEGIC EVALUATION PROGRAM

Marketing strategists need an ongoing evaluation program to keep marketing performance on track. This activity consumes a high proportion of the chief marketing executive's time and energy. Exhibit 18-1 shows the major strategic evaluation activities that occur in any firm. The purpose of evaluation may be to (1) find new opportunities or avoid threats, (2) keep performance in line with management's expectations, and/or (3) solve specific problems that exist. In the Dannon illustration the effectiveness of marketing mix components declined as competition intensified. Management had to adjust the positioning strategy to counter competitive threats.

The major steps in establishing a strategic evaluation program are shown in Exhibit 18-2. Strategic and short-term marketing plans establish the direction and guidelines for the evaluation and control process. First, a strategic marketing audit should be conducted. Next, strategic performance standards, measures, and information needs are

EXHIBIT 18-2 Strategic Marketing Evaluation and Control Process

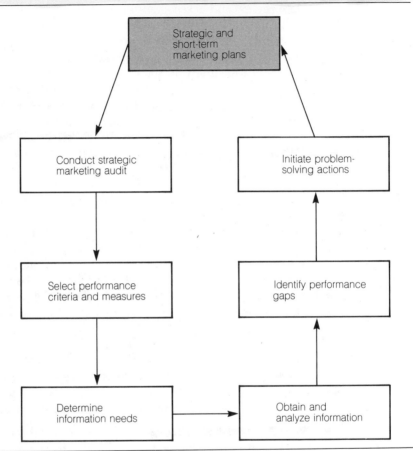

determined, followed by analysis of evaluation and control information, and performance gap identification. Then, if necessary, actions are initiated to pursue opportunities or avoid threats, keep performance on track, or solve a particular problem.

THE STRATEGIC MARKETING AUDIT

Assume that a strategic evaluation program is being established for a business unit in which there has been no previous formal strategic marketing planning and evaluation program. Since evaluation is essentially comparing results with expectations, it is necessary to lay some groundwork before setting up a tracking program. The starting point is the strategic marketing audit.

The Strategic Marketing Audit

This complete review and assessment of marketing operations is similar to the situation analysis discussed in Chapter 16. The major difference is that the audit goes beyond customer and competitive analysis to include all aspects of marketing operations. The audit is larger in scope than the situation analysis and incorporates a more extensive assessment of marketing strategy. The audit can be used to initiate a formal strategic marketing planning program, and then repeated on a periodic basis. Normally, the situation analysis is part of the annual updating of strategic plans. The strategic marketing audit is conducted less frequently—at three- to five-year intervals or even longer.

A guide to conducting the strategic marketing audit is shown in Exhibit 18–3. Although this guide is comprehensive, it can be expanded and adapted to meet the needs of a particular firm. For example, if channels of distribution are not utilized by a company or business unit, this section of the audit guide will require adjustment. Likewise, if the sales force represents the major part of a marketing program, then this section should be expanded to include other aspects of sales force strategy. The audit corresponds to the strategic marketing plan because the main purpose of the audit is to appraise the effectiveness of strategic marketing operations. Exhibit 18–3 contains several questions about the performance of marketing operations. The answers to these questions should be incorporated into the design of the strategic tracking program.

Beyond deciding what should be audited, there are some additional aspects of conducting the audit that management must take into account (refer to other sources for more comprehensive discussion).[2]

Who should conduct the audit? Opinions are mixed on this issue; some advocate use of company personnel and others recommend outside consultants. A combination approach can be used to gain the advantages of both company and external experience, capabilities, and perspectives. Objectivity and professional expertise are the two key prerequisites in selecting an individual or team to plan and conduct the audit.

Planning the audit. Depending on the size and scope of the business unit, proper attention should be given to planning the areas to be audited, defining scope of audit operations, scheduling activities, coordination of participation, and desired results. Auditing costs and expected benefits should be estimated and priorities established regarding various aspects of the audit program.

Using the findings. The results of the strategic marketing audit should contribute to improving strategic performance. Opportunities and problems that are identified should be incorporated into strategic plans.

EXHIBIT 18-3 Guide to Conducting the Strategic Marketing Audit

I. CORPORATE MISSION AND OBJECTIVES
   A. Does the mission statement offer a clear guide to the product-markets of interest to the firm?
   B. Have objectives been established for the corporation?
   C. Is information available for the review of corporate progress toward objectives, and are the reviews conducted on a regular (quarterly, monthly, etc.) basis?
   D. Has corporate strategy been successful in meeting objectives?
   E. Are opportunities or problems pending that may require altering marketing strategy?
   F. What are the responsibilities of the chief marketing executive in corporate strategic planning?

II. BUSINESS COMPOSITION AND STRATEGIES
   A. What is the composition of the business (business segments, strategic planning units, and specific product-markets)?
   B. Have business strength and product-market attractiveness analyses been conducted for each planning unit? What are the results of the analyses?
   C. What is the corporate strategy for each planning unit (e.g., growth, manage for cash, etc.)?
   D. What objectives are assigned to each planning unit?
   E. Does each unit have a strategic plan?
   F. For each unit what objectives and responsibilities have been assigned to marketing?

III. MARKETING STRATEGY (FOR EACH PLANNING UNIT)
   A. Strategic planning and marketing:
      1. Is marketing's role and responsibility in corporate strategic planning clearly specified?
      2. Are responsibility and authority for marketing strategy assigned to one executive?
      3. How well is the firm's marketing strategy working?
      4. Are changes likely to occur in the corporate/marketing environment that may affect the firm's marketing strategy?
      5. Are there major contingencies that should be included in the strategic marketing plan?
   B. Marketing planning and organizational structure:
      1. Are annual and longer range strategic marketing plans developed, and are they being used?
      2. Are the responsibilities of the various units in the marketing organization clearly specified?
      3. What are the strengths and limitations of the key members of the marketing organization? What is being done to develop people? What gaps in experience and capabilities exist on the marketing staff?
      4. Is the organizational structure for marketing appropriate for implementing marketing plans?
   C. Market target strategy:
      1. Has each market target been clearly defined and its importance to the firm established?
      2. Have demand, industry, and competition in each market target been analyzed and key trends, opportunities, and threats identified?
      3. Has the proper market target strategy (mass, niche) been adopted?
      4. Should repositioning or exit from any product-market be considered?
   D. Objectives:
      1. Have objectives been established for each market target, and are these consistent with planning unit objectives and the available resources? Are the objectives realistic?
      2. Are sales, cost, and other performance information available for monitoring the progress of planned performance against actual results?
      3. Are regular appraisals made of marketing performance?
      4. Where do gaps exist between planned and actual results? What are the probable causes of the performance gaps?
   E. Marketing program positioning strategy:
      1. Does the firm have an integrated positioning strategy made up of product, channel, price, advertising, and sales force strategies? Is the role selected for each mix element consistent with the overall program objectives, and does it properly complement other mix elements?
      2. Are adequate resources available to carry out the marketing program? Are resources committed to market targets according to the importance of each?

EXHIBIT 18-3 *(concluded)*

---

3. Are allocations to the various marketing mix components too low, too high, or about right in terms of what each is expected to accomplish?
4. Is the effectiveness of the marketing program appraised on a regular basis?

IV. MARKETING PROGRAM ACTIVITIES
    A. Product strategy:
        1. Is the product mix geared to the needs that the firm wants to meet in each product-market?
        2. What branding strategy is being used?
        3. Are products properly positioned against competing brands?
        4. Does the firm have a sound approach to product planning and management, and is marketing involved in product decisions?
        5. Are additions to, modifications of, or deletions from the product mix needed to make the firm more competitive in the marketplace?
        6. Is the performance of each product evaluated on a regular basis?
    B. Channel of distribution strategy:
        1. Has the firm selected the type (conventional or vertically coordinated) and intensity of distribution appropriate for each of its product-markets?
        2. How well does each channel access its market target? Is an effective channel configuration being used?
        3. Are channel organizations carrying out their assigned functions properly?
        4. How is the channel of distribution being managed? What improvements are needed?
        5. Are desired customer service levels being reached, and are the costs of doing this acceptable?
    C. Price strategy:
        1. How responsive is each market target to price variations?
        2. What role and objectives does price have in the marketing mix?
        3. Should price play an active or passive role in program positioning strategy?
        4. How do the firm's price strategy and tactics compare to those of competition?
        5. Is a logical approach used to establish prices?
        6. Are there indications that changes may be needed in price strategy or tactics?
    D. Advertising and sales promotion strategies:
        1. Have a role and objectives been established for advertising and sales promotion in the marketing mix?
        2. Is the creative strategy consistent with the positioning strategy that is being used?
        3. Is the budget adequate to carry out the objectives assigned to advertising and sales promotion?
        4. Do the media and programming strategies represent the most cost-effective means of communicating with market targets?
        5. Do advertising copy and content effectively communicate the intended messages?
        6. How well does the advertising program measure up in meeting its objectives?
    E. Sales force strategy:
        1. Are the role and objectives of personal selling in the marketing program positioning strategy clearly specified and understood by the sales organization?
        2. Do the qualifications of salespeople correspond to their assigned roles?
        3. Is the sales force of the proper size to carry out its function, and is it efficiently deployed?
        4. Are sales force results in line with management's expectations?
        5. Is each salesperson assigned performance targets, and are incentives offered to reward performance?
        6. Are compensation levels and ranges competitive?

V. IMPLEMENTATION AND MANAGEMENT
    A. Have the causes of all performance gaps been identified?
    B. Is implementation of planned actions taking place as intended? Is implementation being hampered by marketing or other functional areas of the firm (e.g., operations, finance)?
    C. Has the strategic audit revealed areas requiring additional study before action is taken?

There are other reasons for conducting a strategic marketing audit. Organizational changes may bring about a complete review of strategic marketing operations. Major shifts in business involvement such as entry into new product and market areas or acquisitions may require strategic marketing audits. Strategic audits should be conducted at least every three years or more, depending on the company situation.

PERFORMANCE CRITERIA AND INFORMATION NEEDS

Tracking marketing strategy results is essential for Russ Togs Inc., a producer of higher-priced designer fashions for career women.[3] In 1982 management successfully upgraded the firm's marketing strategy from popular-priced women's sportswear. Russ Togs was one of the earliest in the women's apparel industry to separate the design and merchandising functions. Staff for marketing were recruited from retailers. The company has over 15,000 accounts with 73 percent of sales from women's wear, 20 percent from men's wear, and 7 percent from the child and preteen markets. A market segmentation strategy is used, targeting segments in several product and user categories. Department and speciality stores have received increased marketing effort supported by account executives for major accounts, an expanded sales force to improve service to speciality stores, and a toll-free number for smaller stores. These efforts have increased Russ Togs market share and earnings. The firm's apparel lines are merchandised in five selling seasons: spring, summer, transition, fall, and holiday. Performance criteria and information are necessary to track the performance of Russ Tog's various product lines, market segments, selling seasons, and distribution channels.

Selecting Performance Criteria

As strategic and short-term marketing plans are developed, performance criteria should be specified for use in monitoring strategic performance. Specifying the information needed for marketing decision making is important and should receive management's concentrated attention. In the past, some marketing executives could develop and manage successful marketing strategies by relying on intuition, judgment, and experience; successful executives of the 1980s are combining judgment and experience with more formal approaches. Electronic information processing is becoming increasingly important in gaining a strategic edge in industries such as airline services, direct marketing, and wholesaling.

Since objectives indicate the results that are desired, they also serve as the basis for evaluating a strategy's success. Objectives represent standards of performance. (See Exhibit 18–4.) Information on

EXHIBIT 18–4 Excerpts from a Strategic Plan for Product Line X

General strategy: over the next five years expand our sales volume, retain our leading market share position as new competitors enter the product-market, and increase dollar profits by maintaining existing percentage profit margins.

Objectives	1980	1981	1982	1983	1984	1985	1986*	1987	1988	1989	1990
1. Sales ($ millions)	8	10	15	20	30	40	48	60	75	90	110
2. Market share (percent)	100	100	100	98†	95	90	84	73‡	70	70	63
3. Profit margins (percent)	24.6	25.1	27.3	27.1	28.5	25.2	26.0	26.0	26.0	26.0	26.0

*Current year.
†First competitor entered product-market.
‡Second competitor expected to enter product market.

progress toward these objectives and others specified in the strategic and short-term plans should be compiled on a continuing basis. In addition to information on objectives, management will require other kinds of information for use in performance evaluation. Some of this information will be incorporated into regular tracking activities (e.g., advertising expenditures). Other information can be obtained as the need first arises, such as a special study of consumer attitudes and opinions.

Determining Information Needs

Management first has to determine what information it needs. Due to the costs of acquiring, processing, and analyzing information, the potential benefits of needed information must be compared to costs. Normally, needed information falls into two categories: (1) information regularly supplied to marketing management from internal and external sources, and (2) information obtained as needed for a particular problem or situation. Examples of the former are sales and cost analyses, market share measurements, and customer analyses. Information from the latter category includes new product concept tests, brand preference studies, and studies of advertising effectiveness.

There are several types of information that may be needed by management as indicated in Exhibit 18–5. The importance of these categories varies from one firm to another. Information for strategic planning and evaluation can be obtained as a part of four major information acquisition activities:

1. The *internal information system* is the backbone of any strategic evaluation program. These systems may consist of primarily sales and cost reports. Alternatively, an increasing number of firms are developing highly sophisticated marketing information systems for use in strategic and tactical planning, operating, and control activities.

2. Many *standardized information services* are available by subscription or on a one-time basis, often at a fraction of the cost of preparing such information for a single firm. Nielsen's TV rating data service is an example.

3. From time to time marketing decision makers require *special research studies* that may include one or a combination of the types of information shown in Exhibit 18–5. A study of distributor opinions concerning a manufacturer's services is an example.

4. The firm's *strategic intelligence system* is concerned with monitoring and forecasting external, uncontrollable factors that influence the firm's product-markets. These efforts range from formal information activities to informal surveillance of the marketing environment. Product-markets monitored may be those currently served or those the company is interested in.

EXHIBIT 18-5   Information Planning for Strategic Evaluation

Several ways of analyzing marketing information are shown on the right-hand side of Exhibit 18-5. Computers have lowered the cost of processing information, leading to much greater use of statistical analyses and models.

INFORMATION, ANALYSIS, AND ACTION

Management faces a continuing challenge in obtaining information about business performance, analyzing it, and then taking action to realize opportunities and avoid threats. Information provides the basis for identifying performance gaps and determining strategic actions.

Methods for Obtaining Information

While many specific kinds and sources of information are used in strategic evaluation activities, all fall into three broad categories: (1) the internal information system; (2) standardized information services; and (3) special research studies. The relationships among the methods are shown in Exhibit 18-6. Note that standardized information services may be used to supply information for use in strategic intelligence and the internal information system.

The Internal Information System.   This information gathering, analysis, and distribution system is the center of information activities in most firms. Various reports are generated using a variety of company information often supplemented by external information, sales, cost, and operating data. The nature and scope of the internal information system may vary from basic analyses of operating data to elaborate computerized information storage and processing systems. For example, the Quaker Oats Company's sales and marketing information data-

EXHIBIT 18-6 Relationships among the Strategic Information Methods

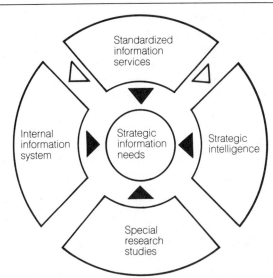

base contains about 500,000 time series and 20 million numbers! The data in the system are described below:

Quaker data:

1. Dollar and pound shipments.
2. Dollar and pound deal shipments.
3. Standard costs.
4. These data are available by item and brand, by Quaker and SAMI markets, and by month for three years.

SAMI data:

1. Dollar and pound withdrawals.
2. These data are available by brand and category, by SAMI market, and by SAMI period for three years.

Advertising data:

1. Ad expenditures from Advertising Information Services.
2. These data are available by brand and category, by SAMI market, and by month for three years.

Socioeconomic data:

1. Various sources.
2. These data are available by population, consumer prices, household income, and food store sales.[4]

The system has a wide range of capabilities for report generation, statistical analyses, retrieval of information, and special studies. Some of the kinds of information that can be supplied to management are shipment data, market shares and trends, advertising performance measures, and socioeconomic analyses (e.g., consumption per capita, brand development indexes, and maps).

Considering the costs of systems such as Quaker's marketing information system (MIS), are the benefits they provide worth the expense? The record over the past decade is mixed. Some users swear by their MIS; others swear at them. On balance, the general trend is clearly toward wider adoption of MIS throughout the business community. B. Dalton Bookseller, the retail bookstore chain owned by Dayton-Hudson Corp., has developed an impressive control system for strategic and tactical planning. Competitors acknowledge that the system is a major advantage for Dalton. It is a computerized book-tracing system that codes each book order and monitors it on a computer. As a result, Dalton's corporate managers can call up weekly sales reports, by title and topic, for every outlet, city, or region, and use the data to restock fast sellers, drop slow movers, and choose new books to buy.[5]

The product mix and the nature of business operations influence what type of internal marketing information system is appropriate in a particular firm. High-volume sales transactions such as those for books, groceries, drugs, and other low-unit price consumer products require computerized tracking and analysis capabilities. In contrast, a producer of low-volume, high-cost products such as ships, steam turbines, large industrial equipment, and similar products may have far less need for systems like Quaker's and Dalton's.

Standardized Information System. A wide variety of marketing information is available for purchase in special publications and on a subscription basis. Suppliers include government agencies, universities, private research firms, industry and trade organizations, and various other groups. Such services offer substantial cost advantages, and many are quite inexpensive (for example, data distributed from the U.S. Census of Population).

Examples of standardized services for consumer and industrial products illustrate the target services available. One computerized information service provides industrial market data. Offered by Economic Information Systems, Inc., of New York, it identifies, measures, and analyzes market potential according to Standard Industrial Classification (SIC) codes. The following are two examples of how the service can be used:

1. A company is interested in acquiring a privately held firm that has sales of $50 million in any one of 15 specific four-digit SIC codes, but whose sales are less than 50 percent of the overall pri-

vate company's total sales. All such companies must be identified and profiles of their sales by industry must be provided.

2. To direct its sales force, a manufacturer of butterfly valves must identify those establishments that account for 80 percent of the butterfly valve consumption within a six-state area.[6]

Using its large data bank organized by SIC code and containing employment, sales volume, and market penetration data, many different analyses can be made, depending on a company's strategic marketing information needs.

The second illustration concerns the use of retail store scanning systems to record purchases by people participating on consumer panels. The use of electronic information systems by IRI is discussed in Exhibit 18–7. The research firm has established its services in several cities like Williamsport.

Standardized information services should be appraised at an early point in the development of a strategic monitoring and evaluation program. Often these sources are cost-effective suppliers of a wide range of external information. However, such sources rarely provide all of the consumer and industry information needed by marketing management.

Special Research Studies. Typically, research studies are initiated in response to problems or special situations. Several examples of these studies are discussed in earlier chapters—segmentation studies, new product concept tests, product use tests, brand name research, and advertising recall tests. They may range in scope from exploratory studies based primarily on published information to field surveys involving personal, phone, or mail interviews with respondents that represent target populations.

Planning and conducting a marketing research study consists of:

1. *Definition of the problem.* The problem formulation should indicate exactly what information is needed to help solve the problem. Caution should be exercised to avoid defining a symptom rather than the decision situation.
2. *Research design.* This involves deciding what type of study to conduct and what sources will be used to obtain the needed information. Most research studies are descriptive in nature, although some are designed to measure the effects of marketing variables such as advertising.
3. *Data collection techniques.* This stage includes decisions as to how contact will be made with respondents (mail, phone, or personal interview) and design of forms to be used for data collection. In some instances, observational techniques are used instead of questioning.

EXHIBIT 18-7 Wired Consumers: Market Researchers Go High-Tech to Hone Ads, Weed Out Flops

WILLIAMSPORT, Pa.—Joann Alter shops at the Weis Market near her home at least four times a week. But even if she's just dashing in for a quart of milk or a dozen eggs, she always remembers to give the cashier her Shopper's Hotline card.

By showing the card, Mrs. Alter gets a chance at a variety of enticing prizes, including vacations in Mexico and Hawaii, small electrical appliances and gift certificates—such as the one she and her husband used for dinner at a fancy local restaurant. "How could I ever forget to show my card, when with so little effort you can gain so much?" she asks.

That's the sort of thing the people at Information Resources Inc. like to hear. The card is a vital link in the Chicago-based company's BehaviorScan test-marketing program. It makes it possible to monitor purchases by consumers like Mrs. Alter and correlate them with information collected by gadgets on their TV sets about what commercials they watch and with other data about what coupons they use.

Weeding Out Flops

Marketers have for years depended on willing consumers in relatively isolated communities to weed out products that are likely to flop and to identify the best ways to promote those that are likely to succeed. But electronic testing techniques—such as those being used here, as well as in several other markets by Information Resources and two major competitors, A. C. Nielson Co. and Burke Marketing Services Inc.—have made it possible to evaluate consumer tastes with much greater precision.

Traditionally, research on buying habits has depended heavily on diaries kept by test participants. But diaries are only as reliable as the people who keep them, and human recall has its frailties.

As an example, Information Resources points to the discrepancies it found when it asked some of the consumers in its BehaviorScan research about what products they had bought in a recent three-month period and compared their answers with their actual purchases. Among the findings: Only about a third of those who reported buying Kellogg's Frosted Flakes had done so; only about one in 10 of those claiming to have purchased Pledge furniture polish had bought the product.

Anthony Adams, director of marketing and research at Campbell Soup Co., says that electronic testing also allows researchers to observe consumers' reactions without tipping them off about what is being studied. That's not possible with questionnaires and focus groups, two other common market-research techniques.

Campbell Soup, which has been a BehaviorScan client since 1980, is one of several companies that use the electronic-testing service to evaluate new products and to determine what marketing strategies will help sell them most effectively. Others include Procter & Gamble Co., Dart & Kraft Inc. and General Foods Corp.

Electronic test marketing is also used to evaluate new advertising campaigns for established products. After the Tylenol poison scare in 1982, for example, Johnson & Johnson retained Information Resources to determine whether consumers would buy safety-sealed Tylenol capsules.

The Williamsport area, with a population of about 93,000 and an average annual discretionary household income of $24,000, provides an unusual opportunity for electronic market testing. Because the community sits in an Appalachian valley at the foot of Bald Eagle Mountain, TV reception is poor, and most residents depend on cable. The extensive network of cable hookups is ideal for Information Resources' purposes.

EXHIBIT 18-7 *(concluded)*

Inside an electronic control room at the local cable-TV franchise, the market-research firm's employees work from 6:30 A.M. until after midnight "cutting" into commercials on the three network affiliates. Clients buy local time to test new ads, or Information Resources can "overlay" a test ad or two in place of the client's national commercial, which the rest of the country is seeing.

Which Is Real?

Local viewers aren't aware which ads are standard and which are being tested. Moreover, families with the same demographic profiles are often shown different ads for the same product. And because the company has gathered detailed information from each household, it can target families that own, say, a cat, a dog, a microwave oven or a personal computer.

Late each night, a computer calls the 3,000 Williamsport households participating in Behavior-Scan to link up with the micro-processor inside each of their cable converters. Information Resources knows exactly what they watch each day and whether family members view an entire show or flip the channel several times.

Meanwhile, at another site three women remove coupons from sandwich-sized plastic bags so that they can be correlated with products bought. Each bag has the Shopper's Hotline number of a BehaviorScan participant. Working shifts around the clock, the women provide the data that lets the computer catalog and analyze about 15,000 coupon transactions a week.

Some of the coupons are tied to advertising pitches for test products; others simply give clients a clearer indication of what competitors are accomplishing.

'Surprisingly Easy'

The Big Brother implications of all this don't seem to concern anyone in Williamsport. "Initially we thought it would be difficult to sign up people," says Gian Fulgoni, president of Information Resources. "But it's surprisingly easy."

Indeed, the little red Shopper's Hotline cards and the research they support seem to have become an accepted part of the local culture. At church choir rehearsals and similar gatherings, residents swap stories about recent prize winners and compare notes on coupons that came in the mail.

"I haven't won yet, but I might win a prize," says Patricia Knapp as she and her husband roll two overflowing shopping carts out of the Giant supermarket here. Adds Mrs. Alter, a 55-year-old grandmother, "I'd really like to win a trip to Disney World."

Information Resources spent about $2 million in start-up costs to establish its electronic network here, equipping nine of the 10 local supermarkets with bar-code scanning equipment that generates a computer file of each consumer's purchases. (One store already had such equipment.)

The company also works hard to keep participants happy. For instance, whenever cable reception at a participant's home goes bad, the company's own repair people investigate without charge.

Still, given the basic purposes of test marketing, there are some drawbacks to being a guinea pig that can't be avoided. Mrs. Alter remembers buying a caramel-tasting cereal that her husband and grandchildren "really loved." But when she went to buy it few months ago, "it had vanished from the shelves."

SOURCE: Michael Days, "Wired Consumers." Reprinted by permission of *The Wall Street Journal.* © Dow Jones & Company, Inc., January 23, 1986, 3. All rights reserved.

4. *Sampling design.* This phase of research planning is concerned with how respondents will be identified in the population of interest. Sample selection is either by probability or nonprobability methods.
5. *Field data collection.* This stage consists of the execution of the decisions made in the first four stages. It involves actual collection and processing of the data obtained from respondents.
6. *Analysis and interpretation of the data.* Finally the data collected must be analyzed using appropriate techniques and then the results studied to determine what has been learned from the research.
7. *Research report.* Normally, study results are communicated to management in a research report. While the purpose of the report is to convey what has been learned from the study, it should also indicate the key aspects of the methodology to allow the user to assess any limitations that may exist.[7]

Opportunities and Performance Gaps

All strategic evaluation activities lead to two basic management responsibilities: (1) identifying opportunities or performance gaps and (2) initiating actions to take advantage of the opportunities or to correct existing and pending problems. Strategic intelligence, internal reporting and analysis activities, standardized information services, and research studies should be developed to meet the information needs of the strategic marketing decision makers. The nature and scope of information gathering and analysis activities vary widely from firm to firm. Some companies develop highly sophisticated marketing information systems, others stick to basic internal financial reporting activities supplemented by special studies and standardized information services. Regardless of the approach to strategic information, the scheme should be carefully evaluated in terms of costs and benefits.

The real challenge in strategic evaluation is to identify opportunities and problems. The best test of the strategic marketing information system is whether it helps marketing management in this area. In carrying out these actions, there are two critical factors that management should take into account in performing strategic evaluation.

Problem/opportunity definition. Strategic analysis should lead to a clear definition of an opportunity or problem since this will be needed to guide whatever strategic action may be taken. Often it is easy to confuse problem symptoms with problem causes.
Interpreting information. Management must also separate normal variations in performance from significant gaps in performance,

since the latter are the ones that require strategic action. For example, how much of a drop in market share is necessary to signal a strategic performance problem? Limits need to be set on the acceptable range of strategic performance.

No matter how extensive the information system may be, it cannot interpret the strategic importance of the information. This is the responsibility of management.

Exhibit 18-8 illustrates how management of the Metropolitan Life Insurance Company links the control function to planning. The company expects gaps between desired and actual results and thus emphasizes analyzing the causes of variances. The description of the three primary control tools highlights what information should be used for comparing performance with the plan. Finally the role of performance reports in the company's overall planning and control process is indicated.

Determining Strategic Action

Many actions are possible, depending on the situation. One objective of this book is to provide a guide to strategic action based upon the opportunity or problem at hand. Management's strategic needs may include divestment strategy, new product planning, target market strategy, adjustments in marketing strategy, or improvements in efficiency.

The tampon market had long been dominated by Tampax, Inc., so top management at Tampax watched carefully as Procter & Gamble test marketed the Rely tampon in 1974. P&G entered the national market in 1980, distributing 60 million tampon samples to 80 percent of U.S. households at an estimated cost of $10 million.[8] While toxic shock findings later in the year caused P&G to remove Rely from the market, it is interesting to review the changes in marketing strategy Tampax management made to counter the intensive competition from P&G and others. In 1979, a vice president for marketing development was hired. He had extensive experience in marketing consumer products at Colgate-Palmolive and American Home Products, plus ad agency experience. Although the television advertising ban was over in 1972, Tampax waited until 1978 to launch its first TV ads due to moral considerations. The new marketing strategist placed strong emphasis on strategic planning and marketing research, brought in consultants, and revised TV commercials. Test marketing of napkins was launched in Europe.

Such major changes in marketing strategy were necessary—by early 1980 the Tampax market share had declined from 70 percent to 40 percent of dollar sales. Playtex held 29 percent, Johnson & Johnson 12 per-

---

EXHIBIT 18-8   Planning Guidelines, Metropolitan Life Insurance Company

---

COMPARING THE PERFORMANCE WITH THE PLAN

Each person, to do a satisfactory job, must achieve his or her portion of the plan. And this is where the concept of control fits in. This section discusses:

1.   The general principles underlying the process of management control.
2.   The Performance Reports we use to implement control.

THE PROCESS OF MANAGEMENT CONTROL

Simply defined, the process of management control consists of seeing that everything is being carried out in accordance with the plans that have been adopted. From this definition, it follows that the primary purpose of the control process is to isolate *variances* from plan so that they can be analyzed, to determine their significance, and to take corrective action as needed.

This does not mean that *variances* from plan are necessarily bad. It simply means that *variances* should be the basis for analysis to determine: (1) whether the *variance* should be accepted as a sound and desirable departure from our plan, (2) whether the *variance* is unavoidable and therefore should serve to sharpen future planning, or (3) whether a different course of action should be taken, such as refocusing of effort or increasing the amount of effort.

The three primary control tools

Control is exercised in a variety of ways, but there are three basic tools or mechanisms which underlie the process.

1.   *Pre-approval of proposed courses of action.* This form of control is implemented by the use of our marketing plan procedure. For example, one of the items we plan is the creation and abolishment of districts in various areas. The effect of such planning is to establish control over changes that will actually be made in the number and location of our districts.
2.   *Direct observation.* This is the basic day-to-day control technique used at the district level. It takes the form of the face-to-face supervision and guidance that district management provides the field force.
3.   *Analysis of formal performance reports and taking required action.* The key control tool of management is the set of performance reports that each manager receives indicating his/her subordinates' performance versus plan. These reports provide the basis for identifying and analyzing *variances* and for taking corrective action as required.

Performance reports

The primary purpose of performance reports are:

1.   To show the *net effect* of many day-to-day decisions and developments.
2.   To provide a check on the adequacy of front-line controls.
3.   To provide a means of continuously motivating down-the-line personnel to take objectives and action programs seriously.
4.   To serve as a further stimulus to continuous sharpening of the planning process.

From all of the above, it follows that performance reports by themselves represent only one aspect of the total control process. Nevertheless, they are an indispensable aspect of the control system, since they provide the basis for evaluating and planning management action.

SOURCE: David S. Hopkins, *The Marketing Plan,* Report No. 801 (New York: The Conference Board, 1981), 127.

---

cent, and P&G 12 percent. Even with P&G out of the market, the future would be a demanding period for Tampax, Inc., calling for the best in strategic marketing planning.

Managing in a changing environment is what strategic marketing is all about. Keeping up with and even anticipating change is the essence of strategic marketing evaluation. Far too many executives develop innovative marketing strategies and then allow them to deteriorate by not monitoring their effectiveness and altering them due to changing conditions.

STRATEGIC INTELLIGENCE

While strategic intelligence could be included as a part of the internal information system, treating it separately demonstrates its scope and importance and highlights its partial reliance on subjective information. The purpose of strategic marketing intelligence activities is monitoring and forecasting changes in *economic, social, technological, governmental,* and *physical* factors that may affect a firm's existing product-markets or those of potential interest. Diebold, Inc., has been in the bank equipment business for over a century and dominates the automatic teller machine market (ATM). Over a decade ago, top management recognized that the company must move into electronics and gear up for the projected ATM boom in order to survive and prosper in the 1980s.[9] This major strategic action involved millions of dollars. ATM technology was completely new to the firm although it had years of experience in marketing bank vaults. The company's name was well known and respected throughout the financial industry, which was an important springboard for entry into the ATM product-market. By the mid-1980s sales of ATMs and other equipment had slowed down. Diebold was dominant in the market, but its sales declined from $474 million in 1984 to around $400 million in 1985. Nevertheless, the future potential was promising.

In retrospect, Diebold's strategy seems obvious although in the early 1970s it was not. Consider, for example, how many U.S. and Swiss watch makers failed to anticipate the impact of quartz crystal technology.

Strategic Marketing Intelligence Plan

Importantly, tracking environmental changes that may affect a firm's product-market requires identifying significant factors. While some corporations, such as General Electric, have well-developed, formal environmental tracking and forecasting groups, many companies rely on trade associations, the intelligence of individual executives, and other informal methods. Thus, in examining Exhibit 18–9, keep in mind that the steps indicated can be used as a guide by individual executives or alternatively as a basis for building a formal strategic marketing intel-

EXHIBIT 18-9 Developing a Strategic Marketing Intelligence Plan

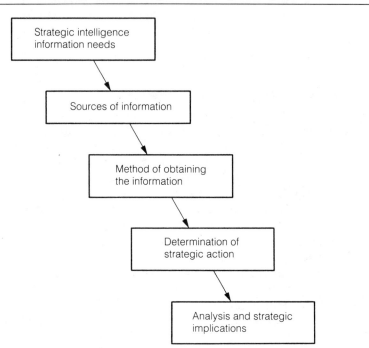

ligence program. Regardless of the approach used, subjective and judgmental information is usually an essential part of strategic intelligence activities. The following corporate intelligence activities were undertaken to assess the impact of federal decisions on business operations:

> Directly or indirectly, corporations deploy hundreds (thousands by some estimates) of agents with widely divergent backgrounds and contrasting methods of operation. Here will be a Ph.D. preparing a scholarly analysis of long-range policy trends, based on private talks with government specialists. There will be a young free-lance lawyer with a phone-answering machine for an office, hustling to make it, not so much as a lawyer, but as a Washington operator. Here a former newspaper reporter worming advance information or an unreleased document out of a carefully cultivated source—but for a private client now, not the reading public. And, of course the high-prestige types—large law firms, well-established information-gathering companies and the official Washington representatives (often bearing a vice president's title) of the nation's major corporations.[10]

Although strategic intelligence activities lack the structure and methodological rigor of formal research and analysis, the two have much in common.

Information needs are related to the areas and problems being monitored by management. Since the alternatives for intelligence gathering are vast, some means of controlling information activities is needed. Information that is gathered is typically used for two major purposes: (1) problem avoidance and opportunity identification; and (2) ongoing strategic management activities. An example of the first category is the monitoring of existing product-markets to identify changes in environmental factors that can alter the attractiveness of a product-market. Subscription to an environmental monitoring information service is an example of the second category.

Major sources of strategic intelligence information are government, competitors, suppliers, customers, professional associations, industry meetings, and other special-purpose sources (e.g., lobbyists and consultants). Using the guide provided in Exhibit 18-9, top management and strategic marketing planners must design a strategic information system to meet the needs of the corporation and each planning unit. A major requirement is setting priorities for needed information. Priorities should be established according to:

1. The importance of becoming aware of an event.
2. The likelihood the event will occur.
3. The costs of anticipation and reaction.[11]

Strategic intelligence is justified if the costs of reacting to the events exceed the costs of anticipating them and responding proactively. Thus, for future events where the stakes are high if they occur, the costs of intelligence efforts may be justified, particularly if responding proactively is possible. Of course, much of the information needed to make these decisions depends heavily on executive judgment and experience. The following example shows how expert judgments can be used in forecasting the likelihood and impact of future events.

An Illustration

Management in a major oil company is interested in assessing the social, political, and economic environment in a country in Southeastern Asia to determine the likelihood of events that could affect its proposed refining investments. Suppose that the venture is commercially attractive based on an evaluation of the market opportunity, the competitive factors, and other relevant influences. Thus, the economic feasibility is attractive unless the overall environment in the country changes substantially in the future. The oil company used a Delphi survey of several acknowledged authorities on the country's economic, social, and political environment. The Delphi method is a procedure whereby experts individually express opinions and estimate the probability of occurrence of future events, the estimates are pooled, and results distributed to each expert. This process is repeated for several rounds until the estimates reach a consensus or a steady state. In the oil company illustration, one key threat was the possibility of expropriation. Participants were surveyed on this and other possible future events. The study results were analyzed, and the strategic implications assessed to help the company determine the proper course of action.

Purchasing the Services of Trend-Spotters

The turbulent, uncertain, and rapidly changing business environment of the last several years has created a new wave of consultants. Hundreds of companies pay trend spotters like the Naisbitt Group *(Megatrends)* retainer fees ranging from $10,000 to $30,000 a year to help management predict the future.[12] While their environmental impact assessments are far from infallible, corporations seem to find the information worth the cost. For example, as a result of the Naisbitt Group's reports of the elderly's growing political and economic influence, Southwestern Bell spent nearly $100 million to launch its Silver Pages directory of businesses catering to the elderly. Others use trend-setters to stimulate management thinking and identify important issues.

The basis for predicting the future is analyzing and interpreting the present according to John Naisbitt, Chairman of the Naisbitt Group:

> Understanding quickly what is happening now and making informed guesses about how it might unfold, the theory goes, provides a measure of predictive power. It can also lead to the obvious. Naisbitt relates that when he tells audiences that Columbus will be Ohio's largest city, they respond, "Wow! Is that true?" Hardly any of his listeners know that Columbus has held that distinction for three years.[13]

The value of intelligence consultants lies in the fact that they monitor the environment on a full-time basis, while busy managers do not have the time to do so. Corporations can obtain important insights and assessments providing they carefully evaluate the inputs from trend-spotters and don't rely on them solely. The usefulness of the consultant should be evaluated on a continuing basis.

DECISION SUPPORT SYSTEMS

An important development for marketing strategy planning and control is the marketing decision-support system (MDSS) which is:

> a coordinated collection of data, systems, tools, and techniques with supporting software and hardware by which an organization gathers and interprets relevant information from business and environment and turns it into a basis for marketing action.[14]

These systems have evolved from marketing information systems, incorporating interactive decision analysis and other advanced capabilities. The vast array of available computer and information processing equipment and software offer exciting opportunities for MDSS development. A brief look at the potential of these advanced systems illustrates their nature and scope.

MDSS Components

Abbott Laboratories Hospital Products Division (HPC) uses its MDSS to forecast sales, perform pricing analyses, track promotion results, and analyze new product plans. Future plans for the system include more powerful tools such as customer segmentation and profiles.[15] MDSS's are both expensive and complex, requiring a substantial investment in time and money. An extensive process of integrating the system with a company's marketing activities and operations may require several years and an investment in software of $200,000 or more plus equipment and time for conceptualizing, developing, and implementing the system. The total cost of the system may be several hundred thousand dollars plus on-going operating costs.

The components of a MDSS consist of the *database,* the *display, models,* and *analysis capabilities.*[16]

Database.   Various kinds of information may be included in the database such as standardized marketing information produced by Nielsen and other research suppliers, sales and cost data, and other forms of internal information, product information, advertising data, price information, and other types of marketing information. The design and updating of the database are vital to the effectiveness of MDSS. The information should be relevant and organized to correspond to the units of analysis used in the system.

Display.   This component of the MDSS enables the user to communicate with the database. Marketing managers and their staff must be able to interact with the database:

> They must be able to extract, manipulate, and display data easily and quickly. Required capabilities range from simple ad hoc retrieval to more formal reports that track market status and product performance. Also needed are exception reports that flag problem areas. Many presentations should have graphics integrated with other materials.[17]

Models.   This component of the MDSS provides mathematical and computational representations of variables and their interrelationships. For example, a sales force deployment model would include an effort to sales response function model and a deployment algorithm for use in analyzing effort deployment alternatives. The models are useful in decision analysis, planning, and control.

Analysis. This capability consists of a portfolio of analysis techniques that may be used in data analysis. Included are various statistical techniques such as regression analysis, factor analysis, time series, and financial analysis. Analysis may be performed on a data set to study relationships, identify trends, prepare forecasts, and other purposes.

The MDSS is more than an information retrieval system. The interactive capabilities using appropriate models and data analysis techniques allow the user to perform "what if" type analyses, adjusting various inputs and evaluating outputs. While the development costs of a MDSS are substantial, the resulting capabilities offer marketing decision makers an exciting potential.

Using the System

Similar to an individual learning to use the capabilities of a personal computer, MDSS capabilities must be learned and developed over time. Managers must understand how to use the system and how to interpret the information generated. Abbott's HPC Division is using the system to meet several information, reporting, and analysis needs.[18] Although Abbott is making only limited use of the system's complex modeling capabilities, marketing management appears pleased with results to date and is excited about its future potential. In one pricing application the system is used to determine how much the company can afford to lower prices in competitive bid situations. The analysis also indicates margins at alternative prices and estimates the impact of the prices on market share.

CONCLUDING NOTE

This final chapter is both an end and a beginning. It forms a vital link in a series of strategic marketing activities. Moreover, it emphasizes that strategic marketing is a continuing process of planning, implementing, evaluating, and adjusting strategies. Strategic evaluation of marketing performance represents the first step in strategic marketing planning and the last step after launching a strategy. The objective is to develop an approach to strategic evaluation, building on the strategic marketing foundations established in Chapters 1 through 17. Strategic evaluation is one of marketing management's most demanding and time-consuming responsibilities. While the activity lacks the glamour and excitement of new strategy development, effective strategic evaluation often separates the winners from the losers.

Much of the actual work of managing involves strategic and tactical evaluation of marketing operations. Yet performing this function depends greatly on management's understanding of the planning process. Strategic evaluation is a continuing cycle of making plans, launching them, tracking performance, identifying performance gaps, and then initiating problem-solving actions. In accomplishing strategic evaluation, management must select performance criteria and measures and then set up a tracking program to obtain the information needed to guide evaluation activities. When first establishing a strategic evaluation program (and periodically thereafter), a strategic marketing audit provides a useful basis for developing the program.

The starting point in developing a strategic evaluation and control program is the strategic marketing audit. It is so easy for practicing managers to become preoccupied with day-to-day activities, neglecting to step back and review overall operations. Regular audits can prevent sudden shocks and can alert management to new opportunities. Building on findings from the strategic marketing audit, the chapter examines the major steps in planning for and acquiring information for strategic analysis. While the execution of the steps will vary by situation, they represent a useful framework for developing a strategic evaluation program in any type of firm. An important part of this process is setting standards for gauging marketing performance. These standards are useful guides for determining what information is needed to monitor performance. There are various alternatives for obtaining information, including strategic intelligence, the internal information system, standardized information services, and special research studies. Information generated in these four categories forms the basis for identifying performance gaps and initiating problem-solving actions.

NOTES

1. This illustration is based on Ronald Alsop, "Dannon Co. Stirs Into Action as Yogurt Competition Grows," *The Wall Street Journal,* December 12, 1985, 35.

2. See for example, Dr. Ernst A. Tirmann, "Should Your Marketing Be Audited?" *European Business,* Autumn 1971, 49–56.

3. Frank W. Campanella, "Stylish Earner," *Barron's,* June 11, 1984, 47–48.

4. George A. Clowes, "Data Management Should Be No. 1 Priority in Developing On-Line MIS," *Marketing News,* December 12, 1980, 10.

5. "Waldenbooks: Countering B. Dalton by Aping Its Computer Operations," *Business Week,* October 8, 1979, 116.

6. A. W. Berger, "How Computer System Provides Accurate Industrial Market Data," *Marketing News,* December 12, 1980, 7.

7. These stages are discussed in greater detail in Gilbert A. Churchill, *Marketing Research,* 3rd ed. (Hinsdale, Ill.: Dryden Press, 1983), chapter 2.

8. This account is based on Bill Abrams, "Tampax, Facing Mounting Competition, Plans Changes in Its Marketing Strategy," *The Wall Street Journal,* May 9, 1980, 34.

9. Larry Marion, "The Early Risers," *Forbes,* October 27, 1980, 68, 72, 75.

10. Roscoe C. Barn, "Corporate CIA," *Barron's*, March 19, 1979, 4.
11. David B. Montgomery and Charles B. Weinberg, "Toward Strategic Intelligence Systems," *Journal of Marketing*, Fall 1979, 42.
12. Myron Magnet, "Who Needs a Trend-Spotter?" *Fortune*, December 9, 1985, 51, 52, 54, 56.
13. Ibid., 52.
14. John D. C. Little, "Decision Support Systems for Marketing Managers," *Journal of Marketing*, Summer 1979, 11.
15. Daniel C. Brown, "The Anatomy of a Decision Support System," *Business Marketing*, June 1985, 80, 82, 84, 86.
16. John D. C. Little and Michael N. Cassettari, *Decision Support Systems for Marketing Managers* (New York: American Management Association, 1984), 12–15.
17. Ibid., 14.
18. Brown, "The Anatomy of a Decision Support System," 86.

QUESTIONS FOR REVIEW AND DISCUSSION

1. Discuss the similarities and differences between strategic marketing *planning* and *evaluation.*

2. Establishing a strategic evaluation program requires completing a series of activities. Beginning with selecting performance criteria and measures, indicate what executives (type of position) and marketing specialists should be responsible for each step.

3. Selecting the proper performance criteria for use in tracking performance is a key part of a strategic evaluation program. Suggest performance criteria that could be used by a fast-food retail chain to monitor strategic marketing performance.

4. What justification is there for conducting a marketing audit in a business unit whose marketing performance has been very good? Discuss.

5. Examination of the various areas of a strategic marketing audit shown in Exhibit 18–3 would be quite expensive and time-consuming. Are there any ways to limit the scope of the audit?

6. Several types of information should be collected for a strategic marketing evaluation. Develop a list of specific kinds of information that would be useful for a strategic evaluation in a life insurance company.

7. Compare and contrast the use of standardized information services and special research studies for tracking the performance of a new packaged food product.

8. Discuss the probable impact of cable television on marketing research methods during the next decade as this medium penetrates an increasing number of U.S. households.

9. What should be the role of industry trade associations regarding the development and distribution of standardized information services? What problems could develop in using trade groups as information sources?

10. Comment on the usefulness and limitations of test market data as a source of marketing information.

11. Suppose the management of a retail wallpaper chain is considering a research study to measure household

awareness of the retail chain and reactions to various aspects of wallpaper purchase and use, and to identification of competing firms. How
could management estimate the
benefits of such a study in order to
determine if the study should be conducted?

12. Are there any similarities between
marketing strategic intelligence and
the operations of U.S. Central Intelligence Agency? Do companies ever
employ business spies?

13. Discuss how manufacturers of U.S.
and Swiss watches could have used a
strategic marketing intelligence program to help avoid the problems that
several firms in the industry encountered in the 1970s.

STRATEGIC APPLICATION 18–1

THE TECHNOLOGY EDGE

Before Saks Fifth Avenue replaced its
old-fashioned cash drawers with computerized cash registers, it often took weeks
for the venerable department store chain
to accurately know what was selling and
what to reorder.

Its technologically advanced competitors, on the other hand, were collecting precise sales data instantaneously,
reordering best sellers within a day. The
message was clear. "If I know during the
day what's selling and you know a week
later, I've got a big advantage over you,"
says Al McCready, a consultant with Arthur Young & Co., New York.

Amid intense competition, more and
more mass retailers are starting to view
computer technology as a powerful strategic tool. "Retailers now compete with
technology the same way they compete
with merchandise, price and store sites,"
says Robert Capone, director of systems
and data processing at J. C. Penney Co.
These systems help merchants cut labor
costs and inventory expenses, quickly
mark down slow-to-move products and
even eliminate mail.

Indeed, the use of technology has become so important that top executives—
once typically merchants or financial

practitioners—now emerge from the
data-processing ranks.

To be sure, general merchandise retailers have used computers for years.
But such equipment was initially the exclusive province of accounting departments, which installed point-of-sale
equipment to track cash and credit purchases. "Times forced a change," explains Chris Schwartz, a vice president
of Dylex Ltd., a Toronto operator of apparel chains. "At one time fashion moved
slowly across the continent. What was
popular in New York took a whole year to
get to Des Moines, Iowa. So merchants
had time to react."

Now, largely because of cable television, Mr. Schwartz continues, "people in rural Iowa know what's selling
in New York and Paris, and they want
the same fashion. Stores have to be
more aware—faster—of what customers
want."

Without state-of-the-art systems,
Norwalk, Conn.-based Caldor could only
collect daily sales data on 30% of its
stores' 80,000 products. "We could track
sales by class," explains James Guinon,
chairman and chief executive officer of
the discount unit of Associated Dry

Goods Corp. "But the class will only tell you cookie jar. It won't tell you it's a cookie jar with a red handle."

The lack of such data can mean shortages of what sells best. Caldor, for instance, stocks about 15 different barbecue grills ranging from Japanese hibachis to multiburner gas models, and "you've got to be very specific about which barbeques you've been selling because during a sale you'll discover you don't have the one the customer wants," Mr. Guinon says.

The computer systems also help control big inventory costs by accurately forecasting each store's merchandise needs. "Fifteen years ago we were paying 6% interest to carry our inventory. Now we're paying 11% to 12% and think we're getting a break," says Mr. Schwartz. "Every item I carry in stock an extra month costs me twice what it used to."

Dylex uses International Business Machines Corp.'s Inforem inventory program, which helps restock more than 1,000 stores from Vancouver to Cornerbrook, Newfoundland. "It allows you to keep track of inventory in each store by size and color and the rate at which it is selling, and then forecasts the estimated inventory," explains Mr. Schwartz. "So if a particular store is in a Chinese neighborhood and sells a lot of small sizes, the computer will know that. And when new merchandise arrives, it will automatically allocate small sizes to that store."

In addition, such systems help retailers adjust quickly when a product is selling poorly, says Gordon Edelstone, a vice president of Dylex's Tip Top division. "We can identify an item that looks like a dog and mark it down immediately and sell it even before (competitors) recognize the product isn't selling well."

Computers also help chains compete by reducing labor costs. Caldor, which plans to invest $15 million in computer hardware and software this year, expects savings equal to the salaries of five full-time employees for each store. "We promote 10,000 to 14,000 items in a weekly flier," explains Mr. Guinon. "In the past you had to mark down all these items manually, take off the old sales tickets and put the new ones on. The human effort was massive, and the error was massive."

During a sale under the new system, price tags are replaced by a single sign placed on a display designating the discount (for instance: "Take 25% off the ticketed price") and the price is filed in the computerized checkout terminal.

This so-called price look-up system also reduces theft by employees, says Stanley Slom, editor of Chain Store Age Executive, a trade magazine. "It prevents employees from charging less, which is one of the biggest areas of theft." Adds Mr. Guinon, "If a store does an average of $20 per customer and a clerk does $14 a sale—bingo, the machine will pick that up."

Electronic mail is another benefit. Bentonville, Ark.-based Wal-Mart Stores Inc. can send messages to 700 stores in less than one workday. Dylex's stores "used to take instructions for markdowns 7 to 10 days later than now," before the company's new point-of-sale terminals were installed recently, Mr. Schwartz says. Caldor expects electronic mail to save $2 million a year. "About 80% to 90% of the mail to keep the company going disappears," Mr. Guinon says.

Retailers also are using computers as an in-store selling device. Shoppers at Nashville, Tenn.-based Service Merchandise Co. stores order products from terminals and pick up their purchases at the checkout counter. Also, Sears, Roebuck & Co., the nation's largest retailer, as an experiment recently installed electronic kiosks in eight stores to provide information on financial services and on merchandise in the stores' window-accessories department.

Retail Technology (percentage of stores surveyed that have recently adopted a new application of technology)

| | Type of Stores | | | | |
Use	Mass Merchandise Stores	Department Stores	Specialty Stores	Combination/ Grocery Stores	All Participants
Point of sale	55%	50%	34%	47%	47%
Sales reporting/ analysis	34	46	34	27	36
Distribution	42	23	31	40	34
Purchase order	40	35	34	20	34
Store-level systems	47	8	19	33	28

SOURCE: Arthur Young, 1985.

Retailers say electronic ordering from suppliers is the next step in the technology of merchandising. It would save time and eliminate many retailers' out-of-stock troubles. A few big chains already are doing some electronic ordering.

In the next three years, K mart Corp., with headquarters in Troy, Mich., expects to spend $300 million to install computerized, laser-scanning registers that will automatically reorder certain merchandise when stock gets low. Wal-Mart reduced the time it takes an order to be delivered to nine days from three weeks because orders are electronically transmitted to more than 500 suppliers. In addition, the company figures that average inventory investment has been reduced by about 17% for some products.

New York-based Penney automatically reorders products accounting for 50% of its $12 billion in annual sales from 281 suppliers, cutting lead time by at least 10 days, says Mr. Capone.

"There are two ways of getting orders into the Penney system," he explains. "Orders are generated automatically based on reorder points and quantities, and other orders are entered into terminals at Penney stores. The order goes directly into the computer and right to the vendor. It isn't approved in New York."

In March, Penney launched an electronic ordering program for its smaller, non-computerized vendors. "There are a lot of suppliers out there that don't have computer facilities. But if one of our suppliers can acquire a personal computer, we'll supply the software to them. They can dial into the Penney system for orders without having a big mainframe," Mr. Capone says.

The growth of retailing technology—and its role in management strategy—eventually may have a big impact on executive suites. "Data processing is now developing management candidates," says Mr. Schwartz of Dylex. "It's one of the most direct paths to get to the top." In 1984, for instance, 24% of data-processing department supervisors reported directly to the company's president, compared with 20% in 1983, according to an Arthur Young survey of retailers.

"The head of the management information-systems pyramid is a senior vice president now—that's new," says Caldor's Mr. Guinon. "This used to be a sub-activity within finance. In another half a generation," he says, the computer chief could be running the company.

SOURCE: Hank Gilman, "The Technology Edge: In Their Drive for Competitive Advantage, Retail Chains Make Strategic Use of Computers." Reprinted by permission of *The Wall Street Journal.* © Dow Jones & Company, Inc., September 16, 1985, 55C, 63. All rights reserved.

DISCUSSION QUESTIONS

1. What strategic evaluation and control issues should be considered by retail chains making strategic use of computers?
2. Discuss the strategic implications for small independents and regional chains of the expanding strategic use of information technology by large retailers.
3. Identify several strategic control applications for the available retail technology.
4. Outline an approach for estimating the costs and returns of proposed new technology applications.

STRATEGIC APPLICATION 18–2

EASTMAN KODAK CO.

ROCHESTER, N.Y.—Eastman Kodak Co.'s 1984 annual report has change written all over it. Behind a slick cover of blue skies and cactus blooms, sections titled "Changing for the Future" and "Charter for Change" portray a company bent on renovation.

Kodak hasn't much choice given the well-publicized slowing growth in its photographic businesses as well as the strong U.S. dollar and vigorous foreign competition. Though Kodak executives have talked about change for several years, it wasn't until recently that the 105-year-old photographic and chemical giant began doing much about it.

In the past 18 months, Kodak entered the floppy-disk and video markets and formed units to produce electronic parts and biological materials. An acquisition binge that brought five new subsidiaries into the corporate fold promises to continue. And, in probably its most dramatic move, Kodak this year reorganized its vast photographic division—which accounted for 80% of its $10.6 billion in 1984 sales—into 17 individual business units.

"We've come out of an environment where we were the single world leader, we had a technology that nobody else could really match, and we were able to dominate that field," says Kodak president Kay R. Whitmore. "The world doesn't allow companies to do that anymore. So we've got to change, and that's a very hard lesson to learn."

Big Challenges

But big challenges face the former model of blue-chip prosperity. First-quarter profit dropped 27%, and the company is cautious about its earnings outlook for the rest of the year. While 1984 profit increased 63% to $923 million or $5.71 a share, it fell short of analysts' expectations and came on 1983's 51% earnings plunge. Still unclear is how successfully Kodak will compete in highly competitive markets, how much growth it can squeeze from its mature businesses

Eastman Kodak Profit and Sales Picture

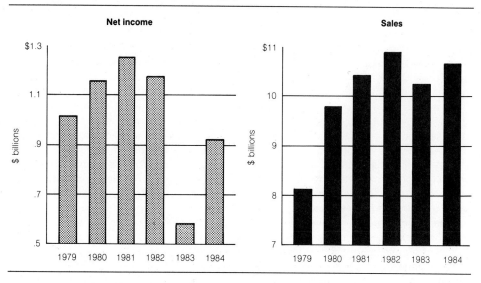

Net income

Sales

and whether it is willing to significantly modify its entrenched compensation and support systems.

"It's not a fat, dumb and happy company; they know what they're up against," says Richard D. Schwarz, an analyst with E. F. Hutton & Co. "I'm optimistic because two years ago they didn't show any signs of being aware of this. But getting consumables to sell that are as proprietary and profitable as film will be difficult."

By reorganizing the photo division, Kodak hopes to spur development of products and speed its responsiveness to the marketplace. While centralized marketing, manufacturing and product development worked well for the single-product company Kodak was, it hobbled Kodak's entry into markets with short product life cycles and aggressive competition—a lesson Mr. Whitmore learned nearly five years ago, when he was assigned to run the Ektachem blood-analyzer program as a separate business.

"I had no marketing force, no manufacturing force; all I had was a planning force," he says. "I'd plan something, but to implement it I had to talk to the marketing organizations." Having to "touch all the bases," he adds, contributed to the 10 years it took to develop Ektachem and to executives' frustration with Kodak's studied pace. "I have been a very frustrated person," Mr. Whitmore said last January when announcing the reorganization.

New Units

As general managers for the 17 new business units, Kodak chose some younger employees described as entrepreneurial, aggressive and decisive, although largely inexperienced and not in line for high-level promotions. Because the positions were new, no older employees were displaced.

Mr. Whitmore, confessing to "a high level of nervousness because we've got these very competent but quite inexperienced managers running off in 17 different directions," says they eventually will operate their units almost as independent companies. Each already has profit and loss responsibility.

That done, observers say Kodak must follow through with changes in compensation and other support functions. "The idea is to decentralize down to the lowest level where you need to manage the business," says Rodman L. Drake, managing director of Cresap, McCormick & Paget Inc., a management consulting firm. "You want to give the general managers the resources and functions to manage their segments effectively, following corporate guidelines and policy."

But so far Kodak executives say they haven't specific plans for further changes in organization or compensation. This sounds somewhat ominous to Ronald M. Schmidt, associate dean at the University of Rochester Graduate School of Management, who believes the 17 units must be free to respond to market competition. "They still have a centralized personnel department with considerable authority over compensation. If that's the case, it's a reorganization on paper and not in substance," he says.

Any reticence to make further changes may result from Kodak's fear of going too far too fast. "The biggest challenge is to develop the sense of urgency across the entire organization and a realization of the intense competitive environment we are in, and at the same time not to give up those elements that really make Kodak a unique company," says Lawrence J. Matteson, vice president and general manager of the commercial and information-systems group.

Known as The Great Yellow Father in Rochester, where it employs 53,200 people—20% of the city's work force—Kodak has a history of providing generous bonuses and lavish benefits. A job at Kodak has been a job for life, with managers counting on orderly if measured progress up the ranks.

That began changing in 1983, when Kodak cut 8,600 workers—8.5% of its U.S. work force. More than 5,000 left voluntarily after the company offered retirement and separation incentives; 3,600 more were laid off. Kodak cited a lagging economy and the strength of the U.S. dollar. Since then, its U.S. work force has shrunk more, to about 85,550 in 1984 compared with 93,350 in 1982.

It was about the same time that Mr. Whitmore joined Colby H. Chandler, chairman and chief executive officer, in the celery-green executive enclave atop Kodak Tower. Mr. Chandler set some ambitious goals: to remain among the country's 25 most profitable companies, to increase real sales by at least twice the gain in real Gross National Product and to post a 20% return on equity. In 1984, return on equity was 12.6% compared to 20.2% in 1980.

Those goals required new strategies. After decades of 8% to 10% annual increases, growth in traditional photography has slowed to about 4% a year. New image-capturing technologies are here, ones that don't require the traditional silver-based film that long has been Kodak's cash cow. More significantly, there are nearly no new products that approach the proprietary position and what analysts say is a minimum 50% profit margin on Kodak's blockbuster color film.

"It's very hard to find anything (with profit margins) like color photography that is legal," says Leo J. Thomas, senior vice president and director of Kodak research.

"It was clear to us that it would take more than a new Kodacolor film or a new disk camera," says Mr. Chandler. "It would take a whole new area—like life sciences—or it would take massive expansions into areas we hadn't participated in very much before."

Five Areas

Kodak is focusing on the following areas: chemicals; life sciences; imaging, including traditional photography, electronic recording of images and hybrid systems of both; and information management. Spending for research and development, traditionally about 6% of sales, increased to 8% in 1984, or $838 million.

Lately, Kodak's push has been in its new life-sciences division and in information management, which it considers important enough to have renamed its reorganized photo division the Photographic & Information Management division. "We're moving into an information-based company," says Mr. Thomas. "A big percentage of our business is in the form of images—to capture, store, manipulate and display them."

With that strategy, Kodak is positioning itself both as a floppy-disk supplier—competing against Minnesota Mining & Manufacturing Co. and Xidex Corp.—and as a disk-drive supplier to original-equipment makers. "We see this as a large market today; media (floppy disks) alone is $4 billion, equipment is equivalent to that, and the growth rates are forecast to be 25% to 35% a year," says William Fowble, vice president and general manager of the diversified technologies group. "I hold no illusions that we're going to go out and get 60% of the market, but if there are five players, we'll have 20% or more."

Kodak last year introduced a new venture program to identify potential growth businesses while fostering entrepreneurship within the corporate monolith. Employees pitch their ideas to a venture board, which makes preliminary grants of as much as $25,000. Four ventures have been approved so far, including Eastman Communications to market proprietary data-communications software and Videk to make machine-vision systems.

Kodak is less certain about its leap into consumer electronics. As executives struggled to define Kodak's role in that volatile market, they decided electronic technology was best applied to an array of products, Mr. Chandler says. Because electronic products like optical disks and video cameras compete with photography for consumer dollars, Kodak is cautious about marketing new technology that will take business from its highly profitable photographic segment.

Vertical Integration

In transforming itself, Kodak is abandoning its history as a stronghold of vertical integration. "One of the things we've learned is that one company can't do everything," Mr. Whitmore says. "We're prepared to acquire if it fits our strategic plan and gets us there sooner, or gives us a technical capacity we don't have in-house, or buys a market share that would be hard to build."

Since 1981, Kodak has acquired makers of electronic-publishing systems, ink-jet printing systems and magnetic data-recording equipment. It recently forged a $45 million joint venture to develop drugs to slow the aging process and antiviral compounds with ICN Pharmaceuticals Co., and last year invested $20 million in Sun Microsystems Inc., a maker of graphics workstations. Earlier this month, it completed its acquisition of Verbatim Corp., a leading maker of floppy disks. Its acquisition of Eikonix Corp., a maker of digital image-processing equipment, is pending, and rumors circulate that Kodak might use its $987.9 million cash hoard to acquire even bigger companies.

Future acquisitions, Kodak promises, will go more smoothly than its 1981 purchase for $79.8 million of Atex Inc., a maker of text-publishing systems that was Kodak's first acquisition in almost ten years. Co-founder Charles Ying says Atex was at a crossroads at the time, with booming sales but few internal controls. But Kodak took a hands-off approach—even when customers who had adhered to Atex's cash-and-carry policy began delaying payments. Kodak provided a succession of managers, some of whom didn't adjust well. "In a company like Atex, you've got to make decisions 10 times more often than equivalent managers at a $10 billion company with 10% growth," says Mr. Ying. "And usually you've got to make decisions with inadequate information."

Kodak still owns Atex and says it remains happy with the acquisition. Adds Mr. Whitmore, however: "If we were to acquire Atex today, we would have done it smarter."

DISCUSSION QUESTIONS

1. Describe Kodak's business composition.
2. Discuss the strategic forces that are causing Kodak to alter its corporate and marketing strategies.
3. Identify the important strategic actions created by changing markets and technologies that Kodak's management must include in future strategic plans.
4. What planning unit is appropriate for developing Kodak's marketing plans for the photographic division?

Index

This book has been set AKI 8600 in 10 and 9 point Century Schoolbook, leaded 2 points. Part numbers are 30 point Century Schoolbook Bold and part titles are 24 point Century Schoolbook Bold Italic. Chapter numbers are 24 point Century Schoolbook Bold and chapter titles are 20 point Century Schoolbook Bold Italic. The size of the type page is 27 picas by 48 picas.